HIDDEN®
Pacific Northwest

"An excellent guidebook that's been made even better in this updated and redesigned edition."
—*Seattle Times & Post-Intelligencer*

"*Hidden Pacific Northwest* lives up to its name with its tips on finding attractions that are off the beaten path."
—*Edmonton Sun*

"Written with an eye for the off-beat, the book is the perfect companion for a jaunt up the Oregon coast, a camping trip on the Olympic Peninsula or even a visit to Vancouver. . . . Fun to read for both the casual visitor and the intrepid traveler."
—*Our World*

"*Hidden Pacific Northwest* spotlights traditional attractions and alternatives in Washington, Oregon and British Columbia. The authors avoid standard hotels and chain restaurants in favor of one-of-a-kind places and locally owned establishments."
—*Ashbury Park Press*

HIDDEN®

Pacific Northwest

FOURTH EDITION

Ulysses Press®

BERKELEY, CALIFORNIA

Published by:
ULYSSES PRESS
P.O. Box 3440
Berkeley, CA 94703-3440

Library of Congress Catalog Card Number 98-84070
ISBN 1-56975-131-5

Printed in Canada by Best Book Manufacturers

10 9 8 7

AUTHORS: Stephen Dolainski, John Gottberg,
    Maria Lenhart, Marilyn McFarlene, Jim Poth,
    Roger Rapoport, Melissa Rivers, Archie Satterfield
UPDATE AUTHOR: Eric Lucas
EDITORIAL DIRECTOR: Leslie Henriques
MANAGING EDITOR: Claire Chun
PROJECT DIRECTOR: Natasha Lay
COPY EDITOR: David Sweet
EDITORIAL ASSOCIATES: Lily Chou, Aaron Newey
TYPESETTER: David Wells
CARTOGRAPHY: Wendy Ann Logsdon, Phil Gardner,
    Mark Rosen
HIDDEN BOOKS DESIGN: Sarah Levin
COVER DESIGN: Leslie Henriques
INDEXER: Sayre Van Young
COVER PHOTOGRAPHY: Front: Dennis Frates
    Circle and back: Terry Donnelly
    Back: Rankin Harvey
ILLUSTRATOR: Catherine Rose Crowther

Distributed in the United States by Publishers
Group West, in Canada by Raincoast Books,
and in Great Britain and Europe by World
Leisure Marketing

For Sarah Levin,
who changed the face of the Pacific Northwest
and all the rest of the hidden world

Write to us!

If in your travels you discover a spot that captures the spirit of the Pacific Northwest, or if you live in the region and have a favorite place to share, or if you just feel like expressing your views, write to us and we'll pass your note along to the author.

We can't guarantee that the author will add your personal find to the next edition, but if the writer does use the suggestion, we'll acknowledge you in the credits and send you a free autographed copy of the new edition.

ULYSSES PRESS
P.O. Box 3440
Berkeley, CA 94703-3440
E-mail: readermail@ulyssespress.com

Acknowledgments

Ulysses Press would like to thank the following readers who took the time to write in with suggestions that were incorporated into this new edition of *Hidden Pacific Northwest*:

Eileen Burlingame of Newburyport, MA; William S. Connell of Durham, NH; O. W. Corman of Ellensburg, WA; J. D. Craddock, III of Munfordville, KY; Barbara L. Davis; Lucy Garzon of Brooklyn, NY; Rita Krishna of London, England; John J. Madison of Arlington, VA; Joyce Maghan of Fayetteville, GA; John and Joan McMillan of New Brighton, MN; Cicely T. Richardson of Orford, NH; Ann Sloan of Burbank, CA; Mary Stumberger of Decatur, IL; Kimberlee J. Trudeau of New Haven, CT.

What's Hidden?

At different points throughout this book, you'll find special listings marked with a hidden symbol:

◄ HIDDEN

This means that you have come upon a place off the beaten tourist track, a spot that will carry you a step closer to the local people and natural environment of the Pacific Northwest.

The goal of this guide is to lead you beyond the realm of everyday tourist facilities. While we include traditional sightseeing listings and popular attractions, we also offer alternative sights and adventure activities. Instead of filling this guide with reviews of standard hotels and chain restaurants, we concentrate on one-of-a-kind places and locally owned establishments.

Our authors seek out locales that are popular with residents but usually overlooked by visitors. Some are more hidden than others (and are marked accordingly), but all the listings in this book are intended to help you discover the true nature of the Pacific Northwest and put you on the path of adventure.

Contents

Maps

OUTDOOR ADVENTURE SYMBOLS

The following symbols accompany national, state and regional park listings, as well as beach descriptions throughout the text.

▲	Camping	🏄	Surfing
🚶	Hiking	🎿	Waterskiing
🚲	Biking	⛵	Windsurfing
🐎	Horseback Riding	🚣	Canoeing or Kayaking
⛷	Downhill Skiing	🚤	Boating
🎿	Cross-country Skiing	🚤	Boat Ramps
🏊	Swimming	🐟	Fishing
🤿	Snorkeling or Scuba Diving		

ONE

The Pacific Northwest

The Pacific Northwest goes by many names, but perhaps "The Evergreen Playground" best captures its enchanting appeal. This is a land of intense beauty: gossamer mists on towering evergreens, icy summits that cast shadows on pastoral valleys and bustling cityscapes, wind-sculpted trees on wave-battered capes and inlets, warm breezes through juniper boughs. Powerful volcanoes, wondrous waterfalls, glistening waterways, even shifting desert sands.

The heavy rainfall for which the Pacific Northwest is famous is truly the heart that gives the region its majestic soul. The drizzle and clouds that blanket the coastal region during much of the winter and spring nourish the incredibly green landscape that grows thick and fast and softens the sharp edges of alpine peaks and jagged sea cliffs. But there's a flip side: Over half the region (meaning points east of the Cascade Range) is actually warm and dry through the year.

"The Evergreen Playground" fairly begs to be explored. While much of it remains undeveloped, vast expanses of wilderness are close by all metropolitan centers. Almost without exception, each city is surrounded by countless outdoor recreational opportunities, with mountains, lakes, streams and an ocean within easy reach. It's no surprise that residents and visitors tend to have a hardy, outdoorsy glow. After all, it is the proximity to nature that draws people here. That remains especially true in Oregon, where development of the land is allowed only in certain areas close to a city center within an "urban growth boundary." The areas outside the towns are protected from the ugly suburban sprawl that has spread throughout much of the West Coast.

Asian populations lend an exotic feel to the bustling commercial centers of Seattle, Portland and Vancouver, while the distinctly British aura of Victoria imparts an entirely different foreign appeal. A montage of tiny ghost towns, towering totem poles, aging wooden forts, Scandinavian and Bavarian communities, stage stops and gold-mining boomtowns and old-time fishing villages adds a frontier feel.

This book will help you explore this wonderful area, tell of its history, introduce you to its flora and fauna. Besides taking you to countless popular spots, it will lead you to off-the-beaten-path locales. Each chapter will suggest places to eat, to stay, to sightsee, to shop and to enjoy the outdoors and nightlife, covering a range of tastes and budgets.

The book starts in Seattle, taking visitors in Chapter Two through this popular city and the surrounding communities spread along Southern Puget Sound. Chapter Three heads up the Sound, taking in some small and some not-so-small coastal towns and the San Juans, an archipelago of evergreen-clad islands. Chapter Four covers the moss-laden rainforests and historic port towns of Washington's Olympic Peninsula and southwestern coast while Chapter Five explores the numerous parks, forests, wildernesses and removed resort communities of the Washington Cascades.

Chapter Six heads to the arid plateau and desert region east of the Cascades in both Washington and Oregon. Portland, the "City of Roses," and the windy Columbia Gorge are the subject of Chapter Seven. Next we go on one of the nation's most scenic drives along the Oregon Coast in Chapter Eight and on to Mt. Hood, Mt. Bachelor, Crater Lake and other majestic peaks of the Oregon Cascades in Chapter Nine. Chapter Ten covers the cultural, learning and political centers lining the Heart of Oregon.

In Chapter Eleven we visit British Columbia, Canada's most westerly province, with stops in exotic Vancouver and the famous Whistler ski resort, followed by a motoring trip up the sleepy Sunshine Coast, an outdoors-lover's paradise. Chapter Twelve rounds out the book with a ferry trip to unspoiled Vancouver Island, its coasts lined with bucolic fishing villages, and to the very proper, very English Victoria, capital of the province.

What you choose to see and do is up to you, but don't delay; things are changing here. The Pacific Northwest is no longer the quiet backwater of a decade ago. Growth and expansion continue in the major population centers strung along the long, black ribbon of Route 5. While Northwesterners are vociferous advocates for preserving nature, rapidly increasing population and growing economic demands are taking a toll.

Sadly, it's becoming difficult to miss the horrid clear-cut swaths through the evergreen background, evidence of the logging industry that feeds the local economies. Salmon that once choked the many streams and rivers have dwindled in number, as have numerous forest creatures such as the spotted owl.

Tourism has also had an impact. As the beauty of the area has been "discovered" by travelers who've taken home tales of this don't-spread-it-around secret vacationland, it's become a hot destination, especially among international visitors. It's getting harder and harder to find those special hidden spots—go soon before "hidden" no longer applies.

▼▼▼▼▼▼▼▼▼▼▼▼

The Story of the Pacific Northwest

GEOLOGY

In terms of geology, the Pacific Northwest is a relatively young land mass formed at the junction of the Juan de Fuca and North American plates. About 200 million years ago, the Klamath-Siskiyou Mountains were created during the Triassic uplift. The Cascade Range

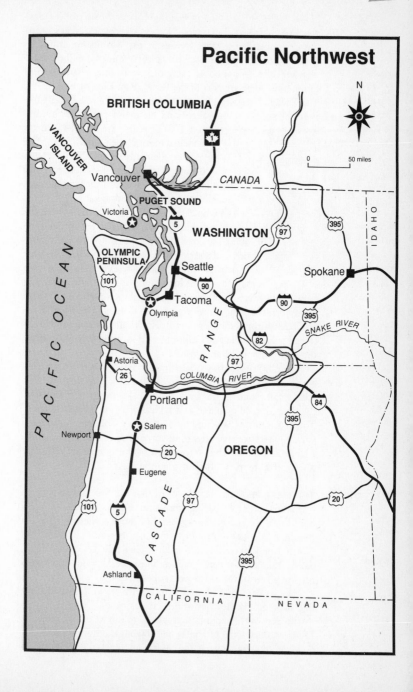

began to rise only 20 million years ago, about the time of the massive Columbia lava flow, second-largest in the world, that formed the Columbia Plateau that spreads across Washington and Oregon. Volcanic eruptions reached a peak about two million years ago with the formation of the Northwest's long chain of "fire mountains" that are part of the Pacific Rim Ring of Fire.

Glaciers have also played a major role within the last million years or so, sculpting valleys and mountain peaks. Within the past 10,000 years, the warmer climate has melted much of the ice mass, adding to the power of already formidable rivers like the Columbia that carved the plateau and continental shelf. Smaller glaciers remain, especially in the high mountains.

The land in the Pacific Northwest continues to shift slowly, as seen in the explosive powers of Mt. St. Helens and the creeping rise of the San Juan Islands from the Pacific.

As a whole, the area can be divided into five distinct geological zones. The Pacific Border zone along the coast includes a chain of coastal mountains and a series of valleys forming what's become known as the Great Trough. The Cascade Sierra zone is made up of the long range of mountains stretching from California across Oregon and Washington and into British Columbia. Reaching down from British Columbia into northeastern Washington is the Northern Rocky Mountain zone, and pushing up from Nevada and California into southwestern Oregon are the arid Basin and Range zones.

Overall features of the Pacific Northwest that most travelers encounter include spectacular sea cliffs, a narrow coastal plain with small estuaries and bays and a major range of mountains, the Cascades, miles inland as is typical of a young coastal region. The coastlines of Washington and British Columbia are highly varied where waves and strong currents have hewn headlands, islands and fjords. The Oregon Coast is fairly regular, with only a few offshore monoliths cut from the jagged cliffs.

HISTORY

THE FIRST PEOPLE   It is believed that the first migrants came from Asia across the Bering Strait land bridge some 25,000 years ago. From the diverse background of those earliest inhabitants descended the many American Indian tribes that populated the North American continent. Kwakiutl, Haida, Bella Coola, Tlingit, Salish, Yakima, Nez Perce, Paiutes, Shoshone, Umpqua and Rogue are but a few of the Northwest tribes.

The verdant land of the Pacific Northwest both provided for and dictated the lifestyles of the various tribes. Those that lived inland east of the mountain ranges were forced to live nomadic lifestyles, depending primarily on foraging and hunting game for survival, moving along as the climate and animal migrations demanded. They generally lived in caves during hunting migration and constructed large pit houses for winter camp.

The mild climate and abundant resources of the valley and coast led to a fairly sedentary life for the tribes that lived west of the mountain ranges. They constructed permanent villages of long-houses from the readily available wood, fished the rich waters of the coast, foraged in lush forests and had enough free time to develop ritualized arts, ceremonies and other cultural pursuits along with an elaborate social structure. The potlatch, a complex ceremony of gaining honor by giving away lavish gifts to the point of bankruptcy, is one of the more renowned ritualized traditions of the Northwest tribes.

Arrival of the white man brought many changes to the generally peaceful natives. Introduction of the horse made life easier for a period, facilitating hunting and travel for the nomadic tribes. However, disease, drugs (namely alcohol) and distrust accompanied the newcomers and eventually added to the decline of the American Indian population. Land grabbing by European settlers forced the tribes onto ever-shrinking reservations.

Resurgence in American Indian arts and crafts is evident in galleries and museums throughout the Northwest. While most natives no longer live on the reservations but have integrated into white society, many have banded together to fight for change. Tribal organizations are now reclaiming lands and fishing rights; nations such as the Sechelt Band in British Columbia have won the legal right to independent self-government. There are even a growing number of native-owned-and-operated resorts such as Ka-Nee-Tah, a hot spring and golf retreat in central Oregon.

EARLY EXPLORATION   In terms of white exploration and settlement, the Pacific Northwest is one of the youngest regions on the continent. The Spanish began to arrive in the Northwest by sea as early as the mid-1500s; the Strait of Juan de Fuca, Heceta Head, Fidalgo Island, Cape Blanco, Quadra Island and other prominent landmarks bear witness to Spanish exploration and influence. Spanish interest waned when other pressing matters required the attention and money needed to chart the Northwest, and all claims to the area were dropped in 1819 as part of the negotiations regarding Florida.

The Russians also made their way into the region beginning with the explorations of Vitus Dane in 1741. Soon afterward, Russian trappers trekked from Siberia down through Alaska and into the Northwest. As a result of losses brought on by the Napoleonic Wars, Russia renounced all claims to the area south of 54° 40′ in 1824.

Sir Francis Drake passed briefly along the Northwest Coast in 1579, but it was explorer James Cook's expedition in the late

1700s in search of the legendary "Northwest Passage" that resulted in British claim to the region. When passing through China on their homeward-bound trip, he and his men discovered the high value of the pelts they carried, leading to an intense interest on the part of the British government in the profitable resources of the Northwest.

The government later commissioned Captain George Vancouver to chart the coastal area between 45° and 60° north latitude which includes Oregon, Washington, British Columbia and Alaska. Mt. Baker, Whidbey Island, Puget Sound, Vancouver Island, Burrard Inlet and many other geographical features retain the names he gave them on his meticulously drawn maps completed between 1791 and 1795.

Captain Robert Gray was also plying Northwest waters at this time, making certain that the United States could lay claim to parts of the lucrative new territory. During his journey, he discovered the mighty Columbia River while searching for the same fabled waterway between the Pacific and Atlantic oceans.

Early explorers like Alexander McKenzie and Simon Fraser were actually the first Europeans to explore land routes, but it was not until Meriwether Lewis and William Clark explored and mapped overland passages, returning with stories of the area's beauty and natural bounty, that interest in settling the Northwest began in earnest.

THE NEWCOMERS   Trading posts were established to facilitate the fur enterprises; large firms like the Hudson Bay Company and the North West Company vied for control of the profitable region. Settlements sprang up around these posts and continued to grow as the trickle of pioneers swelled into a wave with the opening of the Oregon Trail in the mid-1800s.

THE INFAMOUS PIG WAR

Tensions left over from the War of 1812 and the not-yet-forgotten American Revolution caused friction between the Americans and British in the Northwest. The American/British Treaty of 1846 failed to define the border of the British territory, so the Americans and British agreed to use the 49th parallel. However, this latitude divided the San Juan Islands in two, leaving British and American soldiers staring each other down across the makeshift border. The entente was preserved until a lone British pig wandered into the garden of an American settler, who shot and killed the pig—the only bullet fired during the 13-year dispute, a diplomatic struggle for the islands that came to be called the "Pig War." Ultimately the islands were awarded to the United States by a German arbitrator in 1872.

Tensions began to mount between American and British settlers who occupied the same territory and came to a head in the San Juan Islands in what's known as the bloodless "Pig War." An uneasy standoff between the nations held until successful negotiations divided American- and British-controlled territory in 1872.

Homesteading, fishing, logging, ranching and other opportunities kept the flow of settlers coming, as did a series of gold strikes. Stage routes were established, and river traffic grew steadily. There were enough residents to warrant separation of the Oregon Territory by the 1850s, and Washington and Oregon attained statehood by the turn of the century. British Columbia was officially accepted as a Canadian province in 1871. Railroads pushed into the region, reaching Portland and Puget Sound by 1883 and British Columbia in 1885, ushering in the modern age.

Rapid industrial development came with the world wars, and the Northwest emerged as a major player in the shipbuilding and shipping industries. Expansion in lumber, agriculture and fishing continued apace. Growth industries today include banking, high technology and Pacific Rim trade. Modern residents are for the most part rugged individualists, fiercely proud of their natural setting and protective of the environment.

While it's generally the coniferous trees that everyone equates with the Pacific Northwest, there is much more to the flora of the region than its abundance of redwoods, Western hemlock and white pine, red cedar and other evergreens. Each of the distinct geologic zones hosts its own particular ecosystem. **FLORA**

In the moist woodlands of the coastline, glossy madrone and immense Coast redwoods tower over Pacific trilliums and delicate ladyslippers. Bogs full of skunkcabbage thrive alongside fields of yellow Scotch broom and hardy rhododendrons in a riot of color. Unique to the region are pristine rain forests with thick carpets of moss and fern beneath sky-scraping canopies of fir, cedar and spruce.

In the lowland valleys, alders, oaks, maples and other deciduous trees provide brilliant displays of color against an evergreen backdrop each spring and fall. Daffodils and tulips light up the fields, as do azaleas, red clover and other grasses grown by the many nurseries and seed companies that prosper here. Wildberry bushes run rampant in this clime, bringing blackberries, huckleberries, currants and strawberries for the picking. Indian paintbrush, columbines, foxglove, buttercups and numerous other wildflowers are also abundant.

The verdant parks and forests of the mountain chains contain some of the biggest trees in the world, holding records in height and circumference, with fir, pine, hemlock and cedar generally topping the charts. Thick groves filter the sunlight, providing the perfect environment for mushrooms, lichens, ferns and mosses. The elegant tiger lily, beargrass, asters, fawnlily, phlox, columbine, valerian and a breathtaking array of alpine wildflowers thrive in high meadows and on sunny slopes.

With the dramatic decrease in rainfall in the plateaus and deserts zone comes a paralleling drop in the amount of plantlife, although it is still rich in pine, juniper, cottonwood and sagebrush. Flowers of the area include wild iris, foxglove, camas, balsam root and pearly everlasting.

FAUNA

It was actually the proliferation of wildlife that brought about white colonization of the Pacific Northwest, beginning with the trappers who came in droves in search of fur. It turns out that beaver and otter pelts were highly valued in China during the 1800s, so these creatures were heavily hunted. Nearly decimated colonies, now protected by law, are coming back strong. Playful otters are often spotted floating tummy up in coastal waters, while the shy beaver is harder to spot, living in secluded mountain retreats and coming out to feed at night.

Fish, especially salmon, were also a major factor in the economic development of the region, and remain so, though numbers of spawning salmon are dropping drastically. Nonetheless, fishing fanatics are still drawn here in search of the five varieties of Pacific salmon along with flounder, ling cod, rockfish, trout, bass and other varieties of sportfish. Those who don't fish will still be fascinated by the seasonal spawning frenzy of salmon, easily observed at fish ladders in Washington, Oregon and British Columbia.

Watch for the Pacific giant salamander in fallen, rotting logs: it is the largest of its kind in the world, growing up to a foot in length and capable of eating small mice.

Among the more readily recognized creatures that reside in the Pacific Northwest are the orca (killer whales), porpoises, dolphins, seals and sea lions often spotted cavorting in the waters just offshore. Twice-yearly migrations of gray whales on the trip between Alaska and California are much anticipated all along the coastline. Minke whales are more numerous, as are Dall's porpoises, often mistaken for baby orca because of their similar coloration and markings.

Of the varieties of bear living in the Northwest's remote forests, black bear are the most common in Oregon and southern Washington. Weighing upwards of 300 pounds and reaching six feet tall, they usually feed on berries, nuts and fish and avoid humans unless provoked by offers of food or danger to a cub. Grizzly and brown bear are more prevalent farther north. Big-game herds of deer, elk, antelope along with moose, cougar and mountain goats range the more remote mountainous areas. Scavengers such as chipmunks, squirrels, raccoons, opossums and skunks are abundant in the area as well.

Over 300 species of birds live in the Pacific Northwest for at least a portion of the year. Easily accessible mud flats and estuaries throughout the region provide refuge for tufted puffins, egrets, cormorants, loons and other migratory waterfowl making their way along the Pacific Flyway. Hundreds of pairs of bald eagles nest and hunt among the islands of Washington and British Columbia and winter along the Oregon coast, along with great blue herons and cormorants. You might also see red-tailed hawks and spotted owls if you venture quietly into the region's old-growth zones.

With a proliferation of protected refuges and preserves providing homes for great flocks of Canada and snow geese, trumpeter swans, great blue herons, kingfishers, cranes and other species, birdwatchers will be in seventh heaven in the Pacific Northwest, one of the fastest-growing birder destinations on the continent.

On a smaller scale is the slimy slug that thrives in the moist climate. Not quite large enough to be mistaken for a speed bump, they leave telltale viscous trails. While the slug is the bane of gardeners, it is still regarded as a sort of mascot for the region; souvenir shops stock plush toy replicas and gag cans of slug soup.

Where to Go

The number of tourists visiting the Pacific Northwest continues to grow as the secrets of its beauty and sunny summer and fall weather get out. Because the landscape is so widely varied, each area with its own appeal, here are brief descriptions of the regions presented in this book to help you decide where you want to go. To get the whole story, read the more detailed introductions to each chapter, then delve into the material that interests you most. We begin in Washington, head to Oregon, then up to cover British Columbia.

Seattle, recently rated the most liveable city in the United States, offers a comfortable mix of cultural sophistication and natural ruggedness. The clustered spires of its expanding skyline hint at the growth in this busy seaport, the shipping and transportation hub of the Northwest. Nearby communities stretched along Southern Puget Sound, including Tacoma, Olympia (the state's capital) and the Kitsap Peninsula, are also covered.

Northern Puget Sound and the San Juan Islands, regarded in this book as the coastal area stretched between Seattle and Blaine on the Canadian border, is completely enchanting, from sea-swept island chains to pastoral coastline. The entire region is punctuated by rich farming tracts, picturesque, forest-covered islands, quaint fishing villages and a shoreline of sloughs and estuaries. The arts are strong in the region, perhaps because of the preponderance of artists drawn by its natural beauty to live here.

American Indians were probably the first people to discover the beauty and bounty of the **Olympic Peninsula and Washington Coast**, with lush rainforests, stretches of driftwood-cluttered beach, tumbling rivers and snow-capped mountains. Several tribes still live in the area on the outskirts of the massive Olympic National Park alongside fishing villages such as Sequim and Port Angeles and the Victorian-style logging town of Port Townsend.

National parks, forests and wildernesses, including the North Cascades, Snoqualmie and Wenatchee national forests, Mt. Rainier National Park and the Mt. St. Helens National Volcanic Monument, make up the bulk of the spectacular **Cascades and Central Washington**. Fascinating Leavenworth, a Bavarian-style village, and several small resort towns are also important features here.

The majestic Cascade Range parallels the West Coast running through Oregon and Washington and up to British Columbia. Once past the slopes, you'll find sagebrush-filled high desert country with shoot-'em-up Western towns and quiet Indian reservations scattered through Washington and Oregon in the **East of the Cascades** zone. Commercial Spokane, pastoral Yakima and industrial Pendleton (home of the famous Pendleton Wools) are also described in this section.

Bounded by an evergreen forest, productive greenbelt and the mighty Columbia River, **Portland and the Columbia River Gorge** remain as close to nature as a growing metropolis can be. Portland, the "City of Roses," reflects a pleasant mix of historic buildings decorated in glazed terra cotta and modern structures of smoked glass and brushed steel. These buildings lie in the downtown core intersected by the Willamette River and numerous parks. The sense of hustling enterprise dampens as you head east into the gorge where you'll find smaller communities such as The Dalles and Hood River along with breathtaking treasures like Multnomah Falls.

The awe-inspiring beauty of the **Oregon Coast** includes 400 miles of rugged coastline dotted by small, artsy communities such

SO, WHO GIVES A HOOT?

The spotted owl has been the center of controversy in recent years, the focus of the recurring nature-versus-commerce debate. As logging companies cut deeper into the old-growth forests, which have taken 150 years or more to grow, the habitat for this endangered owl—only about 800 pairs survive in Washington today—grows smaller. (These nocturnal birds need thousands of acres per pair to support their indulgent eating habits.) The old-growth forests of the Pacific Northwest provide adequate nesting spots in the protected snags and broken branches of tall trees that shelter their flightless young. Some environmentalists predict the owls' extinction early in the 21st century if logging continues at its present rate.

as Yachats and Bandon and larger fishing villages such as Astoria, Newport and Coos Bay, all connected by Route 101, one of the most beautiful drives in the nation. Foresight on the part of the state legislature preserved the coast from crass commercial corruption, so great stretches remain untouched and entirely natural.

The **Oregon Cascades** hold a bevy of treasures including world-famous rivers like the Rogue and the Umpqua (fishing haunt of Zane Grey), the Mt. Hood and Mt. Bachelor ski resorts and the sapphire splendor of Crater Lake, the deepest lake in the country. As with the Washington Cascades, it is a region of national forests and wildernesses.

Cradled between the Coastal and Cascade mountain ranges is the **Heart of Oregon**, a pastoral valley of historic stage stops, gold-mining boomtowns and small farming communities. Sheep-covered meadows, cloud-shrouded bluffs and striped pastures line Route 5, the primary artery traversing the valley. Salem, the state capital, Eugene, home of the University of Oregon, and Ashland, site of the celebrated Shakespeare Festival, are included in this section.

Stretched above Washington and the United States border, British Columbia boasts delights that are hard to match. Extraordinary natural beauty surrounds **Vancouver and the Sunshine Coast**, seen in the caressing Pacific, soaring, protective mountains and vast tracts of forest. Bustling Vancouver sparkles and excites, with more than enough sightseeing, shopping, dining and entertainment opportunities to please one and all. The scenic Sunshine Coast entices with a broad range of recreational opportunities including hiking, biking, boating, camping, diving and fishing. The glacier-covered peaks of Garibaldi Provincial Park and alluring Whistler resort round out the territory.

Visitors to **Victoria and Vancouver Island** will find civility, gentility and a bit of pomp surrounded by one of the greatest outdoor vacation destinations around. Managing to retain the stately air of the British Empire outpost it once was, charming Victoria, the capital of British Columbia, rests at the southernmost tip of the island. Few roads connect the scattered seaport settlements and rugged provincial parks strewn across the remainder of the island, which is rather wild and wooly.

The Pacific Northwest isn't the rain-soaked, snow-covered tundra many imagine it to be. In fact, summer and fall days (June through September) are generally warm, dry and sunny. Overall temperatures range from the mid-30s in winter to the upper 80s in summer, except east of the Cascade range, where summer temperatures average in the mid-90s. There are distinct seasons in each of the primary zones, and the climate varies greatly with local topography.

▼▼▼▼▼▼▼▼▼▼
When to Go

SEASONS

The enormous mountain ranges play a major role in the weather, protecting most areas from the heavy rains generated over the Pacific and dumped on the coastline. Mountaintops are often covered in snow year-round at higher elevations, while the valleys, home to most of the cities, remain snow-free but wet during the winter months. East of the mountain ranges are temperature extremes and a distinct lack of rain. Travelers spend time at the rivers, lakes and streams during the hot, dry summers and frolic in the snow during the winter.

The mountainous zones are a bit rainy in spring but warm and dry in summer, when crowds file in for camping, hiking and other outdoor delights. Fall brings auto traffic attracted by the changing seasonal colors, while winter means snow at higher elevations, providing the perfect playground for cold-weather sports.

The coastal region is generally soggy and overcast during the mild winter and early spring, making this the low season for tourism. However, winter is high season among Northwesterners drawn to the coast to watch the fantastic storms that blow in across the Pacific. Summer is typically warm and dry in the coastal valleys and along the crisp, windy coast, making it the prime season for travelers. And visitors *do* show up in droves, clogging smaller highways with recreational vehicles.

CALENDAR OF EVENTS

Festivals and events are a big part of life in the Northwest, especially when the rains disappear and everyone is ready to spend time outdoors enjoying the sunshine. Larger cities throughout the region average at least one major event per weekend during the summer and early fall. Below is a sampling of some of the biggest attractions. Check with local chambers of commerce (listed in the regional chapters of this book) to see what will be going on when you are in the area.

JANUARY
Seattle Colorful parades fill the streets of the International District to celebrate **Chinese New Year** in late January or early February.
East of the Cascades In addition to seeing mushing and snowmobiling contests, you'll hear carillon bells and perhaps munch wienerschnitzel at the **Great Bavarian Ice Fest** in Leavenworth. There are also ice sculptures, ski competitions and dogsled races at the **Deer Park Winter Festival**.
Vancouver and the Sunshine Coast A quick plunge into frigid English Bay during the **Polar Bear Swim** on New Year's Day is said to bring good luck throughout the year. **Chinese New Year** lights up Vancouver's Chinatown with fireworks, food and a boisterous dragon parade.

Seattle Fat Tuesday is a week-long Mardi Gras–style festival with parade, arts and crafts and plenty of jazz and food. **Wintergrass** in Tacoma features bluegrass music and a street dance.

Olympic Peninsula and the Washington Coast The **Seafood and Wine Fest** in Newport, the oldest and largest wine fest in the Northwest, promises plenty of seafood, wine and live entertainment. **Hot Jazz Port Townsend** brings jazz greats to the Olympic Peninsula.

Oregon Coast Munch crustaceans to your heart's content at the annual **Crab Feed** in Coos Bay and Charleston.

Washington Cascades There are world-class aerial ski jumpers and snowboarders, snow-castle and sculpture competitions, and workshops and races hosted by Olympic ski champion Phil Mahre at the **White Pass Winter Carnival**.

Portland and the Columbia River Gorge Collectors flock to the Portland Expo Center for **America's Largest Antique & Collectible Show**, where over seven acres of goods are on display.

Oregon Coast Cheer on the crabs at the **Pacific Northwest Crab Races** in Garibaldi. Events in Seaside celebrate the northward migration of gray whales during **Spring Whale Watch Week**.

Vancouver and the Sunshine Coast Vancouver's Granville Island hosts the **Vancouver New Play Festival**, which features experimental productions and new plays by Canadian playwrights.

Victoria and Vancouver Island All eyes are on the water during the **Pacific Rim Whale Watching Festival** in Ucluelet and Tofino.

Seattle Enjoy some of the first blossoms of spring at the **Daffodil Festival Grand Floral Parade**, which passes through Tacoma, Puyallup and nearby communities. And judges under umbrellas count as contestants lure gulls in Port Orchard's **Seagull Calling Contest**.

Puget Sound and the San Juans If you'd rather catch those early-spring colors in all their natural glory, queue up for the drive through the rich farmlands of La Conner and Mount Vernon during the **Skagit Valley Tulip Festival**.

Washington Cascades Enjoy over 40 different apple-oriented events during the 11-day **Washington State Apple Blossom Festival** held in Wenatchee.

East of the Cascades Taste the best of local wines at the **Spring Barrel Tasting** in Yakima Valley.

Portland and the Columbia River Gorge Delicate pink-and-white apple blossoms of the area orchards steal the show during the **Hood River Blossom Festival**.

Victoria and Vancouver Island There's a lot of toe-tapping going on as top entertainers perform at the **TerriVic Dixieland Jazz Party** in Victoria.

MAY

Seattle An international array of crafts and folktales, food, costume, music and dance is the focus of the **Northwest Folklife Festival**. Poulsbo celebrates its Norwegian heritage with entertainment, food, a parade and fun run at the **Viking Fest**.

Puget Sound and the San Juans A salmon barbecue is held in conjunction with the 85-mile **Ski-To-Sea Relay Race** between Mt. Baker and Bellingham. The festivities continue with the **Taste of Whatcom Boat Show & Maritime Festival** and a grand parade.

Olympic Peninsula and the Washington Coast Many of Port Townsend's grand Victorian homes are open to the public during the town's **Historic Homes Tour**.

East of the Cascades The ten-day **Spokane Lilac Festival** features a carnival, bed race, torchlight parade, food booths and more. There's also a **Hot Air Balloon Stampede** with over 50 balloons in Walla Walla. The **Maifest** in Leavenworth celebrates spring with Bavarian maypole dancing, a grand march and oompah bands.

Oregon Coast The **Spring Kite Festival** takes off in Lincoln City, the "Kite Capital of the World."

Heart of Oregon A hydroplane boat race, waterskiing show, parade and skydiving competition are part of the fun at **Boatnik** in Grants Pass.

Vancouver and the Sunshine Coast Vancouver **International Children's Fest**, with food and festivities geared to please the little ones, takes place in Vancouver.

Victoria and Vancouver Island Victoria Days are the big event of the season, topped off by a grand parade in mid-May.

JUNE

Seattle You'll enjoy hearty servings of strawberry shortcake and performances by Norwegian dancers at the **Strawberry Festival** in Poulsbo.

Puget Sound and the San Juans Traditional war-canoe races and ceremonial songs and dances are the highlight of the **Lummi Water Festival** held on the Lummi Reservation northwest of Bellingham. In addition to a range of nautical events, enjoy a carnival, parade, art show and grand pyrotechnics display during Everett's **Salty Sea Days**.

Olympic Peninsula and the Washington Coast Booths sell sausage, doughnuts, ice cream, baskets and dolls made of garlic at the **Garlic Festival** in Ocean Park (Long Beach Peninsula).

East of the Cascades Balloons take to the sky during the **Wallowa Mountain High Balloon Festival** in Enterprise. Fiddlers, banjo players and other musicians from around the region converge in Burns for the **Old Time Country Music Jamboree**.

Portland and the Columbia River Gorge Portland's biggest festival of the year, the **Rose Fest**, is a month-long celebration with parties, pageants and a "Grand Floral Parade" second only to California's Rose Parade. **Fort Vancouver Days**, a citywide celebration with rodeo, chili cook-off and jazz concert takes place in Vancouver, Washington.

Oregon Coast Participants from around the globe come to create a world of perishable marvels at the **Cannon Beach Sandcastle Contest,** ranked one of the top competitions in the world. The **Bite at the Beach** is a weekend-long food and music festival in Lincoln City gathering local restaurants, wineries, breweries, artisans and musicians.

Oregon Cascades The High Cascades play host to the **Sisters Rodeo** in Sisters.

Heart of Oregon Outstanding jazz, bluegrass and gospel performances, as well as classical concerts, mark the month-long **Oregon Bach Festival** at the University of Oregon in Eugene. A similarly outstanding event is the **Peter Britt Music Festival** in Jacksonville which features an array of music, dance and theatrical performances and runs through early September.

Vancouver and the Sunshine Coast Vancouver pulls out all the stops in June with the **North Vancouver Folkfest,** the colorful **Dragon Boat Races** on False Creek and the ten-day **Du Maurier International Jazz Festival** with performances by world-class musicians.

Victoria and Vancouver Island Not to be outdone, Victoria has its fair share of summer events in June including the **Oak Bay Tea Party,** the **Jazz Fest** and the **International Folkfest.**

JULY

Seattle Kimono-clad dancers take center stage in **Bon Odori,** a Japanese festival celebrated in the International District as part of the multicultural events of **Seafair,** one of Seattle's biggest celebrations. Northwest talent is showcased in the **Bellevue Arts and Crafts Fair,** host to over 300 artists, craftspeople and performers.

Olympic Peninsula and the Washington Coast **Splash!** in Aberdeen features a grand parade and street dance.

East of the Cascades At the **Sweet Onion Festival** they celebrate Walla Walla's famous produce. Cowboys and Indians turn out in force to take part in the rodeo and American Indian exhibition that are the centerpieces of the **Chief Joseph Days** in Joseph, Oregon. Gliders come from the world over to take part in the **Hang Gliding Festival** in Lakeview, Oregon.

Portland and the Columbia River Gorge The **Robin Hood Festival** in Sherwood hosts a parade, live music and—what else?—an archery competition.

Oregon Coast The **Astoria Scandinavian Festival** celebrates the area's heritage. The **Dory Festival** in Pacific City offers dory-boat races, a fish fry, parades and lots of crafts and food. Coos Bay and North Bend join forces to present the **Oregon Coast Music Festival.**

Heart of Oregon History comes to life during the **Oregon Trail Pageant** in Oregon City. The **International Pinot Noir Celebra-**

tion, attracting top winemakers from around the world, is held in conjunction with the **Annual Antique Show** in McMinnville. Grants Pass offers arts, crafts and food at the **Artists in Action** festival.

Vancouver and the Sunshine Coast The first of the month brings **Canada Day Celebrations**, which take place throughout the country. The **Whistler Country and Blues Festival** brings music to the mountains. The Sunshine Coast pulls out all the stops during July with the **Halfmoon Bay Country Fair** and the **Sea Cavalcade** in Gibsons, both good, old-fashioned fairs with booths, games, competitions and parades.

Victoria and Vancouver Island The International Sandcastle Competition takes the spotlight in Parksville, while the loggers compete in climbing and chopping in **All Sooke Days**.

AUGUST

Seattle Java aficionados can get their fix at **Coffee-Fest Seattle Style**, where roasters and coffee manufacturers from across the nation gather to ply their goods and demonstrate the behind-the-scene workings of the industry.

Puget Sound and the San Juans Many of the Northwest's finest artists display their work at top local shows like the **Coupeville Arts and Crafts Festival** on Whidbey Island. Friday Harbor is the site of the **San Juan County Fair**, with arts and crafts, agricultural and animal exhibits, a carnival and food booths featuring the bounty of the islands. In addition to great local and international blues music, the **Swinomish Blues Festival** in La Conner has Northwest American Indian food, crafts, drums and dancers.

Olympic Peninsula and the Washington Coast Salmon-fishing competitions, a street fair and a couple of parades highlight the **Derby Days Festival** in Port Angeles. World champions descend on Long Beach to compete in the **International Kite Festival**.

East of the Cascades The Steens Mountain Ten-Kilometer Run is followed by sagebrush roping, a barbecue and beer garden at the **Frenchglen Jamboree**, both in Frenchglen, Oregon.

Portland and the Columbia River Gorge The renowned **Mt. Hood Festival of Jazz** in Gresham is an eagerly awaited weekend of big-name musicians performing in the great outdoors.

Oregon Coast Fresh blackberries and quality arts and crafts draw large crowds to the **Annual Blackberry Arts Festival** held in Coos Bay.

Heart of Oregon A carnival, agriculture and craft exhibits, lots of entertainment and plenty of junk food await at the **Oregon State Fair** in Salem. Junction City's Danish roots are celebrated during the **Scandinavian Festival** with folk dancing, food and crafts.

Vancouver and the Sunshine Coast The popular **International Airshow** takes flight in Abbotsford just above the U.S. border, and the **Pacific National Exhibition**, a massive agricultural and industrial fair with everything from top-name entertainment to lumberjack contests, is a happening from mid-August through Labor Day in Vancouver. In Whistler, the **Whistler Classical Music Festival** brings soothing strains to the mountains. The Sunshine Coast also puts on **Roberts Creek Daze**, a fun-filled fair with games and booths.

Seattle The **Bumbershoot Arts Festival** brings music, plays, art exhibits and crafts to Seattle Center. "Do the Puyallup" is the catch phrase of the **Western Washington Fair** in Puyallup, one of the country's largest agricultural fairs. **Olympia Harbor Days**, one of the largest arts-and-crafts fairs in the Northwest, also offers a fascinating tugboat race.   **SEPTEMBER**

East of the Cascades Bronco busting awaits at the **Ellensburg Rodeo**, ranked among the top ten rodeos in the nation. Tour the biergarten and German food circus at the **Odessa Deutches Fest**. See prize-winning livestock, produce and crafts, nibble cotton candy and enjoy a ride or two at the **Central Washington State Fair** in Yakima. In Oregon, the main event is the **Pendleton Roundup**, a major rodeo along with a historical parade of covered wagons and buggies and a pageant of American Indian culture.

Portland and the Columbia River Gorge Portland's **Artquake** shakes up the city with dance, music, visual-art displays and theater performances.

Oregon Coast Vast quantities of salmon are slow baked over an open alderwood fire at the **Indian Style Salmon Bake** in Depoe Bay. The **Bandon Cranberry Jive** in Bandon celebrates the autumn harvest with a cranberry foods fair, crafts and a parade. Classic cars, planes and boats are showcased in the **Vintage Festival**, held in Newberg.

Vancouver and the Sunshine Coast Alternative performance arts take center stage during the **Vancouver Fringe Festival**. The streets of Whistler fill with clowns, jugglers, musicians and comedians who descend for the **Whistler's Really Big Street Fest**.

Victoria and Vancouver Island There's a flotilla of pre-1955 wooden boats in the **Classic Boat Festival** in Victoria's Inner Harbour. Salmon is king at the **Salmon Festival** in Port Alberni.

Seattle **Salmon Days** in Issaquah features a salmon bake, races, live entertainment, arts and crafts and a parade.   **OCTOBER**

Olympic Peninsula and the Washington Coast There's plenty of seafood and entertainment along with a shucking contest at the **Oysterfest** in Shelton. Make your way through a cranberry bog and enjoy special taste treats at the **Cranberry Festival** in Long Beach.

East of the Cascades Leavenworth is ablaze during the **Washington State Autumn Leaf Festival**, complete with oompah bands and Bavarian costumes.

Portland and the Columbia River Gorge   Pie-eating, pumpkin-carving, apple-peeling and other fruit-related contests highlight the **Hood River Valley Harvest Fest**. The **Mid Columbia River Pow Wow** in Celilo Park (east of The Dalles near Celilo Falls) is celebrated with a traditional salmon bake, ancient rituals, crafts and American Indian music.

Oregon Coast   Stunt flyers compete in the **World Cup Kite Competition** in Seaside.

Vancouver and the Sunshine Coast   Celluloid delights brought from around the world are the focus of the **Vancouver International Film Festival**. **Octoberfest** brews and oompah bands seem right at home in Whistler's Bavarian-style village.

NOVEMBER   **Seattle**   Seattle Center is all decked out with an ice-skating rink, Christmas train display and a few arts-and-crafts booths during **Winterfest**, which runs through early January.

Oregon Coast   Artists, musicians, writers and craftspeople gather for the **Arts Festival** in Cannon Beach.

DECEMBER   **Seattle**   **Zoolights** lends a festive spirit to the famous Tacoma Zoo from early December through Christmas.

Puget Sound and the San Juans   The little town of Lynden is decorated like an old Dutch community during the **Dutch Sinterklaas Celebration**, complete with gingerbread and visits with old St. Nick. **Christmas ships** cruise the Swinomish Channel in La Conner.

East of the Cascades   The Bavarian village of Leavenworth looks like a scenic Christmas card during the **Christmas Lighting Festival**.

Oregon Coast   Victorian teas, lamplighting ceremonies and productions of *A Christmas Carol* are part of the **Dickens Festival** in Cannon Beach.

Heart of Oregon   The works of regional artists are on display in Roseburg at the **Douglass County Christmas Fair**, a good place to pick up those last-minute gifts. Roseburg also celebrates the holiday season with its **Umpqua Valley Festival of Lights**, which features Christmas lights formed into a variety of shapes, from Santa Claus to Mickey Mouse.

Vancouver and the Sunshine Coast   On December 31st there's the alcohol-free **First Night**, a New Year's Eve bash with entertainment on the village square at Whistler.

Victoria and Vancouver Island   **Butchart Gardens** puts on the holiday finery with Christmas light displays throughout the month. A **Christmas Ships Parade** in Victoria's Inner Harbour. Ring in the New Year with the alcohol-free **First Night**, a night-long theatrical and musical series hosted by the merchants of downtown Victoria.

For a free copy of the *Washington State Lodging and Travel Guide*, contact the **Washington Tourism Division**. ~ Department of Trade and Economic Development, 101 General Administration Building, P.O. Box 42500, Olympia, WA 98504-2500; 360-586-2088, 800-544-1800.

Oregon: The Official Travel Guide is available from the **Oregon Tourism Division**. ~ P.O. Box 14070, Portland, OR 97293; 800-547-7842.

Travel information on British Columbia is available from **Supernatural British Columbia**. ~ 865 Hornby Street, Suite 802, Vancouver, BC V6Z 2G3; 604-660-2861, 800-663-6000.

Both large cities and small towns throughout the region have chambers of commerce or visitor information centers; a number of them are listed in *Hidden Pacific Northwest* under the appropriate chapter.

For visitors arriving by automobile, Washington and Oregon provide numerous **Welcome Centers** at key points along the major highways where visitors can pull off for a stretch, grab a cup of coffee or juice and receive plenty of advice on what to see and do in the area. The centers are clearly marked and are usually open during daylight hours throughout the spring, summer and fall.

Comfortable and casual are the norm for dress in the Northwest. You will want something dressier if you plan to catch a show, indulge in high tea or spend your evenings in posh restaurants and clubs, but for the most part your topsiders and slacks are acceptable garb everywhere else.

Layers of clothing are your best bet since the weather changes so drastically depending on which part of the region you are visiting; shorts will be perfectly comfortable during the daytime in the hot, arid interior, but once you pass over the mountains and head for the coastline, you'll appreciate having packed a jacket to protect you from the nippy ocean breezes, even on the warmest of days.

Wherever you're headed, during the summer bring some long-sleeve shirts, pants and lightweight sweaters and jackets along with your shorts, T-shirts and bathing suit; the evenings can be quite crisp. Bring along those warmer clothes—pants, sweaters, jackets, hats and gloves—in spring and fall, too, since days may be warm but it's rather chilly after sundown. Winter calls for thick sweaters, knitted hats, down jackets and snug ski clothes.

It's not a bad idea to call ahead to check on weather conditions. Sturdy, comfortable walking shoes are a must for sightseeing. If you plan to explore tidal pools or go for long walks on the beach, bring a pair of lightweight canvas shoes that you don't mind getting wet.

Text continued on page 22.

High Adventure in the Northwest

Whether you're an expert or a novice, a fanatic or simply curious, there's a sport here with your name written on it. Remember, the Pacific Northwest is known as "Evergreen Playground," not "Evergreen Couch Potato." So if what turns you on is dropping through the sky, paddling alongside whales or keeping your feet firmly on the ground, just do it!

For heart-stopping thrills, the newest madness to hit the Northwest is *bungee jumping*. Jumpers strapped into a full-body harness with three to five connecting bungee cords swan dive off a 180-foot-high bridge, the highest commercial bungee bridge in the Western Hemisphere. If this sounds great until you actually eyeball the 20-story drop, **Bungee Masters** will refund the jump fee. Those who make the plunge are awarded membership in the Dangerous Sports Club. ~ P.O. Box 121, Fairview, OR 97024; 503-520-0303.

Still want to take a flying leap? *Paragliding*, an exercise involving climbing a mountain, stepping off the edge, then gliding down in a parachute-like rig, is growing in popularity, too. In most cases, participants learn to fly in just one day. **Parawest Paragliding** provides qualified instruction and services. ~ Blackcomb Mountain, Whistler, BC V0N 1B0; 604-932-7052.

Heli-sports, from skiing untouched powder or blue glaciers to hiking spongy, moss-covered alpine fields, are currently all the rage in the high reaches of British Columbia. The helicopter ride to inaccessible areas is the highlight for many, while others appreciate the ease of having gear packed in for them. **Mountain Heli-Sports Inc.** can provide further details. ~ P.O. Box 460, Whistler, BC V0N 1B0; 604-932-2070, 800-661-6302.

With so many majestic ranges in the Northwest, *mountaineering* abounds. Rock and ice climbing are big draws in both the Cascades and Rocky Mountains. Climbers should be familiar with cold-weather survival techniques before tackling Northwest heights, which are tricky at best. For climbers' guidelines and further information, turn to the **Outdoor Recreation and Information Center**. ~ REI Building: 222 Yale Avenue North, Seattle, WA 98109; 206-470-4060. The **Outdoor Recreation Council of B.C.** also has information. ~ 1367 West Broadway, Vancouver, BC V6H 4A9; 604-737-3058. Mountaineering clubs like the **Mazamas** (909 Northwest 19th Avenue, Portland, OR 97209; 503-227-2345) and **Ptarmigans** (P.O. Box 1821, Vancouver, WA 98668) conduct classes and lead trips to Northwest peaks.

Mountain bike descents—racing down alpine slopes on two wheels—is a growing sport in resort areas of British Columbia. Participants usually take high-performance mountain bikes on the gondola to the heights, then follow experienced guides down mountain faces that are the winter domain of skiers. **Whistler Outdoor Experience** can tell you more. ~ P.O. Box 151, Whistler, BC V0N 1B0; 604-932-3389.

Rest assured: There are tamer outdoor adventures here. In fact, many swear that the best way to soak in the region's beauty is to travel slowly by bike or foot. Extensive guided *bicycling and walking tours* of the mountains, forests, coastline and islands last anywhere from two days to weeks. Top operators include **Backroads**. ~ 801 Cedar Street, Berkeley, CA 94710; 800-245-3874. The **Sierra Club** also leads tours. ~ Outing Department, 730 Polk Street, San Francisco, CA 94109; 415-977-5630.

In this realm of lakes, streams, rivers and ocean, it's no surprise that many of the top adventure sports are water-related. *Whitewater rafting* is one of the best-known adventure activities in the region, with challenging rapids on the Lewis, Snoqualmie and White rivers in Washington, the Rogue, Deschutes and McKenzie in Oregon and the Fraser and Green rivers in British Columbia. If you aren't acquainted with these rivers join a guided trip or chat with outfitters who know the treacherous spots to look out for. The **Northwest Rafter's Association** is a good source for further information. ~ P.O. Box 19008, Portland, OR 97219.

Kayaking and canoeing are also popular ways to shoot the rapids. Paddlers ready to take on the open ocean gain access to spectacular places like the various marine parks in British Columbia (Desolation Sound and the Pacific Rim National Park) and Washington (numerous protected islands among the San Juans). Other placid bodies of water suitable for kayak and canoe exploration include the Hood Canal in Washington, the Willamette and Columbia rivers in Oregon and the Powell River Canoe Route on British Columbia's Sunshine Coast. The folks at **Ebb & Flow Paddlesports Limited** can tell you more about the waters and area outfitters. ~ 0604 Southwest Nebraska Street, Portland, OR 97201; 503-245-1756.

Squeezed between the border of Washington and Oregon, the breezy Columbia Gorge is reputed to be the *windsurfing* capital of the continent, with championship competitions held annually. English Bay in Vancouver and Washington's San Juan Islands are also popular destinations for the sport, with numerous outfits set up to teach would-be windsurfers or just rent the sailboards and wetsuits. The **Columbia Gorge Windsurfing Association** has information. ~ P.O. Box 182, Hood River, OR 97031; 541-386-9225. The **United States Windsurfing Association** can put you in touch with top schools in the region. ~ P.O. Box 978, Hood River, OR 97031; 541-386-8708.

Scuba divers will probably want to bring their own gear, though rentals are generally available in all popular dive areas. Many places also rent tubes for river floats and sailboards for windsurfing. Fishing gear is often available for rent as well. Campers will need to bring their own basic equipment.

Don't forget your camera for capturing the Pacific Northwest's glorious scenery and a pair of binoculars for watching the abundant wildlife that live here. Pack an umbrella and raincoat, just in case.

LODGING

Lodging in the Northwest runs the gamut, from rustic cabins in the woods to sprawling resorts on the coastline. Chain motels line most major thoroughfares and mom-and-pop enterprises still vie successfully for lodgers in every region. Large hotels with names you'd know anywhere appear in most centers of any size.

Bed and breakfasts, small inns and cozy lodges where you can have breakfast with the handful of other guests are appearing throughout the region as these more personable forms of accommodation continue to grow in popularity. In fact, in areas like Ashland in southern Oregon and the San Juans in Washington, they are the norm rather than hotels and motels.

Whatever your preference and budget, you can probably find something to suit your taste with the help of the regional chapters in this book. Remember, rooms are scarce and prices rise in the high season, which is generally summer along the coastline and winter in the mountain ranges. Off-season rates are often drastically reduced in many places. Whatever you do, plan ahead and make reservations, especially in the prime tourist seasons.

Special museums and exhibits throughout the coastal zone attest to the importance of whales, dolphins and other marine animals in the region.

Accommodations in this book are organized by region and classified by price. Rates referred to are for two people during high season, so if you are looking for low-season bargains, it's good to inquire. *Budget* lodgings are generally less than $50 per night and are satisfactory and clean but modest. *Moderate*-priced lodgings run from $50 to $90; what they have to offer in the way of luxury will depend on where they are located, but they often offer larger rooms and more attractive surroundings. At a *deluxe* hotel or resort you can expect to spend between $90 and $130 for a homey bed and breakfast or a double; you'll usually find spacious rooms, a fashionable lobby, a restaurant and a group of shops. *Ultra-deluxe* properties, priced above $130, are a region's finest, offering all the amenities of a deluxe hotel plus plenty of extras.

Whether you crave a room facing the surf or one looking out on the ski slopes, be sure to specify when making reservations. If you are trying to save money, keep in mind that lodgings a block or so from the waterfront or a mile or so from the ski lift are going to offer lower rates than those right on top of the area's major attractions.

DINING

Seafood is a staple in the Pacific Northwest, especially along the coast where salmon is king. Whether it's poached in herbs or grilled on a stake Indian-style, plan to treat yourself to this regional specialty often. While each area has its own favorite dishes, its ethnic influences and gourmet spots, Northwest cuisine as a whole tends to be hearty and is often crafted around organically grown local produce.

Within a particular chapter, restaurants are categorized geographically, with each entry describing the type of cuisine, general decor and price range. Dinner entrées at *budget* restaurants usually cost under $8. The ambience is informal, service usually speedy and the crowd a local one. *Moderate*-priced restaurants range between $8 and $16 at dinner; surroundings are casual but pleasant, the menu offers more variety and the pace is usually slower. *Deluxe* establishments tab their entrées from $16 to $24; cuisines may be simple or sophisticated, depending on the location, but the decor is plusher and the service more personalized. *Ultra-deluxe* dining rooms, where entrées begin at $24, are often gourmet places where the cooking and service have become an art form.

Some restaurants change hands often while others are closed in low seasons. Efforts have been made to include in this book places with established reputations for good eating. Breakfast and lunch menus vary less in price from restaurant to restaurant than evening dinners. If you are dining on a budget and still hope to experience the best of the bunch, visit at lunch when portions and prices are reduced.

TRAVELING WITH CHILDREN

The Pacific Northwest is a wonderful place to bring the kids. Besides the many museums, boutiques and festivals, the region also has hundreds of beaches and parks, and many nature sanctuaries sponsor children's activities, especially during the summer months. A few guidelines will help make travel with children a pleasure.

Many Northwest bed and breakfasts do not accept children, so be sure of the policy when you make reservations. If you need a crib or cot, arrange for it ahead of time. A travel agent can be of help here, as well as with most other travel plans.

If you're traveling by air, try to reserve bulkhead seats where there is plenty of room. Take along extras you may need, such as diapers, changes of clothing, snacks, toys and books. When traveling by car, be sure to carry the extras, along with plenty of juice and water. And always allow extra time for getting places, especially on rural roads.

A first-aid kit is a must for any trip. Along with adhesive bandages, antiseptic cream and something to stop itching, include any medicines your pediatrician might recommend to treat allergies, colds, diarrhea or any chronic problems your child may have.

When spending time at the beach or on the snow, take extra care the first few days. Children's skin is especially sensitive to sun, and severe sunburn can happen before you realize it, even on overcast days. Hats for the kids are a good idea, along with liberal applications of sunblock. Be sure to keep a constant eye on children who are near the water or on the slopes, and never leave children unattended in a car on a hot day.

Even the smallest towns usually have stores that carry diapers, baby food, snacks and other essentials, but these may close early in the evening. Larger urban areas usually have all-night grocery or convenience stores that stock these necessities.

Many towns, parks and attractions offer special activities designed for children. Consult local newspapers and/or phone the numbers in this guide to see what's happening where you're going.

WOMEN TRAVELING ALONE

It is sad commentary on life in the United States, but women traveling alone must take precautions. It's entirely unwise to hitchhike and probably best to avoid inexpensive accommodations on the outskirts of town; the money saved does not outweigh the risk. Bed and breakfasts, youth hostels, college dorms and YWCAs are generally your safest bet for lodging.

If you are hassled or threatened in some way, never be afraid to scream for assistance. It's a good idea to carry change for a phone call and to know the number to call in case of emergency.

Women alone will usually feel much safer in British Columbia, especially in the well-populated areas. However, it's a good idea to remain cautious just the same.

GAY & LESBIAN TRAVELERS

Information hotlines and social and support groups for gay and lesbians exist in several of the Northwest's larger cities and towns. Information on gay services and events in the Seattle area can be obtained from the **Gay City Health Project**. ~ 206-860-6969. **The Gay and Lesbian Community Service Hotline** has tips on gay activities in Spokane. ~ 509-489-2266.

In Portland, there is the **Lesbian Community Project**. ~ 503-282-8090. Or try the **Asian/Pacific Islander Lesbian and Gay Organization**. ~ 503-232-6408.

AIDS Hotlines are in Seattle (541-205-7837), Spokane (509-326-6070), Portland (800-777-AIDS), Corvallis (541-752-6322) and Eugene (541-342-5088).

The Pacific Northwest is a hospitable place for senior citizens to visit, especially during the cool, sunny summer months that offer respite from hotter climes elsewhere in the country. Countless museums, historic sights and even restaurants and hotels offer senior discounts that can cut a substantial chunk off vacation costs. The national park system's Golden Age Passport, which must be applied for in person, allows free admission for anyone 62 and older to the many national parks and monuments in the region. They are available at any national park, ranger station or park office.

SENIOR TRAVELERS

The **American Association of Retired Persons** (AARP) offers membership to anyone age 50 or over. AARP's benefits include travel discounts with a number of firms and escorted tours with Gray Line buses. ~ 921 Southwest Morrison, Room 528, Portland, OR 97205, 503-227-5268; or 601 E Street Northwest, Washington DC 20049, 800-424-3410.

Elderhostel offers reasonably priced, all-inclusive educational programs in a variety of Pacific Northwest locations throughout the year. ~ 75 Federal Street, Boston, MA 02110; 617-426-7788.

Be extra careful about health matters. In addition to the medications you ordinarily use, it's a good idea to bring along the prescriptions for obtaining more. Consider carrying a medical record with you—including your medical history and current medical status, as well as your doctor's name, phone number and address. Make sure your insurance covers you while you are away from home.

Oregon, Washington and British Columbia are striving to make more destinations accessible for travelers with disabilities. For information on the areas you will be visiting, contact the **Independent Living Resources**. ~ 4506 Southeast Belmont Street, Portland, OR 97215; 503-232-7411; ask for Kathe Coleman.

DISABLED TRAVELERS

For more specific advice on traveling in the Pacific Northwest, turn to *B.C. Accommodations* from **Supernatural British Columbia.**, which lists many wheelchair-accessible lodgings in British Columbia. ~ 1117 Wharf Street, Victoria, BC V8W 9W5; 604-663-6000, 800-663-6000.

The **Society for the Advancement of Travel for the Handicapped** at 347 5th Avenue, Suite 610, New York, NY 10016 (212-447-7284), **Travel Information Service** (215-456-9600) and **Mobility International USA** at P.O. Box 10767, Eugene, OR 97440 (503-343-1284) offer general information.

Flying Wheels Travel is a travel agency specifically for disabled people. ~ 143 West Bridge Street, Owatonna, MN 55060; 800-535-6790. Also providing assistance is **Travelin' Talk**, a networking organization. ~ P.O. Box 3534, Clarksville, TN 37043; 615-552-6670.

FOREIGN TRAVELERS

Passports and Visas Most foreign visitors are required to obtain a passport and tourist visa to enter the United States. Contact your nearest United States Embassy or Consulate well in advance to obtain a visa and to check on any other entry requirements. Entry into Canada calls for a valid passport, visa or visitor permit for all foreign visitors except those from the United States who should carry some proof of citizenship (voter's registration or birth certificate), including two pieces with photo I.D. Officially, driver's licenses are no longer considered proof of citizenship, although they usually let you pass with one. Bring along a passport, voter registration or birth certificate just in case. The necessary forms may be obtained from your nearest Canadian Embassy, Consulate or High Commissioner.

Customs Requirements Foreign travelers are allowed to bring in the following: 200 cigarettes (1 carton), 50 cigars or 2 kilograms (4.4 pounds) of smoking tobacco; one liter of alcohol for personal use only (you must be at least 21 years of age to bring in alcohol); and US$100 worth of duty-free gifts that can include an additional quantity of 100 cigars. You may bring in any amount of currency (amounts over US$10,000 require a form). Americans who have been in Canada over 48 hours may take out $400 worth of duty-free items ($25 worth of duty-free for visits under 48 hours). Carry any prescription drugs in clearly marked containers; you may have to provide a written prescription or doctor's statement to clear customs. Meat or meat products, seeds, plants, fruits and narcotics are not allowed to be brought into the United States. The same applies to Canada, with the addition of firearms.

Driving If you plan to rent a car, an international driver's license should be obtained prior to arrival. United States driver's licenses are valid in Canada and vice versa. Some rental car companies require both a foreign license and an international driver's license along with a major credit card and require that the lessee be at least 25 years of age. Seat belts are mandatory for the driver and all passengers. Children under the age of 5 or 40 pounds should be in the back seat in approved child safety restraints.

Currency American and Canadian money are based on the dollar. Bills in the United States come in six denominations: $1, $5, $10, $20, $50 and $100. Every dollar is divided into 100 cents; in Canada the $1 coin is generally used. Coins are the penny (1 cent), nickel (5 cents), dime (10 cents) and quarter (25 cents). You may not use foreign currency to purchase goods and services in the United States and Canada. Consider buying traveler's checks in dollar amounts. You may also use credit cards affiliated with an American company such as Interbank, Barclay Card, VISA and American Express.

Electricity and Electronics Electric outlets use currents of 110 volts, 60 cycles. For appliances made for other electrical systems, you need a transformer or adapter. Travelers who use laptop computers for telecommunication should be aware that modem configurations for U.S. telephone systems may be different from their European counterparts. Similarly, the U.S. format for videotapes is different from that in Europe; U.S. Park Service visitors centers and other stores that sell souvenir videos often have them available in European format.

Weights and Measurements The United States uses the English system of weights and measures. American units and their metric equivalents are as follows: 1 inch = 2.5 centimeters; 1 foot = 0.3 meter; 1 yard = 0.9 meter; 1 mile = 1.6 kilometers; 1 ounce = 28 grams; 1 pound = 0.45 kilogram; 1 quart (liquid) = 0.9 liter. British Columbia now uses metric measurements.

Outdoor Adventures

CAMPING

Parks in the lush Pacific Northwest rank among the top in North America as far as attendance goes, so plan ahead if you hope to do any camping during the busy summer months. Late spring and early fall present fewer crowds to deal with and the weather is still fine.

Though much of Washington's scenic coastline is privately owned, there are a few scattered parks along the shore and even more situated inland in the mountains. It is possible to reserve campsites at several state parks from Memorial Day through Labor Day; contact the **State Parks and Recreation Commission** for details. ~ 7150 Cleanwater Lane, Olympia, WA 98504; 253-902-8563.

You'll find a multitude of marvelous campsites along Oregon's protected coast and in its green mountain ranges. Twenty-two of the 50 state parks with campgrounds are open year-round. Reservations are accepted at 16 parks and are essential if you hope to get a spot during July and August. The **Oregon Parks and Recreation Department** maintains a **Campsite Information Center** (800-551-6949) to provide updated campsite availability. ~ 1115 Commercial Street Northeast, Salem, OR 97310; 503-378-6305.

For information on camping in the various national parks and forests of Washington and Oregon, contact the **Outdoor Recreation Information Center**. ~ REI Building, 222 Yale Avenue North, Seattle, WA 98174; 206-477-4060.

Many of British Columbia's prime wilderness areas, both marine and interior, are protected as provincial parks. Except for those that are day-use only areas, most parks are set up with some sort of camping facilities, from primitive sites with pit toilets to pull-through recreational vehicle pads (with nearby sani-stations but no electrical, water or sewage hook-ups). There is a minimal fee for use of the campsites available on a first-come, first-served basis year-round. For further information, contact **Ministry of Parks**. ~ 1610 Mount Seymour Road, North Vancouver, BC V7G

1L3; 604-924-2200. Or try the **Outdoor Recreation Council of B.C.** ~ 1367 West Broadway, Vancouver, BC V6H 4A9; 604-737-3058.

For information on camping at the Pacific Rim National Park on Vancouver Island's western shore and other national parks in British Columbia, contact **Parks Canada West Region.** ~ 220 4th Avenue Southeast, Calgary, Alberta T2G 4X3; 403-292-4401.

PERMITS

Wilderness camping is not permitted in the state parks of Oregon and Washington, but there are primitive sites available in most parks. Permits are required for wilderness camping in parts of the Alpine Lakes wilderness area of the Mt. Baker–Snoqualmie and Wenatchee national forests in Washington and in the Mt. Jefferson, Mt. Washington and Three Sisters wilderness areas of Oregon between May 24 and October 31; permits are available at the ranger stations. Campers should check with all other parks individually to see if permits are required.

Follow low-impact camping practices in wilderness areas; "leave only footprints, take only pictures." When backpacking and hiking, stick to marked trails or tread lightly in areas where no trail exists. Be prepared with map and compass since signs are limited to directional information and don't include mileage. Some guidelines on wilderness camping are available from the **Outdoor Recreation Information Center.** ~ REI Building, 222 Yale Avenue North, Seattle, WA 98174; 206-470-4060. In British Columbia, wilderness camping is allowed in Garibaldi, Manning, Strathcona and Cape Scott provincial parks. No permit is required, but it's always best to check in with a ranger station to let someone know your plan before heading into the backcountry. A new BC Parks regulation states that wilderness camping is now permitted in any large provincial park provided that it is done one kilometer inland from any roadway and that campers leave no trace of their overnight stay. Contact the **Ministry of Parks** for further details. ~ 1610 Mount Seymour Road, North Vancouver, BC V7G 1L3; 604-924-2200.

Wilderness camping is also permitted in British Columbia's national parks. Write to the **Canadian Parks Service** for more information. ~ Western Region, #220 4th Avenue Southeast, P.O. Box 2989, Stations M, Calgary, Alberta T2P 3H8.

BOATING

With miles of coastline and island-dotted straits to explore, it's no wonder that boating is one of the most popular activities in the Northwest. Many of the best attractions in the region, including numerous pristine marine parks, are accessible only by water and have facilities set aside for boaters.

Write or call the **State Parks and Recreation Commission** for a boater's guide to Washington. ~ 7150 Cleanwater Lane, KY-11,

Olympia, WA 98504; 800-233-0321. The **Oregon State Marine Board** will furnish information on boating statewide. ~ 435 Commercial Street Northeast, Salem, OR 97301; 503-378-8587.

Boaters heading into B.C. waters from the U.S. must clear customs at the first available port of entry; **Canada Customs** can provide more information on specific policies. ~ 604-666-0545.

There are several waterways suitable for extended canoeing and kayaking trips. The **American Canoe Association** can provide more information. ~ 7432 Alban Station Boulevard, Suite B226, Springfield, VA 22150; 703-451-0141.

Whitewater rafting is particularly popular, especially on the Rogue and Deschutes in Oregon and the Fraser River in British Columbia where you will find outfitters renting equipment and running tours throughout the summer months. The *White Water River Book* (Pacific Research, 1982) is a good guide to techniques, equipment and safety.

WATER SAFETY

The watery region of the Pacific Northwest offers an incredible array of water sports to choose from, be it on the ocean, a quiet lake or stream or tumbling rapids. Swimming, diving, walking the shore in search of clams or just basking in the sun are options when you get to the shore, lake or river. Shallow lakes, rivers and bays tend to be the most populated spots since they warm up during the height of summer; otherwise, the waters of the Northwest are generally chilly. Whenever you swim, never do so alone, and never take your eyes off of children in or near the water.

FISHING

With its multitude of rivers, streams, lakes and miles of protected coastline, the Pacific Northwest affords some of the best fishing in the world. The waters of British Columbia alone hold 74 known

CRUISIN' THROUGH THE PACIFIC NORTHWEST

Nautical adventurers can embark on two week-long cruises through the Northwest offered by **Alaska Sightseeing Cruise West**. The Columbia and Snake Rivers voyage traces Lewis and Clark's search for the Northwest Passage. Departing from Portland, destinations on this scenic, wildlife-infused journey include Hells Canyon in Idaho, Washington's wine country and Hood River. The Canada's Inside Passage cruise follows Captain George Vancouver's expedition along the shore of the Pacific Northwest, taking in the fjords along the British Columbia coast, the towering granite mountains surrounding Princess Louisa Inlet, and the sights and sounds of Victoria and Vancouver. ~ 4th and Battery Building, Suite 700, Seattle, WA 98121; 800-426-7702, fax 206-441-4757.

species, 25 of those sportfish. Salmon is the main draw, but each area features special treats for the fishing enthusiast that are described in the individual chapters of *Hidden Pacific Northwest*.

Fees and regulations vary, but licenses are required for salt- and freshwater fishing throughout the region and can be purchased at sporting-goods stores, bait-and-tackle shops and fishing lodges. You can also find leads on guides and charter services in these locations if you are interested in trying a kind of fishing that's new to you. Charter fishing is the most expensive way to go out to sea; party boats take a crowd but are less expensive and usually great fun. On rivers, lakes and streams, guides can show you the best place to throw a hook or skim a fly. Whatever your pleasure, in saltwater or fresh, a good guide will save you time and grief and will increase the likelihood of a full string or a handsome trophy.

For further information on fishing in Washington concerning shellfish, bottom fish, salmon, freshwater and saltwater sportfish, contact the **Washington State Department of Wildlife**. ~ 600 North Capitol Way, Olympia, WA 98501-1091; 206-753-5700.

The **Oregon Department of Fish and Wildlife** can supply information on fishing in the state. ~ P.O. Box 59, Portland, OR 97207; 503-872-5268.

For updated details and regulations for freshwater fishing in British Columbia, contact the **Fisheries Branch**. ~ Ministry of Environment, 780 Blanshard Street, Victoria, BC V8V 1X4; 250-387-4573. Try the **Recreational Fisheries Division** for saltwater fishing. ~ Department of Fisheries and Oceans, 555 West Hastings Street, Vancouver, BC V6B 5G3; 604-666-6331.

SKIING

As winter blankets the major mountain ranges of the Pacific Northwest, ski season heats up at numerous resorts. Ski enthusiasts head for Mt. Adams, Mt. Rainier and Mt. Baker in Washington, Mt. Hood, Mt. Bachelor and Mt. Ashland in Oregon and Mt. Seymour, Grouse Mountain and the Whistler/Blackcomb mountains in southwestern British Columbia. Specifics on the top resorts are listed in each regional chapter.

For additional information on skiing in Washington and Oregon, contact the **Pacific Northwest Ski Area Association**. ~ P.O. Box 2325, Seattle, WA 98111; 206-623-3777. For information on skiing in British Columbia, obtain a copy of *Ski With Us!* from **Supernatural British Columbia**. ~ 800-663-6000.

TWO

Seattle and
Southern Puget Sound

Rain city? Not today. Last night's storm has washed the air clean, swept away yesterday's curtain of clouds to reveal Mt. Rainier in all its astonishing glory. From your hotel room window you can see the Olympics rising like snow-tipped daggers beyond the blue gulf of Puget Sound. Below, downtown Seattle awakens to sunshine, espresso and the promise of a day brimming with discovery for the fortunate traveler.

The lesson here is twofold: Don't be daunted by Seattle's reputation for nasty weather, and don't limit yourself to anticipating its natural setting and magnificent greenery, awesome as they may be. For this jewel surrounded by water, earning it the nickname "The Emerald City," sparkles in ways too numerous to count after a decade or more of extraordinary growth.

Both greater Seattle and Southern Puget Sound, which we also explore in this chapter, have changed dramatically. The city, squeezed into a lean, hour-glass shape between Elliott Bay and Lake Washington, covers only 92 square miles, and its population is still under 600,000. But the greater metropolitan area, reaching from Everett to Tacoma and east to the Cascade foothills, now boasts some 2.6 million, and the entire Puget Sound basin claims perhaps three million of the state's nearly five million residents.

While most newcomers have settled in the suburbs, Seattle's soaring skyline downtown is the visual focus of a region on the move. No longer the sleepy sovereign of Puget Sound, Seattle today is clearly the most muscular of the Northwest's three largest cities. Its urban energy is admired even by those who bemoan Seattle's freeway congestion, suburban sprawl, crime and worrisome air and water pollution. Growth has been the engine of change, and although the pace has slowed in the '90s, the challenges posed by too rapid an expansion remain persistent topics of discussion.

Seattle offered no hint of its future prominence when pioneers began arriving on Elliott Bay some 140 years ago. Like other settlements around Puget Sound, Seattle survived by farming, fishing, shipbuilding, logging and coal mining. For decades the community hardly grew at all. One whimsical theory has it that because the frontier sawmill town offered a better array of brothels to the region's loggers, miners and fishermen, capital tended to flow into Seattle to fund later investment and expansion.

Whatever the reason, the city quickly rebuilt after the disastrous "Great Fire" of 1889. But it would be another eight years before the discovery of gold in Alaska put Seattle on the map. On July 17, 1897, the ship *Portland* steamed into Elliott Bay from Alaska, bearing its legendary "ton of gold" (actually, nearly two tons), triggering the Klondike Gold Rush. Seattle immediately emerged as chief outfitter to thousands of would-be miners heading north to the gold fields.

Today, Seattle remains tied to its traditions. It's so close to the sea that 20-pound salmon are still hooked in Elliott Bay, at the feet of those gleaming, new skyscrapers. It's so near its waterfront that the boom of ferry horns resonates among its buildings and the cries of gulls still pierce the rumble of traffic. But the city's (and the state's) economy has grown beyond the old resource-based industries. International trade, tourism, agriculture and software giants like Microsoft now lead the way. The spotlight has passed from building ships to building airplanes, from wood chips to microchips, from mining coal to cultivating the fertile fields of tourism.

In the process, one of the nation's most vibrant economies has emerged. You can see that energy in Seattle's highrises, feel it in the buoyant street scene fueled in part by locals' infatuation with espresso. And there is fresh energy beneath your very feet. A "new underground" of retail shops (as distinguished from the historic Pioneer Square Underground) is taking shape around the downtown Westlake stations in the Metro Transit Tunnel, opened in fall 1990.

Civic energy has produced a glorious art museum downtown, a small but lively "people place" in Westlake Park, a spacious convention center and additions to Freeway Park. Private enterprise has added hotels, office towers with grand lobbies brimming with public art, shopping arcades, restaurants, nightclubs and bistros.

During the late '80s, as locals struggled with construction chaos, Seattle's downtown briefly suffered the nickname "little Beirut." Thankfully, that disruption has passed. For now, downtown is relatively peaceful, accessible and rich in discoveries for visitors.

Historically, weather bureau statistics show that mid-July through mid-August brings the driest, sunniest, warmest weather—a sure bet for tourists, or so you'd suppose. But in the last decade or two, that midsummer guarantee all too often has been washed away by clouds or rain. What's the sun-seeking tourist to do?

Consider September. In recent years it has brought modestly reliable weather. Or, simply come prepared—spiritually and practically—for whatever mix of dreary and sublime days that fate delivers. An accepting attitude may be the best defense of all in a region once described in this way: "The mildest winter I ever spent was a summer on Puget Sound."

Have goofy weather, growth, gentrification of downtown neighborhoods and a tide of new immigrants eradicated the old Seattle? Not by a long shot. Pike Place Market's colorful maze is still there to beguile you. Ferry boats still glide like wedding cakes across a night-darkened Elliott Bay. The central waterfront is as clamorous, gritty and irresistible as ever. Pioneer Square and its catacomb-like under-

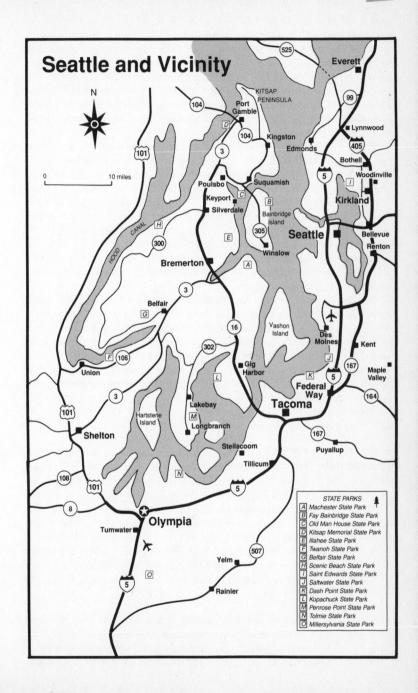

Seattle and Vicinity

N

0 ___ 10 miles

STATE PARKS

A	Machester State Park
B	Fay Bainbridge State Park
C	Old Man House State Park
D	Kitsap Memorial State Park
E	Illahee State Park
F	Twanoh State Park
G	Belfair State Park
H	Scenic Beach State Park
I	Saint Edwards State Park
J	Saltwater State Park
K	Dash Point State Park
L	Kopachuck State Park
M	Penrose Point State Park
N	Tolmie State Park
O	Millersylvania State Park

ground still beckons. The soul of the city somehow endures even as the changes wrought by regional growth accumulate.

It is indeed the changing geography of the wider Puget Sound region that may appear more striking. What nature created here, partly by the grinding and gouging of massive lowland glaciers, is a complex mosaic. From the air, arriving visitors see a green-blue tapestry of meandering river valleys weaving between forested ridges, the rolling uplands dotted by lakes giving way to Cascade foothills and distant volcanoes, the intricate maze-way of Southern Puget Sound's island-studded inland sea.

From on high it seems almost pristine, but a closer look reveals a sobering overlay of manmade changes. Even as Seattle's downtown becomes "Manhattanized," the region is being "Los Angelesized" with the birth of a freeway commuter culture stretching from Olympia on the south to Everett on the north and beyond Issaquah on the east. Some commuters arrive by ferry from Bainbridge Island to the west. Farmlands and wetlands, forests and meadows, are giving way to often poorly planned, hastily built housing tracts, roads and shopping centers.

For the traveler, such rapid growth means more traffic and longer lines for the ferry; more-crowded campgrounds, parks and public beaches; busier bikeways and foot trails; more folks fishing and boating and clam-digging. Downtown parking can be hard to find and expensive.

But despair not. The legendary Northwest may take a bit more effort to discover, but by almost any standard Seattle and its environs still offer an extraordinary blend of urban and outdoor pleasures close to hand. And growth seems only to have spurred a much richer cultural scene in Seattle—better restaurants serving original cuisines, more swank hotels, superb opera and a vital theater community, more art galleries and livelier shopping in a retail core sprinkled with public plazas that reach out to passersby with summer noon-hour concerts.

In this chapter we will point you to familiar landmarks, help you discover some "hidden" treasures and find the best of what's new downtown as we look at a region that reaches from Olympia to Everett, Bremerton to Issaquah.

▼▼▼▼▼▼▼▼▼▼▼▼▼▼
Downtown Seattle

Flying in to Seattle, the central part of this lush region looks irresistible. From the air you'll be captivated by deep bays, harbors, gleaming skyscrapers, parks stretching for miles and hillside neighborhoods where waterskiing begins from the backyard. Central Seattle's neighborhoods offer a seemingly inexhaustible array of possibilities from the International District to Lake Union and the waterfront to Capitol Hill. Eminently walkable, this area can also be explored by monorail, boat and bike. From the lofty heights of the Space Needle to the city's underground tour this is one of the Northwest's best bets.

SIGHTS   Downtown Seattle (Pioneer Square to Seattle Center, the waterfront to Route 5) is compact enough for walkers to tour on foot. Energetic folks can see the highlights on one grand loop tour, or you can sample smaller chunks on successive days. Since downtown is spread along a relatively narrow north–south axis, you can walk from one end to the other, then return by public transit via buses in the new Metro Transit Tunnel or aboard the Waterfront Streetcar trolleys, each of which have stations in both Pioneer Square and the International District. The Alweg Monorail also runs north–south between Westlake Center and Seattle Center.

A good place to orient yourself is the **Seattle-King County Tourism Development Office**. ~ Level 1, Galleria, 800 Convention Place; 206-461-5840.

Pioneer Square and its "old underground" remain one of Seattle's major fascinations. It was at this location that Seattle's first business district began. In 1889, a fire burned the woodframe city to the ground. The story of how the city rebuilt out of the ashes of the Great Fire remains intriguing to visitors and locals alike.

To learn exactly how the underground was created after the new city arose, then was forgotten, then rediscovered, you really need to take the one-and-a-half-hour **Underground Tour**. Several of these subterranean pilgrimages are offered daily to the dark and cobwebby bowels of the underground—actually the street-level floors of buildings that were sealed off and fell into disuse when streets and sidewalks were elevated shortly after Pioneer Square was rebuilt (in fire-resistant brick instead of wood). Admission (reservations recommended). ~ Tour leaves from Doc Maynard's Tavern, 610 1st Avenue; 206-682-4646, 888-608-6337.

Above ground, in the sunshine and fresh air, you can stroll through 88 acres of mostly century-old architecture in the historic district (maps and directories to district businesses are available in most shops). Notable architecture includes gems like the **Grand Central Building**, 1st Avenue South and South Main Street, **Merrill Place**, 1st Avenue South and South Jackson Street, the **Maynard Building**, 1st Avenue South and South Washington Street, the cast-iron **Pergola** in Pioneer Square Park and facing buildings such as the **Mutual Life and Pioneer buildings**, 1st Avenue and Yesler Way.

✔ **CHECK THESE OUT—UNIQUE SIGHTS**

- Explore the **International District**, a polyglot community comprised of immigrants and businesses from many Asian countries. *page 36*
- Join the throng shopping for bargains and fresh seafood at **Pike Place Market**. *page 39*
- Take the elevator on a sunny day to the top of the **Space Needle** for an unsurpassed view of Seattle and Puget Sound. *page 51*
- Spend the day strolling through the many delights of **Washington Park**, including the arboretum and Japanese Garden. *page 58*

More than 30 art galleries are located in the Pioneer Square area. Here you can shop for American Indian art, handicrafts, paintings and pottery.

Yesler Way, located in the heart of the Pioneer Square area, itself originated as the steep "Skid Road" for logs cut on the hillsides above the harbor and bound for Henry Yesler's waterfront mill, and thence to growing cities like San Francisco. Later, as the district declined, Yesler Way attracted a variety of derelicts and became the prototype for every big city's bowery, alias "skid row."

The new city boomed during the Alaska Gold Rush. For a look back at those extraordinary times, stop by the Seattle office of the **Klondike Gold Rush National Historical Park**, where you can see gold-panning demonstrations, a collection of artifacts, films and other memorabilia. ~ 117 South Main Street near Occidental Park; 206-553-7220.

The main pedestrian artery is **Occidental Mall and Park**, a tree-lined, cobbled promenade running south from Yesler Way to South Jackson Street allowing pleasant ambling between rows of shops and galleries (don't miss the oasis of **Waterfall Park** off Occidental on South Main Street).

For an overview of the whole district, ride the rattling old manually operated elevator to the observation level of the 42-story **Smith Tower**, built in 1914. ~ 2nd Avenue and Yesler Way.

Sharp ethnic diversity has always marked the **International District**, next door to Pioneer Square to the southeast. The polyglot community that emerged on the southern fringes of old Seattle always mixed its Asian cultures and continues doing so today, setting it apart from the homogeneous Chinatowns of San Francisco and Vancouver, across the border in British Columbia. ~ South Main to South Weller streets, 5th to 8th avenues South.

Chinese began settling here in the 1880s, Japanese around 1900, and today the "I.D." as it's commonly known is also home to Koreans, Filipinos, Vietnamese and Cambodians. For all its diversity, the district clearly lacks the economic vitality, bustling street life and polished tourist appeal of other major Chinatowns. Yet some find the International District all the more genuine for its unhurried, even seedy, ambience.

A variety of mom-and-pop enterprises predominates here—specialty-food and grocery stores, herbal-medicine shops, dim sum palaces and fortune-cookie factories. You're welcome to poke in for a look at how cookies, noodles, egg rolls and won ton wrappers are made at the **Tsue Chong Company**. Closed Sunday. ~ 801 South King Street; 206-623-0801.

To see a variety of ethnic foodstuffs, drop by **City Produce**, a wholesale vegetable market with retail sales. Closed Sunday. ~ 710 7th Avenue South, at South Lane Street; 206-682-0320.

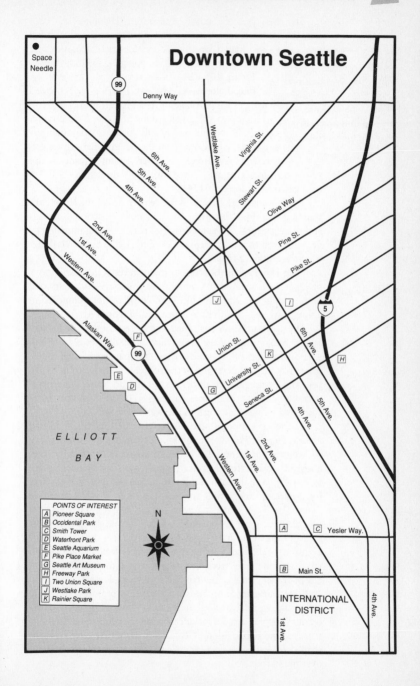

Downtown Seattle

Space Needle

Denny Way

6th Ave.

5th Ave.

4th Ave.

2nd Ave.

1st Ave.

Western Ave.

Westlake Ave.

Virginia St.

Stewart St.

Olive Way

Pine St.

Pike St.

J

I

F

99

E

D

Alaskan Way

6th Ave.

5th Ave.

4th Ave.

2nd Ave.

1st Ave.

Western Ave.

Union St.

University St.

Seneca St.

K

G

H

ELLIOTT

BAY

POINTS OF INTEREST
A	Pioneer Square
B	Occidental Park
C	Smith Tower
D	Waterfront Park
E	Seattle Aquarium
F	Pike Place Market
G	Seattle Art Museum
H	Freeway Park
I	Two Union Square
J	Westlake Park
K	Rainier Square

N

A   C   Yesler Way.

B   Main St.

INTERNATIONAL
DISTRICT

1st Ave.

4th Ave.

The district's single major retail store is **Uwajimaya**; it's not only the largest Japanese department store in the Northwest but also a worthwhile experience of Asian culture even if you're not shopping. ~ 519 6th Avenue South; 206-624-6248.

Seattle was built on seven hills, though only six remain: the seventh hill, Denny, was scraped off and dumped into Puget Sound.

Wing Luke Asian Museum offers a well-rounded look at the Northwest's Asian Pacific history and culture, representing ten groups of Asian Pacific immigrants. Presentations include historical photography and social commentary on the Asian-American experience. You may also see paintings, ceramics, prints, sculpture and other art. Closed Monday. Admission. ~ 407 7th Avenue South; 206-623-5124.

The **Nippon Kan Theater** is the centerpiece of the **Kobe Park Building National Historical Site** and hosts occasional dramas and other cultural presentations. The park and community gardens adjacent to it offer pleasant strolling. ~ 628 South Washington Street; 206-224-0181.

Hing Hay Park is the scene of frequent festivals—exhibitions of Japanese martial arts, Chinese folk dances, Vietnamese food fairs, Korean music and the like. Its colorful pavilion comes from Taipei, Taiwan. ~ South King Street and Maynard Avenue South.

The old **waterfront** beginning at the western edge of Pioneer Square remains one of the most colorful quarters of the city and what many consider Seattle's liveliest "people place." The waterfront grows more interesting by the year, a beguiling jumble of fish bars and excursion-boat docks, ferries and fireboats, import emporiums and nautical shops, sway-backed old piers and barnacle-encrusted pilings that creak in the wash of wakes.

The action's concentrated between Piers 48 and 60, and again around Pier 70. Poking around by foot remains the favorite way to explore, but some folks prefer to hopscotch to specific sites aboard the **Waterfront Streetcar**, which runs from Pioneer Square to Pier 70 (you also can climb into a horse-drawn carriage here for a narrated tour). Still another way to do it is via boat (see "Hey! The Water's Fine" at the end of this chapter). Here's a sampler of attractions: As you stroll south to north, you'll encounter a harbor-watch facility, a dozen historical plaques that trace major events, a public boat landing, the state-ferry terminal at Colman Dock and the waterfront fire station whose fireboats occasionally put on impressive, fountainlike displays on summer weekends. Ye Olde Curiosity Shop houses a collection of odd goods from around the world, Ivar's is the city's most famous fish bar, and cavernous shopping arcades include pier-end restaurants, outdoor picnic areas and public fishing. **Central Waterfront Park** is a crescent-shaped retreat from commercialism presenting sweeping views over the harbor.

The **Seattle Aquarium** allows you to descend to an underwater viewing dome for up-close looks at scores of Puget Sound fish. Admission. ~ Pier 59 at Pike Street; 206-386-4320.

Next to the aquarium is the **Omnidome Theater**. This highly recommended program features the 1980 Mt. St. Helens eruption and an overview of the resulting devastation. Admission. ~ Pier 59; 206-622-1868.

Across Alaskan Way is the 155-step Pike Hillclimb leading past cliff-side shops up to Pike Place Market. If that sounds too daunting, there is also an elevator. You'll also pass some piers whose sheds have been leveled to provide public access, the last vestiges of working waterfront on the central harbor—fish-company docks and such—as well as the Port of Seattle headquarters.

The venerable market, born in 1907, has proved itself one of the city's renewable treasures. Saved from the wrecking ball by citizen action in the early '70s, the market was later revitalized through long-term renovation. Today, the nine-acre **Pike Place Market National Historic District** and the surrounding neighborhood are in many respects better than ever. The main historic market now offers 400 different products in 40 categories, some 600 businesses, about 120 farmers, 200 craftspeople and a good 50 restaurants and eateries. In all, a market experience unparalleled in the nation! To learn more, call for more information or stop at the Info Booth at 1st Avenue and Pike Street. ~ Virginia Street to just south of Pike Street, 1st to Western avenues; 206-682-7453.

There are so many ways to enjoy the market that we can scarcely begin to list them. Come early for breakfast and wake up with the market (at least a dozen cafés open early). Come at noon for the ultimate experience of marketplace clamor amid legions of jostling shoppers, vendors hawking salmon and truck-farm produce, and street musicians vying for your contributions. Come to explore the market's lower level, often missed by tourists, a warrenlike collection of secondhand treasures, old books, magazines, posters and vintage clothing. Come to shop for the largest collection of handmade merchandise in the Northwest on handcraft tables at the market's north end. Come to browse all the "nonproduce" merchandise surrounding the main market—wines, exotic imported foods, French kitchenware, jewelry and avant-garde fashions.

One of the most valuable Pacific Northwest museums of the '90s is the **Seattle Art Museum** south of Pike Place Market, designed by the husband/wife architectural team of Robert Venturi and Denise Scott. The five-story, limestone-faced building highlighted with terra-cotta and marble has quickly become a regional, Post-modern landmark. You'll enter the museum via a grand staircase, but to see the collections, you'll have to ascend by elevator to the galleries. Known for its Northwest Coast American Indian, Asian and African art, the museum also features Meso-American, modern and contemporary art, photography and European masters. Do not miss the superb collection of African masks. Admission. ~ 100 University Street; 206-654-3100.

Opened in 1998 across the street from the Seattle Art Museum, the Seattle Symphony's massive $118 million **Benaroya Hall** gives the symphony its own dedicated concert facility after years of sharing space at Seattle Center with the opera and ballet. The grounds include a memorial garden dedicated to Washington residents who died in military conflicts. ~ 2nd Avenue and University Street; 206-215-4700.

City center, or **Downtown**, has undergone a remarkable rejuvenation. It's a delightful place to stroll whether you're intent on shopping or not. Major downtown hotels are clustered in the retail core, allowing easy walks in any direction. Here's one way to sightsee:

Start at the south end of **Freeway Park**. The park's many waterfalls and pools create a splashy, burbling sound barrier to city noise. Beds of summer-blooming flowers, tall evergreens and leafy deciduous trees create a genuine park feeling, inspiring picnics by office workers on their noon-hour break. Amble north through the park, and take a short detour beneath a street overpass toward University Street (steps next to more waterfalls zigzag up to Capitol Hill and dramatic views of city architecture). ~ 6th Avenue and Seneca Street.

Continue north as the park merges with similarly landscaped grounds of the **Washington State Convention and Trade Center**, which offers occasional exhibits. Maps and information are offered at the Tourist Information Center (206-461-5840) located below the Convention Center. ~ 800 Convention Place; 206-447-5000.

Head west through linking landscaping that leads you past yet more waterfalls and flowers in the main plaza of **Two Union Square**. Cross 6th Avenue and enter **Pacific First Center** on the corner of Union Street. This handsome building's lower levels are lined with upscale shops and a theater complex, bold sculptures and stunning exhibits of colorful art glass. Wander and admire for a bit, stop for a meal or an espresso, then continue by leaving the building at the 5th Avenue and Pike Street exit. Cross 5th Avenue past the striking Coliseum Theater to Nordstrom. Head west on Pike Street to 4th Avenue and turn right, shortly entering triangular **Westlake Park** at 4th Avenue and Pine Street, which offers a "water wall" against street noise, a leafy copse of trees and an intriguing pattern of bricks that replicate a Salish Indian basket-weave design best observed from the terraces on the adjoining Westlake Center.

Westlake Center is an enormously popular, multilevel shopping arcade, a people place offering cafés and espresso bars, a brew pub, flower vendors, handicrafts and access to what's been heralded as downtown's "new underground." The marbled, well-lighted, below-street-level arcades were created as part of the city's new downtown transit tunnel. Metro buses (propelled electrically while underground) rumble by on the lowest level. Just above it are mezzanines full of public art, with vendors and shops, and underground access to a string of department stores.

Walk south on 4th Avenue a few blocks to **Rainier Square**, between 4th and 5th avenues and University and Union streets, and discover another burgeoning underground of upscale enterprises. Follow its passageways eastward past a bakery, restaurants and access to the venerable **Fifth Avenue Theater**. Continue east, up an escalator back to Two Union Square and Freeway Park.

Lodgings vary widely in style and price throughout the Seattle area. Downtown, there's a thick cluster of expensive luxury hotels interspersed with a few at moderate and even budget rates.

LODGING

The **Alexis Hotel** is an elegant little haven two blocks from the waterfront and close to downtown stores and business centers. The 109 rooms have soft colors and contemporary furnishings mixed with a few antiques, all done in good taste. Some of the roomy suites have fireplaces. The service is unmatched in this renovated historic hotel. ~ 1007 1st Avenue; 206-624-4844, 800-426-7033, fax 206-621-9009. ULTRA-DELUXE.

As its name implies, the **Pioneer Square Hotel** is remarkably convenient to Seattle's famed historic district. But location is not the only advantage; the restored turn-of-the-century property offers clean, comfortable, spacious rooms with period furniture, sitting nooks, and blessedly sturdy construction that keeps down the noise common in modern hotels. By downtown standards, the rates are quite reasonable. The Kingdome, ferry terminal and many other attractions are within a few blocks. ~ 77 Yesler Way; 206-340-1234, fax 206-467-0707. MODERATE.

◄ *HIDDEN*

Seattle has only one place to stay that is directly on the waterfront: the **Edgewater Inn**. It began as a top-flight hotel on Pier 67, built in the 1960s for the World's Fair. It later slid into decay and was renovated in 1989 in "mountain lodge" style—meaning plaid comforters and natural-log furniture in the rooms and an antler chandelier in the lobby. Half the 238 rooms and suites have stunning views of Elliott Bay, West Seattle and the Olympic Peninsula. Rooms are comfortable, and the staff is accommodating. The restaurant has a fine water view. ~ 2411 Alaskan Way; 206-728-7000, 800-624-0670, fax 206-441-4119. ULTRA-DELUXE.

A retreat from the throngs in Pike Place Market is **Inn at the Market**. The hotel, several shops and a restaurant are centered by a brick courtyard with a 50-year-old cherry tree. Small (65 rooms), light and airy and furnished in French country style, the inn is one of Seattle's best. Rooms have views of the city, court-yard or water. ~ 86 Pine Street; 206-443-3600, 800-446-4484, fax 206-448-0631. ULTRA-DELUXE.

Pensione Nichols offers European-style lodging within a block of Pike Place Market. Ten rooms on the third floor of a historic building share four baths and a large common space with a stun-ning view of the bay, while two rooms share one bath on the sec-ond floor. The rooms are painted a cheerful yellow; some have windows, while others only have skylights. They are simply fur-nished with antiques. There are also two ultra-deluxe suites that sleep five and have fully equipped kitchens and private baths. A continental breakfast is served. ~ 1923 1st Avenue; 206-441-7125, 800-440-7125. MODERATE TO ULTRA-DELUXE.

The **Hostelling International—Seattle** is a low-priced estab-lishment on the edge of Pike Place Market. In addition to 197 sleeping units, the bright, clean hotel has a kitchen, dining room, lounge, television room and small library. Also available are bike storage and laundry facilities. ~ 84 Union Street; 206-622-5443, 800-622-5443, fax 206-682-2179. BUDGET.

HIDDEN ►

The new downtown location for **Green Tortoise Backpackers Guesthouse** is convenient to most central-Seattle attractions—among them Pike Place Market, just a block away. With func-tional private and dorm rooms, 24-hour check-in, a common room and a fully equipped kitchen, it's much like a hostel, with one extra advantage: a free breakfast. Many guest services, such as tours and discounts at local clubs, pubs and restaurants, add value as well. ~ 1525 2nd Avenue; 206-340-1222, fax 206-623-3207. BUDGET.

The **Four Seasons Olympic** is the place to stay for classic gran-deur and luxury. It offers spacious, well-furnished guest rooms with a subtle oriental flavor. There are three restaurants, a stately marble lobby, meeting rooms and myriad amenities. The Italian Renaissance–style hotel, built in 1924, stands in the heart of the downtown business district. ~ 411 University Street; 206-621-1700, 800-223-8772, fax 206-682-9633. ULTRA-DELUXE.

Considered a luxury hotel some 60 years ago, the **Pacific Plaza Hotel** is now a dignified, quiet downtown classic with 160 rooms. Though updated, it hasn't lost its old-fashioned flavor, with win-dows that open, ceiling fans and traditional furniture in rather small rooms. A continental breakfast and morning newspaper are provided in a lounge off the multitiered lobby. The concierge is very helpful. ~ 400 Spring Street; 206-623-3900, 800-426-1165, fax 206-623-2059. MODERATE TO DELUXE.

The **Seattle** YMCA, a member of the American Youth Hostels Association, offers straightforward, clean accommodations in the heart of downtown. Each of the 198 rooms is plainly furnished with a bed, phone, desk and lamp. Some rooms have TVs, some have private baths. Four people can sleep in each dorm unit. The hotel includes a pool and health club. ~ 909 4th Avenue; 206-382-5000, fax 206-382-7283. BUDGET.

The **West Coast Camlin Hotel**, on the edge of downtown and a block from the convention center, was built in 1926 and has been renovated in recent years. The 140-room hotel has a lovely lobby of marble with oriental carpets, a restaurant and lounge on the 11th floor and a conference room on the lobby level. Most of the oversized, classically furnished rooms have work areas, a popular feature for business travelers. ~ 1619 9th Avenue; 206-682-0100, 800-426-0670, fax 206-682-7415. DELUXE.

Between downtown and Seattle Center is **Sixth Avenue Inn**, a five-story motor inn with 166 rooms. The rooms, done in crisp blue and cream, are a cut above those in most motels. They contain blond furniture and assorted plants and books. Those on the north and in back are the quietest. There's a restaurant overlooking a small garden. ~ 2000 6th Avenue; 206-441-8300, 800-648-6440, fax 206-441-9903. DELUXE.

The **Inn at Virginia Mason** is an attractive, nine-story brick building owned by the medical center next door. On the eastern edge of downtown, it caters to hospital visitors and others looking for a convenient location and pleasant accommodations at reasonable prices. The 79 rooms have been recently remodeled with dark-wood furnishings and teal and gray decor. Two suites have a fireplace and whirlpool tub. There's a small restaurant by a brick terrace. ~ 1006 Spring Street; 206-583-6453, 800-283-6453, fax 206-223-7545. DELUXE.

The **Sorrento Hotel** is known for its personal service and attention to detail. A historic building that has been remodeled,

----

✔ CHECK THESE OUT—UNIQUE LODGING

- *Budget:* Enjoy 24-hour check-in, a free breakfast and discounts at restaurants when you stay at the hostel-like **Green Tortoise Backpackers Guesthouse**. *page 42*
- *Moderate:* Tuck yourself in at an old-style beach house in the nautical village of Gig Harbor at **No Cabbages Bed and Breakfast**. *page 86*
- *Deluxe to ultra-deluxe:* It's walking distance to downtown Seattle from the **Capitol Hill Inn**, a beautifully refurbished 1903 Queen Anne home. *page 54*
- *Ultra-deluxe:* Ascend to a romantic room at the hilltop **Sorrento Hotel**, famous for its attention to your every need. *page 43*

Budget: under $50 Moderate: $50–$90 Deluxe: $90–$130 Ultra-deluxe: over $130

Sorrento is on a hilltop a few blocks above the downtown area. Beyond the quiet, plush lobby are a notable restaurant and an inviting lounge. The Sorrento has been called one of the most romantic hotels in Seattle. All 76 rooms and suites have a warm, traditional, European atmosphere. ~ 900 Madison Street; 206-622-6400, 800-426-1265, fax 206-343-6155. ULTRA-DELUXE.

On a grassy hill in West Seattle, facing east toward Elliott Bay and downtown, is **Hainsworth House**. The impressive, Tudor-style home was built in 1906 and restored in the mid-1980s. It contains antiques, Persian rugs and lots of polished woodwork, but the atmosphere is unassuming. Guests make popcorn in the kitchen, play with the dogs and ask for scrambled tofu for breakfast if they don't want eggs. There are two well-furnished rooms upstairs; both have decks, one has a fireplace and a grand view. ~ 2657 37th Avenue Southwest; 206-938-1020. MODERATE TO DELUXE.

DINING

The fine **al Boccalino** serves some of the city's best Italian dinners. Located in a brick building near Pioneer Square, the restaurant's atmosphere is unpretentious and intimate, the antipasto imaginative, the entrées cooked and sauced to perfection. Saddle of lamb with brandy, tarragon and mustard is a favorite. There are daily specials for every course. ~ 1 Yesler Way; 206-622-7688. MODERATE TO DELUXE.

For a romantic dinner, try **Il Terrazzo Carmine** in the Merrill Place Building. For patio diners, a cascading reflecting pool drowns out some, but not all, of the freeway noise. Entrées include *zuppa di pesce napoletana* (spicy shellfish soup) or veal picatta with capers and lemon. The restaurant also features an extensive Italian wine list. ~ 411 1st Avenue South, Pioneer Square; 206-467-7797. MODERATE TO ULTRA-DELUXE.

White-linen tablecloths, black-rattan furnishings and loads of plants await you at the **Linyen**, an upscale Cantonese restaurant in the International District. In the foyer, the specials such as hot and smokey crab in a spicy sauce, red-pepper beef, fresh fish with vegetables or clams in black-bean sauce are posted on the blackboard. ~ 424 7th Avenue South; 206-622-8181. MODERATE.

Just a few blocks away is **Hanil**, located in the Bush Asia Center, up above a park. The interior of this Korean restaurant is filled with wood paneling, green plants and flowers. The restaurant serves great lunch specials in lovely lacquered boxes and classic Korean barbecue prepared on gas burners at your table. Barbecued chicken, pork or beef are excellent. ~ 409 Maynard Avenue South; 206-587-0464. BUDGET TO MODERATE.

For great Vietnamese food at low prices, try **Saigon Gourmet**. After the green oilcloths and the white-lace curtains, there's no decor to speak of—just hungry patrons eager for a dish of shrimp, Cambodian noodle soup or papaya with beef jerky. Shrimp rolls here are some of the best in town. Closed Sunday. ~ 502 South King Street; 206-624-2611. BUDGET TO MODERATE.

On the outskirts of the International District you'll find **Chau's Chinese Restaurant**, a small, unpretentious restaurant that offers great seafood such as Dungeness crab with ginger and onion, clams in hot garlic sauce, bird's-nest scallops and rock-cod fillets with corn sauce. Choose the fresh seafood entrées over the standard Cantonese entrées. ~ 310 4th Avenue South; 206-621-0006. MODERATE.

It's impossible not to get thoroughly filled at **Zaina**, a friendly, low-key Greek eatery in the midst of the lower downtown business district. The place is packed with office workers at lunch, but the crowd thins out after 1 p.m. The food is not only filling but flavorful. ~ 108 Cherry Street; 206-624-5687. BUDGET.

◀ HIDDEN

Hidden away is **Place Pigalle**. Wind your way past a seafood vendor and Rachel, the brass pig (a popular market mascot), to this restaurant with spectacular views of Elliott Bay. The dark-wood trim, handsome bar and other touches make for a European-bistro atmosphere. The restaurant makes the most of fresh ingredients from the market's produce tables. Dine on fresh Penn Cove mussels in balsamic vinaigrette, gingered calamari in cream or one of the daily fresh salmon specials. The dishes are artfully presented. Closed Sunday. ~ 81 Pike Street, in the Pike Place Market; 206-624-1756. DELUXE.

Ten times more specialty coffees are sold in Seattle than in other U.S. cities, and you'll find espresso stands on almost every corner.

Across the cobbled street, you can observe the eclectic mix of shoppers and artists in the Pike Place Market at **Three Girls Bakery**, a popular hangout. This tiny lunch counter and bakery with just a few seats serves good sandwiches—the meat-loaf sandwich is popular—and hearty soups, including chili and clam chowder. You have more than 50 kinds of bread to choose from. The sourdough and rye breads are recommended. If you don't have room for pastries, buy some to take home. You won't regret it. ~ 1514 Pike Place; 206-622-1045. BUDGET.

The food at **Oriental Mart** is a combination of Filipino and Central American—and it's very good and very inexpensive. Try the pork *adobo* if they have it that day; otherwise, any of the chicken preparations are excellent. There's no better place for lunch at the Market. The lunch counter is in back of the food-and-novelties store. ~ 1506 Pike Place Market; 206-622-8488. BUDGET.

◀ HIDDEN

In Post Alley, behind some of the market shops, you will find more than just a wee bit of Ireland at **Kells**. This traditional Irish pub will lure you to the Emerald Isle with pictures and posters of splendid countryside. A limited menu includes salmon with an Irish dill sauce, leg of lamb, Irish stew and meat pies. From the heavy, dark bar comes a host of domestic and imported beers. Irish music is piped in all the time, and live musicians play Irish tunes Wednesday through Saturday. ~ 1916 Post Alley; 206-728-1916. MODERATE.

HIDDEN ▶   Talk about hidden—this place doesn't even have a sign. You enter through the pink door off of Post Alley. **The Pink Door**, with its Italian kitsch decor, is lively and robust at lunchtime. Especially good are the *lasagna della porta rosa* and a delicious cioppino. In the evening, the pace slows, the light dims and it's a perfect setting for a romantic dinner. In the summer, rooftop dining offers views of the Sound. Closed Sunday and Monday. ~ 1919 Post Alley; 206-443-3241. MODERATE TO DELUXE.

Off a brick courtyard above Pike Place Market, **Campagne** is one of the city's top restaurants. Diners enjoy French country cooking in an atmosphere both warm and elegant. Entrées may include rack of lamb loin brushed with puréed anchovie and garlic sauce or roasted sea bass with tarragon, lemon and tiny herb dumplings. The simply prepared dishes are usually the best: young chicken stuffed with ricotta, spinach and roasted herbs and served with sage-infused jus and rosemary roasted potatoes, for example. ~ 86 Pine Street; 206-728-2800. ULTRA-DELUXE.

Every meal served at **El Puerco Lloron** includes wonderfully fresh tortillas, made by hand while hungry diners watch from the cafeteria line. The *chile rellenos* compares with the best, and the tamales and taquitos are all authentic and of good quality. There's a Mexican fiesta atmosphere in the warm, steamy room. ~ Pike Place Market Hillclimb, 1501 Western Avenue; 206-624-0541. BUDGET.

Tucked into a hillside in Pike Place Market, **Il Bistro** is a cozy cellar spot with wide archways and oriental rugs on wooden floors. Light jazz, candlelight and well-prepared Italian food make it an inviting spot on a rainy evening. Several pastas are served;

▸▸▸

✔ CHECK THESE OUT—UNIQUE DINING

- *Budget:* Feast on fresh fish just off the boat at **The New Day Seafood Eatery**, which overlooks Liberty Bay in Poulsbo. *page 72*
- *Moderate:* Begin a day trip to Vashon Island with brunch at the **Sound Food Restaurant**, an island hangout with a tempting bakery. *page 71*
- *Deluxe:* Overlook Elliott Bay from Pike Place Market as you dine on fresh Penn Cove mussels or gingered calamari at **Place Pigalle**. *page 45*
- *Deluxe to ultra-deluxe:* Savor dishes that are "globally influenced, regionally inspired" at the internationally acclaimed **Fullers**. *page 47*

the entrées include rack of lamb, veal scaloppine, fresh salmon and roasted half-chicken served with wild rice. Dinner only. ~ 93-A Pike Street; 206-682-3049. DELUXE TO ULTRA-DELUXE.

On the Pike Place Market hill, **Takara Restaurant and Sushi Bar** serves Japanese food in a casual atmosphere. Chicken and salmon teriyaki, fried flat noodles with vegetables and pork and sashimi on a bed of grated radish are a few of the delicately flavored dishes. ~ 1501 Western Avenue; 206-682-8609. BUDGET TO MODERATE.

Artists and others without a lot of money for eats hang out at the **Two-Bells Tavern** in Belltown. Local artwork on the walls changes every two months. This funky bar with 25 kinds of beer and a host of inexpensive good food is a busy place. You can always find good soups, sandwiches, burgers, salads and cold plates. Some favorites are the hot beer-sausage sandwich and an Italian-sausage soup. ~ 2313 4th Avenue; 206-441-3050. BUDGET.

A favorite among downtowners is the **Botticelli Café**. The small café is known for its *panini*—little sandwiches made of toasted focaccia bread and topped with olive oil, herbs, cheeses and vegetables. The espresso and ices are good, too. Closed Sunday. ~ 101 Stewart Street; 206-441-9235. BUDGET.

Contemporary, international cuisine prepared with imagination is served at the **Dahlia Lounge** near the shops of Westlake Center. Bright red walls and ceiling, a neon sign and paper-fish lampshades create a celebratory atmosphere. The chef draws upon numerous ethnic styles and uses Northwest products to develop such dishes as potstickers filled with lobster, shrimp and shiitake mushrooms served with sake sauce. ~ 1904 4th Avenue; 206-682-4142. DELUXE.

Original Northwest art hangs above the booths in **Fullers**, an internationally acclaimed restaurant in the Sheraton Seattle Hotel and Towers. The decor is plush and sophisticated and the cuisine still top quality. Chef Monique Barbeau calls her food "globally influenced, regionally inspired." Though the menu changes seasonally, examples may include sea scallops with ginger and risotto, or beef tenderloin served with an herbed bread pudding and truffled asparagus. Closed Sunday. ~ 1400 6th Avenue; 206-447-5544. DELUXE TO ULTRA-DELUXE.

Now at home in the Westin Hotel is **Nikko**, where there's a sushi and hibachi bar and private rooms for groups of six or more. Tempura, sukiyaki, sushi and sashimi are among the Japanese delicacies served. No lunch on Saturday. Closed Sunday. ~ 1900 5th Avenue; 206-322-4905. MODERATE TO ULTRA-DELUXE.

The decor is spare and clean in **Wild Ginger**, and the menu is Chinese and Southeast Asian. Dark-wood booths fill the big, open room; at one end is a satay bar where skewered chicken, beef, fish and vegetables are grilled, then served with peanut and other sauces. The wondrous Seven Elements Soup, an exotic blend of flavors, is a meal in itself. No lunch on Sunday. ~ 1400 Western Avenue; 206-623-4450. MODERATE TO DELUXE.

Spend a perfect summer day at Alki Beach in West Seattle, then take in dinner at the **Alki Bakery & Café**, where a well-rounded menu includes great salads (the wilted spinach and bacon is a favorite), seafood, meat, chicken and pasta dishes. Specials of the evening are listed in the two dining areas. Be sure to leave room for dessert—a lovely fruit torte or delicious cheesecake made in the bakery. Also a popular place for breakfast, the Bakery offers up hearty omelettes, french toast and a host of muffins and cinnamon rolls. Coffee, espressos and lattes are good, too. If you've overindulged, you can always take another stroll on the beach. ~ 2726 Alki Avenue Southwest; 206-935-0616. MODERATE.

SHOPPING   The oldest and loveliest structure in Pioneer Square is the Pioneer Building. Here is Seattle's first electric elevator, and the **Pioneer Square Mall** in the basement has over 10,000 square feet of space devoted to antiques and collectibles and maintained by some 80 dealers. ~ 602 1st Avenue; 206-624-1164.

Grand Central Arcade Building houses 17 shops. Visitors can also enjoy drinks and baked goods at lobby tables adjacent to a brick fireplace. ~ 214 1st Avenue South; 206-623-7417. **Millstream NW** sells Northwest sculpture, prints, pottery and jewelry by local artisans. ~ 112 1st Avenue South; 206-233-9719.

Since 1981, **The Prints and the Pauper** has been dealing in paintings and sculptured works produced by up-and-coming Northwest artists. Prices are reasonable, and you might get a masterpiece with a signature that one day will be highly valued. ~ 112 South Washington Street; 206-624-9336.

In the heart of the Pioneer Square district is the **Elliott Bay Book Company** featuring over 150,000 titles, including an outstanding stock of Northwest books. You're bound to enjoy browsing, snacking in the on-premises café or listening in on frequently scheduled readings by renowned authors. ~ 101 South Main Street; 206-624-6600.

Seattle's connection with the Pacific Rim is legendary, and **Uwajimaya** demonstrates the tie with shoji screens and lamps, kanji clocks and watches, lacquerware music boxes, goldimari ceramic pieces and Japanese, Chinese, Thai, Vietnamese, Filipino and American canned and frozen foods. ~ 519 6th Avenue South; 206-624-6248.

Known as an "Oriental Woolworth's," **Higo Variety Store** has all kinds of small toys, bowls and sundries in the five-and-dime category. Also on hand are some more expensive articles such as hapi coats, kimonos and obi sashes. ~ 604 South Jackson Street; 206-622-7572.

Along the waterfront, Piers 54 through 70 are shoppers' delights. You'll love **Ye Olde Curiosity Shop**, a Seattle landmark where the mummies "Sylvia" and "Sylvester" preside over souvenirs, American Indian totem poles and masks, Russian stacking dolls, lacquerware and Ukrainian eggs. ~ 1001 Alaskan Way, Pier 54; 206-682-5844.

Called the "Soul of Seattle," the **Pike Place Market** has been in business since 1907. Saved from the wrecking ball by citizen action in the early '70s, Pike Place is now a bustling bazaar with 600 businesses, 150 farmers (selling produce and flowers at tables and stalls) and 80 eateries. ~ 85 Pike Street; 206-682-7453.

> It costs less than a dollar to ride the Monorail, which zips between Seattle Center and Westlake Center in two minutes.

A notable establishment within the market is the **Pure Food Fish Market**, which ships fresh or smoked salmon worldwide. ~ 1511 Pike Place Market; 206-622-5765. Also here is **Hands of the World**, where the specialty is ethnic jewelry, masks and home accessories such as carved picture frames and folkloric art. ~ 1501 Pike Place Market; 206-622-1696.

In the downtown area, 5th Avenue, Seattle's fashion street, is lined with shops displaying elegant finery and accessories. **Rainier Square** at 1333 5th Avenue houses several prestigious retail establishments. **Totally Michael's** has contemporary, upscale clothing. ~ 521 Union Street; 206-622-4920. **Biagio** specializes in handsome leather goods—handbags, luggage, business and attaché cases. ~ 1405 4th Avenue; 206-623-3842.

At the **Westlake Center** pushcarts loaded with jewelry, scarves and other small trappings lend a European flavor to the 80 retail establishments here. **Fireworks Fine Crafts Gallery** (206-682-6462) takes its name from unusually fired sculptures. Also offered are a variety of intriguing home accessories and jewelry. ~ 4th Avenue and Pine Street. Located nearby, **Alhambra** deals in Middle Eastern bangles, pendants and other jewelry. ~ 101 Pine Street; 206-621-9571.

NIGHTLIFE

There are many fine nightclubs in Pioneer Square, and on "joint-cover" nights, one charge admits you to nine places within a four-block radius. Among them is **Doc Maynard's**, heavy on rock-and-roll. Cover. ~ 610 1st Avenue; 206-682-4646, 888-608-6337. The **New Orleans Creole Restaurant** offers jazz and blues nightly. Cover. ~ 114 1st Avenue South; 206-622-2563. Over at the **Bohemian Café** there's live blues and reggae Wednesday through Saturday. Cover. ~ 111 Yesler Way; 206-447-1514. And at **Comedy Underground at Swannies**, comics entertain nightly. Cover. ~ 222 South Main Street; 206-628-0303.

Along the waterfront you'll find rock aplenty at **Iguana Cantina at Pier 70**, where you can dance to DJ-spun Top-40 and disco tunes. Cover. ~ Foot of Broad Street and Alaskan Way; 206-728-7071.

Unexpected Productions offers comedy performances and workshops in improvisational theater techniques. ~ The Market Theater, 1428 Post Alley, Pike Place Market; 206-781-9273.

Belltown, near the Pike Place Market, has lots of activity after dark. **The Vogue** features modern dance music. Cover. ~ 2018 1st Avenue; 206-443-0673.

Showbox Variety and Supper Club features comedy and live music. Complete with Italian restaurant and full bar, the Showbox stays open until 4 a.m. from Wednesday to Sunday. Reservations are recommended. Cover. ~ 1426 1st Avenue; 206-628-3151.

Crocodile Café, one of Seattle's legendary spawning grounds for grunge and punk bands, attracts a young crowd for live music. Cover. ~ 2200 2nd Avenue; 206-441-5611.

The **Seattle Symphony's** large, new performance space, Bena-roya Hall, has enabled it to vastly expand its schedule and reper-toire. Noted especially for its attention to American composers under the direction of Gerard Schwarz, the symphony is one of the top recording orchestras in the United States and is renowned for its excellence. ~ 2nd Avenue and University Street; informa-tion: 206-215-4700, tickets: 206-215-4747.

Dimitriou's Jazz Alley is a downtown dinner theater and pre-mier jazz club with international acts. Cover. ~ 6th Avenue and Lenora Street; 206-441-9729.

For satirical/comical revues try the **Cabaret de Paris**. Cover. ~ Rainier Square, 1333 5th Avenue; 206-623-4111.

The renovated **Paramount Theatre**, the elaborate movie pal-ace of the 1920s, now offers Broadway shows and musicals. ~ 9th Avenue and Pine Street; 206-682-1414.

Video games, beer and pub food—sounds like a classic video arcade. But **Gameworks** is much more than that. With the latest in electronic games, Internet access, virtual-reality games and ad-ventures, this has become the highly successful (and highly pub-licized) prototype for what may become a national chain. ~ 1511 7th Avenue; 206-521-0952.

Timberline draws a largely gay crowd, with everyone enjoy-ing country-and-western dancing. Lessons available; cover on the weekends. Closed Monday. ~ 2015 Boren Avenue; 206-622-6220.

▼▼▼▼▼▼▼▼▼▼▼▼▼

Seattle Center–
Queen Anne Area

Northwest of downtown a familiar landmark rises skyward—the Space Needle. This symbol of the city nestles comfortably among museums, cultural centers and a sports arena at the Seattle Center. Just north of the arts and entertainment complex sits the stun-ning Queen Anne area, a hilly neighborhood of fanciful homes and great views. This is the part of Seattle where the downtown bustle starts to give way to the more peaceful charms of the out-lying neighborhoods.

Now, more than thirty years after the 1962 World's Fair, the fair-grounds, long since renamed **Seattle Center**, have been renovated. The 74-acre campus has ten buildings, which house a variety of offices, convention rooms and theaters. Locals and visitors continue to flock to the **Space Needle** (206-443-2111; admission) for the view or a meal, to summer carnival rides at the **Fun Forest**, to the **Food Fair**'s short-order ethnic eateries, to see opera and live theater and to check out wide-ranging exhibits and demonstrations at the **Pacific Science Center** (206-443-2001; admission). The Charlotte Martin Theater is the site of the **Seattle Children's Theater** (206-443-0807), which has jovial performances geared to a young audience. The **Pacific Northwest Ballet** (tickets, 206-292-2787; information, 206-441-9411) has its offices and rehearsal space at the Phelps Center (where the public can watch the corps rehearse through a glass wall). On the grounds is the world's largest Topiary Dinosaur, a life-size 66-foot replica of a mother and baby. There is also a large skateboard park, which is open most of the year just in case you get the urge to hop on a slab of plywood with four wheels and "get radical." ~ Seattle Center: Two miles north of the downtown core between Denny Way and Mercer Street; 206-684-7200.

SIGHTS

Kids will also enjoy visiting the center's **Seattle Children's Museum** on the ground floor of Center House. The collection features a kid's-size neighborhood and multicultural global village, a two-story walk-through re-creation of a mountain forest and mechanically oriented displays. There are also a giant Lego area, a small lagoon for toddlers and a drop-in art studio. Admission. ~ Seattle Center; 206-441-1768.

For a rewarding, spur-of-the-moment visit, drop by the center on a summer evening for a contemplative quarter-hour of gazing at the **International Fountain**. The combination of changing lights and waterworks against a rose-tinted summer sunset can lull you into a dreamy state.

At the **Space Needle Restaurant**, the entertainment—from 500 feet up—in either the restaurant or the observation deck is seeing metropolitan Seattle, its environs, Puget Sound, the Olympic Mountains and Mt. Rainier, the Queen of the Cascade Range, as you rotate in a 360-degree orbit. The restaurant serves various seafood, beef, pasta, poultry and lamb dishes, such as vegetarian pasta and chicken with salsa fresca. ~ 219 4th Avenue North; 206-443-2150. DELUXE TO ULTRA-DELUXE.

DINING

On the plaza at Five Point Square, next to the Chief Seattle statue, the **Five Point Café** is a distinctive Seattle landmark. With

◄ HIDDEN

a sign on the door warning nonsmokers that smokers are welcome, and "Pinball Wizard" inevitably playing on the jukebox, it's a real joint. Why go? The food is good, no-nonsense and quite economical, and no one leaves hungry. Try the fish and chips or the meatloaf sandwich (yes, it's that kind of restaurant). ~ 415 Cedar Street; 206-448-9993. BUDGET.

For sublime breakfast pastries and delectable Mediterranean-inspired lunch items, head for **Macrina Bakery**, a cozy European-style bakery and café where the moss green walls are adorned with scrolls, ironwork, paintings and other work by local artists. Breakfast items include house-made coffee cakes, cereals and fruit pastries, while a changing lunch menu may offer such dishes as tartlet of roast chicken and goat cheese or cheese polenta with red chard. ~ 2408 1st Avenue; 206-448-4032. MODERATE.

Near the Seattle Center and the Queen Anne district, **Thai Restaurant** serves authentic Thai cuisine in a friendly, comfortable setting. There are oriental art objects and an aquarium of exotic, iridescent blue fish to look at while you wait for your order of Bathing Rama (beef or pork in a peanut-chili sauce over spinach) or *tom yum potek* (spicy and sour soup) or another of the menu's 60-plus items. They vary in hotness and are rich with the flavors of coconut, curry, garlic, peanuts and peppers. ~ 101 John Street; 206-285-9000. BUDGET TO MODERATE.

NIGHTLIFE   Home of the 1962 World's Fair, the **Seattle Center** still offers innumerable nighttime diversions. ~ 305 Harrison Street; 206-684-7200.

Sharing facilities at the **Seattle Center Opera House** are the **Seattle Opera Association** (206-389-7676, 800-426-1619), famous for summer performances of Wagner's *Ring of the Nibelung*, and **Pacific Northwest Ballet** (206-441-9411), where the *Nutcracker* is a Christmas tradition. ~ Opera House: Mercer Street at 3rd Avenue North.

The **Seattle Repertory Theatre** plays at the Bagley Wright Theatre. ~ Mercer Street between Warren Avenue and 2nd Avenue North; 206-443-2222. The nearby **Intiman Theatre** presents plays by the great dramatists. ~ 201 Mercer Street at 2nd Avenue North; 206-269-1900.

A Contemporary Theater at 700 Union Street (206-292-7676) and **The Empty Space Theater** at 3509 Fremont Avenue North (206-547-7500) specialize in works by new playwrights.

▼▼▼▼▼▼▼▼▼▼▼▼▼▼▼
Seattle Gay Scene

Seattle's sizable gay population and diverse array of gay inns, clubs and meeting places is one of the many reasons travelers are increasingly flocking to the city. While gay activities and nightlife are found throughout the city, the highest concentration is in Capitol Hill, one of

Seattle's most cosmopolitan neighborhoods. Take a walk down Broadway in Capitol Hill and you'll see one of the most vibrant gay communities in the country.

Capitol Hill is a mixed neighborhood that is a fun place to browse.   **SIGHTS**
Within a block or two you can toss back an exotic wheatgrass drink at a vegetarian bar, slowly sip a double espresso at a side-walk café, shop for radical literature at a leftist bookstore or hit a straight or gay nightclub. If you can't find it on Capitol Hill, Seattle probably doesn't have it. Broadway Avenue is the heart of this region known for its boutiques, yuppie appliance stores and bead shops. Gay clubs and stores are concentrated on Broadway, as well as nearby streets like 15th Avenue East and East Olive Way.

Home of some of the city's finest Victorians, this neighborhood also includes **Volunteer Park**. Be sure to head up to the top of the water tower for a great view of the region. East Ward Street from 11th to 17th avenues.

In August 1994, the building that used to house the Seattle Art Museum reopened as the **Asian Art Museum**. This Arte-Moderne building was a gift to the city in the 1930s by Dr. Richard Fuller, who was the museum's director for the next 40 years. The museum always had a large collection of Asian art, and this new museum has expanded on it. The Japanese, Chinese and Korean collections are the largest, but the museum also has south and southeast Asian collections. Japanese folk textiles, Thai ceramics and Korean screen paintings are some of the highlights. One admission fee will get you into here and the Seattle Museum downtown. Admission. ~ Volunteer Park, 1400 East Prospect; 206-654-3100.

A mother-daughter team runs the **Salisbury House**, a quiet, dig-   **LODGING**
nified, gracious Capitol Hill home two blocks from Volunteer Park. Cathryn and Mary Wiese offer five crisp, clean rooms (all have private baths) furnished with antiques and wicker. Fresh flowers, duvets on the beds, a full (meatless) breakfast and thoughtful innkeepers make this a well-done bed and breakfast. There are fireplaces in the living room and library and a refrigerator guests may use. ~ 750 16th Avenue East; 206-328-8682. MODERATE TO DELUXE.

Also in the popular, busy Capitol Hill area, **Gaslight Inn** is a bed and breakfast with urban flair. The 1906 house is furnished with oak, maple and glass antiques. Various period styles have been effectively combined with modern amenities in the 16 guest rooms. Most have private baths, and six have fireplaces. Gaslight has a heated, outdoor swimming pool (closed in winter) and an outdoor deck that overlooks the city. They serve a continental buffet breakfast. Gay-friendly. ~ 1727 15th Avenue East; 206-325-3654, fax 206-328-4803. MODERATE TO ULTRA-DELUXE.

Expect a friendly welcome and lots of conversation at **Roberta's Bed & Breakfast**. The comfortable, traditional home on Capitol Hill hosts a mixed clientele in four rooms on the second floor and a fifth under the eaves on the third floor. There are cozy window seats, gleaming woodwork, skylights, shelves full of books, a piano and a full, meatless breakfast. Gay-friendly. ~ 1147 16th Avenue East; 206-329-3326, fax 206-324-2149. DELUXE.

From the **Capitol Hill Inn**, it's an easy walk downtown and to the convention center. The Queen Anne–style home dating back to 1903 has been beautifully restored as a bed-and-breakfast inn and furnished with antiques and reproductions of Victorian wallpaper and Tiffany light fixtures. There are six guest rooms, a two-room suite with a jacuzzi and a two-sided fireplace, and two comfortable parlors. An abundant breakfast is served. Gay-friendly. ~ 1713 Belmont Avenue; 206-323-1955. DELUXE TO ULTRA-DELUXE.

On Capitol Hill near Volunteer Park in the Harvard-Belmont Historic District is the landmark **Bacon Mansion**, a 1909 Tudor stucco home. In addition to the two-story carriage house, which has a living room and dining room, there are ten guest rooms in the main house, eight with private bath. The Capitol suite has a sun room with wet bar, fireplace, queen-size four-poster bed, view of the Space Needle and a big bathtub. Gay-friendly. ~ 959 Broadway East; 206-329-1864, 800-240-1864, fax 206-860-9025. MODERATE TO ULTRA-DELUXE.

DINING

When Kaspar Donier moved his acclaimed restaurant to the Seattle Center area, he lost the old location's view atop an office building, but gained a nicer home and a different dinner crowd. Now, symphony, opera, and ballet patrons flock to **Kaspar's** to feast on his intriguing blend of contemporary Northwest cuisine with hearty Swiss cookery. Kaspar's braised lamb shanks, for instance, may be the Northwest's best; his scallops are sumptuous and plentiful. Dinner only. Closed Sunday and Monday. ~ 19 West Harrison Street; 206-298-0123. DELUXE.

HIDDEN ►

Not far from Kaspar's old locale on 1st Avenue, a string of new arrivals has boosted the thriving Belltown shopping, dining and nightlife scene. **Marco's Supperclub** is a little-known purveyor of fine, eclectic multiregional dishes; the deep-fried sage leaves, an appetizer, are a true original. Quite filling meals are reasonable by Belltown standards. ~ 2510 1st Avenue; 206-441-7801. MODERATE.

Ayutthaya is a corner restaurant in Capitol Hill renowned for its Thai cookery. Small, clean-lined and pleasant in blue and lavender, Ayutthaya features plenty of chicken and seafood dishes along with soups and noodles. Flavors blend deliciously in the curried shrimp with green beans, coconut milk and basil. Or try the chicken sautéed in peanut-chili sauce. Closed Sunday. ~ 727 East Pike Street; 206-324-8833. BUDGET.

Near Seattle University, **Kokeb** is a pleasant restaurant offering the hotly spiced dishes of Ethiopia. The finger food is eaten with chunks of a large, flat bread. The atmosphere is rustic, with an open-beamed ceiling. ~ 926 12th Avenue; 206-322-0485. BUDGET TO MODERATE.

Café Septieme is Kurt Timmermeister's re-creation of small Parisian cafés that cater to the literati and students. This eatery carries plenty of reading material and turns out cups of good coffee, lattes and light fare. A favorite luncheon sandwich is eggplant with roasted peppers. Desserts include shortbread, carrot cake, a variety of cookies and other mouthwatering treats. ~ 214 Broadway Avenue East; 206-860-8858. BUDGET.

SHOPPING

If you're in the market for a potato gun, would like to snack on Addams Family candy, crave a glow-in-the-dark squid or are searching for a popping Martian, head on over to **Archie McPhee's** near Lake Union, west of the university. This novelty-and-toy store offers more than 10,000 exotic items from all over the world. ~ 3510 Stone Way North; 206-545-8344.

Capitol Hill's Broadway Market is filled with popular shops like **Urban Outfitters**. Featuring casual urban ware, this shop offers new and vintage clothing, jewelry, housewares and shoes for the hip crowd. ~ 401 Broadway Avenue East; 206-322-1800.

Bailey/Coy Books is well-stocked with reading material, including a wide selection of gay and lesbian literature. ~ 414 Broadway East; 206-323-8842.

Chocoholics can get their fix in the Capitol Hill district at **Dilettante Chocolates**, a combination chocolatier and café. ~ 416 Broadway Avenue East; 206-329-6463.

NIGHTLIFE

Why did celebrity-watchers flock to Capitol Hill in May 1995 to catch a glimpse of Mel Gibson? The Hollywood star was in town for the world premiere of his eventual Oscar winner *Braveheart* —so far, the headiest moment in the 20-year history of the **Seattle International Film Festival**. Each spring, SIFF draws hundreds of thousands of cinema lovers for its weeks-long run in Capitol Hill theaters, and each year one of the SIFF favorites goes on to national acclaim. Besides screenings, lectures and receptions abound. Admission. ~ 206-324-9996.

Capitol Hill also offers a number of popular gay and lesbian clubs and bars including the following:

Night Mary's is a small, intimate bar that attracts a mixed gay and straight crowd. Cover. It's inside **Hamburger Mary's**, a popular restaurant with a mixed clientele. Bar patrons can order from the menu. ~ 1525 East Olive Way; 206-324-8112.

Not your ordinary Seattle café, **Coffee Messiah** beckons you with a large pink neon cross perched on the rooftop. The inside is painted a deep purple, with red velvet curtains and religious images. A pilgrimage to this coffee shrine would not be complete without a trip to its coin-operated discotheque bathroom, decorated to simulate Hell. Pictures of the devil surround a black sink and red toilet equipped with its own heat lamp. Nightly entertainment includes live modern acoustic rock on Friday and Saturday. ~ 1554 East Olive Way; 206-860-7377.

One of the biggest gay clubs in the area is **R-Place Seattle Pub**. Depending on your mood, you can plunk down at the sports bar, throw darts, enjoy a music video, shoot pool, enjoy tunes from the jukebox or play a low-stakes gambling game called pull tabs. ~ 619 East Pine Street; 206-322-8828.

A busy gay bar with a pub atmosphere in the Capitol Hill neighborhood is the **Elite Tavern**. ~ 622 Broadway Avenue East; 206-324-4470.

Another popular spot is **Neighbours Disco** offering deejay dance music seven nights a week. Cover. ~ 1509 Broadway Avenue East; 206-324-5358.

With the largest dancefloor in Seattle, the **Timberline** draws enthusiastic mixed crowds for country line dance sessions and other down-home events. It's located between Capitol Hill and the Space Needle. Cover. ~ 2015 Boren Avenue; 206-622-6220.

BEACHES & PARKS

BOREN/INTERLAKEN PARKS   A secret greenway close to downtown is preserved by these neighboring parks on Capitol Hill; it's just right for an afternoon or evening stroll. Restaurants and groceries are located nearby. ~ The park is located from East Roanoke Avenue to Lake Washington Boulevard East and Washington Park.

HIDDEN ►

▼▼▼▼▼▼▼▼▼▼▼▼▼▼▼▼▼▼▼

Outlying Neighborhoods

While downtown is the city's magnet, some of Seattle's best parks, sightseeing and nightlife can be found in nearby neighborhoods. Arboretums and science museums, lakeside dining and shopping worth a special trip are all in this region.

SIGHTS

Few guidebooks look at the **Lake Washington Ship Canal** as a single unit. Yet it ties together a wondrous diversity of working waterfront and recreational shoreline along eight miles of bay, lake and canal between Puget Sound and Lake Washington. Construction of the locks and canal began in 1911 and created a shipping channel from Lake Washington to Lake Union to Puget Sound.

Along its banks today you can see perhaps the liveliest continuous boat parade in the West: Tugs gingerly inching four-story-tall, Alaska-bound barges through narrow locks; rowboats, kayaks, sailboards and luxury yachts; gill-netters and trawlers in dry dock; government-research vessels; aging houseboats listing at their moorings; and seaplanes roaring overhead.

All in all, the ship canal presents a splendid overview of Seattle's rich maritime traditions. But you'll also discover plenty that's new—rejuvenated neighborhoods like Fremont and south Lake Union's upscale shoreline, a renovated Fisherman's Terminal and a handful of trendy, waterside restaurants. Amid the hubbub of boat traffic and ship chandlers, you'll also encounter quiet, street-end parks for birdwatching, foot and bike paths, the best historical museum in the city and one of the West's renowned arboretums. Here's a summary, west to east.

Hiram M. Chittenden Locks in Ballard is where all boats heading east or west in the ship canal must pass and thus presents the quintessential floating boat show; it's one of the most-visited attractions in the city. Visitors crowd railings and jam footbridges to watch as harried lock-keepers scurry to get boats tied up properly before locks are either raised or lowered, depending on the boat's direction of passage. Terraced parks flanking the canal provide splendid picnic overlooks. An underwater fish-viewing window gives you astonishing looks at several species of salmon, steelhead and sea-going cutthroat trout on their spawning migrations (June to November). Lovely botanical gardens in a parklike setting offer yet more diversion.

Fisherman's Terminal is home port to one of the world's biggest fishing fleets, some 700 vessels, most of which chug north into Alaskan waters for summer salmon fishing. But you'll always be able to see boats here—gill-netters, purse-seiners, trollers, factory ships—and working fishermen repairing nets, painting boats and the like. Here, too, are net-drying sheds, nautical stores and shops selling marine hardware and commercial fishing tackle. One café

LAKE UNION—SPEND THE DAY EXPLORING

The six miles or so of shoreline circling **Lake Union** present a varied mix of boat works and nautical specialty shops, street-end pocket parks, boat-in restaurants, seaplane docks, rental-boat concessions, ocean-research vessels, houseboats and flashy condos. You could spend a day exploring funky old warehouses and oddball enterprises. The lake's south end offers extensive public access to the shore behind a cluster of restaurants, a wooden-boat center and new park.

opens at 6 a.m. for working fishermen; there's a fish-and-chips window and one good seafood restaurant (Chinook's) overlooking the waterway. ~ On the south side of Salmon Bay about a mile east of the locks.

The **Fremont** neighborhood is locally famous for the sculpture *Waiting for the Interurban*, whose collection of lifelike commuters is frequently seen adorned in funny hats, scarves and other castoff clothing. Centered around Fremont Avenue North and North 34th Street at the northwest corner of Lake Union, the district is top-heavy with shops proffering the offbeat (handmade dulcimers, antiques and junk).

Gas Works Park occupies property that dangles like a giant green tonsil from Lake Union's north shore. Until 1956, the park's namesake "gas works" produced synthetic natural gas from coal and crude oil. Some of the rusting congeries of pipes, airy catwalks, spiraling ladders, tall towers and stubby tanks was torn down during park construction, but enough remains (repainted in snappy colors) to fascinate youngsters and old-timers alike. ~ Foot of Wallingford Avenue North off North 34th Street.

On the south side of Union Bay, 175-acre **Washington Park** at Lake Washington Boulevard East and East Madison Street presents enough diversions indoors and out to fill a rich day of exploring in all sorts of weather. Most famous is the **Washington Park Arboretum** (which occupies most of the park), at its best in the spring when thousands of rhododendrons and azaleas—some 10 to 15 feet tall—and groves of spreading chestnuts, dogwoods, magnolias and other flowering trees leap into bloom. Short footpaths beckon from the Visitor Center. But two in particular deserve mention—Azalea Way and Loderi Valley—which wend their way down avenues of pink, cream, yellow, crimson and white blooms. The arboretum's renowned Japanese Garden is especially rewarding in the spring months, and both arboretum and garden present splendid fall colors in October and early November. ~ Visitors Center: 2300 Arboretum Drive East; 206-543-8800.

Miles of duff-covered footpaths lace the park. For naturalists, the premier experience will be found along the one-and-a-half-mile (each way) **Foster Island Trail** at the north end of the park on Foster Island behind the Museum of History and Industry (see below). This footpath takes you on an intriguing bog-walk over low bridges and along boardwalks through marshy wetlands teeming with ducks and wildfowl, fish and frogs and aquatic flora growing rank at the edge of Lake Washington.

In summer, you can join the canoeists paddling the labyrinth of waterways around **Foster Island,** sunbathers and picnickers sprawling on lawns, anglers casting for catfish and trout and the swimmers cooling off on hot August afternoons.

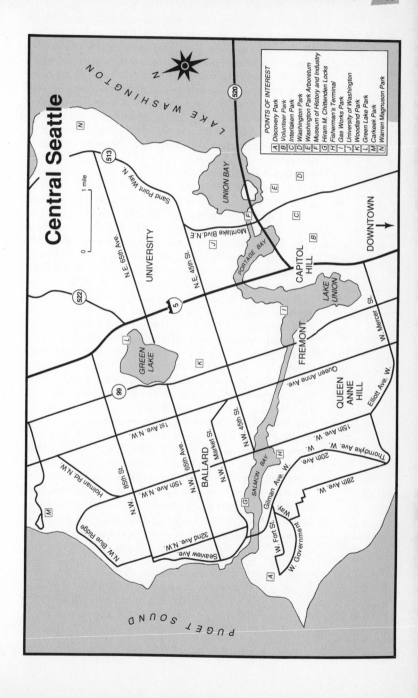

Central Seattle

POINTS OF INTEREST

A Discovery Park
B Volunteer Park
C Interlaken Park
D Washington Park
E Washington Park Arboretum
F Museum of History and Industry
G Hiram M. Chittenden Locks
H Fisherman's Terminal
I Gas Works Park
J University of Washington
K Green Lake Park
L Woodland Park
M Carkeek Park
N Warren Magnuson Park

On rainy days the **Museum of History and Industry** is a fitting retreat. It's the city's best early-day collection and pays special tribute to Puget Sound's rich maritime history, as befits any museum located next door to this vital waterway. Admission. ~ 2700 24th Avenue East; 206-324-1125.

The **University of Washington Campus** borders the canal north of Montlake Cut (part of the waterway) and is a haven for anyone who enjoys the simple pleasure of strolling across a college campus. It boggles the mind to think of what awaits you on its 694 acres—handsome old buildings in architectural styles from Romanesque to modern; Frosh Pond; the **Burke Museum of Natural History and Culture** (206-543-5590) and its famous collection of Northwest Indian Art; the **Henry Art Gallery** (206-543-2280) with its marvelous textiles and contemporary exhibits; red-brick quads and expanses of lawn and colorful summer gardens; canal-side trails on both sides of the Montlake Cut; access to the Burke-Gilman Trail; and a lakeside **Waterfront Activity Center** (206-543-9433) with canoe and rowboat rentals. Pick up a walking tour map at the visitors center. ~ Campus: 45th Street Northeast and 15th Avenue Northeast; 206-543-9198.

A mile or so north of the ship canal, Green Lake Park and Woodland Park straddle Aurora Avenue North (Route 99) and together offer 530 acres of park, lake and zoo attractions.

The star of the parks is **Woodland Park Zoo**, which since 1979 has won praise for its program of converting static exhibits into more natural, often outdoor environments. Most notable are the African Savannah, Gorilla Exhibit, the Marsh and Swamp and the Elephant Forest where you can see Thai elephants working at traditional tasks. There's also a Tropical Rain Forest, heralded as a "journey through different levels of forest," and a seasonal contact yard and family farm. The newest attraction is the Trail of Vines, an Asian rainforest where Indian pythons, lion-tailed macaques, orangutans, Malayan tapirs and siamangs live. Admission. ~ Fremont Avenue North and North 50th Street; 206-684-4800.

Green Lake Park, enormously popular with all ages and classes of Seattlites, is simply the best outdoor people-watching place in the city. Two loop trails circle the shore (the inner trail is 2.8

U-DUB

Exceptional architecture, a garden setting and easy access make a campus tour of the University of Washington (or U-dub, as locals call it) a highlight of a Seattle visit. The university began downtown in 1861; in 1895, it was moved to its present site. The Alaska–Yukon–Pacific Exposition of 1909 was held on the campus, and several of its fine buildings date from that event.

miles long, the outer 3.2 miles) and welcome all comers. On summer days, both paths are filled with strollers and race-walkers, joggers and skaters, bikers and nannies pushing prams. On the lake you'll see anglers, canoeists, sailboarders, swimmers, birdwatchers and folks floating in inner tubes.

Seattle's neighborhoods offer several hotels and numerous bed-and-breakfast accommodations. A bed and breakfast can be a great value, offering a casual atmosphere, home-cooked food included in the room rate and personal contact with an innkeeper who usually knows the city well. Contact **A Pacific Reservation Service.** ~ 206-784-0539, fax 206-431-0932.

LODGING

The MV **Challenger** is a "bunk and breakfast" on Lake Union. The opulent interior of the renovated, 96-foot tugboat is done in mahogany and oak. It has a salon with a fireplace and eight cabins with nautical furnishings. They all overlook the lake and city skyline. Captain's Cabin, the largest, includes the former pilothouse. The Challenger also offers cabin quarters on two yachts beside the main tugboat. ~ 1001 Fairview Avenue North; 206-340-1201, fax 206-621-9208. MODERATE TO DELUXE.

A favorite of visitors to the University of Washington, both gay and straight, the **Chambered Nautilus Bed & Breakfast Inn** is only a block from the campus. Breezily casual, the spacious home has a family atmosphere. Games and books, soft chairs by the fireplace and all-day tea and cookies add to the homeyness. Six guest rooms on the second and third floors have antique furnishings. All have private baths and four feature private porches. A full gourmet breakfast is served, sometimes on the sun porch. ~ 5005 22nd Avenue Northeast; 206-522-2536, 800-545-8459, fax 206-528-0898. MODERATE TO DELUXE.

Also in the University District is **Meany Tower Hotel,** a 15-story tower with 155 corner rooms. All units have views of the mountains or the lake and cityscape. Standard hotel furnishings adorn the spacious, tan-and-green rooms. A handsome restaurant and lounge are on the floor below the lobby. ~ 4507 Brooklyn Avenue Northeast; 206-634-2000, 800-899-0251, fax 206-547-6029. ULTRA-DELUXE.

The **University Plaza Hotel** is a three-story motor hotel adjacent to Route 5, west of the University of Washington. There are 135 comfortably furnished rooms centered around a pool courtyard. Rooms on the freeway side can be noisy. On the ground floor, behind a mock-medieval England facade, are a restaurant, lounge and beauty salon. ~ 400 Northeast 45th Street; 206-634-0100, 800-343-7040, fax 206-633-2743. DELUXE.

Bicycles hang from the rafters. T-shirts are on sale in the lobby. **Cucina! Cucina!** is an open, spacious, noisy Italian restaurant with

DINING

a large deck overlooking Lake Union where you can watch float planes land and take off or see kayakers gently paddling by. Diners can see into the open kitchen to watch the staff making pizzas large and small for baking in the woodburning ovens. One of the most interesting toppings is the barbecue chicken. You will find a variety of pasta dishes, such as linguine with roasted chicken and goat cheese, vegetarian or meat-filled calzones and good caesar salads. ~ 901 Fairview Avenue; 206-447-2782. MODERATE TO DELUXE.

The hillside overlooking Lake Union is a long way from Trinidad, but **Bandoleone** succeeds smashingly at its mix of Caribbean, Central American and Northwest cuisine. Chile-seared fresh fish and roast lamb marinated in plum-pepper sauce typify the highly imaginative offerings. The bar becomes a cigar smokers' haven late in the evening. ~ 2241 Eastlake Avenue East; 206-329-7559. MODERATE.

A colorful and lively Spanish-eclectic restaurant in the Madison Park area, **Cactus** serves a cuisine representative of many different cultures, but mostly influenced by Spanish, Mexican and American Indian food. Start with one of the most unusual items on the menu—a salad of baby field greens topped with beer-battered goat cheese, candied hazelnuts and a roasted-jalapeño-and-green-apple vinaigrette. One of the more unusual entrées is ancho-cinnamon chicken—marinated in ancho chile, cinnamon and Mexican chocolate and glazed with honey. ~ 4220 East Madison Street; 206-324-4140. MODERATE.

Not too far away, in a small house surrounded by gardens, is **Rover's**, which specializes in Northwest cuisine with a French accent and is just the place for those romantic occasions. Chef Thierry Rautureau creates the ever-changing menu based on locally available, fresh produce. In addition to seafood in imaginative sauces, entrées might include rabbit, venison, pheasant and quail. A good selection of Northwest and French wines is available. Service is friendly and helpful, and there is patio seating in summer. ~ 2808 East Madison Street; 206-325-7442. ULTRA-DELUXE.

After visitors watch the ships go through the locks in the Ballard area, they stop at **Pescatore** for Italian seafood and views of the channel. For your comfort the terrace has fireplaces and a retractable awning. Choices include fresh Alaskan halibut, pizzas from a woodburning oven, pennini Gorgonzola, shellfish stew and house-made desserts. ~ 5300 34th Northwest; 206-784-1733. DELUXE.

Scandies is appropriately located in Ballard, a community with Scandinavian roots. Open for breakfast and lunch, Scandies serves such Scandinavian specialties as open-faced sandwiches (pickled herring, Jarlsberg cheese, spiced lamb), crêpe-style pancakes with lingonberries, Denmark's *frickadeller* (pork meatballs) and *scorpa* (cardamom cookies). Beers from Norway and Denmark are available in the informal restaurant. ~ 2301 Northwest Market Street; 206-783-5080. BUDGET.

A favorite seafood place for tourists is **Ivar's Indian Salmon House** with its dugout canoe hung overhead and Northwest American Indian longhouse-style architecture and decor. The restaurant also features views of the kayak, canoe, tugboat, windsurfer and yacht activity on Lake Union. The menu includes prime rib, alder-smoked salmon and black cod, and Northwest American Indian–style. ~ 401 Northeast Northlake Way; 206-632-0767. DELUXE.

When you're nostalgic for a '50s-style coffeehouse with an upbeat, neighborhood flavor, head for **Still Life in Fremont Coffeehouse**. Set in the unpretentious Fremont district, it has high windows, a friendly atmosphere, music, great soups and generous sandwiches. ~ 709 North 35th Street, 206-547-9850. BUDGET.

Near the University of Washington, make a beeline for the **Jitterbug**. Upbeat and lively, this is the place to go for generous portions of well-prepared Northwest regional food with Southwestern and Asian influences. The ever-changing menu may include *huevos rancheros* or grilled ahi. ~ 2114 North 45th Street; 206-547-6313. BUDGET TO MODERATE.

Union Bay Café serves Northwest regional foods with a Mediterranean influence. The seasonal entrées might include grilled sturgeon with roasted garlic, tomato and dill and hazelnut chicken on sautéed spinach with lemon butter. More unusual are the venison medallions served with rosemary, fresh plums and plum chutney. Lighter entrées are available in the simple, classic café. The appetizer list is almost as long as the regular menu. Closed Monday. ~ 3515 Northeast 45th Street; 206-527-8364. MODERATE TO DELUXE.

On a busy commercial street between the University and Ravenna districts is **Ciao Bella Ristorante**. The authentic Italian cuisine has been drawing raves since the little, L-shaped ristorante opened. On the menu are several classic pizzas, veal and chicken

NORTHWEST CUISINE, SEATTLE STYLE

In the Northwest, regional cooking at its best emphasizes the bounty of fresh produce and seafood available; in Seattle, innovative chefs have turned it into a distinctive cuisine showcasing the dazzling variety of ingredients that pour in from farms and boats. Combined with fine wines from Washington's 75-plus wineries, it makes for meals that critics rave about.

entrées and delectable pasta dishes. Chicken breast sautéed with Gorgonzola cheese and fish soup with clams, mussels, calamari and prawns are flavored with artistry. Dinner only. ~ 5133 Northeast 25th Avenue; 206-524-6989. MODERATE.

Guido's Pizza is a funky, unpretentious place, the aromas from which send people walking by into Pavlovian salivation. You can buy pizza by the whole or slice, delicious salads and good cappuccinos. The artichoke pizza is wonderful. ~ 2108 Northeast 65th Avenue; 206-525-3042. BUDGET.

A huge gob of food wrapped in a tortilla is now called a "wrap," and it's all the rage. That's exactly what they've been making for years at **Salsa Colorado Burritos** in West Seattle (on the route to the Vashon–Southworth ferry), and their version is as good as any at hipper joints downtown. The chicken burrito is a meal all by itself. The hot-sauce collection is a wonder; some are of Caribbean-level intensity, unusual for Seattle. ~ 4417 Fauntleroy Way Southwest; 206-935-2441. BUDGET.

Two miles down the road, the **Cat's Eye Cafe** has great coffee, excellent muffins and super sandwiches . . . not to mention plenty of feline pictures and paraphernalia. Soup and sandwich for lunch is an excellent choice. ~ 7302 Bainbridge Place Southwest; 206-935-2229. BUDGET.

SHOPPING **Madison Park Pharmacy** is popular with international travelers. A wide array of cards, world time clocks, cosmetics and guidebooks is found here. ~ 4200 East Madison Street; 206-323-6422.

At the **Washington Park Arboretum Visitor's Center Gift Shop** are gardening books, cards, china, earrings, necklaces, serving trays and sweatshirts. You can also buy plants from the arboretum greenhouse. ~ 2300 Arboretum Drive East; 206-543-8800.

Dominated by the UW campus is the University district, a commercial neighborhood overflowing with a vast array of retail shops. One that attracts many tourists is the **Folk Art Gallery La Tienda**. Here you'll find handpicked craft items from all over the world including those made by 200 selected American artisans. ~ 4138 University Way Northeast; 206-632-1796.

NIGHTLIFE Over in the Ballard district, dance to R&B and hip-hop deejay music at **Sharky's**. Cover. ~ 7001 Seaview Avenue; 206-784-5850. **Conor Byrne's** has live Irish music on the weekends and set dancing every Tuesday evening in the summer. Weekend cover. ~ 5140 Ballard Avenue; 206-784-3640.

Club crawlers frequent the **Ballard Firehouse** for rock, reggae and salsa. ~ 5429 Russell Avenue Northwest; 206-784-3516. **Tractor Tavern** offers a mix of live rock, country and jazz. Cover. ~ 5213 Ballard Avenue Northwest; 206-789-3599.

Near the University of Washington, you'll find an array of clubs and places to park yourself at night.

There are cocktail service, full dinner and comedy shows on Thursday, Friday and Saturday at **Giggles Comedy Niteclub**. Cover. ~ 5220 Roosevelt Way Northeast; 206-526-5347.

At the **University Sports Bar and Grill**, you can dance weekends to local alternative rock bands. Popular with the college crowd, the club features big-screen television, two pool tables, an upstairs deck and darts. Cover. ~ 5260 University Way Northeast; 206-526-1489.

For new renditions of classics, contemporary plays and musicals, try the **Bathhouse Theater** on the shores of Green Lake. ~ 7312 West Greenlake Drive North; 206-524-9108.

SEWARD PARK 🚶 🚴 ⛴ 🏊 🚤 ⚓ On Bailey Peninsula, this 278-acre park jutting into Lake Washington encompasses Seattle's largest virgin forest. Walking through it on one of several footpaths is the prime attraction, but many come to swim and sunbathe, launch a small boat, fish or visit a fish hatchery. Seward Park offers a rare opportunity to see nesting bald eagles in an urban setting. The best introductory walk is the two-and-one-half-mile shoreline loop stroll; to see the large Douglas firs, add another mile along the center of the peninsula. The swimming beaches' gentle surf is ideal for children, and there are lifeguards in summer. You can fish from the pier for crappie and trout. There are picnic areas, restrooms and play areas; restaurants and groceries are nearby. ~ Located on the west shore of Lake Washington, southeast of downtown Seattle, at Lake Washington Boulevard South and South Orcas Street; 206-684-4075.

BEACHES & PARKS

DISCOVERY PARK 🚶 🚴 With two miles of beach trail and nine miles of footpaths winding through mixed forest and across open meadows, this bluff-top preserve (Seattle's largest at 535 acres) protects a remarkable "urban wilderness." Here are sweeping vistas, chances to watch birds (including nesting bald eagles) and study nature, the Daybreak Star Indian Cultural Center (206-285-4425) featuring art and cultural exhibits from various tribes, an interpretive center with environmental displays and educational programs, four miles of road for bicycling and an 1881 lighthouse (oldest in the area). Fort Lawton Historic District includes Officers' Row and military buildings surviving from the park's days as an Army fort. Picnic areas, restrooms and visitors center are at the park's east gate; restaurants and groceries are nearby. ~ It's a quarter-hour drive north of downtown in the Magnolia district; main entrance at 3801 West Government Way and 36th Avenue West; 206-386-4236.

CARKEEK PARK 🚶🚲 Tucked into a woodsy canyon reaching toward Puget Sound, this 224-acre wildland protects Piper's Creek and its resurrected runs of salmon and sea-going trout. Signs explain how citizens helped clean up the stream and bring the salmon back. Trails lead past spawning waters, to the top of the canyon and through a native-plant garden. Picnic areas, restrooms, play areas, beachcombing and pioneer orchard are the facilities here; restaurants and are groceries nearby. ~ Take 3rd Avenue Northwest to 110th Street Northwest, turn and follow the signs; 206-684-0877.

WARREN G. MAGNUSON PARK 🏊 🚤 ⛴ This 212-acre site carved from the Sand Point Naval Air Station presents generous access to Lake Washington and wide views across the lake. It's a favorite place to launch a boat, swim or toss a frisbee. You'll find picnic areas, restrooms, softball fields, tennis courts and swimming beaches with summer lifeguards; restaurants and groceries are nearby. ~ Located on Lake Washington, northeast of downtown Seattle, at Sand Point Way Northeast and 65th Avenue Northeast; 206-684-4075.

▼▼▼▼▼▼▼▼▼▼
Seattle North Heading north from Seattle, you'll cross the county line (into Snohomish County) toward the less urban and more maritime cities and villages lining Northern Puget Sound. You don't have to travel far to catch a glimpse of the region's past, before Seattlemania lured businesses and families to relocate here. North of Seattle you'll find a slower pace and strong reminders of Washington's history.

SIGHTS To the northeast of Seattle is **Edmonds**, a longtime mill town. A historic walk will take you past the site of the old shingle mills, Brackett's Landing, where the earliest pioneers settled, and numerous homes and buildings constructed in the late 1800s or early 1900s. The **Edmonds Chamber of Commerce and Visitors Information Bureau** has a brochure covering the historic sites around town. ~ 120 5th Avenue North, Edmonds; 425-776-6711.

A visit to the **Edmonds Historical Museum** with its working shingle-mill model, maritime heritage exhibits and collections of logging tools and household furnishings will give you a better understanding of the pioneer heritage and industrial history of Edmonds. Closed Monday and Tuesday. ~ 118 5th Avenue, Edmonds; 425-774-0900.

You'll find tidepools, three stretches of public beach, a long fishing pier, an underwater park and summer beach walks led by the Edmonds Beach Rangers (425-771-0230) on the **Edmonds waterfront**.

Rooms in the **Travelodge**, a three-story motel, are comfortably
appointed and clean, with dark blue carpets, curtains and bedspreads and cable television. There are even a few kitchenette and
jacuzzi units. Other amenities include hot tubs and continental
breakfast. ~ 23825 Route 99, Edmonds; phone/fax 425-771-
8008, 800-771-8009. MODERATE.

LODGING

If you venture up to Edmonds, try **Ciao Italia**. This small restaurant on the main drag doesn't look like much from the outside—
thankfully the lace curtains block out most of the traffic view.
Best choices include spaghetti *mirechiaro* (a garlicky seafood pasta
in white-wine sauce) and veal piccata. Dinner only. ~ 546 5th Avenue South, Edmonds; 425-771-7950. MODERATE.

DINING

A café and bakery, **Brusseau's** features country-style breakfasts, homemade meatloaf sandwiches, homemade soups and a
wide variety of desserts. The restaurant has a pleasant courtyard
with planters and picnic tables. Try their quiche Lorraine or omelette special. ~ 117 5th Avenue South, Edmonds; 425-774-4166.
BUDGET.

There are a number of good shops in the renovated **Old Mill
Town** in Edmonds. Within it, check out the **Edmonds Antique
Mall** (425-771-9466) with toys, dolls, glasses and antique furni-
ture. ~ 201 5th Avenue South, Edmonds.

SHOPPING

Over 200 dealers sell their wares at the **Aurora Antique Pavilion**. ~ 24111 Route 99, Edmonds; 425-744-0566.

▼▼▼▼▼▼▼▼▼▼
Seattle West

Seattle West offers some rare treasures such as a company
town operating in the time-honored manner, a fascinating
Indian cultural show, a marine-science center and inns that
look like they were created for a James Herriott book. From the
islands of Puget Sound west to Hood Canal, this is also a region
rich in parks and natural areas. You'll also want to tour the Kitsap
Peninsula, Bremerton's Naval Heritage and the parks of Southern
Puget Sound.

Since you can reach pastoral **Vashon Island** by state ferry from the
Fauntleroy dock in West Seattle (a 15-minute crossing), we include
it in this section of the book. However, Vashon stretches south for
13 miles toward Tacoma (accessible by another 15-minute ferry
from Tahlequah), creating a lovely Seattle-to-Tacoma country-road
alternative to Route 5. The ferry to Tacoma lands next to one of
the city's highlights, splendid Point Defiance Park (see "Tacoma
and Olympia" below).

SIGHTS

◄ HIDDEN

The Vashon Island Highway will take you fairly directly down
the island, through the town of Vashon. Just south of town is the

Country Store and Gardens, where you can peruse merchandise grown or produced on the island—fruit and syrups, berries and preserves, a nursery stocked with perennials and a variety of gardening tools, natural-fiber clothing, kitchenware and such. ~ 20211 Vashon Highway Southwest; 206-463-3655.

Side roads beckon from the highway to a handful of poorly marked state beaches and county parks. **Point Robinson County Park** on Maury Island (linked to Vashon via an isthmus at the hamlet of Portage) is easier to find and particularly interesting since it's next door to the Coast Guard's picturesque Point Robinson Lighthouse (not open to the public).

Looking like a lane in faraway Scandinavia, the main street of Poulsbo is lined with wonderful galleries and boutiques.

To the north, **Bainbridge Island** offers a much more attractive destination for most travelers, and you can see it on foot. The picturesque town is located on an island of the same name, just a 35-minute ferry ride from Coleman Dock. To see more than obvious attractions (restaurants, shops, a winetasting room), head for the mile-long waterfront footpath called **Walkabout** to the left of the ferry landing. Follow it along the shoreline, past shipyards and hauled-out sailboats under repair, to **Eagle Harbor Waterfront Park** and its fishing pier and low-tide beach. Carry on to a ship chandler and pair of marinas. Return as you came, or through the town's business district.

Another interesting loop trip west of Seattle begins in the Navy town of Bremerton. You can explore some of the region's history, as well as the remote reaches of southern Puget Sound.

If you take the ferry or drive to Bremerton, you'll pass by the **Puget Sound Naval Shipyard**. The best way to get here is the Washington State Ferry (cars and walk-ons; one hour) or state foot-ferry (50 minutes) from Seattle's Colman Dock (Pier 52) through Rich Passage to Bremerton. The shipyard houses the famous World War II battleship U.S.S. *Missouri*, on whose decks the peace treaty ending the war with Japan was signed. Although the shipyard is not open for public tours, it's an amazing sight even from a distance. ~ Burwell Street and Pacific Avenue, near the ferry dock, Bremerton; 360-476-3711.

Bremerton Naval Museum looks back to the days of Jack Tar and square-riggers. ~ 130 Washington Avenue, a half-block north of the ferry dock, Bremerton; 360-479-7447.

In the small town of Keyport, off Route 308 between Poulsbo and Silverdale, you'll find the **Naval Undersea Museum**. Historical exhibits here focus on the Navy's undersea activities from the Revolutionary War to the present. Diving and defense displays explore such subjects as nautical archaeology and the history of the submarine. There's also an interactive installation on the ocean environment. ~ 610 Dowell Street, Keyport; 360-396-4148.

Only an hour from the heart of Seattle, the Kitsap Peninsula is framed on the east side by Puget Sound and the west by Hood Canal. Historic company towns, naval museums and remote parks make this area a fine retreat from the city.

A good place to learn about the region's American Indian heritage is the town of **Suquamish**. Chief Seattle and the allied tribes he represented are showcased at the **Suquamish Museum**. There's an outstanding collection of photographs and relics, along with mock-ups of a typical American Indian dwelling and the interior of a longhouse. Two award-winning video presentations are shown in a small theater. Admission. ~ 15831 Sandy Hook Road off Route 305, Suquamish; 360-598-3311.

◄ HIDDEN

Chief Seattle's Grave, set under a canopy of dugout canoes in a hillside graveyard overlooking Seattle (his namesake), is just a few miles down Suquamish Way. Follow the road signs.

"Velkommen til **Poulsbo**" is an oft-repeated phrase in "Washington's Little Norway." There are some wonderful samples of historic architecture on a **walking tour** of town; the **Poulsbo Chamber of Commerce** can provide more information. ~ 19131 8th Avenue Northeast, Poulsbo; 360-779-4848.

At the **Marine Science Center**, you can learn about the various forms of marine life that inhabit the waters of Southern Puget Sound; they even have touch tanks of friendly sea creatures. ~ 18743 Front Street Northeast, Poulsbo; 360-779-5549.

One of the West's last company towns, **Port Gamble** is a favored visitor stop. Situated on a bluff at the intersection of Admiralty Inlet and Gamble Bay, this century-old community is owned by the Pope and Talbot lumber firm.

◄ HIDDEN

The oldest running lumber mill in the U.S. (operating since 1853) was just closed in 1995. Although all the sawmill workers were laid off, Pope and Talbot announced that they will keep the town running. The town had long been home to about 150 sawmill workers and their families, who rented homes by the company. Picturesque frame houses, towering elms and a church with Gothic windows and a needle spire give the community a New England look. Don't miss the mock-ups of Captain Talbot's cabin and A. J. Pope's office at the **Pope and Talbot Historical Museum**. Admission. ~ Route 3, Port Gamble; 360-297-3341.

Also worth seeing is the **Sea and Shore Museum** (360-297-2426) on the second floor of the quaint, 1853 **Port Gamble Country Store**. Other historic homes and buildings are occupied by former Pope and Talbot employees but can be seen from the outside; a walking-tour guide can be obtained at the Country Store. ~ Rainier Avenue, Port Gamble.

SOUTHERN PUGET SOUND   On a map, Southern Puget Sound looks like a fistful of bony fingers clawing at the earth. This maze of inlets, peninsulas and islands presents plentiful saltwater ac-

cess and invites days of poking around. Here are three representative experiences in the area:

HIDDEN ►   South of Bremerton is the **Longbranch Peninsula**, a showcase
of Southern Puget Sound's outdoor treasures. Quiet coves and
lonely forests, dairy farms, funky fishing villages with quiet cafés,
shellfish beaches and oyster farmers, a salmon hatchery, fishing
piers and wharves all await leisurely exploration. Take Route 16
to Route 302, proceeding west until you reach Key Center. The
Key Peninsula Highway, running south from this community, is
the main road bringing you to most attractions.

To visit the hamlet of **Lakebay** on Mayo Cove, turn east from
Peninsula Highway three-and-a-half miles south of Home (the
town, not your Home Sweet) onto Cornwall Road and follow it
to Delano Road. On the south side of the cove is **Penrose Point
State Park** with 145 acres of forest, two miles of beaches, hiking
trails, fishing, picnicking and camping. ~ 253-884-2514.

At the end of the highway is another bayside village, **Longbranch**, on the shores of Filucy Bay, one of the prettiest anchorages in these waters.

HIDDEN ►   **Hartstene Island** (northeast of Shelton via Route 3 and Pick-
ering Road) is connected to the mainland by a bridge, providing
auto access to a quintessential Southern Puget Sound island experience.

Many of the island's public beaches are poorly signed, but
Jarrell Cove State Park and a marina on the other side of the cove
are easily found at the island's north tip. You'll see plenty of
boats from both sides of the cove, and at the park you can stroll
docks, fish for perch, walk bits of beach or explore forest trails.
Main roads loop the island's north end, or head for the far southern tip at Brisco Point with views overlooking Peale Passage and
Squaxin Island. ~ Foot of Wingert Road, off North Island Drive;
360-426-9226.

HIDDEN ►   The eastern shore of **Hood Canal** is located a mere mile or
two from the western side of the channel, but in character it's
worlds apart. Beach access is limited, but views across the canal
to the Olympic Mountains are splendid, settlements few and quiet
and back roads genuine byways—few tourists ever get here. This
is also where the canal bends like a fishhook to the east, which
has been nicknamed the "Great Bend."

To see the east shore in its entirety, begin at Belfair, leaving
Route 3 for Route 300. At three miles, watch for Belfair State Park
on the left. The road now narrows and traffic thins on the way
to the modest resort town of Tahuya; shortly beyond, the canal
makes its great bend. The road dives into dense forest, bringing
you in about 11 miles to a T-junction; bear left, then left again
to the ghost town of Dewatto. Take Dewatto Bay Road eastward
out of town, then turn north and follow signs 12 miles to a left

turn into the little town of Holly, or continue north 15 miles more to **Seabeck**, founded in 1856 as a sawmill town and popular today with anglers, scuba divers and boaters.

On Bainbridge Island, **The Beach Cottage Hideaways** is a complex of four cottages, one of which may be rented by the night. This cottage is built over the water and has a kitchen (with breakfast ingredients in the refrigerator), a private deck, a fireplace and views of Eagle Harbor and the Olympic Mountains. It accommodates up to four people. ~ 5831 Ward Avenue Northeast, Bainbridge Island; 206-842-6081. ULTRA-DELUXE.

LODGING

Serenity and comfort in the countryside characterize **Bombay House**, a 1907 Victorian set on a hilltop. The five-room bed and breakfast has a bright, cheery atmosphere. The rooms, which vary in size and decor, view the sea or the lavish flower and herb gardens. ~ 8490 Northeast Beck Road, Bainbridge Island; 206-842-3926. MODERATE TO ULTRA-DELUXE.

Rooms at Poulsbo's **Holiday Inn Express** are modern and comfortably furnished with big beds, satellite television, individual air conditioning and other basic amenities; a few are equipped with kitchenette or jacuzzi. There is a seasonal outdoor pool and continental breakfast is included. ~ 19801 7th Avenue Northeast, Poulsbo; 360-697-4400, 800-465-4329, fax 360-697-2707. MODERATE.

If you can afford the high tariff, a stay at the **Manor Farm Inn** is like stepping onto the set of *All Creatures Great and Small*. Seven plush rooms are country cozy, and the food can't be beat, but the best thing about this place is the chance to stroll among the chickens, pig, sheep, rabbits, doves and horses in the farm's white-fenced pastures or the opportunity to pull on a pair of rubber boots and head to the quiet trout pond to drop a line and wait for a nibble. The inn offers pure quietness: no one under 16, no pets and no telephones or TVs can be found, nor is smoking permitted. Reservations required; book well in advance. ~ 26069 Big Valley Road Northeast, Poulsbo; 360-779-4628. ULTRA-DELUXE.

◄ HIDDEN

Turtle Island Cafe, in the heart of downtown Vashon, has a new expanded menu that offers an eclectic choice of Italian, Pacific Rim and Asian food. Entrées here include *linguine puttanesca* and sautéed prawns in pesto-cream sauce. Don't forget to save room for a piece of homemade apple pie or chocolate mousse. Children under 10 eat free. ~ 9924 Southwest Bank Road, Vashon Island; 206-463-2125. MODERATE.

DINING

The old island hangout is **Sound Food Restaurant**. The restaurant is known for its casual atmosphere—windows overlooking the gardens and lots of wood inside. Saturday and Sunday brunches result in long waits, but the food—whole-wheat waffles, blintzes with fresh fruit, potato pancakes, omelettes with wonderful sauces and breads and pastries from the bakery—is usually worth it. A variety of soups, salads and sandwiches of baked bread is available for lunch. Dinner entrées include pasta primavera, seafood dishes and a number of large salads. Desserts—sigh—come fresh from the bakery. ~ 20312 Vashon Highway Southwest, Vashon Island; 206-463-3565. MODERATE.

In a large Tudor house nestled in the trees is the **Pleasant Beach Grill**. The white-linen tablecloths and low lighting bespeak a comfortable island elegance. The chef specializes in Northwest seafood but includes a couple of succulent chicken dishes, pastas and aged-beef entrées. The leg of lamb, served with roasted garlic, fresh herbs and shallot–rose cabernet sauce, comes recommended. Dinner only. ~ 4738 Lynwood Center Northeast, Bainbridge Island; 206-842-4347. MODERATE TO DELUXE.

Exotic flavors and innovative sauces are what you'll find at the **Four Swallows**, an upscale Italian restaurant located in a spacious 1880s farmhouse. The kitchen staff, utilizing fresh Northwest ingredients, whips up gourmet, thin-crust pizzas and zesty pastas. The entrées show the chef's creativity, and include grilled veal chops with porcini-mushroom sauce and *brodetto*, a fresh fish-and-shellfish stew in a rustic saffron-tomato-fennel broth. Dinner only. Closed Sunday and Monday. ~ 481 Madison Avenue, Bainbridge Island; 206-842-3397. MODERATE TO DELUXE.

Locals swear by the sandwiches and clam chowder at **Judith's Tearoom and Rose Café**, but we found the staff to be abrupt to the point of rudeness. Anyway, try something from the daily dessert tray where the selections often include fruit, nut or cream pies, bread pudding and cheesecake. They also have homemade soups. The Black Forest soup is a meal to contend with—including cabbage, potatoes, mushrooms and German sausage. Lunch and formal tea. ~ 18820 Front Street, Poulsbo; 360-697-3449. BUDGET.

The New Day Seafood Eatery is actually the outlet for the fresh catch brought in every day by the vessel *New Day* and features fast and cheap fish and chips (or clams, shrimp, scallops, oysters or chicken and chips). Diners choose from booths inside or picnic tables on the large deck overlooking Liberty Bay and the wharf. Lunch and dinner. ~ 325 Northeast Hostmark Street, Poulsbo; 360-697-3183. BUDGET.

SHOPPING In Poulsbo, you'll find paintings, pottery, weavings, cards, rosemaling, baskets, even food products created by local artists at the **Verksted Co-operative Gallery**. ~ 18884 Front Street Northeast; 360-697-4470. Also in Poulsbo, the **Potlatch Gallery** carries a fine selection of prints, glasswork, pottery and jewelry by Northwest artists. ~ 18830-B Front Street Northeast; 360-779-3377.

For fine collectibles including Lladro, nutcrackers and plates, visit **Loretta's Gifts**. ~ 18924 Front Street Northeast, Poulsbo; 360-779-7171. Right next door is **Sluys Bakery** where you'll get your fill of pastries and cookies. ~ 18924 Front Street Northeast; 360-779-2798.

MANCHESTER STATE PARK 🚶 🚲 ⚓ 🚤 ⛵ This one-time fort overlooking Rich Passage includes abandoned torpedo warehouses and some interpretive displays explaining its role in guarding Bremerton Navy Base at the turn of the century. The park is infamous for its poison oak—stay on the two miles of hiking trails, or try the 3400 feet of beach. The rocks off Middle Point attract divers. There are picnic areas, restrooms and showers; restaurants and groceries are nearby. ~ Located at the east foot of East Hilldale Road off Beach Drive, east of Bremerton; 360-871-4065.

▲ There are 50 developed sites for tents and RVs ($10 per night, no hookups; $15 per night with hookups) plus three walk-in sites ($5 per night).

BEACHES & PARKS

FAY BAINBRIDGE STATE PARK 🚶 ⚓ ⛵ A small park (17 acres), it nevertheless curls itself around a long sandspit to present some 1400 feet of shoreline. The only campground on Bainbridge Island is here. Facilities include picnic areas, restrooms, showers, a play area, horseshoe pits and volleyball courts; restaurants and groceries are nearby. ~ At Sunrise Drive Northeast and Lafayette Road about six miles north of the town of Bainbridge Island at the island's northeast tip; 206-842-3931.

▲ There are 11 developed sites, ten walk-in sites ($10 per night) and 25 RV sites with partial hookups ($15 per night).

OLD MAN HOUSE STATE PARK ⚓ ⛵ This day-use-only park was once the site of a longhouse used as a meeting place by Chief Seattle and the Suquamish Indians. Check out the interpretive and historical displays. A small, sandy beach overlooks the heavy marine traffic that cruises through Agate Passage. There are pit toilets and picnic tables; groceries are nearby. ~ On the Kitsap Peninsula north of Agate Pass off Route 305; 206-842-3931.

POINT NO POINT BEACH RESORT 🎣 ⚓ 🏊 ⛵ This private resort with beach access sits on the northern tip of the Kitsap Peninsula overlooking Admiralty Inlet and mid-Puget Sound. The waters off the point teem with salmon, attracting anglers from the world over to these outstanding waters. Other sites of interest include the Point No Point Lighthouse and the 3.5-acre Point No Point Nature Park with trails, viewpoints for watching eagles and a beach for clam digging. It's possible to swim here, but the water is very cold. You'll find restrooms, showers, a laundromat

◄ HIDDEN

and picnic tables; boat rentals, launch and groceries are nearby in Hansville. ~ 8708 Northeast Point No Point Road; from Kingston follow Route 104 to Hansville Road, then to Point No Point Road just east of Hansville; 360-638-2233.

▲ Four cabins are available in the summer and 38 RV hookup sites ($15 per night) are available on Friday and Saturday. Call for reservations.

BUCK LAKE COUNTY PARK Near Hansville on the northern tip of the Kitsap Peninsula, picturesque Buck Lake is a good spot for quiet, contemplative fishing or a relaxing summer swim. Fishing is excellent on the lake or from the shore. Facilities include restrooms, bathhouse, picnic tables and a playground. ~ Located on Buck Lake Road; take Route 104 from Kingston to Hansville Road and follow it north; 360-692-3655.

SALISBURY POINT This tiny, six-acre park with small stretch of saltwater beach is next to Hood Canal Floating Bridge and gives views of the Olympic Mountains across the canal. Though camping here is limited, this is the closest you'll come to accommodations near historic Port Gamble, just seven miles west. There are restrooms, picnic shelters and a playground; restaurant and groceries are located nearby. ~ North of Hood Canal Floating Bridge, turn left on Wheeler Road and follow the signs.

KITSAP MEMORIAL STATE PARK This 58-acre park four miles south of Hood Canal Floating Bridge has a quiet beach well suited for collecting oysters and clams. Between the canal, beach and playground facilities there's plenty to keep the troops entertained, making this a good choice for family camping. Fishing is excellent off the beach. You'll find restrooms, showers, shelter, tables and stoves, boat moorage, a playground with horseshoe pits and baseball diamond; restaurant and groceries are nearby. ~ From Kingston take Route 104 (which turns into Bond Road) to Route 3, then follow it north until you reach the park; 360-779-3205.

▲ There are 25 sites for tents and RVs ($10 per night, no hookups); trailer dump ($3).

ILLAHEE STATE PARK Wooded uplands and 1700 feet of saltwater shoreline are separated by a 250-foot bluff at this site. A steep hiking trail connects the two park units. On the beach is a fishing pier; at the south end are tide flats for wading. Facilities include a picnic area, restrooms, showers, a baseball field, a play area and horseshoe pits. ~ Located at the east foot of Sylvan Way (Route 306) two miles east of Route 303 northeast of Bremerton; 360-478-6460.

▲ There are 24 tent/RV sites (no hookups); $10 per night.

TWANOH STATE PARK 🧍 🛶 ⛵ ⚓ 🏕 🚤 🛥 🚣 With many amenities of a city park, Twanoh's 182 acres also include the forests, trails and camping of a more remote site. A two-mile hiking trail takes you through a thick forest of second-growth conifers next to Twanoh Creek; or explore a half-mile of saltwater beach that attracts divers. There are picnic areas, restrooms, showers, tennis, horseshoe pits and a concession stand. ~ Eight miles southwest of Belfair on Route 106; 360-275-2222.

▲ There are 25 tent sites ($11 per night) and 22 full hookup sites ($16 per night); closed in winter.

BELFAIR STATE PARK 🏊 🚣 Two creeks flow through the 63-acre park en route to Hood Canal, affording both fresh and saltwater shorelines. Along its 3700 feet of beach the saltwater warms quickly across shallow tide flats, but pollution makes swimming here risky; many instead swim in a lagoon with a bathhouse nearby. Shellfish are usually posted off-limits. Facilities include picnic areas, restrooms and showers; restaurants and groceries are nearby. ~ Located three miles west of Belfair on Route 300; 360-275-0668.

▲ There are 138 tent sites ($11 per night) and 47 full hookup sites ($16 per night); dump station ($3).

SCENIC BEACH STATE PARK 🧍 🛶 ⛵ ⚓ 🛥 🚣 Well named it is, with glorious views across Hood Canal to the Olympics and north up Dabob Bay. Nearly 1500 feet of cobblestone beach invites strolls; scuba divers also push off from here. Every year in May, 88 acres of native rhododendrons burst into bloom. Anglers try for salmon and bottom fish at the nearby artificial reef, and there's a boat launch next to the park. There are picnic areas, restrooms, showers, a play area, a horseshoe pit, volleyball and a community center; restaurants and groceries are nearby. ~ Located just west of Seabeck on Miami Beach Road Northwest about nine miles northwest of Bremerton; 360-830-5079.

▲ There are 50 tent/RV sites and two hike- or bike-in sites ($11 per night, no hookups).

Seattle East, extending from the eastern shore of Lake Washington to the Cascade foothills, blends the urban and rural assets of this metropolitan region. Here you'll find wineries and archaeological sites, prime birdwatching areas and homey bed and breakfasts.

Seattle East

Located just south of Woodinville, **Château Ste. Michelle** is the state's largest winery with daily tasting and tours. Situated on a turn-of-the-century estate, it also has greenswards, duck and trout ponds, experimental vineyards and outdoor concerts on summer weekends. ~ Route 202; 425-488-1133.

SIGHTS

Renowned as Seattle's foremost suburb, **Bellevue** boasts a surprisingly diverse network of parks embedded within its neighborhoods. **Mercer Slough Nature Park**, stretching north from Route 90 off Bellevue Way with the entrance at 2102 Bellevue Way Southeast, is the biggest and may be the best with some 300 acres of natural wetland habitat and ten miles of trails. **Wilburton Hill Park** is centered around a botanical garden of native and ornamental Northwest plants. The park covers over 100 acres and has more than three miles of hiking trails and softball and soccer fields. ~ 12001 Main Street off 116th Avenue Northeast, Bellevue; 425-452-2750.

Evergreen Point Floating Bridge, crossing Lake Washington between Seattle and Bellevue, is the world's longest floating bridge (1.4 miles).

To see what Bellevue used to be like before freeways, commuters and office towers, stroll the short stretch of shops along Main Street westward from 104th Avenue Southeast in **Old Bellevue**.

Seattle's rock legend Jimi Hendrix is buried south of Bellevue. A caretaker can show you the guitarist's grave at **Greenwood Memorial Park**. ~ 350 Monroe Avenue Northeast, Renton; 425-255-1511.

LODGING   The **Shumway Mansion** is a historic mansion with a New England flavor. To save it from demolition, the present owners had it moved to a knoll in north Kirkland, where it now stands as a bed-and-breakfast inn and accommodates guests, weddings and social functions. When a group takes over, overnight visitors can retreat to a tiny reading alcove on a second floor. The formal inn contains European furnishings, rugs out of the Orient, lace curtains and silk floral arrangements. Each of the eight rooms has a queen-size bed and antiques and easy chairs. The innkeepers serve a full breakfast on crystal and china. ~ 11410 99th Place Northeast, Kirkland; 425-823-2303. MODERATE TO DELUXE.

Set on three-plus acres, **A Cottage Creek Inn** has its own creek, pond and gazebo on the grounds. The English Tudor house features two guest rooms, one with a brass bed, the other with an antique bed, each with its own bathroom. There's a pleasant sitting room with a piano, which guests are encouraged to play. Continental breakfast included. ~ 12525 Avondale Road Northeast, Redmond; 425-881-5606. MODERATE TO DELUXE.

The **Bear Creek Inn** is a Cape Cod house set among trees on an acre of land. There's a large rock fireplace in the sitting room, a patio and a deck with a hot tub. The three rooms feature wood furniture with oak and pine trim painted with flowered designs. ~ 1950 Northeast 144th Place, Woodinville; 425-881-2978. MODERATE.

HIDDEN ▶   In a quiet wooded area southeast of Seattle is the **Maple Valley Bed and Breakfast**. The two-story contemporary home has open-beamed ceilings, peeled-pole railings, cedar walls and detailed-wood trim. Guests like to relax on the antique furniture on the front porch. The two guest rooms are individually decorated and color coordinated with French doors that open onto a large deck. On cool nights, heated, sand-filled pads ("hot babies") are used to warm the beds. A full breakfast is served on country-stencil pottery in a dining area that overlooks trees, wandering peacocks and ponds with ducks. ~ 20020 Southeast 228th Street, Maple Valley; 425-432-1409. MODERATE.

DINING

The open kitchen at **Andre's Bistro** is as entertaining as the food. This restaurant offers a menu with Vietnamese specialties like spring rolls or chicken with lemongrass, as well as Continental selections, such as lamb with garlic. Vietnamese chef Andre Nguyen comes with experience from some of Seattle's best restaurants. Closed Sunday. ~ 14125 Northeast 20th Street, Bellevue; 425-747-6551. MODERATE.

You wouldn't expect to find a good restaurant in this little shopping strip, but here it is. At **Pogacha**, a Croatian version of pizza is the mainstay. The pizzas, crisp on the outside but moist inside, are baked in a brick oven. Because the saucing is nonexistent or very light, the flavor of the toppings—pesto and various cheeses, alone or over vegetables or meat—is more apparent. Other entrées include grilled meats and seafood, salads and pastas. Closed Sunday. ~ 119 106th Avenue Northeast, Bellevue; 425-455-5670. MODERATE.

One of the best Japanese restaurants in all of Puget Sound is hidden in the Totem Lake West shopping center in suburbia. **Izumi** features an excellent sushi bar. Entrées are fairly standard —beef, chicken sukiyaki and teriyaki and tempura—but the ingredients are especially fresh and carefully prepared. Service is friendly. Closed first and third Monday of each month. ~ 12539 116th Avenue Northeast, Kirkland; 206-821-1959. MODERATE TO DELUXE.

◄ HIDDEN

A couple of local residents who grew up in Pakistan and Bangladesh have opened **Shamiana**. The food is cooled to an American palate but can be spiced to a full-blown, multistar *hot*. A buffet of four curries, salad, *nan* and *dal* is offered at lunch. Dinners are a la carte, and include entrées such as lamb curry with rice *pulao* or chicken *tikka*. ~ 10724 Northeast 68th Street, Kirkland; 425-827-4902. MODERATE.

SHOPPING

Bellevue Square has 200 unique shops, department stores and restaurants. **Domus** (425-454-2728) carries ever-changing design items for the home. Expect extensive selections of bric-a-brac, paintings, furniture, chinaware and some jewelry. ~ Northeast 8th Street and Bellevue Way, Bellevue.

One of the most elegant shops in town is **Alvin Goldfarb Jewelers**. Specializing in 18-carat gold pieces crafted by an in-house goldsmith who also works with precious and semiprecious gems, this is a mecca for discriminating people who desire a one-of-a-kind item. ~ 305 Bellevue Way Northeast, Bellevue; 425-454-9393.

Just five miles north of Bellevue is the downtown **Kirkland Square**, a minimall easily identified by its handsome, ten-foot-high clock. If you're tired of shopping 'til you drop, kids (and some adults) rave about **Quarters** (425-889-2555), where you can play video games. ~ 215 Main Street, Kirkland; 425-889-2555.

Excellent Northwest pottery, ceramics, jewelry and blown glass make **Lakeshore Gallery** a fine place to stop even if you have no intention of buying. The carved woodwork is especially well done. ~ 15 Lake Street, Kirkland; 425-827-0606. Around the corner, **The Tobacco Patch** has the East Side's best selection of cigars and pipe tobaccos, plus many tobacco-related gifts. ~ 125 Central Avenue, Kirkland; 425-739-4782.

Refurbished farmhouses, a barn and a feed store are stocked with handicrafts and artful, designer clothing at Issaquah's **Gilman Village**. Among the 40-plus shops clustered in these historic structures is **Northwest Gallery of Fine Woodworking** (425-889-1513), owned by 30 woodworkers and stocked with fine hand-crafted furniture, custom cabinetry, boxes and screens. **Made in Washington** (425-392-4819) handles pottery, specialty foods and wine, dinnerware and wood carvings. ~ 317 Northwest Gilman Boulevard.

Satisfy your sweet tooth at **Boehm's Candies**, where hundreds of chocolates are hand-dipped every day. You can tour the factory (reservations are advisable; this is a popular spot) and watch the skilled workmanship that goes into making candies of this quality. ~ 255 Northeast Gilman Boulevard, Issaquah; 425-392-6652.

NIGHTLIFE **Daniel's Broiler** has a jazz guitarist on Monday, piano Tuesday through Saturday and a Sunday jazz showcase. ~ Bellevue Place, 10500 Northeast 8th Avenue, 21st Floor, Bellevue; 425-462-4662.

Live sports events via satellite plus an extensive bar menu are on tap at **Chadfield's Sports Pub**. ~ Hyatt Regency Bellevue, 900 Bellevue Way Northeast, Bellevue; 425-462-1234.

New Jake O'Shaughnessey's is a grill and bar with four televisions in the lounge. ~ 401 Bellevue Square, Bellevue; 425-455-5559.

With a welcoming fireplace, the **West Coast Bellevue Hotel** features live piano music every night in the lounge. ~ 625 116th Avenue Northeast, Bellevue; 425-455-9444.

Enjoy live jazz on Monday and blues on Friday and Saturday at **Forecasters Redhook Ale Brewery**. ~ 14300 Northeast 145th Avenue, Woodinville; 425-483-3232.

Good things come in small packages, and the **Village Theater** proves it. The local casts here will tackle anything, be it Broadway musicals, dramas or comedy. ~ 303 Front Street North, Issaquah; 425-392-2202.

SAINT EDWARDS STATE PARK 🏃🚴⛵⚓ This former Catholic seminary still exudes the peace and quiet of a theological retreat across its 316 heavily wooded acres and 3000 feet of Lake Washington shoreline. Except for a handful of former seminary buildings, the park is mostly natural, laced by miles of informal trails. To reach the beach, take the wide path just west of the main seminary building. It winds three-fourths mile down to the shore, where you can wander left or right. Side trails climb up the bluff for the return loop. There's also a beach (no lifeguard) and year-round indoor pool (fee). Facilities include picnic areas, restrooms, tennis court, a horseshoe pit and soccer and baseball fields. ~ Located on Lake Washington's eastern shore, between Kenmore and Kirkland on Juanita Drive Northeast; 425-823-2992.

MARYMOOR COUNTY PARK 🏃🚴🐎 This roomy, 520-acre preserve at the north end of Lake Sammamish in Redmond is a delightful mix of archaeology and history, river and lake, meadows and marshes, plus an assortment of athletic fields. A one-mile footpath leads to a lakeside observation deck, and there's access to the eight-mile Sammamish River Trail. The circa-1904 Marymoor Mansion houses a historical museum, with a pioneer windmill nearby. You'll find picnic areas, restrooms, play areas, baseball and soccer fields, tennis courts, a model-airplane airport, a bicycle velodrome with frequent races, a climbing wall and an archaeological site; restaurants and groceries are nearby. ~ Located on Westlake-Sammamish Parkway (Route 901) off Route 520 just south of Redmond city center; 206-296-2964.

LAKE SAMMAMISH STATE PARK 🏃⛵🚤🛥 A popular, 431-acre park at the southern tip of Lake Sammamish near Issaquah, it offers plenty to do, including swimming (no lifeguard), boating, picnicking, hiking and birdwatching along 6858 feet of lake shore and around the mouth of Issaquah Creek. Look for eagles, hawks, great-blue heron, red-wing blackbirds, northern flickers, grebes, kingfishers, killdeer, buffleheads, widgeon and Canada geese. Facilities include picnic areas, restrooms, showers, soccer fields and a jogging trail; restaurants and groceries are nearby. ~ Located at East Lake Sammamish Parkway Southeast and Southeast 56th Street, two miles north of Route 90 in Issaquah (15 miles east of Seattle) via Exit 17; 425-455-7010.

BEACHES & PARKS

LUTHER BURBANK COUNTY PARK 🏃 🏊 ⚓ At the northeast corner of Mercer Island in Lake Washington, this little jewel presents some 3000 feet of shoreline to explore along with marshes, meadows and woods. The entire 77-acre site is encircled by a loop walk. You can fish from the pier for salmon, steelhead, trout and bass, and in summer swim at the beach. Picnic areas, restrooms, play area, tennis courts and amphitheater with summer concerts are all available here; restaurants and groceries are nearby. ~ Entrance is at 84th Avenue Southeast and Southeast 24th Street, via the Island Crest Way exit from Route 90 on Mercer Island, east of Seattle; 206-296-4232.

GENE COULON BEACH PARK 🏊 🚤 ⛵ ⚓ At the south tip of Lake Washington in Renton, this handsomely landscaped site is most notable for the loads of attractions within its 55 acres: one-and-a-half miles of lakeside path, the wildfowl-rich estuary of John's Creek and a "nature islet," a lagoon enclosed by the thousand-foot floating boardwalk of "Picnic Gallery," a seafood restaurant, a fast-food restaurant, and interesting architecture reminiscent of old-time amusement parks. A logboom-protected shoreline includes a fishing pier. There's a boat harbor with an eight-lane boat launch, and good fishing from the pier for trout and salmon. The bathing beach is protected by a concrete walkabout with summer lifeguard. Facilities include picnic grounds and floats, restrooms, play areas, volleyball and tennis courts, and a restaurant. ~ Bordered by Lake Washington Boulevard North in Renton, north of Route 405 via Exit 5 and Park Avenue North; 425-235-2568.

▼▼▼▼▼▼▼▼▼▼
Seattle South

Meander from the heart of the city south to the Tacoma line and you'll find one of the world's great aviation museums, the historic coal-mining town of Black Diamond and beautiful river gorges. Inviting fresh and saltwater beaches provide a convenient retreat from urban living. With an ample array of outdoor activities, Seattle South serves as the city's back door to the wilderness.

SIGHTS

About ten miles to the south of downtown Seattle, off Route 5 at Boeing Field, you'll encounter the **Museum of Flight**. Centered in a traffic-stopping piece of architecture called the Great Gallery, the museum is a must. In the glass-and-steel gallery, 22 aircraft hang suspended from the ceiling, almost as if in flight. In all, some 50 aircraft (many rare) trace the history of more than 70 years of aviation. You'll see a 1916 B&W float plane, 1917 Curtis Jenny biplane, 1929 Boeing 80-A biplane, 1932 Yakima Clipper sail plane, 1935 DC-3, 1962 A-12 Blackbird, 1944 B-29 Superfortress and many homebuilts. The 1909 **Red Barn** houses one wing of the museum. The so-called barn was originally the Boeing Co.'s boat-building factory on the banks of the nearby Duwamish River. Later it was converted to aircraft production, the company's original plant. Relocated several times, the Red Barn now houses exhibits on Boeing's early days in the airplane business, a far cry from today's mammoth factories. Visitors can also tour the operating air traffic control tower. Admission. ~ 9404 East Marginal Way South; 206-764-5720.

Green River Gorge is less than an hour from downtown Seattle but is worlds away from the big city. Just 300 feet deep, the steep-walled gorge nevertheless slices through solid rock (shale and sandstone) to reveal coal seams and fossil imprints and inspire a fine sense of remoteness. State and county parks flank the gorge (see "Beaches & Parks" below).

LODGING

A stone's throw from Sea-Tac Airport, the **Seattle Marriott** is a wonderfully luxurious hotel featuring a 20,000-square-foot tropical atrium five stories high. Around it are 459 renovated guest rooms. A restaurant, lounge, whirlpool, health club and gameroom round out the amenities. Airport shuttle is provided. ~ 3201 South 176th Street, Sea-Tac; 206-241-2000. ULTRA-DELUXE.

DINING

An excellent Thai restaurant convenient to Sea-Tac Airport is **Bai Tong**. Located in a former A&W drive-in, this eatery is known for its steamed curry salmon, grilled beef with Thai sauce and marinated chicken. The carpeted dining room is lush with potted plants, and the walls are adorned with photos of mouthwatering dishes. ~ 15859 Pacific Highway South, Sea-Tac; 206-431-0893. BUDGET.

◀ HIDDEN

When Thai Airways served Seattle, crews visited **Erawan** for the best Thai food near the airport. Thai Airways overflies Seattle now, but the restaurant is still there, serving especially good

BLACK DIAMOND—COAL AND BREAD

Black Diamond (about 35 miles southeast of Seattle on Route 169) is an old coal-mining town with the odds and ends of its mining, logging and railroading history on display at the **Black Diamond Historical Society Museum**. ~ Baker Street and Railroad Avenue; 360-886-1168. This intriguing museum is housed in an 1884 railroad depot. But the real reason most folks stop here—on their way to Mt. Rainier, the Green River Gorge or winter ski slopes—is the famous **Black Diamond Bakery**. At last count, the bakery and its wood-fired ovens produced some 30 varieties of bread. ~ 32805 Railroad Avenue.

soups and curries. This restaurant is really hidden—it's a block off Pacific Highway South, on the ground floor of the Orchid Inn. ~ 3423 South 160th Street; 206-244-5404. BUDGET TO MODERATE.

BEACHES & PARKS

The **Green River Gorge Conservation Area** includes three state parks and some 50 miles of hiking trails. Here we pick the two developed parks at the entrance and exit of the gorge and one nearby state park on a lake. ~ 206-931-3930.

FLAMING GEYSER STATE PARK 🏃 ⚓ 🚣 Once a resort, this 667-acre park downstream from the exit of Green River Gorge offers ten miles of hiking trails and nearly five miles of riverbank. Pick up a trail map and brochure in the main parking lot. Fish for steelhead in season (check the posted regulations). There are picnic areas, restrooms, play areas, volleyball courts and horseshoe pits; restaurants and groceries are in Black Diamond. ~ Located on Green Valley Road three miles west of Route 169, south of Black Diamond; 253-931-3930.

KANASKAT-PALMER STATE PARK 🏃 ⚓ 🚣 ⚓ Lovely walking on riverside paths, especially in summer, is the hallmark of this 320-acre park upstream from the entrance to Green River Gorge. During fishing season, try for steelhead (check posted regulations). You'll find picnic areas, restrooms, showers, volleyball courts and horseshoe pits. ~ Located on Cumberland-Kanaskat Road off Southeast 308th Street, 11 miles north of Enumclaw and Route 410; 360-886-0148.

▲ There are 31 developed sites and 19 with partial hookups ($11 to $16 per night).

NOLTE STATE PARK 🏃 🚲 ⚓ 🚣 ⚓ Surrounding Deep Lake, 117-acre Nolte Park is famous for its huge Douglas firs, cedars and cottonwoods. A one-and-a-half-mile path circles the lake taking you around nearly 7200 feet of shoreline and past the big trees; a separate nature trail interprets the forest. You can swim at the lake (no lifeguards); motorboats are prohibited. There's a small picnic area; groceries and restaurants are in Enumclaw. ~ Located on Veazie-Cumberland Road just south of Southeast 352nd Street, six miles north of Enumclaw and Route 410; 360-825-4646.

ED MUNRO SEAHURST COUNTY PARK 🏃 ⚓ 🎣 ⚓ 🚣 A well-designed, 140-acre site where landscaping divides 4000 feet of saltwater shoreline into individual chunks just right for private picnics and sunbathing. A nature trail and some three miles of primitive footpath explore woodsy uplands and the headwaters of two creeks. An artificial reef just offshore is popular with divers and anglers with boats. Picnic areas, restrooms, showers, playground and marine laboratory with fish ladder and outdoor viewing slots are the facilities here; restaurants and groceries are nearby. ~ Located at 16th Avenue Southwest and Southwest 144th Street, via Exit 154B from Route 5; 206-244-5662.

SALTWATER STATE PARK 🏃 ⛵ You'll share this busy park with lots of locals, nearly 800,000 visitors a year, so don't expect solitude. But among the 88 acres, do revel in the fine views, some 1500 feet of shoreline and quiet woods with two miles of hiking trails. There's tolerable swimming in saltwater tide flats at the south end of beach (no lifeguard). A sunken barge about 150 yards offshore from a prominent sandspit attracts a variety of fish and divers. Facilities include picnic areas, restrooms, showers, play areas and a concession stand; restaurants and groceries are nearby. ~ Located on Marine View Drive (Route 509) about halfway between Seattle and Tacoma, west of Route 5 via Exit 149; 800-233-0321.

▲ There are 47 sites for tents and RVs ($11 per night, no hookups).

WEST HYLEBOS WETLANDS STATE PARK 🏃 A rare chunk of urban wetland tucked between industrialization and subdivisions, the 68-acre park offers examples of all sorts of wetland formations along a one-mile boardwalk trail—springs, streams, marshes, lakes, floating bogs and sinks. You'll also see remnants of ancient forest, plentiful waterfowl, more than a hundred species of birds and dozens of mammals. You won't find any amenities—just portable toilets; restaurants and groceries are nearby. ~ Located on South 348th Street at 4th Avenue South, northeast of Tacoma just west of Route 5 and Exit 142; 800-233-0321.

◀ HIDDEN

▼▼▼▼▼▼▼▼▼▼▼▼▼
Tacoma and Olympia

The Tacoma/Olympia region southwest of Seattle is rich in history, parks, waterfalls and cultural landmarks. Tacoma features numerous architectural gems; nearby villages like Gig Harbor are ideal for daytrippers. One of the nation's prettier capital cities (and here you may have thought Seattle was the capital of Washington!), Olympia is convenient to the wildlife refuges of Southern Puget Sound, as well as to American Indian monuments and petroglyphs.

Despite a lingering mill-town reputation, Tacoma, the city on Commencement Bay, has experienced a lively rejuvenation in recent years and offers visitors some first-rate attractions. Charles Wright, president of the Great Northern Railroad, chose it as the western terminus of his railroad, and he wanted more than a mill town at the end of his line. Some of the best architects of the day were commissioned to build hotels, theaters, schools and office buildings.

Today, Tacoma is the state's "second city" with a population of 179,000. The city jealously protects its treasure trove of turn-of-

SIGHTS

the-century architecture in a pair of historic districts overlooking the bay on both sides of Division Avenue. The 1893 **Old City Hall** was modeled after Renaissance Italian hill castles. ~ South 7th and Commerce streets. A classic example of a triangular Victorian "flatiron" is the 1889 **Bostwick Hotel**. ~ South 9th Street and Broadway. The 1911 **Union Depot** was designed by the same architects who created New York's Grand Central Station. ~ Pacific Avenue and South 19th Street.

Designed by Marcus Priteca in 1918, the restored **Pantages Theater** is a classic of the vaudeville circuit (W. C. Fields, Mae West, Will Rogers and Houdini all performed here) and offers dance, music and theater productions. ~ 901 Broadway, Tacoma; 206-591-5894.

Without a doubt, Tacoma's prettiest garden spot is the **W. W. Seymour Botanical Conservatory**, a graceful Victorian domed conservatory constructed at the turn of the century with over 12,000 panes of glass. Inside are exotic tropical plants, including bird-of-paradise, ornamental figs, cacti and bromeliads; seasonal displays of flowers; and a fish pond with waterfall. ~ 316 South G Street, Tacoma; 206-591-5330.

Washington State History Museum has a respected collection of Northwest Indian art. Admission. ~ 1911 Pacific Avenue, Tacoma; 253-272-3500.

A treat for the kids as well as adults is **Point Defiance Park**, which offers an outstanding aquarium and zoo featuring polar bears you can watch from an underwater window. You'll also see an outdoor railroad museum with steam engine; Fort Nisqually, a reconstruction of the original 1833 Hudson's Bay Company post; a children's fantasy land; rhododendron, rose, Japanese and native Northwest gardens; and numerous scenic overlooks (see "Beaches & Parks" below). ~ North 54th and Pearl streets, Tacoma; 253-305-1000, 253-591-5337 (zoo).

HIDDEN ▶   **Steilacoom** about five miles south of Tacoma is a quiet counterpoint to Gig Harbor's bustle. Founded by Yankee sea captains in the 1850s, it exudes a museum-like peacefulness and preserves a New England look among its fine collection of clapboard houses. Get a self-guiding brochure at **Steilacoom Historical Museum**. Closed Monday and the month of January. ~ 112 Main Street, Steilacoom; 253-584-4133.

Don't miss the **Pioneer Orchard**; it surrounds the **Nathaniel Orr Home** (closed for renovation). ~ 1811 Rainier Avenue. At the 1895 **Bair drugstore**, you can order an old-fashioned float from the 1906 soda fountain. ~ Lafayette Street near Wilkes Street.

At the southern tip of Puget Sound, **Olympia**'s state capitol dome rises boldly as you approach on Route 5, a tempting landmark for travelers and an easy detour from the busy freeway. But this community of some 35,800 offers visitors more to peruse than government buildings and monuments. Nevertheless, the capitol campus may be the best place to begin your explorations.

You can take a guided tour through the marbled halls of the remodeled Romanesque **Legislative Building** (360-586-8687) and see other buildings on the grounds—**Temple of Justice, Governor's Mansion** and **State Library**.

The nearby **State Capitol Museum** includes a fine collection of Northwest Coast Indian artifacts. Closed Monday. Admission. ~ 211 West 21st Avenue, Olympia; 360-753-2580.

Downtown, the handsomely restored **Old Capitol**, at 7th Avenue and Washington Street across from stately Sylvester Park, will catch your eye with its fanciful architecture. But most of downtown is a potpourri of disparate attractions—the **Washington Center for the Performing Arts** at 512 Washington Street Southeast, galleries, the **Capitol Theater** at 5th Avenue and Washington Street with its old films and local theater, and a bit of Bohemia along 4th Avenue West.

Percival Landing is an inviting, harborside park with observation tower, kiosks with historical displays, picnic tables, cafés and boardwalks next to acres of pleasure craft. ~ At the foot of State Avenue at Water Street. For a longer walk, head south on Water Street, cross 4th and 5th avenues, then turn west and follow the sidewalk next to the Deschutes Parkway (or get in your car and drive) around the park-dotted shores of manmade **Capitol Lake**, which is two-and-a-half miles from the town of Tumwater.

◄ HIDDEN

Tumwater marks the true end of Puget Sound. Before Capitol Lake was created, the sound was navigable all the way to the Deschutes River. **Tumwater Historical Park**, at the meeting of river and lake, is rich in both history and recreation. One of two pioneer houses here was built in 1860 by Nathaniel Crosby III (Bing Crosby's grandfather). Down by the river you can fish, have a picnic, explore fitness and hiking trails, watch birds in reedy marshes and see more historical exhibits. Across the river, a handsome, six-story, brick brew house built in 1906 marks an

THE BEST BOAT WATCHING GIG—HARBOR, THAT IS

Gig Harbor across the Tacoma Narrows off Route 16 is a classic Puget Sound small town. The community that arose around the harbor was founded as a fishing village by Croatians and Austrians. Today you're more likely to see every sort of pleasure craft here; it's one of the best boat-watching locales on Puget Sound. The tight harbor entrance funnels boats single-file past dockside taverns and cafés where you can watch the nautical parade. Or, rent a boat from **Rent-A-Boat** and join the flotilla. ~ 8829 North Harborview Drive; 206-858-7341.

early enterprise that lives on in a 1933 brewery a few hundred yards south. ~ 777 Simmons Avenue, Tumwater; 360-754-4160.

Follow Deschutes Parkway south to **Tumwater Falls Park**, a small park that's a nice spot for a picnic lunch and whose main attraction is the namesake "falls," twisting and churning through a rocky defile. Feel the throb of water reverberating through streamside footpaths. Listen to its sound, which the Indians called "Tumtum." You'll find plenty of history in the headquarters exhibit, including an American Indian petroglyph and a monument recounting the travails of the first permanent settlement north of the Columbia River here in 1845.

Before the Alaska Gold Rush thrust Seattle into prominence at the turn of the century, Tacoma was Puget Sound's leading city.

Ten miles south of Olympia are **Mima Mounds**, an unusual group of several hundred hillocks spread across 450 acres. Scientists think they could have been created by glacial deposits or even, believe it or not, giant gophers. There is a self-guided interpretive trail offering a close look at this geologic oddity, as well as several miles of hiking trails. ~ Wadell Creek Road, Littlerock; 360-748-2383.

LODGING

No Cabbages Bed and Breakfast is a comfortable, old-fashioned beach house built against a wooded hillside. It has two guest rooms, which have their own entrance and share a bath. They feature knotty-pine walls and great views of the deck terrace and harbor. A third, moderately priced room is open in the summer. The house is filled with eclectic art and interesting conversation. The innkeeper serves an outstanding breakfast. ~ 7712 Goodman Drive Northwest, Gig Harbor; 206-858-7797. MODERATE.

HIDDEN ►

On a hillside overlooking Puget Sound, **The Pillars** offers views of Mt. Rainier and Vashon Island. The gracious home has three attractive rooms, two with water views and one giving a bird's-eye look at the garden. Guests may play the piano in the large living room, relax and read by the stone fireplace, swim in the covered heated pool or soak in the covered jacuzzi. The hosts offer a warm welcome but don't intrude on their visitors' privacy. Their breakfast includes home-baked breads. ~ 6606 Soundview Drive, Gig Harbor; 206-851-6644. DELUXE.

The **Harbinger Inn** is a restored, 1910 mansion with period antiques and a manicured lawn and garden. The living room, a first-floor porch with wicker furniture and a second-floor veranda overlook the marina, capitol building and the Olympic Mountains. Four of the five well-furnished rooms also have views. All units have private baths. The owners lend bicycles, as this is a choice area for bicycling, and serve a continental breakfast. ~ 1136 East Bay Drive, Olympia; 360-754-0389. MODERATE.

Do you enjoy good tempura? Then don't walk, run to **Fujiya** in downtown Tacoma. Masahiro Endo, owner and chef, is a great entertainer with his knife at the sushi bar. Chicken sukiyaki is delicious. Closed Sunday. ~ 1125 Court C, Tacoma; 206-627-5319. MODERATE.

If you've a hankering for barbecued ribs, fried chicken or catfish, try **Gloria's Southern Kitchen**. This is no antebellum mansion, just a plain, well-lighted café with good food. Just as good as the entrées are the greens, grits, yams, fried okra, biscuits and melt-in-your-mouth corncakes served up alongside. Gloria is Southern stock herself, so you can count on this fare being authentic. Breakfast is served all day. ~ 1716 6th Avenue, Tacoma; 206-627-4282. BUDGET.

One of the best views in Olympia is from **Falls Terrace**, through huge windows overlooking the Tumwater Falls on the Deschutes River. A good way to start your meal is with some Olympia oysters. The menu features pasta dishes, an excellent bouillabaisse and an array of chicken, lamb and beef entrées. Desserts are more ice-cream theatrics than tasty morsels. ~ 106 South Deschutes Way, Olympia; 360-943-7830. MODERATE TO DELUXE.

Hidden across from the Farmer's Market is **Gardner's Seafood and Pasta**. It is no secret to locals, who flock to this small restaurant. While seafood is the specialty here, there are several pastas that are very good, too. Try the pasta primavera. The Dungeness crab casserole is rich with cream, chablis and several cheeses. Homemade ice cream fills out the meal. Dinner only. Closed Sunday and Monday. ~ 111 West Thurston Street, Olympia; 360-786-8466. MODERATE TO DELUXE.

◄ *HIDDEN*

Patrons don't usually go to a restaurant for the water, but at **The Spar** it truly is exceptional because it comes from the eatery's own artesian well. Once a blue-collar café, the restaurant features large photographs of loggers felling giant Douglas firs. On the menu are thick milkshakes, giant sandwiches, prime rib and Willapa Bay oysters. ~ 114 East 4th Avenue, Olympia; 360-357-6444. BUDGET TO MODERATE.

In downtown Olympia, the **Urban Onion** serves sizable breakfasts, good sandwiches and hamburgers and a thick, hearty lentil soup. Dinners include chicken, seafood and *gado gado*, a spicy Indonesian dish of sautéed vegetables in tahini and peanut sauce. They also offer several vegetarian specials. The restaurant is part of a complex of shops in the former Olympian Hotel. ~ 116 Legion Way, Olympia; 360-943-9242. MODERATE.

The Olympia area isn't the place you'd expect gourmet French-Northwest cuisine, but chef Jean-Pierre Simon exceeds expectations at **Jean-Pierre's Garden Room**. Located in a historic old home near the Olympia Brewery, Simon serves up luscious crêpes, pastas and fish entrées that meld French Provincial influences with local ingredients—such as Dungeness crab. ~ 316 Schmidt Place, Tumwater; 360-754-3702. MODERATE TO DELUXE.

SHOPPING   In the Proctor District in north Tacoma you can find souvenirs, gifts and handmade clothing at the **Pacific Northwest Shop**. ~ 2702 North Proctor Street, Tacoma; 253-752-2242. Fine Irish imports are in stock at **The Harp & Shamrock**. ~ 2704 North Proctor Street, Tacoma; 253-752-5012. The **Old House Mercantile** offers a variety of gifts. ~ 2717 North Proctor Street, Tacoma; 253-759-8850. Educational toys are found at **Teaching Toys**. ~ 2624 North Proctor Street, Tacoma; 253-759-9853. The **Washington State Historical Museum** features gifts, jewelry, games and books. ~ 315 North Stadium Way, Tacoma; 253-798-5880.

Tacoma's best bookstores include **Fox Book Company**, which stocks used books. ~ 737 St. Helens Street, Tacoma; 253-627-2223. **O'Leary's Books** has both new and used titles. ~ 3828 100th Street Southwest, Tacoma; 253-588-2503. If science fiction is your interest, try **Lady Jayne's Comics and Books** at the Highland Hills Shopping Center. ~ 6th and Pearl streets, Tacoma; 253-564-6168.

For sportswear and outdoor gear in Tacoma, try **Sportco**. ~ 4602 East 20th Street, Tacoma; 206-922-2222. The **Duffle Bag** has similar merchandise. ~ 8207 South Tacoma Way, Tacoma; 206-588-4433.

In Gig Harbor, **The Beach Basket** features, of course, baskets and other gifts. ~ 4102 Harborview Drive, Gig Harbor; 206-858-3008. Scandinavian utensils, books and gifts can be found at **Strictly Scandinavian**. ~ 7803 Pioneer Way, Gig Harbor; 206-851-5959. **Kelly's Toys & Gifts** features stuffed animals and games. ~ 7806 Pioneer Way, Gig Harbor; 206-851-8697. **Mostly Books** stocks books (you're kidding) and gift items. ~ 3126 Harborview Drive, Gig Harbor; 206-851-3219.

In Olympia, contemporary women's clothing and accessories are found at **Juicy Fruits**. ~ 113 West 5th Avenue, Olympia; 360-943-0572. **Olympic Outfitters** is housed in a restored, brick-and-metal building and is stocked with everything from backpacking to waterskiing and cross-country ski gear. ~ 407 East 4th Avenue, Olympia; 360-943-1114.

NIGHTLIFE   Pete's BBQ **Rib and Steak House**, or "Barbecue Pete's" as locals know it, has dancing Thursday through Sunday to DJ-spun Top-40 or house music. ~ 1602 South Mildred Street, Tacoma; 206-565-7427. **Christie's Lounge** features live bands playing Top-40 music Tuesday through Saturday. Cover. ~ Best Western Executive Inn, 5700 Pacific Highway East, Fife; 206-922-0080.

In the Lakewood area try **Happy Days Diner and Time Tunnel Lounge,** which has deejayed Top-40 tunes. Cover. ~ 11521 Bridgeport Way Southwest, Tacoma; 206-582-1531. The **Lakewood Chop House** features a DJ playing Top-40, country-and-western and alternative music. Cover. ~ 10009 59th Avenue Southwest, Tacoma; 206-589-6950.

Drake's Downtown Café & Cabaret offers karaoke, happy-hour specials and deejay dancing on weekends. Cover. ~ 734 Pacific Avenue, Tacoma; 206-572-4144. **Katie Downs Tavern** is an adults-only pub overlooking Commencement Bay with a menu featuring local microbrews, seafood and pizza. ~ 3211 Ruston Way, Tacoma; 206-756-0771. Boasting one of the largest selections of draught beer in the state is the **Ale House Pub**. ~ 2122 Mildred Street West, Tacoma; 206-565-9367.

The **Tacoma Little Theater** is a community theater producing six plays a year. ~ 210 North I Street, Tacoma; 253-272-2281.

The **Tides Tavern** in Gig Harbor features live bands on weekends playing '50s and '60s rock and some rhythm-and-blues. Cover for live shows. ~ 2925 Harborview Drive, Gig Harbor; 206-858-3982.

The **Piper's Lady** features a number of good, locally brewed beers and live bluegrass or Irish folk music. ~ 200 West 4th Avenue, Olympia; 360-943-5575.

BEACHES & PARKS

DASH POINT STATE PARK Nearly 500 acres of forested wildland with 3300 feet of saltwater shoreline preserve a bit of solitude just barely outside the Tacoma city limits. Seven-and-a-half miles of trail ramble through mixed forest of second-growth fir, maple and alder. The park's beach is one of the few places on Puget Sound where you'll find enjoyable saltwater swimming—shallow waters in tide flats are warmed by the summer sun. Tides retreat to expose a beachfront nearly a half-mile deep. There's fishing from the pier at Brown's Point Park south of Dash Point State Park, and swimming in tide flat shallows (no lifeguard). Facilities include picnic areas, restrooms and showers; restaurants and groceries are nearby. ~ Located just northeast of Tacoma on Southwest Dash Point (Route 509); 800-233-0321.

▲ There are 100 developed sites ($10 per night) and 38 sites with hookups ($15 per night).

POINT DEFIANCE PARK Jutting dramatically into Puget Sound, this 700-acre treasure is hailed by some as the finest saltwater park in the state, by others as the best city park in the Northwest. Here are primeval forests, some 50 miles of hiking trails, over three miles of public shoreline and enough other attractions to match almost any visitor's interests. Five Mile Drive loops around the park perimeter with access to trails, forest, beach, views, attractions and grand overlooks of Puget Sound. The park is also known for its zoo and aquarium, particularly the shark tank (fee). Popular with boaters, there's a fully equipped marina with boat rentals, a boathouse and a restaurant. You can fish from the pier or in a rented boat. You'll find picnic areas, restrooms, play areas, tennis courts, snack bar, restaurant at boathouse; other restaurants and groceries nearby. ~ The entrance is on North 54th and Pearl streets; 253-305-1000.

KOPACHUCK STATE PARK 🏃 🛶 ⛵ 🚤 Spectacular views across Carr Inlet toward the Olympic Mountains from a half-mile of shoreline gives Kopachuck much to boast about. Many car-top boaters launch from the beach near the park to fish or paddle out to Cutts Island Marine State Park a half-mile away. There are picnic areas, restrooms and showers; restaurants and groceries are nearby. ~ Located on Kopachuck Drive Northwest at Northwest 56th Street about seven miles west of Gig Harbor and Route 16; 253-265-3606.

▲ There are 41 sites for tents and RVs ($11 per night); no hookups are available.

PENROSE POINT STATE PARK 🏃 🚲 🛶 🛶 🚤 ⛵ With nearly two miles of saltwater shoreline, this 152-acre park provides some of the most accessible public clamming in Southern Puget Sound. Try the half-mile of sandspit in Mayo Cove exposed at low tide. You can also hike along two miles of trail, launch a canoe or kayak for shoreline explorations, picnic, swim in shallow-water beaches and camp. You'll find picnic areas, restrooms and showers; restaurants and groceries are nearby. ~ Located off Delano Road at the foot of 158th Avenue near Lakebay on the Longbranch Peninsula west of Tacoma; 253-884-2514.

▲ There are 83 tent/RV sites ($11 per night, no hookups).

NISQUALLY NATIONAL WILDLIFE REFUGE 🏃 This 3780-acre refuge's ecosystem is a diverse mix of conifer forest, deciduous woodlands, marshlands, grasslands and mud flats and the meandering Nisqually River (born in Mt. Rainier National Park). Here, the river mixes its fresh waters with the salt chuck of Puget Sound. An important stop for migratory wildfowl on the Pacific Flyway, the refuge also is home to mink, otter, coyote and some 50 other species of mammals, over 200 kinds of birds and 125 species of fish. Trails thread the refuge; longest is the five-mile, dike-top loop that circles a pioneer homestead long since abandoned. There's an education center as well as pit toilets; restaurants and groceries are nearby. Entrance fee, $2 per family. ~ Located about 25 miles south of downtown Tacoma via Exit 114 from Route 5; 360-753-9467.

TOLMIE STATE PARK 🏃 🛶 🛶 A salt marsh with interpretive signs separates 1800 feet of tide flats from forested uplands overlooking Nisqually Reach. The sandy beach is fine for wading or swimming; at low tide you may find clams. A two-and-a-half-mile perimeter hiking trail loops through the park's 106 acres. An artificial reef and three sunken barges 500 yards offshore and almost-nonexistent current make the underwater park here popular for divers. Picnic areas, restrooms and showers are available; restaurants and groceries are nearby. ~ Located on Hill Road Northeast, northeast of Olympia via Exit 111 from Route 5; 360-456-6464.

MILLERSYLVANIA STATE PARK 🏃 ⛵ 🚤 🛶 Some 840 acres of primeval conifer forest and miles of foot trail are this park's big appeals. But visitors also come to enjoy its 3300 feet of shoreline along Deep Lake, where you can swim, launch a small boat or fish for trout. Picnic areas and restrooms; restaurants and groceries are nearby; private resort across the lake. ~ The park is located at Exit 95 just east of Route 5, ten miles south of Olympia; 360-753-1519.

▲ There are 135 developed sites ($11 per night) and 50 sites with hookups ($16 per night).

▼▼▼▼▼▼▼▼▼▼▼▼▼▼
Outdoor Adventures

SPORT-FISHING

Salmon, of course, is the big draw for anglers on Puget Sound. State hatchery programs see to it that the anadromous fish are available year-round, but the months from midsummer to midfall bring the bulk of salmon—and anglers—to these waters. From mid-July to late August, chinook salmon are king; by Labor Day coho take over, until October. Then chum arrive, but since they tend to be plankton eaters they don't bite. Pink salmon return in odd numbered years, in August, and are most plentiful in the Sound north of Seattle, near Everett. Sockeye used to be plentiful, but there hasn't been a good run since the summer of 1988, and fisheries in Lake Washington are now "very depressed," according to an official with the state Fish and Wildlife.

Several charter companies operate fishing trips on the Sound. The cost, which can range from $35 to $80 and up, usually includes everything except lunch and the fishing license (which you can purchase through the charter company).

SEATTLE AREA Ballard Salmon Charters offers full-day salmon-fishing trips on 36-foot boats. ~ Shilshole Marina, Seattle; 206-789-6202.

SEATTLE WEST The family-run **Emerald City Salmon Charter** has a 40-foot boat that accommodates up to 12 people for winter weekend and daily summer trips on the Sound. Dad skippers the boat while kids help out as deck hands. ~ 253-630-3150.

SEATTLE NORTH Father and Son Charters operates a 24-foot boat and caters to small parties, usually of three people. A deck hand goes out on all trips, which permits a lot more individual attention. Besides salmon charters, Father and Son runs charters for ling cod in April, for shrimp and crab in April, for early chinook in May and June, and for halibut in June. ~ Everett; 360-568-7514.

All Seasons Charter Service operates five boats, of either 24 or 50 feet, for salmon or bottomfish. Charter trips last about eight hours. ~ Port of Edmonds; 425-743-9590.

KAYAKING & SMALL BOATING   If your nautical knowhow extends no further than a good row across a lake, then head for Lake Union, on the northern edge of Seattle's downtown center. On a bright summer day, the waters of Lake Union are dotted with kayaks, small wooden rowboats and sailboats. And if you're in Tacoma, you can fish from a dinghy in Puget Sound off Point Defiance Park.

SEATTLE AREA   To rent a single, double or triple kayak, call **Northwest Outdoor Center** to reserve ahead. Kayaking on Lake Union is very popular, and it's not unusual for all the center's 120 kayaks to be rented on a nice day. Classes and guided trips are also available. ~ 2100 Westlake Avenue North; 206-281-9694. At the **Center for Wooden Boats**, not only can you rent one of several different kinds of classic wooden rowboats, you can also learn a bit about their history. There are also several small sailboats for rent, but only experienced boaters can rent one. The center is a nonprofit, hands-on museum that also offers sailing instruction and occasional guest speakers. ~ 1010 Valley Street; 206-382-2628.

> The heart of Green River Gorge covers only some six miles on the map but is so twisted into oxbows that it takes kayakers 14 river miles to paddle through it.

TACOMA AND OLYMPIA   Located near the tip of the peninsula in Point Defiance Park, the **Boathouse Marina** has three dozen 14-foot dinghies for rent. Most of the time they're rented by anglers, but you can row around in the Sound if you prefer. Also for rent are 14 motors to power the boats. ~ 253-591-5325.

SCUBA DIVING   Although the water temperature in Puget Sound averages a cool 45° to 55°, diving is quite popular, especially from October through April, when there's no plankton bloom because of reduced sunlight during those months. With several dive clubs in the Seattle-Tacoma area, there are usually many dives scheduled each weekend: a wall dive off Fox Island perhaps, or a shore dive at Three Tree Point (near Federal Way) or Sunrise Beach (near Gig Harbor). Southern Puget Sound and the area around Vashon Island are considered the best places to dive—you'll see starfish, crabs, ling cod, scallops and many more species. Be prepared, however. Because currents are extremely strong south of Seattle you'll need to check the tides and currents carefully before diving. The dive shops listed below can provide details about these hazards as well as information on local dive spots. If you're not an experienced diver, you can arrange lessons with these shops, although it takes several days to complete training for certification.

With 12 locations between them, **Underwater Sports Inc.** and **Lighthouse Diving Centers** are convenient to most Seattle-area locations. They offer lessons and rent and repair equipment.

SEATTLE NORTH **Underwater Sports Inc.** has shops in Seattle, Edmonds and Everett. ~ Seattle: 10545 Aurora Avenue North; 206-362-3310, 800-252-7177. Edmonds: 264 Railroad Avenue; 425-771-6322. Everett: 205 East Casino Road; 425-355-3338.

Lighthouse Diving Centers offers outposts in Seattle and Lynnwood. ~ Seattle: 8215 Lake City Way Northeast; 206-524-1633. Lynnwood: 5421 196th Street Southwest; 425-771-2679.

SEATTLE SOUTH In Federal Way, rent from **Underwater Sports Inc.** ~ 34428 Pacific Highway South; 253-874-9387. **Lighthouse Diving Centers** has a shop in Midway. ~ 24860 Pacific Highway South; 253-839-6881.

SEATTLE EAST You'll find local branches of **Underwater Sports** in Bellevue and Kirkland. ~ 12003 Northeast 12th Street, Bellevue, 425-454-5168; 11743 124th Avenue Northeast, Kirkland, 206-821-7200.

In Bellevue, **Silent World** has gear and rentals. ~ 13600 Northeast 20th Street; 425-747-8842.

TACOMA AND OLYMPIA In Tacoma, you can try **Lighthouse Diving.** ~ 3630 South Cedar Street; 253-475-1316. In Gig Harbor, contact **Tagert's Dive Locker** for equipment, lessons and licenses. ~ 3226 Harborview Drive; 253-857-3660.

Underwater Sports Inc. is found in both Tacoma and Olympia. ~ Tacoma: 9606 40th Avenue Southwest; 253-588-6634. Olympia: 3330 Pacific Highway; 360-493-0322.

Except when the occasional snowstorm closes them down, golf courses in the area are open year-round.

GOLF

SEATTLE NORTH **Kayak Point Golf Course**, about 30 miles north of Seattle, is hilly and overlooks the Olympic Mountains and Puget Sound. This championship course is worth the drive. They also have an 18-hole putting course. ~ Marine Drive, Stanwood; 800-562-3094, 360-652-9676.

SEATTLE EAST **Bellevue Municipal Golf Course** is one of the most active courses in the state, probably because it's a good walking course with moderate hills. ~ 5500 140th Avenue Northeast; 425-451-7250.

TACOMA AND OLYMPIA **Lake Spanaway Golf Course** is in Pierce County Park. The 18-hole public course was cut out of a forest, so it's treelined but fairly open. It has a putting green and a pro shop. ~ 15602 Pacific Avenue; 253-531-3660.

TENNIS

Northwest precipitation practically turns tennis into an indoor sport. You'll have to call a few days in advance to reserve an indoor court at one of these public facilities.

SEATTLE SOUTH It helps to mention that you're an out-of-town visitor when you call—at least six days in advance—to reserve one of the ten indoor courts at **Seattle Tennis Center**. The center also has four outdoor courts. ~ 2000 Martin Luther King Jr. Way South; 206-684-4764.

SEATTLE EAST The City of Bellevue operates the public courts at **Robinswood Tennis Center**. There are four indoor and four outdoor lighted courts; call six days in advance (start dialing at 8 a.m.). (Fee.) ~ 2400 151st Place Southeast at Southeast 22nd Street; 425-455-7690.

TACOMA AND OLYMPIA Call two or three days in advance to reserve one of the four indoor courts (or five racquetball courts) at **Sprinker Recreation Center**. (Fee.) ~ 14824 South C Street at Military Road; 253-537-2600.

RIDING STABLES

Take off on a guided ride to the top of a mountain east of Seattle or a slow meander through a wooded tract near Tacoma.

SEATTLE EAST On a clear day, you can see more than 100 miles atop Tiger Mountain near Issaquah. **Tiger Mountain Outfitters** will get you there in a three-hour trail ride that will let you see Mt. Rainier 65 miles away in the distance and possibly black bear, deer and cougar within several yards. Call for reservations. ~ 24508 Southeast 133rd Street, Issaquah; 425-392-5090.

TACOMA AND OLYMPIA **Su Dara Riding** offers a "tranquil, peaceful" one-hour ride for up to seven people through woodland thick with firs and maples. On a clear day, there are two views of Mt. Rainier. Su herself says, "We ride rain or shine." ~ Puyallup; 253-531-1569.

✔ **CHECK THESE OUT—UNIQUE OUTDOOR ADVENTURES**

- Bring your clam bucket when you amble along the shoreline in Southern Puget Sound's Penrose Point State Park. *page 90*
- Experience the thrill of a whitewater quest as you kayak through the Green River Gorge. *page 92*
- Don your wetsuit and explore the underwater park at Tolmie State Park. *page 92*
- Cycle the Burke-Gilman Trail with its 12 flat miles through downtown Seattle—including the University of Washington and the shore of Lake Union. *page 95*

It takes about an hour to skate around Seattle's **Green Lake** on the paved multi-use trail. You can rent inline skates at **Gregg's Greenlake Cycle**. ~ 7007 Woodlawn Avenue Northeast; 206-523-1822.

SKATING

It's no surprise to learn that Seattle has earned a nod from *Bicycling* magazine as one of the top bicycling cities in the country. Bicycle programs are administered by state, city and county transportation agencies, which has resulted in a network of bicycle lanes and trails throughout the region, many of them convenient for visitor recreational use. Helpful information, including bicycle route maps, is available from several agencies. The Washington Department of Transportation operates the **Bicycle Hotline** to request a route map and informative brochure. ~ P.O. Box 47393 Olympia, WA 98504-7393; 360-705-7277. **The Seattle Bicycling Guide Map** is available from the Seattle Engineering Department and can usually be found in bike stores and public libraries. ~ 600 4th Avenue, Seattle 98104; 206-684-5349. **King County** publishes a bicycling guide map; it's distributed through REI stores and Metsker Maps stores. Or call the King County Bike Hotline at 206-689-4741. The **Cascade Bicycle Club** is an all-purpose club, serving riders of all skill levels. The club operates a hotline, which provides general information about bicycling in the area and club-sponsored weekend rides. ~ 206-522-2453.

BIKING

SEATTLE AREA   Although the central city is fairly hilly, especially if you're biking in an east–west direction, there are trails within Seattle that run near the water and on lower and flatter terrain that are ideal for recreational bicyclists. The most famous, of course, is the multi-use **Burke-Gilman Trail**, popular with bikers, walkers and joggers. It's flat, paved and, following an old railroad right of way, it extends from Gas Works Park on Lake Union, through the university campus, past lovely neighborhoods next to Lake Washington and on to Kenmore. In Kenmore, it links up with the **Sammamish River Trail**, which winds through Woodinville (and its wineries) and on to suburban Redmond. It's a lovely city-to-farmlands tour. In west Seattle, the **Alki Bike Route** (6 miles) offers shoreline pedaling—half on separated bike paths—from Seacrest Park to Lincoln Park. Besides changing views of the city and Puget Sound, you should have great views of the Olympic Peninsula mountains.

TACOMA AND OLYMPIA   When it comes to bicycling in Tacoma and Pierce County, "things are just getting going," according to one of the city's public works planners. The area does not yet have the extensive network of lanes and trails that they have up in Seattle, but continues to develop its bicycle and pedestrian plan.

Meanwhile, the **Pierce County Department of Public Works** puts out a bike route map. ~ 2401 South 35th Street, Tacoma; 253-798-7250. The **Tacoma Wheelman's Bicycle Club** operates a recorded Ride Line. ~ 253-759-2800.

Among the more popular and convenient places to ride in the city is a two-mile lane along the **downtown waterfront**. Beginning at Schuster Parkway and McCarver Street, this multi-use lane (it's separated from traffic, however) extends to Waterview Street near Ruston and Point Defiance Park. Within **Point Defiance Park**, a shoulder lane of Five Mile Drive loops around the peninsula. The drive is closed to vehicular traffic every Saturday morning until 1 p.m. Call the Metropolitan Parks District for more information. ~ 253-305-1000.

Bike Rentals   **Gregg's Greenlake Cycle** rents children's, mountain and road bikes. ~ 7007 Woodlawn Avenue Northeast, Seattle; 206-523-1822. The **Bicycle Center of Seattle**, near the Burke–Gilman Trail, has mountain bikes, hybrids and tandems. ~ 4529 Sand Point Way Northeast, Seattle; 206-523-8300.

For mountain-bike and hybrid rentals in Tacoma, contact **Northwest Mountain Bike**. The shop can also give you information about the large network of trails near Victor Falls and in Capital Forest, near Olympia. ~ 6304 6th Avenue, Highland Hill; 253-565-9050.

HIKING   Nearly every park mentioned in the "Beaches & Parks" sections of this chapter offers at least a few miles of hiking trail through forest or along a stream or beach. Some are outstanding, such as Nisqually National Wildlife Refuge, Green River Gorge, Point Defiance Park in Tacoma and Discovery Park in Seattle.

DOWNTOWN SEATTLE   For short strolls in downtown Seattle, try **Freeway Park** and the grounds of the adjoining Washington State Convention Center (.5 mile) and **Myrtle Edwards** and **Elliott Bay parks** (1.25 miles) at the north end of the downtown waterfront. Just across Elliott Bay, West Seattle offers four miles of public shoreline to walk around Duwamish Head and Alki Point.

SEATTLE NORTH   For a longer walk, the **Burke-Gilman Trail** (12 miles) extends from Gas Works Park in Seattle to Logboom Park in Kenmore.

The **Shell Creek Nature Trail** (.5 mile) in Edmonds' Yost Park, at 96th Avenue West and Bowdoin Way, is an easy walk along a stream. Contact Edmonds Parks and Recreation for a guide to the area. ~ Edmonds Parks Department: 700 Main Street; 425-771-0230

SEATTLE WEST   Located southwest of Bremerton, **Gold Mountain Hike** (4 miles) is a moderate-to-strenuous climb with a 1200-

Hey! The Water's Fine

Even if you're a diehard landlubber, do not fail to go sightseeing here by boat at least once. Simply put, if you leave Seattle without plying its surrounding waters your trip will be incomplete. So don't hesitate, dear traveler: Head to the downtown central waterfront and make some waves.

On a clear day you can see forever, or so it would seem aboard one of the **Washington State Ferries**. Headquartered at Colman Dock, the ferries make frequent departures to Bremerton and to Bainbridge Island, both across Puget Sound to the west. But getting there is much of the fun because from your watery perch you'll be treated to grand views of Mt. Rainier, Mt. Baker and the Olympics (the Mountains, not the Games, silly). Up closer you'll see pleasure boats and other craft, and you may even catch a glimpse of an orca (killer) whale. To Bremerton, you can ride the car-and-passenger ferry or the passenger-only boat. At Pier 50 next door, you can board a passenger-only ferry to Vashon Island. ~ Pier 52; 206-464-6400.

This is your captain speaking. That's just part of the show on **Argosy Cruises**, which offer at least one tour every day year-round and more in midsummer. On the harbor spin you'll get grand mountain views and see boat traffic like you won't believe: freighters, tugboats, sailboats, ferries, you name it. The live narrator spices up the trip. ~ Pier 55; 206-623-1445.

Argosy and **Gray Line Water Sightseeing** join forces for their "locks tour." The tour goes north to Shilshole Bay, eastward through the Hiram M. Chittenden Locks into the Lake Washington Ship Canal and then on to the south tip of Lake Union. You return to the waterfront by bus. Going through the locks is an experience in itself, plus you'll get to see zillions of other boats doing the same. And along the way you might even see salmon jumping. ~ Pier 57; 206-623-4252.

For something different, **Spirit of Puget Sound** presents half-hour "minicabaret" performances as the highlight of its cruises, all of which serve meals. Lunch, dinner and moonlight cruises go throughout the week. Longer tours feature live music and dancing. ~ Pier 70; 206-443-1442.

A narrated harbor tour is included in the **Tillicum Tours-Blake Island** four-hour excursion to 55-acre Blake Island Marine State Park, which has tons of things to see and do. ~ Piers 55 and 56; 206-443-1244.

S.S. Virginia V is the last authentic operating steamboat of the legendary "Mosquito Fleet," the motley flotilla of steamboats that once carried foot-passengers and cargo around Puget Sound before the coming of highways and autos. Today, the *Virginia V* offers evening tours that include appetizers or dinner, live music (mostly jazz) and dancing. Historical tours around Lake Union and Lake Washington sail on Sunday in the summer season. ~ 206-624-9119.

foot elevation gain. You will survey the twisting waterways of Southern Puget Sound and Hood Canal from a 1761-foot point that also offers vistas from the Olympics to the Cascades and Edmonds to Olympia. The walk begins at a gate on Minard Road, about one-and-a-half miles from old Belfair Valley Road, five-and-a-half miles west of Route 3.

SEATTLE EAST   Three foothills peaks nicknamed the "Issaquah Alps" (Cougar Mountain County Park, Squak Mountain State Park and Tiger Mountain State Forest) south of Issaquah (about 15 miles east of Seattle) include miles and miles of trail and road open to hikers year-around. **Cougar Mountain Regional Wildland Park** (206-296-4281) is the best bet for visitors. Call for trail maps. Another good resource is the **Issaquah Alps Trails Club** (206-328-0480), which publishes several hiking guidebooks and offers excursions, group hikes and general hiking information. One representative hike is the **West Tiger 3 Trail** (2.5 miles), which meanders to an elevation of 2500 feet at the summit of West Tiger 3 for stunning aerial views. Leave Route 90 at the High Point exit (the first exit east of Issaquah) and you will see the small parking lot where the trailhead is located.

SEATTLE SOUTH   The trail along **Big Soos Creek** (4.5 miles), now protected in two parks, is an inviting ramble on a blacktop path next to one of the few wetland streams still in public ownership hereabouts. The trail winds from Kent-Kangley Road to Gary Grant Park. In Kent, south of Seattle, follow signs off Route 516 (Kent-Kangley Road) at 150th Avenue Southeast.

TACOMA AND OLYMPIA   A wonderful river-delta walk, **Farm Dike Trail** (5 miles), which starts on the Brown Farm Road, loops through the Nisqually National Wildlife Refuge. You may see bald eagles, coyotes, deer, great blue heron, red-tail hawks and a variety of waterfowl such as wood, canvasback and great-scalp ducks, as well as mallards and pin tails. Views stretch from Mt. Rainier to the Olympics. You'll also see many of the islands in the south, Steilacoom and the Tacoma Narrows Bridge.

▼▼▼▼▼▼▼▼▼▼
Transportation

CAR

Seattle lies along Puget Sound east of the Olympic Peninsula in the state of Washington. **Route 5** enters Seattle from Olympia and Tacoma to the south and from Everett from the north. **Route 90** from Eastern Washington goes near Snoqualmie and through Bellevue on its way into Seattle. **Route 405** serves the Eastside suburban communities of Bellevue, Kirkland and Redmond. **Route 169** leads from Route 405 southeast of Renton to Maple Valley, Black Diamond and Enumclaw. **Route 16** leads north from Tacoma, across the Tacoma Narrows Bridge toward Gig Harbor and further north toward Bremerton. On Bainbridge Island, the main thoroughfare is **Route 305** that goes from Bainbridge Island northwest across the island and onto the Kitsap Peninsula to Poulsbo.

About 20 miles south of downtown Seattle is **Seattle-Tacoma International Airport,** also called Sea-Tac, which is served by Aeroflot, Air B.C., Alaska Airlines, Alaska Commuter, American Airlines, America West Airlines, British Airways, Canadian Regional Airlines, China Eastern Airlines, Continental Airlines, Delta Air Lines, EVA (Evergreen), Harbor Airlines, Hawaiian Airlines, Horizon Air, KLM, Mark Air, Northwest Airlines, SAS, Southwest Airlines, Trans World Airlines, United Airlines, USAir and several smaller charter airlines. For general information, call 206-431-4444.

AIR

Shuttle service to the northern Kitsap Peninsula is available through the **Bremerton-Kitsap Airporter.** ~ 360-876-1737.

The **Washington State Ferry System** serves Seattle, Port Townsend, Tacoma, Southworth, Vashon Island, Bainbridge Island, Bremerton, Kingston, Edmonds, Mukilteo, Clinton, the San Juan Islands and Sidney, B.C. Most are car ferries. ~ 206-464-6400.

FERRY

The **Victoria Clipper** passenger catamaran service operates daily trips between Seattle and Victoria, B.C. ~ 206-448-5000.

Ferry service between Seattle and Victoria on the 190-car, 900-passenger *Queen of Bandy* is offered by **Victoria Line** from mid-May to mid-September. ~ 206-448-5000.

Greyhound Bus Lines serves Seattle. The terminal is at 8th Avenue and Stewart Street. ~ 800-231-2222.

BUS

Rail service in and out of Seattle is provided by **Amtrak** on the "Empire Builder," "Coast Starlight" and "Pioneer." Call for more information on connections from around the country. ~ 800-872-7245.

TRAIN

Most major car-rental businesses have offices at Seattle-Tacoma International Airport. Rental agencies include **Avis Rent A Car** (800-331-1212), **Budget Rent A Car** (800-527-0700), **Dollar Rent A Car** (800-800-4000), **Hertz Rent A Car** (800-654-3131) and **Thrifty Car Rental** (800-367-2277). XtraCar Discount Rentals (800-227-5397) offers low rates and shuttle service to the airport.

CAR RENTALS

Bus transportation provided by **Metro Transit** is free in downtown Seattle. Metro Transit provides service throughout the Seattle-King County area. ~ 206-553-3000.

PUBLIC TRANSIT

Deemed transportation for the future, the **Monorail** was built for the 1962 World's Fair. It runs between downtown and the Seattle Center every 15 minutes. ~ 206-441-6038.

Waterfront Streetcar trolleys run along the waterfront from Seattle's historic Pioneer Square to Pier 70. ~ 206-553-3000.

In the Kitsap Peninsula area, the **Poulsbo-Kitsap Transit** provides routed service in all of Kitsap County. ~ 360-373-2877.

TAXIS

In the greater Seattle area are **Checker Cab** (206-622-1234), **Farwest Taxi** (206-622-1717), **North End Taxi** (206-363-3333) and **Yellow Cab** (206-622-6500).

THREE

Northern Puget Sound and the San Juan Islands

"Every part of this land is sacred to my people. Every shining pine needle, every sandy shore, every mist in the dark woods, every clearing and humming insect is holy in the memory and experience of my people . . . . We are part of the earth and it is part of us. The perfumed flowers are our sisters; the deer, the horse, the great eagle, these are our brothers. The rocky crests, the juices in the meadows, the body heat of the pony, and man—all belong to the same family." This was part of Chief Seattle's poignant reply when, in 1854, the "Great White Chief" in Washington pressed to purchase some of the land around Puget Sound then occupied by several Northwest Indian tribes. And those sentiments still ring true today as the natural beauty and appeal of Northern Puget Sound and the San Juan Islands remain undiminished.

The Indians had good reason to hold this awe-inspiring land in such high regard. It supported them, providing for all their needs with verdant woods full of deer and berries and crystal waters full of salmon, letting them live in peaceful coexistence for hundreds of years. Even the weather was kind to them here in this "rain shadow," shielded by the Olympic and Vancouver mountain ranges.

Things slowly began to change for the Northwest Indian tribes and the land with the arrival of Juan de Fuca in 1592, who came to explore the coastline for the Spanish. The floodgates of exploration and exploitation weren't fully opened, however, until Captain George Vancouver came in 1792 to chart the region for the British, naming major landmarks such as Mt. Baker, Mt. Rainier, Whidbey Island and Puget Sound after his compatriots.

Establishment of trade with the Indians and the seemingly inexhaustible quantity of animals to supply the lucrative fur trade drew many pioneers. Before long, industries such as logging, mining, shipping and fishing began to flourish, supporting the early settlers (and still supporting their descendants today).

The geographical layout of the 172 islands of the San Juan Archipelago made for watery back alleys and hidden coves perfect for piracy and smuggling, so the history of the area reflects an almost Barbary Coast–type of intrigue where a man could get a few drinks, a roll in the hay and be shanghaied all in one night. Chinese laborers were regularly brought in under cover of night to build up coastal cities and railroads in the 1800s. This big money "commodity" was replaced by opium and silk, and then booze during Prohibition.

Smuggling has since been curbed, and while things are changing as resources are diminished, logging and fishing are still major industries in the region. However, current booms in real estate and tourism are beginning to tilt the economic scale as more and more people discover the area's beauty.

The area referred to as Northern Puget Sound begins just beyond the far northern outskirts of Seattle, where most visitors first arrive, and extends northward up the coast to the Canadian border. Coastal communities such as Everett, Bellingham and Blaine tend to be more commercial in nature, heavily flavored by the logging and fishing industries, while other small towns such as La Conner and Mount Vernon are still very pastoral, dependent on an agriculturally based economy. Springtime along this stretch of land is particularly lovely, especially in the Skagit Valley when the fields are ablaze in daffodils, iris and tulips.

Of the 172 named islands of the San Juans, we concentrate on the four most popular. These also are very pastoral, with rich soil and salubrious conditions perfectly suited to raising livestock or growing fruit. The major islands are connected to the mainland by bridges or reached by limited ferry service, an inhibiting factor that helps preserve the pristine nature here.

Although it's not considered part of the San Juans, serpentine Whidbey Island, with its thick southern tip reaching toward Seattle, is the largest island in Puget Sound. Situated at Whidbey's northern tip is Fidalgo Island, home of Anacortes and the ferry terminal gateway to the San Juans. Lopez is by far the friendliest and most rural of the islands, followed closely by San Juan, the largest and busiest. Shaw Island is one of the smaller islands, and lovely Orcas Island, named after Spanish explorer Don Juan Vincente de Guemes Pacheco y Padilla Orcasitees y Aguayo Conde de Revilla Gigedo (whew!) rather than orca whales, is tallest, capped by 2400-foot Mt. Constitution.

The ferry system is severely overtaxed during the busy summer season when the San Juans are inundated with tourists, making it difficult to reach the islands at times and absolutely impossible to find accommodations if you haven't booked months in advance. The crowds drop off dramatically after Labor Day, a pleasant surprise since the weather in September and October is still lovely and the change of seasonal color against this beautiful backdrop is incredible.

Northern Puget Sound

Stretched along the fertile coastline between the Canadian border and the outer reaches of Seattle, communities along Northern Puget Sound are dependent on agriculture, logging and fishing, so the distinct pastoral feel of the area is no surprise. Verdant parks and vista spots taking in the beauty of the many islands not far offshore head the list of sightseeing musts in the region.

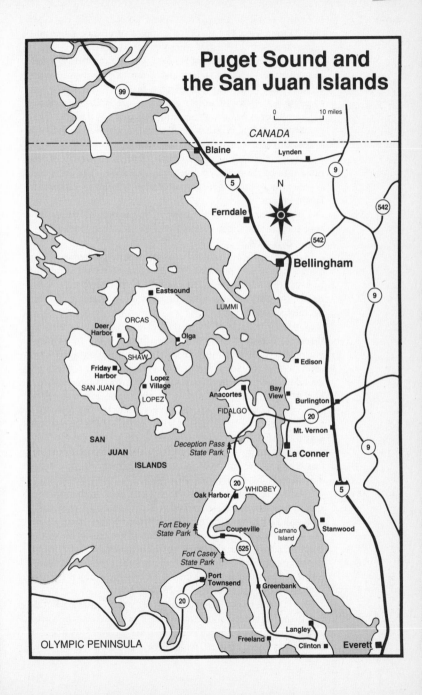

Puget Sound and the San Juan Islands

0 _____ 10 miles

CANADA

Blaine
Lynden
99
5
N
9
542
Ferndale
542
Bellingham
9
Eastsound
LUMMI
ORCAS
Deer Harbor
Olga
SHAW
Edison
Friday Harbor
Lopez Village
SAN JUAN
Bay View
Anacortes
LOPEZ
Burlington
FIDALGO
20
Mt. Vernon
SAN
Deception Pass State Park
La Conner
JUAN
9
ISLANDS
20
WHIDBEY
Oak Harbor
5
Fort Ebey State Park
Coupeville
Camano Island
Stanwood
525
Fort Casey State Park
Port Townsend
Greenbank
20
Langley
OLYMPIC PENINSULA
Freeland
Clinton
Everett

SIGHTS   In Everett you'll find your best vantage point from the dock behind **Marina Village**, a sparkling complex of upscale shops and restaurants. ~ 1728 West Marine View Drive, Everett.

The boxy little temporary building opposite the marina serves as an interpretive site and information center for the popular summertime Jetty Island Days, when a free ferry ride will shuttle you to picturesque **Jetty Island** for guided nature walks, birdwatching, campfires, a hands-on "Squirmy, Squiggly and Squishy" program to teach children about small marine animals and one of the only warm saltwater beaches on the Sound.

The **Firefighter's Museum** offers a storefront display of antique turn-of-the-century firefighting equipment. The collection is set up for 24-hour, through-the-window viewing. ~ 13th Street Dock, Everett.

The **Everett/Snohomish County Convention and Visitor Bureau** can provide more information. ~ 1710 West Marine View Drive, Everett; 425-252-5181.

On the hillside above the marina, ornate **mansions** of the lumber barons that once ruled the economy here line Grand and Rucker streets from 16th Street north. None are open to tour, but a slow drive up and down these avenues will give you a feel for the history of the city.

On the south side of town you'll find a free industrial tour at **Boeing**, a massive facility (the largest in the world by volume) where they construct those gigantic commercial airplanes that carry over one million passengers every day. The 90-minute tours include films on the history of flight and growth at Boeing followed by a narrated walk viewing the production lines where they build the 747 and 767 models. Reservations for these popular tours are available for groups of ten or more; otherwise, the best way to obtain tickets is to be in line at the tour center by 7:30 a.m. during the busy summer months. Call for directions and tour times; no children under 45 inches tall admitted. ~ Tour Center, State Road 526, Everett; 800-464-1476.

HIDDEN ►   Visitors to **Bieringer Farm** can not only pick fresh strawberries, raspberries, vegetables and other delights, they can get a good look at how a farm operates. Kids can ride a trolley-train; adults can learn about organic gardening and food preserving; the whole family can take a hayride. But the prime reason to visit remains the incomparable fresh fruits, vegetables and berries. Watch carefully for direction signs off Route 5 north of downtown Everett. ~ 4625 40th Place, Everett; 425-259-0253.

If you plan to catch the Mukilteo ferry to Clinton on Whidbey Island, be sure to allow enough time to visit the historic **Mukilteo Lighthouse** built in 1905. There are picnic tables above a small rocky beach cluttered with driftwood and a big grassy field for kite-flying located adjacent to the lighthouse in little Mukilteo State Park. Open April through September, weekends only, from noon to 5 p.m. ~ Mukilteo; 425-355-9656.

La Conner, built on pilings over the banks of Swinomish Channel, got its start in the 1880s as a market center for farmers in the Skagit Flats. It remains a fine example of American life at the turn of the century, with many well-preserved homes and buildings from the late 1800s. For information call or visit the **La Conner Chamber of Commerce.** ~ Morris Street between 3rd and 4th streets, La Conner; 360-466-4778.

Many of those historic structures along the waterfront now house boutiques, galleries and restaurants, while others in town such as the **Gaches Mansion,** a grand Victorian structure filled with period furnishings, are preserved as museums. Open Friday through Sunday. Admission. ~ 703 South 2nd Street, La Conner; 360-466-4446.

A walk through the collection of automobiles, farm and fishing equipment, vintage clothing, household furnishings and photographs at the **Skagit County Historical Museum** gives a further lesson on the history of the region. Closed Monday. Admission. ~ 501 South 4th Street, La Conner; 360-466-3365.

Each spring, the fields between La Conner and neighboring Mount Vernon are alive with color as the tulips and daffodils begin to appear. **The Skagit Valley Tulip Festival Office** provides a guide to the festival that runs the first two weeks of April; the guide lists events and includes a tour map of the nurseries and display gardens. ~ 117 North 1st Street, Suite 4, Mount Vernon; 360-428-5959.

There are interesting gardens to view year-round. The prettiest is **RoozenGaarde** with display gardens and a great little gift shop. ~ 1587 Beaver Marsh Road, Mount Vernon; 360-424-8531.

SCENIC SKAGIT VALLEY

The Skagit Valley has become a year-round retreat for city visitors, as nourishing to the soul in winter as it is inspiring to the adventurous spirit in summer. Indeed, artists and writers have been gathering in the Skagit for decades, including members of the famed "Northwest School" beginning in the 1930s—Mark Tobey, Morris Graves, Kenneth Callahan, Clayton James, Guy Anderson and many others. They were drawn by the Skagit's enchanting blend of meandering river levees and farm fields, bayous and bays, nearby islands and distant misty mountains, along with the extraordinary quality of the valley's ever-changing light.

Located just south of Bay View, **Padilla Bay National Estuarine Research Reserve** is the place to find bald eagles, great blue herons and dozens of other species of waterfowl and raptors. The interpretive center offers exhibits on the region's natural and maritime history. ~ 1043 Bay View Edison Road, Bay View; 360-428-1558.

Early growth in **Bellingham** centered around the industries of mining and logging. To this day, the city retains an industrial nature with thriving ports that are home to a large fishing fleet and, more recently, the Alaska Marine Highway Ferry System terminal, tempered by a firm agricultural base. Perhaps it is because of this outward appearance that visitors are often amazed at the array of cultural arts and international dining experiences to be enjoyed here.

Bellingham has two noteworthy museums. The first is the **Whatcom Children's Museum**, which has several hands-on exhibitions to delight the kids (ages 2–10). Admission. ~ 227 Prospect Street, Bellingham; 360-733-8769.

Just down the street, the red-brick Victorian architecture of the **Whatcom Museum** is as interesting as the fine collections of contemporary American art, Northwest art and regional history featured inside. It's also a good point to start a walking tour of the many outdoor sculptures scattered around downtown. Closed Monday. ~ 121 Prospect Street, Bellingham; 360-676-6981.

A Sculpture Walk route guide is available from the **Bellingham/Whatcom County Visitor and Convention Bureau**. ~ 904 Potter Street, Bellingham; 360-671-3990.

At the **Maritime Heritage Center** you can tour the hatchery, watch fish make their way up the ladder, learn about the life cycle of salmon, or just toss a line into the abutting creek for steelhead, cutthroat trout or salmon. ~ 1600 C Street, Bellingham; 360-676-6806.

✔ **CHECK THESE OUT—UNIQUE SIGHTS**

- Watch bald eagles and great blue herons fly freely at the **Padilla Bay National Estuarine Research Reserve**. *page 106*
- Delve into the past on Whidbey Island—from Indian artifacts to pioneer forts—at America's first historical reserve, **Ebey's Landing**. *page 115*
- Get to know Anacortes by taking in some of downtown's 40 **murals** reproducing turn-of-the-century photographs of the town. *page 120*
- Find out what distinguishes Puget Sound's 90 species of orca whales at San Juan Island's **Whale Museum**. *page 135*

No visit to Bellingham is complete without a trip to the **Big Rock Garden**, a fantastic, open-air gallery of Northwestern and Japanese art set in a serene Japanese garden with patio and deck areas where visitors can sit and take it all in. ~ 2900 Sylvan Street at Illinois Avenue, Bellingham; 360-676-6985.

◄ HIDDEN

Don't miss the opportunity to stroll through the grounds of **Western Washington University** on the Western Sculpture Tour to enjoy the many fountains, sculptures and tremendous variety of architecture to be found on this rich green campus. ~ McDonald Parkway, Bellingham; 360-650-3000.

Immediately adjacent to the campus is **Sehome Hill Arboretum**, 165 acres laced with six miles of hiking trails and fern-lined footpaths under a cool green canopy of moss covered trees; only the hum of traffic and the view from the observation tower remind you that you're in the city rather than some forest primeval. ~ 25th Street, Sehome Hill Neighborhood, Bellingham; 360-676-6985.

Hovander Homestead Park features a 19th-century farmhouse and handsome Victorian residence. Laced by the Nooksak River, the 720-acre park also includes **Tennant Lake**, where you'll find a boardwalk leading out over the lake and a fragrance garden with braille signs. There's also an interpretive center. Admission. ~ 5299 Neilsen Road, Ferndale; 360-384-3444.

To see the largest collection of original log homes in the state, stop by **Pioneer Park**. Each of the 14 buildings is a minimuseum. You'll see a post office, stagecoach inn, granary, veteran's museum, schoolhouse and a residence. Look for the little log church. Open May to September. Closed Monday. ~ 1st Avenue at Cherry Street, Ferndale; 360-384-6461.

Another site in the Northern Puget Sound area worth taking in is **Peace Arch State Park**. The large, white arch, flanked by American and Canadian flags, is surrounded by bountiful formal gardens and symbolizes the ongoing friendship between the two neighboring countries. The park is meticulously groomed, and spills across the international boundary. ~ Follow the signs to the park off Route 5; 360-332-8221.

In addition to its outstanding waterfront location, the friendly 26-room **Marina Village Inn** is loaded with special touches. The spacious harborside rooms have sunken sitting areas with custom sleeper sofas, cushioned seats built into large bay windows and personal telescopes for viewing Whidbey, Hat and Jetty islands. Some rooms have private decks and jacuzzi tubs. Reservations are required. ~ 1728 West Marine View Drive, Everett; 425-259-4040, 800-281-7037, fax 425-252-8419. MODERATE TO ULTRA-DELUXE.

LODGING

The Hotel Planter, originally built in 1907, is right in the thick of things when it comes to shopping and dining in downtown La

Conner. The 12 rooms have sunlights, light paint and carpeting, floral chintz comforters and pine furnishings. There's also a jacuzzi under the gazebo on the garden terrace out back. ~ 715 1st Street, La Conner; 360-466-4710, 800-488-5409, fax 360-466-1320. MODERATE TO DELUXE.

White Swan Guest House offers accommodations in a country setting. The rooms are country casual and there's a superb collection of samplers spread across the house. The English country garden features a big orchard where you're welcome to pick your own apples and plums, as well as pears. A separate cottage offers kitchen facilities. Country continental breakfast and homemade chocolate chip cookies are included. ~ 1388 Moore Road, Mount Vernon; 360-445-6805. MODERATE TO DELUXE.

Built in 1914, the **Benson Farmstead Bed and Breakfast** is a four-room charmer in the heart of "north valley" farms. Some guests come for the homemade desserts, big farm breakfasts and cozy rooms full of country antiques. Others come for the chance to stay on a working farm that's been in operation for more than eight decades. Still others stay for the proximity to some of the state's best country bicycling. ~ 1009 Avon-Allen Road, Bow; 360-757-0578. MODERATE.

HIDDEN ▶ As you might guess from the name, **Schnauzer Crossing** is presided over by a delightful pair of schnauzers. Choose from a spacious master suite with fireplace, garden sitting room, jacuzzi tub and double shower, a smaller lakeview room done in iris motif or a recently completed cottage, perfect for families or couples seeking romantic seclusion. Well-thought-out amenities in each room include thick terry robes for the trip to the hot tub in the Japanese garden. Gourmet breakfast included. ~ 4421 Lakeway Drive, Bellingham; 360-733-0055, 800-562-2808, fax 360-734-2808. DELUXE TO ULTRA-DELUXE.

Tucked into the rose garden near the north end of picturesque Chuckanut Drive is the **Hostelling International—Bellingham**. You will find this your typical hostel environment: men's and women's dorms, showers and laundry facilities. All the action of the Fairhaven district is within walking distance. ~ 107 Chuckanut Drive, Bellingham; 360-671-1750. BUDGET.

Housed in the old Blaine Air Force Base a few miles from the Canadian border, the **Hostelling International—Birch Bay** provides 40 beds in bare shared or private rooms. Pluses here include a sauna and the hostel's proximity to Birch Bay State Park. Reservations required from October through April. ~ 7467 Gemini Street, Blaine; 360-371-2180. BUDGET.

There is something for everyone at the sumptuous **Inn at Semiahmoo**, located on the tip of the sandy spit stretched between Semiahmoo Bay and Drayton Harbor. History buffs will enjoy browsing through the inn's collection of early photography, romantics will delight in a walk on the beach or a leisurely sunset meal in one of the restaurants or lounges, and sports fanatics will flip over the array of activities, including charter boats, parasailing and jet skiing. The 196 guest rooms are spacious and nicely appointed; some rooms have decks or patios, and others have fireplaces. ~ 9565 Semiahmoo Parkway, Blaine; 360-371-2000, 800-770-7992, fax 360-371-5490. ULTRA-DELUXE.

DINING

◄ HIDDEN

The history of **Charles at Smugglers Cove** is as good as the food, making it doubly worth the drive out to Mukilteo. This red-brick mansion-turned-restaurant was purportedly owned at one time by Mafia kingpin Al Capone. Today the owners traffic in fresh seafood and steaks with French flair; their bouillabaisse, châteaubriand, rack of lamb, prawns in tarragon butter and baked Alaska are outstanding, and the setting in the elegant dining rooms or on the sheltered deck is splendid. Closed Sunday. ~ 8340 53rd Avenue West, Mukilteo; 206-347-2700. DELUXE.

Anthony's Home Port is the spot for seafood when it comes to waterfront dining in Everett. Prime picks on the menu include six varieties of fresh oysters, steamed Discovery Bay clams or Whidbey Island mussels, grilled steak and prawns, Dungeness crab cakes and pan-fried scallops sprinkled with gremolada. Their four-course Sunset Dinner (served from 4:30 to 6 p.m.) is a bargain and includes everything from appetizer to dessert. You can dine alfresco on the deck or pick a spot in the considerably less breezy dining room or lounge. ~ 1725 West Marine View Drive, Everett; 206-252-3333. MODERATE.

The same people own and operate the **Lighthouse Inn** in nearby La Conner, so you can expect extra-large servings here as well, though the fare of this waterfront location is primarily seafood and pasta. Favorites include lobster, fresh barbecued fish, clam strips and prime rib, with fish and chips and burgers thrown in to please the little ones. The simple nautical decor leaves something to be desired, but the fresh flowers and dim lamps on the tables lend a slight air of romance. ~ 512 South 1st Street, La Conner; 360-466-3149. MODERATE.

Best bet for breakfast or lunch in La Conner is the **Calico Cupboard** at the south end of the main drag, where they serve hearty and wholesome baked goods, soups, salads, sandwiches and vegetarian fare as good for the heart as for the taste buds. Don't be surprised if there is a line to get in to this modest café. ~ 720 South 1st Street, La Conner; 360-466-4451. BUDGET.

The Norwegian proprietors of the **Farmhouse Inn**, a large restaurant with country decor dominated by heavy oak tables and chairs, believe in serving up solid, old-country-style portions of meat and potato classics—fried chicken and french fries, roast turkey with mashed potatoes and gravy, rib eyes and baked potatoes—along with a hearty selection of daily baked goods like their famous pies thrown in for good measure. The lunch buffet and children's menu are great bargains. ~ 1376 La Conner–Whitney Road, Mount Vernon; 360-466-4411. BUDGET TO MODERATE.

> The greatest concentration of wintering bald eagles can be found in the Skagit River Bald Eagle Natural Area.

In addition to coffees and teas, the coffee shop in **Tony's Coffees & Teas** serves up fresh daily soups, salads, sandwiches and pastries to an eclectic crowd of regulars. It's almost too bohemian, but the bagels with cream cheese and sprouts, Greek salad and cocoa mocha make it worth the trip. ~ 1101 Harris Avenue, Bellingham; 360-738-4710. BUDGET.

Paper lanterns and fans add a dash of color to liven up the bare-bones decor of the new **Tokyo House** with its industrial-style tables and chairs. Patrons don't come here for the atmosphere but for tasty Japanese standards with interesting additions to the menu such as kim chee. Service is prompt and the eatery is as neat as a pin. ~ 1222 North Garden Street, Bellingham; 360-733-6784. BUDGET.

HIDDEN ►

Warm reds and yellows in the dining room decor and walls decorated with banners and paintings by local artists give an inviting and relaxed atmosphere to **Il Fiasco**. The seasonal menu features a variety of salads, antipasti, pastas and *piatti forti* (usually fish, veal or duck) highlighted by whatever special the imaginative chef creates each day. Ask any resident and they'll invariably tell you that this is *the* place for fine dining in Bellingham. ~ 1309 Commercial Street, Bellingham; 360-676-9136. MODERATE TO DELUXE.

The tables at **Café Toulouse** are always full, a testament to the quality breakfast, lunch and dessert selections served here. Favorites include fresh fruit pancakes, curried chicken salad, roast pork loin with mint jelly or smoked turkey with cranberry-apple cream cheese sandwiches. You will also find pizzas and calzones from their wood-fire stove, and many selections from the fresh daily dessert board accompanied by piping espresso or latte to finish the meal. ~ 114 West Magnolia Street, Crown Plaza Building, #102, Bellingham; 360-733-8996. BUDGET.

For Mexican dining, try **Chihuahua**. Decorated with Mexican murals, paintings and parrot sculptures, the dining room offers booth and table seating. There's also dining in an enclosed patio. Popular specialties are fajitas, carne asada and a wide variety of combination plates. ~ 5694 3rd Avenue, Ferndale; 360-384-5820. BUDGET TO MODERATE.

HIDDEN ►

Since it is always so busy, locals would probably prefer not to share the **Vista Pizza, Rib and Steak House**. Rumor has it that the amazingly low-priced one-pound steak dinner brings in enough business to this smoke-filled little diner to generate $1.4 million a year. Though it's not made clear on the menu, the generously proportioned luncheon special of lasagna, spaghetti or pizza and a trip to the salad bar is still available in the evenings, making it possible to get a substantial meal for under $7 per person, tip included. ~ 442 Peace Portal Drive, Blaine; 360-332-5155. BUDGET.

For romantic waterfront dining, it's hard to beat the Inn at Semiahmoo's elegant dining room, **Stars**. Soft piano music fills the room as diners feast on deluxe-priced filet of salmon roasted on an alder plank, venison in a red currant sauce, Dungeness crab-cakes, wok-charred sea scallops and other rich entrées. For lighter fare, try the livelier, budget-priced **Packers Oyster Bar** just down the corridor for fresh steamer clams, a salmon sandwich, shrimp caesar salad or homestyle burgers. ~ 9565 Semiahmoo Parkway, Blaine; 360-371-2000. BUDGET TO DELUXE.

SHOPPING

Antique hounds will want to make the quick 15-minute trip east of Everett to Snohomish, home to **Star Center Antique Mall**, a five-level mall with over 165 dealers and dozens of other antique shops to browse through. ~ 829 2nd Street, Snohomish; 360-568-2131.

Shopping is a major drawing card of little La Conner, with most of the boutiques and galleries concentrated along 1st and Morris streets. Focus on **Earthenworks** at 713 1st Street (360-466-4422) and **The Scott Collection** in the Pier 7 Building on 1st Street (360-466-3691) for fine art. **Bunnies by the Bay** carries collectibles and unique gifts. ~ 617 East Morris Street; 360-466-5040. **The Wood Merchant** features handcrafted gifts and custom furniture by Northwest woodworkers. ~ 709 South 1st Street, La Conner; 360-466-4741. Ethnic folk art as well as fine art and crafts by regional artists are sold at **Janet Huston Gallery**. ~ 413 Morris Street, La Conner; 360-466-5001. The historic **Tillinghast Seed Company** has been in business for over 100 years. Besides a variety of seeds for sale, there is a flower shop, a garden store, kitchen supplies and a Christmas attic. ~ 623 East Morris Street, La Conner; 360-466-3329.

At **Go Outside**, the owners' remarkable taste is reflected in an appealing collection of garden tools, clothing and art selected with great care. ~ 111 Morris Street, La Conner; 360-466-4836.

Don't miss **Cascade Candy**—it produces first-class truffles and other chocolate concoctions at about half the price of similar candy-makers in Seattle or Vancouver, B.C. ~ 605 South 1st Street, La Conner; 360-466-2971.

The best shops and galleries in Bellingham are generally located in the Fairhaven District. You'll find an eclectic collection of goods including steins, beerabilia and 200 varieties of beer, as well as food and cocktails, at **Bullie's Restaurant, Cocktail Lounge and Oyster Bar**. ~ Marketplace Building, 12th Street and Harris

Avenue, Bellingham; 360-734-2855. **Artwood,** a co-op gallery of fine woodworking by Northwest artists, is also in Bellingham. ~ 1000 Harris Avenue, Bellingham; 360-647-1628. Try **Inside Passage** for gifts of the Pacific Northwest. ~ 355 Harris Avenue, Suite 103, Bellingham; 360-734-1790.

NIGHTLIFE   Everett's **Club Broadway Entertainment Center** offers several after-hours options under one roof, including a sports bar, dance club, jazz club and country-and-western bar. ~ 1611 Everett Avenue, Everett; 206-259-3551. Things are jumping at **Anthony's Homeport,** with great happy-hour prices and a nice sheltered deck overlooking the marina. ~ 1725 West Marine View Drive, Everett; 206-252-3333.

The **La Conner Tavern,** housed in a waterfront structure that was at one time Brewster's Cigar Store, is the primary watering hole in La Conner and does a booming business through the wee hours of the morning. ~ 702 1st Street, La Conner; 360-466-9932.

There are a half-dozen other country taverns scattered across the Skagit Valley, well known to locals but nearly unknown to tourists, which also serve up terrific burgers, microbrewery ales and bitters and weekend jazz and dancing. The **Conway Tavern and Eatery** is best for burgers. ~ 1667 Spruce Street, Conway; 360-445-4733. The **Old Edison Inn** is also very popular. ~ 583 Cains Court, Edison; 360-766-6266.

HIDDEN ►   You'll find great happy-hour specials and the best sunset views in the little bar of **Le Chat Noir.** ~ 1200 Harris Avenue, Sycamore Square, Suite 306, Fairhaven; 360-733-6136.

BEACHES & PARKS   **MUKILTEO STATE PARK** 🚶 🛶 ⛽ 🏖 🎣 ⚓ A swath of beach adjacent to the Whidbey Island–Mukilteo Ferry facilities on Puget Sound, Mukilteo State Park is a day-use-only facility known primarily as a prime fishing spot with public boat launch. Noble little Elliott Point Lighthouse, also known as Mukilteo Lighthouse, on the tip will keep shutterbugs happy; it's also a fine spot for beachcombing or picnicking while waiting for the ferry to Whidbey Island. Facilities include restrooms, picnic grounds and floats. ~ Take the Mukilteo exit off Route 5 and follow the signs to the ferry; 206-353-2923.

BAY VIEW STATE PARK 🚶 🚲 ⚓ 🎣 🏖 ⚓ This tiny park on the north side of the town of Bay View overlooks the **Padilla Bay National Estuarine Research Reserve,** an 11,600-acre ecological pocket of marsh and tidelands tucked between the north Skagit Valley at Bay View and March Point. The Breazeale Padilla Bay Interpretive Center, half a mile north on Bay View–Edison Road, is a good place to get better acquainted with the many forms of wildlife that inhabit the area. A nature trail winds through parts of the wildlife habitat area just beyond the center. There are rest-rooms, showers, fireplaces, picnic tables and shelter and a kitchen; restaurants and groceries are in Burlington. ~ Take Exit 230 off Route 5 in Burlington, follow Route 20 west to Bay View–Edison Road. Turn right, then follow the signs to the park; 360-757-0227.

▲ There are 76 sites (RV hookups available); $11 to $16 per night.

LARRABEE STATE PARK 🏃 🚲 🏖 🛶 🚤 🛥 🚣 This 2683-acre park on Samish Bay offers nine miles of hiking trails, including two steep trails to small mountain lakes (Fragrance and Lost lakes), and a stretch of beach with numerous tidepools for views of the local marine life. There's good freshwater fishing in either of the mountain lakes and saltwater fishing in Chuckanut and Samish bays. You'll find restrooms, showers, picnic tables and shelters, barbecue grills and kitchens; restaurant and groceries are nearby. ~ Located seven miles south of Bellingham on scenic Chuckanut Drive (Route 11); 360-676-2093.

▲ There are 59 tent sites and 26 hookups; $11 to $16 per night.

TEDDY BEAR COVE 🏖 This secluded, narrow stretch of white sand bordered by thick trees just south of the Bellingham city limits is a public beach that was once a well-hidden haunt for nudists. There are no facilities and the water is very cold in case you are thinking of swimming. The beach area curves out around the shallow cove, like a thumb jutting out toward Chuckanut Bay. ~ There's a well-signed parking lot along Chuckanut Drive, Route 11, at the intersection of California Street. The trail to the beach is marked with signs at the parking lot and meanders down a steep bank for 100 yards or so from the road; 360-733-2900.

◄ HIDDEN

BIRCH BAY STATE PARK 🏃 🏖 🛶 🚣 🚣 The highlight of this 192-acre park with 6000 feet of shoreline is the warm, shallow bay, suitable for wading up to half a mile out in spots, bordered by a mile-long stretch of driftwood and shell-strewn beach edged by grassland. Swimming and fishing are both excellent here. The camping area is inland in a stand of old-growth cedar and Douglas fir; nestled in the lush greenery it's hard to tell that the park sits in the shadow of Arco's Cherry Point Refinery. Birdwatchers frequent the park to visit the marshy estuary at the south border that attracts over 100 varieties of birds. You'll find restrooms, fireplaces, picnic tables, shelters, trails and an underwater park; some facilities for disabled; restaurants, groceries and a boat launch are nearby. ~ It's eight miles south of Blaine off Birch Bay; 360-371-2800.

▲ There are 167 sites here, some with RV hookups; $11 to $16 per night.

SEMIAHMOO PARK 🚲 🏊 🚤 This long, slender spit dividing Semiahmoo Bay and Drayton Harbor is a favorite among beach lovers, who can comb sandy, narrow beaches on both sides of the spit, and of birdwatchers who come here to observe bald eagles, loons, herons and other species supported by this protected, nutrient-rich habitat. You'll encounter outstanding clamming on both sides of the spit. The spit was once home to the Semiahmoo Indians and later the site of a fish cannery; the history of both are reviewed in the park's museum. There are restrooms, picnic tables, fire pits and a bike path. ~ Take the Birch Bay–Lynden Road exit west off Route 5, turn north onto Harbor View Road then west onto Lincoln Road, which becomes Semiahmoo Parkway and leads into the park; 360-733-2900.

Whidbey Island

▼▼▼▼▼▼▼▼▼▼▼▼

Whidbey Island, stretching north to south along the mainland, is the longest island in the continental United States. This slender, serpentine bit of land is covered in a rolling patchwork of loganberry farms, pasturelands, sprawling state parks, hidden heritage sites and historic small towns. The artistic hamlet of Langley near Whidbey's southern tip is a current hot spot for weekend escapes from Seattle.

SIGHTS

Most of the sights in **Langley** are concentrated along 1st and 2nd streets, where falsefront shops house small galleries, boutiques and restaurants. There's a lovely stretch of public beach flanked by a concrete wall adorned in Northwest Indian motifs just below **Seawall Park** (look for the totem pole on 1st Street), and a wonderful bronze statue by local artist Georgia Gerber above a second stairwell leading down to the beach.

In the spring months, you'll find a colorful tulip display at **Holland Gardens**. During the balance of the year come to see the beautiful floral displays that make this small garden a local favorite. ~ 500 Avenue West and 30th Street Northwest, Oak Harbor.

Beautiful greenery typifies Whidbey Island, and two Greenbank area establishments offer visitors a close look at cultivating the landscape. The famous **Meerkerk Rhododendron Gardens** feature hundreds of varieties of these showy bushes—with 2000 native and hybrid species spread across 53 acres—which find Whidbey's climate one of the best on earth. Magnolia, maple and cherry trees add to the beauty of this spot, which is also a test garden. May and June are the peak months for blooms. The nursery has rhodies for sale. ~ Just off Route 525 south of Greenbank; 360-678-1912.

Nearby **Sassafras Farm** is devoted to herbs, with dozens of examples of how rosemary, thyme, oregano, sage and other plants can be both ornamental and useful. Its nursery offers plants for sale, too. ~ 3223 Day Road, Greenbank; 360-678-7135.

Only a few wine grapes ripen in Puget Sound's cool climate; **Whidbey Island Vineyard & Winery** specializes in clean, crisp vintages, such as Madelaine Angevine and Siegerrebe, that are rarely grown elsewhere. ~ 5237 South Langley Road; 360-221-2040.

The **Ebey's Landing National Historical Reserve,** the first such reserve in the country, lies midway up Whidbey Island. The reserve takes in 17,400 acres that include Fort Ebey and Fort Casey state parks and the historic town of Coupeville, where falsefront buildings line Front Street above the wharf. Here you'll find **Alexander Blockhouse** (Alexander and Front streets) and **Davis Blockhouse** (Sunnyside Cemetery Road), built by early settlers for protection against possible Indian attacks, and a good collection of pioneer agricultural displays and artifacts in the **Island County Historical Museum** at 908 Northwest Alexander Street in Coupeville (360-678-3310). ~ Ebey's Landing National Historical Reserve: P.O. Box 774, Coupeville, WA 98239; 360-678-6084.

Built in 1901, **Admiralty Head Lighthouse** at Fort Casey State Park features an interpretive center offering history on the region's military past. You'll also enjoy excellent views of Puget Sound. ~ 1280 South Fort Casey Road, Coupeville; 360-678-4519.

The beautiful **Inn at Langley** has perfected the fine art of hospitality at a polished property worthy of its magnificent waterfront setting. With a decorator's color palette taken directly from the beach, rooms in shades of gray, cream, tan and brown accented by lots of natural wood are elegant, presenting a delicate balance of modern art and furnishings, and are decked out with every possible amenity (fireplace, jacuzzi, Krups coffee set and large deck to take advantage of the view). A serene oriental garden set in front of the grand dining room is an added touch. If you can afford the tariff, this is the most luxurious selection available on the island. ~ 400 1st Street, Langley; 360-221-3033. ULTRA-DELUXE.

LODGING

◄ *HIDDEN*

✔ **CHECK THESE OUT—UNIQUE LODGING**

- *Budget to deluxe:* Relax in a mineral bath or three-tiered sauna before retiring to a rustic cabin at **Doe Bay Village Resort.** *page 130*
- *Moderate:* Chow down on a big farm breakfast after toiling on **Benson Farmstead Bed and Breakfast's** working farm. *page 108*
- *Deluxe:* Check into the **Wharfside Bed and Breakfast,** a 60-foot two-masted sailboat docked on San Juan Island. *page 126*
- *Ultra-deluxe:* Be pampered at Whidbey Island's **Inn at Langley** as you unwind on a deck overlooking Puget Sound. *page 115*

Budget: under $50   Moderate: $50–$90   Deluxe: $90–$130   Ultra-deluxe: over $130

HIDDEN ►

Gallery Suite overlooks Saratoga Passage and includes a bedroom, parlor, kitchen and great views from a private deck. Furnished with contemporary pieces and an antique Japanese chest, this inn is convenient to good shopping and restaurants in turn-of-the-century Langley. Gay-friendly. ~ 302 1st Street, Langley; 360-221-2978. MODERATE TO DELUXE.

Though it's only a few miles north of downtown Langley, the **Log Castle Bed and Breakfast** somehow feels like a retreat hidden away on a gorgeous, sandy beach far from everything. This colossal log home crowned by an eight-sided turret was built bit by bit over the years. The four rooms are warm and inviting, with private baths and comfortable furnishings, and private decks with grand views. ~ 4693 Saratoga Road, Langley; 360-221-5483, fax 360-221-6249. DELUXE.

Cliff House is an architecturally stunning two-story structure of wood and sweeping panes of glass set on a wooded bluff overlooking Admiralty Inlet. Guests have the run of the entire two-bedroom house, with its open central atrium, wonderful gourmet kitchen, sunken sitting area with fireplace and wrap-around cedar deck with large jacuzzi. There is also a separate small cottage with one bedroom. ~ 5440 Windmill Road, Freeland; 360-331-1566. ULTRA-DELUXE.

Of Washington State's nearly 400 bed-and-breakfast inns, almost 25 percent are on Whidbey Island.

The **Captain Whidbey Inn**, a well-preserved and maintained log inn on Penn Cove, is a fine example of the type of Northwest retreat all the rage 50 years ago and now coming back into fashion. This walk into the past offers several cozy, antique furnished rooms that share two baths and waterfront views; more recent additions to the property include two rows of spacious, pine-paneled rooms with baths and a few private cottages with fireplaces. A full breakfast is served in the dining room where the wooden floors creek nostalgically and the massive stone fireplace chases away the chill. This is one of only a handful of waterside accommodations in the region; to enjoy the water fully, arrange for an afternoon sail with Captain John Colby Stone, the third-generation descendant of the original innkeeper. ~ 2072 West Captain Whidbey Inn Road, Coupeville; 360-678-4097, 800-366-4097, fax 360-678-4110. DELUXE TO ULTRA-DELUXE.

The **Auld Holland Inn** is a moderately priced roadside motel with flair, from the flowering window boxes on the European exterior to the immaculately clean, antique-filled rooms. Some rooms even have fireplaces and princess canopied beds. For those seeking budget prices, there are 24 mobile home units with two or three bedrooms tucked behind the full-sized windmill housing the motel's office. If you're looking for more luxurious surroundings, there are six deluxe-priced units furnished with jacuzzis and fire-places. ~ 33575 Route 20, Oak Harbor; 360-675-2288, 800-228-0148, fax 360-675-2817. BUDGET TO ULTRA-DELUXE.

Since 1989, **Café Langley** has served Greek favorites like spani-kopita, moussaka, dolmades and lamb shish kabobs along with fresh seafood (Penn Cove mussels, grilled salmon and halibut), pastas and steaks. The atmosphere here is airy Mediterranean, with stucco-like walls, exposed beams and an assortment of ex-otic fish etched on a glass partition. There are often people wait-ing in the park across the street for a table in this popular café. ~ 113 1st Street, Langley; 360-221-3090. MODERATE.

DINING

The **Doghouse Tavern** is the place to go for great ribs, ham-burgers, fish-and-chips and chowder. A totem on the side of this waterfront building points the way to their separate family din-ing room in case you've got the kids along. ~ 230 1st Street, Lang-ley; 360-221-9825. BUDGET.

The **Star Bistro Café and Bar**, a trendy little café with art deco decor, is a popular meeting spot for lunch, dinner and drinks. Their pastas, salads and espressos are particularly good, and the grilled pesto King salmon on a french roll is inventive and tasty. On a calm day you can dine alfresco on the second-floor deck with a great view of the Saratoga Passage. ~ 201½ 1st Street, Lang-ley; 360-221-2627. MODERATE.

Toby's Tavern serves up a cheeseburger that was rated tops by actress Kathleen Turner, who starred in the film *War of the Roses*, which was filmed partly in and around Coupeville in 1989. Good fish-and-chips, Penn Cove steamed mussels and an upscale atmos-phere add a touch of class to this waterfront watering hole. ~ 8 Northwest Front Street, Coupeville; 360-678-4222. MODERATE.

Award-winning **Rosi's Garden** serves a blend of Northwest and gourmet Italian cuisine. On the menu you'll find Penn Cove mussels, garlic-and-black-pepper–crusted prime rib, halibut flo-rentine and poached salmon in hollandaise. Save room for the decadent desserts. Seating in the front room of this tiny, historic Victorian seaside cottage is very limited, so reservations for din-ner, the only meal they serve, are highly recommended. There is live classical music Wednesday and Friday nights. ~ 606 North Main Street, Coupeville; 360-678-3989. MODERATE.

At **Kasteel Franssen**, lace table dressings, antiques, tapestries and fine art reproductions of Rembrandt and other masters set a romantic European tone well suited to this Northwest French res-taurant. Special dishes include ostrich in pinot noir–shallot tar-ragon demi-glace, Ellensburg rack of lamb and specials that fea-ture venison, pheasant and other wild game. Dinner only. ~ 33505 Route 20, Oak Harbor; 360-675-0724. MODERATE.

SHOPPING   There's plenty to keep shoppers and browsers busy on Whidbey Island, especially in artsy Langley and historic Coupeville. The best art galleries are concentrated in Langley. **Museo Piccolo** specializes in art glass made by the owner and other regional artists. ~ 215 1st Street, Langley; 206-221-7737. The **Childers/Proctor Gallery** showcases bronzes, paintings, sculpture and pottery. ~ 302 1st Street, Langley; 360-221-2978. **Soleil** carries Nambe ware, double-sided aluminum pieces by Arthur Court and jewelry by local craftspeople. ~ 308 1st Street, Langley; 360-221-0383. The **Hellebore Glass Studio** has fine handblown glass and a studio where you can watch them work. ~ 308 1st Street, Langley; 360-221-2067.

Another noteworthy shop in town is **The Star Store**, a modern mercantile selling fun clothing and housewares. ~ 201 1st Street; 360-221-5222. You can also browse the two shops of **Whidbey Island Antiques**. ~ 2nd Street and Anthes Avenue, Langley; 360-221-2393.

Blackfish Gallerio offers women's clothing with handpainted designs on raw silk. Check out the gallery for Northwest photography, jewelry, handwovens and pottery, all made by local artists. ~ 111 Anthes Street, Langley; 360-221-1274.

There's an array of charming shops in the revitalized waterfront district of Coupeville. You'll find wonderful antiques and collectibles at **Elk Horn Truck Antiques**. ~ 15 Front Street, Coupeville; 360-678-2250. Fine imported clothing and jewelry from Scotland and Ireland are the specialties at **Tartans and Tweeds**. ~ 4 Front Street, Coupeville; 360-678-6244. Nautical gifts, artifacts and sportswear can be found at **Nautical 'N' Nice**. ~ 22 Front Street, Coupeville; 360-678-3565.

NIGHTLIFE   **Hong Kong Gardens** has a pool table and karaoke. ~ 4643 East State Highway 525, Clinton; 360-341-2828.

For local color in a friendly tavern try the cozy pub in the **Captain Whidbey Inn**, where the walls are adorned with university pennants and business cards. ~ 2072 West Captain Whidbey Inn Road, Coupeville; 360-678-4097.

BEACHES & PARKS   **SOUTH WHIDBEY STATE PARK** 🕴 🏊 🛶   There are 340 acres with 4500 feet of rocky shoreline to explore in this lovely state park. Hikers here will enjoy the one-and-a-half-mile loop trail through an old-growth stand of fir and cedar. Black-tailed deer, bald eagles and osprey are among the many creatures here. Only the hardy will venture into the cold waters of Admiralty Inlet for a dip. There are restrooms, showers, picnic tables and shelter and fireplaces; restaurants and groceries are nearby. ~ Take Route 525 nine miles north of Clinton to Bush Point Road, which after six miles becomes Smuggler's Cove Road; 360-331-4559.

▲ There are 54 standard sites and 3 primitive ones; $10 per night. Sites on the wooded bluff above the beach are secluded.

FORT CASEY STATE PARK History buffs and children will enjoy exploring the military fortification of this 137-acre park. While most of the big guns are gone, you'll still find panoramic views of the Olympic Mountains across the Strait of Juan de Fuca from the top of the concrete bunkers built into the escarpment. Wild roses and other flowers line the paths to the museum housed in pretty Admiralty Head Lighthouse and the beachside campground that overlooks the Keystone Harbor ferry terminal. Scuba enthusiasts swarm to the underwater trail through the park's marine wildlife sanctuary off Keystone Harbor, and anglers try for salmon and steelhead. You'll find restrooms, showers, picnic tables, fireplaces and an underwater marine park; restaurants and groceries are nearby. ~ At Coupeville turn south off Route 20 onto Engle Road and follow the Keystone Ferry signs to the park; 360-678-4519.

▲ There are 35 sites; $10 to $11 per night.

FORT EBEY STATE PARK The massive guns are long gone from this coastal World War II fortification, but there are still bunker tunnels and pillboxes to be explored. The picturesque beach at Partridge Point is the hands-down favorite of the islanders; at low tide it's possible to walk the five-mile beach stretch to Fort Casey. Anglers cast a rod for bass on Lake Pondilla. Facilities include restrooms, showers, picnic tables, fireplaces and nature trails; restaurants and groceries are nearby. ~ From Route 20 turn west onto Libbey Road, then south onto Hill Valley Drive and follow the signs; 360-678-4636.

▲ There are 50 sites; $10 to $11 per night. The secluded campsites under a canopy of Douglas fir are much nicer than the crowded sites at nearby Fort Casey.

OAK HARBOR CITY BEACH PARK A full-scale windmill and an A-6 Intruder, first used in Vietnam and donated by the Navy, are just two of the features of this day-use park on Oak Harbor Bay next to the sewage processing plant (not a deterrent, believe it or not). A sandy beach slopes down from the lighted walking path bordering expansive green fields suitable for flying kites or playing frisbee. There's a wading pool and protected swimming area. You'll find bathhouses, picnic tables, ball fields, tennis and volleyball courts and a playground. ~ Located in downtown Oak Harbor off Pioneer Parkway, east of Route 20; watch for the windmill; 360-679-5551.

DECEPTION PASS STATE PARK The most popular state park in Washington, it encompasses over 4800 acres laced with eight-and-a-half miles of hiking trails through forested hills and wetland areas and along rocky headlands. There are several delightful sandy stretches for picnics or beachcombing. Breathtaking views from the 976-foot steel bridge spanning the pass attract photographers from around the world. At Cranberry Lake's south shore you'll find beaver dams and muskrats. There's swimming on Cranberry Lake in the summer and flyfishing for trout on Pass Lake. Facilities include restrooms, showers, a bathhouse, picnic tables, kitchens, shelters, fireplaces, a concession stand, an environmental learning center and an underwater park; restaurants are nearby. ~ Take the Mukilteo ferry to Whidbey Island and follow Route 525 and Route 20 to the park on the northern tip of the island; 360-675-2417.

▲ There are 255 sites at Deception Pass and 16 at Bowman Bay; $11 per night.

Fidalgo Island

A two-hour drive northwest of Seattle, Anacortes on Fidalgo Island is a good place to enjoy folk art, ride a charming excursion train and see impressive murals. Quiet inns and waterfront restaurants make this town a pleasant retreat.

But Anacortes is only the beginning of adventures on this charming island. Often called the first of the San Juans, Fidalgo is actually linked to the mainland by the Route 20 bridge over Swinomish Channel in the Skagit Valley, and to Whidbey Island by another bridge. Access is easy. Nevertheless, you can still find quiet beaches and parks to explore. Lonely trails wind through an enormous forest reserve to superb viewpoints. A mini "Lake District" clusters more than half-a-dozen splendid lakes. And a marvelous new resort complex—Scimitar Ridge Ranch—combines a working Northwest horse ranch and a deluxe campground that includes covered wagons outfitted for camping.

SIGHTS

Because of its ferry terminal, **Anacortes** is known as "the gateway to the San Juans," but don't just zip on through because there's plenty to see and do here. One of the best ways to get acquainted with the city and its history is to make a walking tour of downtown to view the 40 life-size murals attached to many of the historical buildings. As part of the **Anacortes Mural Project,** these murals are reproductions of turn-of-the-century photographs depicting everyday scenes and early pioneers of the town. A tour map of the murals is available from the **Anacortes Chamber of Commerce.** ~ 819 Commercial Avenue, Anacortes; 360-293-3832.

Another reminder of earlier days is the **W. T. Preston,** a drydocked sternwheeler that once plied the waters of the Sound breaking up log jams. ~ 7th Street and R Avenue, Anacortes; 360-293-1900.

Next door is the refurbished **Burlington Northern Railroad Depot,** now a community arts center and the spot to catch the **Anacortes Railway,** an elaborate miniature steam locomotive with three passenger cars built by a local resident. The train is operated on summer weekends. ~ 6th Street and R Avenue, Anacortes; 360-293-2634.

At the **Anacortes Museum**, you'll find an entertaining collection of memorabilia from Fidalgo and Guemes islands. In front of the building there's a highly amusing drinking fountain with varying levels suited for dogs, cats, horses and humans, which was donated to the city by the Women's Temperance Union. Closed Tuesday and Wednesday. ~ 1305 8th Street, Anacortes; 360-293-1915.

Even if you don't plan to stay in Anacortes at the **Majestic Hotel**, stop by for a 360-degree view of Fidalgo and surrounding islands from the fantastic cupola above fourth-floor suites and ogle the amazing skylight and collection of art and antiques. ~ 419 Commercial Avenue, Anacortes; 360-293-3355.

◄ HIDDEN

If you have an interest in **totems**, drive by 2102 9th Street to see the display in front of the home of former State Senator Paul Luvera, Sr., who carved thousands of totems during his retirement before passing away several years ago.

At the **Holiday Motel** one of the only motels that keeps its prices low even during high season, you get what you pay for. Aging rooms are very basic but tidy, with nicked furnishings in both the cramped bedroom and separate sitting room. ~ 2903 Commercial Avenue, Anacortes; 360-293-6511. BUDGET.

LODGING

A lot of care and expense went into the painstaking renovation of the historic 1889 McNaught Building, now the **Majestic Hotel** which specializes in European elegance, from the plush feather bedding and antique furnishings of each highly individual guest room to the warm and inviting mahogany-paneled library and grand English garden. Guests are treated to croissants and coffee each morning. ~ 419 Commercial Avenue, Anacortes; 360-293-3355, 800-588-4780, fax 360-293-5214. DELUXE TO ULTRA-DELUXE.

◄ HIDDEN

At the **Nantucket Guest House Inn** the proprietress was welcoming weary travelers into her home long before bed and break-

DECEPTION PASS BRIDGE

Spanning the "Grand Canyon of Puget Sound," Deception Pass Bridge links Whidbey with Fidalgo Island. Most visitors just drive slowly by, taking in the sights. But for a little more excitement, stroll out onto the bridge for vertigo-inducing views—straight down into the swift, churning currents of Deception Pass. You can also walk down to the shore on the footpaths of Pass Island to watch the streaming waters up close and personal.

fasts came into fashion. Each of the comfortable guest rooms is furnished in lovingly polished family antiques and cozy quilts; of the seven rooms, three have private baths. ~ 3402 Commercial Avenue, Anacortes; 360-293-6007, 888-293-6007, fax 306-299-4399. MODERATE.

DINING

Gisela's **Bridgeway Café** serves a mix of German and American cuisine. In addition to the traditional hand-breaded oysters and prawns, grilled burgers and mouth-watering pies that have kept the original Bridgeway in business for over 50 years, the new owners now serve schnitzel and German sausages. Look for this un-pretentious roadside establishment located on the hill four miles north of Deception Pass. Closed Monday and Tuesday. ~ 1541 Route 20, Anacortes; 360-293-9250. BUDGET.

Although it's not particularly well decorated or romantic, **La Petite** is the only dinner spot in town fancy enough to have table-cloths. The fare here is solid Dutch gourmet, with often repeated favorites such as *gemarinder de lam* (marinated lamb in herbs and red wine) and *kippige knoflock* (chicken breast over parmesan pasta). The traditional Dutch breakfast of egg cup, thinly sliced ham and cheese and piping hot loaves of bread draws a crowd. ~ 3401 Commercial Avenue, Anacortes; 360-293-4644. DELUXE.

Potted plants, taped classical music and tablecloths soften the rough edges of **Charlie's**, a roadside hash house overlooking the ferry terminal and water. Captive diners, here during the long wait for the ferry, choose from soups, salads, sandwiches and seafood at lunch and pasta, steak and seafood for dinner. ~ 5407 Ferry Terminal Road, Anacortes; 360-293-7377. MODERATE.

SHOPPING

At the fascinating and fun **Bunnies by the Bay** you can tour the workshop where they create designer stuffed animals to comple-ment any decor scheme. ~ 3115 V Place, Anacortes; 360-293-

---

✔ **CHECK THESE OUT—UNIQUE DINING**

- *Budget:* Dig into a wood-fired calzone as you survey the local scene at **Café Toulouse**. *page 110*
- *Budget to moderate:* Enjoy a hearty meal of American classics like roast turkey and fried chicken at the **Farmhouse Inn**. *page 109*
- *Moderate:* Watch a lingering sunset as you dine on today's catch of fresh fish pulled from Puget Sound at **Islander Lopez Restaurant**. *page 125*
- *Deluxe:* Make a detour to **Charles at Smugglers Cove**, a red-brick mansion purportedly once owned by Al Capone. *page 109*

Budget: under $8   Moderate: $8–$16   Deluxe: $16–$24   Ultra-deluxe: over $24

8037. The same business also has a retail outlet store at 2320 Commercial Avenue.

Most of the great shops on Fidalgo Island are scattered along Anacortes' Commercial Avenue. **Left Bank Antiques**, housed in a renovated church, absolutely bulges with American and European antiques and gift items. ~ 1904 Commercial Avenue, Anacortes; 360-293-3022. At **Sylvia's Garden**, you'll find an intriguing collection of wares from local artisans and farmers, including handwoven baskets, celtic jewelry, fresh and dried flowers, herb-flavored vinegars and oils, gardening items and more. ~ 812 Commercial Avenue, Anacortes; 360-293-8359. The historic **Marine Supply and Hardware** is packed to the rafters with nautical antiques and memorabilia. ~ 202 Commercial Avenue, Anacortes; 360-293-3014.

Resist the temptation to buy smoked salmon to take home until you visit **SeaBear Specialty Seafoods** for alderwood smoked oysters and king, North Pacific or sockeye salmon. Discount prices are terrific at the difficult-to-locate warehouse (take 22nd Street east toward the Anacortes Marina, turn right onto T Avenue and you'll find the warehouse in an industrial complex a block down on the right). ~ 605 30th Street, Anacortes; 360-293-4661.

◄ HIDDEN

If a quiet conversation over drinks in refined surroundings is your style, visit the **Rose and Crown Pub**. ~ Majestic Hotel, 419 Commercial Avenue, Anacortes; 360-293-3355.

NIGHTLIFE

Life on pastoral Lopez Island is slow and amiable; residents wave to everyone and are truly disappointed if you don't wave back. Lopez didn't earn its nickname as the "Friendly Island" for nothing. Even better, it remains much less developed than San Juan and Orcas islands.

▼▼▼▼▼▼▼▼▼
Lopez Island

The history of the island is well mapped out at the **Lopez Historical Museum** with its exhibit of pioneer farming and fishing implements. While you're here, pick up a historical landmark tour guide to the many fine examples of Early American architecture scattered around the island. Open May through September. ~ Lopez Village; 360-468-2049.

SIGHTS

Stroll out to **Agate Beach Park** on MacKaye Harbor Road to watch the sunset. Another good sunset view spot is **Shark Reef Park** on Shark Reef Road, where you might see some harbor seals, heron and, if you're lucky, a whale or two.

If you like horses, pull off the road at the bend on Center Road between Cross and Hummel Lake roads to admire the large herd of **Shetlands** frolicking in rolling pastures.

Shaw Island is one of only four of the San Juan Islands that can be reached by ferry, but most visitors to the San Juans miss it. You need to stay on the ferry from Anacortes and get off at Shaw, one stop beyond Lopez Island. Those who do make the trip are in for a treat. Stop by the general store near the ferry landing (both operated by Franciscan nuns) for picnic supplies before heading out to **South Beach County Park** on Squaw Bay Road, two miles to the south.

Afterward, continue east along Squaw Bay Road, turn north on Hoffman Cove Road and make your way to the picturesque little red schoolhouse. Park by the school and cross the street to see the **Shaw Island Historical Museum**, a tiny log cabin housing a hodgepodge of pioneer memorabilia. ~ Schoolhouse Corner, Shaw Island; 360-468-4068.

LODGING

HIDDEN ▶

The best bet on Lopez Island is the **Inn At Swifts Bay**, a delightful bed and breakfast in an elegant Tudor home. Posh best describes the interior, with a comfortable mix of modern, Williams-Sonoma–style furnishings and antique reproductions adorned in crocheted antimacassars and needlepoint pillows. There are two rooms sharing one bath, as well as three suites with private entrances and baths. There is a hot tub on the premises and a gas-lit fireplace in each of the rooms. The leisurely gourmet breakfast is without a doubt the most delicious morning repast available in the islands. Gay-friendly. ~ Port Stanley Road, four miles north of Lopez Village; 360-468-3636, fax 360-468-3637. DELUXE TO ULTRA-DELUXE.

Edenwild, the newest addition to the scant list of lodgings on the island, is a two-story Victorian. The eight guest rooms are pretty, with blond-wood floors, claw-foot tubs and antique furnishings; three rooms have romantic fireplaces, one is handicap accessible and four have views of Fisherman's Bay or San Juan Channel. Included in the room rates is breakfast, served in the sunny dining nook or on the delightful garden terrace. Apéritifs and truffles are served in the rooms. ~ Lopez Village; 360-468-3238, fax 360-468-4080. DELUXE TO ULTRA-DELUXE.

There are few low-priced rooms on the island. The **Lopez Lodge** above Lopez Video in the village has two no-frills, motel-like rooms with a shared bath across the hall. One room has a private bath. ~ 360-468-2500. MODERATE TO DELUXE.

The **Island Farm House** offers a more cozy and comfortable room (with bath) overlooking a pasture and pond as well as a private cabin near the main house. ~ Route 2, Box 3114, Hummel Lake Road; 360-468-2864. BUDGET TO MODERATE.

DINING

The **Bay Café** has an imaginative menu of ethnic cuisine featuring fresh Northwest products. There are always daily specials to choose from, with often-repeated favorites like scallops in Thai curry, rack of lamb, tiger prawns with chili corn cakes and pork tenderloin with Indonesian coconut sauce. Reservations are essential, especially during summer. Winter hours vary. Dinner only. ~ Lopez Village Road; 360-468-3700. MODERATE TO DELUXE.

Set off to one side within the **Lopez Island Pharmacy** is an ◄ HIDDEN
old-fashioned, pink and gray soda fountain, the best spot for lunch on Lopez. Grab a stool at the bar and order a sandwich, bowl of soup or chili or slice of pie to go with your phosphate, malt, float or other fountain treat. ~ Lopez Village; 360-468-2644. BUDGET.

The **Islander Lopez Restaurant** is a true waterfront restaurant, looking west across Fisherman Bay to spectacular evening sunsets. In summer, ask for a table on the outdoor dining patio. Specialties of the house include an award-winning clam chowder, cajun chicken and a daily fresh sheet of local seafood—salmon, halibut, shark and mahi mahi, for example. ~ Fisherman Bay Road, Lopez Village; 360-468-2234. MODERATE.

For the most part, shopping here is limited to those establishments **SHOPPING**
located in sleepy little Lopez Village. **Archipelago** sells natural fiber clothing and a line of tourist T-shirts. ~ 360-468-3222. **Panda Books** stocks an admirable selection of new and used books and regional music. ~ 360-468-2132. For fine art, visit **Chimera Gallery**, the cooperative showcase for prints, paintings, weaving, pottery, handblown glass and jewelry produced by local artists. ~ 360-468-3265.

SPENCER SPIT STATE PARK 🚶 🚴 ⛵ 🛶 This long stretch of **BEACHES**
silky sand on Lopez Island encloses an intriguing saltwater lagoon. **& PARKS**
The mile-long beach invites clamming, crabbing, shrimping, bottom fishing, wading and swimming during warm summer months. There are restrooms, beach bonfire pits and picnic shelters; restaurants and groceries are nearby in Lopez Village. ~ Take the ferry from Anacortes to Lopez Island, then follow the five-mile route to the park on the eastern shore of the island; 360-468-2251.

▲ There are 35 sites, ten of which are walk-in only; $11 per night.

San Juan Island, the namesake of the archipelago, is a ▼▼▼▼▼▼▼▼▼▼
popular resort destination centered around the town **San Juan Island**
of Friday Harbor. This 20-mile-long island has a colorful past stemming from a boundary dispute between the United States and Great Britain. The tension over who was entitled to the islands was embodied in American and British farmers whose warring over, get this, a pig, nearly sent the two countries to the battlefield. When an American farmer shot a British homesteader's pig caught rooting in his garden, ill feelings quickly escalated. Fortunately, cooler heads prevailed so that what is now referred to as the "Pig War" of 1859 only resulted in one casualty: the pig.

SIGHTS   The history of this little-known war is chronicled through interpretive centers in the **San Juan Island National Historical Park** (360-378-2240), which is divided into **English Camp**, West Valley Road, on the north end of the island, with barracks, a formal garden, cemetery, guardhouse, hospital and commissary left intact, and **American Camp**, Cattle Point Road, on the south end of the island where the officers and laundress' quarters, a cemetery and the Hudson Bay Company Farm Site remain.

San Juan Historical Museum is a charming turn-of-the-century frame building that gathers within its walls a good collection of American Indian baskets and stone implements, an antique diving suit, period furniture and clothing. A great place to learn about the region's maritime history, the museum also features an excellent collection highlighting the region's proud past. Closed Sunday through Wednesday. ~ 405 Price Street, Friday Harbor; 360-378-3949.

HIDDEN ▶   Oyster lovers and birdwatchers should make the trip down the dusty road to **Westcott Bay Sea Farms**, where they'll find saltwater bins of live oysters and clams and an array of birds attracted to the oyster beds that stretch out into the bay. ~ 4071 Westcott Drive, Friday Harbor; 360-378-2489.

Afterglow Vista is the mausoleum of one of the region's wealthy families. The structure itself is fascinating; an open, Grecian-style columned complex surrounds six inscribed chairs, each containing the ashes of a family member, set before a round table of limestone. A seventh chair and column have obviously been removed, some say as part of Masonic ritual, others believe because a member of the family was disinherited. ~ Roche Harbor Resort, 4950 Reuben Tarte Memorial Drive, Roche Harbor.

LODGING   Named for its view, **Olympic Lights** is a remodeled 1895 farmhouse set on five grassy, breeze-tossed acres overlooking the Olympic Peninsula across the Strait of Juan de Fuca. Guests kick off their shoes before heading up to the cream-carpeted second floor with four comfortably appointed, pastel-shaded rooms sharing two baths; a fifth room on the ground floor has a private bath. You'll find no frilly, Victoriana clutter here, just a peaceful night snuggled under down comforters topped off by a farm-fresh breakfast. ~ 4531-A Cattle Point Road, Friday Harbor; 360-378-3186, fax 360-378-2097. MODERATE TO DELUXE.

If you've dreamed of life on the water, you'll appreciate the **Wharfside Bed and Breakfast**, a 60-foot, two-masted sailboat with two guest rooms. The forward stateroom with double bed and two bunks feels a bit cramped, while the aft stateroom with queen bed seems roomier. The rates include a three-course breakfast. ~ Port of Friday Harbor; 360-378-5661. DELUXE.

Friday's is a renovated bed and breakfast with eleven individually decorated rooms, all with down comforters and wildlife art. You can stay in the Rose Room and watch the sunset or the Orca Room and soak in the private jacuzzi. The most popular is the Eagle Cove Room with a private jacuzzi, kitchen and balcony. And all this romance is conveniently located in the heart of Friday Harbor. ~ 35 1st Street, Friday Harbor; 360-378-5848, 800-352-2632, fax 360-378-2881. DELUXE TO ULTRA-DELUXE.

Set in the rolling West Valley near British Camp National Park and surrounded by a working ranch, **States Inn** is a bit of Sleepy Hollow in San Juan. Each of the ten rooms has a decor that hints at its namesake state—tiny Rhode Island comes closest, with shells and brass dolphins on the fireplace mantle, various renditions of ships on the walls and copies of the New England publication *Yankee* to peruse. The friendly and informative innkeeper and the multicourse country breakfasts make up for the slight sulphur odor that emanates from the tap water. The inn is also handicap accessible, hard to find in the islands. ~ 2039 West Valley Road, Friday Harbor; 360-378-6240, fax 360-378-6241. DELUXE.

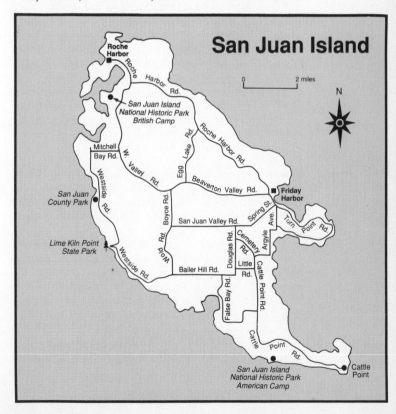

San Juan Island

Roche Harbor Resort has something for everyone. You can check in to the century-old **Hotel de Haro**, where gingerbread trim, parlor beds, antiques and a roaring fireplace bring back memories of the good old days. In addition to this three-story, 20-room establishment, nine former workers' cottages have been converted into two-bedroom units, ideal for families. Furnished with Salvation Army pieces, the cottages are convenient to the swimming pool. For contemporary lodging, choose one of the condominiums. ~ 4950 Reuben Tarte Memorial Drive, Roche Harbor; 360-378-2155, 800-451-8910, fax 360-378-6809. MODERATE TO ULTRA-DELUXE.

DINING

Named for the ancient elm tree shading its front entrance, **Springtree Café** exudes a southern Mediterranean ambience with its earth-tone textured walls and adjoining outdoor patio. The chef makes good use of local seafood and fresh herbs in such dishes as salmon and Dungeness crab cakes with cilantro-pesto aioli and ginger shrimp with mango sauce. ~ 310 Spring Street, Friday Harbor; 360-378-4848. DELUXE.

HIDDEN ►

Roberto's sits on the hill overlooking the ferry landing. You'll find no fancy decor, but the Italian fare served here is a culinary escape. Try the Sicilian salmon in capers, followed up by homemade cheesecake or fresh fruit tarts. Closed December through February. ~ 1st and A streets, Friday Harbor; 360-378-6333. MODERATE TO DELUXE.

Another welcome addition to Friday Harbor's dining scene is **The Blue Dolphin**, an unpretentious diner serving hearty portions of home-cooked breakfast and lunch favorites like biscuits and gravy, blueberry pancakes, chicken-fried steak and burgers. ~ 185 1st Street, Friday Harbor; 360-378-6116. BUDGET.

SHOPPING

Most of the shops are located within blocks of Friday Harbor, giving you plenty to do while waiting for the ferry. Cannery Landing, next to the ferry terminal on Front Street, houses **Dolphin Art** (360-378-3531), selling original screenprint art on cotton sportswear.

Art lovers visiting Friday Harbor will want to stop by several galleries. **Waterworks Gallery** features a collection of contemporary eclectic Northwest art in media such as glass, pottery, oil and watercolor. ~ Spring and Argyle streets, Friday Harbor; 360-378-3060. **Garuda & I** carries an amazing selection of ethnic arts, beads, crafts, musical instruments as well as jewelry from Indian, Asian and local artisans. ~ 60 1st Street, Friday Harbor; 360-378-3733. The **Sunshine Gallery** offers locally produced basketry, sculptures, watercolors, ceramics and jewelry. ~ 85 Nichols Street, Friday Harbor; 360-378-5819.

On San Juan Island, **Herb's Tavern** is the local sidle-up-to-the-bar joint with the only pool tables in town. ~ 80 1st Street, Friday Harbor; 360-378-7076. You'll find occasional live music, a game room and six big-screen TVs at **Hailey's Bait Shop**, a smoke-free sports bar and grill. ~ 175 Spring Street, Friday Harbor; 360-378-4747. The **Roche Harbor Resort Lounge** also has weekend dancing to live music in the summer. ~ 4950 Reuben Tarte Memorial Drive, Roche Harbor; 360-378-2155.

NIGHTLIFE

SAN JUAN COUNTY PARK Orca whales frequently pass by the rocky shoreline of this 10-acre park on the western edge of San Juan Island. Because of its location on Smallpox Bay, the park is a haven for kayakers and scuba divers who enjoy the easy waters in the shallow bay or the more challenging shelf that drops steeply off about 80 feet out. Swimming is good in the shallow, protected bay; fishing is fair. Restrooms, picnic tables and fire pits are the only facilities here. ~ On Westside Road just north of Lime Kiln Point State Park; 360-378-2992.

BEACHES & PARKS

▲ There are 20 standard sites and one for groups; $15 per night.

LIME KILN POINT STATE PARK   Situated on a rocky bluff overlooking Haro Strait, this is the prime whale-watching spot on San Juan Island. A footpath takes you to picturesque Lime Kiln Lighthouse, listed on the National Register of Historic Places. The site is named for an early lime kiln operation, with remnants of old structures still visible to the north of the lighthouse. Facilities include restrooms, picnic tables and interpretive displays. ~ It's just off Westside Road on the western shore of San Juan Island; 360-378-2044.

CATTLE POINT PICNIC AREA   Though it takes a precarious scramble down a rocky ledge to reach it and picnic tables on the bluff above lend little privacy, this gravelly half-moon is arguably the prettiest public beach on San Juan Island. There are picnic tables, shelter, restrooms, interpretive signs and a nature trail. ~ Follow Cattle Point Road through American Camp and on to the southern tip of the island.

◄ HIDDEN

FOURTH OF JULY BEACH   This secluded, sandy crescent is where the locals head when they're looking for privacy. There are often bald eagles nesting in the nearby trees, a poignant sign of this aptly named stretch. The shallow, little bay area extends out a long way and is suitable for wading on hot days. You'll find pit toilets, picnic tables and a fenced grassy area off the parking lot suitable for frisbee. ~ Located on the northeastern edge of American Camp; 360-378-2240.

▼▼▼▼▼▼▼▼▼▼
Orcas Island

Trendy, artsy-craftsy and lovely to look at, Orcas Island is a resort that caters to everyone from backpackers to the well-to-do. A nature sanctuary pocketed with charming towns, the island also boasts more sun than some of its neighbors.

SIGHTS

One of Orcas Island's leading landmarks is Rosario Resort. Even if you're not planning to stay here during your trip, make sure to visit **Moran Mansion** for a fantastic evening show that includes music performed on a 1910 Steinway grand piano and an amazing pipe organ along with entertaining narration and slides of life on the island in the early 1900s. ~ 1 Rosario Way; 360-376-2222.

HIDDEN ►

Of the many small historical museums in the San Juans, the **Orcas Island Historical Museum** is our favorite. A fine assemblage of relics and antiques, American Indian art and local contemporary art stored in six interconnected log cabins of prominent early settlers maps the history and growth of industry on the island. Closed Monday and Tuesday. Admission. ~ North Beach Road, Eastsound; 360-376-4849.

HIDDEN ►

Madrona Point, a pretty madrone-tree–dotted waterside park saved from condo development by the Lummi Indians, is a fine spot for a picnic. It's at the end of the unmarked road just past Christina's Restaurant in Eastsound.

LODGING

A stay at **Turtleback Farm Inn** is like stepping into the much-loved story *Wind in the Willows*, surrounded as it is by acres of forest and farm tracts full of animals as far as the eye can see. Rooms in this lovely, 100-year-old farmhouse vary in size and setup, but all 11 guest rooms have a charming mix of contemporary and antique furniture, cozy quilts and antique fixtures in private baths. Prices include a full breakfast. ~ Route 1, Box 650, Eastsound, WA 98245; 360-376-4914, 800-376-4914. DELUXE TO ULTRA-DELUXE.

It's not unusual to find semitame deer roaming around the ample grounds of **Rosario Resort**, tucked away on Cascade Bay on the east side of the horseshoe of Orcas Island. The motel-style rooms scattered along the waterfront or perched on the hillside overlooking the bay are clean and comfortable, and many have been recently renovated to imitate the original state of the resort. ~ 1 Rosario Way, Eastsound; 360-376-2222, 800-562-8820, fax 360-376-2289. DELUXE TO ULTRA-DELUXE.

Accommodations at the funky **Doe Bay Village Resort** range from bunk houses to rustic cabins to tents with 33 units total. There are shared central bathrooms, a community kitchen and a small café on the grounds of this large retreat along with a splendid three-tiered sauna and three mineral baths perched on a covered deck. ~ Star Route 86, Olga; 360-376-2291, fax 360-376-5809. BUDGET TO DELUXE.

La Famiglia, an inviting, wood-paneled restaurant decorated with local prints, has been the preferred choice of islanders since opening in 1976. The lunch and dinner menus feature Italian classics with island flair—pasta primavera with salmon, seafood linguine Orcas Island steamer clams in garlic and wine. There are even pizza and sandwiches to please the younger set. ~ A Street, Eastsound; 360-376-2335. MODERATE.

DINING

Bilbo's Festivo specializes in Tex-Mex fare. A margarita or cerveza on the tiled garden patio surrounded by adobe walls rounds out the experience. Bilbo's serves dinner only, but opens **La Taqueria**, a lunch outlet in the courtyard, during the summer months. ~ North Beach Road, Eastsound; 360-376-4728. MODERATE.

The Deer Harbor Inn, tucked away in an expanse of orchard grove overlooking Deer Harbor and the Olympic Range, is where locals come for that special night out. The daily menu is chalked on the board; rock cod, coho salmon and choice steaks are prime picks. For diners on the deck, this is a great spot to watch the sunset. Dinner only; reservations recommended. ~ Deer Harbor Road, Deer Harbor; 360-376-4110. MODERATE TO DELUXE.

You'll find several interesting shops in Eastsound. **Darvill's Rare Print Shop** (360-376-2351) carries antique maps, etchings and fine prints and has a connected bookstore. **Artifacts** (360-376-3810) features local artists' sculptures, woodwork, stained glass, stone and work in other media. Charts, maps, local music and original T-shirts can be found at **Gulls & Buoys Gifts** (360-376-2199).

SHOPPING

Don't spend all your time and money in Eastsound because you won't want to miss **Orcas Island Pottery**, the oldest existing craft studio on Orcas. You can even watch potters at work through the windows of the studio. ~ Off West Beach Road; 360-376-2813.

◄ HIDDEN

The Right Place has more pottery strewn about the garden and in the showroom. ~ Off Enchanted Forest Road; 360-376-4023. An intriguing spinning and weaving shop, **The Naked Lamb**, is also on the grounds. ~ West Beach Road; 360-376-4606.

At a bend in Horseshoe Highway as you reach Olga is **Orcas Island Artworks**, the cooperative art gallery showcasing fine arts, handicrafts and furniture all produced by local hands. ~ 360-376-4408. Tucked away in the attic is the **Temenos Bookstore**, with metaphysical books, crystals and incense. ~ 360-376-5645.

◄ HIDDEN

Moran Lounge is the place to go for live entertainment and great sunsets. ~ Rosario Resort, 1 Rosario Way, Eastsound; 360-376-2222.

NIGHTLIFE

MORAN STATE PARK 🚶 🚴 ⛵ 🎣 🏊 🛶 Washington's fifth-largest park consists of 5000 verdant acres flanked by 1800 feet

BEACHES & PARKS

of saltwater shoreline and crowned by sweeping Mt. Constitution. The view from the stone tower at the peak takes in the San Juans, Mt. Baker and Vancouver, B.C. There are miles of forest trails connecting the four mountain lakes, numerous waterfalls and five campgrounds. There is fishing on several lakes, with boat rentals available. Other facilities include restrooms, showers, kitchen shelters and picnic tables; restaurants and groceries are nearby. ~ Located near Eastsound, accessible by state ferry from Anacortes; 360-376-2326.

▲ There are 135 developed sites and 15 primitive sites; $11 per night; reservations are recommended.

HIDDEN ►   **OBSTRUCTION PASS STATE PARK** 🏃 🛶 🎣 This primitive, heavily forested locale on the southeastern tip of Orcas Island is tricky to get to, so the crowds are kept to a minimum, a reward for those who care to search it out. The area is laced with hiking trails, has several free campsites and a beach. There are vault toilets, picnic tables, buoys and trails; restaurants and groceries are located in Eastsound. ~ From the town of Olga follow Doe Bay Road east, turn right on Obstruction Pass Road and keep right until you hit the parking area. From there it's a half-mile hike to the campground; 360-856-3500.

▲ There are nine free primitive sites; hike-in only.

OTHER PARKS   Many of the smaller islands are preserved as state parks including **Doe, Jones, Clark, Sucia, Stuart, Posey, Blind, James, Matia, Patos** and **Turn.** They are accessible by boat only and in most cases have a few primitive campsites, nature trails, a dock or mooring buoys off secluded beaches, but no water or facilities except for pit toilets. Costs are $5 for mooring buoys, $5 for camping and $11 for boats to dock overnight.

▼▼▼▼▼▼▼▼▼▼▼▼▼▼
Outdoor Adventures

SPORT-FISHING

Catching some salmon is the hoped-for reward when you head out on a fishing charter through Northern Puget Sound and the San Juan Islands. As a bonus, you're also likely to encounter seals, eagles and whales as you sail past islands wooded with red-bark madrone trees.

In winter, of course, the temperature on the water can get chilly and the water a bit choppy. All the charter fishing services listed here provide boats with heated, enclosed cabins to keep you comfortable. Charter fees include bait and tackle, but do not include a fishing license or food and drink.

NORTHERN PUGET SOUND   Jim's Salmon Charter specializes in arranging trips to fisheries in the San Juan and Canadian islands for small groups of no more than six people. Jim has three decades of experience and operates year-round. ~ Marine Drive, Blaine Harbor; 360-332-6724.

In Everett, Gary Krein is president of the Puget Sound Charter Boat Association and owner of **All Star Charters**. He operates two boats of up to six people each, and encourages "angler participation" on his trips (two daily in summer, one in winter). ~ Port of Everett; 206-252-4188.

Mike Dunnigan is the skipper of **Sea Hawk Salmon Charters**. He runs year-round, exclusive charters for up to four people to fish for salmon, bottom fish and halibut. ~ Skyline Marina, Anacortes; 360-424-1350.

SAN JUAN ISLANDS Trophy Charters will pick anglers up from the other islands before heading out on a four- to six-hour fishing trip. Captain Monty runs a fast boat (up to 30 mph), so travel time is reduced. ~ Friday Harbor; 360-378-2110.

RIVER FISHING

Several rivers in the area—the Snohomish, Skykomish, Skagit and Sauk, for example—provide year-round catches, notably steelhead and all species of salmon except sockeye (it's not permitted to take this fish from rivers). **Washington Fishing Adventures** specializes in highly personalized fishing trips for a maximum of five people. Ken Elsea tries to help anglers both catch fish and sharpen their skills. His jet boat lets him take anglers onto sections of rivers inaccessible to boats with conventional motors. ~ Marysville; 360-653-5924.

SEA KAYAKING

For nonadventurers who want an outdoor experience that's a lot of fun but not extremely challenging, a guided water excursion in a sea kayak may be just the thing. No previous kayaking experience is necessary to join one of these groups for a paddling tour on the gentle waters of Chuckanut Bay, with its sandstone formations near Bellingham; of sea caves around Deception Pass State Park on Whidbey Island; or off San Juan Island, where you're likely to see whales, seals and other marine wildlife. Unless noted, the operators listed here generally offer a regular schedule of excursions from April–May to September–October. Cost for a sea kayak excursion ranges from $30 to $60. Most operators can also arrange overnight or longer trips.

NORTHERN PUGET SOUND Moondance Sea Kayaking Adventures escorts up to 12 people in double sea kayaks for day trips to nearby locations such as Chuckanut Bay and Clark's Point (where you'll see a fossil of the entire trunk of a palm tree). A bit longer trip to see sea caves heads down to Deception Pass State Park, where the wave action is rougher. ~ Bellingham; 360-738-7664.

WHIDBEY ISLAND During the winter, **Northwest Sea Ventures** works with the Breazeale Interpretive Center to run a four-hour Saturday excursion of nearby Padilla Bay Estuarine Sanctuary. One of center's naturalists accompanies the group for an exploration of the estuary and tidal marshes. During the summer, Northwest Sea Ventures operates on San Juan Island (see San Juan Island, below). ~ Anacortes; 360-293-3692.

LOPEZ ISLAND Lopez Kayaks offers morning and afternoon sea-kayaking tours to MacKaye Harbor, which is also popular with seals. If you have experience, you can also rent a kayak for your own use without joining a tour. ~ Fisherman Bay; 360-468-2847.

SAN JUAN ISLAND Since the waters just off the west side of San Juan Island are in the main whale-migration corridor, your chances of seeing whales are good. If not, there's plenty of other wildlife to view, notably seals and bald eagles. (The highest density of bald-eagle nestings in the lower 48 states is in the San Juan Islands.) There are also kelp forests, jutting cliffs, sea caves and rocky outcroppings. A biologist or scientist accompanies the day excursions led by **Sea Quest Kayak Expeditions** for groups of four to twelve, in double kayaks. ~ Friday Harbor; 360-378-5767. **Crystal Seas Kayaking** escorts up to eight people on morning or afternoon sunset excursions that last up to six hours. ~ Friday Harbor; 360-378-7899. **Northwest Sea Ventures** takes up to 12 people out in single and double kayaks for morning and sunset trips. ~ Anacortes; 360-293-3692.

ORCAS ISLAND Osprey Tours brings a different, historical twist to half-day and full-day sea-kayaking tours. Following the Alaskan Eskimo tradition, owner Randy Monge makes these wood-frame kayaks with bifurcated (T-shaped) bows, which, he says, split the water and provide lift going through waves. Monge also gives each kayaker an Aleutian whale-hunter's hat, shaped like a conical visor that resembles a bird's beak. The hats helped disguise Aleutian hunters and, acting like a hearing aid, collected sound. ~ West Beach; 360-376-3677.

SCUBA DIVING

The protected waters of Puget Sound hold untold treasures for the diver: craggy rock walls, ledges and caves of this sunken mountain range and enormous forests of bull kelp provide homes for a multitude of marine life. Giant Pacific octopus thrive in these waters, as do sea anemones and hundreds of species of fish. "Within fifteen minutes of Friday Harbor on San Juan Island, there are hundreds of great dive spots," says one local diver who grew up in the area. The west side of San Juan Island and the south side of Lopez Island are particular favorites, largely because the absence of silt means the water is cleaner and therefore clearer. There are also lots of ledges along these rocky coasts, which abound with exceptional wall-dive spots. Acres of bull kelp forests, with their teeming marine life, are also popular dive spots. But just as these waters hold great beauty, they can also be treacherous with tremendous tidal changes and strong currents.

Whale Watching in the San Juan Islands

Here in the waters of the San Juan archipelago there are three resident pods, or extended families, of *Orcinus Orca*, otherwise known as "killer" whales. Because they are so frequently and easily spotted in the protected waters, these gentle black and white giants have been carefully studied by scientists since 1976.

Their research is documented at the **Whale Museum**, where you can learn more about whales and other marine animals found in the area. A photo collection with names and pod numbers will help you identify some of the 90 or so resident orcas, distinguished by their grayish saddle patches and nicks, scars or tears in the dorsal fins and tails. Displays and videos explain the difference between breaching, spy hopping, tail lobbing and other typical orca behavior and the many vocalization patterns that scientists can only guess at the significance. Admission. ~ 62 1st Street North, Friday Harbor; 360-378-4710.

The Whale Museum also has an orca adoption program set up to help fund the ongoing research and all sorts of whale-related educational material, art and souvenirs available in their gift shop. They operate a 24-hour hotline (800-562-8832) for whale sightings and marine mammal strandings as well.

From May to September you can often see the whales from shore when they range closest to the islands to feed on migrating salmon. The best shoreline viewing spots are **Lime Kiln Point** on San Juan Island or **Shark Reef Park** on Lopez Island. Sightings drop dramatically in the winter as the pods travel up to 100 miles per day out to the open ocean for food.

If you want to get a closer look, put on your parka and sunglasses, grab your binoculars and camera and climb aboard one of the **wildlife cruises** that ply the waters between the islands. Even if you don't see any orca during the trip, you will almost certainly spot other interesting forms of wildlife such as sleek, gray minke whales, Dall's porpoises (which look like miniature orca), splotchy brown harbor seals, bald eagles, great blue heron, cormorants or tufted puffin.

Island Mariner Cruises offers day-long nature and whale-watching expeditions with commentary on the history, flora and fauna of the San Juans as you cruise through the islands. ~ 5 Squalicum Esplanade, Bellingham; 360-734-8866.

Western Prince Cruises has similar naturalist-accompanied wildlife tours on a half-day basis. ~ Friday Harbor; 360-378-5315, 800-757-6722. You can also try **San Juan Boat Rentals and Tours** for a three-hour whale-sighting excursion. ~ Friday Harbor; 360-378-3499.

Happy spotting!

NORTHERN PUGET SOUND   Besides complete rental and diving services, **Washington Divers, Inc.**, operates a full schedule of diving activities year-round. A one-day dive charter to the San Juan Islands is the most popular trip. In the summer, extended daylight hours make it possible to make up to three dives during the six- to seven-hour trip. The shops also runs a free "come along" beach dive at least two weekend days a month. ~ 903 North State Street, Bellingham; 360-676-8029.

WHIDBEY ISLAND   Besides air fills, diving lessons and rental of wetsuits and other equipment, **Whidbey Island Dive Center** offers dive charters for up to six people. One popular spot for experienced divers is under the bridge at Deception Pass State Park, where currents reach seven knots—"a diving rush." For the less experienced, the charter to the diving sanctuary off Keystone Jetty, an excellent spot to view marine life, is "pretty swell." ~ 1020 Northeast 7th Avenue #1, Oak Harbor; 360-675-1112.

SAN JUAN ISLAND   **Emerald Seas Aquatics** is a full-service dive shop, retail and rental. It specializes in daily half-day charters, guaranteeing you at least two dives in different locations during the trip. One might be a vertical wall dive, another may be in the kelp forest. Groups are kept small—two to six people. ~ 2-A Spring Street Landing, Friday Harbor; 360-378-2772.

RIDING STABLES   Saddle up for a gentle, leisurely ride around an 85-acre ranch or take in the scenic beauty of the San Juan Islands.

NORTHERN PUGET SOUND   A year-round operation, **Lang's Pony and Horse Farm** takes up to 20 riders on a slow, leisurely paced guided trail ride around the hilly and wooded ranch, which is about 30 miles south of Bellingham. Call for reservations. ~ 4565 Little Mountain Road, Mount Vernon; 360-424-7630.

WHIDBEY ISLAND   Put on jeans and a pair of sturdy leather shoes (leave your Birkenstocks and sneakers at home) for a guided trail ride through the hilly, heavily forested **Madrona Ridge Ranch**. Please call ahead (evenings are best) to arrange a ride, which are limited to only three people at a time. ~ Madrona Way, Coupeville; 360-678-4124.

ORCAS ISLAND   You'll have to call ahead for an appointment to ride one of Jeri Smart's Tennessee walking horses at **Walking Horse Country Farm**. These horses can walk fast and keep their backs flat so you won't flop around. Following a brief orientation, a guided ride takes in the farm's hilly woodlands and ponds. Only six riders at a time; reservations necessary. ~ Eastsound; 360-376-5306.

GOLF   Award-winning design, lush scenery and the Northwest's only par-five to an island green are among the distinctions of golf courses in this part of the state.

NORTHERN PUGET SOUND Dakota Creek was named Washington's most challenging nine-hole course by the Pacific Northwest Golf Association. Carved out of a mountain, this par-35 course is quiet, well maintained and hilly. ~ 3258 Haynie Road, Custer; 360-366-3131.

The 18th hole at **Homestead Golf Course** is the Northwest's only par-five to an island green. The par-72 course is flat, but has lots of water. ~ 115 East Homestead Boulevard, Lynden; 360-354-1196.

There's a hilly back nine at **Lake Padden Municipal Golf Course**, located in Lake Padden Park. It's a tight, densely treed course. ~ 4882 Samish Way, Bellingham; 360-676-6989.

The most expensive course (up to $70 greens fees) in the area is the semiprivate **Semiahmoo Golf and Country Club**. It's ranked as one of nation's best resort courses and was designated as a sectional qualifying course for the 1996 U.S. Amateur and the 1997 U.S. Open. The 18-hole par-72 course was designed by Arnold Palmer. ~ 8720 Semiahmoo Parkway, Blaine; 360-371-7005.

SAN JUAN ISLAND It's only nine holes, but the **San Juan Golf and Country Club** "plays like eighteen." Private, but open to the public, the course is set on a wooded, rolling tract next to Griffin Bay. ~ 2261 Golf Course Road, Friday Harbor; 360-378-2254.

BIKING

For biking in the Bellingham area, the best map is "Bicycling in Bellingham and Whatcom County," which outlines trails according to traffic volume, surface status (gravel, paved, etc.) and hill difficulty; it also categorizes trails as City Ride, City Trail or Country Ride. The map is available in many bicycle stores and during the summer from the **Bellingham/Whatcom County Convention and Visitors Bureau**. ~ 904 Potter Street, Bellingham; 360-671-3990, 800-487-2032.

If you plan to bike on the San Juan Islands, it's important to remember that the islands' narrow roads don't have special lanes or other provisions for cyclists. Lopez Island is probably the best

✔ **CHECK THESE OUT—UNIQUE OUTDOOR ADVENTURES**

- Scuba dive off Lopez Island and explore underwater rocks, ledges and caves. *page 134*
- Cycle the steep, forested Horseshoe Route on Orcas Island, with a challenging side trip up 2000-foot Mt. Constitution. *page 138*
- Ascend from the beach on a hiking trail through pine and fir forest on Ebey's Landing Loop Trail on Whidbey Island. *page 140*
- Go clamming on the slender sandspit at Semiahmoo Park or observe the area's protected wildlife. *page 113*

bet for the occasional bicyclist: you'll be able to bike long, flat country roads, rather than the steeper, twisting roads of some of the other islands. You can rent a bike on the island or in Anacortes before ferrying over for the day.

The hardy cyclist might prefer a 20-mile hilly and winding route around San Juan Island or 16 miles of steep, twisting roads beginning at the ferry landing on Orcas Island.

In February 1996, San Juan County outlawed jet skis. Locals complained that the serenity of the San Juans was disrupted by the incessant buzzing of cityfolk zipping around on their waterfront.

For bike trails here and in other parts of the state, contact the **Washington Department of Transportation** to request a route map and informative brochure, or call 360-705-7277 for the Bicycle Hotline. ~ P.O. Box 47393, Olympia, WA 98504-7393.

NORTHERN PUGET SOUND Bellingham offers several bike routes, some arduous, some easy, all highlighting the scenery and history of the area. One is the moderate **Interurban Trail** (also known as the Chuckanut Trail). The seven-mile trail, which follows an old trolley route, begins at the Fairhaven Parkway and ends at Larrabee State Park. The best of the bunch is the fairly easy, 45-minute **Lake Padden Loop** in Lake Padden Park. It connects to series of trails on **Mt. Galbraith**, a local "hot spot" for mountain biking.

LOPEZ ISLAND The easiest and most popular bike route here is the **Lopez Island Perimeter Loop**, 32 miles of gently rolling hills and narrow, paved roads passing by Fisherman's Bay, Shark Reef Park, MacKaye Harbor and Agate Beach on the west side of the island and Mud Bay, Lopez Sound and Shoal Bay on the east side.

SAN JUAN ISLAND The slightly difficult, 30-mile **San Juan Island Loop** leads along hilly, winding roads through Friday Harbor, Roche Harbor, San Juan Island National Historical Park and along the San Juan Channel.

ORCAS ISLAND The **Horseshoe Route** is by far the most difficult island bike route, with 16 miles of steep, twisting roads beginning at the ferry landing in Orcas, continuing through Eastsound, then on to Olga. An alternative route for the very hardy starts in Olga, passes through Moran State Park and ends in Doe Bay, with a possible challenging 3.5-mile side trip up and back down Mt. Constitution.

Bike Rentals For year-round mountain-bike rentals in the Bellingham area, try **Fairhaven Bicycle and Ski**. ~ 1103 11th Street, Bellingham; 360-733-4433. North of Bellingham, rent a mountain or hybrid bike at **Semiahmoo Marina** for a leisurely ride around the adjacent resort or golf course. ~ 9540 Semiahmoo Parkway, Blaine; 360-371-5700.

If you're planning a trip out to the San Juan Islands and you'd like to ferry a bike over with you, call ahead to reserve a mountain or 21-speed bike at **Ship Harbor Inn Bicycle Rental**. A lock, tool kit, patch kit and water bottle come with the cost of the rental (and you can keep the water bottle). ~ 5316 Ferry Terminal Road, Anacortes; 360-293-5177, 800-235-8568.

Most people coming to Lopez Island who want to bicycle bring their own bikes. If you want to follow suit, you can rent a bike in Anacortes and ferry it over to Lopez. If not, head for **Bike Shop on Lopez,** which is open year-round for rentals of hybrids, mountain bikes, ten speeds, touring bikes and children's bikes. The shop will even deliver a bike to any location on the island, including the ferry landing. ~ Lopez Village; 360-468-3497.

Lopez Bicycle Works also rents mountain bikes, touring bikes and hybrids and will let you drop off the bike at the ferry landing when you leave for the day. ~ Fisherman's Bay Road; 360-468-2847.

For mountain bike rentals on San Juan Island, contact **Island Bicycles**. ~ 380 Argyle Avenue, Friday Harbor; 360-378-4941.

Rent mountain bikes and hybrids on Orcas Island at **Dolphin Bay**. ~ Ferry Landing; 360-376-3093. Mountain bikes can also be found on the island at **Wildlife Cycles**. ~ Box 1048, Eastsound; 360-376-4708.

All distances listed for hiking trails are one way unless otherwise noted.

HIKING

NORTHERN PUGET SOUND On the **Langus Riverfront Park Nature Trail** (2.5 miles) in Everett, hikers are likely to spot red-tailed hawk or gray heron as they make their way through towering spruce, red cedar and dogwood trees along the banks of the Snohomish River, past Union Slough and on toward Spencer Island, a protected haven for nesting ducks.

The Padilla Bay National Estuarine Sanctuary (360-428-1558) in the tiny town of Padilla Bay a few miles north of Mount Vernon offers the best hikes in the area. Stringent rules on noise guide hikers on the **Padilla Bay Shore Trail** (2.2 miles) so that they do not disturb the migratory waterfowl that nest in the estuary, mudflat, sloughs and tidal marsh viewed along this path. An additional interpretive route tying into the roadside trail takes you to the Breazeale Interpretive Center, bringing the distance to 6 miles. Binoculars and field guides can be checked out at the center to aid your exploration of the forest and meadow habitat of the **Upland Trail** (.8 mile).

There are several good choices for hikes in Bellingham. The **Interurban Trail** (6 miles) begins near the entrance to Larrabee State Park, hugs the crest above Chuckanut Drive overlooking the bay and the San Juan Islands, then passes the rose gardens of Fairhaven Park into the revitalized Fairhaven District of the city.

There are 5.3 miles of rolling trails through the lush **Sehome Hill Arboretum**, crowned by incredible views of Mt. Baker and the San Juans from the observation tower at the summit. Since no motorized boats are allowed on **Lake Padden**, the path (2.6 miles) around the glistening lake and through some of the park's 1008 acres is both peaceful and rejuvenating.

In Birch Bay State Park in Blaine, the gently sloping **Terrell Marsh Trail** (.5 mile) winds through a thickly wooded area of birch, maple, red cedar, hemlock and fir, home to pileated woodpeckers, bald eagle, ruffed grouse, muskrats and squirrel, and on to Terrell Marsh, the halfway point on the loop, before passing back through the forest to the trailhead. Pick up a flora and fauna guide to the interpretive trail at the contact station just inside the park gate.

WHIDBEY ISLAND The most picturesque hikes on Whidbey Island are found in and around Fort Ebey State Park. The **Ebey's Landing Loop Trail** (3.5 miles) has some steep sections on the bluff above the beach, but carry your camera anyway to capture the views of pastoral Ebey's Prairie in one direction and Mt. Rainier and the Olympic Mountains framed by wind-sculpted pines and fir in the other. Trimmed in wild roses, the trail swings around Perego's Lagoon and back along the driftwood-strewn beach. Be aware that the trail passes over some private property.

The **Partridge Point Trail** (3.5 miles) in Fort Ebey State Park climbs through a mix of coastal wildflowers on a windswept bluff rising 150 feet above the water with wide views of Port Townsend, Admiralty Inlet, Protection Island and Discovery Bay. A fenced path at the southern end drops down the headland to the cobbly beach below.

There are numerous trails to choose from in Deception Pass State Park. Locals prefer **Rosario Head Trail** (.3 mile) on the Fidalgo Island side, stretching over the very steep promontory between Rosario Bay and Bowman Bay with sweeping views of the San Juans, Rosario Strait and the Strait of Juan de Fuca, and continuing on the **Lighthouse Point Trail** (1.5 miles), which extends farther along the rocky bluff, past the lighthouse and into a dense stand of fir and cedar. On the Whidbey Island side of the bridge, climb the steep switchback on **Goose Rock Perimeter Trail** (3.5 miles) and you might see great blue heron on Coronet Bay, then follow the path down under the bridge next to the swirling waters of the pass and on to quiet North Beach to see the totem pole located at West Point where North and West beaches converge. Heartier hikers might want to tackle the **Goose Rock Summit Trail** (.5 mile), with an altitude gain of some 450 feet for an unparalleled view of Deception Pass and the Cascades.

FIDALGO ISLAND   In Anacortes, your best bet is to head for the **Washington Park Loop Road** (2.7 miles), located on Fidalgo Head at the end of Sunset Avenue four miles west of downtown. Rewarding views on this easy, paved path with a few moderate slopes include incredible glimpses of the San Juans, Burrows Pass and Burrows Island. You'll also find quiet, cool stretches through dense woods and access to beaches and romantic, hidden outcroppings suitable for a glass of champagne to toast the breathtaking sunsets.

LOPEZ ISLAND   On Lopez, ideal hiking choices include the **Shark Reef Park Trail** (.5 mile), a mossy path that meanders through a fragrant forest area and along a rock promontory looking out over tidal pools, a large kelp bed, a jutting haul out spot for seals and across the channel to San Juan Island. Spencer Spit State Park's **Beach Trail** (2 mile) travels down the spit and around the salt marsh lagoon alive with migratory birds; at the end of the spit is a reproduction of a historic log cabin built by early settlers, a fine spot for a picnic or brief rest stop with a nice view of the tiny islands offshore.

SAN JUAN ISLAND   Two of the best hiking alternatives on San Juan are the established hiking trails of the San Juan Island National Historical Park. The **Lagoon Trail** (.5 mile) in American Camp is actually two trails intertwined, starting from a parking area above Old Town (referred to on maps as First) Lagoon and passing through a dense stand of Douglas fir connecting the lovely, protected cove beaches of Jakle's Lagoon and Third Lagoon. The highlight of the short but steep **Mt. Young Trail** (.75 mile) in English Camp are the plates identifying the many islands dotting the waters as far as the eye can see. If you want a closer view of the water, you can take the flat, easy **Bell Point Trail** (1 mile), also in English Camp, which runs along the edge of the coast.

ORCAS ISLAND   Unless you plan to spend an extended period of time here, there's little chance of covering the many hiking trails that twist through Moran State Park on Orcas Island connecting view spots, mountain lakes, waterfalls and campgrounds. The **Mountain Lake Trail** (3.6 miles) takes you from the summit of Mt. Constitution along a rocky ledge to Twin Lakes and the Mountain Lake Campground, with occasional views glimpsed through the thick trees. The **Around-the-Lake Trail** (3.6 miles) is fairly easy and takes in sights such as drooping log cabins and a dam and footbridge at the south end of Mountain Lake; for a little more challenge, try the **Twin Lakes Trail** (2.1 miles) that heads up the valley at the north end of Mountain Lake. If you're a waterfall lover, take the **Cascade Creek Trail** (2.7 miles) from the south end of Mountain Lake past Cascade and Rustic falls and on to Cascade Lake.

▼▼▼▼▼▼▼▼▼▼▼▼
Transportation

CAR

Route 5, also known as the Pacific Highway, parallels the Northern Puget Sound coastline all the way up to the Canadian border. Route 20 from Burlington takes you into Anacortes, the main jump-off point for ferry service to the San Juan Islands. Route 16 leads from Tacoma across The Narrows and onto the Kitsap Peninsula where it connects to Route 3 skirting the Sinclair Inlet and continuing north to Port Gamble.

AIR

Visitors flying into the Northern Puget Sound area usually arrive at either Bellingham International Airport (360-676-2500) or the much larger and busier Seattle-Tacoma International Airport (see Chapter Two for further information). Carriers serving the Bellingham airport include Alaska Airlines, Horizon Air and United Express.

The Bellingham/Sea-Tac Airporter provides express shuttle service between Bellingham, Mount Vernon, Stanwood, Anacortes, Oak Harbor and the Sea-Tac airport. ~ 360-733-3600.

Charter and regularly scheduled commuter flights are available into the tiny Friday Harbor Airport through Harbor Airlines and West Isle Air. ~ 360-378-4724. Small commuter airports with limited scheduled service include Anacortes Airport, Eastsound Airport and Lopez Airport; all are served by West Isle Air.

FERRY

Washington State Ferries, which are part of the state highway system, provide transportation to the main islands of the San Juans —Lopez, Orcas, Shaw and San Juan—departing from the Anacortes Ferry Terminal (Ferry Terminal Road; 800-843-3779 in Washington). Schedules change several times per year, with added service in the summer to take care of the heavy influx of tourists. The system is burdened during peak summer months, so arrive at the terminal early and be prepared to wait patiently (sometimes three hours or more) in very long lines if you plan to take your car along; walk-on passengers seldom wait long. ~ 206-464-6400.

Island Shuttle Express runs between Bellingham and the San Juan Islands. ~ 355 Harris Avenue, Bellingham; 360-671-1137.

BUS

Greyhound Bus Lines (800-231-2222) provides regular service into Bellingham, Everett and Mount Vernon. ~ Bellingham: 401 Harris Street, in Fairhaven Station; 360-733-5251. Everett: 1503 Pacific Avenue; 425-252-2143. Mount Vernon: 1101 South 2nd Street; 360-336-5111.

TRAIN

Amtrak offers service into Everett on the Puget Sound shoreline via the "Empire Builder," which originates in Chicago and makes its final stop in Seattle before retracing its route. West Coast connections through Seattle on the "Coast Starlight" are also available. ~ 2900 Bond Street, Everett; 800-872-7245.

At the Bellingham International Airport, you'll find **Avis Rent A Car** (800-331-1212), **Budget Rent A Car** (800-527-0700), **Hertz Rent A Car** (800-654-3131), **National Interrent** (800-328-4567). **U-Save Auto Rental** (800-272-8728), located downtown, offers free airport pickup.

Less expensive local rental agencies include the **Inn at Friday Harbor Rentals** (360-378-4351) and **U-Save Auto Rental** (800-272-8728) in Anacortes.

Whatcom County Transportation Authority provides public transit in Lynden, Bellingham, Blaine, Birch Bay, Ferndale and Gooseberry Point. ~ 360-676-7433. **Skagit Transit** services the Mount Vernon, Cedar Wooley, Anacortes and Burlington areas and is free. ~ 360-757-4433. In Everett you can get just about anywhere for 75 cents via **Everett Transit**. ~ 425-353-7433. **Island Transit** covers Whidbey Island, with scheduled stops at Deception Pass, Oak Harbor, Coupeville, the Keystone Ferry, Greenbank, Freeland, Langley and the Clinton Ferry. ~ 360-678-7771. In smaller towns like La Conner and Mount Vernon and on most of the islands there are no public transportation systems set up; check the yellow pages for taxi service.

A cab company serving the Bellingham International Airport is **City Cab** (360-733-8294). For service from the Friday Harbor Airport contact **Primo Taxi Service** (360-378-3550). **Triangle Vans** (360-293-3979) serves the Anacortes Airport.

FOUR

Olympic Peninsula and Washington Coast

One of the most spectacular sights for many Pacific Northwest visitors is sitting on the dock of the bay (Seattle's Elliott Bay, that is) watching the sun set behind the stark profile of the Olympic Mountains. The area is even more memorable looking from the inside out.

The Olympic Peninsula is a vast promontory bounded on the east by Puget Sound, the west by the Pacific Ocean and the north by the Strait of Juan de Fuca. With no major city—the largest town is Port Angeles, a community of only 19,000 people—it retains a feeling of country living on the edge of wilderness, which indeed it is. The Olympic National Park, which dominates the peninsula, is a primeval place where eternal glaciers drop suddenly off sheer rock faces into nearly impenetrable rainforest, where America's largest herd of Roosevelt elk roams unseen by all but the most intrepid human eyes, where an impossibly rocky coastline cradles primitive marine life forms as it has done for millions of years. No fewer than five Indian reservations speckle sections of a coast famed as much for its shipwrecks as for its salmon fishing.

South of the national park, the Washington coast extends down the Northwest's finest sand beaches and around two enormous river estuaries, to the mouth of the Columbia River and the state of Oregon. In this region, two towns have become major resort centers: Ocean Shores and Long Beach.

The Washington coast is known for its heavy rainfall, and justifiably so. Although the Olympics are not high by many standards—its tallest peaks are under 8000 feet—they catch huge amounts of precipitation blowing in from the Pacific Ocean. So much snow falls that more than 60 glaciers survive at elevations as low as 4500 feet. Even greater amounts fall on the windward slopes: 140 inches a year and more in the Forks area. Not only does this foster the rapid growth of mushrooms and slugs, but it has also led to the creation of North America's greatest rainforest in the soggy Hoh River valley. Yet a mere 40 miles away as the raven flies, Sequim—in the Olympic rain shadow—is a comparative desert with only about 15 inches of rain per year.

The first residents of the peninsula and coast were tribes like the Makah, Ozette and Quileute, whose descendants still inhabit the area today. A seafaring people noted for their woodcarving, they lived in a series of longhouses facing the sea and are known to have inhabited this region for as long as 2500 years.

Their first contact with Europeans came in 1775, when they massacred a Spanish landing party. Three years later, the ubiquitous British captain James Cook sailed the coast and traded for sea otter furs with Vancouver Island natives; his report opened the gates to the maritime fur trade.

American entrepreneur John Jacob Astor established a fort at the mouth of the Columbia River in 1803, and two years later Meriwether Lewis and William Clark led a cross-country expedition that arrived at Cape Disappointment, on the Washington side of the Columbia, in late 1806. White settlement was at first slow, but by the mid-19th century Port Townsend had established itself as Puget Sound's premier lumber-shipping port, and other communities sprang up soon after.

Olympic National Park was annexed to the national park system in 1938. But long before that, Washingtonians had discovered its natural wonders. A fledgling tourism industry grew, with lodges constructed at several strategic locations around the park, including lakes Crescent and Quinault, Sol Duc Hot Springs and Kaloch, overlooking the Pacific. Coastal communities were also building a visitor infrastructure, and quiet beach resorts soon emerged.

Today, typical Olympic Peninsula visitors start their tour in Port Townsend, having traveled by ferry and car from Seattle or Whidbey Island, and use Route 101 as their artery of exploration. Port Townsend is considered the most authentic Victorian seacoast town in the United States north of San Francisco, and its plethora of well-preserved 19th-century buildings, many of them now bed and breakfasts, charms all visitors. Less than an hour's drive west, the seven-mile Dungeness Spit (a national wildlife refuge) is the largest natural sand hook in the United States and is famed for the delectable crabs that share its name. Port Angeles, in the center of the north coast, is home to the headquarters of Olympic National Park and is its primary gateway. The bustling international port town also has a direct ferry link to Victoria, Canada, across the Strait of Juan de Fuca.

Neah Bay, the northwesternmost community in the continental United States, is the home of the Makah Indian Museum and Cultural Center and an important marina for deep-sea fishing charters. Clallam Bay, to its east, and La Push, south down the coast, are other sportfishing centers. The logging town of Forks is the portal for visitors to the national park's Hoh Rainforest.

Route 101 emerges from the damp Olympic forests to slightly less moist Grays Harbor, with its twin lumber port towns of Aberdeen and Hoquiam. Though these towns combined have a population of over 25,000, they have limited appeal to travelers, who typically head over the north shore of Grays Harbor to the hotels of Ocean Shores, or down the south shore of the harbor to the quaint fishing village of Westport.

Serene Willapa Bay is another huge river estuary south of Grays Harbor. The resort strip of 28-mile-long Long Beach Peninsula, which provides a seaward dike for the bay, is older and less contrived than the Ocean Shores area. Wildlife refuges, oyster farms and cranberry bogs lend it a sort of 1950s Cape Cod ambience.

Port Townsend Area

Before either Seattle or Tacoma were so much as a tug on a fisherman's line, Port Townsend was a thriving lumber port. Founded in 1851, it has retained its Victorian seacoast ambience better than any other community north of San Francisco. Much of the city has been designated a National Historic Landmark district, with more than 70 Victorian houses, buildings, forts, parks and monuments. Many of the handsomely gabled homes are open for tours and/or offer bed-and-breakfast accommodations.

SIGHTS

The best way to see Port Townsend is on foot. When you drive into town on Route 20, you'll first want to stop at the **Port Townsend Chamber of Commerce** visitors center. Then continue east on Route 20 as it becomes Water Street. ~ 2437 Sims Way, Port Townsend; 360-385-2722.

At the corner of Madison Street, opposite the city dock, you'll find the **Jefferson County Historical Museum** in City Hall, with Victorian antiques, artifacts and hundreds of photos of Port Townsend's early days. ~ 210 Madison Street, Port Townsend; 360-385-1003.

Heading west on Water Street by foot, note the elegant stone and wood-frame buildings on either side of the street, most of them dating from the 1880s and 1890s. Turn right on Adams Street; halfway up the block on the right is the **Enoch S. Fowler Building**, built in 1874, the oldest two-story stone structure in Washington. A former county courthouse, it now houses the weekly newspaper.

Turn left at Washington Street and five blocks farther, on your right, you'll see the **James House**, built in 1889. It has five chimneys and a commanding view of the harbor—and in 1973 became the Northwest's first bed and breakfast. ~ 1238 Washington Street, Port Townsend; 360-385-1238.

Turn right up Harrison Street, then right again at Franklin Street. Two blocks farther, the **Captain Enoch S. Fowler Home**, built in 1860, is the oldest surviving house in Port Townsend and is typical of New England–style homes. ~ Franklin and Polk streets, Port Townsend.

Two more blocks ahead, you'll encounter the **Rothschild House**, built in 1868 by an early Port Townsend merchant. Notable for its outstanding interior woodwork, it's maintained by the State Parks Commission for public tours. Admission. ~ Franklin and Taylor streets, Port Townsend; 360-379-8076.

A block north, **Trinity Methodist Church** (1871) is the state's oldest standing Methodist church. Its small museum contains the Bible of the church's first minister. ~ Jefferson and Clay streets, Port Townsend.

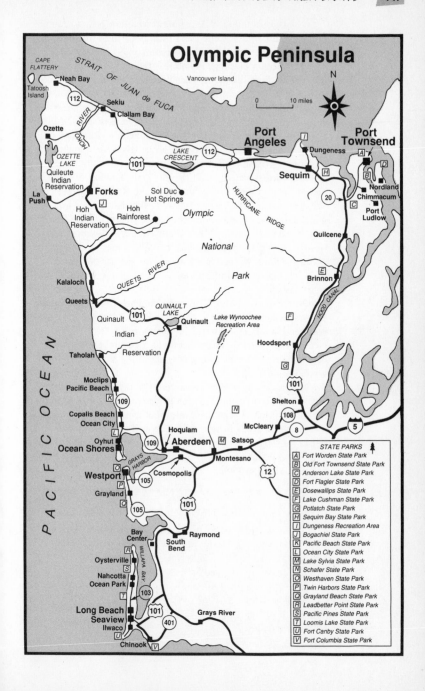

Olympic Peninsula

CAPE FLATTERY

STRAIT OF JUAN de FUCA

Vancouver Island

N

0   10 miles

Tatoosh Island

Neah Bay

112

Ozette

Sekiu

Clallam Bay

HOKO RIVER

OZETTE LAKE

Quileute Indian Reservation

La Push

Forks

J

Hoh Indian Reservation

Hoh Rainforest

101

LAKE CRESCENT

112

Sol Duc Hot Springs

Olympic

National

Park

Port Angeles

I

Dungeness

Sequim

H

20

Port Townsend

A

B

D

B

Nordland

Chimmacum

C

Port Ludlow

HURRICANE RIDGE

Quilcene

E

Brinnon

HOOD CANAL

Kalaloch

Queets

QUEETS RIVER

QUINAULT LAKE

Quinault

Lake Wynoochee Recreation Area

F

Quinault Indian

Reservation

Taholah

Hoodsport

G

101

Moclips

Pacific Beach

K

109

Copalis Beach

Ocean City

L

Oyhut

Ocean Shores

109

Hoquiam

Aberdeen

M

Satsop

Montesano

N

Shelton

108

McCleary

8

5

GRAYS HARBOR

Westport

O

105

Cosmopolis

12

US 101

Grayland

P

Q

105

Bay Center

Raymond

South Bend

R

Oysterville

S

Nahcotta

Ocean Park

T

103

101

Long Beach

Seaview

Ilwaco

401

Grays River

U

Chinook

V

WILLAPA BAY

PACIFIC OCEAN

STATE PARKS
A Fort Worden State Park
B Old Fort Townsend State Park
C Anderson Lake State Park
D Fort Flagler State Park
E Dosewallips State Park
F Lake Cushman State Park
G Potlatch State Park
H Sequim Bay State Park
I Dungeness Recreation Area
J Bogachiel State Park
K Pacific Beach State Park
L Ocean City State Park
M Lake Sylvia State Park
N Schafer State Park
O Westhaven State Park
P Twin Harbors State Park
Q Grayland Beach State Park
R Leadbetter Point State Park
S Pacific Pines State Park
T Loomis Lake State Park
U Fort Canby State Park
V Fort Columbia State Park

A block east, the 1889 **Ann Starrett Mansion**, now a bed-and-breakfast inn, offers public tours from noon until three. Admission. ~ 744 Clay Street, Port Townsend; 360-385-3205.

The **Lucinda Hastings Home** was the most expensive house ever built in Port Townsend when it was erected in 1889 at a cost of $14,000. ~ Clay and Monroe streets, Port Townsend.

Turn right here, and return down Monroe to Water Street and your starting point at City Hall. Get back in your car and drive north on Monroe Street. (The arterial staggers a half-block right at Roosevelt Street onto Jackson Street, then turns right onto Walnut Street.) All roads flow into W Street, the south boundary of **Fort Worden State Park**. If the fort looks familiar, it could be because it was used in the filming of the Richard Gere–Debra Winger movie, *An Officer and a Gentleman.* Authorized in 1896, it includes officers' row and a refurbished **Commanding Officer's House** (admission), the **248th Coast Artillery Museum** (admission), gun emplacements, a concert pavilion, marine interpretive center and **Point Wilson Light Station**. Fort Worden offers stretches of beach that command impressive views of the Cascades and nearby islands. ~ Port Townsend; 360-385-4730.

On the dock at Fort Worden is the **Port Townsend Marine Science Center**. Of special interest are its four large touch tanks, representing different intertidal habitats, and a "wet lab" where creatures like starfish, anemones and sea cucumbers can be handled by curious visitors. Closed Monday. Admission. ~ Port Townsend; 360-385-5582.

Visitors driving to Port Townsend typically cross the one-and-a-half-mile **Hood Canal Floating Bridge** on Route 104 from the Kitsap Peninsula. Located 30 miles southeast of Port Townsend, it is the world's only floating bridge erected over tidal waters and one of the longest of its kind anywhere. Constructed in 1961, the bridge was washed away during a fierce storm in February 1979, but was rebuilt in 1982.

✔ CHECK THESE OUT—UNIQUE SIGHTS

- Learn about the early Indian inhabitants of the Olympic Peninsula at the **Makah Cultural and Research Center** in Neah Bay. *page 160*
- Drive along knife-edge coastal cliffs at **Cape Flattery**, the northwesternmost corner of the contiguous United States. *page 162*
- Join the million birds—yes, literally 1,000,000—that flock to **Grays Harbor National Wildlife Refuge**. *page 168*
- Soar to the skies with the exhibits at Long Beach's **World Kite Museum and Hall of Fame**. *page 175*

Traveling south from Port Townsend, Route 20 joins Route 101 at Discovery Bay. Twelve miles south of the junction is the town of **Quilcene** on the Hood Canal, a serpentine finger of Puget Sound. The town is especially noted for its oyster farming and processing and is the location of a state shellfish research laboratory (not open to the public). The **Mount Walker Observation Point**—five miles south on Route 101, then another five miles on a gravel road that starts at Walker Pass—offers a spectacular view of the Hood Canal and surrounding area.

LODGING

The James House claims to have been the Pacific Northwest's first bed and breakfast. Just a few steps from shops and restaurants at the foot of the bluff that stands behind lower downtown, it dates from 1889, though it's only been a bed and breakfast since 1973. The house is unmistakable for its five chimneys; inside, the floors are all parquet. Most of the 13 rooms have private baths. There are a fireplace and a library, and a full breakfast is served. Save a few moments to enjoy the English gardens with an impressive view of the water. Kids are welcome, but only if they're over 12 years old. ~ 1238 Washington Street, Port Townsend; 360-385-1238, 800-385-1238, fax 360-379-5551. DELUXE TO ULTRA-DELUXE.

For those less than enthralled with bed and breakfasts, the **Palace Hotel** provides historic accommodation in a former seafarers' bordello. Though nicely renovated, this is a bit rustic: After checking in at the main lobby you must climb a long flight of stairs (or two) to your room. There are 15 guest chambers, each with antiques recalling the red-light flavor of the past. Three of the rooms, including the madam's former room, even have kitchenettes. ~ 1004 Water Street, Port Townsend; 360-385-0773, 800-962-0741, fax 360-385-0780. MODERATE TO ULTRA-DELUXE.

The renowned **Ann Starrett Victorian Mansion Bed and Breakfast Inn**, a National Historic Landmark built in 1889, is a classic mansion in Victorian style. High on a bluff overlooking downtown Port Townsend and Puget Sound, it combines diverse architectural elements—frescoed ceilings, a free-hung spiral staircase, an eight-sided dome painted as a solar calendar, the requisite gables and dormer window—into a charming whole. The 11 guest rooms all have private baths and are furnished with antiques, of course. The gourmet breakfast menu changes daily. ~ 744 Clay Street, Port Townsend; 360-385-3205, 800-321-0644, fax 360-385-2976. MODERATE TO ULTRA-DELUXE.

With so many heritage choices, few visitors actually opt for a motel stay. If you're in that minority, check out **The Tides Inn**, along the waterfront at the south end of town. Among the 21 units are five efficiencies and nine with hot tubs; most units have balconies overlooking the bay. ~ 1807 Water Street, Port Townsend; 360-385-0595, 800-822-8696, fax 360-385-7370. MODERATE TO DELUXE.

For students and backpackers, there are two **youth hostels** in eastern Jefferson County. The first is at **Fort Worden State Park**, open year-round. ~ Port Townsend; 360-385-4730. BUDGET.

The other is at **Fort Flagler State Park**, open mid-March through September. ~ Located three miles north of Nordland; 360-385-1288. BUDGET.

South of town about 20 miles, **Port Ludlow Resort and Conference Center** is one of the Northwest's premier family resorts. It boasts a championship golf course, tennis courts, swimming pools, a marina, hiking and bicycling trails and 1500 acres of land. There are 180 suites with fireplaces, kitchens and decks and a restaurant with marvelous views of water and mountains. ~ 9483 Oak Bay Road, Port Ludlow; 360-437-2222, 800-732-1239, fax 360-437-2482. DELUXE TO ULTRA-DELUXE.

> The Whitney Gardens in Brinnon, on Route 101, boast an extensive collection of rhododendrons, Washington State's official flower.

DINING

For an evening of fine dining, it would be hard to top the **Manresa Castle**. Located in an 1892 hilltop inn that overlooks the town and bay like a German castle on the Rhine River, it combines an elegant restaurant and an Edwardian pub. The menu offers everything from curry chicken and bouillabaisse to tiger prawns. ~ 7th and Sheridan streets, Port Townsend; 360-385-5750. MODERATE TO DELUXE.

Ask locals where to eat, and chances are they'll recommend the **Fountain Café**. You'll probably have to stand in line for a seat, but the wait will be worth it. Occupying the ground floor of a historic building, the Fountain serves outstanding seafood and pasta dishes, including oysters as you like 'em. Soups and desserts are homemade. The decor is in keeping with the eclectic penchant of many young local artists. Dinner only. Closed Tuesday and Wednesday. ~ 920 Washington Street, Port Townsend; 360-385-1364. MODERATE.

Breakfasts draw full houses at the **Salal Café**. Huge omelettes and various seafood and vegetarian recipes get *oohs* and *ahs*. Lunch features gourmet home-style cooking, along with pastas and sandwiches. ~ 634 Water Street, Port Townsend; 360-385-6532. BUDGET.

Some say the **Shanghai Restaurant** serves the best Chinese food this side of Vancouver's Chinatown. Forget the view of the RV park across the street, and enjoy the spicy Szechuan and northern Chinese cuisine. ~ Point Hudson, Port Townsend; 360-385-4810. BUDGET.

HIDDEN ►

The **Chimmacum Café**, nine miles south of Port Townsend, is a local institution. This is food like grandma should have made

—country-fried chicken dinners, baked ham and so forth, followed, of course, by homemade pies brimming with fresh fruit. Breakfast, lunch and dinner are served. ~ 9253 Rhody Drive, Chimmacum; 360-732-4631. BUDGET.

SHOPPING

Port Townsend offers the most interesting shopping on the peninsula with its array of galleries, antique and gift shops, bookstores, gourmet restaurants and cafés and all-purpose emporiums. Proprietors have paid particular attention to historical accuracy in restoring commercial buildings. Many of the shops feature the work of talented local painters, sculptors, weavers, potters, poets and writers.

For antiques, try any of the many other shops along the 600 through 1200 blocks of Water or Washington streets. Or you can try the **Port Townsend Antique Mall** on Washington Street. ~ 802 Washington Street, Port Townsend; 360-385-2590.

NIGHTLIFE

In Port Townsend, you'll find two rustic establishments, popular with locals. Live rock music or rhythm-and-blues is featured weekends at the **Back Alley**. Cover. ~ 923 Washington Street, Port Townsend; 360-385-2914. Jazz, opera and Celtic harp accompany dinner at **Lanza's** on the weekend. ~ 1020 Lawrence Street, Port Townsend; 360-379-1900.

BEACHES & PARKS

FORT WORDEN STATE PARK A 433-acre estate right in Port Townsend, this turn-of-the-century fort includes restored Victorian officers houses, barracks, theater, parade grounds and artillery bunkers. A beach and a boat launch are on Admiralty Inlet, at the head of Puget Sound. Try the dock or beach for fishing. There are restrooms, picnic areas and lodging; restaurants and groceries are in town. ~ The entrance is located on W Street at Cherry Street, at the northern city limits of Port Townsend; 360-385-4730.

▲ There are 80 sites with RV hookups; $16 per night. Reservations are strongly recommended year-round.

KAH TAI LAGOON NATURE PARK This midtown park, which features 50 acres of wetlands and 35 acres of grasslands and woodlands, is a great place for birdwatching: more than 50 species have been identified here. There are two-and-a-half miles of trails, a play area for kids, interpretive displays, restrooms and picnic areas; restaurants and groceries are in town. ~ On 12th Street near Sims Way in Port Townsend; 360-385-2722.

OLD FORT TOWNSEND STATE PARK Decommissioned in 1895 when Indian attacks on Port Townsend (the town) were no longer a threat, the park has seven miles of trails and a beach on Port Townsend (the inlet). You can fish from the shore.

Facilities include restrooms and picnic areas; restaurants and groceries are in town. ~ Located on Old Fort Townsend Road, three miles south of the town of Port Townsend off Route 20; 360-385-3595.

▲ There are 40 sites; $10 per night.

FORT FLAGLER STATE PARK 🚶 🚲 🏊 🎣 🚣 ⛵ 🛥️ 🚤 🛶 The long-abandoned fort building, which dates from 1898, is a minor attraction here: bigger is the saltwater beach on Admiralty Inlet, popular for clamming, beachcombing and fishing for salmon, halibut, sole, crab and shellfish. There are also a boat launch, hiking trails, restrooms, picnic areas and lodging; gas and groceries are in Nordland, three miles south; restaurants are in Hadlock. ~ Located on north tip of Marrowstone Island, eight miles northeast of Hadlock off Route 116; 360-385-1259.

▲ There are 116 developed sites for tents or RVs; prices range from $11 to $16 per night.

DOSEWALLIPS STATE PARK 🚶 🚲 🛶 At the mouth of the Dosewallips River on the Hood Canal, a long, serpentine arm of Puget Sound, this 425-acre park is especially popular among clam diggers and oyster hunters during shellfish season. There are hiking trails, a mudflat beach, restrooms, showers and picnic areas; restaurants and groceries are in nearby Brinnon. ~ Located in Brinnon, 37 miles south of Port Townsend on Route 101; 360-796-4415.

▲ There are 87 developed sites and 40 RV sites with hookups; $10 to $16 per night. For reservations call 800-452-5687.

OLYMPIC NATIONAL FOREST 🚶 🚲 🏊 🛥️ 🛶 Surrounding Olympic National Park on its east, south and northwest sides, this national forest provides ample recreational opportunities, including good fishing in the forest's many lakes and rivers. It includes five wilderness areas on the fringe of the park. You'll find restrooms and picnic areas; restaurants and groceries are in towns around perimeter of forest. ~ Numerous access roads branch off Route 101, especially south of Sequim, and between Quilcene and Hoodsport, on the east side of the Olympic Peninsula; 360-956-2300.

▲ There are 19 campgrounds throughout the forest. Camping costs up to $14, though some spots are free.

▼▼▼▼▼▼▼▼▼▼▼
Port Angeles Area
The northern gateway to Olympic National Park as well as a major terminal for ferries to British Columbia, the Port Angeles area is one of northwest Washington's main crossroads. Sequim on Route 101, 31 miles west of Port Townsend, and nearby Port Angeles are two of the peninsula's more intriguing towns. On the Strait of Juan de

Fuca at the foot of the Olympic Mountains, this region often may be dry when it's pouring rain just a few miles south.

The town of **Sequim** (pronounced "Squim") is graced with a climate that's unusually dry and mild for the Northwest: it sits in the Olympic rain shadow. A major attraction just north of town is the **Olympic Game Farm**, whose animals—lions, tigers, bears, buffalo and many others—are trained for film roles. Driving tours of the farm are available year-round; walking tours, including a studio barn, are offered during the summer. Admission. ~ 1423 Ward Road, Sequim; 360-683-4295.

SIGHTS

In the Sequim–Dungeness Valley area, the **Museum and Art Center** preserves the native and pioneer farming heritage of Sequim and showcases the work of local artists. ~ 175 West Cedar Street, Sequim; 360-683-8110.

For visitor information, contact the **Sequim–Dungeness Valley Chamber of Commerce**. ~ Route 101 and Rodefer Street, Sequim; 360-683-6197.

North off Route 101, the Dungeness Valley is dotted with strawberry and raspberry fields. Weathered barns left over from the area's dairy farming days are still visible. Pay a visit to the **Cedarbrook Herb Farm**, where 300 different varieties of herbs and spices fill the air with a marvelous (but undefinable!) aroma and inspire many a gourmet chef to go on a culinary buying spree. ~ 1345 Sequim Avenue South, Sequim; 360-683-7733.

Opposite the mouth of the Dungeness River is one of the Olympic Peninsula's most remarkable natural features: the **Dungeness Spit**, almost seven miles long and the largest natural sand hook in the United States. A short trail within the adjacent Dungeness Recreation Area provides access to this national wildlife refuge. The spit and the surrounding bay and estuary are teeming with wildlife, including seabirds, seals, fish, crabs and clams.

Seventeen miles west of Sequim on Route 101 is the fishing and logging port of **Port Angeles**, the Olympic Peninsula's largest town. A major attraction here is the **City Pier** (360-457-0411). Adjacent to the ferry terminal, it boasts an observation tower, promenade decks and a picnic area.

The **Arthur D. Feiro Marine Laboratory**, where visitors can observe and even touch samples of local marine life, is also found at the City Pier. Admission. ~ 360-452-9277.

As the gateway to Olympic National Park, Port Angeles is home to national park headquarters. At the **Olympic National Park Visitor Center**, you'll find an excellent slide show and exhibits on the natural and human history of the park. Open seven days a week. ~ 3002 Mount Angeles Road, Port Angeles; 360-452-0330.

The **Clallam County Museum** in the old county courthouse building has a variety of interesting regional historical displays. Closed Saturday and Sunday. ~ 223 East 4th Street, Port Angeles; 360-417-2364.

For tourist information, contact the **North Olympic Peninsula Visitor & Convention Bureau.** ~ 338 West 1st Street, Port Angeles; 360-452-8552.

LODGING

You'll feel good right down to your cockles—as well as your steamer clams, butter clams and horse clams—after shellfishing on the saltwater beach outside the **Sequim Bay Resort**. The eight fully equipped housekeeping cottages here are suitable for vacationing families and shoreline lovers. There are no pets allowed in the cottages. There are also guest laundry facilities and hookups for RVs. ~ 2634 West Sequim Bay Road, Sequim; 360-681-3853. BUDGET.

HIDDEN ▶

Just a spit from the Spit—Dungeness, that is—is the **Groveland Cottage,** by the coast north of Sequim. The turn-of-the-century building has four rooms above a country craft shop, two with private baths. There is also a private cottage with a queen-size bed and private bath. The rooms may be simple, but service is not: coffee is delivered to your room in anticipation of the four-course gourmet breakfast. They also rent 17 vacation cottages in the area. ~ 4861 Sequim-Dungeness Way, Dungeness; 360-683-3565, 800-879-8859, fax 360-683-5181. MODERATE TO DELUXE.

Sequimvalley room

Perhaps the nicest motel-style accommodation in these port communities is the **Doubletree Hotel.** A modern tan building that extends along the Strait of Juan de Fuca opposite the ferry dock, it offers rooms with private balconies overlooking the water. A private strand of beach and swimming pool beckon bathers. ~ 221

✔ CHECK THESE OUT—UNIQUE LODGING

- *Budget to moderate:* Sleep next to a rolling river on the threshold of the Hoh Rainforest at the **River Inn on the Bogachiel.** *page 162*
- *Moderate to deluxe:* Relax on a private balcony 132 steps up from the beach at the **Ocean Crest Resort** in Moclips. *page 166*
- *Deluxe to ultra-deluxe:* Check into the oldest continually operating hotel in Washington (dating back to 1896) at **The Shelburne Country Inn.** *page 176*
- *Ultra-deluxe:* Play the handcrafted harpsichord at the **Domaine Madeleine Bed and Breakfast,** a charming inn with stunning views of the San Juan Islands. *page 155*

Budget: under $50   Moderate: $60–$90   Deluxe: $90–$130   Ultra-deluxe: over $130

North Lincoln Street, Port Angeles; 360-452-9215, 800-222-8733, fax 360-452-4734. DELUXE.

Situated on the water with spectacular views of the San Juan Islands, the **Domaine Madeleine Bed and Breakfast** excels in both comfort and hospitality. There are five rooms including a honeymoon cottage at this charming inn: the Renoir Room with impressionist art and feather beds; the Monet Room with Monet prints and a jacuzzi; and the Ming Room, with 19th-century antiques, an array of French perfumes, a jacuzzi and a large private balcony. Relax in front of the 14-foot-high basalt fireplace or try your hand at the handcrafted harpsichord. The full gourmet breakfast is elegantly presented—don't miss it. Gay-friendly. ~ 146 Wildflower Lane, Port Angeles; 360-457-4174, fax 360-457-3037. ULTRA-DELUXE.

Victoria, across the strait on Vancouver Island, is said to be "more British than the British"—but the same slogan could almost apply to **The Tudor Inn**. Mother and daughter hosts Jane and Katy Glass serve a traditional English breakfast and afternoon tea in the restored Tudor-style home. Most of their antique collection is Old English, and the well-stocked library will steer you to books on the United Kingdom. All five bedrooms have private baths; one has a gas fireplace and small balcony. ~ 1108 South Oak Street, Port Angeles; 360-452-3138. MODERATE TO DELUXE.

DINING

El Cazador is a casual, family-run restaurant with red and green table linens, whitewashed walls and Mexican artwork. What sets it apart is its use of fresh seafood in traditional Mexican dishes that consistently win local "best of" awards. The burrito Veracruz stuffed with baby shrimp is a standout. ~ 531 West Washington Street, Sequim; 360-683-4788. BUDGET.

◄ HIDDEN

If retired physicist Tom Wells and his Cambodian-born wife, Lay Yin, aren't off studying a solar eclipse somewhere around the globe, you'll find them at the **Eclipse Café**. Yin's culinary touch dominates: Southeast Asian taste tempters stand out. This one's for hungry adventurers. Breakfast and lunch only. Closed Wednesday to Friday. ~ 139 West Alder Street, Sequim; 360-683-2760. BUDGET.

The undisputed winner in the northern Olympic Peninsula fine-dining sweepstakes is **C'est Si Bon**. The decor is modern and dramatic, with handsome oil paintings and full picture windows allowing panoramas of the Olympic Range. The cuisine, on the other hand, is classical French: tournedos with crabmeat and a shallot sauce, coquilles St. Jacques, veal Normande with apples and calvados. There are French wines and desserts, too. Dinner only. Closed Monday. ~ 23 Cedar Park Drive, four miles east of Port Angeles; 360-452-8888. DELUXE.

Haguewood's Restaurant, located in the Red Lion Bayshore Inn, offers sweeping waterfront views in a casually elegant decor of etched glass and tapestry-covered booth seating. Simple and straightforward seafood dishes such as cracked Dungeness crab and grilled salmon are the specialties. ~ 221 North Lincoln Street, Port Angeles; 360-457-0424. MODERATE TO DELUXE.

Practically next door is the **First Street Haven,** one of the best places around for quick and tasty breakfasts and lunches. Have a homemade quiche and salad, along with baked goods and the house coffee, and you'll be set for the day. Breakfast and lunch only. ~ 107 East 1st Street, Port Angeles; 360-457-0352. BUDGET.

SHOPPING   Sequim is full of antique dealers. A good one is **Country Cottage Antiques.** ~ 243 West Washington Street; 360-683-8983.

Today's and Yesterday's is a women's clothing boutique that doubles as a hair salon. ~ 131 East Washington Street, Sequim; 360-683-5733.

NIGHTLIFE   You didn't come to this part of the state for its nightlife, and that's good. What little there is usually exists only on Friday and Saturday nights.

The **Hurricane Ridge Lounge** in the Red Lion Bayshore Inn features daily drink specials. ~ 221 North Lincoln Street, Port Angeles; 360-457-0424.

BEACHES & PARKS   **SEQUIM BAY STATE PARK** 🏃 🚣 🛶 🚤 🛥️ 🎣 Water sports and hiking, both along the shore and up the Jimmycomelately River (that's its name, honest), are the main attractions at this park on Sequim Bay, sheltered from rough seas by two spits at its mouth and from heavy rains by the Olympic rain shadow. There are restrooms, picnic areas and a beach; restaurants and groceries are located in Sequim. ~ Located on Route 101, four miles east of Sequim; 360-683-4235.

▲ There are 60 tent sites, 26 RV sites, 3 hiker/biker sites; $10 to $15 per night.

DUNGENESS RECREATION AREA 🏃 🚴 🐎 🎣 The Dungeness Spit is a national wildlife refuge, but a recreation area trail provides access. Marine birds and seals are among the impressive wildlife to be seen; the Dungeness crab is internationally famous as a fine food. Facilities include restrooms, showers and picnic areas; restaurants and groceries are in Dungeness three miles east, or Sequim eight miles southeast. ~ Located at the base of the Dungeness Spit, five miles west of Sequim on Route 101, then four miles north on Kitchen-Dick Road; 360-683-5847.

▲ There are 66 sites; $10 per night.

HIDDEN ▶   **SALT CREEK RECREATION AREA** 🏃 🚴 🏊 🎣 One of the finest tidepool sanctuaries on the Olympic Peninsula is this three-mile stretch of rocky beach. Starfish, sea urchins, anemones, mussels, barnacles and other invertebrate life can be observed . . . but not removed. You'll find restrooms, picnic areas, a playground and hiking trails; restaurants and groceries are in Joyce. ~ Located three miles north from Joyce (or 15 miles west from Port Angeles) on Route 112, then another three miles north on Camp Hayden Road; 360-928-3441.

▲ There are 92 sites; $8 to $10 per night.

The Olympic Peninsula's main attraction —in fact, the reason most tourists come here at all—is Olympic National Park. Rugged,

Olympic National Park

glaciated mountains dominate the 1400-square-mile park, with rushing rivers tumbling from their slopes. But the rainier western slopes harbor an extraordinary rainforest, and a separate 57-mile-long coastal strip preserves remarkable tidepools and marvelous ocean scenery. Wildlife in the park includes the rare Roosevelt elk, as well as deer, black bears, cougars, bobcats, a great many smaller mammals and scores of bird species.

The most direct route into the park from Port Angeles is the Heart of the Hills/Hurricane Ridge Road. It climbs 5200 feet in just 17 miles to the **Hurricane Ridge Lodge**, where there are breathtaking views to 7965-foot Mt. Olympus, the highest peak in the Olympic Range, and other glacier-shrouded mountains. Visitors to Hurricane Ridge can dine in the day lodge, picnic, enjoy nature walks or take longer hikes. In winter, enjoy the small downhill ski area here and many cross-country trails. ~ 360-928-3211.

SIGHTS

Twenty miles west of Port Angeles on Route 101 is **Lake Crescent**, one of three large lakes within park boundaries. Carved during the last Ice Age 10,000 years ago, it is nestled between steep forested hillsides. A unique subspecies of trout lures many anglers to its deep waters. There are several resorts, restaurants, campgrounds and picnic areas around the lake's shoreline. From National Park Service–administered Lake Crescent Lodge, on the southeast shore, a three-fourth-mile trail leads up Barnes Creek to the beautiful Marymere Falls.

West of Lake Crescent, the Sol Duc River Road turns south to **Sol Duc Hot Springs**, 14 miles off of Route 101. Long known to the Indians, the therapeutic mineral waters were discovered by a pioneer in 1880 and like everything else the white man touched, soon boasted an opulent resort. But the original burned to the ground in 1916 and today's refurbished resort, nestled in a valley of old-growth Douglas fir, is more rustic than elegant. The springs remain an attraction. Sol Duc is a major trailhead for backpacking trips into Olympic National Park; also located here is a ranger station. ~ 360-327-3534.

On the west side of the national park are three more major points of entry. The **Hoh Rainforest** is 19 miles east of Route 101 via the Hoh River Road, 13 miles south of Forks. For national park information here, call the Forks Ranger Station (360-374-5450). There's a less well-known rainforest at the end of the **Queets River Road**, 14 miles off Route 101, 17 miles west of Quinault. Finally, **Quinault Lake**, on Route 101 at the southwestern corner of Olympic National Park, is the site of several resorts and campgrounds, including the venerable Lake Quinault Lodge. Watersports of all kinds are popular at this glacier-fed lake, surrounded by old-growth forest. For general information on the park, call the **Olympic National Park Visitor Center.** ~ 360-452-0330.

LODGING

The rustic **Log Cabin Resort** is a historic landmark on the shores of gorgeous Lake Crescent along Route 101. Budget-watchers can stay in the main lodge; more upscale are lakeshore chalets and cabins. There is also an RV park with full hookups on Log Cabin Creek. The handsome log lodge has a restaurant and a gift shop; all manner of boats are rented at the marina. ~ 3183 East Beach Road, 21 miles west of Port Angeles; 360-928-3245, fax 360-928-2088. BUDGET TO DELUXE.

The **Sol Duc Hot Springs Resort** is another historic property, this one built in 1910 around a series of hot sulphur pools 12 miles south of Route 101. The 33 cabins (six with kitchens) have undergone occasional renovations since then, including indoor plumbing! The best plunge, however, after a day of hiking or fishing, remains the natural mineral springs, kept at 98 to 104°. There is also a full-size swimming pool. Camping sites and RV hookups are available. The resort is open May to October. ~ Sol Duc Hot Springs Road, 44 miles west of Port Angeles; 360-327-3583, fax 360-327-3593. DELUXE.

DINING

The best choice for dining in the park is the **Log Cabin Resort**. Enjoy the view of beautiful Lake Crescent, where anglers dip their lines for the unique crescenti trout, a subspecies of rainbow trout that may wind up on your platter in the restaurant. Northwest cuisine is a specialty. ~ 3183 East Beach Road, 21 miles west of Port Angeles; 360-928-3325. MODERATE.

There's another dining room at the **Sol Duc Hot Springs Resort**, just behind the hot sulphur springs. As at the Log Cabin, the food is solid Northwest fare, including Dungeness crab from the north Olympic Coast. Open May to October. ~ Sol Duc Hot Springs Road, 44 miles west of Port Angeles; 360-327-3583. MODERATE.

A mile high in the Olympic Range, 17 miles south of Port Angeles, the **Hurricane Ridge Lodge** frames glaciers in the picture

The Hoh
Rainforest

No matter where you go on this earth, there's only one Hoh Rainforest. It's said to be one of the only coniferous rainforests in the world. Graciously spared the logger's blade, it's been undisturbed since time began. In other words, it's a natural wonder to be embraced and cherished.

Reached by traveling 13 miles south from Forks on Route 101, then 19 miles east on Hoh River Road, this is the wettest spot in the contiguous 48 states. In fact, wet isn't the word: even the air drips like a saturated sponge, producing over 30 inches of fog drip in the summer. The average annual precipitation due to rainfall is 145 inches, more than 100 inches of which fall between October and March. But temperatures at this elevation, between 500 and 1000 feet, rarely fall below 40° in winter or rise above 85° in summer. The legacy of this mild climate is dense, layered canopies of foliage.

The forest floor is as soft and thick as a shag carpet, cloaked with mosses, bracken ferns, huge fungi and seedlings. Hovering over the lush rug are vine maple, alder and black cottonwood, some hung with moss, stretching wiry branches to taste any slivers of sunlight that may steal through the canopy. Above them, Douglas fir, Sitka spruce, Western hemlock, Western red cedar and other gigantic conifers rise 200 to 300 feet, putting a lid on the forest. In all, over 300 plant species live here, not counting 70 epiphytes (mosses, lichens and such).

Some compare this environment to a cathedral. Indeed, the soft light is like sun filtered through stained glass, and the arching branches could pass for a vaulted apse. To others, it's simply mystical. The ancient coastal Indians would have agreed.

Though there are similar rainforests in Washington, the rainforest ecology is most conveniently studied at the **Hoh Rainforest Visitor Center** (360-374-6925) and on the nature trails that surround it. The **Hoh River Trail** extends for 19 miles to the river's source in Blue Glacier, on the flank of Mt. Olympus, but the rainforest can be appreciated by most visitors on one of two loop hikes that are both about a mile long. About three-fourths of a mile in, you'll see enormous old-growth firs, some over nine feet in girth and at least 500 years old. At about one mile, the trail drops down to Big Flat, the first of several grassy open areas. The winter grazing of Roosevelt elk, whose survival was a major reason for the creation of Olympic National Park, has opened up the forest floor.

Keep your eyes open, too, for wildlife. Besides the elk, you may spot river otter or weasel. Black bears and cougars also inhabit these forests. Bald eagles and great blue heron feed on the salmon that spawn seasonally in the Hoh.

windows of its coffee shop. Come for the view, but the standard American fare served here isn't half-bad either. Open daily mid-May through September, weekends mid-December to April. ~ Hurricane Ridge Road; 360-928-3211. MODERATE.

BEACHES & PARKS

OLYMPIC NATIONAL PARK 🏃‍♂️🚴🐎🎣🚣⛵🛶 This spectacular national park, 900,000 acres in area and ranging in elevation from sea level to nearly 8000 feet, contains everything from permanent alpine glaciers to America's lushest rainforest (the Hoh) to rocky tidepools rich in marine life. Wildlife includes goats in the mountains, elks in the rainforest, steelhead and trout in the rivers and colorful birds everywhere. Three large lakes, Crescent (near Port Angeles), Ozette (on the coast) and Quinault (on the southwestern edge), are especially popular visitor destinations. Facilities are restrooms, picnic areas, hotels, restaurants and groceries. ~ Route 101 circles the park. The numerous access roads are well marked; 360-452-4501 (Port Angeles); ranger stations in Forks (360-374-5450), Quilcene (360-765-3368) and Sol Duc (360-327-3534).

▲ There are 16 campgrounds; $10 to $12 per night.

▼▼▼▼▼▼▼▼▼▼

Olympic Coast

Largely undeveloped, the rough-and-tumble Olympic Coast is one of the Northwest's hidden gems. Home to America's finest American Indian research centers, this region is also famous for its archaeological preserves, maritime sanctuaries and pristine beaches. It features some of the finest wilderness hiking in the region.

SIGHTS

Fifty miles west of Port Angeles via Route 112, where the Strait of Juan de Fuca approaches the Pacific Ocean, are the sister communities of **Clallam Bay** and **Sekiu** (pronounced "C-Q"). These are prime sportfishing grounds for salmon and huge bottom fish, especially halibut. If you're spending time at a fishing resort in one of these towns, don't miss the wonderful tidepools northeast of Clallam Bay at **Slip Point**. Just west of Sekiu, at the mouth of the Hoko River, visitors can view the remains of a 2500-year-old Makah Indian fishing village at the **Hoko Archeological Site**.

For more than 2500 years, **Neah Bay**, located in the Makah Indian Reservation 18 miles west of Sekiu on Route 112, has been the home of the Makah tribe. Visitors can enjoy excellent charter-fishing excursions from the harbor, which is also home to a commercial fishing fleet.

The **Makah Cultural and Research Center** houses the prehistoric artifacts discovered at the Hoko and Lake Ozette digs, including baskets, whaling and sealing harpoons, canoes and a replica of a 15th-century longhouse. Admission. ~ Bay View Avenue, Neah Bay; 360-645-2711.

Returning on Route 112 toward Sekiu, Lake Ozette Road branches south at the Hoko River. The road leads 20 miles to the northernmost of three tiny Indian reservations (the Ozette) surrounded by the coastal strip of Olympic National Park. **Ozette Lake** is the largest of the national park's three lakes; a strip of land just three miles wide separates it from the ocean. Two trails lead from here to the sea.

The Indian Village Trail to **Cape Alava**, the westernmost point of the continental United States, leads to the **Ozette Dig**, a 500-year-old Indian village excavated by archaeologists in the 1970s.

Much of the Olympic coastline remains undeveloped. Hikers can wander along the high-water mark or on primitive trails, some wood-planked and raised above the forest floor. Offshore reefs have taken many lives over the centuries since European exploration began, and two memorials to shipwreck victims are good destinations for intrepid hikers. Nine miles south of Ozette, the **Norwegian Memorial** remembers seamen who died in an early 20th-century shipwreck. Six miles farther south, and about three miles north of Rialto Beach opposite La Push, the **Chilean Memorial** marks the grave of 20 South American sailors who died in a 1920 wreck.

The Ozette Loop Trail weaves past 56 petroglyphs that depict various aspects of historic Makah life.

Return to Sekiu to continue your drive south down the coast. Twenty-seven miles south of Clallam Bay on Route 101 is **Forks**, with 3000 people the largest town between Port Angeles and Hoquiam. (It's also Washington's rainiest town, with well over 100 inches a year.) Steelhead fishing, river rafting and mushroom gathering are major activities here, but the one most evident to visitors is the timber industry. Some days, in fact, there seem to be more log trucks on the roads than passenger cars.

The **Forks Timber Museum** is filled with exhibits of old-time logging equipment and historical photos, as well as pioneer and Indian artifacts. ~ Route 101 North, Forks; 360-374-9663.

On the coast 14 miles west of Forks is the 800-year-old Indian fishing village of **La Push**, center of the **Quileute Indian Reservation**. Sportfishing, camping and beach walking are popular year-round. An abandoned Coast Guard station and lighthouse here are used as a school for resident children. ~ 360-374-6163.

A national park road eight miles west of Forks branches off the La Push Road and follows the north shore of the Quileute River five miles to **Rialto Beach**, where spectacular piles of driftwood often accumulate. There are picnic areas and campgrounds here, and a trailhead for hikes north up the beach toward Cape Alava.

The **Hoh Indian Reservation** is 25 miles south of Forks, off Route 101. Of more interest to most visitors is the **Kalaloch**

Lodge, 35 miles south of Forks on Route 101. A major national park facility, it affords spectacular ocean views at the southern-most end of the park's coastal strip. ~ Kalaloch Lodge: 157151 Route 101; 360-962-2271.

LODGING The hamlet of Sekiu flanks Route 112 on the protected shore of Clallam Bay, on the Strait of Juan de Fuca. The lone waterfront hotel here is **Van Riper's Resort and Charters**. Family owned and operated, it's a cozy getaway spot. More than half of the 16 rooms have great views of the boats on the picturesque strait. ~ Front and Rice streets, Sekiu; 360-963-2334, fax 360-963-2776. BUDGET TO DELUXE.

Open year-round, **The Cape Motel and RV Park** has eight motel rooms and two cottages; the latter all have kitchens. ~ Bay-view Avenue, Neah Bay; 360-645-2250. MODERATE.

The main population center on the Olympic Coast, and the nearest to the Hoh Rainforest, is the lumber town of Forks. Among several low-priced bed and breakfasts here is the **River Inn on the Bogachiel**, an A-frame chalet on the banks of the Bogachiel River two-and-a-half miles from town. Two bedrooms share a bath and sundecks; one has a private bathroom and stairs leading to the hot tub. You can fish from the shore or relax in the hot tub while keeping your eyes open for elk, deer and river otter. ~ 2596 West Bogachiel Way, Forks; 360-374-6526, fax 360-374-6590. BUDGET TO MODERATE.

HIDDEN ►

Sixteen miles west of Forks in the Quileute Indian Reservation, surrounded by the coastal strip of Olympic National Park, is the **La Push Ocean Park Resort**. The driftwood-speckled beach is just beyond the lodgings, which fall into four categories: cabins with fully supplied kitchenettes and fireplaces; older townhouse units with balconies overlooking the beach; 20 motel units with either full kitchens or kitchenettes; and rustic A-frames with wood stoves (haul your own fuel from the woodshed) and toilets (show-ers are in a communal washroom). ~ 700 Main Street, La Push; 360-374-5267, 800-487-1267. BUDGET TO DELUXE.

FLATTERY WILL GET YOU NOWHERE, BUT THE VIEW'S TERRIFIC

A winding, scenic coastal drive to the end of Route 112 climaxes at **Cape Flattery**, the northwesternmost corner of the contiguous United States. The road at times runs within feet of the water, providing spectacular blufftop views of the Strait of Juan de Fuca and Tatoosh Island—a great location for whale watching between March and May. A short trail leads to the shore. Beach hikers can find some of the last wilderness coast in Washington south of here.

Forks also has a youth hostel: the **Rain Forest Hostel**. As with other lodgings of its ilk, it offers dorm bunks and community bathrooms and kitchen. The common room is a bonus with its fireplace and library. There is also one room for a couple and one room for a family. ~ 169312 Route 101 North, 23 miles south of Forks; 360-374-2270. BUDGET.

Back in Olympic National Park, one of the most picturesque spots found on the Washington coastline is the **Kalaloch Lodge**. Accommodations here include eight lodge units, ten motel units, 20 log cabins with kitchenettes (but no utensils provided) and 18 units atop the bluff, six of which are duplexes. The lodge has a dining room and lounge overlooking the Pacific Ocean, as well as a general store, gas station and gift shop. ~ 157151 Route 101, 35 miles south of Forks; 360-962-2271, fax 360-962-3391. MODERATE TO ULTRA-DELUXE.

If you're planning a stay in the corner of Olympic National Park that includes beauteous Lake Quinault, consider the **Lake Quinault Lodge**—especially if you can get a lakefront room in the historic cedar-shingled lodge itself. The huge building arcs around the shoreline, a totem-pole design on its massive chimney facing the water. Antiques and wicker furniture adorn the main lobby, constructed in the 1920s. There is also a sun porch, dining room and bar. There are nice rooms in a newer wing, but they lack the lodge's historic ambience. You can rent boats in the summer, hike year-round or relax in the pool or sauna. ~ 345 South Shore Road, Quinault; 360-288-2571, fax 360-288-2901. DELUXE TO ULTRA-DELUXE.

DINING

Sunsets from the **Kalaloch Lodge**, high on a bluff overlooking the ocean in the national park's coastal strip, can make even the most ordinary food taste good. Fortunately, the fresh salmon and oysters served here don't need the view for their rich flavor. A lounge adjoins the dining room. ~ 157151 Route 101, 35 miles south of Forks; 360-962-2271. MODERATE.

The restaurant at the park's **Lake Quinault Lodge** faces a gorgeous lake surrounded by lush cedar forests. As you've come to expect along this coast, the seafood is excellent. ~ 345 South Shore Road, Quinault; 360-288-2571. MODERATE TO DELUXE.

Other than the national park lodges, pickings are slim in the restaurant department along this stretch of highway. A mile north of Forks, the **Smoke House Restaurant** is located on the Calabash River and serves a superb alder-smoked salmon. You can also get generous portions of other seafood and meats, plus a salad bar. ~ Route 101 at La Push Road; 360-374-6258. MODERATE.

SHOPPING

For authentic Northwest Indian crafts, you won't do better than the gift shop at the **Makah Cultural and Research Center** on the

Makah Indian Reservation near Cape Flattery at the end of Route 112. ~ Bayview Avenue, Neah Bay; 360-645-2711.

BEACHES & PARKS

BOGACHIEL STATE PARK 🏃 ⛵ Not far from the Hoh Rainforest, this eternally damp park sits on the Bogachiel River, famous for its salmon and steelhead runs. Hiking and hunting in the adjacent forest are popular activities. Facilities include restrooms, showers and picnic areas; restaurants and groceries are in Forks. ~ Located on Route 101 six miles south of Forks; 360-374-6356.

▲ There are 34 standard sites, six RV hookups and two primitive sites; $5 for primitive sites, $10 to $15 for other sites.

▼▼▼▼▼▼▼▼▼▼▼
Ocean Shores–Pacific Beach

A six-mile-long, 6000-acre peninsula, Ocean Shores was a cattle ranch when a group of investors bought it for $1 million in 1960. A decade later, its assessed value had risen to $35 million. Today, it would be hard to put a dollar figure on this strip of condominium-style hotels and second homes, many of them on a series of canals. The main tourist beach destination on the Grays Harbor County coastline, it's located along Route 115 three miles south of its junction with Route 109.

SIGHTS

Folks come to Ocean Shores for oceanside rest and recreation, not for sightseeing. One of the few "attractions" is the **Ocean Shores Environmental Interpretive Center** four miles south of the town center near the Ocean Shores Marina. Open only on Saturday in the summer, it has exhibits describing the peninsula's geological formation and human development. ~ Point Brown Avenue, Ocean Shores; 360-289-4617.

The 22-mile beach that parallels Routes 115 and 109 north to Moclips is an attraction in its own right. Beyond Moclips, however, the coastline gets more rugged. Eight miles past Moclips, the **Quinault Indian National Tribal Headquarters** in the village of Taholah, on the Quinault Indian Reservation, offers guided fishing trips on reservation land and tribal gifts in a small shop. ~ 360-276-8215.

LODGING

The nearest ocean beach area to the Seattle-Tacoma metropolitan area, Ocean Shores' condominiums and motels are frequently booked solid during the summer and on holiday weekends, even though prices can be high. At other times, it can be downright quiet . . . and inexpensive.

Like almost every other lodging on this stretch of shoreline, **The Polynesian Resort** is as close to the water as you can get—a good mile trek across the dunes to the high-tide mark. The four-story building has 71 rooms ranging from motel units to three-bedroom penthouse suites. It has a restaurant, lively lounge, indoor pool and spa, outdoor games area and indoor game room popular with families. ~ 615 Ocean Shores Boulevard Northwest, Ocean Shores; 360-289-3361, 800-562-4836, fax 360-289-0294. DELUXE TO ULTRA-DELUXE.

Across the street from the Polynesian is Ocean Shores' largest property, with 83 units, and one of its least expensive: the **Gitche Gumee Motel**. Basic sleeper units are small, but kitchen units (many with fireplaces) are good-sized. Rooms have televisions and phones; everyone can use the sauna and indoor and outdoor pools. ~ 648 Ocean Shores Boulevard Northwest, Ocean Shores; 360-289-3323, 800-448-2433, fax 360-289-3320. BUDGET TO ULTRA-DELUXE.

Neighboring units at **The Grey Gull** are fewer in numbers (36), but they're all studios or suites with fireplaces, microwave ovens, videocassette recorders and private decks or balconies. The Gull has an outdoor pool and jacuzzi guarded by a wind fence. ~ 647 Ocean Shores Boulevard, Ocean Shores; 360-289-3381, 800-562-9712, fax 360-289-3673. DELUXE TO ULTRA-DELUXE.

The **Caroline Inn** offers four bi-level townhouse suites just steps from the water. Decorated in soft rose colors, the rooms are furnished with sleigh beds and other antiques. Each suite offers all the comforts of home and then some: fireplaces, jacuzzis, complete kitchens and living areas with entertainment centers. ~ 1341 Ocean Shores Boulevard, Ocean Shores; 360-289-0450, fax 360-289-9682. DELUXE TO ULTRA-DELUXE.

One of few accommodations away from "the strip" is the **Discovery Inn**, a condo motel close to the Ocean Shores Marina near the cape's southeast tip, five miles from downtown. Rooms are built around a central courtyard with a seasonal pool. There is an indoor jacuzzi and family game room. A private dock on Ocean Shores' grand canal encourages boating and fishing. ~ 1031 Discovery Avenue Southeast, Ocean Shores; 360-289-3371, 800-882-8821. MODERATE.

North up the coast from frenetic Ocean Shores are numerous quiet resort communities and accommodations. At Ocean City, four miles north, the **Pacific Sands Motel** is one of the top economy choices on the coast. There are just nine units, but they're well kept; seven have kitchens and three have fireplaces. The extensive grounds include a nice swimming pool, playground, picnic tables and direct beach access across a suspension bridge. ~ 2687 Route 109, Ocean City; 360-289-3588. BUDGET.

◄ HIDDEN

The **Iron Springs Resort** has 29 units in 25 cottages built up a wooded hill and around a handsome cove at the mouth of Iron Springs Creek. The beach here is popular for razor clamming, crabbing and surf fishing; the cottages are equally popular for their spaciousness and panoramic views. All have kitchens and fireplaces. There are an indoor pool, playground and gift shop.

~ 3707 Route 109, Copalis Beach; 360-276-4230, fax 360-276-4365. MODERATE TO DELUXE.

Ocean Crest Resort may be the most memorable accommodation on this entire stretch of beach. It's built atop a bluff, so getting to the beach involves a 132-step descent down a staircase through a wooded ravine. But the views from the rooms' private balconies are remarkable, and all but the smallest rooms have fireplaces and refrigerators. There are exercise facilities with a swimming pool, jacuzzi and weight room open to all guests free of charge. ~ Sunset Beach, Route 109, Moclips; 360-276-4465, 800-684-8439, fax 360-276-4149. MODERATE TO DELUXE.

DINING

The **Home Port Restaurant** is appointed like the private garden of a sea captain home from the waves. Steaks, seafood and pasta dominate the menu. ~ 854 Point Brown Avenue opposite Shoal Street, Ocean Shores; 360-289-2600. MODERATE TO DELUXE.

Numerous Ocean Shores restaurants appeal to more casual diners. **Flipper's Fish Bar** has excellent fish-and-chips. ~ Chance a la Mer at Ocean Court; 360-289-4676. BUDGET. The **Sand Castle Drive-in** is the in-spot for hamburgers. ~ 788 Point Brown Avenue, north of Chance a la Mer; 360-289-2777. BUDGET.

A bit of Manzanillo on the Washington coast, **Las Maracas** feels like the tropics with its bright tropical colors and profusion of plants. All the usual Mexican specialties are on the menu, but the best bets are the fajitas, crab and prawn enchiladas and seafood chimichangas. ~ 729 Point Brown Avenue, Ocean Shores; 360-289-2054. BUDGET.

Authentic Irish and Scottish pub fare is dished up at **Galway Bay Irish Restaurant and Pub** where you can ward off the coastal chill with Irish stew, beef sautéed in Guinness, and chicken and mushroom pasties. The pub decor is authentic, with wainscoted walls adorned with Irish prints and memorabilia. ~ 676 Ocean Shores Boulevard, Ocean Shores; 360-289-2300. MODERATE.

Fresh oysters anyway you want them—stewed, fried or on the half shell—are in abundance at **Copalis Beach Surf and Sand Restaurant**, a rustic wood-framed eatery dating back to the 1920s. Picture windows overlook the ocean. Creamy clam chowder, prawns and grilled local fish are longtime favorites. ~ 29 Heath Road, Copalis Beach; 360-289-2240. MODERATE.

Mariah's provides a spacious, relaxing cedar dining room with a domed ceiling and skylights. Specialties include honey-baked salmon, prime rib and chicken baked with artichoke hearts. Dinner only. ~ 615 Ocean Shores Boulevard, Ocean Shores; 360-289-3315. MODERATE TO DELUXE.

For a gourmet continental dinner in spectacular surroundings, check out the **Ocean Crest Resort**. Attentive service and superb meals (with a focus on seafood and Northwest regional cuisine), amid an atmosphere of Northwest Indian tribal art, only add to the enjoyment of the main reason to dine here: the view from a bluff, through a wooded ravine, to Sunset Beach. ~ Sunset Beach, Route 109, Moclips; 360-276-4465. MODERATE.

SHOPPING

The most interesting galleries in Grays Harbor County are, not surprisingly, in the beach communities. For a wide range of works by regional artists, including oil paintings, watercolors, ceramics and textile crafts, make sure to seek out **The Cove Gallery**. ~ Route 109, Iron Springs; 360-276-4360. The **Gallery Marjuli** also exhibits recent works by local artists. ~ 865 Point Brown Avenue, Ocean Shores; 360-289-2858.

NIGHTLIFE

In Ocean Shores, at the Polynesian Hotel, **Mariah's** is a nice place to enjoy a nightcap. ~ 615 Ocean Shores Boulevard; 360-289-3315.

The **Legend Inn** is a sports bar and tavern with big screen TV, pool tables, extensive burger menu and some 18 brews on tap. ~ 105 Chance a la Mer, Ocean Shores; 360-289-3095.

BEACHES & PARKS

PACIFIC BEACH STATE PARK Broad, flat, sandy North Beach, extending 22 miles from Moclips (just north of Pacific Beach) to the north jetty of Grays Harbor at Ocean Shores, is the *raison d'être*. Beachcombing, kite flying, jogging and (in season) surf fishing and razor clam digging are popular activities. Swimming is not recommended because of undertow and riptides. There are restrooms and picnic areas; restaurants and groceries are in downtown Pacific Beach. ~ Located along Route 109 in Pacific Beach; 360-276-4297.

▲ There are 64 sites, 33 with RV hookups; $10 to $15 per night.

OCEAN CITY STATE PARK Stretching for several miles along the Pacific coastline, this North Beach park offers a dozen access points. Popular activities include clamming and surf fishing (in season), horseback riding and surf kayaking in summer, kite flying when the wind blows, birdwatching especially during migratory periods, and beachcombing year-round. Swimming is not recommended because of undertow and riptides. This flat, sandy beach is the same broad expanse that stretches 27 miles north to Pacific Beach, and you can drive on some sections of the beach! Restrooms and picnic areas are found here; restaurants and groceries are in Ocean Shores and Ocean City. ~ Located off Route 115 and Route 109 north of Ocean Shores; campground is two miles north of Ocean Shores off Route 115; 360-289-3553.

▲ There are 178 sites, 29 with RV hookups; $11 to $16 per night.

Grays Harbor Area

Industrial towns are not often places of tourist interest. The twin cities of Aberdeen and Hoquiam, on the northeastern shore of the broad Grays Harbor estuary, are an exception. A historic seaport, a rich assortment of bird life and numerous handsome mansions built by old timber money make it worthwhile to pause in this corner of Washington.

Aberdeen has about 16,750 people, Hoquiam around 9000, and the metropolitan area includes some 33,000. Wood-products industries provide the economic base; in fact, more trees are harvested in Grays Harbor County than in any other county in the United States. Boat building and fisheries, both more important in past decades, remain key businesses.

SIGHTS

If you're coming down Route 101 from the north, it's wise to follow the signs and make your first stop a guided tour of **Hoquiam's Castle**. A stately, 20-room hillside mansion built in 1897 by a millionaire lumber baron, it has been fully restored with elegant antiques like Tiffany lamps, grandfather clocks and a 600-piece, cut-crystal chandelier. With its round turret and bright red color, the house is unmistakable. Open weekends only in winter. Admission. ~ 515 Chenault Avenue, Hoquiam; 360-533-2005.

Also in Hoquiam is the **Arnold Polson Museum**. Built in the early 1920s by a pioneer timber family and furnished with pieces donated by Hoquiam and Grays Harbor County residents, the 26-room home represents the history of the area. It is surrounded by native trees and the Burton Ross Memorial Rose Gardens. Open weekends only in winter. Admission. ~ 1611 Riverside Avenue at Route 101, Hoquiam; 360-533-5862.

A couple miles west of Hoquiam on Route 109, at Bowerman Basin on Grays Harbor, next to Bowerman Airfield, is the **Grays Harbor National Wildlife Refuge**, one of four major staging areas for migratory shorebirds in North America. Although this basin represents just two percent of the intertidal habitat of the estuary, fully half the one million shorebirds that visit each spring make their stop here. It's the last place to be flooded at high tide and the first to have its mudflats exposed, giving the avians extra feeding time. April and early May are the best times to visit. ~ 360-532-1924.

A major attraction in neighboring Aberdeen, just four miles east of Hoquiam on Route 101, is the **Grays Harbor Historical Seaport**. Craftspersons at this working 18th-century shipyard have constructed a replica of the *Lady Washington*, the brigantine in which Captain Robert Gray sailed when he discovered Grays Harbor and the Columbia River in 1783. There are also two 18th-century longboat reproductions, as well as informational and hands-on exhibits. Visitors can stay and watch the shipbuilders at work or go for a sail on the *Lady Washington*. Call ahead for schedules. ~ 813 East Heron Street, Aberdeen; 360-532-8611.

A few blocks west, the **Aberdeen Museum of History** offers exhibits, dioramas and videos of regional history in a 1922 armory. Displays include several re-created turn-of-the-century buildings: a one-room school, a general store, a church, a blacksmith's shop and more. Closed Monday and Tuesday from June through Labor Day and Monday through Friday the rest of the year. ~ 111 East 3rd Street, Aberdeen; 360-533-1976.

Route 105 follows the south shore of Grays Harbor west from Aberdeen to the atmospheric fishing village of **Westport**, at the estuary's south head. Perhaps the most interesting of several small museums here is the **Westport Maritime Museum**, housed in a Nantucket-style Coast Guard station commissioned in 1939 but decommissioned in the 1970s. Historic photos, artifacts and memorabilia help tell the story of a sailor's life. The museum also has exhibits of skeletons of marine mammals (including whales), a beachcombing exhibit and a children's discovery room. ~ 2201 Westhaven Drive, Westport; 360-268-0078.

Other spots of interest in Westport include the **Westport Aquarium**, with tanks of fish and other ocean creatures. Admission. ~ 321 Harbor Street; 360-268-0471. Also in Westport is **Shellflair**, featuring displays of sea shells, crustacea and fossils. Admission. ~ 102 South Forest Street, Westport; 360-268-9087.

For more information on the Grays Harbor area and the coastal route, visit the **Grays Harbor Chamber of Commerce**. ~ Duffy Street at Route 101, Aberdeen; 360-532-1924, 800-321-1924.

LODGING

There's considerable character at the **Lytle House Bed & Breakfast**, a three-story Victorian hillside mansion. Each of the eight guest rooms, six of which have private bathrooms with clawfoot tubs, has a different theme, such as nautical (Harbor View room) and equestrian (Esquire). Guests choose a full gourmet breakfast from a menu offered the previous night. The house hosts murder-mystery parties by guest appointment. ~ 509 Chenault Street, Hoquiam; 360-533-2320, 800-677-2320, fax 360-533-4025. MODERATE TO DELUXE.

Like any regional center, the twin cities of Aberdeen and Hoquiam have a strip of look-alike motels along Route 101. Though it's hard to choose one above another, the **Olympic Inn Motel** is notable for its modern, spacious rooms. Decor in the 55 units is simple but pleasant. ~ 616 West Heron Street, Aberdeen; 360-533-4200, 800-562-86 18, fax 360-533-6223. MODERATE.

Just southeast of Aberdeen, the **Cooney Mansion** is located in a secluded wooded area on a golf course with an adjoining tennis court and park. A National Historic Landmark built in 1908 by a lumber baron, its interior was designed to show off local woods. Now a bed and breakfast, it has nine bedrooms, five with private baths, as well as a jacuzzi, sauna, sundeck and exercise room. Full lumber baron's breakfast included. ~ 1705 5th Street, Cosmopolis; 360-533-0602. MODERATE TO ULTRA-DELUXE.

East of Grays Harbor in the county seat of Montesano is the **Abel House**. This stately 1908 home has five bedrooms, two with private baths. There are also a game room and reading room and an exquisite English garden. A full breakfast, afternoon tea and dessert are included with the room. ~ 117 Fleet Street South, Montesano; 360-249-6002, 800-235-2235. MODERATE TO DELUXE.

Farther east—halfway from Montesano to Olympia, in fact, but still in Grays Harbor County—**The Old McCleary Hotel** maintains antique-laden rooms that seem to be especially popular with touring bicyclists. ~ 42 Summit Road, McCleary; 360-495-3678. BUDGET.

In Westport, at the mouth of Grays Harbor, the largest motel is the **Château Westport**. Many of the 108 units have balconies and fireplaces, and a third are efficiency studios with kitchenettes. The upper floors of the four-story property, easily identified by its gray mansard roof, have excellent ocean views. Dip into the indoor pool and hot tub. ~ 710 West Hancock Avenue, Westport; 360-268-9101, 800-255-9101, fax 360-268-1646. MODERATE TO ULTRA-DELUXE.

For serious wallet-watchers, **The Islander Motel & RV Park** offers simple but clean and spacious motel units. Fifty-seven RV spaces are also available, some overlooking the harbor. ~ 421 West Haven Street, Westport; 360-268-9166, 800-322-1740, fax 360-268-0902. BUDGET.

More atmospheric Westport accommodations are found at the **Glenacres Inn**, which will celebrate its 100th anniversary in 1998. Appointments are still turn-of-the-century in style, and all 12 units—five spacious guest bedrooms, three deck rooms and four cottages (each of which sleep four to twelve)—have private baths. Outdoor recreation on nine wooded acres centers around a huge deck with a gazebo-covered hot tub. ~ 222 North Montesano Street, Westport; 360-268-9391. MODERATE TO ULTRA-DELUXE.

You can catch a fish, clean it and cook it for dinner all without straying from the **Grayland Motel and Cottages**, located on the beach. The grounds offer a fish- and clam-cleaning shed, children's play area, motel units and self-contained cottages with tiled kitchens, pine furnishings and small living/dining areas. ~ 2013 Route 105, Grayland; 360-267-2395, 800-292-0845. BUDGET TO MODERATE.

DINING   It's a comfort to know that Grays Harbor has more memorable restaurants than memorable accommodations. The best of the best is **The Levee Street**, which extends over the Hoquiam River on pilings. Though it's just a block off Route 101, it has a nondescript entrance that's easy to miss. Inside, though, it's a real charmer, with fresh seafood, steaks and an excellent wine list. Closed Sunday and Monday. ~ 709 Levee Street, Hoquiam; 360-532-1959. MODERATE.

When chef Pierre Gabelli moved to the Washington coast from his native Italy, it was only natural that he should open the **Parma Ristorante Italiano**. Dine on gourmet pastas like gnocchi and tortelli d'Erbetta, as well as several outstanding meat dishes. Best of all are the homemade desserts. Closed Sunday and Monday. ~ 116 West Heron Street, Aberdeen; 360-532-3166. MODERATE.

◀ HIDDEN

Bridges Restaurant is a handsome, garden-style restaurant with one dining room that's actually a greenhouse. As the size of its parking lot attests, it's very popular locally, for its lounge as well as its cuisine. Local seafood, steaks, chicken and pasta highlight the menu. ~ 112 North G Street, Aberdeen; 360-532-6563. MODERATE.

For historic flavor, you needn't look further than **Billy's Bar and Grill**. Named for an early 20th-century ne'er-do-well notorious for mugging loggers and shanghaiing sailors, Billy's boasts an ornate century-old ceiling, huge antique bar and wall murals that are colorful if not downright bawdy. This is the place to settle back with a burger and a beer and soak up the past. ~ 322 East Heron Street, Aberdeen; 360-533-7144. BUDGET.

Elsewhere in the area, the **Hong Kong Restaurant** is surprisingly authentic for a town so far removed from China! It has chop suey and egg foo yung, yes, but it also has egg flower soup, moo goo gai pan and other tastes from the old country. Closed Monday. ~ 1212 East 1st Street, Cosmopolis; 360-533-7594. BUDGET.

✔ CHECK THESE OUT—UNIQUE DINING

- *Budget:* Feast on homestyle meals like grandma might have whipped up at the **Chimmacum Café.** *page 150*
  - *Moderate:* Suck down some fresh oysters on the half-shell (unless you prefer them cooked) at the rustic **Copalis Beach Surf and Sand Restaurant.** *page 166*
    - *Moderate to deluxe:* Sample fresh Willapa Bay oysters and locally picked mushrooms and cranberries at **The Ark Restaurant and Bakery.** *page 178*
      - *Deluxe:* Dine on mussel chowder or country rabbit sausage in turn-of-the-century surroundings at **The Shoalwater Restaurant.** *page 177*

Budget: under $8   Moderate: $8–$16   Deluxe: $16–$24   Ultra-deluxe: over $24

There aren't many restaurant choices in McCleary, but if you appreciate a good old-fashioned hamburger, head for **M & M Burger House**. An authentic 1950s burger stand with drive-up service and a tiny inside dining area, the M & M makes burgers to order with heated buns, quality beef and a variety of toppings. Other specialties are homemade soups, fresh salads and soda fountain treats. ~ 301 Simpson Avenue, McCleary; 360-495-3822. BUDGET.

Out in Westport, whose resemblance to a New England fishing village may be coincidental, is **Constantin's**, whose similarity to Greek restaurants in the Aegean is no accident. The specialties revolve around fresh seafood and seafood-meat combinations including lamb chops, filet mignon and crab and black tiger prawns. There is also an extensive wine list featuring local and imported wines. ~ 320 East Dock Street, Westport; 360-268-9353. MODERATE TO DELUXE.

HIDDEN ►   The **Corral Drive In** claims its Tsunami is the world's largest hamburger—and who's to argue with a four-pounder on an 18-inch bun? Not only is it huge (better have the whole family along), it's actually quite good. The place also has regular-sized burgers, fries, milkshakes and such. ~ North Pacific Highway and 95th Street North, Long Beach; 360-642-2774. BUDGET TO MODERATE.

SHOPPING   For a sampling of creations by regional artisans visit the **Pacific Center of the Arts and Crafts**, which features pottery, original art, prints and gift items. ~ 1767 Route 105, Grayland; 360-267-1351.

NIGHTLIFE   Folks in the Grays Harbor area show a predilection for **Sidney's Restaurant and Sports Bar**, where a deejay spins disks regularly. Cover on weekends. ~ 512 West Heron Avenue, Aberdeen; 360-533-6635.

Also check out the Victorian bar at **Billy's Bar and Grill**. ~ 322 East Heron Avenue, Aberdeen; 360-533-7144. The posh lounge at **Bridges Restaurant** is also a happenin' spot for drinks. ~ 112 North G Street, Aberdeen; 360-532-6563.

BEACHES & PARKS   **LAKE SYLVIA STATE PARK** 🏃 🚴 ⚓ 🎣 ⛵ 🛶 ↲ Visitors can circumambulate this narrow, forest-enshrouded lake on a two-mile hiking trail. Also here are trout fishing (from boat or shore), a swimming beach and boat rentals in season. There are restrooms, picnic areas and groceries; restaurants are in Montesano. ~ Located two miles north of Montesano off Route 12, via North 3rd Street; 360-249-3621.

▲ There are 35 sites; $11 per night.

SCHAFER STATE PARK 🏃 ⚓ ↲ Once a family park for employees of the Schafer Logging Company, this tranquil 119-acre site on the East Fork of the Satsop River is still popular with families. This heavily forested park is ideal for picnics, hikes and fishing. You can fish in the river, although swimmers may find the water too cold. You'll find restrooms and picnic areas; groceries and restaurants are in nearby Satsop and Brady. ~ West 1365 Schafer Park Road, 12 miles north of Elma, off Route 12 via Brady; 360-482-3852.

▲ There are 42 sites, six with hookups; $10 to $15 per night.

WYNOOCHEE LAKE RECREATION AREA An Army Corps of Engineers project, this four-and-a-half-mile-long lake was created in 1972 by a water-supply and flood-control dam on the Wynoochee River. The visitors center has interpretive displays. A 15-mile trail winds around the lake, past a beach and designated swimming area. Trout fishing, water-skiing, swimming (the water is cold, though) and wildlife watching are also popular. Restrooms and picnic areas are some facilities here; groceries and restaurants are located in Montesano. ~ Located off Route 12 about 35 miles north of Montesano on West Valley Road. Take a left on Forest Service Road 22 and a right on Forest Service Road 2294; 360-877-5254.

▲ There are 56 sites and ten primitive sites in the Coho campground; $12 per night.

WESTHAVEN & WESTPORT LIGHT STATE PARKS Westhaven State Park, which occupies the southern headland at the mouth of Grays Harbor, is a great place for watching birds and wildlife, including harbor seals and whales during migratory periods. Surfing is excellent here (try the jetty) and there are yearly competitions. Surfers and swimmers should be very careful of riptides. Westhaven is adjacent to Westport Light State Park, from which you can see a historic lighthouse that's warned coastal ships of the entrance to Grays Harbor since 1897. There's a multi-use paved trail connecting the two parks that's open for hiking, bicycling, roller-blading and other nonmotorized forms of transportation. You can fish from the shores of both parks or the jetty of Westhaven. There are restrooms and picnic areas; groceries and restaurants are located in town. ~ Both parks are located close to downtown Westport; Westhaven is about one and a half miles from downtown on East Yearout Drive; Westport Light is half a mile from downtown at the end of Ocean Avenue; 360-268-9565.

TWIN HARBORS STATE PARK The Washington coast's largest campground dominates this 168-acre park. It also includes the Shifting Sands Nature Trail with interpretive signs for dunes explorers. Beachcombing, kite flying and clamming are popular activities on the broad, sandy beach. There's fishing in the surf or from a boat (which you can charter at Westport), but swimming is not recommended because of riptides. Facilities include restrooms and picnic areas; groceries and restaurants are in Westport and Grayland. ~ Located along Route 105, four miles south of Westport and four miles north of Grayland; 360-268-9717.

▲ There are 307 sites, three of which are for campers with disabilities, 49 with RV hookups; $11 to $16 per night.

GRAYLAND BEACH STATE PARK 𝄞 ⌇ Like other coastal beaches, this 400-acre park is broad and flat and ideal for surf fishing, clam digging, beachcombing, kite flying and other seaside diversions. Swimming is discouraged due to riptides. Restrooms, groceries and restaurants are in Grayland. ~ Located on Route 105, one mile south of Grayland; 360-267-4301.

▲ There are 60 sites with full RV hookups, two of which are equipped for handicap use; $16 per night.

▼▼▼▼▼▼▼▼▼▼

Long Beach–Willapa Bay

The largest "unpopulated" estuary in the continental United States, this region's pristine condition makes it one of the world's best places for farming oysters. From Tokeland to Bay Center to Oysterville, tiny villages that derive their sole income from the shelled creatures display mountains of empty shells as evidence of their success. Begin your visit on Route 105 south from Westport, then head east along the northern shore of Willapa Bay.

SIGHTS

Thirty-three miles from Westport, Route 105 rejoins Route 101 at **Raymond**. This town of 3000, and its smaller sister community of **South Bend** four miles south on Route 101, are lumber ports on the lower Willapa River.

You'll find murals—43 of them, to be exact—on walls from Ocean Shores to the Columbia River, Elma to Ilwaco. Chambers of commerce and other visitor information centers have guide pamphlets. But no mural is larger than the 85-foot-wide painting of an early logger on the **Dennis Company Building**. The company's outdoor display of old-time farm equipment is across the street. ~ 5th Street, Raymond.

Attractions in South Bend include the **Pacific County Museum**, with pioneer artifacts from the turn of the century. ~ 1008 West Robert Bush Drive, South Bend; 360-875-5224.

Also have a look at South Bend's 1911 **Pacific County Courthouse**, noted for its art-glass dome and historic foyer wall paintings. ~ 300 Memorial Drive off Route 101, South Bend; 360-875-9300.

The **Long Beach Peninsula**, reached via Route 101 from South Bend (43 miles), has had a significant flow of vacationing Northwest urbanites for over a century. But its economy is more strongly founded in fish processing and cranberry growing. Information is available from the **Long Beach Peninsula Visitor Bureau.** ~ Route 101 and Route 103, Seaview; 360-642-2400.

Route 103, which runs north-south up the 28-mile-long, two-mile-wide peninsula, is intersected by Route 101 at **Seaview.** The town of **Long Beach** is just a mile north of the junction. Its principal attraction is a 2300-foot wooden **boardwalk,** South 10th to Bolstad streets, elevated 40 feet above the dunes, enabling folks to make an easy trek to the high-tide mark. The beach, incidentally, is open to driving on the hard upper sand, and to surf fishing, clamming, beachcombing, kite flying and picnicking everywhere.

Kite flying is a big thing on the Washington coast, so it's no accident that the **World Kite Museum and Hall of Fame** is in Long Beach. The museum has rotating exhibits of kites from around the world—Japan, China, Thailand and so on—with displays of stunt kites, advertising kites and more. Admission. ~ 3rd Street Northwest at Route 103, Long Beach; 360-642-4020.

The **Pacific Coast Cranberry Museum** provides a historic view of the West Coast cranberry industry. Exhibits include hand tools, cranberry boxes, labels, pickers, sorters and separators. Open weekends. ~ Pioneer Road, Long Beach; 360-642-2891.

North of Long Beach ten miles is **Ocean Park**, the commercial hub of the central and northern Long Beach Peninsula. Developed as a Methodist camp in 1883, it evolved into a small resort town. Older yet is **Oysterville**, another three miles north via the Peninsula Highway. Founded in 1854, this National Historic District boasts the oldest continuously operating post office in Washington (1858) and 17 other designated historic sites. Get a walking-tour pamphlet from the **Old Church** beside the Village Green on Territory Road.

South of Seaview just two miles on Route 103 is **Ilwaco**, spanning the isthmus between the Columbia River and the Pacific Ocean. Local history is featured at the impressive **Ilwaco Heritage Museum**. A series of galleries depicts the development of southwestern Washington from early Indian culture to European voyages of discovery, from pioneer settlement to the early 20th

------

CRANBERRY CENTRAL

In October and early November, the cranberry harvest takes precedence over all else on the Long Beach Peninsula. Most fields are owned by the folks from Ocean Spray. The **Pacific Coast Cranberry Research Foundation** offers free self-guided tours of the cranberry "bogs" during harvest, and other times by appointment. ~ Pioneer Road, Long Beach; 360-642-2891.

century. Admission. ~ 115 Southeast Lake Street, Ilwaco; 360-642-3446.

About eight miles southeast, a short distance before Route 101 crosses the Columbia River to Astoria, Oregon, **Fort Columbia State Park** is a highly recommended stop for history buffs. Two buildings at the site are museums: the **Fort Columbia Interpretive Center**, exhibiting artifacts of early 20th-century military life in a former coastal artillery post, and the **Columbia House**, which the Daughters of the American Revolution have restored to depict the everyday lifestyle of a military officer of the time. The state park is open summer only. ~ Route 101, Chinook; 360-777-8221.

LODGING

Possibly the most delightful accommodation anywhere on the Washington coast is **The Shelburne Country Inn**. The oldest continually operating hotel in the state, it opened in 1896 and is still going strong. Fifteen guest rooms are furnished with Victorian antiques and fresh flowers. All have private baths and most have decks. A hearty country breakfast is served in the morning, as well as freshly-baked cookies upon arrival. ~ 4415 Pacific Way, Seaview; 360-642-2442, 800-466-1896, fax 360-642-8904. DELUXE TO ULTRA-DELUXE.

HIDDEN ►

Another one-of-a-kinder, but for very different reasons, is **The Sou'wester Lodge, Cabins and Tch! Tch!** It's a place much beloved by youth hostelers who, well, grew up. Proprietors Len and Miriam Atkins have intentionally kept the accommodation simple and weathered. They advertise it as a B&MYODB—"bed and make your own damn breakfast." Kitchen rights extend to the living room, including the fireplace and library. Sleeping options include rooms in the historic lodge, cedar-shingled housekeeping cabins, a dozen-or-so vintage TCH! TCH! mobile homes ("Trailer Classics Hodgepodge") and an area for RVs and tent campers. The historic lodge draws an artistic clientele and often hosts cultural events such as poetry readings or evenings of chamber music. ~ Beach Access Road, 38th Place, Seaview; 360-642-2542. BUDGET TO MODERATE.

Nestled in the sand dunes three miles north of Long Beach, **Land's End Bed and Breakfast** is an "upside down" house with two bedrooms on the first floor and a sitting room with a huge picture window on the second floor where guests can relax and enjoy a panoramic ocean view. The larger of the two guest rooms features a spectacular 1850s quilt wallhanging, a Dutch ceramic stove and its own mini-library of books. Call ahead for directions. ~ P.O. Box 1199, Long Beach, WA 98631; 360-642-8268. DELUXE.

Numerous beachfront cabin communities speckle the shoreline of the Long Beach Peninsula north from the towns of Ilwaco and Seaview. One of the best is the **Klipsan Beach Cottages**. Each of the ten cottages, in a lovely wooded setting eight miles north of the town of Long Beach, has a kitchen and fireplace or wood-burning stove (with free firewood). There is also a two-bedroom and a three-bedroom unit. ~ 22617 Pacific Highway, Ocean Park; 360-665-4888. MODERATE.

Shakti Cove is a located just five minutes from the water. Ten rustic cabins all are fully equipped with kitchens and sleep up to four guests. The units are furnished with queen-size beds, older couches and feature eclectic decor. Pets are welcome. Gay-friendly. ~ 253rd Place and Park Avenue, Ocean Park; 360-665-4000. BUDGET TO MODERATE.

A hideaway on a pristine stretch of beach near Ocean Park, **Coast Watch Bed & Breakfast** has two suites where unobstructed views of dunes and the sea take center stage. Each suite has a queen-size bed and sitting area and is decorated in subtle earth tones and wicker furnishings. Breakfasts of fresh fruit and muffins are served in the suite. Call ahead for directions. ~ P.O. Box 841, Ocean Park, WA 98640; 360-665-6774. DELUXE.

Willapa Bay oyster lovers frequent the beds near the north end of the Long Beach Peninsula, and this is where they'll find the **Moby Dick Hotel**. An 11-room bed-and-breakfast inn that first opened its doors in 1930, it maintains a country nautical atmosphere, with rambling grounds, its own vegetable garden and oyster farm. A fireplace and piano beckon on rainy days. ~ Sandridge and Bay avenues, Nahcotta; 360-665-4543, fax 360-665-6887. MODERATE.

◄ HIDDEN

Hostelling International—Fort Columbia occupies the former Coast Artillery Infirmary. There are two dorms—a 13-bunk room for men, a five-bunk room for women—and a single family room. Guests share kitchen, bathroom and living facilities. A pancake breakfast is served every morning. Open April through September. ~ Route 101, Chinook; 360-777-8755. BUDGET.

For a unique dining experience, visit the **Blue Heron Inn**, on an off-the-beaten-track peninsula that juts into Willapa Bay 12 miles south of South Bend just off Route 101. Oysters, of course, are a specialty at this café-tavern; they even serve them for breakfast, along with other seafood omelettes. The fish market here also sells fresh crab and smoked salmon. ~ Bay Center Road at 2nd and Bridge streets, Bay Center; 360-875-5130. BUDGET TO MODERATE.

DINING

◄ HIDDEN

Expensive, but worth it. Everything is exquisite in **The Shoalwater Restaurant**, one of Washington's most highly acclaimed country restaurants. From the seafood mousseline to the mussel chowder, the country rabbit sausage to the sautéed Willapa Bay oysters with a Thai-style wild mushroom sauce and the creative preparations of the day's fresh catches, a meal here is one to savor. The turn-of-the-century ambience adds an element of comfort. ~ Shelburne Inn, 4415 Pacific Way, Seaview; 360-642-4142. DELUXE.

Opposite the restaurant entrance is **The Heron & Beaver Pub**, with light meals produced by the same kitchen as the Shoalwater Restaurant. ~ Shelburne Inn, 4415 Pacific Way, Seaview; 360-642-4142. MODERATE.

Owned and operated by the former chef and manager of the renowned Shoalwater Restaurant, the **42nd St. Café** is fast making its own reputation. Hand-cut ravioli sauced with sun-dried tomato cream, iron skillet fried chicken, pot roast with vegetables and other down-home fare are prepared with a gourmet hand. The café is located in a converted army barracks. The dining room is bright and casual with blue and green cloth napery, candles and fresh flowers. ~ 4201 Pacific Way at 42nd Place, Seaview; 360-642-2323. MODERATE.

My Mom's Pie Kitchen has great pies—from wild blackberry to chocolate almond to sour-cream raisin—but that's not the only reason to eat at this charming double-wide trailer. Other dishes including soups, chowders, salads and sandwiches are served for lunch, and the chicken-almond pot pie is a mouth-watering delight. ~ 4316 Route 101, Seaview; 360-642-2342. BUDGET.

For possibly the best and certainly the most innovative pizza on the coast, try **Bubba's Pizza**. This is where a traditional New York–style hand-spun pie meets up with Northwest seafood, fresh spinach, pine nuts, goat cheese and other unusual toppings. Bubba's has a cheerful interior accented with changing displays by local artists. ~ 115 Route 101 at Bolstad Street, Long Beach, 360-642-8700. MODERATE.

Mountains of oyster shells surround **The Ark Restaurant and Bakery**, located near the north end of the Long Beach Peninsula on oyster-rich Willapa Bay. In fact, the restaurant has its own oyster beds—as well as an herb and edible-flower garden and a busy bakery. Nearby are cranberry bogs and forests of wild mushrooms. All these go into the preparation of creative dishes like pan-fried salmon with wild mushrooms, sun-dried tomatoes and balsamic creme sauce and beef tenderloin with pinenuts and caramelized garlic sauce. Dinner Tuesday through Saturday; Sunday brunch and dinner. Call ahead for winter hours. ~ 270 3rd Street and Sandridge Road, Nahcotta; 360-665-4133. MODERATE TO DELUXE.

Dining at **The Sanctuary** is a sacred ritual to some folks. And well it should be: The restaurant occupies the premises of the historic Methodist Episcopal Church of Chinook (1906–1978). Few renovations have been made to the building, although wine is taken much more often than during communion, and sundaes can sometimes be sinful. The varied menu includes Swedish meatballs and fish cakes, steaks and fresh seafood. Dinner only. ~ Route 101 and Hazel Street, Chinook; 360-777-8380. MODERATE.

There's wonderful bric-a-brac at **Marsh's Free Museum**, from the world's largest frying pan (so they say) to antique music boxes. ~ 409 Pacific Avenue South, Long Beach; 360-642-2188.

SHOPPING

The souvenir most typical of beach recreation here, perhaps, would be a colorful kite. Look for them in Long Beach at **Ocean Kites** located at 511 Pacific Avenue South (360-642-2229) and **Long Beach Kites** at 104 Pacific Avenue North (360-642-2202).

Noted watercolorist Eric Wiegardt displays his work at the **Wiegardt Studio Gallery**. ~ 2607 Bay Avenue between Route 103 and Sandridge Road, Ocean Park; 360-665-5976.

The Lightship Restaurant has the Long Beach Peninsula's only ocean-view restaurant from its fourth-story loft; come for a sunset drink. ~ Nendel's Edgewater Inn, 409 Southwest 10th Street, Long Beach; 360-642-3252. Quiet beers are best quaffed at **The Heron & Beaver Pub** in the Shelburne Inn. ~ 4415 Pacific Way, Seaview; 360-642-4142.

NIGHTLIFE

LEADBETTER POINT STATE PARK 🚶🚴🛶 Shifting dunes and mudflats, ponds and marshes, grasslands and forests make this northern tip of the Long Beach Peninsula an ideal place for those who like to observe nature. As many as 100 species of migratory birds stop over here. There are numerous hiking trails. Surf fishing is popular, but riptides discourage swimming. You'll find pit toilets, restrooms and picnic areas; groceries are in Oysterville, restaurants at Nahcotta and farther south on peninsula. ~ Located three miles north of Oysterville on Stackpole Road, via Route 103 and Sandridge Road; 360-642-3078.

BEACHES & PARKS

PACIFIC PINES STATE PARK 🚶🛶 This day-use park offers beach access for appropriate activities, like beachcombing, kite flying, jogging, surf fishing and razor clam digging in season. You can drive on the uppermost sand, but be sure it's hard-packed; more than one car owner has needed a tow after getting bogged in the sand. There are restrooms and picnic areas; restaurants and groceries are in Ocean Park. ~ Located on Park Road, a mile north of Ocean Park; 360-642-3078.

LOOMIS LAKE STATE PARK 🚶🛶 Situated south of Klipsan Beach, this day-use park offers ocean beach access with good fishing from the shore and good clamming on the beach. Swimming is not recommended. Facilities include restrooms and picnic areas; restaurants and groceries are in Ocean Park. ~ Located on Park Road, via 199 Place off Route 103, four miles south of Ocean Park; 360-642-3078.

FORT CANBY STATE PARK 🚶 🚲 🚗 🚤 🎣 The point where the Columbia River meets the Pacific Ocean has been a crossroads of history for two centuries. The Lewis and Clark expedition arrived at this dramatic headland in 1805 after 18 months on the trail. Two 19th-century lighthouses—at North Head on the Pacific and at Cape Disappointment on a Columbia sandbar —have limited the number of shipwrecks to a mere 200 through 1994. The fort was occupied from the Civil War through World War II. Today, the 1800-acre park contains the Lewis and Clark Interpretive Center (with exhibits and a multimedia program), numerous forest, beach and clifftop trails, a boat launch, a swimming beach, fishing (in the surf, from the jetty or from a boat), summer interpretive programs, lighthouse tours, restrooms and picnic areas; groceries and restaurants are in Ilwaco. ~ Located two and a half miles southwest of Ilwaco on Route 101; 360-642-3078.

▲ There are 250 sites, 90 with RV hookups; $11 to $16 per night.

▼▼▼▼▼▼▼▼▼▼▼▼▼▼

Outdoor Adventures

SPORT-FISHING

Despite charter operators' complaints that government restrictions hinder their operations, the Strait of Juan de Fuca is still one of the nation's great salmon grounds, with chinook, coho and other species running the waters during the summer months. From April to September, halibut is also big in these waters—literally: one local operator holds the state record, 268 pounds. Bottom fish like ling cod, true cod, red snapper and black bass round out the angling possibilities.

OLYMPIC COAST When **Big Salmon Charters** isn't breaking state records for halibut (268 pounds), it runs half-day charters for salmon and bottom fish, using nine boats for between six and twelve people. ~ Bay View Avenue (or Front Street), Neah Bay; 360-645-2374.

Olson's Resort runs six-hour trips in the Strait of Juan de Fuca for salmon, halibut, ling cod and bottom fish, accommodating up to six people on a 38-foot boat. ~ Sekiu; 360-963-2311.

GRAYS HARBOR AREA **Deep Sea Charters** operates seven boats for one-day charters for salmon, bottom fish and halibut, and for overnight tuna charters. ~ Across from Float 6, Westport; 360-268-9300.

LONG BEACH–WILLAPA BAY At the mouth of the Columbia River, Ilwaco is another center for deep-sea fishing. Salmon and sturgeon are caught near the river mouth, while tuna, rockfish, cod and sole are in deeper waters. **Seabreeze Charters** arranges daylong charters, operating four boats, and carrying up to 16 people. Large engines cut down run times for deep-bottom trips. ~ 185 Howerton Way Southeast, Ilwaco; 360-642-2300.

It's not just the fish—salmon, steelhead, trout—that attract anglers to the mountain streams flowing from the Olympic Mountains. Spectacular scenery and glimpses of eagles, deer, elk and other wildlife sweeten the deal.

RIVER FISHING

PORT ANGELES AREA An hour or two away are several destinations for river fishing: the Sol Duc, Bos, Hoh, Queets and Calawah rivers. Contact **Olympic Raft & Guide Service**, which operates year-round. ~ 239521 Route 101 West, Port Angeles; 360-452-1443.

OLYMPIC COAST The lower Quinault River is not "overpacked" with fishermen—yet—partly because nontribal people may not fish rivers on the reservation without a Quinault guide. Contact the **Quinault Indian Nation Fish and Game Department** to receive information about available guides for drift boat or walk-in fishing. ~ 1214 Aalis Street, Taholah; 360-276-8211 ext. 227. Between Forks and La Push, **3-River Resort & Guide Service** operates two drift boats for two anglers (plus guide) on the Sol Duc, Bogachiel and Hoh rivers (another "quiet" spot). Tackle and lunch are included. ~ 7764 La Push Road, Forks; 360-374-5300.

Folks who like to shellfish will be happy in Washington. There are clams (littleneck, butter, Manila and razor), scallops, oysters (Willapa Bay is famous for its oysters), mussels and crab (Dungeness Spit, north of Sequim, is the home of the renowned Dungeness crab). Then, of course, there's that Northwest oddity, the geoduck (say "gooey-duck"), whose huge foot cannot fit within its shell.

SHELL-FISHING

Before you start digging up clams or other shellfish, please remember that just like other forms of fishing, a license is required for this activity. You can pick one up at tackle shops and other locations that sell fishing licenses. Recreational harvesting of shellfish is permitted on public beaches, but you should double-check, because much of the state's tideland is privately owned. Generally, shellfishing is permitted year round; one exception is razor clams, which are restricted by season and location. Call the **Washington State Department of Fish and Wildlife** for information. ~ 360-902-2200. You must also check with the Health Department's **Red Tide Hotline** to find out which waters are unhealthy for shellfish harvesting. ~ 800-562-5632 from inside Washington; 360-753-5992 from outside the state.

The Elwha River flows from the Olympic Mountains into the Strait of Juan de Fuca. Along the way, there are some Class II whitewater rapids—not quite a thrill ride, but enough excitement for good family fun (it's the only commercially rafted whitewater on the peninsula). Besides that, there's plenty of wildlife to see—elk, osprey, bald eagles, deer, harlequin ducks—as well as a view of a glacier. **Olympic Raft and Guide Service** runs a couple of

RIVER RUNNING

trips daily, each lasting about two-and-a-half hours. Inflatable kayaks are run on parts of the Hoh River. ~ 239521 Route 101 West, Port Angeles; 360-452-1443.

KAYAKING   Experienced or novice, kayakers who paddle around a mountain lake, through coastal marshlands or under sea cliffs will be rewarded not only with good exercise but also with the opportunity to observe abundant wildlife in a wilderness setting. Companies offering guided tours generally operate during the warmer months (May through September). But think about this: Many kayakers swear the best time to paddle is in the rain.

PORT TOWNSEND AREA   Nearby Bird Island is a popular half-day sea-kayaking destination for the guided tours operated by **Kayak Port Townsend**. Trips, for up to nine people, can be extended to full day or longer. ~ Water Street at Monroe Street, Port Townsend; 360-385-6240.

PORT ANGELES AREA   Bring your favorite bird book when you join one of **Pedal 'N' Paddle**'s half-day kayak tours of Dungeness Bay. You'll need it to help you identify all the waterfowl you're likely to see. ~ 120 East Front Street, Port Angeles; 360-457-1240.

You may have Lake Aldwell all to yourself, aside from the waterfowl nesting along its shores, when you join a two-hour guided tour of this clear blue lake. **Olympic Raft and Guide Service** uses the more stable sea kayaks for these lake tours. ~ 239521 Route 101 West, Port Angeles; 360-452-1443.

GRAYS HARBOR AREA   **NorthWest Experiences, Inc.**, will give you a lighter composite paddle to use on its guided tours (which often include lunch) of the sloughs and marshes fed by several rivers in the Grays Harbor area. A favorite kayaking spot of owner Jeff Beard is the Black River, so-called for the tea-colored water (a high tannin content) of this slow-moving stream east of Cosmopolis. Paddling on the Black, which feeds into the Chehalis River, is like skimming over a carpet of vegetation. Beard also rents kayaks to individuals who may want to set out on their own. ~ Aberdeen; 360-532-9176.

KITE FLYING   Several miles of wide, flat beach make the beaches at Ocean Shores and Long Beach ideal kite-flying spots. A nationally sanctioned kite-flying festival in June brings some of the sport's best fliers to Ocean Shores; the same month, competing stunt kites fill the sky over Long Beach. In August, Long Beach hosts the weeklong Washington State International Kite Festival, said to be the biggest kite festival in the country (about 100,000 people attend). You don't have to be up to championship standards, though, to buy a kite and fly it or to visit a museum about kite flying.

OCEAN SHORES–PACIFIC BEACH   Pick up a kite and some tips on how to fly it at **Ocean Shores Kites**. Besides dozens of different kites, the store sells windsocks and other wind toys (Frisbees, etc.). ~ Shores Mall, 120 Chance a la Mer, Ocean Shores; 360-289-4103.

LONG BEACH–WILLAPA BAY The beach is about 200 yards away from **Long Beach Kites,** where you can buy a variety of kites as well as windsocks and flags. ~ 104 Pacific Highway North, Long Beach; 360-642-2202. Also in Long Beach is the **World Kite Museum and Hall of Fame,** which has probably the largest collection of Chinese and Japanese kites outside Asia. ~ 3rd Street Northwest at Route 103; 360-642-4020.

California gray whales head back up to Alaskan waters between March and May, and we land-based mammals can't seem to get enough of the spectacle. Many fishing charter operators convert to whale-watching cruises during these months.

WHALE WATCHING

GRAYS HARBOR AREA Two-and-a-half hour whale-watching cruises generally head offshore toward the whales' migration path, but occasionally the whales wander into Grays Harbor and the boats never get out to sea. In Westport, contact **Ocean Charters.** ~ Across from Float 6, 360-268-9144. In the same harbor is **Deep Sea Charters.** ~ Across from Float 6, 360-268-9300.

OLYMPIC NATIONAL PARK The only skiing on the Olympic Peninsula is **Hurricane Ridge Ski Area,** 17 miles south of Port Angeles, in Olympic National Park. Here skiers will find a few downhill runs and several cross-country trails starting from the day lodge. There are three rope tows and a T-bar lift on site. The Hurricane Hill Road cross-country trail (1.5 miles one way) is probably the easiest of the area's six trails; the most challenging is the Hurricane Ridge Trail to Mt. Angeles, a steep three-mile route that's often icy. Rentals of downhill, cross-country and snowshoeing equipment are also available. Open December through March, weekends only. Contact the **Olympic National**

SKIING

◆◆

✔ **CHECK THESE OUT—UNIQUE OUTDOOR ADVENTURES**

- Walk through the misty and lush Hoh Rainforest, the wettest spot in the continental United States. *page 158*
    - Surf the breaks near the mouth of Grays Harbor at Westhaven State Park. *page 173*
        - Cast a line for coho salmon in the Strait of Juan de Fuca. *page 180*
        - Harness the power of Mother Nature as you fly a kite in the benevolent ocean breezes of Ocean Shores and Long Beach. *page 182*

Park Visitor Center. ~ 3002 Mount Angeles Road, Port Angeles; 360-452-0330. For road conditions, call 360-452-0329.

RIDING STABLES

On the Olympic Peninsula, it's possible to saddle up for a guided mountain ride through forests of towering trees or a ride along the beach at sunset.

OCEAN SHORES–PACIFIC BEACH   The year-round guided rides at **Nan-Sea Stables** stick to the hilly, wooded property (but never follow paved trails). In the summer, you'll cross a small stream to reach the beach for the sunset beach rides. ~ 255 State Route 115, Ocean Shores; 360-289-0194.

GOLF

Bay views, ocean views, mountain views—take your pick. They're part and parcel with the courses in this region.

PORT TOWNSEND AREA   The public 18-hole **Chevy Chase Golf Club** is set in the woods above Discovery Bay. It's a fairly flat course that can get a bit mushy after winter rains. ~ 7401 Cape George Road, Port Townsend; 360-385-0704. The double-teed, nine-hole **Port Townsend Golf Club** is located in town. It's considered the best winter course in the area (it gets only 17 inches of rain), with rolling terrain, small greens and a driving range. ~ 1948 Blaine Street, Port Townsend; 360-385-4547. *Golf Digest* has named the 27-hole semiprivate **Port Ludlow Golf Course** one of the best in the country. Although housing flanks one section, the spectacular views of Ludlow Bay and abundant wildlife prompt comments like "Amazing" and "It's like golfing in a national park" from local duffers. ~ 751 Highland Drive, Port Ludlow; 360-437-0272, 800-455-0272.

PORT ANGELES AREA   Although the 18-hole, semiprivate **Sunland Golf and Country Club** goes through a housing development, it's well treed and fairly flat. Call for public hours. ~ 109 Hilltop Drive, Sequim; 360-683-6800.

OCEAN SHORES–PACIFIC BEACH   The front nine of the municipal **Ocean Shores Golf Course** has a links-like layout in the dunes; the back nine wanders into the trees. ~ 500 Canal Drive Northeast at Albatross Street, Ocean Shores; 360-289-3357.

GRAYS HARBOR AREA   An old farming tract was turned into an 18-hole golf course in the early 1920s, so **Oaksridge Golf Course** is very flat. It gets pretty wet in the winter, but drains fast. The front nine is long. ~ 1052 Monte–Elma Road, Elma; 360-482-3511.

BIKING

Except along the southwestern shore areas, biking this part of Washington requires strength and stamina. There's spectacular beauty here, but there's also rain—lots of it—and challenging terrain.

PORT TOWNSEND AREA Recreational bicyclists will probably enjoy a ride through **Fort Worden State Park**, which overlooks the Strait of Juan de Fuca, in Port Townsend, or the paved six-mile trail that loops the Port Angeles waterfront. The trail is flat, mostly following the shoreline, with picnic tables and other stopping spots along the way. On a clear day, you can see across the strait to Victoria.

OLYMPIC COAST A recommended road tour is the 85-mile **Upper Peninsula Tour** from Sequim to Neah Bay. The 55-mile trip down Route 101 from **Port Angeles to Forks** is also recommended.

OCEAN SHORES–PACIFIC BEACH One of the gentlest biking opportunities in the area is the 14-mile **Ocean Shores Loop** from North Beach Park.

GRAYS HARBOR AREA The 69-mile **Aberdeen-Raymond-Westport** loop on Routes 101 and 105 is worth a long ride. A new paved trail has been built in Westport along the beach. It runs for a mile and a half between two small state parks.

LONG BEACH–WILLAPA BAY The 42-mile **Seaview-Naselle** loop in Pacific County is popular.

Bike Rentals In Port Townsend, rent mountain bikes, tandems, running strollers, bike trailers and road bikes at **Port Townsend Cyclery**. ~ 100 Tyler Street, Port Townsend; 360-385-6470. In Port Angeles, **Pedal 'N' Paddle** carries hybrids and mountain bikes. ~ 120 East Front Street, Port Angeles; 360-457-1240. **Westport Family Fun Center** rents cruisers (with the wide tires for beach riding). ~ 1600 North Montesano Street, Westport; 360-268-0700.

All distances listed for hiking trails are one way unless otherwise noted.

HIKING

PORT TOWNSEND AREA **Mount Walker Trail** (2 miles) ascends the Olympics' easternmost peak (2804 feet) through a rhododendron forest. The view from the summit, across Hood Canal and the Kitsap Peninsula to Seattle and the Cascades, is unforgettable. The trailhead is one-fifth mile off Route 101 at Walker Pass, five miles south of Quilcene.

PORT ANGELES AREA **Dungeness Spit Trail** (5 miles) extends down the outside of the longest natural sandspit in the United States, and back the inside. The spit is a national wildlife refuge with a lighthouse at its seaward end. The trail begins and ends at the Dungeness Recreation Area.

OLYMPIC NATIONAL PARK Olympic National Park and adjacent areas of Olympic National Forest are rich in backpacking opportunities. Most trails follow rivers into the high country, with its peaks and alpine lakes. **Obstruction Point Trail** (8 miles) leads from the Deer Park Campground to Obstruction Point, following a 6500-foot ridgeline.

An unnamed trail (28.5 miles) starts at the Dosewallips Ranger Station on the park's eastern boundary, follows the Dosewallips River to its source in the Anderson Glacier, then goes down the East Fork of the Quinault to the Graves Creek Campground.

Seven Lakes Basin Loop (22.5 miles) has several trail options, starting and ending at Sol Duc Hot Springs.

Hoh River Trail (18.5 miles) wanders through North America's most famous rainforest from the Hoh Ranger Station, to Glacier Meadows, at the base of the Blue Glacier on 7965-foot Mt. Olympus, the park's highest point.

OLYMPIC COAST   Coastal areas of the Olympic Peninsula have hiking trails as well. **Cape Alava Loop** (9 miles) crosses from the Ozette Ranger Station to Cape Alava; follows the shoreline south to Sand Point, from which there is beach access to shipwreck memorials farther south; and returns northeast to the ranger station. Prehistoric petroglyphs and an ancient Indian village can be seen en route.

GRAYS HARBOR AREA   **Wynoochee Lake Shore Trail** (12 miles) circles this manmade reservoir in Olympic National Forest north of Montesano.

Shifting Sands Nature Trail (.5 mile) teaches visitors to Twin Harbors State Park, south of Westport, about plant and animal life in the seaside dunes.

LONG BEACH–WILLAPA BAY   Along the southwestern Washington coast there are few inland trails, but the long stretches of flat beach appeal to many walkers. **Leadbetter Point Loop Trail** (2.5 miles) weaves through the forests and dunes, and past the ponds, mudflats and marshes, of the wildlife sanctuary/state park at the northern tip of the Long Beach Peninsula. Accessible from Oysterville, it's of special interest to birdwatchers.

The **Trail of the Ancient Cedars** (3.2 miles) goes through an important grove of old-growth red cedar, some as large as 11 feet wide and 150 feet tall, on Long Island. You must find your own boat access to Long Island. The Willapa Bay National Wildlife Refuge offers an interpretive brochure of the trail. ~ Milepost 24, Route 101; 360-484-3482.

▼▼▼▼▼▼▼▼▼▼
Transportation

CAR

Route 101 is the main artery of the Olympic Peninsula and Washington coastal region, virtually encircling the entire land mass. Branching off Route 5 in Olympia, at the foot of Puget Sound, it runs north to Discovery Bay, where Route 20 turns off to Port Townsend; west through Port Angeles to Sappho; then zigzags to Astoria, Oregon, and points south. Remarkably, when you reach Aberdeen, 292 miles after you start traveling on 101, you're just 36 miles from where you started!

Traveling from Seattle, most Olympic Peninsula visitors take either the Seattle–Winslow ferry (to Route 305) or the Edmonds-Kingston ferry (to Route 104), joining 101 just south of Discovery Bay. From Tacoma, the practical route is Route 16 across the Narrows Bridge. From the north, the Keystone ferry to Port Townsend has its eastern terminus midway down lanky Whidbey Island, off Route 20. Northbound travelers can reach the area either through Astoria, on Route 101, or via several routes that branch off Route 5 north of Portland.

Fairchild International Airport, near Port Angeles, links the northern Olympic Peninsula with major cities throughout the United States and western Canada via Horizon Air Lines. ~ 360-417-3433.

AIR

Washington State Ferries serves the Olympic Peninsula directly from Whidbey Island to Port Townsend and indirectly across Puget Sound (via the Kitsap Peninsula) from Seattle and Edmonds. ~ 260-464-6400. The **Black Ball Transport** offers direct daily service between Port Angeles and Victoria, B.C. ~ 360-457-4491. **Victoria Rapid Transit** provides foot-passenger service mid-May through October. ~ 360-452-8088. Some smaller cruise lines may make stops in Port Angeles.

FERRY

Bus service in Port Townsend and vicinity is offered by **Jefferson Transit** (360-385-4777), which connects with **Clallam Transit** (360-452-4511) serving the Port Angeles area. For getting around in the Grays Harbor and Ocean Shores areas, there is **Grays Harbor Transit** (360-532-2770, 800-562-9730).

Two-day bus tours of the Olympic Peninsula are offered by **Gray Line** departing from downtown Seattle hotels. ~ 206-624-5813.

BUS

In Port Angeles, **Budget Rent A Car** (800-527-0700) can be found at or in town. In Forks, there is **Dan Wilder Auto Center** (800-927-9372). In Aberdeen, you'll find **U-Save Auto Rental** (800-272-8728).

CAR RENTALS

For local bus service in the northern Olympic Peninsula, including Port Angeles and Sequim, contact **Clallam Transit System** in Port Angeles. ~ 360-452-4511. Port Townsend, Sequim and eastern Jefferson County are served by **Jefferson Transit**. ~ 360-385-4777. The **Grays Harbor Transportation Authority** offers bus service to Aberdeen, Ocean Shores and the surrounding region. ~ 360-532-2770.

Bus service between Raymond, Long Beach and Astoria, Oregon, is provided by the **Pacific Transit System**. ~ 360-642-9418.

PUBLIC TRANSIT

FIVE

The Cascades
and Central Washington

Perhaps without even realizing it, many Americans have a burning image of this region. For it was here, in the Cascade Range, that Mt. St. Helens blew its top in 1980. But the area has a lot more going for it than one hyperactive mountaintop. Indeed, think of the Cascades and Central Washington as one wild place for anyone who loves the outdoors.

The Cascade Range contains some of the most beautiful mountain scenery in the United States, much of it preserved by two major national parks, several national recreation areas and numerous wilderness areas that make this a major sports haven. There are also glaciers galore; 318 are in the North Cascades National Park alone. Thousands of miles of trails and logging roads lace the Cascades, leading to mountaintop lookout towers, old gold mines, lakes, streams and gorgeous sights.

The hand of man has done little to alter the Cascades. Not until 1952 did a highway cross the state north of Route 2. And when the North Cascades Highway (Route 20) was completed, it was with the understanding that it would be closed during the heavy snows, usually from October until May. Thus, most of the Cascades are still wild and remote, seen and experienced by humans but not transformed by them.

The range, about 700 miles long, begins at the Fraser River in southern British Columbia and extends southward through Washington and Oregon and into California just beyond Lassen Peak. The most dominant features of the Cascades are its 15 volcanoes. Washington lays claim to five, with Mt. Rainier the granddaddy at 14,411 feet. Most peaks are under 10,000 feet, and Harts Pass, the highest pass in the state, is only 6197 feet.

Although the range is not a comparatively high one, it served as an effective barrier to exploration and development until well into the 20th century. The pioneers who came over the Oregon Trail avoided it, choosing instead to go down the Columbia River to the Cowlitz River, travel up to present-day Toledo, then move overland to Puget Sound at Tumwater and Olympia.

Mining has always been part of the Cascades story. Although no major gold strikes have been found, several smaller ones have kept the interest alive, and there's probably never been a day since the mid-1870s when someone wasn't panning or sluicing in the mountains.

The range supports a wide variety of plants and wildlife because it has so many climatic zones. Naturalists have given names to eight distinct ones: Coastal Forest Zone, Silver Fir Zone, Sierran Mixed-Conifer Zone, Red Fir Zone, Subalpine Zone, Alpine Zone, Interior Fir Zone and Ponderosa Pine Zone. Each zone has its own community of plants, animals and birds.

Although most of the range is under the stewardship of the Forest Service, which by law has to practice multiple-use policies, most people think of the Cascades as their very own. It is used by mushroom hunters, hikers, runners, bird-watchers, anglers, hunters, photographers, painters, skiers, horse riders, loggers and miners. Whichever of these apply to you, enjoy.

▼▼▼▼▼▼▼▼▼▼▼▼

North Cascades

Extending from the Canadian border south into the Mt. Baker–Snoqualmie National Forest, the North Cascades region has over 300 glaciers, valleys famous for their spring tulip fields and some of the best skiing in the Pacific Northwest. Backroads wind through old logging towns past mountain lakes to unspoiled wilderness areas. The North Cascades National Park forms the core of this realm that includes Rainy and Washington passes, two of the Cascades' grandest viewpoints.

SIGHTS

Beginning at the northernmost approach, **Route 542** enters the Cascades from Bellingham, a pleasant, two-lane, blacktop highway that is shared by loggers, skiers, anglers and hikers. Much of the route runs through dense forest beside fast streams and with only rare glimpses of the surrounding mountains. The road dead-ends just beyond the Mt. Baker day-use lodge for skiers. In clear weather you will see 9127-foot **Mt. Shuksan**, one of the most beautiful peaks in the Cascades. It can't be seen from any other part of the range, but it probably appears on more calendars and postcards than its neighbor Mt. Baker or even Mt. Rainier.

The **Mt. Baker** ski slopes usually open in November and run all the way into April, making it the longest ski season of any area in Washington. During the summer the mountain is popular with day hikers and backpackers, who often hike over Austin Pass between Mt. Shuksan and Mt. Baker and down to Baker Lake, an artificial lake behind Seattle City Light's Lower Baker Dam.

Mt. Baker was named by George Vancouver on April 30, 1792, in honor of James Baker, a lieutenant on his ship. It was first climbed on August 17, 1868, by a party of four led by an experienced alpinist named Edward T. Coleman. Although it is listed as an active volcano and occasionally steam is seen rising from it, Mt. Baker hasn't erupted for nearly 10,000 years.

Route 20, one of America's premier scenic routes, goes through the North Cascades National Park and along the way provides hiking trails, roadside parks, boat launches and one of the more unusual tours in the Cascades, the **Seattle City Light Skagit Tours**. This four-hour tour tells how Seattle built three dams on the Skagit to produce its electricity. The tour begins at Diablo with a boat ride up the lake to the dam, then a ride up the side of a mountain on an antique Incline Stairway Lift to another boat, which takes you to the powerhouse. After the tour, guests are taken to the cookhouse for an all-you-can-eat chicken dinner. Reservations are required. Admission. ~ 206-684-3030.

Because the highway is enclosed by the Ross Lake National Recreation Area, new development is virtually nonexistent, and the small company towns of Newhalem and Diablo look frozen in the pre-World War II days. **Ross Lake**, created by the hydro-electric project, is a fjordlike lake between steep mountains that eventually crosses over into British Columbia.

When driving on Route 20, be forewarned: No gasoline is available between Marblemount and Mazama, a distance of more than 70 miles, and there are few places to buy groceries. Fill your tank and bring your lunch.

Ross Lake on the Skagit River was formed by Ross Dam. Diablo Dam was built a short distance downstream, creating the much smaller Diablo Lake. Ross Lake is an international body of water because its backwaters cross the border into Canada, and when the timber was being cleared before the lake was formed, the work was done via a road in from British Columbia.

An alternate way to reach Route 20 is over what is locally known as the **Mountain Loop Highway**, a favorite weekend drive for years before Route 20 was completed across the mountains. The Mountain Loop begins in Granite Falls with Route 92, which goes along the South Fork of the Stillaguamish River past the one-store towns of Robe, Verlot and Silverton. The road is crooked and slow driving because it follows the river route closely. It is always closed in the winter and sometimes landslides close it for much of the summer. Near the old mining town of Monte Cristo, the road turns north along the Sauk River and emerges in the logging town of Darrington. Here you can drive due north to catch Route 20 at Rockport or turn west on Route 530 and return to Route 5.

Route 20 plunges into the Cascades and goes over two passes—**Rainy Pass**, 4860 feet, and **Washington Pass**, 5477 feet —before descending into the Methow Valley. Stop at each viewpoint and turnout for stunning views of the region. One viewpoint

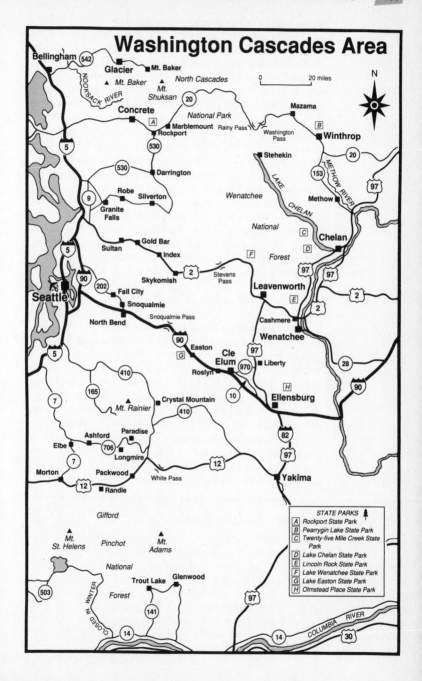

Washington Cascades Area

Bellingham
542
Glacier
Mt. Baker
▲ Mt. Baker
North Cascades
Mt. Shuksan
20
Concrete
National Park
Mazama
A
Marblemount
Rainy Pass
Washington Pass
B
Winthrop
Rockport
530
Stehekin
20
530
Darrington
153
Methow
9
Robe
Silverton
Wenatchee
97
Granite Falls
National
C
Chelan
5
Sultan
Gold Bar
D
F
Forest
97
97
5
Index
2
Stevens Pass
Leavenworth
Skykomish
E
90
202
Fall City
2
Seattle
Snoqualmie
Cashmere
North Bend
Snoqualmie Pass
Wenatchee
90
Easton
97
5
G
Cle Elum
97
28
410
Roslyn
970
Liberty
7
165
10
H
Crystal Mountain
Ellensburg
▲ Mt. Rainier
410
90
Ashford
Paradise
Elbe
706
82
7
Longmire
97
Morton
Packwood
12
12
White Pass
Yakima
12
Randle

Gifford

▲ Mt. St. Helens
Pinchot
▲ Mt. Adams
National
503
Trout Lake
Glenwood
Forest
141
14
97
14
COLUMBIA RIVER
30

0   20 miles

N

NOOKSACK RIVER

LAKE CHELAN

METHOW RIVER

CLOSED IN WINTER

STATE PARKS 🌲

A Rockport State Park
B Pearrygin Lake State Park
C Twenty-five Mile Creek State Park
D Lake Chelan State Park
E Lincoln Rock State Park
F Lake Wenatchee State Park
G Lake Easton State Park
H Olmstead Place State Park

above Ross Lake shows miles of the long, narrow lake, and another just beyond Washington Pass gives a grandstand view of the jagged mountains behind the pass.

The only way to visit the resort town of **Stehekin**, at the tip of Lake Chelan, is by boat, plane or hiking. Most visitors take the trip up the lake on the **Lady of the Lake**, the tour-mail-supply boat for Stehekin and points between. The schedule allows you three-and-a-half hours in Stehekin, and you can buy lunch either on the boat or at the Stehekin landing. Reservation suggested. Admission. ~ 509-682-4584.

The best way to get to Stehekin, though, is also an incomparably scenic way to see Lake Chelan and its surroundings. **Chelan Airways** has been flying the lake for more than a half-century, and its experienced floatplane pilots not only give passengers the best views, they know every nook and cranny of the lake and all the stories that accompany them. Roundtrip passage is not too expensive, but it's worth a flight just to see the sights even if you don't stay "uplake." ~ 1328 West Woodin Avenue (one mile west of Chelan on Route 97A); 509-682-5555.

LODGING   The nearest public lodging to Mt. Baker is the **Snowline Inn**, a condominium complex with 37 units. Half of these are studios and half have sleeping lofts. The pseudo-chalet, two-story building is set back in the trees away from the busy highway. The units with sleeping lofts can sleep from two to five people and have a full bath. Some units have a foldout couch and bunk beds just inside the front door. The smaller units are also designed for up to four persons. All have completely equipped kitchens, and some units have microwaves. ~ 10433 Mt. Baker Highway, Glacier; 360-599-2788, 800-228-0119, fax 360-599-2772. MODERATE.

The **Glacier Creek Lodge** earns its description of rustic. It is a motel with nine units and 12 blue-and-white cabins. In addition to a hot tub, there is a large lobby with an espresso bar and a few café tables. The cabins are one or two bedrooms, with a

✔ **CHECK THESE OUT—UNIQUE SIGHTS**

- Watch the salmon at **Rocky Reach Dam** struggling up the Columbia River to reach their spawning grounds. *page 202*
- Revel in the fun ticky-tack of cuckoo clocks and lederhosen in the Bavarian-themed burg of **Leavenworth**. *page 206*
- Chug through forest and across high bridges near Washington's tallest mountain on the **Mt. Rainier Scenic Railroad**. *page 214*
- Explore the remains of lakes and forests flattened by the 1980 blast of **Mt. St. Helens**. *page 218*

bath, a kitchen, double bed and tired furniture. The motel units are so small there's no room for a table. ~ 10036 Mt. Baker Highway, Glacier; 360-599-2991. BUDGET TO MODERATE.

One of the larger lakeside resorts is **Baker Lake Resort**, 20 miles north of Concrete on Baker Lake Road. It is a mixture of RV sites and eight rustic cabins on the lake. The cabins have bathrooms and showers, a refrigerator, dishes and cooking utensils, but guests must bring their own linen and towels. Boating and fishing are popular on the lake; boat rentals are available. Open seven days a week in the summer and only on weekends in the winter. ~ P.O. Box 100, Concrete, WA 98237; 360-757-2262. MODERATE.

A motel with bed-and-breakfast ambience, the **North Cascade Inn** is a vintage Northwest cedar-shake hostelry with an adjoining restaurant and lounge. There are 14 individually decorated, wood-paneled rooms, some with antique and hand-carved furnishings. All rooms come with modern comforts such as telephones and televisions. Guests can have breakfast or dinner in the restaurant or on an adjoining outdoor patio adorned by a three-tiered fountain and dozens of hanging flower baskets. ~ 4284 Route 20, Concrete; 360-853-8870, 800-251-3054. MODERATE.

Rustic reigns in remote Stehekin. The most outdoorsy is the **Stehekin Valley Ranch**, owned and operated by the Courtneys, the major family in the valley. The ranch is nine miles from town, up the Stehekin River Valley. Guests are housed in tent cabins with wooden walls and canvas-covered roofs. Showers and toilets are in the main building. Guests are encouraged to bring their own sleeping bags and towels to save $5 per person. All meals are included and served in the dining room, which has split logs for tables and seats. Horseback rides, river float trips, scenic flights and day hikes are offered. Closed October through mid-June. ~ P.O. Box 36, Stehekin, WA 98852; 509-682-4677, 800-536-0745. MODERATE.

The fanciest Stehekin lodging is **Silver Bay Inn**, at the head of the Stehekin River a short distance from the village. In the owners' home there are two rooms with private baths and one large suite that includes a private bath and soaking tub, two decks and a breakfast that features Devonshire cream for your fresh fruit and scrambled eggs with cashews. Outside are two cabins that will sleep six and are complete with kitchens and dishwashers. Closed mid-October to mid-May. ~ 10 Silver Bay Road, Stehekin; 509-682-2212. MODERATE TO ULTRA-DELUXE.

A popular place along the Mt. Baker Highway is **Milano's Market and Deli**, a combination small restaurant and deli. With its black-and-white tile floor and café tables, it offers a hearty supply of soups, salads, fresh pasta dishes and homemade desserts.

DINING

This is a good place to have a picnic lunch made up. If the weather is right, the deck is open for outside dining. ~ 9990 Mt. Baker Highway, Glacier; 360-599-2863. BUDGET TO MODERATE.

A mile east of Glacier, near the Snowline Inn, is a much larger restaurant with more of a rural flavor. **The Chandelier** is built in the chalet style and divided into two sections with a large fireplace in the entrance hall. To the left is a large bar with the obligatory big-screen television set and wooden chairs and tables. The restaurant serves straightforward American food, large burgers, steaks, seafood, barbecued chicken, fresh strawberry pie and homemade cheesecakes. You can also have them make up box lunches for day trips. Closed Monday and Tuesday. ~ 10453 Mt. Baker Highway, Glacier; 360-599-2233. MODERATE.

On the western edge of Concrete, **North Cascade Inn** has established a local reputation for good, plain American food (steaks, chops, seafood) and delicious pie (made by a local woman especially for the restaurant). The exterior is decorated with farm and logging equipment, but the interior decor is softened a bit with antique furnishings and decorations. There's also a full-service bar. ~ 4284 Route 20, Concrete; 360-853-8771, 800-251-3054. BUDGET TO MODERATE.

SHOPPING If you're in Concrete on Saturday during the summer months, hit the **Saturday Market** in the **North Cascades Visitor Center** on Route 20 for arts and crafts and baked goods.

For nostalgic atmosphere as well as the largest variety of goods in town, take a stroll through the **Concrete Department Store**. With its wooden floors and counters, it has remained almost unchanged since the 1920s and has been used as a backdrop for several Hollywood films. Closed Sunday. ~ 138 Main Street, Concrete; 360-853-8700.

Potter Stephen Murray is known for his wood-fired ceramic dinnerware that comes in a variety of lustrous glazes. Individual pieces are sold at his **Sauk Mountain Pottery** store east of Concrete. ~ 4865 Route 20, Concrete; 360-853-8689.

NIGHTLIFE The Cascades isn't the place to go for stellar nightlife. After a day traipsing around in the mountains, most people return to town tired and only want to eat and go to bed. Consequently, only the busiest areas even have live music.

Near Mt. Baker, **The Chandelier** has dancing and occasional live music. ~ 10453 Mt. Baker Highway, Glacier; 360-599-2233.

PARKS **MT. BAKER–SNOQUALMIE NATIONAL FOREST** 🚶🚴🐎🛶 ⛺🎣🏊🛶🚤🛶♪ This 1.7-million-acre forest begins at the Canadian border and goes south along the western slopes of the Cascades to Mt. Rainier National Park. It is dominated on the north by the inactive volcano, 10,778-foot Mt. Baker. Another inactive volcano, 10,568-foot Glacier Peak, lies in the middle of the forest. The Forest Service controls the land for the ski areas at Crystal Mountain, Mt. Baker and Snoqualmie Pass. Its best-known wilderness area is Alpine Lakes Wilderness, but it also includes the Glacier Peak and Mt. Baker Wilderness areas. Within the forest is excellent fishing for rainbow trout in Baker Lake and many other streams and lakes. Facilities include picnic areas, restrooms and showers; restaurants and groceries are in area towns. Parking fee, $3 to $5 per day. ~ Four east–west highways cross the national forest: Routes 90, 20, 2 and 410; 206-775-9702.

▲ Camping is permitted (unless otherwise posted) along the highways, trails and the Pacific Crest Trail, as well as at established campsites. Most of the 40-plus campgrounds are primitive with pit toilets and vary from walk-in to drive-in sites; RV sites are available; over half the sites are by reservation only (800-280-2267), $6 to $10 per night.

ROCKPORT STATE PARK 🏃 🚲 This park is essentially a large campground in a grove of old-growth Douglas fir. Most of the camping areas are shielded from one another by thick undergrowth. It is within easy walking distance of the fish-laden Skagit River, which makes it popular with steelheaders. There are picnic areas, restrooms, showers and five miles of footpaths; restaurants and groceries are a mile away in Rockport. ~ Located on Route 20 one mile west of Rockport; 360-853-8461.

▲ There are 62 sites: 50 RV with hookups, eight walk-in and four three-sided Adirondack shelters; $10 to $15 per night.

HOWARD MILLER STEELHEAD COUNTY PARK 🏃 🚲 🎣 🚣 🛶 🚤 One of the most popular parks on the Skagit River for steelheaders and travelers alike, it covers 93 acres and has museum exhibits of a historic cabin, an old river ferry and dugout canoe. The clubhouse is a popular hangout for local anglers. Facilities include picnic areas, a volleyball court, a playground, a clubhouse, restrooms, showers and a trailer dump; restaurants and groceries are nearby. ~ Located in the middle of Rockport at the junction of Routes 20 and 530; 360-853-8808.

▲ There are 10 tent sites at $12 and 50 RV sites at $16, which have partial hookups. Campground, including showers, is wheelchair-accessible. Reservations: 360-853-8808, fax 360-853-7315.

NORTH CASCADES NATIONAL PARK 🏃 🐎 🚣 🛶 🚤 Covering 505,000 acres in the north-central part of the state, this park is divided into two units. The northern unit runs from the Canadian border to **Ross Lake National Recreation Area**. The southern unit continues on to the **Lake Chelan National Recreation Area**. Much of its eastern boundary is the summit of the

Cascade Range, and the western boundary is the Mt. Baker–Snoqualmie National Forest. It is the most rugged and remote of the national parks in Washington and has the fewest roads. All visitor facilities and roads in the northern portion are inside the Ross Lake National Recreation Area. On the southern end, the Lake Chelan National Recreation Area covers the heavy-use area on the north end of the lake, including the city of Stehekin. Try for rainbow trout in Ross Lake, steelhead in the Skagit River downstream from Newhalem and rainbow and eastern brook trout in high lakes. There are interpretive trails, boardwalk trails and restrooms; a visitors center is in Newhalem. No restaurants or grocery stores; rangers sometimes lead nature walks from the Colonial Creek and Newhalem campgrounds. ~ Only Route 20 goes through North Cascades National Park, and it is closed in winter, generally from mid-November to April; 360-856-5700.

▲ There are over 400 campsites at four campgrounds. You can camp year-round at Goodell Creek. Some sites are free; others are up to $10 per night. The adjacent Okanogan Forest has more sites, including the popular Lone Fir and Early Winter campgrounds.

▼▼▼▼▼▼▼▼▼▼▼▼
Methow Valley

The scenery changes quickly and dramatically once you have crossed Washington Pass into the Methow Valley. Located along Route 20 between Mazama and Pateros, this region includes the tourist center of Chelan, gateway to one of the state's most popular lake-resort areas.

SIGHTS

As you descend the east slope of the Cascades, the thick, fir forest gives way to smaller pine with almost no underbrush. The mountains become bare, and you can see for miles. And by the time you arrive in **Winthrop**, you will wonder if you are in Colorado or Wyoming because the small town is all falsefronts, saloon doors, hitching rails and wooden porches.

The Shafer Museum is in the cabin built by town founder Guy Waring in 1897 and has exhibits from the valley's early days, including a stagecoach and antique automobiles. Open weekends and some weekdays from April through October. ~ One block up the hill off Route 20, Winthrop; 509-996-2712.

HIDDEN ►

There are several areas around Winthrop worth driving to, including 6197-foot **Harts Pass** a short distance from town. This is the highest point to which you can drive in Washington and is only an hour's drive on a gravel Forest Service road. The views from the summit are spectacular.

Not long after driving south on Route 153, the last of the timbered mountains are left behind, and the Methow Valley flattens into a series of irrigated ranches with broad hayfields. The valley is gaining popularity with people from Puget Sound looking for more space, so houses are beginning to line the low hills on both sides.

When you reach the **Columbia River** at Pateros, the landscape is one of basaltic cliffs on both sides of the river. Instead of a fast-flowing river there is a chain of lakes behind dams all the way past Wenatchee. Route 97 hugs the west side of the Columbia, then swings away from the river to go through the resort town of Chelan, which sits at the end of **Lake Chelan**.

Thousands of acres of apple orchards climb the hills along Route 150 northwest of Chelan.

The lake is a remnant of the Ice Ages. Scoured out of the mountains by glaciers, it is one of the deepest lakes in the region, more than 1500 feet deep in at least one place, which places its bed at 400 feet below sea level. It is 55 miles long but quite narrow, and the mountains rising from its shores give it the appearance of a Norwegian fjord.

Chelan is a small town that has been given over almost entirely to tourism. Woodin Avenue is the main drag and the lakefront is lined with resorts, but the small-town atmosphere is retained so a farmer can come to town and still buy a two-by-four or a cotter pin.

The **Lake Chelan Museum** displays American Indian artifacts, early farming and orchard equipment. One room depicts a miner's cabin, and another shows a typical country kitchen. Closed Sunday and from October through May. ~ Woodin Avenue and Emerson Street, Chelan; 509-682-5644.

LODGING

If you want to get up close and personal with the North Cascades, head for the **Early Winters Cabins/Freestone Inn**. The six cabins sit across the highway from the Forest Service/National Park Service information center at the foot of the mountains. Small and widely spaced apart, the newly renovated cabins are heated with propane fireplaces, and there are fire pits outside. Electric heaters warm the bathrooms. All cooking utensils are provided for the stove. **Jack's Hut** offers cross-country ski rentals in the winter and mountain-bike rentals in the summer for adventurers who want to explore the Methow Valley Nordic Ski Trails—a 175-kilometer network of trails running through the property. ~ 17798 Route 20, Mazama; 509-996-2355, 800-639-3809. DELUXE TO ULTRA-DELUXE.

The most elaborate place in the Methow Valley, and one of the best resorts in the Pacific Northwest, is **Sun Mountain Lodge**. Built at the 3000-foot level atop a small mountain, this low-rise, stone-and-timber resort gives a 360-degree view of the Cascades, Pasayten Wilderness, Okanogan Highlands and Methow Valley. The 115 units are spread over three buildings atop the mountain and down the road in thirteen rustic, cozy cabins. The resort has just about everything: several miles of hiking trails that become cross-country ski trails in the winter, two pools, three hot tubs, an exercise room, the largest string of saddle-and-pack horses in the state, mountain-bike rentals, canoe and sailing on the lake, heli-skiing and tennis. It also has a great restaurant. Rooms feature bentwood furniture, a fireplace (only the suites have real-wood fireplaces), coffee, the thickest, softest towels and robes you can hope for and no television. ~ Patterson Lake Road, Winthrop; 509-996-2211, 800-572-0493, fax 509-996-3133. ULTRA-DELUXE.

Right in the heart of Western-themed Winthrop you'll find the **Trails End Motel** with its tall falsefront and wooden porch. The 12 units, which have VCRs (you can choose from among 50 free videos), are simply furnished, and big windows look down onto Main Street. In season, the area's oldest irrigation canal runs behind the motel. A bookstore anchors one end of the building. ~ 130 Riverside Street, Winthrop; 509-996-2303. MODERATE.

On the south edge of Winthrop is the **Virginian Motel and Restaurant**. Located on the high bank of the Methow River, the riverfront rooms in this 39-unit motel have balconies. Cedar was used extensively, and most units retain the pleasant aroma. There are also seven cabins, which are a bit more expensive, but several have fireplaces and room enough for six. Kitchens are large and well equipped. ~ 808 North Cascades Highway, Winthrop; 509-996-2535, 800-854-2834. MODERATE.

The oldest and most reliable resort in Chelan is **Campbell's Resort**, which has been in business since 1901. With 172 rooms, it is still growing along the lakeshore in the heart of town. It has two heated pools, an outdoor jacuzzi, good beach and boat moorage. The larger rooms have kitchenettes and one king or two queen beds, and are decorated in softer pastels, or earth tones. ~ 104 West Woodin Avenue, Chelan; 509-682-2561. ULTRA-DELUXE.

One of the most complete resorts inside the Chelan city limits is **Darnell's Resort Motel**, a few blocks southwest of the city

✔ CHECK THESE OUT—UNIQUE LODGING

- *Budget to moderate:* Bed down in a rustic blue-and-white cabin at **Glacier Creek Lodge** after a relaxing soak in the hot tub. *page 192*
- *Moderate:* Escape to **The Shepherd's Inn**, nestled on 40 wooded acres between Mt. Rainier and Mt. St. Helens. *page 219*
- *Moderate to deluxe:* Begin your day with a cowboy-size breakfast before riding the range at the **Hidden Valley Guest Ranch**. *page 212*
- *Ultra-deluxe:* Check into **Salish Lodge at Snoqualmie Falls'** fantasy-like setting, familiar to fans of *Twin Peaks*. *page 210*

Budget: under $50   Moderate: $50–$90   Deluxe: $90–$130   Ultra-deluxe: over $130

center on Route 150. It has a heated pool and hot tub, putting greens, lighted tennis courts, swimming beach, boats and bicycle rentals, waterskiing, volleyball, badminton and conference rooms. The resort is divided into two three-story buildings. All rooms have balconies with views of the lake. All units are suites; some have two bedrooms, and the larger units have sleeping lofts. The penthouse suites have two fireplaces and private jacuzzi. ~ 901 Spader Bay Road, Chelan; 509-682-2015, 800-967-8149, fax 509-682-8736. MODERATE TO ULTRA-DELUXE.

Mary Kay's Romantic Whaley Mansion is actually a bed and breakfast. This white Edwardian house trimmed in pink has six rooms decorated with antiques from the family collection. A footstool has antlers for legs; ribbons and garlands of artificial flowers are everywhere. The guest rooms, on the second and third floors, are decorated with flowered wallpaper and have old-fashioned beds and private baths, TVs and VCRs with a selection of free movies. There is also a full library for sitting. In addition to a gourmet breakfast that includes hand-dipped chocolates, Mary Kay will sing with the player piano accompanying her. Gay-friendly. ~ 415 3rd Street, Chelan; 509-682-5735, 800-729-2408, fax 509-682-5385. DELUXE TO ULTRA-DELUXE.

On the eastern edge of Chelan is the clean and comfortable **Apple Inn Motel** with white stucco walls and black wood trim. The 41 rooms are small and clean; some have kitchenettes. The heated outdoor pool is open in the summer, and a hot tub is open year-round. ~ 1002 East Woodin Avenue, Chelan; 509-682-4044. MODERATE.

DINING

One of the newest restaurants to get statewide attention is the **Sun Mountain Lodge Dining Room**. The room is cantilevered with views down into the Methow Valley and Winthrop 5000 feet below. All seats here have a view. The menu features wonderful seafood and creatively prepared grilled or roasted meats. ~ Sun Mountain Lodge, Patterson Lake Road, Winthrop; 509-996-2211. DELUXE.

One of Winthrop's most trendy restaurants is the oddly named **Duck Brand Cantina** in the hotel of the same name. The menu reflects an effort to please several palates, including Mexican, Continental, American and vegetarian. The restaurant is divided into two areas: a dining room with several old, oak tables and hanging greenery, and a deck overlooking Winthrop's sole street. ~ 248 Riverside Avenue, Winthrop; 509-996-2192. MODERATE.

Decorated in rustic western style with wooden tables, hardwood floors, and elk heads mounted on the walls, **Three Fingered Jack's Saloon and Restaurant** offers fresh meats and vegetables, homemade soups, salads and desserts. The New York steaks are cut in-house in this family-run establishment. Try the vegetarian mixed grill with risotto or the fettuccine with garlic parmesan sauce. ~ 176 Riverside Avenue, Winthrop; 509-996-2411. BUDGET TO MODERATE.

Although Campbell's Resort is so large that it overwhelms some people, it is hard to find a better place in the area than the resort's **Campbell House** for a good meal. The large room seats about 130 and is pleasantly decorated in Early American furnishings with walls covered with an eclectic collection of prints, documents and paintings. The menu is large: prime rib, medallions of pork, prawns Provençal, the catch of the day and a variety of pasta. Closed November to mid-March. ~ 104 West Woodin Avenue, Chelan; 509-682-2561. MODERATE TO DELUXE.

A few doors down from Campbell's on the lakefront is **Peter B's Bar and Grill**. It has two floors—with open-air seating on the top level—and specializes in lunches of sandwiches (some are purely vegetarian), soups and salads. Dinner offers a series of specials throughout the week, seafood, steak and several pastas. ~ 114 East Woodin Avenue, Chelan; 509-682-1031. BUDGET TO MODERATE.

SHOPPING   Art is big, and often very good, in Winthrop, especially at **Hildabob's Gallery** where you will find paintings, sculpture and hand-knit apparel. Closed January to mid-April. ~ 231 Riverside Avenue, Winthrop; 509-996-3279. Other artwork, some by nationally known artists such as Richard Beyer, is usually on exhibit in the public rooms at **Sun Mountain Lodge**. ~ Patterson Lake Road, Winthrop; 509-996-2211. For photographs by the area's best-known photographer, Bob Spiwak, visit **Winthrop Mountain Sports**. ~ 257 Riverside Drive, Winthrop; 509-996-2886.

Art is also a growth industry in the Chelan area. Beyer and Rod Weagant exhibit at the **Manson Gallery**. It is open only by appointment. ~ Washington and Ford streets, Manson; 509-687-3959. Another is the **Wapato Studio**, featuring watercolors, oils and sculpture by local artists. Closed Sunday during the winter. ~ 108 East Woodin Avenue, Chelan; 509-682-2423.

However, the apple is king in Chelan, and the **Harvest Tree** is a mail-order store for packaged apples and other Northwest-produced food items. ~ 109 East Woodin Avenue, Chelan; 509-682-3618.

NIGHTLIFE   The **Winthrop Palace** offers live rock and R&B most nights during the summer. ~ 918 Riverside Avenue, Winthrop; 509-996-2245.

Chelan has a few more choices, nearly all featuring live disco, rock and country music and dancing during the summer months. **Chelan House** has karaoke on weekends during the summer and occasionally in the winter. ~ 502 East Woodin Avenue, Chelan;

509-682-2013. For occasional dancing to live or deejay music on Friday, try the **Goochi Restaurant**. Cover for live shows. ~ 104 Woodin Avenue, Chelan; 509-682-2436.

PEARRYGIN LAKE STATE PARK This is a popular park for travelers in RVs because it is close to Winthrop and has a sandy beach on a small lake surrounded by mountains. There are picnic areas, restrooms and showers; restaurants and groceries are in Winthrop. Closed from late October through March. ~ Located five miles north of Winthrop off Route 20; 509-996-2370.

PARKS

There are 30 RV hookups and 53 tent/RV sites; $11 to $16 per night. Reservations, 800-452-5687.

LAKE CHELAN STATE PARK This is a favorite park for Puget Sound youths yearning for sunshine, and in July and August the beach looks more like California than Washington with its broad, sandy beach (great swimming) and play area. Because it has docks and launching areas for skiers, it is equally popular with powerboaters and waterskiers. Anglers fish in Lake Chelan as far away from the powerboats as possible. You'll find picnic tables, restrooms and showers. ~ Located nine miles west of Chelan on Route 971; 509-687-3710.

By reservation; 111 tent sites and 34 RV hookup sites; $11 to $16 per night. Reservations, 800-452-5687.

TWENTY-FIVE MILE CREEK STATE PARK More remote than Lake Chelan State Park but popular with those more interested in mountain scenery than body scenery, it is quiet, with the Chelan Mountains behind and the jagged peaks of the Sawtooth Wilderness across the lake. The small beach is mostly for wading, though boaters fish in the lake. Open April through September only. Facilities include picnic areas, restrooms, showers and moorage at the marina; concession offers snacks, groceries and fishing supplies. ~ Located 20 miles up-lake from Chelan on Route 971; 509-687-3610.

There are 61 tent sites and 19 RV hookups; $11 to $16 per night. Reservations, 800-452-5687.

LINCOLN ROCK STATE PARK Named for a rock outcropping that resembles Abraham Lincoln's profile, this is a heavily used state park in the Columbia River canyon a short distance north of Wenatchee. There is swimming, fishing and boating and several species of wildlife residing in the park, including marmots, rabbits, beaver, nighthawks and swallows. There are picnic shelters, restrooms, showers, volleyball courts, a playfield and play equipment for children. ~ Located six miles north of East Wenatchee on Route 97/2; 509-884-8702.

▲ There are 27 tent sites and 67 RV hookup sites, 35 of which have full hookups; $11 to $16 per night. Reservations, 800-452-5687.

Wenatchee Area

Famous for its apple orchards, the sunny Wenatchee Area is located in the heart of Washington. Popular with rafters and gold panners, this region is also home to one of the state's most picturesque gardens.

SIGHTS

You have a choice of two highways when leaving Chelan: You can continue along Route 97, which cuts through the Cascade foothills back to the Columbia River and south to Wenatchee, or cross the Columbia at Chelan Falls, hardly more than a junction, and follow the lesser-used Route 151 south through the orchard town of Orondo to East Wenatchee. Stop at **Rocky Reach Dam** to visit the Fish Viewing Room where healthy numbers of migratory salmon and steelhead swim past the windows. The dam also has two museums, one showing the natural and human history of the Columbia River, complete with a handcarved American Indian canoe, parts of steamboats and orchard equipment. The Gallery of Electricity also has hands-on exhibits that let you create electricity. ~ Located 28 miles south of Chelan; 509-663-7522.

Wenatchee is the largest town in this region and directed more toward orchards than tourists, although you will certainly feel welcome. On the northern edge of town, overlooking the Columbia River, Wenatchee and Rocky Reach Dam, is **Ohme Gardens**. You'll find nine acres of alpine gardens built by an orchardist on the steep, rocky outcroppings at the edge of his property overlooking the Columbia River. Admission. ~ 3327 Ohme Road, Wenatchee; 509-662-5785.

Downtown, the **North Central Washington Museum** has several permanent exhibits including a 1919 Wurlitzer theater pipe organ and an apple-packing shed featuring an apple wiper, sizing machine and a 1924 orchard truck. In the gift shop area is an original WPA mural by Peggy Strong depicting the change of the postal service from its pioneer days to a modern, organized unit. Admission. ~ 127 South Mission Street, Wenatchee; 509-664-3340.

On the western edge of town is the **Washington Apple Commission Visitor Center**, which has an interpretive center offering apple tasting; samples are given of the different varieties of apples that are in season. The gift shop sells sweatshirts and other items with the commission message. Closed weekends from Christmas through May. ~ 2900 Euclid Avenue, Wenatchee; 509-663-9600.

Ten miles west via Routes 2 and 97, **Cashmere**, so-named because it reminded a pioneer of Kashmir, India, has an Early American theme to its downtown buildings. The **Chelan County Historical Museum and Pioneer Village** has more than two dozen original buildings from Chelan and Douglas counties assembled to re-create a pioneer village, including a blacksmith shop, school, gold mine and hotel. Closed Monday and November through March. ~ 600 Cottage Avenue, Cashmere; 509-782-3230.

From Cashmere, Routes 2 and 97 follow the swift Wenatchee River into the Cascades. Shortly before reaching Leavenworth, Route 97 turns south toward the Route 90 Corridor towns of Cle Elum and Ellensburg by going over 4101-foot **Swauk Pass**. An alternative route, in the summer only, is to follow the **Old Blewett Pass Highway**, which has been preserved by the Wenatchee National Forest. The old highway is a series of switchbacks with sweeping views of the Cascades. No services are available until you reach Cle Elum and Ellensburg, other than a small grocery store at **Liberty**, a gold-mining town just off the highway that is making a comeback as people move into its modest cabins along a single street.

Most hotels in Wenatchee are along North Wenatchee Avenue. The largest hotel in this part of the state is the **WestCoast Wenatchee Center**, at nine stories one of the tallest buildings along the eastern edge of the Cascades. The 147 rooms are larger than at most other hotels in town and suites have double sofas and potted plants. A large lobby has a baby grand piano. There is a restaurant, an indoor-outdoor pool and a fitness center. ~ 201 North Wenatchee Avenue, Wenatchee; 509-662-1234, 800-426-0670, fax 509-662-0782. DELUXE TO ULTRA-DELUXE.

LODGING

For a low-priced place, try the **Orchard Inn**. It has 103 rooms on three floors decorated with subtly flowered bedspreads, unobtrusive furniture and wallhangings. There is a heated pool and hot tub. ~ 1401 North Miller Street, Wenatchee; 509-662-3443, 800-368-4571, fax 509-662-3443 ext. 150. MODERATE.

If you want to be close to Routes 2 and 97, the best place is across the Columbia River in the **Rivers Inn**. With 55 units on two floors that surround the heated pool and hot tub, it is unpretentious but has basic, comfortable rooms with cable television, and there's always coffee in the office (after 7 a.m. free rolls are available). ~ 580 Valley Mall Parkway, East Wenatchee; 509-884-1474, 800-922-3199, fax 509-884-9179. MODERATE.

The **Cashmere Country Inn** is putting the town of Cashmere on the map. Owners Dale and Patti Swanson are unofficial ambassadors for this town, having remodeled an old farmhouse into a five-bedroom inn that follows an early French country style. All rooms have private baths. An area has been set aside for guests' lounging. Or relax in the hot tub or solar-heated pool. Breakfasts are imaginative with several kinds of fruit, crêpes, pastries and a main entrée. ~ 5801 Pioneer Avenue, Cashmere; 509-782-4212, 800-291-9144. MODERATE.

More impersonal is the **Village Inn Motel** in the heart of town. The white-and-green motel has 21 units, six with refrigerators. Clean, quiet and reasonably priced. ~ 229 Cottage Avenue, Cashmere; 509-782-3522, fax 509-782-2619. BUDGET TO MODERATE.

DINING

Want Italian? Try **Viscounti's Italian Restaurant.** Both Southern and Northern Italian dishes are offered in a family-friendly atmosphere. Their new wood-fired oven is used to "broil-roast" seafood and prime cuts of meat. ~ 1737 North Wenatchee Avenue, Wenatchee; 509-662-5013. MODERATE TO DELUXE.

A top-notch steakhouse is **The Windmill**. It is down to earth, with waitresses who have been there for years. A blackboard keeps a running total of the number of steaks sold there since 1982, when the present owners took over. Châteaubriand and lobster are now offered, in addition to a wide selection of seafood dishes. Fresh-baked pies round out the meals. ~ 1501 North Wenatchee Avenue, Wenatchee; 509-665-9529. MODERATE TO DELUXE.

One of Wenatchee's apple-pioneer homes has become a popular restaurant. The owners of the **John Horan's Steak and Seafood House** have turned three upstairs bedrooms into rooms for private parties, and the downstairs dining room has a fireplace that is welcome on chilly evenings. The menu boasts a large selection of seafood, steak, chicken, pasta and lamb dishes. Save room for the homemade desserts. ~ 2 Horan Road, Wenatchee; 509-663-0018. MODERATE TO DELUXE.

As a reflection of Central Washington's growing Hispanic population, **Tequila's** is owned by former residents of Mexico. The refried beans are homemade, and the salsa is as tangy as you'd

---

✔ CHECK THESE OUT—UNIQUE DINING

- *Budget:* Bring the kids to **The Gingerbread Factory** in Leavenworth for cookies, pastries and gingerbread houses. *page 207*
- *Moderate:* Embark on a dining adventure if not an outdoor one at **Adventures Restaurant**, where the Caribbean jerk-spiced chicken salad will surely electrify your tastebuds. *page 220*
- *Deluxe:* Relish the plunging views of Winthrop and Methow Valley from the **Sun Mountain Lodge Dining Room** before sitting down to a creatively prepared meal. *page 199*
- *Ultra-deluxe:* Prepare for a stunning culinary treat at **The Herbfarm**, where dinner starts with a tour of the gardens. *page 213*

Budget: under $8   Moderate: $8–$16   Deluxe: $16–$24   Ultra-deluxe: over $24

get in Guadalajara. ~ 800 North Wenatchee Avenue, Wenatchee; 509-662-7239. BUDGET TO MODERATE.

A wide range of Washington souvenirs and products, everything **SHOPPING** from jam to table linens, can be found at **Pack-it-Right**. ~ 517 South Wenatchee Avenue, Wenatchee; 509-663-1072.

Victorian Village is a small mall constructed in the best of the Victorian Carpenter Gothic style—round towers, falsefronts and steeples. You will find fabrics, antiques and, interestingly for a Victorian theme, a Mexican restaurant. ~ 611 South Mission Street; Wenatchee. If you need a fix for an urban-size mall, the **Valley Mall** has 47 stores, making it the largest shopping center you'll encounter in the shadow of the Cascades. ~ 511 Valley Mall Parkway, East Wenatchee.

Nearby Cashmere is the place to shop for a wide range of apple-based food products and gifts. Especially tempting is **Liberty Orchards**, which has been making fruit gelatin confections since 1920. Known for their Aplets and Cotlets, fruit-and-nut concoctions sprinkled with powdered sugar, Liberty Orchards also sells a wide variety of apple-themed gifts. Tours of the candy-making process are offered on weekdays. ~ 117 Mission Street, Cashmere; 509-782-2191.

It seems simple enough, the combination of apple and cherry juices. Why **Woodring Orchards'** preparation is better than almost any other fruit juice you can buy is hard to explain, but it's definitely worth a stop when you're in the area. You can also tour the orchards, buy fresh fruit in season, and take home gift packs of preserves, jams, butters and other fruit preparations from the gift shop. ~ 5420 Woodring Canyon Road, Cashmere; 509-782-2178.

◄ *HIDDEN*

Although Wenatchee is the largest town in the Cascades, it doesn't **NIGHTLIFE** have a wider choice than its smaller neighbors. The Chieftain's **Pow Wow Room** is a sports bar offering pull-tab machines Monday through Saturday. ~ 1005 North Wenatchee Avenue, Wenatchee; 509-663-8141.

WENATCHEE NATIONAL FOREST 🚶🚴🐎🎿⛷🏔🏊🎣🚣 ⛵🛶🚤🛥 At 2.1 million acres, Wenatchee is one of the largest national forests in the United States. It encompasses seven wilderness areas, hundreds of lakes, downhill-ski areas and 2500 miles of trails for hiking, riding and biking (including the Pacific Crest National Scenic Trail). Salmon, steelhead, searun cutthroat trout, Dolly Varden, bass, crappie, walleye and sturgeon are among the fish found in streams and lakes. There are picnic areas and restrooms; restaurants and groceries are in towns nearby. ~ The forest is crossed by Routes 12, 97/2 and 90; 509-662-4335.

PARKS

▲ There are more than 60 campgrounds; RVs accommodated in some campgrounds (no hookups); prices range from free to $10. Most campgrounds do not take reservations; the six that do can be reached at 800-280-2267.

▼▼▼▼▼▼▼▼▼▼▼▼▼▼
Leavenworth Area

Think Bavarian! If you like cuckoo clocks, fancy woodwork, beer steins and alpenhorns, you'll love making a stop in Leavenworth.

SIGHTS   One of the major tourist spots in the Cascades, **Leavenworth** welcomes visitors with oompah bands, specialty stores and impressive alpine scenery. Almost everything here—architecture, hotels, restaurants, annual events—is centered around the Bavarian theme. Mountains are on three sides, and a river rushes through town. During most of the summer, free concerts and dancing exhibitions are given in the City Park, and outdoor art exhibits are held on weekends.

Just west of Leavenworth, Route 2 enters **Tumwater Canyon**, which follows the Wenatchee River some 20 miles. It is marked by sheer canyon walls, plunging river rapids and deciduous trees along the riverbank that turn into brilliant colors in autumn.

Route 2 continues over **Stevens Pass**, a popular ski area and where the **Pacific Crest National Scenic Trail** (see "Hiking" below) crosses the highway. Soon after crossing the summit and passing Skykomish, the **Skykomish River** parallels the highway. This is one of Western Washington's most popular whitewater rivers. Most trips originate in the small alpine village of **Index**, a short distance off the highway. The sheer-faced, 5979-foot **Mt. Index** looms behind the town. From there, the river rumbles down past the small towns of Gold Bar and Sultan, then flattens out onto the Puget Sound lowlands.

LODGING   One of the most pleasant spots in Leavenworth is the **Pension Anna**. It has 15 rooms with furniture and decor imported from Austria and has been decorated in the theme of a farmhouse. Heavy, wooden bed frames and cupboards are used throughout, along with feather beds and down comforters. Three suites come with fireplace and jacuzzi, and all rooms have private baths. Breakfast is included. ~ 926 Commercial Street, Leavenworth; 509-548-6273, 800-509-2662, fax 509-548-4656. MODERATE TO ULTRA-DELUXE.

A Bavarian wood carver was imported to fashion the rails and ceiling beams of the **Enzian Inn**, and the entire 104-room motel with its turret and chalet-styled roofs shows similar touches. The seven suites have king-size beds, spas and fireplaces. It has indoor and outdoor pools and hot tubs. During the winter, free cross-country ski equipment is available to guests. The complimentary buffet breakfast is served in the big solarium on the fourth floor. ~ 590 Route 2, Leavenworth; phone/fax 509-548-5269, 800-223-8511. MODERATE TO ULTRA-DELUXE.

For a change of pace, try renting one of the townhouses at the **Linderhof Motor Inn**, next door to the Enzian Inn. The ten townhouses are divided into one- and two-bedroom units that sleep six and eight respectively. They have cathedral ceilings with balcony bedrooms and full kitchens with all appliances. There are 22 additional units, some with fireplaces and spas, all with handcrafted furniture. There is an outdoor pool and hot tub. Continental breakfast is included. ~ 690 Route 2, Leavenworth; 509-548-5283, 800-828-5680. MODERATE TO DELUXE.

More and more bed and breakfasts and inns are opening outside town. One is **Run of the River**, a mile east of Icicle River from Route 2. The building is made of logs and has cathedral ceilings with pine walls and handmade log furniture. The six rooms come with private baths and cable television. Three of the rooms have woodstoves and three have jacuzzis. Stay here, kick back and just contemplate the beautiful setting. There are complimentary mountain bikes for exploring the many surrounding trails and backroads. Breakfasts are country-style. (For the health-conscious, this inn is for nonsmokers only.) ~ 9308 East Leavenworth Road, Leavenworth; 509-548-7171, 800-288-6491, fax 509-548-7547. DELUXE TO ULTRA-DELUXE.

Located in a wooded setting on the banks of the Wenatchee River, the **All Seasons River Inn** offers spacious rooms and suites, all with private decks overlooking the river and some with fireplaces and jacuzzis. The inn provides full breakfasts and bicycles for touring the nearby Icicle Loop. ~ 8751 Icicle Road, Leavenworth; 509-548-1425, 800-254-0555. DELUXE TO ULTRA-DELUXE.

Farther down the mountain you'll find the **Dutch Cup Motel**, which is popular with skiers. The two-story motel has 21 units with queen-size beds and cable television. ~ 918 Main Street, Sultan; 360-793-2215, 800-844-0488, fax 360-793-2216. MODERATE.

DINING

Lorraine's Edel Haus offers an outdoor patio overlooking the Wenatchee River and an intimate dining room with candlelit tables, ceiling fans and Victorian furnishings. The menu offers an eclectic assortment of northwest dishes, ranging from grilled wild king salmon to buffalo sausage linguine. Dinner only. Closed Tuesday. ~ 320 9th Street, Leavenworth; 509-548-4412, 800-487-3335. MODERATE TO DELUXE.

The Gingerbread Factory is a delight for children and parents alike with all the cookies and gingerbread houses. The café sells pastries, salads, espresso and all sorts of gifts related to gingerbread. ~ 828 Commercial Street, Leavenworth; 509-548-6592. BUDGET.

The first place to eat after coming down off Stevens Pass is the **Sky Chalet**. Serving country breakfasts all day, this large restaurant has roomy booths with high backs as well as open tables. Lunch specials might be Swedish meatballs or chicken-fried steak. The dinner menu is unembellished—Swedish dishes, steaks, pork chops and chicken. ~ Route 2, Skykomish; 360-677-2223. BUDGET TO MODERATE.

In Index, the best place to eat is in the **Bush House Country Inn**. Here, in the century-old hotel dining room you will find a big, stone fireplace and gourmet country cuisine that uses very fresh meat, seafood, fish, fruits and vegetables. The Sunday breakfast is served until 3 p.m. and includes omelettes, homemade pastries and fresh fruit. ~ 300 5th Street, Index; 360-793-2312. MODERATE.

The Dutch Cup Restaurant is one of the most popular restaurants on the Stevens Pass route. It opens at 6 a.m. to catch the ski crowd as they head up the highway and stays open until 11 p.m. to get them on the way home. The home-cooking menu includes country breakfasts, burgers, soups and sandwiches for lunch, and offers steaks, prime rib and chicken and weekend specials for dinner. There is also a lounge. ~ 927 Main Street, Sultan; 360-793-1864. BUDGET TO MODERATE.

SHOPPING   Leavenworth has the best selection of specialty shops in the Cascades; about 100 are crammed into a two-block area. **A Different Drummer** sells international greeting cards, other paper supplies and children's books. ~ 725 Front Street, Leavenworth; 509-548-5320. Train buffs will love the **Train Store at Leavenworth** for its railroad memorabilia, which includes pen-and-ink drawings, pins and artwork. ~ 217 9th Street, Leavenworth; 509-548-7246. **Village Book** has a good selection of new and used regional titles. Their emphasis is on Northwest history, hiking and flyfishing. ~ 205 Commercial Street, Leavenworth; 509-548-5911.

NIGHTLIFE   Leavenworth has almost no nighttime entertainment; its movie theater collapsed beneath a heavy snowfall several years ago and has not been replaced, and only one place offers live music after dark. One such establishment is the **Leavenworth Brewery**. They have live rhythm-and-blues and jazz on Saturday throughout the year. ~ 636 Front Street, Leavenworth; 509-548-4545.

Leavenworth's major sports bar is the **Old Post Office Tavern**, which offers TVs, pool tables and karaoke on Friday and Saturday nights. ~ 213 9th Street, Leavenworth; 509-548-6573.

PARKS   **LAKE WENATCHEE STATE PARK** 🏃 🚴 🐎 ⛺ 🏕 🏞 🎣 🚤 ⛵
The lake is tucked away near Stevens Pass and is popular in summer for canoeing, kayaking, sailing, swimming

and fishing and in the winter for cross-country skiing and snow-mobiling. The secluded, wooded campsites are great. You'll find picnic areas, restrooms, showers and evening interpretive programs. ~ Eighteen miles north of Leavenworth and four miles off Route 2 on Route 207; 509-763-3101.

▲ There are 197 tent and RV sites (no hookups); $11 per night. Reservations, 800-452-5687.

▼▼▼▼▼▼▼▼▼▼▼▼▼
Route 90 Corridor

This pristine area remains one of America's scenic icons. From snow-capped peaks to dramatic waterfalls, the corridor is one of the Northwest's hidden treasures. It extends from Snoqualmie across the Cascades to Ellensburg and the Kittitas Valley. Fasten your seat belts for a breathtaking ride past volcanic peaks, fir forests and rivers where you're likely to land tonight's dinner.

SIGHTS

The Cascades begin rising only a half-hour's drive east of Seattle. The town of **Snoqualmie** has an ornate, old railroad depot that is home to the **Snoqualmie Valley Railroad,** which makes a ten-mile trip through the Snoqualmie Valley on weekends (April or May through October) and runs a special Christmas train. ~ 38625 Southeast King Street, Snoqualmie; 425-746-4025.

Nearby is **Snoqualmie Falls,** a thundering cataract with a small park, observation platform and trails leading to the river below the 268-foot falls.

The town of **North Bend** has adopted an alpine theme for its downtown buildings, but it hasn't caught on with the vigor of Winthrop and Leavenworth. Fans of the television show *Twin Peaks* will recognize Mt. Si, which looms behind town, from the show's opening credits.

An integral part of the show was the **Mar-T Café,** which served as the model for the *Twin Peaks* diner. The faux gas lamps, wood paneling and neon tubes that run across the ceiling create a fitting atmosphere in which to enjoy a cup of "damn good coffee" and their famous cherry pie. ~ 137 North Bend Way, North Bend; 425-888-1221.

The summit of **Snoqualmie Pass** has four major ski areas, for both downhill and cross-country, and a Forest Service combination museum and information center where you can pick up brochures and outdoor-recreation information. The small collection of artifacts relate to pioneers of the pass and antique ski equipment.

In **Cle Elum,** an American Indian name meaning "swift water," you will find the unusual **Cle Elum Historical Telephone Museum** where old telephones, switchboards and other equipment from the area are displayed. Open Friday to Sunday during the summer. ~ 221 East 1st Street, Cle Elum; 509-674-5702.

At the foot of 4th Street is the access point for the 25-mile-long **Iron Horse State Park**, a section of the former railroad right of way with the rails and ties removed and the roadbed smoothed over for walking, jogging and cross-country skiing. It is part of the **John Wayne Pioneer Trail** that will eventually run the width of the state.

Three miles away is the tiny town of **Roslyn**, used as the set for television's *Northern Exposure*. It was formerly a coal-mining town with a large population of Italian, Croatian and Austrian immigrants who worked in the mines. There are separate cemeteries —23 in fact—for these nationalities.

As you drive through the Kittitas Valley to Ellensburg, notice that the prevailing wind off the Cascades gives trees a permanent lean toward the east. When you reach Ellensburg, you're out of the Cascades and entering the arid climate that characterizes most of the eastern side of Washington. **Ellensburg** is perhaps best known for its rodeo each Labor Day weekend, and in keeping with the Western legacy, the Western Art Association has its headquarters there and holds an annual show and sale each fall.

The **Clymer Museum Gallery** displays work by the famous Western artist, who lived in Ellensburg. ~ 416 North Pearl Street, Ellensburg; 509-962-6416.

The **Kittitas County Historical Museum** displays American Indian artifacts and pioneer tools and has extensive rock and doll collections. Closed Sunday. ~ 114 East 3rd Avenue, Ellensburg; 509-925-3778.

Three miles east of town is the **Olmstead Place State Park**, a working farm that uses pioneer equipment. The 217-acre farm and all its buildings were deeded to the state. Weekend tours are offered from Memorial Day to Labor Day. ~ 921 North Ferguson Road, Ellensburg; 509-925-1943.

LODGING   *Twin Peaks* aficionados will recognize the **Salish Lodge at Snoqualmie Falls**. But it deserves better than the way it was shown in the spooky opening credits. The Salish perches on the cliff overlooking the spectacular falls, one of the more dramatic settings for a hotel and restaurant in the Northwest. The 91 rooms and suites are decorated in an upscale-country motif with down comforters, wicker furniture, woodburning fireplaces and jacuzzis. Only a few rooms have views of the falls, but the interiors are so well done that most visitors console themselves by watching the falls from the lounge or observation deck. There is also a full-service spa. ~ 6501 Railroad Avenue Southeast, Snoqualmie Falls; 425-888-2556, 800-826-6124, fax 425-888-2420. ULTRA-DELUXE.

A less pricey place to stay is the **Edgewick Inn**. It is a straightforward motel with 44 clean and quiet units three miles east of

Snow
Bound

It's all downhill from here: Yes, friends, we are going to take you skiing. Whether you are into slopes or cross-country, the best ski areas in Washington are stretched along the Cascades from Mt. Baker to Mt. Rainier.

Beginning at the northernmost ski area and working south toward the Columbia River, **Mt. Baker** is 56 miles east of Bellingham and has an elevation range from 3500 to 5040 feet. ~ Route 542; 360-734-6771. The state's only helicopter skiing is **North Cascade Heli-Skiing**, which operates out of Mazama. ~ 509-996-3272

Some skiers prefer **Stevens Pass**, located on Route 2 about 80 miles east of Everett, because at times it has more powdery snow than spots at the summit of Snoqualmie Pass. ~ 360-973-2441.

Probably the best powder snow at a large ski area is at **Mission Ridge**, 13 miles southwest of Wenatchee. ~ Mission Ridge Road, up Squilchuck Canyon; 509-663-6543; Snowline, 800-374-1693. But the largest operation of all is at Snoqualmie Pass 47 miles east of Seattle. Four major ski areas are to be found in a space of two miles: **Alpental, Ski Acres, Snoqualmie** and **Hyak**. For information on all areas, call 206-434-7669. The average summit elevation is 5400 feet and the average base is 3000 feet. For information on snow conditions, call 206-236-1600.

Way up in the sky is **Crystal Mountain**. Forty miles east of Enumclaw just off Route 410 and in the shadow of Mt. Rainier, the summit has an elevation of 7000 feet. Crystal has 32 major runs and 1000 acres of back country for cross-country skiing. ~ 360-663-2265. In the same general area, **White Pass** is 20 miles east of Packwood on Route 12 southeast of Mt. Rainier. ~ 509-453-8731.

Cross-country skiing is particularly popular on the eastern slopes of the mountains. Some of the best is in the Methow Valley where 90 miles of trails are marked, the majority of which are groomed. The **Methow Valley Sport Trail Association** has a hotline for ski-touring information (800-682-5787) and a brochure showing the major trails. ~ P.O. Box 147, Winthrop, WA 98862; 509-996-3287.

Echo Valley offers downhill and limited cross-country skiing. It is ten miles northwest of Chelan on a dirt road off Route 150 and has elevations of 3000 to 3500 feet. ~ 509-687-3167. The Leavenworth area maintains several ski trails, including the **Icicle River Trail** (5 miles), **Ski Hill** (3 miles) and **Leavenworth Golf Course** (6 miles). You can actually ski from your hotel in downtown Leavenworth to the golf course trails. ~ 509-548-5115.

town. ~ 14600 468th Avenue Southeast, North Bend; 425-888-9000, fax 425-888-9400. MODERATE.

About the only place to stay at Snoqualmie Summit is the **Best Western Summit Inn**. Outfitted for skiers, its 82 rooms come with king- or queen-size beds, and it has a complimentary ski-storage area and coin-operated laundry. The large lobby is large and is stocked with comfortable sofas and wing-back chairs set around the native-stone fireplace. ~ P.O. Box 163, Snoqualmie Pass, WA 99607; 206-434-6300, 800-557-7829, fax 206-434-6396. MODERATE TO ULTRA-DELUXE.

A former Milwaukee Railroad crew house and recognized in the National Historic Register, **The Moore House** has been converted into one of the state's best inns. The 12 rooms, half with shared baths, are named for former roomers. All are decorated in turn-of-the-century antiques—with an emphasis, not surprisingly, on railroad trinkets and tools. There are two remodeled cabooses sporting queen-size beds, refrigerators and sundecks with hot tub. The Moore House is adjacent to the Iron Horse State Park Trail, where cross-country skiing, bicycling, horseback riding and walking are popular. ~ 526 Marie Street, South Cle Elum; 509-674-5939, 800-228-9246. MODERATE TO DELUXE.

HIDDEN ▶ Although this is supposedly the state's oldest dude ranch, it is one of those places that keeps being "discovered." **Hidden Valley Guest Ranch** is eight miles from Cle Elum nestled at the edge of a broad valley and at the base of low mountains. In addition to the main building, where guests gather for trail rides, hikes and the community meals, the ranch has a total of 14 cabins and rooms that haven't had all the rustic removed, so don't expect sound- or cold-proofing. However, the fireplaces are great for taking off the chill as are the new heated pool and communal hot tub. All meals, and they are very large meals, are eaten in the buffet-style dining room. There are no telephones or TVs on this ranch; instead there is a sport court, horseback riding and 750 acres of nature to explore. Two-night minimum stay. ~ 3942 Hidden Valley Road, Cle Elum; 509-857-2322, 800-526-9269, fax 509-857-2130. MODERATE TO DELUXE.

For more impersonal lodgings, the **TimberLodge Inn**, on the western edge of town, has 35 bright, clean rooms far enough off the street to deaden the noise of the busy main drag. Amenities include an exercise room and hot tub. ~ 301 West 1st Street, Cle Elum; 509-674-5966, fax 509-674-2737. BUDGET TO MODERATE.

Murphy's Country Bed and Breakfast, four miles west of Ellensburg, has two rooms in a ranch home built in 1915. It has a broad porch made of local stone with views across the valley. The large rooms have antique furnishings, and share one-and-a-half baths. A full country breakfast is served. ~ 2830 Thorp Highway South, two miles from Exit 106 off Route 90, Ellensburg; 509-925-7986. MODERATE.

The **Salish Lodge at Snoqualmie Falls** offers spectacular views over the falls and canyon below, and the food is first rate. The menu leans toward what has become known as Northwest cuisine: lots of seafood, fresh fruits and vegetables, game, the largest wine list in the state and a dessert list almost as long. ~ 6501 Railroad Avenue Southeast, Snoqualmie Falls; 206-888-2556. DELUXE TO ULTRA-DELUXE.

DINING

Nearby in Fall City is **The Herbfarm**. What began as a roadside stand selling herbs has grown into one of the region's most unusual and successful restaurants. The menu changes constantly because it is built around seasonal herbs. Each meal takes at least three to four hours and begins with a tour of the herb gardens. Then during the meal the owners go from table to table discussing herbs with the patrons and explaining how they were used in the dishes. Reservations are strongly recommended. The Herbfarm is rebuilding after a devastating fire and plans to reopen in summer 1998. ~ 32804 Issaquah–Fall City Road, Fall City; 206-784-2222. ULTRA-DELUXE.

Cle Elum is better known for its inns and small hotels, but it has at least one good restaurant, **Mama Vallone's Steak House and Inn**. Tables are placed in most of the downstairs rooms, and you never have to wait for someone to replenish your water or bring more bread. A specialty is *bagna cauda*, a fondue-style mixture of olive oil, anchovy and garlic served with dipping strips of steak or seafood. ~ 302 West 1st Street, Cle Elum; 509-674-5174. MODERATE.

Pub Minglewood's owner John Herbert, from the Isle of Jersey, has a menu of salads, pasta and sandwiches for lunch, and steak, seafood, lamb, fish, chicken and light entrées for dinner. Closed Sunday. ~ 402 North Pearl Street, Ellensburg; 509-962-2260. MODERATE TO DELUXE.

A short walk away is the **Valley Café**. Food is American with a Northwest flair. Fish (frequently salmon) and chicken dominate the dinner menu. There is also lamb, steak and pasta on the menu. ~ 105 West 3rd Street, Ellensburg; 509-925-3050. MODERATE.

Hedges Cellars is a Yakima Valley winery that has opened a full-fledged tasting room on the West side of the Cascades; some aging is done here. Hedges is known for its reds, especially Cabernets and Merlots. ~ 195 Northeast Gilman Boulevard, Issaquah; 425-391-6056.

SHOPPING

Antique hunters will enjoy Ellensburg, which has at least half a dozen antique stores in a three-block area, including a mall.

Anchor in Time has antiques and rare books. ~ 310 North Main Street, Ellensburg; 509-925-7067. The **Showplace Antique Mall** is a restored art deco theater with up to 40 antique dealers displaying at a time. ~ 103 East 3rd Street, Ellensburg; 509-962-9331.

NIGHTLIFE   Cle Elum has almost nothing in nightlife other than taverns with jukeboxes, although occasionally **Moore House** guests will bring their own instruments for a sing-along. ~ 526 Marie Street, Cle Elum; 509-674-5939.

In Ellensburg between the rodeos there is little entertainment, but **The Mint Tavern** keeps 'em at the bar with beer and jukebox music. There's also a dancefloor and a deejay on weekends. ~ 111 West 3rd Street, Ellensburg; 509-962-5448. **Pounder's**, a bar and grill, occasionally has live or canned rock music on the weekend. ~ 315 North Main Street, Ellensburg; 509-962-4141.

PARKS   **LAKE EASTON STATE PARK**
On Route 5 and near Snoqualmie Pass, this lakeside park with forested trails is used as a base for skiers and snowmobilers in winter, as a lunch stop for travelers, and for hiking, swimming and fishing in the summer. The lake is stocked with trout. There are picnic areas, a swimming beach and restrooms. ~ Located on Route 90 a mile west of Easton; 509-656-2230.

▲ There are 91 tent sites and 45 RV hookups here plus two primitive walk-in-only sites; $11 to $16 per night. Reservations, 800-452-5687.

Mt. Rainier Area

It is always a dramatic moment when Mt. Rainier suddenly appears ahead of you (in the Northwest it is often called just The Mountain). You could spend weeks in this area and only sample a small portion of its recreational possibilities. Whether you approach from the east or the west, the forest gets thicker and thicker and the roadside rivers get swifter and swifter. The national park is almost surrounded with national forest wilderness areas as buffer zones against clear-cut logging. Located southeast of Seattle, this peak is the site of the aptly named town of Paradise.

SIGHTS   If you arrive via Route 706 you will have to go through Elbe, which has the **Mt. Rainier Scenic Railroad**, a steam-powered train that makes a 14-mile trip through the forest and across high bridges to Mineral Lake. It runs daily in the summer, on Saturday and Sunday in September and on special holidays. A four-hour dinner train is offered Friday through Sunday in the summer and on Saturday the rest of the year. ~ P.O. Box 921, Elbe, WA 98330; 360-569-2588, 888-783-2611, 888-773-4637 (dinner train only).

Once inside the park you may be almost overwhelmed by the scenery. **Mt. Rainier** is so monstrous (14,410 feet) that it makes everything around it seem trivial. **Mt. Rainier National Park** has numerous visitor centers and interpretive exhibits along winding roads.

In **Paradise**, head to the **Henry M. Jackson Visitor Center** (360-569-2211 ext. 2328), which has several exhibits and audio-visual shows. Paradise is one of the most beautiful places in the park, and the visitors center one of the busiest. It has a snack bar and gift shop. Open daily from May to October; open weekends and holidays only the rest of the year. The **Longmire Museum** (360-569-2211 ext. 3314) emphasizes the natural history of the park with rock, flora and fauna exhibits. It is also an information center for hikers, and next door at the National Park Inn you can rent cross-country skis or snowshoes. The **Ohanapecosh Visitor Center** (360-494-2229), down in the southeast corner near a grove of giant, ancient cedar trees, has history and nature exhibits. Closed mid-October through May. The **Sunrise Visitor Center** (360-663-2425) has geological displays and at 6400 feet is the closest you can drive to the peak. Numerous trails fan out from the center for day hikes but be aware that even into July, there is often snow on the trails. For park information, call the National Park Service (360-569-2211).

> Mt. Rainier is the tallest mountain in the Northwest and has more glaciers—26—than any other mountain in the conterminous 48 states.

Nearby, at the intersection of Routes 410 and 12 east of the mountain, you can watch elk and bighorn sheep being fed by game officials during the middle of winter at the **Oak Creek Wildlife Recreation Area**.

LODGING

Two inns are located inside Mt. Rainier National Park, and several other places to stay are found around the park in Ashford, Packwood, Elbe, Crystal Mountain, Morton and the White Pass area.

The most popular is **Paradise Inn**. Nineteen miles into the park, this inn has 117 rooms and a lobby that boasts exposed beams, peeled-log posts, wooden furniture, Indian-made rugs and two huge fireplaces. The views are grand, but the rooms are ordinary, and most of the bathrooms are museum pieces. Open May to October. ~ Paradise, WA 98398; 360-569-2275. MODERATE TO DELUXE.

The other in-park hotel is the **National Park Inn**, seven miles from the Nisqually entrance. Built in 1884, the inn offers much of the rustic charm of the Paradise Inn, yet is much smaller with only 25 rooms, half with private baths. Some rooms have views of the mountain. In keeping with the rustic theme, there are no telephones or televisions. The lobby has an enormous stone fireplace. ~ Longmire, WA 98397; 360-569-2275, fax 360-569-2770. MODERATE.

Equally popular with lovers of old inns is **Alexander's Country Inn**. This inn was built in 1912 as a small hotel designed to look like a manor with turret rooms and grand entrance hall. It retains the Old World look while adding modern conveniences such as a hot tub. Breakfast is included, as is champagne in the evening. ~ 37515 Route 706 East, Ashford; 360-569-2300, 800-654-7615, fax 360-569-2323. DELUXE.

In Packwood on the southern flank of the national park is the **Cowlitz River Lodge**. It is notable for clean, brightly decorated rooms and views of the mountains, although not "The Mountain." It is set back from the busy Route 12 far enough for the logging trucks to be a distant hum rather than an immediate roar. ~ 13069 Route 12, Packwood; 360-494-4444, 888-881-0379, fax 360-494-2075. MODERATE.

On the northeast boundary of the park is **Crystal Mountain Resort**, a year-round resort that is best known for its skiing. Visitors can choose from a number of places to stay, ranging from condominiums to inexpensive hotels, all of which are nonsmoking. Don't expect much charm because skiing, not hotel amenities, is the focus. Typical is **Silver Skis Chalet Condominiums**, which has a cluster of one- and two-bedroom units, some with fireplaces and views. All have kitchens and television and can sleep up to four persons. They are decorated in the traditional rental-condo manner of plastic furniture and durable fabrics. ~ Resort headquarters: P.O. Box 1, Crystal Mountain, WA 98022; 360-663-2558, fax 360-663-0145. ULTRA-DELUXE.

A bit farther east toward Yakima is the White Pass ski area with **The Village Inn Condominiums**. The complex has 50 rental units designed for large groups, up to eight in many units, and they have a bit of variation in decor since all are privately owned. Some have fireplaces and sleeping lofts, while all have full-kitchen facilities. ~ P.O. Box 3035, White Pass, WA 98937; 509-672-3131. ULTRA-DELUXE.

DINING

Good restaurants are hard to find around Mt. Rainier. Some of the best are:

Wild Berry Restaurant is a mile outside the park, and lunch items on the menu will be packed to-go on request. As the name suggests, it tends toward ferns and granola (the owners call it "mountain yuppie") but the food is imaginative: quiche, pizza and wild blackberry pie. ~ 37720 Route 706 East, Ashford; 360-569-2628. BUDGET TO MODERATE.

Casual family dining and great mountain views are staples of **Rainier Overland**, a cedar-sided restaurant in a forested setting. A beer garden is found out back. Good menu choices here are steaks, hamburgers, fresh grilled halibut and house-made soups and pies. The restaurant is open only during the summer; the saloon serves from a limited menu the rest of the year. ~ 31811 State Route 706, Ashford; 509-569-0851. BUDGET TO MODERATE.

Set on three wooded acres, which also include log cabin units and an RV park, the **Gateway Inn** offers a wood-paneled coffee shop–style restaurant serving breakfast, lunch and dinner. The standard road fare of burgers, steaks and omelettes is enhanced by such items as local trout and freshly baked breads and fruit pies. ~ 38820 State Route 706, Ashford; 360-569-2506. MODERATE.

One of the most popular restaurants between Mt. Rainier and Mt. St. Helens is **Peters Inn**, a large, old-fashioned place where they serve burgers, steaks, veal and some seafood and have a large salad bar. Pies and cinnamon rolls are made locally. ~ 13051 Route 12, Packwood; 360-494-4000. BUDGET TO MODERATE.

The **Whistlin' Jack Lodge** is a rustic, 50-year-old mountain lodge 20 miles east of Mt. Rainier National Park that offers a sophisticated level of dining unusual in these parts. Panfried rainbow trout boned tableside and a signature appetizer of crab-stuffed artichoke hearts served with garlic toast points are among the specialties. Prime rib, lobster and "bubbleberry" pie (a blend of apples, cherries, raspberries and huckleberries) round out the menu. Breakfasts are also exceptional, with items such as huckleberry coffee cake. The spacious dining area is set with white linen napery and features a huge fireplace fashioned from local river rock. Picture windows overlook the Naches River. ~ 20800 State Route 410, Naches; 509-658-2433, 800-827-2299. DELUXE TO ULTRA-DELUXE.

Nightlife is meager. Try **Crystal Mountain Resort**, which has an occasional small group of revelers in spite of skiers' notorious reputation for going to bed early. During the winter, live bands play on weekends and holidays. ~ Crystal Mountain; 360-663-2558.

NIGHTLIFE

MT. RAINIER NATIONAL PARK 🚶 🚴 🐎 🦌 🛶 The most heavily used national park in Washington, Mt. Rainier is everybody's favorite because the mountain can be approached from so many directions and the area around it is glorious no matter the time of year. The mountain is open for climbing for individuals or groups under the leadership of Rainier Mountaineering (mid-May to September: 360-569-2227; October to mid-May: 253-627-6242), a concessionaire. The park charges a climbing fee of $15 per person, per climb above 10,000 feet. Otherwise, you can hike the lower stretches of the mountain on your own for free. The lower elevations are notable for the vast meadows that are covered with wildflowers from late June until August and have

PARKS

dramatic fall colors in September and October. Numerous trails lead day hikers to viewpoints, and backpackers can explore the lower elevations on a first-come, first-serve permit system. It is open year-round with special areas set aside for wintersports at Paradise. Fishing is permitted without a state license. Check with a ranger for regulations. Facilities include picnic areas, restrooms, four information centers, museums and self-guided nature trails. ~ Entrances to the park are located on Route 165 on the northwest, Route 410 on the northeast, Route 706 on the southwest and Route 123 on the southeast; 360-569-2211.

▲ There are four car campgrounds, a few walk-in sites and overnight hike-in backcountry areas on a first-come, first-serve basis; RVs allowed (no hookups); $10 to $12 per night.

Mt. St. Helens Area

▼▼▼▼▼▼▼▼▼▼▼▼▼▼▼

There are few certitudes in travel writing, but here's one: Don't miss Mt. St. Helens. At the southern end of the Washington Cascades an hour north of Portland, this peak might best be described as a cross between a geology lesson and a bombing range. East of this landmark is Gifford Pinchot National Forest and Mt. Adams Wilderness, the heart of a popular recreation area ideal for rafting and fishing.

On May 18, 1980, Mt. St. Helens, dormant for 123 years, blew some 1300 feet off its top and killed 59 persons, causing one of the largest natural disasters in recorded North American history.

Today, access to the volcano remains limited because the blast and resulting mudslides and floods erased the roads that formerly entered the area.

SIGHTS

A major sightseeing destination, **Mt. St. Helens National Volcanic Visitor Center** (360-274-2100) is on Route 504 at Silver Lake, five miles east of Route 5. The center is elaborate and includes a walk-in model of the inside of the volcano. A 22-minute film on the eruption plays almost continuously, and an equally dramatic nine-minute slide show runs every 30 minutes. There is also the new **Coldwater Ridge Visitors Center** (360-274-2131), 38 miles farther east on Route 504. It is located near the area where the volcano erupted and offers guided walks. Good for three days, the admission fee allows you access to these two visitors centers and Johnston Ridge Observatory.

Windy Ridge is the closest you can get to the volcano, and it is reached by driving south from Randle on a series of Forest Service roads. Hourly talks are given by rangers in the amphitheater there. **Meta Lake Walk** is on the way to Windy Ridge, and rangers tell how people survived the blast. A 30-minute talk is given in **Ape Cave** on the southern end of the monument. It includes a walk into the 1900-year-old lava tube that got its name from a reputed confrontation between some miners and what they believed were the legendary, apelike creatures known as Sasquatches by Northwest Indians.

East of Mt. St. Helens, continue south through **Gifford Pinchot National Forest** on paved logging roads that are better maintained than many state or county roads. First, buy a copy of the national forest map at the visitors' center or from a ranger station. You can drive to the edge of **Indian Heaven Wilderness Area** and hike through peaceful meadows and acres of huckleberry bushes, or continue east to the edge of **Mt. Adams Wilderness** with views of that mountain reflected in lakes. Day and overnight permits are required to enter Mt. Adams Wilderness. This whole area is known for wild huckleberries, and there are two seasons for them; in the higher elevations they ripen in July and into August, then a week or two later the lower-elevation berries ripen. ~ For information, call the Ranger Station (509-395-2501).

During salmon runs, American Indians still fish with their traditional dip nets from the Fisher Hill Bridge near Klickitat.

The logging roads will eventually take you to **Trout Lake**, a small town close to a lake of the same name that reflects Mt. Adams in clear weather. Here you'll find all services and a Forest Service Ranger Station. Just west of town is a vast lava flow called the Big Lava Bed and a lava tube called Ice Cave, which is chilly all through the summer. Both are reached on Forest Service roads.

From Trout Lake, drive east 16 miles to the small cowboy town of **Glenwood**. There's not much more than a country tavern and post office to the town, but in the Shade Tree Inn tavern you can get directions to some of the more unusual sights in the area, such as a group of quartz crystals more than 200 feet in diameter and what is locally called "volcano pits," a series of small craters left behind by cinder cones.

◀ HIDDEN

From Glenwood, take the Glenwood-Goldendale Road to the junction with Route 142 and drive back southwest to Klickitat and the Columbia Gorge at Lyle. This takes you through the deep, winding Klickitat River Canyon with views of the river, a steelheaders' favorite. Mt. Adams often frames the scene.

The **Seasons Motel**, about halfway between Mt. Rainier and Mt. St. Helens, has 50 rooms in a slate-blue, two-story, frame building at the intersection of Routes 12 and 7. All beds are queen-size, and the clean, odor-free rooms have flowered drapes and bedspreads. ~ 200 Westlake Avenue, Morton; 360-496-6835, fax 360-496-5127. MODERATE.

LODGING

Located 17 miles west of Morton in the tiny town of Salkum, **The Shepherd's Inn** is about an hour and a half away from both Mt. Rainier and Mt. St. Helens. Set on 40 acres of wooded land, guests can enjoy the region's natural beauty on any of the numer-

◀ HIDDEN

ous walking trails that web through the property. The inn's five rooms offer country Victorian furnishings and brass beds. If you have the urge to tickle the ivories, you may do so on the grand piano. There's also a jacuzzi. Full breakfast includes wild huckleberry crêpes. ~ 168 Autumn Heights Drive, Salkum; 360-985-2434, 800-985-2434. MODERATE.

The Farm Bed and Breakfast is situated on six acres in Trout Lake, the closest town to Mt. Adams. Two rooms decorated in antiques with cozy quilts are available in this three-story 1890 farmhouse. Surrounding the B&B are perennial gardens, a barn, sheep and a vegetable garden. Hosts Rosie and Dean Hostetter serve a full farm breakfast. ~ 400 Sunnyside Road, Trout Lake; 509-395-2488, fax 509-395-2127. MODERATE.

HIDDEN ►

Also on the southwestern edge of Mt. Adams is the outdoor-oriented **Flying L Ranch**. Originally a working ranch, since 1960 the Flying L has been a guest ranch but now without horses. Hiking is popular here as are photography and fishing in the nearby Klickitat River. Bikes are available free of charge to get around the mostly flat roads in the area. In the winter, cross-country skiing and snowshoeing access is nearby. The main lodge has six rooms, half with shared bath; a two-story guest house has five rooms with private baths, and three separate cabins sleep up to five. Full breakfast is provided and served in the cookhouse. The main lodge has a large common kitchen where guests can prepare their own lunches and dinners. ~ 25 Flying L Lane, Glenwood; 509-364-3488, 888-682-3267, fax 509-364-3634. MODERATE TO DELUXE.

DINING

The **Wheel Café** has long been a local fixture in downtown Morton, with its wood paneling and burgundy booths. Breakfast specialties include blueberry or strawberry pancakes, while dinner choices are a large salad bar, steaks, prime rib, burgers, fish and chips and house-made pies. There is also an adjoining bar area with dart boards, pool table and pull tabs. ~ 185 Main Street, Morton; 360-496-3240. BUDGET TO MODERATE.

Adventures Restaurant has a motif true to its name. A hang glider is suspended from the ceiling and the walls are adorned with photographs of skydiving, skiing and African safari scenes. Dining here is a gourmet adventure, with tasty menu choices that include fresh salmon poached in an herb-infused broth and a salad of Caribbean jerk-spiced chicken with house-made poppyseed dressing. ~ 200 Westlake Avenue, Morton; 360-496-6660. MODERATE.

In Trout Lake, the most popular place to eat is **Trout Lake Country Inn**. Fresh seafood (including grilled halibut with cream sauce), steaks, salads and homemade huckleberry pie top the menu. The inn's large hall runs dinner theater shows in the summer. Closed Monday and Tuesday. ~ 15 Guler Road, Trout Lake; 509-395-2894. MODERATE.

MT. ST. HELENS NATIONAL VOLCANIC MONUMENT 🚶 🚴 🐎 🏕

PARKS

The monument covers 110,000 acres and was created to preserve and interpret the area that was devastated by the eruption. Interpretive centers and overlooks show the destroyed Spirit Lake, vast mud flows and the forests that were flattened by the blast. Access to the east side of the monument is limited to a few Forest Service and county roads, most of which are closed in the winter. Guided tours are provided by several operators departing from Seattle, Olympia and Vancouver. Scenic flights in planes and helicopters operate out of area airports. Fishing is excellent for bass and trout in nearby Silver Lake and good for trout in lakes behind dams on the Lewis River, south of the monument. There are interpretive centers, picnic areas, scenic overlooks and self-guided nature walks; view points on the east side are closed during the winter; restaurants and groceries are available in nearby towns. ~ From the north, Forest Service roads branch off Route 12 at Randle. From the west, Route 504 from Route 5 leads five miles to the Mt. St. Helens National Volcanic Visitor Center on the shores of Silver Lake, and Route 503 leads up the Lewis River to the town of Cougar and the southern flank of the monument; 360-247-3900.

GIFFORD PINCHOT NATIONAL FOREST 🚶 🚴 🐎 🏕 ⛵ 🚤

This 1.3-million-acre forest covers most of the southern Cascades to the Columbia River, marked by the Mt. St. Helens National Monument on the west and Mt. Adams on the east. Enclosing seven wilderness areas, most of its forest roads have been paved and are used almost equally by logging trucks and recreationists. Of particular interest are the **Big Lava Beds**, 14 miles west of Trout Lake, where unusual formations of basalt are found, and the **Ice Cave**, six miles southwest of Trout Lake, a lava tube where ice remains until late summer. Rivers and frequently stocked lakes offer excellent fishing. Picking huckleberries is very popular in late summer. You'll find picnic areas and restrooms; restaurants and groceries are in nearby towns. ~ The easiest way to reach the forest is by Route 12 from the north. There is also access on smaller roads such as Route 14, State Route 503 off Route 5 at Woodland, and Route 504 off Route 5 at Castle Rock; 360-891-5000, fax 360-891-5245.

▲ There are over 50 campgrounds, a number of which allow reservations; $6 to $22 per night. For reservations call 800-280-2267.

▼▼▼▼▼▼▼▼▼▼▼▼▼▼
Outdoor Adventures

FISHING

Winter steelhead, Dolly Varden, rainbow trout, eastern brook trout, walleye, sturgeon, catfish, bass, perch and crappie all can be caught in the interior and along the flanks of the Cascade Range. Fishing is typically done from the banks or on private boats, but most resorts on lakes and rivers have boats and fishing tackle for rent.

The other Cascade rivers, such as the Methow, Wenatchee, Yakima, Snake and Klickitat, drain into the Columbia River. All have good trout, walleye and steelhead fishing. The Klickitat River has an excellent summer steelhead run as does the Columbia. As their numbers continue to dwindle, fewer and fewer salmon can be caught upstream from the Bonneville Lock and Dam, the first of 14 dams on the river.

NORTH CASCADES Several rivers in the area—Snohomish, Skykomish, Skagit and Sauk, for example—provide year-round catches, notably steelhead and all species of salmon except sockeye (it's not permitted to take this fish from rivers). **Washington Fishing Adventures** specializes in highly personalized fishing trips for a maximum of five people. Ken Elsea tries to help anglers both catch fish and sharpen their skills. His jet boat lets him take anglers onto sections of rivers inaccessible to boats with conventional motors. ~ Marysville; 360-653-5924.

RIVER RUNNING

"Mild to wild"—that's how one outfitter describes the range of whitewater-rafting experiences in the Cascades. From the easy Class I and II rapids on the Skagit, to the steady Class II and III staircase rapids on the Suiattle, to the Skykomish's Class IV and the Tieton's Class IV–plus rapids, whitewater-rafting trips are fun and popular throughout the Cascades. In the Wenatchee-Leavenworth area, the Wenatchee River, which has a relatively easy Class III rapid, makes a great trip for families with children. If you're nervous about whitewater rafting, a scenic float is the way to go. Depending on the river, outfitters generally operate April through October. From mid-December through January, the Skagit is the place for float trips to observe bald eagles, who migrate to the area to feed on salmon from the river.

NORTH CASCADES **Downstream River Runners** rafts the Skagit, Sauk and Suiattle rivers in the North Cascades region, as well as several others elsewhere in the state and in Oregon. They do one-day and multiple-day trips at all levels of difficulty. Daytrips can accommodate up to 150 people. Eagle-viewing trips are also offered. ~ Monroe; 360-805-9899, 800-234-4644.

WENATCHEE AREA Besides whitewater trips, **All Rivers** offers eagle-viewing and scenic floats (accompanied by a naturalist) and can arrange rafting trips for individuals using wheelchairs or with other special needs. Trips are one-day or overnight, on all classes of rivers. ~ Cashmere; 509-782-2254, 800-743-5628.

LEAVENWORTH AREA   **Alpine Adventures** concentrates its operation on rivers found within the Cascade Loop (the Route 2–Route 20 driving loop), including the Wenatchee, Methow and Skagit. They also run trips on the Tieton River in September. Alpine's trips range from scenic floats to all classes of rivers. ~ Cashmere; 509-782-7042, 800-926-7238.

Experienced guides at Leavenworth Outfitters lead whitewater rafting trips on the Class III Wenatchee River. There's hardly an outdoor activity the company can't arrange an excursion or provide gear for: canoeing, kayaking, mountain biking, hiking and cross-country skiing are among the activities they outfit. ~ 21312 Route 207, Leavenworth; 509-763-3733, 800-347-7934.

RIDING STABLES

Seen from atop a horse, the Cascades wilderness areas—deep mountain valleys, alpine meadows ablaze with wildflowers, heavily forested slopes and high peaks—take on new beauty. Winter weather limits horseback riding to the warmer months, from mid-April through October. Besides guided rides, some outfitters also schedule pack trips that last overnight or longer. Always call ahead to make arrangements.

NORTH CASCADES   For a two-and-one-half-hour "nose-to-tail" guided ride through a pine forest to Coon Lake, which is in the North Cascades Wilderness Park, contact **Cascade Corrals**. ~ Stehekin; 509-682-4677.

METHOW VALLEY   Guided rides at **Sun Mountain Lodge** are open to the public. The lodge's stable of 35 horses is one of the largest in the Cascades. The 90-minute ride is perfect for beginners; a four-hour trip through the aspen, pine and fir trees of the valley up to a lookout ridge is popular with more experienced riders. Specialty rides include dinner or breakfast trips. Reservations are a good idea. ~ Patterson Lake Road, Winthrop; 509-996-2211 ext. 735, 800-572-0493.

LEAVENWORTH AREA   At **Eagle Creek Ranch**, a guided ride into Wenatchee National Forest follows a trail through alpine

◆◆◆

✔ **CHECK THESE OUT—UNIQUE OUTDOOR ADVENTURES**

- Ski some of the 90 miles of cross-country trails (many of which are groomed) in the Methow Valley. *page 211*
  - Scale the Northwest's tallest mountain, Mt. Rainier, to elevations over 10,000 feet high. *page 217*
    - Shoot the rapids under skies filled with bald eagles and osprey on the Skagit River. *page 222*
      - Hike one of the most scenic stretches of the Pacific Crest National Scenic Trail between Stevens Pass and Snoqualmie Pass. *page 225*

meadows blooming with dozens of varieties of wildflowers before reaching a lookout peak for a spectacular view of the Cascades. The ranch also puts on western barbecues year-round and horsedrawn sleighrides in the winter. ~ 7951 Eagle Creek Road, Leavenworth; 509-548-7798, 800-221-7433.

SKIING

In the winter, the Cascades turn into a wonderland for all types of skiing—cross-country, downhill and snowboarding. Several locations have night skiing. See the sidebar "Snow Bound" for more information. ~ Recorded information about cross-country conditions, 206-632-2021; Forest Service's Avalanche Center, 206-526-6677.

GOLF

It seems that nearly every community in the foothills has a golf course. And the courses are as varied as the individual communities that host them.

NORTH CASCADES   In the foothills near Mt. Baker, the semi-private **Peaceful Valley Country Club**, which once was pastureland, is a nice walking course without any water hazards. The nine-hole course is open year-round, weather permitting. ~ 8225 Kendall Road, Maple Falls; 360-599-2416.

METHOW VALLEY   Along the eastern slopes of the North Cascades, in the Methow Valley, the public **Lake Chelan Golf Course** is a fairly challenging 18-hole course, with small elevated greens and a tenth-hole canyon to hit over. The course is open March through November, weather permitting. ~ 1501 Golf Course Drive, Chelan; 509-682-8026, 800-246-5361.

WENATCHEE AREA   **Three Lakes Golf Course** is a pretty tough par 69, set on rolling terrain with plenty of water hazards. Weather permitting, it's open year-round. ~ 2695 Golf Drive; 509-663-5448.

LEAVENWORTH AREA   The Wenatchee River flows through the **Leavenworth Golf Club**, a semiprivate golf course that is closed to the public for a few hours each week. But the course's spectacular mountain valley setting makes it worth the effort to get a tee time at this short, tight 18-hole course. The club is open April through October. ~ 9101 Icicle Road; 509-548-7267.

ROUTE 90 CORRIDOR   Although it's relatively flat, **Cascade Golf Club**, with its good drainage, is probably the best winter course in the area. The nine-hole course has three sets of tees and easy access from Route 90, Exit 32. ~ 14303 436th Avenue Southeast, North Bend; 206-888-0227.

BIKING

For the most part, bicycling in the Cascades is not for the faint of heart or inexperienced. Besides that, unless you bring your own bike, it's hard to find bikes to rent. One exception is the Leavenworth area, where a relatively easy seven-mile loop will take you along the river and through town. You can pick up a free map at the **Leavenworth Chamber of Commerce**. ~ 894 Route 2; 509-548-5807.

Bike Rentals You can rent mountain bikes by the hour or the day at **Leavenworth Ski & Sports Center**, located in the Icicle Junction Family Fun Center. ~ Corner of Route 2 and Icicle Road.

Leavenworth Outfitters rents mountain bikes and offers guided tours. They can also arrange to shuttle you and your rental up into the Cascades for a downhill cruise back into town. ~ 21312 Route 207, Leavenworth; 509-763-3733, 800-347-7934.

The Cascades are a backpacker's paradise laced with thousands of miles of maintained trails. All distances listed for hiking trails are one way unless otherwise noted.

HIKING

NORTH CASCADES The **Pacific Crest National Scenic Trail** (480 miles) has its northern terminus in Washington. It is a hard hike in many places but can be broken into easier chunks, such as from Stevens Pass to Snoqualmie Pass. Contact the Outdoor Recreation Information Center in Seattle for further details. ~ 206-470-4060.

The **Heliotrope Ridge Trail** (2 miles) leads to a precipice where you can look down on Coleman Glacier. This popular hike is accessed on Road 39 at Heliotrope Ridge, just east of the town of Glacier. Purchase a one-day trail parking pass before parking at the trailhead. Contact the visitors center (360-856-5700) for more information.

In the Baker Lake area, try the hike up Desolation Peak on the **East Bank Trail** (9 miles) to the lookout tower where the Beat Generation writer Jack Kerouac spent a summer. The views of the surrounding mountains and Ross Lake are spectacular.

Perhaps the most historic route in the North Cascades is **Cascade Pass Trail** (3.5 miles), the American Indians' route across the mountains for centuries. It is also a route from Marblemount to Stehekin (9 miles), if you want to really make a trip of it.

All along **Route 20** are signs denoting trailheads, and all are worth exploring. They tell the destination of the trail and the distance.

For a long trip—allow three or four days—**Image Lake** (16 miles) is considered one of the most beautiful in the Central Cascades. The lake mirrors Glacier Peak, the most remote and inaccessible of the Washington volcanoes.

METHOW VALLEY **Goat Peak Trail** (2.5 miles) leads to a 7100-foot summit that has a staffed lookout tower. The fairly steep trail starts from a Forest Service road near Mazama; it is hikeable only from July through September. Contact the Methow Valley Visitors Center (509-996-4000) for information.

LEAVENWORTH AREA **Icicle Gorge Trail** (3.5 miles roundtrip) is an interpretive loop trail a short distance west of Leavenworth.

Enchantment Lakes (18 miles) is Washington's most beloved backpacking trip because the lakes are so otherworldly. They are approached from Icicle Creek near Leavenworth. The hike is a hard one, and permits must be obtained through the Leavenworth Ranger Station (509-782-1413).

ROUTE 90 CORRIDOR **Iron Horse Trail State Park** (113 miles) is a former railroad right-of-way that is used by hikers, horse riders, cross-country skiers and bicyclists. No motorized vehicles are allowed on the trail, which goes from North Bend over Snoqualmie Pass to Vantage.

MT. RAINIER AREA For information on trails around the mountain, call 360-569-2211 ext. 3317. **Naches Wagon Trail** (10 miles), west of Yakima, is a good historical hike because this was one route pioneers used on their way to Puget Sound. They left behind blazed trees and other evidence of crude road building. Call 360-825-6585 for information.

Wonderland Trail (93 miles) goes entirely around Mt. Rainier and can be made in stages ranging from the 6.5-mile section between Longmire and Paradise to the 39-mile section from Carbon River to Longmire.

Northern Loop Trail (34 miles roundtrip) runs through the wilderness with frequent views of the mountain between Carbon River and Sunrise.

MT. ST. HELENS AREA **Klickitat Trail** (17 miles) runs through a remote part of the Gifford Pinchot National Forest and is believed to be part of an old American Indian trail network. For information contact the Randle Ranger Station, one mile east of Randle on Route 12, 360-497-1100.

Conboy Lake National Wildlife Refuge Trail (3 miles) wends through the refuge just south of Glenwood with interpretive signs showing you nesting sites, migratory patterns and discussions on the ecology of the lava and desert area.

Indian Heaven (3.3 miles) is a beautiful section of the Pacific Crest National Scenic Trail that people return to again and again. It is near Trout Lake and goes past numerous lakes reflecting the surrounding mountains.

▼▼▼▼▼▼▼▼▼▼▼

Transportation

CAR

Route 542 travels east from Bellingham through Glacier to dead-end at Mt. Baker Lodge. **Route 20**, also known as the North Cascades Highway, is one of the state's most popular highways and goes east from Route 5 at Burlington to the Methow Valley. **Route 2**, one of the last intercontinental, two-lane, blacktop highways, runs from Everett to Maine and is called the Stevens Pass Highway in Washington. From Seattle, **Route 90** goes over Snoqualmie Pass to Cle Elum and Ellensburg.

Only one airport, **Pangborn Field** in Wenatchee, serves this large area, and only two carriers offer scheduled service: Horizon Air and United Express. The roadless Lake Chelan area is served by Chelan Airways, which makes scheduled and charter flights between Chelan and Stehekin.

The Lady of the Lake provides daily transportation between Chelan, Manson, Fields Point, Prince Creek, Lucerne, Moore and Stehekin. Reduced service from November through mid-March. ~ 1318 West Woodin Avenue, Chelan; 509-682-2224.

Greyhound Bus Lines (800-231-2222) offers service to Leavenworth and Wenatchee and a stop in Cashmere. ~ Wenatchee station: 300 South Columbia Street.

   Link Transit serves Ardenvoir, Cashmere, Chelan, Dryden, East Wenatchee, Entiat, Leavenworth, Malaga, Manson, Monitor, Orondo, Peshastin, Rock Island, Waterville and Wenatchee. ~ 509-662-1155.

Amtrak travels from Seattle, Portland and Spokane to Wenatchee via the "Empire Builder." ~ 800-872-7245.

At the Wenatchee airport are **Budget Rent A Car** (800-527-0700) and **Hertz Rent A Car** (800-654-3131). In Wenatchee is **U-Save Auto Rental** (800-972-2298). Ellensburg has **Budget Rent A Car** (800-527-0700).

SIX

East of the Cascades

If state boundaries were determined by similar geography, customs and attitude, Washington and Oregon as we know them would simply not exist. Instead, they'd be split into two more states using the crest of the Cascades as the dividing line or would run vertically from California on the south to Canada on the north with one state taking either side of the mountain range.

Well, who ever said life was perfect? So what we have are two states whose eastern and western halves bear almost no resemblance to each other. From the Cascades west, the land is damp, the forests thick and the climate temperate. The eastern side of the range is almost exactly the opposite: Very little rain falls and most crops are irrigated by water from the Columbia Basin Project created by Grand Coulee Dam, or by water from deep wells. Here, the winters are cold and the summers are hot.

Even the people are as different as east and west. While those in the western halves tend to be liberal and innovative, the eastern residents are more conservative and content with the status quo. And since we're in a status-quo frame of mind now, we take you through both Eastern Washington and Oregon in this chapter. Other chapters look at the western sides of the states. So buckle up!

In contrast, only bits and pieces of Eastern Oregon are irrigated because it has not been blessed with any large rivers other than the Snake. It remains mostly arid, the northern reaches of the Great American Desert that runs north from Mexico through Arizona, California and Nevada. It is land more suitable for cattle grazing than growing crops, although in some valleys ranchers have drilled wells or dammed small streams to enable them to irrigate meadows. This kind of open and sparsely populated countryside doesn't appeal to all travelers, so you tend to see more recreational vehicles and truck stops than hotels and restaurants.

If urban amenities such as hotels, finer restaurants, theater and shopping centers are what you're after, head to Washington's larger cities—Spokane, Walla Walla, the Tri-Cities and Yakima—and to Pendleton in Eastern Oregon. Elsewhere you'll find RV parks and inexpensive but clean motels. On the lakes and streams are rustic resorts, some with log cabins.

Away from the cities, hunting and fishing abound. Deer, elk and an occasional black bear are popular quarry, as are waterfowl, pheasant, grouse and quail. Don't be startled while driving along a mountain road during hunting season if you spot someone in camouflage clothing carrying a rifle emerge from the forest. In the high desert of Eastern Oregon you'll sometimes see antelope and wild horses, usually in the distance since they justifiably avoid human encounters. Many streams and lakes are stocked regularly with trout, and a few sturgeon are still caught in the Snake and Columbia rivers.

Some of the most interesting geology in North America can be found in this region due to its tortured creation by volcanoes, lava flows through vast fissures and floods gigantic beyond imagining. Throughout the two states' eastern sides you will find vivid reminders of this creation process. In Oregon it is shown by hundreds if not thousands of dead volcanoes and cinder cones, the lava flows that have not yet been covered by windblown soil, the brilliantly colored volcanic ash deposits, and sheer canyons whose basalt walls were created by these lava flows. In Washington it is the dramatic Coulee Country along the Columbia River and the beautiful Palouse Country with its steep, rolling hills.

The forests are mainly pine with very little underbrush. Along some parts of the eastern slope of the Cascades you will find larch, the only species of coniferous trees that are deciduous. They are brilliantly colored in the fall and stand out as vividly as sumac and maples in the dark green forest.

One stretch of landscape of unusual origin is the Channeled Scablands south and west of Spokane, which was created by floods from a lake formed at the end of the Ice Age in the valley around Missoula, Montana.

In Oregon you will find the painted hills of the John Day Fossil Beds National Monument, the dramatic canyons of the Owyhee River and the vast Alvord Desert, barren of vegetation and flat as an airport. In both states east of the mountains is another treasure: peace and quiet. There are lonesome roads undulating off into the distance, small rivers stocked with trout, open pine forests, vast lakes made by man, working cowboys and mornings so tranquil you can hear a door slam.

As is true elsewhere in America, the general rule is the smaller the town the friendlier the people, so don't be surprised if folks stop to talk about anything or nothing in particular. Also, nearly everything is less expensive than along the coast.

Traveling these remote areas you will have a continual sense of discovery as you visit places barely large enough to get themselves onto state maps. And you will find small towns that don't bother opening tourist bureaus but have a clean motel, a good café, friendly people to talk to and a small city park for your picnic.

Compared with the rest of the country, the Northwest's history is both recent and benign. The Northwest is so new that East Coast visitors look askance when they find that the major cities weren't founded until the latter part of the last century. Very little recorded history goes back before 1800; the Lewis and Clark Expedition of 1804–1806 was the first overland crossing between the original 13 states and the Pacific Coast, and they were the first to describe the lower Snake River.

While the Indian wars had less bloodshed than in other parts of the West, one campaign has become almost legendary for the skill with which the Nez Perce tribe eluded the white army, and for the "humane" manner in which the war was fought. This was the running battle of 1877, when Chief Joseph led his band of a few warriors and a lot of women, children and elderly people on a brilliant retreat from their ancestral home in the Wallowa Valley 1400 miles across Idaho and Montana, only to be captured a few miles south of their goal, the Canadian border.

A few remnants of the pioneer years still remain standing in Eastern Oregon and Washington. Here and there you'll see the remains of a cabin with the tall tripod of a windmill where a homesteader tried but failed to "prove up" the land given him by the Homestead Act. You'll also see remains of ghost towns (although some have been rediscovered and are peopled again). Most of these towns were built at or near mines and abandoned when the mines began coughing up only rocks and sand.

For your own exploration of this fascinating region, this chapter is divided into six sections:

The Okanogan Highlands, often called the Okanogan Country or simply the Okanogan, has boundaries that are fairly easy to determine: Route 97 to the west, the Canadian border to the north, the Columbia River on the east and the Colville Indian Reservation on the south.

Grand Coulee Area includes all the Columbia River system from where it swings west at the southern end of the Colville Indian Reservation and follows past Grand Coulee Dam south to the Vantage–Wanapum Dam area, where the Columbia enters the Hanford Nuclear Reservation.

The Spokane Area covers the only true metropolitan center east of the Cascades.

Southeastern Washington encompasses the famed Palouse Hills between Spokane and Pullman; the Snake River town of Clarkston; Walla Walla; the Tri-Cities of Pasco, Kennewick and Richland; and Yakima and the agricultural and wine-producing valley of the same name.

Northeastern Oregon covers the Pendleton and La Grande areas, the Blue Mountains, the beautiful Enterprise and Joseph area on the edge of the Eagle Cap Wilderness, and across the Wallowa Mountains to the few entrances to Hells Canyon on the Snake River. The centerpiece of this region is the Wallowas, a broad valley in the Enterprise and Joseph area where Wallowa Lake, one of the most beautiful in America, reflects the mountains of the Eagle Cap Wilderness.

Southeastern Oregon is the largest area covered and the least populated. It includes the cowboy country of the vast high desert that occupies most of the region, as well as the lava wasteland near La Pine and the multicolored John Day Fossil Beds National Monument.

▼▼▼▼▼▼▼▼▼▼▼▼▼▼▼▼

Okanogan Highlands

One of the pleasures of touring the Okanogan Country is simply driving down country roads to see where they lead. A number of ghost towns, some no more than a decaying log cabin today, dot the map.

Most visitors enter the Okanogan Country from Route 97, the
north–south corridor that runs up the Columbia River Valley to
Bridgeport, then follows the Okanogan River Valley north toward
Canada. This is desertlike country with irrigated orchards on either side of the highway and open range climbing back up the
mountains. First, contact the **Omak Visitor Information Center** for
brochures and maps. ~ 401 Omak Avenue, Omak; 509-826-1880.

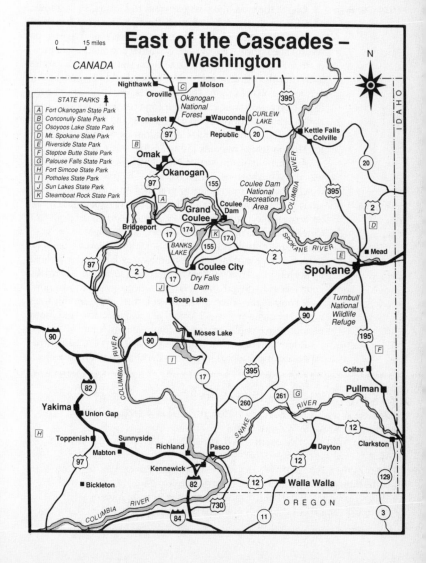

The **Okanogan County Historical Museum**, also headquarters for the county historical society, is on Okanogan's Main Street and has a collection of American Indian artifacts, pioneer farm and ranch implements and historical photos. This is also a good place to start your travels because members of the volunteer staff have lived in the region for many years and know where everything is, including skeletons in the county's closets. ~ 1410 2nd Street, Okanogan; 509-422-4272.

HIDDEN ► One of the most interesting drives is to **Molson**, a ghost town 12 miles northeast of Tonasket off Route 97 near the Canadian border; follow the highway signs in downtown Tonasket. Molson was founded when a nearby mine was attracting hundreds of prospectors and workers. Owing to a land-claim mix-up, a farmer took over the whole town, so a new one had to be built and it was named New Molson. The two towns, less than a mile apart, fought over everything except education for their children. They built a school halfway between the towns, and it became Center Molson. Today **Old Molson** is an outdoor museum, and the **Center Molson school building** (509-485-9921) is a museum.

Another popular drive is to **Nighthawk**, just west of Oroville, which was a ghost town until recently. The paved county road, which heads west from Route 97 near the Canadian border, curves along the Similkmeen River Valley, then swings south into a valley between the mountains of the Pasayten Wilderness of the North Cascades National Park and a series of steep ridges to the east. This area is dotted with old mines, some still worked from time to time, but most of the land along the valley floor and stretching up the hillsides a few hundred feet has been turned into orchards and vineyards. Nighthawk is far from being a ghost town now, as is **Loomis**, the other mining town farther south on this loop drive. The highway passes Palmer Lake and Spectacle Lake, both of which have public beaches, before rejoining Route 97.

Route 20 is one of Washington's best highways for leisurely rural driving, especially as it traverses the Okanogan Country on its

✔ **CHECK THESE OUT—UNIQUE SIGHTS**
- Marvel at one of America's most impressive public works projects, Washington's **Grand Coulee Dam**. *page 237*
- Join the residents of Spokane at **Riverfront Park**, the pride of the city that opened for the 1974 World's Fair. *page 242*
- Tour **Eastern Washington's vineyards**, which locals note are at the same latitude as France's top winegrowing regions. *page 248*
- Bring your camera and color film to capture the brilliant hues of Oregon's **John Day Fossil Beds National Monument**. *page 258*

way to the Idaho border. It comes in from the Cascades to Omak-Okanogan, joins Route 97 north to Tonasket, swings east across the heart of the highlands through Wauconda and Republic, crosses the Columbia River at Kettle Falls and continues on to Tiger, where it follows the Pend Oreille River south to the Idaho border at Newport. There it disappears. The highway follows the path of least resistance beside streams and along valleys where ranches stretch off across rolling hills that disappear in pine forests.

Heading east from Tonasket, the first notable town you'll come to is **Republic**. The **Stonerose Interpretive Center** lets visitors dig for fossils on a hillside on the edge of Republic. The site is named for an extinct rose fossil found there. The center is closed November through April. ~ Republic; 509-775-2295.

◄ HIDDEN

Continue eastward and you'll reach a historical site called **St. Paul's Mission** in **Kettle Falls** where Route 395 crosses the Columbia River. It was built as a chapel for American Indians in 1845 and operated until the 1870s. A modest museum is also here.

In **Colville**, three miles southeast of Kettle Falls, several buildings make up the **Keller Historical Park**. Sponsored by the Stevens County Historical Society, the complex has a museum, a fire lookout tower, Colville's first schoolhouse, a trapper's cabin and the home of the pioneer Keller family. ~ 700 North Wynne Street, Colville; 509-684-5968.

Surrounded by 178 acres of meadows, woods and orchards, **Amy's Manor** provides bed-and-breakfast lodging in a 1928 gray stucco home with green shutters. Three guest rooms upstairs provide river views and are adorned with queen-size beds. Small sitting areas are furnished with antiques from the home's original owner. Downstairs is a living area with a fireplace where breakfasts made with ingredients picked from the surrounding orchards and organic vegetable garden are served. ~ 435 Route 153, four-and-a-half miles north of Pateros; 509-923-2334, 888-923-2334, fax 509-923-2691. MODERATE.

LODGING

The most modern motel in Okanogan is the **Cedars Inn**. It has 78 rooms (including two suites and four rooms with kitchenettes), an unpretentious dining room and heated swimming pool. ~ Appleway Street and Route 97, Okanogan; 509-422-6431, fax 509-422-4214. MODERATE.

A cheaper Okanogan motel is the **Ponderosa Motor Lodge** downtown, an older but clean one-story motel of basic design with a pool. ~ 1034 South 2nd Avenue, Okanogan; 509-422-0400, 800-732-6702, fax 509-422-4206. BUDGET.

The **U and I Motel** has nine small "cabinettes" with rustic paneling; each unit has a kitchen. They come with deck chairs, so you can sit and look across a lawn and flower garden to the Okanogan River. ~ 838 2nd Avenue, Okanogan; 509-422-2920. BUDGET.

In Omak are several small, budget-priced motels including the **Thrift Lodge.** ~ 122 North Main Street, Omak; 509-826-0400, 800-578-7878, fax 509-826-5635. BUDGET. There's also the **Leisure Village Motel.** ~ 630 Okoma Drive, Omak; 509-826-4442, 800-427-4495. BUDGET.

Several small resorts are scattered along lakes in the area. Among them is the **Bonaparte Lake Resort.** This resort, 26 miles from both Republic and Tonasket, has ten airy and clean log cabins along the lake shore. Three bathrooms have bedding, towels and kitchen supplies. There are public showers and bathroom. ~ 695 Bonaparte Lake Road, Tonasket; 509-486-2828, fax 509-486-1987. BUDGET.

A mile east of Kettle Falls on Route 395 is **My Parent's Estate Bed and Breakfast**, one of the first bed and breakfasts in this part of the state. It formerly was a Catholic mission with a convent added later, then a boys' school. It offers three rooms with baths, queen-size beds and central air conditioning, plus a suite with a kitchenette. Each room is named for its period decor and furnishings: Queen Anne Lace, English Cottage and French Country. Included on the 47 acres are a gazebo, gymnasium, pond and a trail to the Colville River. ~ 719 Route 395, Kettle Falls; 509-738-6220. MODERATE TO DELUXE.

DINING

Basic, standard fare is pretty much the order of the day here. For starters, there is the **Cedars Inn Restaurant and Lounge**, which serves adequate, straightforward lunches and dinners and farmer-sized breakfasts. ~ Appleway Street and Route 97, Okanogan; 509-422-6431. MODERATE.

For some local color and reasonable prices, try the **Double J**. This is a place where you can have an old-fashioned breakfast and lunch—complete with homemade soups and famous burgers —while listening to the auctioneer selling horses and cattle. ~ Okanogan Livestock Market, Okanogan; 509-422-3660. BUDGET.

The choices are fewer in Omak, but one café and bakery that rates high is the antique-decorated **Breadline Café**, where lunch features big sandwiches on whole-grain breads and dinner includes shrimp Creole, jambalaya, mushroom marinara over pasta and pork loin medallion. ~ 102 South Ash Street, Omak; 509-826-5836. MODERATE.

Omak's **North Country Pub** serves nothing fancy—burgers, steaks, tacos and barbecue—but it's solid, filling food. The lunch specials are usually pretty good, and if you're there on a Thursday night, the steak special is a bargain. ~ 15 South Main, Omak; 509-826-4271. BUDGET TO MODERATE

One of the few deluxe dining choices in the region is provided by **Hidden Hills Resort**. The contemporary hotel has created a dining room built to resemble an 1890s mansion. The large room overlooks a mountain range and is handsomely decorated with oak furnishings, Oriental rugs and fringed lamps. The menu offers just one multicourse dinner selection that changes nightly. Roast turkey, steaks or steak and seafood combinations are among the possibilities. ~ 144 Fish Lake Road, Tonasket; 509-486-1895. DELUXE.

Created by a gold rush in the late 1890s, the town of Republic still hosts operative gold mines, such as the Echo Bay mine a short distance outside town.

One of the more interesting places to stop for a snack or down-home American meal is **Wauconda**, the one-store town on Route 20 east of Tonasket. A lunch counter to the left of the door is crammed between the cash register and a smaller dining room with a few booths overlooking a valley and low mountains beyond. The food is uncomplicated and hearty, and the portions are generous, especially the prime rib that is the house special on Friday and Saturday. ~ 2360 Route 20, Wauconda; 509-486-4010. BUDGET TO MODERATE.

Omak's Main Street provides a few good browsing spots such as **Mustard Seed Gallery & Gifts**, which features artwork by local artists, crafts and collectibles. ~ 21 North Main Street, Omak; 509-826-2463. In the same block is **Lampe Jewelers**, known for custom-made gold and silver jewelry. ~ 26 North Main Street, Omak; 509-826-1280.

SHOPPING

Western wear of all kinds plus handcrafted silver jewelry, Pendleton blankets and saddles are stock and trade at the **Triangle L Western Store**, a few miles north of Omak in Riverside. ~ Main Street, Riverside; 509-826-2200.

You don't have many retail options in the small town of Oroville. However, **Prince's Center** may be all you need (or find). Half of Prince's is devoted to groceries; the other side carries general merchandise—everything from footwear and apparel to toys and garden tools. ~ 1000 23rd Avenue, Oroville; 509-476-3651.

Most nightlife in this cowboy and fruit-picking area is limited to taverns, a few of which have live bands on weekends and during the Omak Stampede, the rodeo held each August.

NIGHTLIFE

The **Caraboo Inn** hosts one of the few nightspots in the region, a restaurant with adjoining cocktail lounge featuring dancing with live country-rock music on weekends and karaoke music on Wednesday and Thursday. ~ 223 Queen Street, Okanogan; 509-422-6109.

Big-screen TV, pool, darts, and beer on tap are provided by **Shorthorn Tavern** in downtown Omak. ~ 3 North Main Street, Omak; 509-826-0338.

CONCONULLY STATE PARK 🚶 ⛴ 🛶 🎣 ⛵ ⛵ Strung along the edge of the town of the same name, this site is popu-

PARKS

lar with boaters, swimmers, families and anglers. For hikers, there is a nature trail. You'll also find picnic areas, restrooms and a wading pool. ~ Located 22 miles northwest of Omak on Conconully-Okanogan Highway; 509-826-7408.

▲ There are 81 sites: 71 developed sites, 10 with hookups; $10 per night.

OSOYOOS STATE PARK This lakeshore park is one mile north of Oroville and stretches along the southern end of Osoyoos Lake. It has some of the few trees in the area for shade while picnicking and camping and is the most popular state park in the area. It is heavily used by Canadians and Americans alike since it is almost on the Canadian border. For nature lovers, the lake is a prime nesting area for Canadian geese; for anglers, this is a year-round spot for trout and spiny ray. There are picnic areas and restrooms. ~ Located on the northern end of Oroville on Route 97; 509-476-3321.

▲ There are 86 developed sites; $11 per night.

CURLEW LAKE STATE PARK This 128-acre setting is on the southeastern shore of a lake in a pine forest with several islands. Remnants of homesteaders' cabins can be seen near the park, and a large variety of animals, including chipmunks, squirrels and deer, lives in the area. Several species of birds also can be seen. The park is surrounded by Colville National Forest. You'll find a picnic area and restrooms; restaurants and groceries are in nearby resorts. ~ Located ten miles north of Republic on Route 21; 509-775-3592.

▲ There are 64 standard sites and 25 with RV hookups; $10 to $15 per night.

▼▼▼▼▼▼▼▼▼▼▼▼▼▼

Grand Coulee Area

The centerpiece of the Grand Coulee Area, not surprisingly, is Grand Coulee Dam with its spectacular laser light shows during the summer. The sheer mass of the dam is almost overwhelming and for decades was the largest concrete structure in the world.

Also of interest are the many lakes created by the dam that have become some of the Northwest's most popular recreation areas. The backwaters of the dam itself, named in honor of President Franklin D. Roosevelt, reach far north nearly to the Canadian border and east into the Spokane River system. A chain of lakes and some smaller dams were built to hold irrigation water for distribution south and east of the dam. These include Banks Lake and the Potholes Reservoir, known as the Winchester Wasteway. Don't be put off by the name—wasteway refers to the water that has been used for irrigation and has seeped along bedrock to emerge again ready for reuse. These lakes continue south to the Crab Creek Valley before re-entering the Columbia River below Vantage.

Grand Coulee Dam was built in the 1930s and memorialized by **SIGHTS**
the songs of Woody Guthrie. The area that became known as the
Columbia Basin was so barren before the dam that locals liked to
say you had to prime yourself to spit and that jackrabbits crossing the basin had to carry canteens. The dam was the largest concrete pour in the world for many decades after its completion at
the beginning of World War II. It stands 550 feet above bedrock,
as tall as a 46-story building, and at 5223 feet is nearly a mile long.
While its 12 million cubic yards of concrete may be difficult to
imagine, the Bureau of Reclamation points out that this is enough
to build a standard six-foot-wide sidewalk around the world at
the equator. ~ 509-633-9265.

In addition to the 151-mile-long Roosevelt Lake used to power
the hydroelectric system, the dam serves the additional purpose
of irrigating more than 500,000 acres. Water is pumped 280 feet
up the canyon wall to fill Banks Lake's reservoir, from which the
water is moved through canals and pipes to the area's farmland.

Visitors are welcome at the dam and can go on self-guided
tours. One of the most popular events is the nightly **laser show**,
a free, 40-minute demonstration that uses the spillway of the dam
for its screen. It is shown from Memorial Day through September.

In Coulee Dam, the **Colville Tribal Museum and Gift Shop**
displays authentic village and fishing scenes, coins and metals
dating from the 1800s and many ancient artifacts. The gift shop
sells local beadwork and other artwork by tribal members. ~ 512
Mead Way, Coulee Dam; 509-633-0751.

The best way to appreciate the stark beauty of the Grand
Coulee Area is to drive south from the dam on Route 155 along
Banks Lake. The artificial lake is used for all water sports, and
its color and character change dramatically with the time of day
and weather.

At Coulee City you come to the **Dry Falls Dam**, which holds
Banks Lake water and sends it on south into a system of canals.
Pinto Ridge Road heads due south from Coulee City and passes
Summer Lake, a favorite picnic spot. The falls are created by the
irrigation water from Banks Lake.

The main route out of Coulee City is across Dry Falls Dam,
then south on Route 17 past Dry Falls and Sun Lakes State Park,
along a series of smaller lakes in the coulees—Park Lake, Blue
Lake, Lake Lenore (where you can see the form of a small rhi-
noceros that was trapped in a prehistoric lava flow) and finally
to Soap Lake.

Soap Lake was so named because the water forms foam, or
"soap suds," along the shore when the wind blows. The water is
rich in minerals—sodium, chloride, carbonate, sulfate, bicarbon-
ate and several others—so it has attracted a number of motels that
pump water for use in the rooms or into spas where people go to

soak themselves seeking comfort from a variety of skin, muscle and bone afflictions.

South of Soap Lake the coulees flatten out, and the landscape away from the Columbia River becomes the gently rolling wheat-growing region. **Moses Lake** is the last town of any size connected with the Columbia Basin and is better known as a hub for farmers of the basin than as a tourist destination. The lake for which the town is named joins the Potholes Reservoir to the south.

LODGING   If you want a room with a view, there are two good places near the dam. The **Ponderosa Motel** is right across the street from Grand Coulee Dam. Most rooms have a view of the spillway and the nightly laser light shows in the summer. The recently remodeled motel has 34 rooms and an outdoor pool with a hot tub. Two rooms have jacuzzis, and you pay for it. ~ 10 Lincoln Street, Coulee Dam; 509-633-2100, 800-633-6421, fax 509-633-2633. MODERATE.

The other is **Coulee House Motel**, which is up a steep hill and provides a top-notch view. It has clean, unremarkable rooms and a swimming pool and hot tub. ~ 110 Roosevelt Way, Coulee Dam; 509-633-1101, 800-715-7767, fax 509-633-1416. MODERATE.

Four Winds Guest House is a large, wood-frame Cape Cod–style bed and breakfast across the street from City Hall. It was built as a rooming house for engineers while the dam was being built in the 1930s. All guest rooms have furniture from that period, and all have washbasins. Two rooms have a shared bath and one room has a private bath; otherwise, the bathrooms are at the end of the hall. ~ 301 Lincoln Street, Coulee Dam; 509-633-3146, 800-786-3146, fax 509-633-2454. MODERATE.

Several budget-priced motels and resorts are located near Banks Lake and Roosevelt Lake. **Ala Cozy**, a mile and a half from the marina at the end of Banks Lake, offers ten motel-style units with private bathrooms and refrigerators. There's a pool on the premises. ~ 9988 Route 2 East, Coulee City; 509-632-5703. BUDGET.

In Soap Lake, **Notaris Lodge** is the best-known and most modern motel in town. It also boasts unusual decor in its rooms with names like the "Bonnie Guitar" room (the entertainer grew up in the area). Another room is called the "Ben Snipes" in honor of a pioneer cattleman and has cowboy gear for decoration. The accommodations are spacious and equipped with microwave ovens, refrigerators and breakfast nooks. Massages, whirlpool therapy and mineral baths in Soap Lake water are available. ~ 242 Main Street, Soap Lake; 509-246-0462, fax 509-246-1054. MODERATE TO DELUXE.

Moses Lake is one of the most popular RV destinations in the central part of the state because several lakes are in the immediate vicinity, and hot, sunny weather is almost guaranteed. Several motels are also along the Route 90 corridor and the lake, including the **Best Western Hallmark Inn**, which has 161 units right on Moses Lake. In addition to boating and waterskiing, right off the dock, the motel has tennis courts, a heated pool and sauna. ~ 3000 West Marina Drive, Moses Lake; 509-765-9211, 800-235-4255, fax 509-766-0493. MODERATE TO ULTRA-DELUXE.

The **Lakeshore Motel** is also on the lake, where a marina and waterskiing are available. The motel has 24 units, nine housekeeping cabins and a heated pool. ~ 3206 West Lakeshore Drive, Moses Lake; 509-765-9201, fax 509-765-1800. BUDGET TO MODERATE.

DINING

A well-known eatery in this region is the **Melody Restaurant & Lounge**. With views of the Grand Coulee Dam and its summer laser light show, the Melody offers standard American fare, seafood and pasta. ~ 512 River Drive, Coulee Dam; 509-633-1151. BUDGET TO MODERATE.

For a cozy dinner, stop by **The Country Goose**. Have a latte at the oak-trimmed coffee bar, then move over to the Spanish-style dining room and order country-fried steak or an omelette that hangs over the edge of its plate. ~ 113 Midway Avenue, Grand Coulee; 509-633-3683. BUDGET.

In Grand Coulee, try the **Sage Inn** for diner-style food such as soups, sandwiches and pie. ~ 413 Midway Avenue, Grand Coulee; 509-633-0550. BUDGET.

If you want Asian food, **Siam Palace** will have it. Thai, Chinese and American dishes are served. Closed Monday. ~ 213 Main Street, Grand Coulee; 509-633-2921. BUDGET.

A light-filled, contemporary restaurant built of native stone, **Michael's at the Lake** offers both indoor and outdoor dining. A spacious deck overlooks Moses Lake. Open for both lunch and dinner, prime rib, hamburgers, Oriental chicken salad and homestyle desserts like apple crisp are especially popular here. ~ 910 West Broadway, Moses Lake; 509-765-1611. MODERATE.

SHOPPING

The **Colville Tribal Museum, Gallery and Gift Shop** sells local beadwork and other artwork crafted by the tribal members. ~ 512 Mead Way, Coulee Dam; 509-633-0751.

NIGHTLIFE

Moses Lake has a series of free concerts, all beginning at 8 p.m., on most Saturdays from May to September, in its 3000-seat outdoor amphitheater on the lakeshore. Nationally known musicians perform here. ~ Route 17 out of Coulee City; 509-765-7888.

PARKS

LAKE ROOSEVELT NATIONAL RECREATION AREA This area stretches 151 miles along the entire length of Roosevelt Lake, including parts of the Spokane and Kettle rivers. Owing to the arid climate, the lake has miles and miles of sandy beaches and outcroppings of dramatic rocks. Only when you get close to the Spokane River do trees begin appearing along the shoreline. It is a particular favorite for waterskiers. Sailing and windsurfing are also popular activities. More than 30 species of fish are found here, including walleye, rainbow trout, sturgeon, yellow perch and kokanee, the land-locked salmon. There are picnic areas; restaurants and groceries are nearby. ~ Located 26 miles north of Coulee City on Route 155; 509-633-9441.

▲ There are 27 campgrounds with over 200 sites; $10 per night.

STEAMBOAT ROCK STATE PARK 🚶 🐎 🎿 🏊 🐟 🎣 🛶 🚣 🚤 ⚓ This is one of Washington's most popular state parks and thus is one of the dozen parks where camping-space reservations are a necessity. The park is on the shores of Banks Lake at the foot of the butte by the same name. The ship-shaped butte rises 700 feet above the lake and has a good trail to the 640-acre flat top. Fishing is good year-round, and it's a popular place to ice fish. Picnic tables, playground equipment, a bathhouse and a snack bar are the facilities here. ~ Located 13 miles south of Grand Coulee on Route 155; 509-633-1934.

▲ There are 80 primitive campsites, 26 developed sites, 12 boat-access sites and 100 sites with hookups. Fees are $8 to $16 per night plus a $6 reservation fee per site. Reservations must be obtained by contacting Reservations Northwest. ~ 800-452-5687.

SUN LAKES STATE PARK 🚶 🐎 🚣 🚤 This park is located on the floor of the coulee that was scoured out when the Columbia River's normal course was blocked by ice and debris at the end of the Ice Age. The river, three miles wide, flowed over nearby 400-foot-high Dry Falls, which was the original name of the state park but was changed because of the lakes and recreation. It is now home to boating, riding, hiking and golfing. Picnic areas and restrooms are here. Included in the park is Camp Delaney, an environmental learning center complete with 80 air-conditioned cabins. ~ Located seven miles southwest of Coulee City on Route 17; 360-632-5583.

▲ There are 174 sites including 18 with RV hookups; $11 to $16 per night. Note: A private concessionaire, Sun Lakes Park Resort, operates a portion of the park and rents cabins ($59 to $67 per night for three to four people), mobile homes ($91 per night for up to six people) and 112 full hookups ($16 to $17 per night). Sun Lakes has a general store, a snack bar, heated swimming pool, boat rentals, laundry and a nine-hole golf course. ~ 34228 Park Lake Road Northeast, Coulee City; 509-632-5291.

POTHOLES STATE PARK 🚶 🚣 🚤 ⚓ The potholes were created when water from the Columbia Basin Project seeped in to fill depressions around the coarse sand dunes in the area. Now the dunes stand above the water level and are used for campsites, bird blinds and picnic areas. The area supports a large population of waterfowl and other birds, including blue herons, white pelicans, sand-hill cranes, hawks and eagles. A lawn and shade trees, tables and stoves are beside the lake. Rainbow trout, bass, perch, crappie, bluegill and walleye are found in the park. The park has restrooms and showers. ~ Route 262, 17 miles southwest of Moses Lake; 509-346-2759.

▲ There are 126 sites: 66 for tents, 60 with RV hookups; $8 to $16 per night.

GINKGO PETRIFIED FOREST STATE PARK 🏃 More than 200 species of fossilized trees have been identified in this area of barren hillsides and lava flows, making it one of the largest fossil forests in the world. The park has an interpretive center overlooking the Columbia River with a wide selection of petrified wood. No camping, fishing or swimming are permitted at Ginkgo, but you can head four-and-a-half miles south on the Columbia River to the **Wanapum Recreation Area**. It also has hiking trails, and there is a one-mile interpretive trail at Ginkgo, as well. Facilities here are picnic areas and restrooms. ~ Located on the edge of Vantage, a tiny town on Route 90 where it crosses the Columbia River; 509-856-2700.

▼▼▼▼▼▼▼▼▼▼

Spokane

The northeastern corner of Washington is an area of pine forests, sparkling lakes, sprawling wheat farms and urban pleasures in a rural setting. Spokane is where the Midas-rich miners from Idaho came to live in the late 19th century, so the city has an abundance of historic homes, museums, bed and breakfasts and inns, and one of the most beautiful city park systems in the West.

SIGHTS

The best way to become acquainted with Spokane is to take the self-guided "City Drive Tour" outlined in a brochure from the city that is available in all hotels and at the **Spokane Convention and Visitors Bureau**. ~ 926 West Sprague Avenue, Spokane; 509-747-3230, 800-248-3230.

Another useful brochure is the self-guided tour of historic architecture in downtown Spokane. The "City Drive Tour" takes you along Cliff Drive where many of the finest old homes stand and through **Manito Park**, one of the city's largest parks. Manito Park includes the Japanese Garden built by Spokane's sister city in Japan and the **Duncan Formal Gardens**, whose lush scenery looks like something out of a movie set in 18th-century Europe. ~ Stevens Street and 5th Avenue.

The tour continues past **Coeur d'Alene Park**, off 2nd Avenue, and the stately **Patsy Clark Mansion** at 2nd Avenue and Hemlock Street. It goes on to the **Cheney Cowles Museum** with its major collection of regional history and fine art. Closed Monday. Admission. ~ 2316 West 1st Avenue; 509-456-3931.

Next is **Finch Arboretum**, which features an extensive collection of trees from all over the world. From there the tour leads you back to the downtown area. ~ 3404 West Woodland Boulevard, off Sunset Boulevard; 509-625-6657.

The city is most proud of its **Riverfront Park** located in the heart of downtown and known for the natural beauty of its waterfall and island. A glorious addition to Spokane built for the 1974 World's Fair, the park has the restored 1909 Looff Carrousel, a gondola skyride over Spokane Falls, various other rides, food concessions and the 70mm IMAX Theater. It also has footpaths, natural amphitheaters, lawns and hills, and always the roar of the waterfall for a backdrop. Admission. ~ 509-625-6600.

Another must see is the château-style **Spokane County Courthouse** across the river from downtown. Oddly enough, it was designed in the 1890s by a young man whose only formal training in architecture came from a correspondence course. It is a magnificent conglomeration of towers and turrets, sculpture, iron and brickwork in the French Renaissance manner. ~ Broadway just off Monroe Avenue; 509-456-5790.

Spokane has several wineries with sales and tasting rooms. **Worden Winery** is one of the largest in the area with a capacity of 50,000 gallons. ~ 7217 West 45th Avenue; 509-455-7835.

Arbor Crest Wine Cellars is in a building designated as a National Historic Site on a bluff overlooking the Spokane River. ~ 4705 North Fruithill Road; 509-927-9894.

Latah Creek Wine Cellars has a Spanish-style building with a large courtyard and a tasting room decorated with oak. ~ 13030 East Indiana Avenue; 509-926-0164.

LODGING

Spokane has some pleasant hotels that don't carry big-city rates like those found in Seattle and Portland. You won't find deluxe or luxury accommodations here, but the down-home hospitality of the hotel staffs more than makes up for it.

Two of the largest offer perhaps the best rooms and service. The **West Coast Ridpath** is an old, yet newly renovated, establishment downtown divided into two buildings across the street from each other with a second-story skywalk connecting them. The second building has the larger rooms, which all look inside to the courtyard and large swimming pool. The lobby is small, but the staff is cheerful. There are two restaurants and a newly added weight room. ~ 515 West Sprague Avenue; 509-838-2711, 800-426-0670, fax 509-747-6970. MODERATE TO DELUXE.

The **Doubletree Spokane Hotel** was built for Spokane's 1974 World's Fair and has the best location, right along the Spokane

River and on Riverfront Park. The lobby is impressive, and most rooms have good views of the river, park and downtown. It also has a covered pool and two restaurants. ~ 322 North Spokane Falls Court; 509-455-9600, 800-222-8753, fax 509-455-6285. MODERATE TO DELUXE.

The **Roadway Inn** is a favorite of many who visit Spokane frequently. Built on a hill west of town, it is roughly halfway between the airport and downtown, is quiet and affords good views of the city's growing skyline. ~ 4301 West Sunset Highway; 509-838-1471, 800-228-2000. BUDGET.

A newer downtown establishment is **Cavanaugh's Inn at the Park**. It has 402 rooms and is across North River Drive from the Riverfront Park. Unfortunately, it is just far enough away from the river to lose some of the waterfront charm. The inn is walking distance from downtown, and some of the rooms have private decks. ~ 303 West North River Drive; 509-326-8000, 800-843-4667, fax 509-325-7329. DELUXE.

The **Fotheringham House** is Spokane's best bed and breakfast, and, for that matter, one of the best in the state. The fully restored Fotheringham House is in the Browne's Addition, Spokane's equivalent of San Francisco's Nob Hill, where many of the mining barons built their homes. There are four guest rooms with Victorian furnishings in keeping with the architecture. ~ 2128 West 2nd Avenue; 509-838-1891, fax 509-838-1807. MODERATE.

DINING

Spokane's most popular Asian cuisine comes from the two **Mustard Seed Oriental Cafés**. The menu offers specialties from several provinces in China, as well as Japanese and American dishes. The downtown location is open, airy and the service brisk and friendly. ~ 245 West Spokane Falls Boulevard, 509-747-2689; and 9806 East Sprague Avenue, 509-924-3194. MODERATE.

✔ CHECK THESE OUT—UNIQUE LODGING

- *Budget:* Discover a hidden gem—that is **Hotel Diamond**, which doubles as general store and post office. *page 262*
- *Budget to moderate:* Unwind in an antique-filled room at **Apple Country B&B**, a 1911 house set on a working farm. *page 252*
  - *Moderate:* Sleep in a Victorian-era mansion in Spokane's most exclusive neighborhood at the **Fotheringham House**. *page 243*
    - *Moderate to deluxe:* Roam 47 acres of grounds, including a trail down to the Colville River, at **My Parent's Estate Bed and Breakfast**. *page 234*

Budget: under $50   Moderate: $50–$90   Deluxe: $90–$130   Ultra-deluxe: over $130

The most striking restaurant in town is **Patsy Clark's**. It is in the mansion designed for a millionaire miner and has marble from Italy, wood carvings from England and an enormous, stained-glass window from Tiffany's. Meals are served in several rooms, and during good weather you can have drinks served on the second-story veranda. The restaurant maintains a high standard for steaks, seafood, duckling, lamb and veal. There is also a champagne buffet brunch on Sunday. ~ 2208 West 2nd Avenue; 509-838-8300. MODERATE TO DELUXE.

A favorite lunch and dinner spot is **The Onion**. Occupying a vintage downtown building, The Onion has a 1904 mahogany bar, 1890s prints and brass accents. A wide menu of appetizers and entrées includes onion rings, deep-fried mozzarella, burgers, caesar and taco salads, vegetable stir-fries and baby back ribs. ~ 302 West Riverside Street; 509-747-3852. BUDGET TO MODERATE.

SHOPPING The Skywalk in the downtown core, a series of weatherproof bridges that connects 15 blocks on the second level, makes downtown shopping pleasant year-round. It leads to the major downtown department stores such as **Nordstrom** at Post Street and Main Avenue (509-455-6111) and **Bon Marché** at Wall Street and Main Avenue (509-626-6000), several specialty shops, restaurants and art galleries.

With more and more Canadians driving just over a hundred miles to Spokane, where nearly all goods are less expensive, the city has had a surge of discount stores, from national chain stores to the West Coast warehouse stores. Shopping centers have sprung up on the north and northeast edges of town. Covered shopping areas include **Northtown Mall** at Division Street and Wellesley Avenue, **Franklin Park Mall** at Division Street and Rowan Avenue and **University City** at Sprague Avenue and University Street.

The **Flour Mill** is one of the more charming places to shop. It was built as a flour mill but was turned into a specialty shopping center in 1974 with more than 20 shops, including bookstores, clothing and gift stores and cafés and restaurants. ~ 621 West Mallon Avenue; 509-459-6100.

Fresh vegetables, fruit and berries are some of the Spokane area's best buys. The **Green Bluff Growers**, a marketing cooperative, publishes a map each year with directions to its member orchards, vegetable farms and Christmas-tree farms. ~ 9807 East Bay Road, Mead; 509-238-4709.

NIGHTLIFE You'll find live jazz and Top-40 music and dancing at **Ankeny's** on the top floor of the West Coast Ridpath hotel Thursday through Saturday. ~ 515 West Sprague Avenue; 509-838-2711.

Fort Spokane Brewery serves pub food and brews their own beers daily. Live blues is featured on weekends, and occasionally during the week. Cover on nights with live music. ~ 401 West Spokane Falls Boulevard; 509-838-3809.

One of the city's liveliest sports bars is **Finnerty's Red Lion,** which offers sports events on 20 screens. A bar menu features barbecue ribs. ~ 126 North Division Street; 509-624-1934.

The **Park Place Lounge** has a deejay playing classic rock every night. On Saturday there is live comedy; cover on comedy nights only. ~ Cavanaugh's Inn at the Park, 303 West North River Drive; 509-326-8000.

Dempsey's Brass Rail is a popular gay and lesbian nightspot with a dancefloor and cabaret performances. Cover Friday and Saturday. ~ West 909 1st Street; 509-747-5362.

The **Spokane Symphony Orchestra** performs a number of times throughout the year. ~ 601 West Riverside Avenue; 509-624-1200.

The **Spokane Civic Theater** presents musicals, dramas and comedies year-round. ~ 1020 North Howard Street; 509-325-1413.

RIVERSIDE STATE PARK 🚶 🚲 🐎 🚣 🛥 ⛴ 🎣 On the edge of Spokane, this 7655-acre park includes nearly eight miles of Spokane River shoreline (perfect for rainbow trout fishing), odd basaltic formations in the river and Indian paintings on rocks. It houses the Spokane House interpretive center, which tells the history of Spokane. It also has picnic areas with shelters, restrooms, hot showers and horse trails. ~ Located six miles northwest of Spokane at junction of Route 291, Rifle Club Road and Aubrey L. White Parkway; 509-456-3964.

▲ There are 101 standard sites; $11 per night.

PARKS

MT. SPOKANE STATE PARK 🚶 🚲 🐎 ⛷ 🏂 This 5881-foot mountain is used as much or more in the winter as it is in summer, but warm-weather visitors will find its views spectacular; Idaho, Montana, Canada and much of Washington can be seen from the summit. It is especially pretty during the spring when its slopes are blanketed with flowers and in the fall when the fields are brown and the leaves have turned. For those into winter sports, there are downhill and cross-country skiing, as well as snowmobiling. During warm weather, the park has some of the best mountain biking in Washington. There are picnic areas and restrooms. ~ Located at the end of Route 206, 30 miles northeast of Spokane; 509-238-4258.

▲ There are 8 primitive sites; $10 per night.

TURNBULL NATIONAL WILDLIFE REFUGE 🚶 🚲 🏂 One of the most popular natural places for day trips in the Spokane area, the refuge was established in 1937 primarily for waterfowl. It has several lakes and undisturbed wooded areas and a marked, self-guided auto-tour route. You will also find hiking trails and cross-country skiing areas as well as restrooms. ~ Located 20 miles south of Spokane on Plaza Highway; 509-235-4723.

▼▼▼▼▼▼▼▼▼▼▼▼▼▼▼▼▼▼▼▼▼
Southeastern Washington

The drive from Spokane south into Oregon is one of unusual beauty, especially early or late in the day, or in the spring and fall. The entire region between the wooded hills around Spokane to the Blue Mountains is known as the Palouse Country. Here the barren hills are low but steep, and wheat is grown on nearly every acre. In fact, it is acknowledged as the best wheat-growing land in the world.

SIGHTS

Proceeding south from Spokane along Route 195, you'll find that the two best places to view the Palouse Hills are **Steptoe Butte State Park** (see "Parks" below) and **Kamiak Butte County Park**. Kamiak Butte stands 3360 feet high and offers bird's-eye views of the Palouse Hills. The park has picnic areas, a hiking trail and, unlike Steptoe Butte, a fringe of trees on its crest and over 100 kinds of vegetation, including the Douglas fir more common to the damp, coastal climate. Kamiak Butte is 18 miles east of Colfax and 15 miles north of Pullman just off Route 27.

The town of **Pullman** is almost entirely a product of Washington State University, although a few agricultural businesses operate on the edge of town. Continuing south from this campus town, Route 195 gains elevation through the small farming communities of Colton and Uniontown, then crosses over into the edge of Idaho just in time to disappear into Route 95 and then take a dizzying plunge down the steep Lewiston Hill, where you drop 2000 feet in a very short time over a twisting highway. The old highway with its hairpin turns is still passable and is exciting driving if your brakes and nerves are in good condition.

Clarkston, Washington, and Lewiston, Idaho, are separated by the Snake River, which flows almost due north through Hells Canyon before taking a sudden westward turn where Idaho's Clearwater River enters in Lewiston. Most of the Snake River boat operators are headquartered in these two towns. For more information, contact the **Clarkston Chamber of Commerce**. ~ 502 Bridge Street, Clarkston; 509-758-7712.

The population has followed the Snake on its way west to join with the Columbia, but it is a tamed river now, a series of slackwater pools in deep canyons behind a series of dams: Lower Granite, Little Goose, Lower Monumental and Ice Harbor. The main highway doesn't follow the Snake River because of the deep canyon it carved, so from Clarkston you follow Route 12 west through the farming communities of Pomeroy and Dayton to

Walla Walla, then on to the Tri-Cities area around Richland, where the Snake enters the Columbia River. Along the way is Dayton, an agricultural town with a large asparagus cannery. The town raised funds to preserve the beautiful **Dayton Depot**, a classic Victorian building that had an upper floor for the stationmaster's quarters. ~ Depot: 222 East Commercial Street, Dayton; 509-382-4825.

Walla Walla looks much like a New England town that was packed up and moved to the rolling hills of Eastern Washington, weeping willows, oak and maple trees included. Best known for its colleges, Whitman and Walla Walla College, the town with a double name has many ivy-covered buildings, quiet streets lined with old frame houses, enormous shade trees and, rather incongruously amid this Norman Rockwellian beauty, the state penitentiary. Contact the **Walla Walla Chamber of Commerce**. ~ 29 East Sumach Street, Walla Walla; 509-525-0850.

> The cemetery at Fort Walla Walla contains victims from both sides of the first conflicts with the Indians.

At **Whitman Mission National Historic Site** one of the Northwest's worst tragedies occurred because of a basic misunderstanding of American Indian values by an American missionary, Marcus Whitman. He and his wife, Narcissa, founded a mission among the Cayuse Indians in 1836 to convert the Cayuse to Christianity. As traffic increased on the Oregon Trail, the mission became an important stop for weary travelers. Eleven years later the Cayuse felt betrayed by Whitman because his religion hadn't protected them from a measles epidemic that killed half the tribe. On November 29, 1847, the Cayuse killed both Whitmans and nine others and ransomed 50 to the Hudson's Bay Company. The site is seven miles west of Walla Walla on Route 12 and is run by the National Park Service. There's a visitors center, memorial monument, millpond and walking paths to sites where various buildings once stood. None of the original buildings remain. Admission. ~ 509-529-2761.

The Tri-Cities are best known for the nuclear-power plant and research center in nearby Hanford. It was here that the components for the first atomic bombs were assembled. Two nuclear-related visitors centers tell the nuclear story. The **Columbia River Exhibition of History, Science and Technology** is operated by Westinghouse for the Department of Energy and tells of the various sources of energy. The exhibits and historical displays focus on people's interaction with the environment, such as agricultural production, hydroelectric power, nuclear energy and environmental restoration. Admission. ~ 95 Lee Boulevard, Richland; 509-943-9000.

Another nuclear facility for visitors is the **Washington Public Power System Plant 2 Visitor Center**, which offers information

Text continued on page 250.

Washington Wine

For a long time, Washington's liquor laws were so restrictive that it was illegal to bring wine into the state; you had to buy it from the state-run stores. The best Washington wine in those days was made by an Italian immigrant, Angelo Pelligrini, who taught Shakespeare at the University of Washington and made wine in his basement—illegally.

That has changed completely. Some 80 wineries are spread across the state, most in Eastern Washington, and many of those in the Puget Sound region own vineyards in Eastern Washington or buy their grapes there. The soil and climate are excellent for wine grapes, and the **Washington Wine Commission** likes to remind us that Eastern Washington is at the same latitude as some of France's great winegrowing regions. The wine commission publishes a free guide to wineries. ~ 1932 1st Avenue, Suite 510, Seattle; 206-728-2252.

Washington has four viticultural regions: Columbia Valley, which extends southward from the Okanogan Country into Oregon and east to Idaho; Yakima Valley, which runs from the foothills of the Cascades east to the Kiona Hills near Richland and is bisected by Interstate 82, making it the most convenient for visits; the Walla Walla Valley region, which straddles the Oregon–Washington border, taking in some vineyards in the Milton-Freewater area; and the Puget Sound region, which covers areas from Olympia in the south to Bellingham in the north, and includes various Puget Sound and San Juan islands in between.

In keeping with the French adage that the best grape vines "like to be in sight of the water but don't want to get their feet wet," some of the best vineyards in Eastern Washington are on south-facing slopes above the Columbia, Yakima and Snake rivers, where they get as much as 16 hours of sunlight a day and fresh irrigation water on well-drained soil. As with all wine-producing areas, many wineries have been built in palatial settings.

One of the most dramatic is the **Columbia Crest Winery**. Built on a hillside overlooking the Columbia River, it produces more than a million gallons of wine annually and has a reflecting pool, fountain and courtyard, a luxurious lobby and tasting-and-sales room. ~ Route 221, Paterson; 509-875-2061.

Running a close second is the eastern branch of **Château Ste. Michelle**. This is the state's oldest continuously operating winery and is the red-wine facility for the large winery best known for its Woodinville palace. ~ 205 West 5th Street, Grandview; 509-882-3928.

Located in an old converted gasoline station, **White Heron Cellars** emphasizes a natural winemaking process, leaving as much of the ecosystem undisturbed as possible. ~ 101 Washington Way North, George; 509-785-5521.

A wine that keeps gaining new fans is the **Covey Run** label. The tasting room stands on a hill overlooking the winery's 100 acres of grapes. ~ 1500 Vintage Road, Zillah; 509-829-6235.

The quirky **L'Ecole No. 41** got its name from the retired schoolhouse near Walla Walla in which it was built. It is open Wednesday through Sunday. ~ 41 Lowden School Road, Lowden; 509-525-0940.

Wine is only one of several agricultural products produced by Hogue Ranches. But the **Hogue Cellars** wines have been getting much more attention than their asparagus. ~ Wine Country Road, Prosser; 509-786-4557.

Hunter Hill Vineyards is named for the well-known bird-hunting area around the nearby Potholes Reservoir. The tasting room is in the original farmhouse, which gives a feeling of a country home to visitors who come by to taste. ~ 2752 West McMannaman Road, Othello; 509-346-2736.

The most homey of the wineries is probably **Kiona Vineyards**. It is a family operation, with the tasting room, winery and the Kiona Vineyard at the home of John and Ann Williams. The winery was one of the originals to produce lemberger. ~ Sunset Road, Benton City; 509-588-6716.

Staton Hills is located in a French-country building set on a rolling hillside. The two-story tasting room features a stone fireplace and cathedral ceilings. ~ 71 Gangl Road, Wapato; 509-877-2112.

Pontin del Roza came into being because the Pontin family's Italian heritage included a love of wine. They decided to add wine grapes to the crops they had been growing on their Prosser farm for two decades and produce both reds and white. ~ McCreadie and Hinzerling roads, Prosser; 509-786-4449.

Cheers!

on the state's first commercial nuclear-power plant. Closed Monday through Wednesday. ~ Off Stevens Drive, 12 miles north of Richland; 509-372-5000.

From the Tri-Cities, the population follows the Yakima River, which flows into the Columbia at the Tri-Cities. The **Yakima Valley** is the state's richest in terms of agriculture: Yakima County ranks first nationally in the number of fruit trees, first in the production of apples, mint and hops and fifth in the value of all fruits grown. It is also the wine center of the state: Some 40 wineries have been built between Walla Walla and Yakima, and they have helped create a visitor industry that has encouraged the growth of country inns and bed and breakfasts. Brochures listing the wineries and locations are available in visitors centers and many convenience stores, and once you're off Route 82, signs mark routes to the wineries.

Fort Simcoe State Park is probably the best-preserved frontier army post in the West and was one of the few forts where no shots were fired in anger. It was used in the late 1850s during the conflict with the local American Indian people. There's a museum/interpretive center (closed Monday and Tuesday). Four of the original buildings are still standing, including the commanding officer's home. ~ End of Fort Simcoe Road, about 35 miles south of Yakima; 509-874-2372.

If you are a rail buff, you can ride the rails on **Yakima Interurban Lines** that runs from 3rd Avenue and Pine Street in downtown Yakima five miles to Selah on weekends and holidays. It is the oldest continuous interurban electric railway in the West operating on its original track, which dates back to 1907. ~ 509-575-1700.

Three important museums are in the Yakima Valley. One is the **Yakama Nation Cultural Center**. Here, the history of the tribe is told in dioramas and writings by and about the tribe preserved in a large library. The center also has a theater for films and concerts and a restaurant that serves traditional dishes. Admission. ~ Route 97, 100 Spil-yi Loop, Toppenish; 509-865-2800.

The Central Washington Agricultural Museum has a large collection of early farm machinery including a working windmill, a

THAT DAMMED RIVER

The Columbia River runs free for about 60 miles through Hanford Reservation, but when it swings through the Tri-Cities (Richland, Pasco and Kennewick) it becomes Lake Wallula, thanks to McNary Dam. Several city parks with picnic and boating facilities are along the river, such as Columbia Park in Kennewick.

blacksmith shop, a furnished log cabin and a tool and artifact collection. ~ 4508 Main Street, Union Gap; 509-457-8735.

The **Yakima Valley Museum** has a comprehensive collection of horse-drawn vehicles, an extensive collection of furniture and other belongings of the late Supreme Court Justice William O. Douglas, a fine pioneer photo collection and special agricultural and American Indian exhibits. There is also a new interactive children's museum. Admission. ~ 2105 Tieton Drive, Yakima; 509-248-0747.

The main road leading from the Yakima Valley to the beautiful Columbia River Gorge (see Chapter Seven, "Portland and the Columbia River Gorge") is Route 97, which runs south from Toppenish, crosses Satus Pass (3107 feet) and reaches the Gorge just past Goldendale. An alternate route from the Yakima Valley down to the Columbia River is the **Mabton-Bickleton Road,** which heads south from the small town of Mabton through the even smaller Bickleton. An unincorporated town with a scattering of Victorian houses and falsefront store buildings, Bickleton's claim to fame is hundreds of houses for (are you ready for this?) bluebirds. Maintained by residents, the houses are on fence posts along the highway and country lanes and literally all over town. The one in front of the community church is a miniature copy of the church itself.

◄ HIDDEN

Twelve miles outside Bickleton sits the funky **Whoop N Holler Museum.** The owners showcase a vast array of turn-of-the-century pioneer memorabilia, much of which was handed down through their families. Highlights are the large classic auto collection and various horse-drawn vehicles, including an antique hearse on sled runners. Admission. ~ 1 Whitmore Road at East Road, Bickleton; 509-896-2344.

It's difficult to find anything other than your basic, cookie-cutter motel in Southeastern Washington, although Yakima shows some imagination.

LODGING

Pullman has about half a dozen motels, none particularly distinguished, and all budget or moderate in price. The best view is offered by the **Best Western Heritage Inn,** about a half mile from WSU. ~ 928 Olson Street at Davis Way, Pullman; 509-332-0928, 800-528-1234, fax 509-334-5275. MODERATE. The **Quality Inn** is near both the campus and the airport and offers 66 rooms. ~ 1050 Bishop Boulevard, Pullman; 509-332-0500, 800-669-3212, fax 509-334-4271. MODERATE.

Walla Walla has about ten motels, most of them in the budget to moderate range. The **Tapadera Budget Inn** offers a continental breakfast. ~ 211 North 2nd Street, Walla Walla; 509-529-2580, 800-722-8277, fax 509-522-1380. BUDGET.

Dayton seems to be out in the middle of nowhere—gateway to the Blue Mountains and an agricultural center. The **Purple House B&B** is thus an unexpected pleasure. This elegant inn is housed in an 1882 Queen Anne mansion built by a pioneer physician. Two upstairs bedrooms share a bath; the master suite downstairs has a private bath. All rooms are furnished in period antiques; there's a library and heated outdoor pool. The full breakfast is cooked to order. ~ 415 East Clay Street, Dayton; 509-382-3159, 800-486-2574. MODERATE TO DELUXE.

The Tri-Cities have several fair-size motels, many with meeting rooms since the Hanford Nuclear Center is nearby. One of the largest is the **Ramada Inn on Clover Island**, built on an island in the Columbia River. Half of the rooms have a view of the river, and the restaurant is open 24 hours a day. It has a pool, hot tub and lounge. ~ 435 Clover Island, Kennewick; 509-586-0541, 800-272-6232, fax 509-586-6956. MODERATE TO ULTRA-DELUXE.

Built of materials shipped west by railroad, the **Von Hellstrum Inn** was slated for demolition until its current owners bought and restored the 1908 farmhouse. Perched on a knoll overlooking the Yakima Valley, the inn has four bedrooms with private baths; they're furnished in antiques, some 200 years old. The Rose Room has a Victorian sitting room; it and the Chippendale Room have private balconies. Full breakfast is included. ~ 51 Braden Road, Sunnyside; 509-839-2505. MODERATE TO DELUXE.

Peace and quiet are the overwhelming virtues of the **Apple Country B&B** outside Yakima. With two antique-furnished bedrooms in a 1911 house on a working farm, hard-working hostess Shirley Robert wants her guests to feel as serene as the setting suggests. Sit outside your antique-furnished rooms overlooking the back yard and orchards beyond, sipping lemonade, and peace prevails. ~ 4561 Old Naches Highway, Naches; 509-965-0344, fax 509-965-1591. BUDGET TO MODERATE.

Yakima does a lively convention business, and one of the best places to stay is next door to the convention center. **Kavanaugh's** has 152 large, comfortable rooms with colorful furnishings and spacious bathrooms, two heated pools, dining room and coffee shop. ~ 607 East Yakima Avenue, Yakima; 509-248-5900, 800-843-4667, fax 509-757-8975. DELUXE.

DINING

In Pullman, *the* most popular place to eat is **The Seasons**, on the hill near Washington State University. It is an elegant setting in a renovated house and has a menu that changes frequently. Closed Sunday and Monday. ~ 205 Southeast Paradise Street, Pullman; 509-334-1410. MODERATE.

The **Hilltop Steakhouse** shares the steep hill with the Hilltop Motor Inn. It caters to the local trade with thick steaks, Sunday brunches and afternoon dinners. ~ 920 Olson Street at Davis Way, Pullman; 509-334-2555. MODERATE.

If you're good at what you do, so goes the saying, the world will beat a path to your door. This could be the slogan for **Patit Creek Restaurant**. It has been in business since 1978 and has built a national reputation for excellent dishes in what is most accurately described as French country cuisine. Meat is the specialty —beef and lamb. Most of the food is grown locally, some by the staff, and since some of the luxurious plants inside and around the outside are herbs, they may one day season your food. Closed Sunday and Monday. ~ 725 East Dayton Avenue, Dayton; 509-382-2625. MODERATE TO DELUXE.

If you're feeling nostalgic for New York delis, **Merchant's Ltd.** will help. It has a wide choice of foods and a sidewalk café ideal for Walla Walla's mostly sunny weather. ~ 21 East Main Street, Walla Walla; 509-525-0900. BUDGET.

The Cedars is one of the Tri-Cities' most striking restaurants. It is cantilevered over the Columbia River with boat-docking facilities. The specialties are steaks, seafood and prime rib. Favorites include the bier garten steak and the pepper steak. ~ 7 Clover Island, Kennewick; 509-582-2143. MODERATE TO DELUXE.

Emerald of Siam serves authentic Thai food in a former drugstore that has a combination of French, Thai and American decor and menu. A buffet lunch is served on weekdays, or you may order from the menu. Closed Sunday. ~ 1314 Jadwin Avenue, Richland; 509-946-9328. BUDGET.

Prosser is a farm town, pure and simple. But what better place for fine, gourmet country cuisine? At **The Blue Goose**, local wine and produce form the basis for a Tuscan/Northwest menu that ranges from veal marsala to chicken-fried steak (well, it is a country restaurant). The wine list features more than 50 local

---

✔ **CHECK THESE OUT—UNIQUE DINING**

- *Budget:* Witness a horse-and-cattle auction while having an old-fashioned breakfast at **Double J.** *page 234*
- *Budget to moderate:* Carbo-load before rafting Hells Canyon at the German-Hungarian **Vali's Alpine Delicatessen and Restaurant.** *page 260*
- *Moderate to deluxe:* Order duckling at the cosmopolitan **Patsy Clark's**, set in a mansion designed for a millionaire miner. *page 244*
- *Deluxe:* Feast on specialties featuring locally grown Yakima Valley fruits and vegetables at the **Birchfield Manor.** *page 254*

Budget: under $8   Moderate: $8–$16   Deluxe: $16–$24   Ultra-deluxe: over $24

wines, some of them superb vintages, at prices you'll never see in any urban restaurant. ~ 306 7th Street, Prosser; 509-786-1774. MODERATE.

Over the years, **Birchfield Manor** has won more magazine awards than any other Washington restaurant outside the Puget Sound region. The owners restored an old farmhouse and filled it with antiques, then opened the restaurant with a menu including fresh salmon in puff pastry, filet mignon, rack of lamb and chicken breast scallopine. Local fruit and vegetables are used, and the fixed menu includes an appetizer, a salad and a homemade chocolate treat. Closed Sunday through Wednesday. ~ 2018 Birchfield Road, Yakima; 509-452-1960. DELUXE.

SHOPPING   **Yesterday's Village** is a collection of shops in the former Fruit Exchange Building. Most of the interior has been left intact so you can see how fruit was cooled and processed, but the old building houses some 110 shops that sell antiques, glassware and jewelry. ~ 15 West Yakima Avenue, Yakima; 509-457-4981.

Yakima offers several intriguing shopping areas. One is the **North Front Street Historical District**, where the city's oldest buildings, some of them made of rough-hewn local rock, now house an assortment of boutiques, restaurants and brew pubs. The former train depot is now the site of the **Paper Station**, where you can shop for books, cards and custom stationery. ~ 10 North Front Street, Yakima; 509-575-1633.

NIGHTLIFE   **Walla Walla** has several restaurants with dancefloors and a few with live entertainment. The **Red Apple Restaurant and Lounge** has entertainment and dancing on weekends. ~ 57 East Main Street, Walla Walla; 509-525-5113.

Yakima has one of the widest selections of nightlife in southeastern Washington, ranging from cultural events to country-and-western taverns. **Grant's Brewery Pub** serves British pub food and frequently offers live music. ~ 32 North Front Street, Yakima; 509-575-2922. The **Golden Kayland Chinese Restaurant** has live music. ~ 40th Avenue and Summitview Street, Yakima; 509-966-7696.

In addition, Yakima has frequent concerts by the **Yakima Symphony Orchestra**. ~ Yakima; 509-248-1414.

Square dancing is very popular in the Yakima Valley, and numerous clubs welcome travelers to their dances. For information, contact Daron Tandberg of the Square Dance Club of Yakima (509-576-4249). Dances are held Saturday nights at the Yakima Valley Square Dance Center. ~ 207 East Charron Road, Moxee.

PARKS   **STEPTOE BUTTE STATE PARK** 🏃 This park consists of the butte and a picnic area at the base but has no amenities at all. The reason for the park's existence is the butte itself, which rises to an

elevation of 3612 feet out of the rolling Palouse Hills with panoramic views that are popular with photographers. The butte is
actually the top of a granite mountain that stands above the lava
flows that covered all the other peaks. The word "steptoe" has
entered the international geological vocabulary to represent any
similar remnant of an earlier geological feature standing out from
the newer feature. There is a picnic area at the foot of the butte;
no water. ~ Located 33 miles south of Spokane just off Route
195; 509-549-3551.

FIELDS SPRING STATE PARK 🚶 🚲 🎿 This 800-acre park is
in forested land on the eastern slope of the Blue Mountains. It is
just below Puffer Butte, a 4450-foot mountain that overlooks the
Grand Ronde River Canyon. For hikers, there is a one-mile trail
to the summit of Puffer Butte. Winter-sports enthusiasts will find
cross-country skiing, snowshoeing and tubing. There are restrooms, showers and two lodges where groups or individuals can
stay for just $6 per night. ~ Located four-and-a-half miles south
of Anatone on Route 129; 509-256-3332.

▲ There are 20 developed sites; $10 per night.

FORT WALLA WALLA PARK AND MUSEUM 🚶 🚲 This collection of pioneer buildings is located on a 208-acre former Army
fort and cemetery containing victims from both sides of the first
conflicts with the Indians. It also has 20 buildings, some authentic and others replicas, of pioneer homes, schools and public buildings. One of the largest collections of horse-drawn farm equipment
in the Northwest is also owned by the museum (509-525-7703;
admission). There are also nature and bicycle trails in the park.
Other facilities include picnic areas, restrooms, play equipment
and volleyball courts. ~ Located on southwest side of Walla Walla
on Dalles Military Road at Myra; 509-527-3770.

▲ There are 55 developed sites and 21 sites with hookups;
$10 to $13 per night.

PALOUSE FALLS/LYONS FERRY STATE PARK 🚶 🏊 🚤 🐟 🛶
This two-part, remote park is out in the rugged Channeled Scablands. The Lyons Ferry section consists of a pleasant, grassy area
with boat ramps at the confluence of the Snake and Palouse rivers.
About four miles up the Palouse River is the Palouse Falls section, with a dramatic picnic area and viewpoint overlooking the
thundering Palouse Falls. You'll find picnic areas and restrooms;
wheelchair-accessible hiking trail at Lyons Ferry. ~ Located 36
miles southeast of Washtucna on Route 261; 509-646-3252.

▲ Palouse Falls has ten primitive, walk-in sites ($7 per night)
while Lyons Ferry has 50 standard sites ($10 per night).

McNARY NATIONAL WILDLIFE REFUGE 🚶 🛶 This is one of the
major resting areas in the Pacific Flyway for migratory water-

fowl, especially Canada geese, American widgeon, mallards, pintails and white pelicans. The population peaks in November, and the few summer migratory birds, such as the pelicans and long-billed curlews, arrive in the spring and summer. The refuge covers 3600 acres along the Snake River just before it enters the Columbia River at Pasco. Hunters look for waterfowl and upland birds, while anglers cast a rod for largemouth black bass, catfish and crappie. There is a self-guided wildlife trail through the marsh and croplands. ~ Located southeast of Pasco just off Route 395 on the Snake River; 509-547-4942.

▼▼▼▼▼▼▼▼▼▼▼▼▼▼▼▼

Northeastern Oregon

For the most part, Northeastern Oregon remains the parched land so inhospitable to settlers nearly two centuries ago. Nowadays, towns are still few and far between, leaving plenty of room for viewing the wagon ruts left by the original pioneers. Also a part of the Northeastern Oregon experience are the vividly colored earthscapes at the John Day Fossil Beds National Monument and the whitewater rafting opportunities in the tremendous Snake River along the Idaho border. Capping it off in the state's northeastern corner is a surprisingly lush area surrounding the Wallowa Mountains that reminds many visitors of the Swiss Alps.

SIGHTS   At the Oregon–Washington border Route 129 heading south from Clarkston, Washington changes to Route 3 and runs along high ridges and through ponderosa-pine forests until it enters the **Wallowa River Valley**. This valley is postcard perfect with the jagged Wallowa Mountains providing an ideal backdrop to the broad valley with the lush farms and ranches, rail fences, ranch buildings and the small, winding Wallowa River. Once you've seen it you'll understand why it is becoming a haven for artists and writers.

The twin towns of **Enterprise** and **Joseph** can be used as a base for exploratory trips around Wallowa Lake and backpacking into the Eagle Cap Wilderness. The **aerial tramway** that runs from Wallowa Lake to the 8200-foot summit of Mt. Howard is a popular way to spend part of a day. Another good day trip is the 30-mile drive from Joseph on a good road to Imnaha on the edge of **Hells Canyon National Recreation Area** (see "Parks" below).

HIDDEN ▶   A gravel road takes you another 25 miles to **Hat Point** for a grand view across one of the most rugged stretches of Hells Canyon.

The last miles of the **Oregon Trail**, which began in St. Joseph, Missouri, run along the same general route taken by Route 84 from the city of Ontario northwest through Baker City, La Grande, Pendleton and along the Columbia River until hitting the rapids in

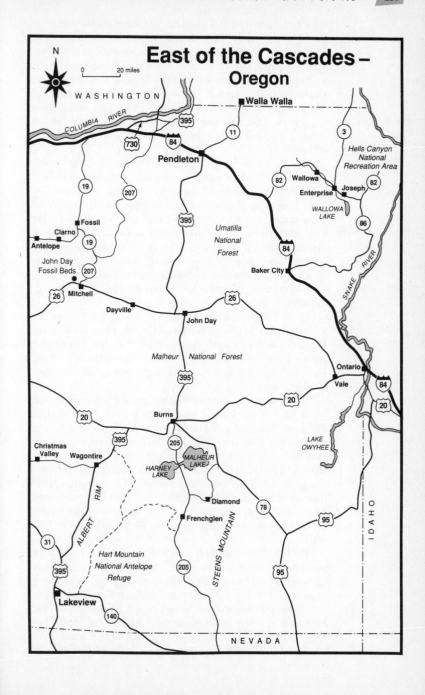

the Cascades. Several sites have been set aside that show ruts made by the wagons along the trail. You can see them at Vail, west of Ontario, and along the route near Baker City in Burnt River Canyon, Gold Hill, Durkee, Pleasant Valley and Baker Valley.

Don't miss the **National Historic Oregon Trail Interpretive Center** on top of Flagstaff Hill on Route 86 east of Baker City. The center has a permanent collection of artifacts found along the trail, a theater for stage productions and outdoor exhibits showing a wagon-train encampment and mine operation. ~ 541-523-1843.

You also can visit a number of **ghost towns**, all visible records of the boom-and-bust nature of the mining industry—with broken windmills, abandoned shacks and fireplaces surrounded by ashes from burned houses that bear witness to failed homesteads. Some of these towns are making a comeback. Neighboring Baker City are such falsefronted old-timers as Greenhorn, Sumpter, Granite, Whitney, Bourne, Sparta and Cornucopia, which have colorful remains of the original towns and mining equipment standing among the summer homes that have taken root. Most of these towns are along Route 7 or on Forest Service roads leading off it.

Route 7 leads from Baker City southwest to Route 26, which you can stay on heading west to **John Day** and **Canyon City**, twin towns that look very much like the Old West. In fact, twice a year the main street of John Day is closed to vehicular traffic so that a local rancher can drive his cattle through town to and from their summer range.

The best-known museum in these parts was a store owned for decades by two Chinese immigrants, Ing Hay and Lung On. The **Kam Wah Chung & Co. Museum**, next to the city park in the center of John Day, began as a trading post on the military road that ran through the area. Then the Chinese laborers in the mines bought the building for a community center, general store and an herbal doctor's office. The museum has thousands of artifacts related to the building's history and more than a thousand herbs, some from China and others from the immediate area. Closed in winter. Admission. ~ Ing Hay Way, John Day; 541-575-0028.

The **John Day Fossil Beds National Monument** is a three-part preserve that attracts serious and amateur photographers from all over the world to capture the vivid colors of the volcanic-ash deposits and the fossils of plants and animals. **Sheep Rock**, eight miles west of Dayville where Routes 26 and 19 intersect, has the main visitors center and the best fossil collection at the monument. **Painted Hills**, at the end of a three-mile paved access road northwest of Mitchell, is popular for the brilliantly colored ash deposits found there that range from rose to pink, gold and bronze. **Clarno** is on the John Day River 20 miles west of Fossil and 30 miles east of Shaniko on Route 218. It has a good collection of plant fossils. The monument has self-guided loop trails. ~ 541-987-2333.

In Pendleton, the best hotel is the **Doubletree Hotel,** just off Route 84 on a hill above the city. Rooms have picture windows and balconies overlooking the wheat fields rolling off to the north and west. It has a formal dining room with a window wall, coffee shop, pool and a duck pond. ~ 304 Southeast Nye Avenue, Pendleton; 541-276-6111, 800-547-8010, fax 541-278-2413. MODERATE.

LODGING

In the downtown area, the **Longhorn Motel** has most of the usual amenities, except a pool. ~ 411 Southwest Dorion Avenue, Pendleton; 541-276-7531. BUDGET.

Most of the hotels in the Enterprise-Joseph area are in the budget category. The lone exception is **Wallowa Lake Lodge,** an aging lodge on the lakeshore with adjoining cabins that have kitchens in all units. ~ 60060 Wallowa Lake Highway, Joseph; 541-432-9821, fax 541-432-4885. DELUXE.

An alpine look was adopted by builders of the **Chandler's Bed, Bread and Trail Inn,** which has five simply furnished rooms at the top of a log staircase. Three rooms have private baths and the other two share one-and-a-half baths off of a common sitting room. ~ 700 South Main Street, Joseph; 541-432-9765, 800-452-3781. MODERATE.

In Enterprise, **The Wilderness Inn** is a basic motel: clean and uncomplicated. ~ 301 West North Street; 541-426-4535. BUDGET TO MODERATE. Or try the **Country Inn.** ~ 402 West North Street; 541-426-4022. BUDGET TO MODERATE.

Baker City has about ten motels, most with the basic goodies of highway stopovers. The **Best Western Sunridge Inn,** just off Route 84, has 156 rooms, pool, dining room, coffee shop and a lounge. ~ 1 Sunridge Lane, Baker City; 541-523-6444, 800-233-2368, fax 541-523-6446. MODERATE.

The selection is thin in the area of John Day Fossil Beds National Monument. The town of John Day has several motels in the budget range. The **Best Western John Day Inn** has 39 units. ~ 315 Main Street, John Day; 541-575-1700, 800-243-2628, fax 541-575-1558. BUDGET. You can also try the similar but smaller **Budget Inn.** ~ 250 East Main Street, John Day; 541-575-1751, 800-854-4442. BUDGET.

One small motel is in Mitchell, the town nearest to the Painted Hills portion of the monument: the **Sky Hook Motel,** with only six units. ~ Route 26, Mitchell; 541-462-3569. BUDGET TO MODERATE.

DINING   Red meat is almost required eating in cowboy towns, but in Pendleton you can find a wider variety at **Raphael's Restaurant and Lounge,** a restaurant and cocktail lounge that displays the work of local American Indian artists. The menu has beef (of course), but seafood items are also common, such as shrimp and bottom fish. Closed Sunday and Monday. ~ 233 Southeast 4th Street, Pendleton; 541-276-8500. MODERATE.

Good food is making inroads in the Wallowa Valley, and one of the first notable eateries was **Vali's Alpine Delicatessen and Restaurant.** German-Hungarian dishes such as goulash, chicken paprikas and wienerschnitzel are served, but for the nonadventurous there is also plain old American fare. The decor is also German-Hungarian. Open for continental breakfast and dinner only. Between Memorial Day and Labor Day, open every day except Monday; otherwise, open only Saturday and Sunday. ~ 59811 Wallowa Lake Highway, Joseph; 541-432-5691. BUDGET TO MODERATE.

The Anthony is an unusual place—offbeat paintings, weird statues and busts of the famous—with a large menu of standard beef dishes and broiled and poached fish and chicken. ~ 2820 Broadway, Baker City; 541-523-4475. MODERATE.

SHOPPING   **Hamley's Saddlery** is a Pendleton institution where generations of folks have bought their saddles, clothes and various cowboy needs. They also have a gallery section featuring Western art. ~ 30 Southeast Court Street, Pendleton; 541-276-2321.

Baker City has become an antique mecca. You'll find items dating back to the pioneer years of the town, including oak furniture bought at estate sales, glass, rock collections, kitchen utensils and tools. **Memory House Antiques** specializes in depression glass. ~ 1780 Main Street, Baker City; 541-523-6227.

NIGHTLIFE   Live music is hard to come by except on special occasions, such as rodeos and patriotic holidays. An exception is in Pendleton. **Crabby's Underground Saloon and Dance Hall** has live country music by local talent on Friday and Saturday night. It's located in a basement beneath several small shops, and in addition to the music and dancefloor has darts and pool tables. Cover on weekends. ~ 220 Southwest 1st Street, Pendleton; 541-276-8118.

PARKS   **WALLOWA LAKE STATE PARK** 🚶 ⛵ 🎣 🏕 🚐 🛥 ⛴ On the southern end of the lake with large playground areas surrounded by trees, this park stretches from the lakeshore well back into the pine and spruce timber. Hiking trails are on the grounds. There's good rainbow trout fishing north of the park. Closed from November to April. There are day-use areas, a marina, a boat dock and a concessionaire. ~ Located at the southern end of Wallowa Lake on Route 82; 541-432-4185.

▲ There are 89 tent sites and 121 RV sites with hookups; $14 to $16 per night.

HELLS CANYON NATIONAL RECREATION AREA 🏃 ⛵ 🛥 🛶

This 652,488-acre monument protects the Snake River Gorge, a 20-mile-long canyon that has an average depth of 6000 feet, the deepest river gorge in the world. It is one of the most popular whitewater-rafting trips in the United States. Rafts can be launched from Hells Canyon Dam in Oregon and Pittsburg Landing on the Idaho side of the river. The Snake River is very swift, and swimming is allowed only in certain spots. There's fishing access from 18 sites; smallmouth bass, catfish and crappie are best. There is also sturgeon (catch-and-release only). Facilities include day-use picnic areas, scenic overlooks and restrooms. ~ You can reach the area two ways: by taking Route 86 from Baker City through Halfway and Oxbow to Forest Service Road 39; or by heading east on Route 350 from the town of Joseph south to Forest Service Road 39; 541-426-4978.

▲ There are 17 campgrounds with numerous sites. Indian Crossing (14 tent/RV sites) is the starting point for some of the area's horseback riding and hiking trails, making it an ideal place to set up camp. Ollokot Campground, with 12 tent/RV sites, is also popular. Some campgrounds charge $4 per night when water is made available (during the summer only); otherwise there is no charge to camp. There is also primitive camping along the river for rafters and backpackers.

Southeastern Oregon

If you thought Northeastern Oregon seemed lonely, you probably haven't yet experienced Southeastern Oregon. To travel in this part of the state you need a sturdy, reliable car, a cooler for cold drinks and snacks, and it might not be a bad idea to take along camping equipment because hotels/motels are few and far between. Harney County is the largest county in the United States, larger in fact than many Northeastern states, but this part of the country is really wide open. Harney is the largest of the three counties in southeastern Oregon at 10,228 square miles and has the smallest population, just over 7000. One town, Wagontire on Route 395, has a population that hovers around seven. Some say it depends on how many children are home for the holidays.

Few roads run through this area: Route 395 from California and Route 95 from Nevada are the main north–south corridors. Route 20 goes across the center from Idaho to the Cascades, and Route 140 runs across the bottom from northern Nevada through Lakeview to Klamath Falls. In Malheur County you will find evidence of its diverse culture as Basque shepherds, Mexican cowboys and laborers, Japanese-American laborers and various Europeans came through and left their marks.

In Harney County are wildlife refuges around Malheur Lake and Steens Mountain. The only real population center is Burns. Crane, a tiny town southeast of Burns on Route 78, has the only public boarding school in the country.

SIGHTS   **Sycan Marsh** is north of Lakeview off Route 31. It was purchased by the Nature Conservancy, which is using it as a research center for the effects of grazing on native grasses. Sycan Interpretive Center leads trips to the marsh with guests sleeping in tents and eating food cooked on a wood stove. ~ P.O. Box 1267, Lakeview, OR 97630; 541-947-2691.

Northeast of Lakeview on Route 395 is **Abert Rim**, at 30 miles the largest exposed fault in North America. The massive fault juts up into the desert sky like a continuous cliff on the east side of Route 395, while on the west side of the highway is the talcum-white wasteland around **Lake Abert**.

The three counties that make up the southeastern corner of Oregon cover 28,450 square miles, with a population of only 12,400.

Northwest of Lakeview just off Route 31 on county roads in Christmas Valley is **Crack in the Ground**, a 700-foot-deep crack caused by an earthquake. In the same area, **Fort Rock** is the remnant of a volcano crater and ocean shoreline that looks like one side of a destroyed fort. Indian sandals found there were carbon-dated and found to be 10,000 years old.

About 25 miles northeast of Christmas Valley is **Lost Forest**, a 9000-acre ponderosa-pine forest that has managed to survive in the middle of the harsh desert. The forest is surrounded by shifting sand dunes, which are popular with the all-terrain-vehicle set.

Oregon's longest lake, manmade **Lake Owyhee**, has miles of striking desert topography along its shores. It is reached by taking Route 201 south from Nyassa to the small town of Owyhee, then a county road that dead-ends at the lake. Farther down in the desert where the Owyhee River still runs free is some of the state's best whitewater for river runners.

LODGING   Down in the desert, Burns has four or five motels, including the **Best Western Ponderosa Motel**. It has 52 ordinary but clean rooms that don't smell of disinfectant, and a swimming pool. ~ 577 West Monroe Street, Burns; 541-573-2047, 800-303-2047, fax 541-573-3828. BUDGET.

HIDDEN ►   **Hotel Diamond** is located 30 miles northeast of Frenchglen. Built in 1898 as a hotel, the wood structure also serves as a general store and post office, so if you stay there you will probably meet all the locals. Because the roads can be difficult, it also has a gas station and a tire changer. The hotel has six small, wallpapered rooms with shared baths and one room with private bath.

Meals are available. ~ 10 Main Street, Diamond; 541-493-1898.
BUDGET.

There are only three places to stay in the area around Steens
Mountain, Alvord Desert and Malheur and Harney lakes, so
reservations are strongly recommended. A historic place is the
Frenchglen Hotel, a classic ranch house with screened porch built
in 1924. Frenchglen has eight guest rooms decorated with rustic
pine and patchwork quilts and has two shared baths. The man-
agers serve a family-style dinner. Closed from mid-November
through March. ~ Frenchglen, OR 97736; 541-493-2825. BUDGET.

Two miles north of Lakeview is **Hunter's Hot Springs Resort,**
which owns one of Oregon's two geysers. Named Old Perpetual,
it shoots water and steam 60 feet into the air every 30 seconds.
The resort has a thermal pool, and the hot water is reputed to have
healing powers. The resort's 30 units are simply decorated in what
the owner calls country style. For the athletically minded, the resort also offers a fitness center and racquetball court. ~ Route
395 North, Lakeview; 541-947-2127, 800-979-4350, fax 541-
947-5496. BUDGET TO MODERATE.

DINING

Almost everyone's favorite place to eat in Burns is the **Pine Room
Lounge.** The family that owns this restaurant has a secret recipe
for potato-dumpling soup, cuts all their own meat and makes their
own bread. Closed Sunday and Monday. ~ Monroe Street and
Egan Avenue, Burns; 541-573-2672. MODERATE.

SHOPPING

More than 50 local artists display their works at **Tuning Studio
& Gallery,** where items include iridescent raku pottery, horseshoe
sculptures, handcarved carousel horses, landscape paintings, wood
carvings and historic Harney County photographs from the original negatives. ~ 21 North Burns Street, Burns; 541-573-2435.

PARKS

MALHEUR NATIONAL WILDLIFE REFUGE   At 183,000
acres, Malheur covers an interesting and diverse wildlife population and geological features. Malheur Lake is a major resting area
for migratory birds on the Pacific Flyway. Fishing is permitted at
Krumbo Reservoir, and hunting is allowed at certain times of the
year. Malheur Field Station (541-493-2629) has dormitory and
family housing and meals available. ~ Located 26 miles south of
Burns on Route 205, then 6 miles on Princeton-Narrows Road;
541-493-2612.

HART MOUNTAIN NATIONAL ANTELOPE REFUGE
This 275,000-acre refuge 65 miles northeast of Lakeview protects a large population of antelope, bighorn sheep, mule deer,
coyotes, a variety of smaller animals and a bird population. Hart
Mountain, the centerpiece of the refuge, rises to 8065 feet and

has deep gorges, ridges and cliffs on the west side. The east side of the mountain climbs more gradually. For rockhounds, collections are limited to seven pounds per person. Fishing is permitted in Rock and Guano creeks depending on conditions. No facilities. ~ Located 65 miles northeast of Lakeview on county roads off Routes 395 and 140; 541-947-3315.

▲ There is a site designated for primitive camping; free of charge; no water.

▼▼▼▼▼▼▼▼▼▼▼▼▼▼
Outdoor Adventures

FISHING

Although eastern Washington is not, as one local guide puts it, "blue ribbon" fishing territory for most of the year, the region has its moments: come August, some big salmon show up in the Klickitat River; September starts the steelhead run in the Snake River; and trout in June and July make the Yakima River the most popular flyfishing stream in the Northwest. Some outfitters can also arrange hunting trips for game like elk, deer and bighorn sheep.

OKANOGAN HIGHLANDS   Although his primary activity is arranging horse-drawn wagon camping adventures, Donald Super of **Highland Stage Company** also guides one-day fishing trips for trout in nearby Bonaparte Lake and multiday pack trips to wilderness areas for fishing and hunting. ~ Tonasket; 509-486-4699.

SPOKANE AREA   G. L. Britton has been flyfishing since he was a boy; he now guides visiting anglers for walk-and-wade fishing on the Spokane during June and July, and in August on the Wenatchee. The rest of the year, which is not necessarily peak fishing season in eastern Washington, Britton will take you out to one of the local lakes for fishing that's more "teach-you" than "trophy." ~ Spokane; 509-466-4635.

SOUTHEASTERN WASHINGTON   If you would "rather be fishing," then call Dan Little at RBF Excursions to arrange a day of catch-and-release flyfishing for trout on the Yakima River. RBF also guides summer steelhead trips to the Klickitat River, about 65 miles away; for part of the year, Dan guides on Olympic Peninsula rivers as well. ~ Yakima; 509-965-6308.

NORTHEASTERN OREGON   Hells Canyon Adventures operates one-day charters for steelhead and sturgeon fishing on the Snake River. If you'd like to head out on your own, you can hitch a ride on one of the charter boats, which will drop you off downriver in the morning and pick you up on the return later in the afternoon. ~ Oxbow; 541-785-3352, 800-422-3568.

RIVER RUNNING

In September on the Tieton River, in southeastern Washington, water is released from the dam that controls the flow, creating Class III and some Class IV rapids and drawing ever-increasing crowds of rafters. It may not be a "hidden" spot, but it's still a thrill. Whitewater thrills come on the Snake River in Northeastern Oregon, where it cuts through walls of black basalt, forming Hells Canyon, the deepest gorge in the country.

SOUTHEASTERN WASHINGTON   Chinook Expeditions offers day and overnight guided trips here. ~ P.O. Box 324, Index, WA 98256; 206-793-3451. **Rivers, Inc.** also offers guided trips on paddle rafts. ~ P.O. Box 2092, Kirkland, WA 98083; 425-822-5296.

Snake Dancer Excursions provides one-day jet boat tours down the Snake River and through Hells Canyon, with a stop at Kirkwood Ranch. ~ P.O. Box 635, Clarkston, WA 99403; 509-758-8927, 800-234-1941.

Another popular location for rafting is the Snake River between the Washington and Idaho border. Contact **O.A.R.S. Dories** for information on outfitted trips. ~ P.O. Box 216, Altaville, CA 95221; 209-736-0811, 800-877-3679.

NORTHEASTERN OREGON   Operating from Memorial Day to mid-September, **Hells Canyon Adventures** offers wild whitewater-rafting adventures as well as gentle scenic float trips through the canyon on a raft or jet boat. ~ Oxbow; 541-785-3352, 800-422-3568.

For a list of other outfitters licensed to operate raft or float trips in Hells Canyon, you can write or call the **park ranger headquarters** in Enterprise. ~ 88401 Route 82, Enterprise, OR 97828; 541-426-4978.

GOLF

Mountain valleys and high desert vistas give golfers satisfying course options, and greens fees that are lower than in urban areas sweeten the deal. Winter weather closes many courses for two to five months.

OKANOGAN HIGHLANDS   Hilly terrain makes a cart rental highly recommended at nine-hole **Oroville Golf Club**. The scenic course runs beside a river. ~ Nighthawk Road, two miles west of Oroville; 509-476-2390. Another option is the nine-hole **Okanogan Valley Golf Club**, between Omak and Okanogan. ~ Pogue Road off the Okanogan–Conconully Route, 509-826-9902.

GRAND COULEE AREA   Banks Lake Golf and Country Club offers nine holes for golf enthusiasts. The course is next to Banks Lake, and offers a few canyons and wide fairways. Both electric and pull carts are available for rent. ~ Two-and-a-half miles south of Grand Coulee on Route 155; 509-633-0163.

SPOKANE AREA   If you've seen San Francisco's Lincoln Park Municipal Golf Course with its view across the city skyline, Spokane's **Indian Canyon Golf Course** will seem familiar. Set on a hillside that undulates downward toward Spokane, the 18-hole course is well known throughout the region. ~ West 4304 West Drive; 509-747-5353.

SOUTHEASTERN WASHINGTON In Yakima, **Suntides Golf Course** is fairly flat, so it's very walkable, making it popular with seniors and junior golfers. There's water on 13 of the holes. ~ 231 Pence Road, Yakima; 509-966-9065. The 17th hole at public **Apple Tree Golf Course** is called Apple Island, and is shaped like an apple and surrounded by water (this is apple country, after all). The 9th and 18th greens are double holes. ~ 8804 Occidental Road, Yakima; 509-966-5877.

In Pasco, **Sun Willows Golf Course** is a public, 18-hole course that's very playable for all handicaps. It's fairly flat, but has several lakes. Carts are available for rent. ~ 2035 North 20th Avenue, Pasco; 509-545-3440. In Kennewick, a canyon runs through **Canyon Lakes Golf Course**, which makes for plenty of interesting shots on this 18-hole public course. Rated one of the top ten courses in the Northwest, Canyon Lakes also has a champion putting course and full practice facilities. ~ 3700 Canyon Lakes Drive, Kennewick; 509-582-3736.

NORTHEASTERN OREGON Golf courses are scarce in eastern Oregon simply because there aren't that many people around. A pleasant surprise is the nine-hole **Echo Hills Golf Course**. The course is par 36 and rather challenging, with hills and gullies. It's 23 miles northwest of Pendleton. ~ Take the Echo exit off Route 84; 541-376-8244. For 18 holes, try **Pendleton Country Club**. It's fairly flat, but very attractive. ~ Route 395 between Pendleton and Pilot Rock; 541-278-1739.

South of Pendleton, you'll find only nine-hole courses, such as the **Baker City Golf Course**, a fairly easy par-35 course. ~ 2801 Indiana Avenue; 541-523-2358. Near Hells Canyon is the nine-hole **Alpine Meadows**. The par-72 course is surrounded by beautiful mountains and has a laid-back atmosphere. ~ 66098 Golf Course Road, Enterprise; 541-426-3246. **John Day Golf** is a nine-hole course in the crossroads town where Route 365 meets Route 26. ~ West Highway, John Day; 541-575-0170.

✔ CHECK THESE OUT—UNIQUE OUTDOOR ADVENTURES

- Cut a trail through the winter snow on your snowmobile or cross-country skis at Mt. Spokane State Park. *page 245*
- Hike to the top of a granite mountain rising above its surrounding Palouse Hills at Steptoe Butte State Park. *page 254*
- Raft, fish or hike the Snake River at Hells Canyon National Recreation Area, home of a gorge deeper than the Grand Canyon. *page 261*
- Bicycle a traffic-free road of the Wallowa National Forest near Hells Canyon *page 267*

NORTHEASTERN OREGON Several outfitters are licensed to **PACK TRIPS**
lead overnight horse pack trips into the **Hells Canyon National
Recreation Area** and **Eagle Cap Wilderness**. A few offer day rides
and llama pack trips. For a list, write or call park headquarters.
~ 88401 Route 82, Enterprise, OR 97828; 541-426-4978.

Ski areas in this part of the state, particularly the southeast part, **SKIING**
are little farther away from the hustle and bustle of the larger,
more popular spots elsewhere.

OKANOGAN HIGHLANDS Downhill and cross-country skiing
are both popular in this region, particularly the latter because there
is so much open country and powdery snow. Cross-country trails
are maintained at most downhill areas, but any country road,
most golf courses and parks may be used by skiers. **Loup Loup**
between Okanogan and Twisp on Route 20 has a 1240-foot drop
for downhill skiing and snowboarding and a groomed area for
Nordic skiers. Its three lifts serve over a dozen runs; 30 percent are
for beginners, 40 percent intermediate and 30 percent advanced.
There is a small half-pipe for snowboarders, and 25 kilometers
of groomed trails for cross-country skiers. The resort has a full-
service rental and repair shop. Closed Monday, Tuesday and
Thursday. ~ 509-826-2720.

   Sitzmark, 20 miles northeast of Tonasket, has a base elevation of 3900 feet and a modest 650-foot drop. There is one chair
lift and one rope tow. The runs break down to 20 percent for beginners, 70 percent intermediate and 10 percent expert. The ski
shop rents downhill skis and snowboarding equipment, lessons
are also available. ~ 509-486-2700. **49° North**, ten miles east of
Chewelah, has five chairlifts on 1900 feet as well as a snowboard
park. The runs are 30 percent beginner, 40 percent intermediate
and 30 percent expert. They also offer free lessons for beginning
skiers. ~ 509-935-6649.

SOUTHEASTERN WASHINGTON **Ski Bluewood**, 22 miles southeast of Dayton at the end of a Forest Service road, has 1125 vertical feet of downhill skiing and a ski school. A quarter of the
slopes are beginner, 40 percent intermediate and 35 percent expert. A full ski shop sells and rents all equipment. ~ 509-382-
4725.

For the most part, automobile traffic is sparse in these regions, **BIKING**
so bicyclists have little trouble finding long stretches of road that
are practically deserted, and scenically beautiful. But they're also
challenging and attract avid cross-country bicyclists, especially
along Routes 3 and 86 in the Wallowa National Forest near Hells
Canyon. Recreational bicyclists, however, have a couple of options. Along the bank of the Spokane River, the paved **Centennial**

Trail connects Spokane with Coeur d'Alene, Idaho, about 35 miles away. The trail is a relatively flat, easy ride (and nobody says you have to go the full distance; you might just want to go as far as Plantes Ferry Park, where you'll find some interesting basalt rock formations in the water). Also in Spokane is the forested Riverside State Park, which has several gravel trails for mountain biking. Mt. Spokane, which rises some 5800 feet, is another recommended destination.

In the Yakima area, besides an easy five-mile multi-use route along the **Yakima Greenway**, which meanders along the river, there are several possible routes through the local **wine country**. The **Yakima Valley Visitors and Convention Bureau** has information and maps. ~ 509-575-3010.

In some cities, you'll find some bicycle routes that double as hiking trails (see "Hiking" below).

Bike Rentals   There are three bike shops located along Spokane's main street. Rent a bike or buy equipment at **North Division Bicycle Shop**. They rent everything—tandems, mountain bikes, racks and trailers. A full-service bike shop, they also organize a variety of bike treks. ~ 10503 North Division Street; 509-467-2453. Mountain bikes are rented at **Spoke 'N Sport**. ~ 212 North Division Street; 509-838-8842.

In the Yakima area, contact the **Yakima Valley Visitors and Convention Bureau** for a map of bike routes through the local wine country. ~ 509-575-3010. Mountain-bike rentals are available at **Valley Cycling and Fitness**. ~ 1802 West Nob Hill Boulevard, Yakima; 509-453-6699. **Sagebrush Cycles** also has bikes for rent. ~ 1406½ Fruitvale Boulevard, Yakima; 509-248-5393.

HIKING   All distances listed for hiking trails are one way unless otherwise noted.

OKANOGAN HIGHLANDS   Backpackers and day hikers alike enjoy this area because the weather is often clear and dry and the forest is more open than in the Cascades and Olympics. A number of established hiking trails are shown on Forest Service maps and in free brochures given out at the ranger station in Tonasket. ~ 509-486-2186.

A good walk for a family with small children is the one-mile trail leading from Bonaparte Campground just north of the one-store town of Wauconda to the viewpoint overlooking the lake. Another easy one is the **Big Tree Trail** (.7 mile roundtrip) from Lost Lake Campground, which is only a short distance north of Bonaparte. This one goes through a signed botanical area.

One of the most ambitious highlands trails is the **Kettle Crest Trail** (13 miles). The trek begins at the summit of Sherman Pass on Route 20 and winds southward past Sherman Peak and several other mountains. The trail is through mostly open terrain, and you'll have great views of the mountains and Columbia River Valley. ~ 509-775-3305.

GRAND COULEE AREA A system of paths and trails connects the four towns clustered around Grand Coulee Dam. The Bureau of Reclamation built a paved route called the **Community Trail** (2 miles), which connects Coulee Dam and Grand Coulee. An informal system of unpaved paths connects these two towns to Elmer City and Electric City.

The newest is the walking-biking trail called the **Down River Trail** (6.5 miles). It runs north along the Columbia River from Grand Coulee, beginning in the Coulee Dam Shopping Center. It is accessible for wheelchairs.

Bunchgrass Prairie Nature Trail (.5 mile roundtrip) begins in the Spring Canyon Campground, which is three miles up Roosevelt Lake by water and two miles from Grand Coulee. The trail starts in the campground, and self-guided booklets are at the trailhead. It goes through one of the few remaining bunchgrass environments here. ~ 509-633-9441.

SOUTHEASTERN WASHINGTON **Cowiche Canyon** (3 miles) starts five miles from Yakima. The trail is actually an old railroad bed that ran through the steep canyon. The canyon has unusual rock formations, and you can expect to see some wildlife.

Noel Pathway (10 miles) is a trail inside the city limits of Yakima that follows the Yakima River. The pathway is used by bicyclists, as well.

NORTHEASTERN OREGON The **Eagle Cap Wilderness** can be entered south of Enterprise and Joseph or from Lostine and has about a dozen major routes. One popular hike is from Wallowa Lake State Park seven-and-a-half miles to Ice Lake. It is heavily used during the summer months.

The **Hells Canyon National Recreation Area** straddles the Snake River and offers some of the most rugged landscape in the canyon. About a dozen trails have been established here, with ratings from easy to difficult. The **Western Rim Trail** (34 miles) gives great views of the canyon and has the advantage of going from the end of one Forest Service road to another. The **HC Reservoir Trail** (4.8 miles) runs along the river between Copper Creek and Leep Creek.

▼▼▼▼▼▼▼▼▼▼
Transportation

CAR

Eastern Washington and Oregon are served by a network of roads that range from interstates to logging roads that have been paved by the Forest Service. **Route 97** serves as the north–south dividing line between the Cascade Mountains and the arid, rolling hills that undulate to the eastern boundaries of the states.

Route 90 runs through the center of the Washington, from Spokane southwest through Moses Lake, George and across the

Columbia River at Vantage, where the highway turns almost due west for its final run to Puget Sound.

Route 82 begins near Hermiston, Oregon, crosses the Columbia River to the Tri-Cities (Richland, Kennewick and Pasco) and runs on up the Yakima Valley to join Route 90 at Ellensburg. **Route 84** runs almost the entire length of the Columbia River Gorge in Oregon before swinging southeast at Hermiston and connecting Pendleton, La Grande and Baker City with Ontario on the Idaho border.

Other major highways are **Route 395**, starting south of Lakeview, Oregon, and continuing into Washington at the Tri-Cities to Ritzville. It joins with Route 90 at Ritzville only to emerge again at Spokane, where it continues north into British Columbia. Smaller but important highways include **Route 12** between Clarkston and Walla Walla, and **Route 195** running between Spokane and the Clarkston-Lewiston area.

Perhaps the most beautiful of all the highways in Washington is **Route 20**, which starts at Whidbey Island and continues to the North Cascades, through the Methow Valley, then straight through the Okanogan Highlands to Kettle Falls, where it merges with Route 395. It becomes Route 20 again at Colville, and continues southeast to Newport on the Idaho border. Oregon's **Route 26** is another lovely drive. It runs from Astoria over the Coast Range to Portland, then over the Cascades at Mt. Hood into the desert at Prineville and through the John Day Fossil Beds National Monument to Ontario on the Snake River.

Certainly the loneliest major highway in the Northwest is **Route 95**, which comes up from McDermitt, Nevada, to cross the Oregon desert for nearly 150 miles before arriving at the first town, Burns Junction. From there it heads northeast into Idaho.

AIR

Spokane International Airport is by far the busiest in Eastern Washington with eight airlines serving the area: Alaska Airlines, America West Express, Delta Airlines, Horizon Air, Northwest Airlines, Southwest Airlines, United Airlines and United Express.

Airport Shuttle Service offers transportation from your door to the airport by appointment. ~ 509-535-6979.

Other airports with scheduled service in Washington are **Moses Lake, Pullman, Wenatchee, Yakima,** the **Tri-Cities** and **Walla Walla.** All of these smaller cities are served by either Horizon Air, United Express or both. In addition, Delta Airlines serves the Tri-Cities. Empire Airlines serves the Tri-Cities and Yakima.

The only Oregon city in this region with scheduled air service is **Pendleton,** served by Horizon Air.

BUS

Three bus lines operate in the region. From the Spokane terminal at 221 West First Street are **Greyhound Bus Lines** (509-624-

5255, 800-231-2222) and **Northwestern Trailways** (509-838-4029). Greyhound also serves Yakima at the depot at 602 East Yakima Avenue.

Operating from Medical Lake (just southwest of Spokane) is **Alpha Omega Tours and Charters**. ~ 419 North Jefferson; 509-624-4116.

Eastern Oregon is served primarily by **Greyhound**. ~ 320 Southwest Court, Pendleton; 541-276-1551, 800-231-2222.

TRAIN

Washington is one of the few states to have two **Amtrak** (800-872-7245) routes. Both start in Spokane. The first route runs from Spokane due west with stops in Ephrata, Wenatchee, Everett and Edmonds before arriving in Seattle. The other route runs southwest from Spokane to the Columbia River Gorge with stops in Pasco, Wishram, Bingen and Vancouver, and ultimately goes to Portland, Oregon.

In Oregon, Amtrak follows the same route pioneers took coming into Oregon, from Ontario to Baker City, La Grande, Pendleton and Hermiston before going down the Columbia Gorge to Portland. ~ 800-872-7245.

CAR RENTALS

Car-rental agencies in Spokane include the following: **Affordable Rent A Car** (800-722-9732), **Budget Car and Truck Rental** (800-527-0700), **National Interrent** (800-227-7368), **Thrifty Car Rental** (800-367-2277) and **U-Save Auto Rental** (800-272-8728).

Agencies in the Tri-Cities include **Avis Rent A Car** (800-331-1212), **Budget Rent A Car** (800-527-0700), **Hertz Rent A Car** (800-654-3131) and **National Interrent** (800-227-7368). Walla Walla is served by **Budget Rent A Car** (800-527-0700).

The agency at the Pendleton airport is **Hertz Rent A Car** (800-654-3131). Other, smaller airports served by scheduled airlines will have rental cars available, often from a local automobile dealer.

PUBLIC TRANSIT

The Tri-Cities area (Pasco, Kennewick and Richland) has **Ben Franklin Transit** (509-735-5100). **Valley Transit** (509-525-9140) serves Walla Walla and College Place, and Prosser has its own **Rural Transit** (509-786-1707). Pullman has **Pullman Transit** (509-332-6535). Yakima has **Yakima Transit** (509-575-6175).

TAXIS

Major taxi companies in the area are **Budget Taxi** (509-326-8294) and **Spokane Cab** (509-535-2535).

SEVEN

Portland and the Columbia River Gorge

But for the flip of a coin, Portland could have been called Boston. Our story begins with two pioneers, Asa Lovejoy of Massachusetts and Francis Pettygrove of Maine, hitting the Oregon Trail in search of the American Dream. On a fall 1843 canoe journey up the Willamette River from Fort Vancouver to Oregon City, Tennessee drifter William Overton (traveling with Lovejoy) thought the land was perfect for a settlement. Lacking the 25-cent filing fee, he split the claim with Lovejoy in return for the money. Overton soon grew tired of working the land, and sold his half to Francis W. Pettygrove.

Soon, Lovejoy found himself partners with Pettygrove at "The Clearing," what native guides called the area. Lovejoy wanted to call the new town Boston, but Pettygrove preferred to appropriate the name of Maine's Portland. True gentlemen, they settled the matter with a coin toss at Oregon City's Francis Ermatinger House.

Pettygrove won, but it was years before Portland began to rival Oregon City, the immigrant hub at the end of the overland trail. Even today, with a metropolitan population of more than 1.5 million, many visitors wonder how this city emerged as Oregon's centerpiece. Unlike the largest cities of the Pacific Northwest or California, it is not located on a major coast or sound. Although it is midway between the equator and the North Pole, Portland is not central to the geography of its own state. Yet from the arts and winter recreation to architecture and vineyards, this city is an admirable metropolis, one that merits inclusion on any Northwest itinerary.

The community boasts a rich cultural life, has a popular National Basketball Association franchise, is blessed with some of the prettiest urban streets in the Northwest, is a veritable haven for antique lovers, runners, cyclists and garden aficionados and has an impressive array of jazz clubs, bistros and offbeat museums.

And yet the legacy of "The Clearing" is very much intact as the city remains intimately connected to the great outdoors. Near the entrance to the fabled Columbia River Gorge, Portland is just 65 miles from the nearest glacier and 110 miles from the ocean. Riverfront greenspace, the 5000-acre Forest Park and the wonderful wetlands of Sauvie Island all demonstrate why this city has been named "best" on the Green Index, a study of pollution, public health and environmental policy.

When the weather turns very wet, as it does in the winter months, residents head for the powder-packed slopes of Mt. Hood or start gearing up for a bit of steelheading on the nearby coastal rivers. Winter is also the height of the cultural season, enjoyed at the Portland Center for the Performing Arts and dozens of other venues around town.

Portland's emergence as a major city owes much to emigrant New England ship captains who decided, in the mid-19th century, that the town's deep riverfront harbor was preferable to the shallows of Oregon City. Easy ocean access via the Columbia made the new port a convenient link to the emerging agrarian economy of the Willamette Valley, as well as the region's up-and-coming lumber mills. Like San Francisco, Portland flourished as an international shipping hub and as a gateway for the 1852 gold rush that began in the Jacksonville region.

As the Northwest's leading port and economic center, the town soon attracted the state's new gentry, the lumber barons, shipping titans, traders, mercantilists and agribusiness pioneers. They drew heavily on the architectural legacy of the Northeast and Europe, erecting Cape Cod–style homes, Victorian mansions, villas and French Renaissance–style mini-châteaus complete with Italian marble and virgin-redwood interiors.

A city that started out in life as a kind of New England–style village crafted out of native fir was made over with brick office blocks sporting cast-iron facades. Florentine, Italianate, gothic, even Baroque architecture began to emerge along the main drags. City fathers worked hard to upgrade the town's agrarian image, often with mixed results.

To unify the community, planners added a 25-block-long promenade through the heart of town. Lined with churches, office blocks, apartments and homes, these "Park Blocks" offered a grassy median ideal for contemplating the passing scene. Like a Parisian boulevard, this was the place where one might come for the hour and stay for the day. Brass water fountains, known as Benson Bubblers and left on 24 hours a day, brought the pure waters of the Cascades to street level.

While the city's New England quality made Bostonians feel right at home, Portland also attracted a significant Chinese community that labored long and hard on railroad lines and in salmon factories. Badly persecuted, they were just one of many victims of intolerance in this city that became a Ku Klux Klan center. Blacks, Jews and Catholics were also victimized at various times. But as Portland grew, this deplorable bigotry was replaced by a new egalitarianism. The city's intellectual life flourished thanks to the arrival of several major universities and prestigious liberal arts colleges.

As Portland modernized, it developed into a manufacturing center famous for everything from swimsuits to footwear. But as the city flourished as a center for high-tech industry, it did not forget its roots. Visitors eager to discover the Northwest flock here and to the Columbia River Gorge in pursuit of outdoor activities from windsurfing to birding. An ideal home base, this city has also drawn many famous artists, musicians and writers from larger, more congested and expensive communities like New York and Los Angeles.

Although much of Portland's best is within easy walking distance of downtown, the city's outer reaches are also well worth your time. The touchstones of great urban centers—science museums, zoos, children's museums and craft centers—are all found here. Amid its 50 museums, 23 theater companies and countless other amenities, Portland also offers many pleasant surprises such as a strong used-book-seller community, America's only advertising museum, the sole extinct volcano within the limits of a continental U.S. city and the world's smallest park.

At a time when many major American urban centers are fighting hard to preserve their quality of life, Portland has been named the "Most Livable U.S. City" by the U.S. Conference of Mayors. Careful restoration of the downtown core and historic old town, a beautiful riverfront area and thriving nightlife make this town a winner. Neighborhoods such as Nob Hill, Hawthorne and Sellwood all invite leisurely exploration. And when it comes to parks you can choose from more than 80 spanning 37,000 acres.

In this chapter we have divided the city into three geographic regions. The Central Portland region encompasses downtown, the Skidmore Old Town District and the Yamhill Historic District. Portland West covers the balance of the city and metropolitan region west of the Willamette River. Portland East explores the metro area east of the Willamette River including Lloyd Center, Burnside, Sellwood and southerly destinations like Oregon City.

Because of its proximity to Portland, we have included the Columbia River Gorge region in this chapter. Even if you only have a couple of hours to cruise up to Multnomah Falls, by all means go. The Gorge extends about 60 miles east to Hood River and White Salmon, Washington. It was the final leg of the journey west for many Oregon pioneers; imagine how it felt for them to glide through this verdant, waterfall-lined canyon after 2000 miles of hardscrabble, blazing desert and treacherous mountain passes. This fir-clad valley really was Valhalla, the light at the end of the tunnel some people call the American Dream. We think you'll enjoy it as much as they did.

▼▼▼▼▼▼▼▼▼▼▼▼▼
Central Portland

The urban renaissance is clearly a success in Portland. A walkable city with perpetually flowing drinking fountains, this riverfront town is a place where commerce, history, classic architecture and the arts flourish side by side. Even when the weather is foul, Portland is an inviting place.

Downtown Portland *does* have its sleek towers, but it also contains plenty of low-lying delights as well. It's easy to tell that the city has spent a lot of time and money on parks and public art projects—Portland, after all, is the city whose mayor dreamed up the "Expose Yourself to Art" campaign in the 1970s (and that was mayor Bud Clark himself clad in an open trench coat on the famous poster).

A city that focuses so much on user-friendly public spaces certainly is welcoming to visitors. Whether you're taking a slow stroll

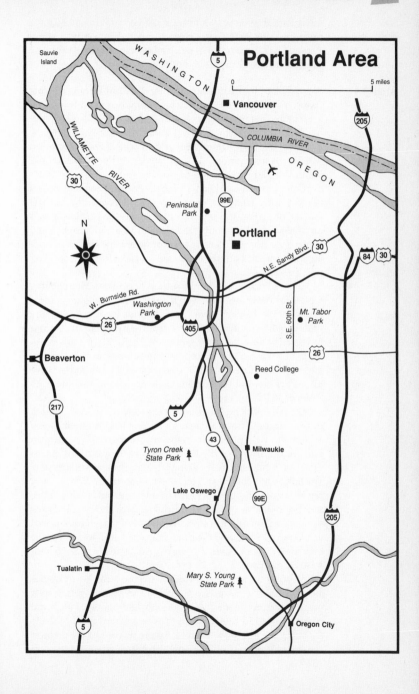

Portland Area

Sauvie Island

WASHINGTON

5

0   5 miles

■ Vancouver

205

COLUMBIA RIVER

OREGON

WILLAMETTE RIVER

30

Peninsula Park

99E

Portland ■

N.E. Sandy Blvd.

30

84   30

N

W. Burnside Rd.

Washington Park

26

405

S.E. 60th St.

Mt. Tabor Park

26

■ **Beaverton**

Reed College

217

5

43

Tyron Creek State Park

■ Milwaukie

Lake Oswego ■

99E

205

■ Tualatin

Mary S. Young State Park

5

■ Oregon City

along Park Avenue or shopping the markets of Portland's China-town (once the West Coast's largest Chinese community), Central Portland will impress you as much more than just the place where the populace clocks in from 9 to 5.

SIGHTS

A good place to orient yourself is the **Portland/Oregon Visitors Association**. Here you can pick up helpful maps and brochures. ~ Front and Salmon streets; 503-222-2223, 800-345-3214.

Walk west on Main Street to Justice Center and learn about the history of local law enforcement at the **Portland Police Historical Museum**. Closed Friday through Sunday. ~ Room 1682, 1111 Southwest 2nd Avenue; 503-823-0019.

Continue west on Main Street to the **Portland Building**, a post-modern office landmark opened in 1982. Designed by Michael Graves, this whimsical skyscraper represents the Northwest with an American Indian motif making extensive use of turquoise and earth tones. Above the entrance is **Portlandia**, the world's second-largest hammered-bronze sculpture. ~ 1120 Southwest 5th Avenue; 503-823-4000.

HIDDEN ▶

On the Portland Building's second floor is the **Metropolitan Center for Public Art**. Here you'll find *Portlandia* molds and renderings of the building, as well as pieces from the *Visual Chronicle of Portland*, a continually evolving series of works on paper meant to represent how the city views itself. The center is unstaffed—it's more an exhibition space than a museum—but it has assembled a walking-tour book that is available at the information desk on the first floor of the Portland Building. ~ 1120 Southwest 5th Avenue; 503-823-5111.

Continue west on Madison Street to South Park and turn left to the **Oregon History Center**. Home of the Oregon Historical Society, this is the place to learn the story of the region's American Indians, the arrival of the Europeans and the westward migration. You'll find sea chests from early voyages and artifacts documenting the political and social evolution of the West. A vast repository of Oregon history full of manuscripts and photographs, the Historical Society has a wonderful research library. Handsome trompe l'oeil murals, featuring the coming of the pioneers as well as Lewis and Clark and their Indian guide, Sacajawea, grace the building's exterior. Closed Monday. Admission. ~ 1200 Southwest Park Avenue; 503-222-1741.

Adjacent to the Oregon History Center is the **First Congregational Church**, dating from 1895. This Venetian gothic–style basalt structure, modeled on Boston's Old South Church and crowned by a 175-foot tower, is at its best in the fall. Elms shade the street in front of the church, making this one of the prettiest corners in Portland. ~ 1126 Southwest Park Avenue; 503-228-7219.

Directly across the street is the **Portland Art Museum**, known for its collection of Asian and European art as well as 20th-century American sculpture. The vast collection of American Indian art and artifacts showcases excellent tribal masks and wood sculptures. The pre-Columbian pieces, box drums, potlatch dishes and cones are all notable, and the Cameroon collection is nationally known. Don't miss the skylit sculpture courtyard. A new wing will be completed in the fall of 1998. Admission. ~ 1219 Southwest Park Avenue; 503-226-2811.

Head west to 11th Avenue and then turn south to **The Old Church**. Built in 1883, this gothic classic is one of the city's oldest and best-loved buildings. Noon concerts are held Wednesday. Closed weekends. ~ 1422 Southwest 11th Avenue; 503-222-2031.

Return to Park Avenue and continue north to Yamhill Street and turn right. Walk two more blocks to **Pioneer Courthouse Square**, a popular Portland gathering point. A waterfall and 64,000 red bricks inscribed with the names of local residents who donated money for the square's construction are all here. Named for adjacent **Pioneer Courthouse**, the oldest public building in Oregon (completed in 1873), which you may want to explore, the square offers a variety of special events including concerts and, at Christmas time, a ceremonial Christmas-tree lighting and tuba concert. ~ 701 Southwest 6th Avenue; 503-223-1613.

Continue walking east on Yamhill past the 19th-century Victorian Italianates and the shops, food stands and outdoor produce stalls of **Yamhill Marketplace**. ~ 110 Southwest Yamhill Street; 503-224-3450.

Proceed onward to **Tom McCall Waterfront Park**, on Front Avenue, which is notable for being the green river frontage that 20 years ago replaced a busy, ugly stretch of freeway blocking the Willamette. Go south past **Mill Ends Park**, located in the median at Southwest Front Avenue and Taylor Street. Just two feet wide, this is the smallest park in the world.

•••

✔ CHECK THESE OUT—UNIQUE SIGHTS

- Experience Portland's revitalized **waterfront** from a deck chair of a moonlight river cruiser. *page 278*
  - Relive the old-time atmosphere of a vintage carnival and theme park at the riverside **Oaks Amusement Park**. *page 288*
    - Escape the bustle of downtown Portland in the serenity of Washington Park's **Japanese Strolling Pond Garden**. *page 295*
      - Blaze a trail to **Fort Vancouver**, the original fur-trading post of the first British settlers in the area. *page 302*

Walk south to **Salmon Springs Fountain**, Salmon Street at Front Avenue, a synchronized fountain that is a favorite downtown meeting place. Kids and dogs love to play in its cool water on hot days. Farther south, past the Hawthorne Bridge on Harbor Way, you'll come to the sloped-roof buildings of **RiverPlace**, a popular shopping, hotel, restaurant and nightclub complex on the water. A promenade overlooks the Willamette River and the marina's many plush yachts.

Then return north to the **Oregon Maritime Center and Museum**. Here's your chance to learn Northwestern maritime history and see models of early ships, historical photographs and interpretive displays. Closed Monday and Tuesday in the summer and Monday through Friday the rest of the year. Admission. ~ 113 Southwest Naito Parkway; 503-224-7724.

When you're ready to take a break, head to the **Ira Keller Memorial Fountain**, located across from the Civic Auditorium. Situated in a pretty little park, this is a lovely spot to rest your weary feet. ~ Clay Street between 3rd and 4th avenues.

To fully experience the Portland waterfront consider boarding an excursion boat; the following companies depart from RiverPlace Marina at 1510 Southwest Harbor Way behind the RiverPlace Alexis Hotel. For a dramatic trip on the Willamette River, board the **Sternwheeler Cascade Queen**. ~ 503-223-3928. For summer cruises on the Columbia, board the **Sternwheeler Columbia Gorge** from Cascade Locks. ~ 503-223-3928. **Rose City Riverboat Cruises/Yachts-O-Fun Cruises** offers harbor, brunch, dinner and evening trips. ~ 503-234-6665. **Sternwheeler Rose** departs from the Oregon Museum of Science and Industry and offers scenic Willamette River cruises. ~ 503-286-7673. Another possibility is Portland's newest cruise ship, **Portland Spirit**, with year-round lunch, brunch, dinner and moonlight cruises. ~ 503-224-3900.

Now go north to Skidmore Fountain. Your gateway to the Skidmore Historic District, the fountain area is the site of the **Portland Saturday Market**, held on weekends from March through Christmas. Ankeny Park and the district beneath the Burnside Bridge is a great place to shop for arts and crafts, sample savory specialties served up by vendors and enjoy performances by musicians, street performers and clowns. ~ 108 West Burnside Street; 503-222-6072.

The **Skidmore/Old Town** area illustrates Portland's commitment to adaptive reuse. This area between Front and Third streets both north and south of Burnside Street boomed in the later 19th century when the harbor was bustling. The look of the buildings from that era derives from Florentine civic palaces: broad, strong, imposing facades constructed of brick and cast iron. Eventually

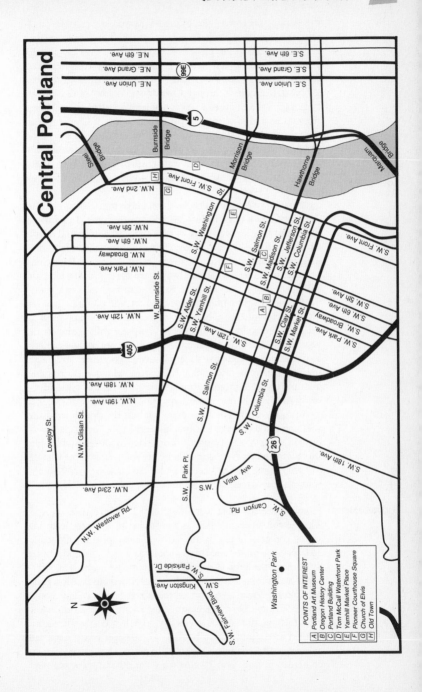

Central Portland

POINTS OF INTEREST

A	Portland Art Museum
B	Oregon History Center
C	Portland Building
D	Tom McCall Waterfront Park
E	Yamhill Market Place
F	Pioneer Courthouse Square
G	Church of Elvis
H	Old Town

this became the rowdy part of town where sailors caroused, and polite society began to keep away as the buildings fell into disrepair. But interest has grown in the waterfront over the past 30 years, and historic commercial buildings and warehouses have been reborn as trendy shops, galleries, restaurants and nightclubs.

Next, head north through **Chinatown** on 4th Avenue. Not as large as it was a hundred years ago, it is still packed with Chinese restaurants and markets. The ornate entry gate to Chinatown at the corner of Burnside Street and 4th Avenue looks a bit out of place among the neighboring adult bookstores. At Glisan Street head west to 6th Avenue. Then walk north to **Union Station**, Portland's marble-walled Amtrak Station. ~ 800 Northwest 6th Avenue; 503-273-4865.

HIDDEN ►

Finally, we believe everyone should take time out to visit the 24-hour **Church of Elvis**. Just head down 6th Avenue to Burnside Street and take a right. Walk one block to Broadway and take a left; proceed one block to Ankeny Street, take a right and this theological automat, also known as the world's first 24-hour coin-operated art gallery, will be halfway down the block. The ultimate storefront parish fuses religion, rock and metaphysics in a multimedia window presentation likely to keep you plunking quarter after quarter into the church's coin slot. Yes, it's cash up front to get the Commodore 64 ministerial computer rolling and set up your direct line to Graceland. Because there are no pews, much less a sanctuary, you have to stand outside, communicating with the interactive monitor behind the store window. By pushing multiple-choice buttons on the doorframe, you can respond directly to the computer screen's questions about Elvis, God, life, death and so forth. For a few extra quarters the church will issue wedding and divorce certificates. Inside there's a "tragic and spectacular" tour of the Church's World Headquarters—and a gift shop. Remember, every donation makes you a saint in the Church of Elvis. Come for the Elvis. Stay for the cookies. ~ 720 Southwest Ankeny Street; 503-226-3671.

LODGING

From its paneled lounge to a collection of 250 film classics on tape, **The Heathman** exemplifies Portland's charm. A library featuring signed copies of books by authors who have spent the night and 151 spacious rooms and suites appointed with contemporary art are some of the lures. Contemporary furniture, king beds and mirrored and marble baths make this refurbished landmark a good bet. Jazz is performed nightly on the lounge Steinway, and a popular café supplements the main dining room. How far does The Heathman go to make its guests happy? When Luciano Pavarotti wanted to sleep in after a late arrival, manager Mary Armistad asked a contractor across the street to postpone the start of noisy construction from 7 to 10 a.m. They agreed and the tenor slept soundly. ~ 1001 Southwest Broadway at Salmon Street; 503-241-4100, 800-551-0011, fax 503-790-7110. ULTRA-DELUXE.

A grand hotel and a registered historic landmark, **The Benson Hotel** offers casual fireside elegance in the lobby and 287 comfortably large rooms with understated gray decor, oak furniture, armoires and Early American prints. Like a good English club, the walnut-paneled lobby court contains easy chairs, comfortable sofas and a mirrored bar. Marbled halls, chandeliers, brass fixtures, a grand staircase and grandfather clock add an elegant touch. The stamped-tin ceiling, a common architectural feature in the late 19th and early 20th centuries, is one of the finest we've seen. Amenities include a health club and two restaurants. ~ 309 Southwest Broadway; 503-228-2000, 800-426-0670, fax 503-226-4603. ULTRA-DELUXE.

A good value is the 136-room **Imperial Hotel**. Floral-pattern spreads, small sitting areas and modern prints have brightened up this venerable hotel. Convenient to popular shops, cafés and clubs, the Imperial also has a full lounge and restaurant. ~ 400 Southwest Broadway; 503-228-7221, 800-452-2323, fax 503-223-4551. MODERATE TO DELUXE.

Boutique hotels are one of the fastest-growing trends in the lodging industry and now Portland has one of its own, **Hotel Vintage Plaza**. A remake of the historic Wells Building, this hotel features a ten-story atrium. Each of the 107 guest rooms and expansive suites is named for a local winery. Rooms with burgundy and green color schemes come with cherry-wood armoires, neoclassical furniture, columned headboards, black-granite nightstands and Empire-style column bedside lamps. On the top floor, there are some "Starlight" rooms, with light-sand beach motifs and one-way solarium windows for stargazers. Local fine wines can be sampled at the complimentary tasting held each evening in front of the fireplace in the lobby. ~ 422 Southwest Broadway; 503-228-1212, 800-243-0555, fax 503-228-3598. ULTRA-DELUXE.

An excellent value, the **Riverside Inn** is the place to enjoy views of boat traffic on the Willamette. The rooms have a contemporary feel, with oak furniture and earth-toned decor. Enjoy the sunset from the comfort of your deck. The 140-room inn is within walking distance of Portland's business and shopping district. A café and bar are also here. ~ 50 Southwest Morrison Street; 503-221-0711, 800-899-0247, fax 503-274-0312. DELUXE.

Enjoying one of the best locations in town, **RiverPlace Hotel** offers 84 rooms, suites and condos, many with views of the Willamette. In the midst of the Esplanade area featuring bookstores, antique shops and restaurants, this establishment is a short walk from the downtown business district. Wing-back chairs, teak tables, writing desks, fireplaces and pastel decor make the rooms inviting. A health club, whirlpool baths and indoor track are all available. ~ 1510 Southwest Harbor Way; 503-228-3233, 800-227-1333, fax 503-295-6161. ULTRA-DELUXE.

For reasonably priced rooms and suites head for the **Mallory Hotel**. This 143-unit establishment has a mirrored lobby, leaded skylights, a chandelier and grandfather clock. The eclectic rooms here come with floral-print spreads, oak furniture, contemporary couches and, in some cases, small chandeliers. There is also a classy dining room with marble pillars supporting the embossed gold-leaf ceiling. ~ 729 Southwest 15th Avenue; 503-223-6311, 800-228-8657, fax 503-223-0522. MODERATE.

Portland also has many bed and breakfasts. To book a room in or near the city contact **Northwest Bed and Breakfast Travel Unlimited**. They handle bed and breakfasts from British Columbia through California. ~ 1067 Hanover Court South, Suite 606, Salem; 503-243-7616.

DINING

The brick pizza oven, trattoria ambience, dark-wood booths and gleaming bar make **Pazzo Ristorante** a welcome addition to the Portland restaurant scene. Dip a little of the fresh-baked bread in the special-press extra virgin olive oil, hoist a glass of the red and survey the Mediterranean menu. Pizza, grilled beef T-bone with red onion relish over white beans, creamy polenta with rosemary and parmesan, and pasta tubes with lamb sausage, Swiss chard, marinara and ricotta are some of the popular entrées. ~ 627 Southwest Washington Street; 503-228-1515. MODERATE TO DELUXE.

A veritable designer showcase with Asian, art deco, nautical and brass-and-glass furnishings, **Atwater's** looks like an exclusive private club. That's precisely what it is by day. At night the public is welcome to dine in this 30th-floor restaurant. Appetizers prepared in the display kitchen might include thyme-roasted quail with potato, smoked bacon, leeks and pinot noir ver jus and spinach and Gorgonzola ravioli. After a salad of organic mixed greens, try the grilled ahi, marinated salmon or roasted ten-vegetable stew. Dinner Only. ~ 111 Southwest 5th Avenue; 503-275-3600. MODERATE TO ULTRA-DELUXE.

A favorite in Portland is **The Heathman Restaurant**. The seasonally changing menu features traditional dishes using Northwest ingredients, seafood and game meats. Some specialties include grilled lightly smoked salmon, seared ahi tuna wrapped in prosciutto and roast rack of lamb. This spacious dining room and adjacent brass and marble bar is a great place to watch the passing scene on Broadway. The walls are graced with a classy collection of contemporary art. ~ Southwest Broadway at Salmon Street; 503-241-4100. MODERATE TO DELUXE.

Pass the retsina and toast **Alexis**. This family-style taverna brings the Aegean to the Columbia in the time-honored manner. Belly dancing on the weekend, wallhangings and long tables upstairs with checkered blue-and-white tablecloths add to the ambience. Lamb souvlaki, moussaka, charbroiled shrimp and vegetarian specialties are all on the menu. Be sure to try the dolmas and share an order of hummus and homemade pita. ~ 215 West Burnside Street; 503-224-8577. MODERATE.

A memorable dining room is **Jake's Famous Crawfish**. This mahogany-paneled, century-old landmark has a grand bar, big tables and a seafood menu that seems to stretch from here to Seattle. Inevitably packed, the restaurant offers good chowder, smoked and fresh salmon, halibut, oysters and a good bouillabaisse. For the non-seafood lover, they also offer pasta and steak dishes. Despite the crowds, service is terrific. ~ 401 Southwest 12th Avenue; 503-226-1419. MODERATE TO DELUXE.

B. Moloch Heathman Bakery and Pub is an ideal downtown stop for a light lunch or dinner, snacks, coffee or a drink at the full bar, supplied by one of 14 Oregon microbreweries. Exposed concrete columns, pine floors and tables give the place the ambience of a college student union. Order an individual pizza, Pacific seafood salad or herb roast beef and potted cheddar on dark rye. ~ 901 Southwest Salmon Street; 503-227-5700. MODERATE.

A vast menu offering Asian, Cajun, Italian and Oregon cuisine, **Harborside** is a kind of culinary United Nations. Window tables on the river and paneled booths on the upper levels provide great views of the harbor traffic. Excellent seafood salads, pasta dishes, stir frys, steaks, hamburgers and pizza are served. ~ 0309 Southwest Montgomery Street; 503-220-1865. MODERATE TO DELUXE.

A display kitchen, stained-glass ceiling, mahogany tables and booths make **Opus Too Bar and Restaurant** one of the city's more stylish restaurants. The restaurant serves up mesquite-broiled seafood, steaks, chicken and a wide variety of pasta dishes. Other highlights include pan-fried oysters, garlic prawns and a chocolate decadence cake that lives up to its name. After dinner enjoy live jazz in the lounge. ~ 33 Northwest 2nd Avenue; 503-222-6077. MODERATE TO DELUXE.

Obi is the place for sushi, *yaki soba*, shrimp tempura, salmon teriyaki and dozens of other Japanese specialties. The dark dining room has modest plastic tables and displays silk-screen art, watercolors and traditional costumes. Closed Sunday. ~ 101 Northwest 2nd Avenue; 503-226-3826. MODERATE.

Couch Street Fish House is an elegant Old Town restaurant located in a skylit brick storefront graced with historic photos and seascapes. Liveried waiters and comfortable booths and tables make the restaurant a good choice for a big night out. Seafood fettuccine, Pacific oysters, live Maine lobster, rack of lamb and crab legs toscana are a few of the specialties. Top them off with one of their distinctive flambéed desserts. Dinner only. Closed Sunday. ~ 105 Northwest 3rd Avenue; 503-223-6173. MODERATE TO ULTRA-DELUXE.

The setting alone justifies a trip to **Accuardi's Old Town Pizza Company**. A landmark commercial building with stained glass, wicker furniture, enough antiques to furnish a store and old root beer advertising signs make this two-level establishment a genuine period piece. More than two dozen toppings from goat cheese to roasted garlic give you plenty of options. Focaccia, antipasti, lasagna and salads are also available. ~ 226 Northwest Davis Street; 503-222-9999. BUDGET.

From the fresh flowers to the big red chairs, **Wilf's Restaurant and Piano Bar** is one of the most elaborate dining rooms in Portland. In this elegant setting along the tracks you can enjoy Northwest salmon filet, pepper steak, Dungeness crab legs, rack of lamb and, for dessert, bananas Foster or crêpes Suzette. Dinner only on Saturday. Closed Sunday. ~ 800 Northwest 6th Avenue; 503-223-0070. MODERATE TO DELUXE.

SHOPPING   The **Oregon History Center Museum Store** has an outstanding collection of local and regional history titles. From American Indian culture to walking tours of Portland, this admirable shop is definitely worth a look. Souvenir books, guides, children's literature, historical toys as well as regional gifts, are all found in abundance. ~ 1200 Southwest Broadway; 503-306-5230.

Don't walk, run to **Nike Town**. Featuring a statue of Michael Jordan, this store—the first—is a monument to conditioning. Two floors of museum-like galleries hawk the Nike line, while the latest models zoom through the store on a series of high-speed tubes connected to the basement warehouse. ~ 930 Southwest 6th Avenue; 503-221-6453.

Classic newsstands are rare these days. Fortunately, century-old **Rich's Cigar Store** continues this grand tradition. Browse for your favorite magazine or out-of-town newspaper in this beautiful wood-paneled shop. ~ 820 Southwest Alder Street; 503-228-1700.

A favorite used-book option in Portland is **David Morrison Books**. The shop focuses on rare photography, architecture and art books. Its bland storefront and unmarked red door give no hint of the wealth of out-of-print and antique books within. The back room houses an extensive photography collection, with more than a thousand titles. A generous assortment of books outside the focus area is guaranteed to amuse any browser. ~ 1420 Southeast 37th Avenue; 503-233-5868.

Bigger than many libraries, **Powell's City of Books** is only one of Portland's many fine bookstores. What makes it unique is its size—it would be hard to dispute its claim of being the world's largest bookstore. With over a million new and used titles, this

Goliath encourages customers to pick up a large map, indexed into hundreds of categories ranging from abortion to Zen. Somewhere in between you're likely to find the title you want. They also host guest readings by well-known authors.

Along the way, stop by the Anne Hughes Coffee Room for a break and a leisurely read. ~ 1005 West Burnside Street; 503-228-4651, 800-878-7323.

Powell's also has **Powell's Travel Store** at 701 Southwest 6th Avenue. ~ 503-228-1108.

When it comes to parks, Portland offers more than 80 spanning 37,000 acres.

Several major malls are in the downtown area. **The Galleria** is a fine example of adaptive reuse that has transformed a historic building into a three-story retail center. ~ 921 Southwest Morrison Street. **Pioneer Place** boasts 80 stores spread across a three-block area. ~ Southwest 5th Avenue and Morrison Street.

One of the region's best-known apparel makers offers its line at **The Portland Pendleton Shop**. Skirts, shirts, slacks, jackets and blankets are sold at this popular shop. While its reputation was built on woolens, it also sells high-quality apparel in silk, rayon and other fabrics. ~ 4th Avenue at Salmon Street; 503-242-0037.

Elizabeth Leach Gallery presents an array of regional and national painters, sculptors, photographers and print makers. ~ 207 Southwest Pine Street; 503-224-0521.

Oregon Mountain Community is the ultimate shop for recreational equipment and supplies. In addition to a full line of outdoor wear, there's skiing, backpacking and climbing gear. ~ 60 Northwest Davis Street; 503-227-1038.

Nearly 300 artisans display handcrafted glass, jewelry, gyroscopes, hats, sweaters, furniture, rugs, music boxes and folk and fine art at the **Portland Saturday Market**. There's also live entertainment. Closed January and February. ~ Between Front and 1st streets just south of Burnside Street; 503-222-6072.

The **Attic Gallery** features paintings, sculpture, prints and ceramics by major Northwest artists. ~ 206 Southwest 1st Avenue; 503-228-7830.

The city's cultural hub is the **Portland Center for the Performing Arts**. Included are the Arlene Schnitzer Concert Hall and the Intermediate and Winningstad theaters. The center is home of the **Oregon Symphony Orchestra** (503-228-1353), the **Civic Auditorium** and **Portland Center Stage** (503-274-6588). ~ 1111 Southwest Broadway; 503-248-4335.

NIGHTLIFE

Portland Repertory Theater stages contemporary drama. A professional equity company, The Rep frequently sells out. ~ 25 Southwest Salmon Street; 503-224-4491.

Artists Repertory Theater is the place for off-Broadway productions. ~ 1516 Southwest Alder Street; 503-241-1278.

Both the **Oregon Ballet Theater** (503-227-6867) and **Portland Opera** (503-241-1802) perform at the Civic Auditorium, located at 222 Southwest Clay Street.

At **The Heathman Lobby Lounge,** musicians like Dave Firshberg play jazz on the Steinway. ~ Southwest Broadway at Salmon Street; 503-241-4100.

Enjoy a cocktail to the strains of live pop and jazz piano at **The Benson Hotel's Lobby Court.** This elegant setting includes plush sofas and wing chairs and walnut paneling. The lounge is a great place to impress your friends—or yourself. ~ 309 Southwest Broadway; 503-228-2000.

Brasserie Montmartre is another good jazz venue. This artdeco establishment, where patrons are encouraged to draw on their paper tablecloths, even has a strolling magician. Contemporary drawings, comfortable banquettes, chandeliers and a checkered black-and-white floor all add to the café's charm. ~ 626 Southwest Park Avenue; 503-224-5552.

The **Portland Art Museum—After Hours** is the perfect way to spend a Wednesday evening, October through April. Take a seat or explore the collection while the halls resonate to jazz or blues. Beer, wine and hors d'oeuvres are served. Admission. ~ 1219 Southwest Park Avenue; 503-226-2811.

One of the coolest clubs in town is **Jazz de Opus**. This lowslung lounge adjacent to a popular restaurant offers a full bar. Live music is offered seven days a week. Cover Friday and Saturday. ~ 33 Northwest 2nd Avenue; 503-222-6077.

There's no cabaret in Portland quite like **Darcelle XV**. Female impersonators perform nightly in this small theater where dinner is also available. Cover. ~ 208 Northwest 3rd Avenue; 503-222-5338.

For rhythm-and-blues, rock, jazz, folk and pop in a faux tropical setting head on down to **Key Largo**. This red-brick commercial building with an exposed beam ceiling, casablanca fans, wicker furniture and hanging plants is at its best in the summer. Then you can head out back to party on the patio. Dinner and munchies are served. Cover. ~ 31 Northwest 1st Avenue; 503-223-9919.

A drag bar at **Embers** features drag shows nightly. In the rear of this brick building is **On The Avenue**, home of Portland's largest gay dancefloor. With neon-lit walls, two bars and deejay music, this room is always jumping. Cover Thursday through Saturday. ~ 110 Northwest Broadway; 503-222-3082.

With male strippers five nights a week, neon bar signs and a swinging dancefloor, **Silverado** has plenty of action. Deejay music, a long bar and dining room. Cover Friday and Saturday. ~ 1217 Southwest Stark Street; 503-224-4493.

The Pilsner Room is an upscale bar attached to a micro-brewery, serving fish-and-chips, hamburgers and the like. ~ 0309 Southwest Montgomery Street; 503-220-1865.

▼▼▼▼▼▼▼▼▼▼

Portland East

Just across the Willamette from the frenzied downtown core are some of Portland's most inviting neighborhoods. The city planners have emphasized good public transportation throughout the entire metropolitan area, keeping the neighborhoods east of the river unified with the downtown core. But only here can you glimpse Portland's lower-key charms: a shipping area devoted exclusively to antiques, a city park featuring an extinct volcano and a religious retreat doubling as a peaceful garden. Portland East is also home to a rare heirloom, a classic old-time amusement park.

This section of Portland also includes such suburbs as Oregon City and Milwaukie, the former of which once welcomed settlers who had made the arduous trek overland on the Oregon Trail. Today, Portland East is a network of streets and parks designed, like much of Portland, for maximum use by its residents.

SIGHTS

Cross the Willamette via MAX lightrail and disembark at the beautiful **Oregon Convention Center** plaza, landscaped with terraced planters. Stroll over for a look at the 490,000-square-foot center crowned by a matching pair of glass-and-steel spires soaring 250 feet above the hall. The center's interior contains art, dragon boats, a bronze pendulum and inspirational quotes about the state. Everywhere you go, even in the restrooms, you'll find talented artists and craftspeople have left their decorative touch. ~ 777 Northeast Martin Luther King Jr. Boulevard; 503-235-7575.

A mile south of the convention center, the **Oregon Museum of Science and Industry** (OMSI) is a 220,000-square-foot science education center. Four exhibition halls offer displays on the physical, earth, life and information sciences, while another deals with space and a sixth has traveling exhibits. In addition, you'll find an

◆◆◆

A PEACEFUL PLACE TO TAKE SANCTUARY

No visit to the city's east side is complete without a stop at **The Grotto**. Near the Portland airport, this 62-acre Catholic sanctuary and garden is a peaceful refuge that seems to have as much in common with a Zen retreat as it does with the Vatican. Beautiful ponds and shrines, paths leading through flower gardens and expansive views of the mountains and the Columbia River make The Grotto a local favorite. ~ Northeast 85th Avenue and Sandy Boulevard; 503-254-7371.

OMNIMAX motion picture theater and the Murdock Sky Theater presenting astronomy and laser light shows. Special exhibits focus on biotechnology, computers, engineering for kids, communications and chemistry. Closed Monday from September through May. Admission. ~ 1945 Southeast Water Avenue; 503-797-4000.

To the south are two popular Portland shopping districts. **Hawthorne Boulevard** from 30th to 40th avenues has become one of the city's more intriguing commercial districts. A great place to browse, shop and eat, this district is known for its used bookstores and offbeat boutiques. Another popular neighborhood is **Sellwood**, an antique center extending along 13th Avenue from Clatsop to Malden streets.

While cities across the land have scrapped these period pieces, Portland has held on to the **Oaks Amusement Park**, located just west of the Sellwood district. In addition to vintage thrill rides, you can enjoy roller skating to the strains of a Wurlitzer organ. This pretty park is part of the **Oaks Bottom Wildlife Sanctuary**, a major Portland marsh habitat. Closed Monday. ~ Amusement park: foot of Southeast Spokane Street; 503-236-5722.

One of the nation's most progressive liberal arts institutions, **Reed College** has a forested, 98-acre campus cloaked in ivy. Reed's gothic buildings and old dorms are close to Crystal Springs Rhododendron Garden at 28th Avenue and Woodstock Boulevard (see "Beaches & Parks" below for more information). ~ 3203 Southeast Woodstock Boulevard; 503-771-1112, 800-547-4750.

LODGING

An exceptional value, **The John Palmer House Bed and Breakfast Inn** is a circa-1890 Victorian that takes the bed-and-breakfast experience to the limit. Lace, oak headboards, stained glass and gingerbread detailing galore are all here. You can take advantage of the moderately priced Beethoven room or Schumann suite or go

---

✔ **CHECK THESE OUT—UNIQUE LODGING**

- *Budget:* Enjoy a barbecue at the **Condon House** when you check into one of the hunter-green rooms with a brass or iron bed. *page 309*
- *Moderate:* Retreat to a rarity—an affordably priced room in the center of Portland—at the **Mallory Hotel**. *page 282*
- *Deluxe:* Elect to stay at **Portland's White House**, a replica of the president's residence minus the Secret Service agents. *page 289*
- *Ultra-deluxe:* Join the likes of Luciano Pavarotti at Portland's most glamorous downtown address, **The Heathman**. *page 280*

Budget: under $50 Moderate: $50–$90 Deluxe: $90–$130 Ultra-deluxe: over $130

for the upscale Rossini suite. All come with a continental breakfast. Carriage rides, baskets of fruits or flowers, a private maid or butler, massage service, gardenias on the pillows and serenades from the veranda can all be arranged for a reasonable fee. ~ 4314 North Mississippi Avenue; 503-284-5893, 800-518-5893, fax 503-284-1239. BUDGET TO DELUXE.

Hail to the Chief! **Portland's White House** strongly resembles the other White House in Washington, D.C. The stately Greek columns, circular driveway, crystal chandeliers and French windows would all make the First Family feel right at home. The difference here is that you don't have to stand in line for a tour, and there are no Secret Service agents to hustle you along. Originally built as a lumber baron's summer home, this White House features handpainted murals of garden scenes and oak-inlaid floors. Canopy and brass beds, clawfoot tubs and leaded glass adorn the six rooms. Three additional rooms in an adjacent carriage house feature bronze feather beds and stained glass. The price of a room includes a full breakfast. ~ 1914 Northeast 22nd Avenue; 503-287-7131. DELUXE.

◄ HIDDEN

In the Hawthorne neighborhood, **Hostelling International— Portland** offers dorm accommodations for men and women and a family room. This older home also has a self-serve kitchen and all-you-can-eat pancakes in the morning. Guests are asked to do easy chores that take just a few minutes. Check-in begins at 4 p.m. Quiet time starts at 11 p.m. ~ 3031 Southeast Hawthorne Boulevard; 503-236-3380. BUDGET.

In Oregon City, the 1851 Greek Revival **Captain Ainsworth House Bed and Breakfast** offers cozy elegance. Each of the four guest rooms has a private bath and is decorated in burgundy, forest green and gold, with antiques and reproductions. ~ 19130 Lot Whitcomb Drive, Oregon City; 503-655-5172, fax 503-722-2099. MODERATE TO DELUXE.

One of Portland's better breakfasts is found at **Tabor Hill Café**. This small, red-brick establishment with eclectic decor features modern art, gray carpet and red tables. The apple-walnut pancake (that's singular, not plural) is large enough to blanket your entire plate. Other choices include chicken omelettes and a fresh fruit cup. Lunch specialties include turkey breast, avocado-and-bacon sandwich, burgers, marinated chicken breast and blackened-snapper salad. Closed Monday. ~ 3766 Southeast Hawthorne Boulevard; 503-230-1231. BUDGET.

DINING

It's not easy to find a three-course Sunday brunch these days, but we did it at **Bread and Ink Café**. The coffee is strong, the lox are beautiful and the children are kept content with crayons and paper. In addition to bagels and cream cheese, challah and a

Text continued on page 292.

Oregon City— The Trail's End

Wagons, ho!

So you missed out on the 19th-century move west? (Well, at least we weren't around then.) To get a sense of what it must have been like, head to Oregon City. Just a half-hour south of Portland, this community built along the 40-foot-high Willamette River waterfalls is one of the best places in the Pacific Northwest to understand and appreciate manifest destiny. For this was the destination that launched the migration of over 300,000 Americans to a blank slate known as the promised land.

The center of human endeavor for more than 10,000 years, the Willamette Falls was an important place long before the first white immigrants arrived. But once they did show up, things moved quickly. In 1818, just five years after the British took control of the Northwest region from the Astorians, the Americans and British agreed to jointly occupy Oregon Country. In 1829, Dr. John McLoughlin, the shrewd operator of the Hudson's Bay Company base at Fort Vancouver, built three homes at the Willamette Falls. Although the American Indians responded by burning these buildings, McLoughlin forged ahead with a new sawmill and flour mill.

American settlers began trickling in, and by 1841 the first wagon trains started to arrive. Pouring in by boat and by land, the pioneers soon spread across the Willamette Valley in search of farmsteads. Thankfully, you don't have to retrace the entire trail to learn of this riveting history. Just head to Oregon City's museums, homes, farms and cemeteries.

The place to begin your visit is the **End of the Oregon Trail Interpretive Center and Historic Site**. The center offers guided tours featuring living history presentations, a multimedia show and exhibits displaying notable artifacts, photographs and maps. You'll gain a well-rounded perspective on American Indian, missionary and immigrant history. You can also pick up helpful walking and driving tour guides to the community. Admission. ~ 1726 Washington Street; 503-657-9336.

Among the major highlights are the **McLoughlin House**, where the Hudson's Bay Company leader and "Father of Oregon" retired. Although his employer was British, John McLoughlin generously aided the new settlers and helped lay the groundwork for Americanization. Regular tours show off this home, which was a social hub in pioneer days. Highlights include a Chilkoot Indian ceremonial robe, banjo-shaped clock and Hudson's Bay Company sideboard. The home is closed on Monday and during the month of January. Incidentally, you can learn the rest of the McLoughlin story by visiting Fort Vancouver across the Columbia River from Portland. Admission. ~ 713 Center Street; 503-656-5146.

Also of special interest is the **Frances Ermatinger House**, a Federal-style residence showcasing antiques and memorabilia. Admission. ~ 6th and John Adams streets. The **Stevens Crawford House**, a historically preserved turn-of-the-century site, has a small collection of American Indian artifacts. Closed Monday. Admission. ~ 603 6th Street; 503-655-2866.

Well worth your time is the **Rose Farm**, one of the state's oldest residences. The first territorial governor was inaugurated at this home surrounded by rose plantings. A two-tiered piazza and second-story ballroom are highlights of this restored residence, now on the National Register of Historic Places. ~ 536 Holmes Lane.

The **Clackamas County Historical Society Museum of History** explores the history of Clackamas County with exhibits covering geology, traders and trappers, immigration, government and religion. Admission. ~ 211 Tumwater Drive; 503-655-5574.

Also of special interest is the **Oregon City Municipal Elevator**. Founded in 1916, this ride was designed to make it easy for residents to journey from the riverfront to the upper part of town. One of only four municipal elevators in the world, the 90-foot ride is a great way to enjoy views of Willamette Falls, particularly at sunset. Admission. ~ 7th and Main streets.

variety of omelettes, you'll enjoy the family-style atmosphere. Set in an elegant commercial building adorned with terra cotta, this weekly happening is a Portland original. The restaurant is also famous for its burgers. ~ 3610 Southeast Hawthorne Boulevard; 503-239-4756. MODERATE.

Located in the Sellwood district known for its antique stores, **Papa Haydn** is a yummy storefront café where fans twirl from the ceilings, watercolors grace the gray walls and bentwood furniture accommodates guests who don't come to count calories. Sunday brunch includes a bay-shrimp-and-salmon omelette, pear brioche french toast and salmon cakes. Dinner entrées include a salmon pepper pot and scallops carbonara. An extensive wine list and espresso drinks are found here along with one of the longest dessert menus in the Pacific Northwest. Closed Sunday night and Monday. ~ 5829 Southeast Milwaukie Avenue; 503-232-9440. MODERATE.

SHOPPING   Death can be proud at **Murder by the Book**. Mystery addicts will get their fix here and also become acquainted with many well-known Northwest authors. ~ 3210 Southeast Hawthorne Boulevard; 503-232-9995.

Even if you hate Garfield, you'll be charmed by **The Cat's Meow**. From shirts and cards to ceramics and lamps, everything sold here has a feline theme. ~ 3538 Southeast Hawthorne Boulevard; 503-231-1341.

NIGHTLIFE   The Moorish **Baghdad Theater and Pub** has a fairy-tale decor with painted walls and a fountain in the lobby. Every other row of theater seating has been removed to accommodate tables where patrons can order food and drinks and enjoy second-run films. Customers under 21 years of age are welcome for the Saturday and Sunday matinees only when accompanied by a parent. ~ 3702 Southeast Hawthorne Boulevard; 503-236-9234, 505-230-0895 (movie line).

The **Echo Theater** is the home of **Do Jump Movement Theater**. Shows include acrobatic and trapeze acts. Visiting dance troupes also use the theater's stage. ~ 1515 Southeast 37th Avenue; 503-231-1232.

Parchman Farm offers some of Portland's finest blues in an intimate setting. Etched glass, wood detailing, a full bar and a good dinner menu make this blues club and restaurant an excellent spot for a night on the town. Closed Sunday. Cover Friday and Saturday. ~ 1204 Southeast Clay Street; 503-235-7831.

One of the city's finest classical programs is **Chamber Music Northwest** (503-223-3202). Nationally known groups perform during June and July in the beautiful settings at Reed College and Catlin Gabel School.

The 9000-square-foot **Egyptian Club**, located in a former milk plant, features three different rooms in an Egyptian motif, with a bar, a dancefloor, pool tables and a restaurant. The crowd is primarily lesbian. Cover Thursday through Saturday. ~ 3701 Southeast Division Street; 503-236-8689.

KELLEY POINT PARK 🏃 🏊 ⛵ At the confluence of the Willamette and Columbia rivers, this forested site is popular for swimming (watch for the large drop-offs), biking and hiking. The park, largely undeveloped, is busy during the summer months but wide open the rest of the year. There are restrooms. ~ Located in northernmost Portland at the west end of Suttle Road off Northeast Marine Drive; 503-823-2223.

PENINSULA PARK 🏊 This 16-acre park features beautiful sunken rose gardens highlighted with fountains and a charming gazebo. Extensive recreational facilities and a small pond make Peninsula popular with families. Facilities include picnic tables, a basketball court, horseshoe pits, a pool, a soccer field, tennis courts and restrooms. ~ Located at North Albina Street and Portland Boulevard; 503-823-2223.

POWELL BUTTE NATURE PARK 🏃 🚴 🐎 This rustic, 570-acre park centers around a 630-foot-high volcanic mound that offers great views of the city and the Cascades. If you can, circle this volcanic butte via a two-mile loop route at day's end and take advantage of the sunset. Facilities are limited to restrooms and picnic tables. ~ Located at Southeast 162nd Avenue and Powell Boulevard; 503-823-2223.

LAURELHURST PARK Bordered by rhododendron, a pretty lake is the heart of this 34-acre park in a historic residential district. Along the way you're likely to spot geese, ducks, swans and turtles. Forested with fir and oak, the park also features glens, gardens and contemporary sculpture. You'll find restrooms, picnic tables, a playground and tennis courts. ~ Located on Southeast 39th Avenue and Stark Street; 503-823-2223.

MT. TABOR PARK 🏃 The only extinct volcano within the limits of an American city, Mt. Tabor was uncovered during excavations in 1912. While the cinder cone is the park's star attraction, it also offers an extensive network of trails for hiking and jogging. This forested setting affords smashing views of the city. There are picnic tables, restrooms, horseshoe pits, a playground, tennis courts and basketball courts. ~ Located at Southeast Salmon Street and 60th Avenue; 503-823-2223.

LEACH BOTANICAL GARDEN These nine acres are home to 1500 flowers and plants, including many native species, and is laced by a small creek. You can explore the grounds of this one-time estate on your own or via a guided tour. You'll find a manor house, restrooms and self-guiding brochures. ~ 6704 Southeast 122nd Avenue; 503-761-9503.

CRYSTAL SPRINGS RHODODENDRON GARDEN   Seven acres of flora and fauna, this park is at its best in May. The colorful panorama of more than 2000 rhododendron and azalea is enhanced by a waterfall and two bridges spanning a creek that flows into Crystal Lake. Ducks and other waterfowl are found year-round at this refuge near Reed College. There are restrooms. Admission. ~ Located at Southeast 28th Avenue north of Woodstock Boulevard; 503-823-2223.

CLACKAMETTE PARK   A haven for ducks and geese, Clackamette's 22 acres border the Willamette River in the Oregon City area. It's also a prime spot to see blue herons nesting on Goat Island. Restrooms are available. ~ Take Exit 9 from Route 205 toward Oregon City and Gladstone. Go west on Clackamette two-tenths of a mile; 503-657-8299.

▲ There are 38 RV sites (water/electric hookups); $12 per night.

▼▼▼▼▼▼▼▼▼▼▼▼
Portland West   From vineyards to Japanese gardens, Portland's west side has many of the city's best parks, major museums and wildlife preserves. Charming Victorians line many streets and the city's fabled Pittock Mansion reminds visitors of Portland's glamorous past. Washington Park, the city's beloved green oasis, presides over Portland West in much the same way that Central Park does in New York. Most of the other worthwhile attractions here also involve the outdoors: just half an hour from downtown, you can enjoy wilderness areas or cycle along placid sloughs, in addition to other delights.

Heading south from downtown along the western side of the Willamette, you'll pass residential 'burbs like Tigard and Beaverton before encountering the vineyards that comprise Oregon's wine country. The original settlers believed the Willamette Valley to have some of the best soil in the world, and the area just beyond the city limits does maintain a rural flavor. But Portland's populace has also worked hard not to overdevelop all of its own land, and this section of the city definitely benefits as a result.

SIGHTS   Still, the area closest to downtown does maintain a cosmopolitan air. We begin our tour in one of the trendiest areas in Portland, **Nob Hill**. The district was given its name by a 19th-century San Franciscan who saw a similarity to his old neighborhood. At the Portland/Oregon Visitors Association downtown you can pick up the walking guide to this district focused around Northwest 23rd Avenue, north of Burnside Street. Home of many of the city's finest restaurants, bookstores and antique and art shops, Nob Hill also has noteworthy turn-of-the-century Victorian and Georgian homes, as well as churches and commercial buildings. Among them are the **Charles F. Adams House**, 2363 Northwest Flanders Street, and the **Ayer-Shea House** at 1809 Northwest Johnson Street.

When the roses are in bloom (from late June through early September), it's hard to find a better vantage point for the city below than at the International Rose Test Garden.

This tree-lined district is also convenient to **Washington Park**, a 332-acre refuge created by the Olmsted brothers, from the family of landscape architects who gave the world Central Park in New York and Golden Gate Park in San Francisco. Home to several museums, gardens and the zoo, this park is one of Portland's most worthy destinations. ~ Southwest Park Place and Vista Avenue; 503-823-3635.

Begin your visit at the **International Rose Test Garden**. Consisting of three terraces, this four-and-a-half-acre gem has over 8000 bushes, enough to make this park a true mecca for rose aficionados worldwide. In addition to the test area, visitors are welcome to see the Royal Rosarians and Gold Medal Award Garden. ~ 400 Southwest Kingston Avenue; 503-823-3636.

Directly west of the Rose Garden is the **Japanese Garden Society of Oregon**. Five traditional gardens spread across seven acres make this tranquil spot a great place for a quiet walk. The Flat Garden is reminiscent of Kyoto's Zen shrines. The Sand and Stone Garden is a simple geometric arrangement of sea and stone. The Tea Garden contains a Japanese teahouse, while the Natural Garden has a fine miniature arrangement. Don't miss the Strolling Pond Garden with its waterfalls, pools and beautiful wooden bridge. There's also a pavilion overlooking Mt. Hood, Oregon's answer to Mt. Fuji. Admission. ~ 611 Southwest Kingston Street; 503-223-4070.

Follow Kingston Street until you see signs leading to 61-acre **Metro Washington Park Zoo**. Also accessible by a steam train from the Japanese and International Rose Test gardens during the summer months, the zoo features an African rainforest as well as a savannah roamed by giraffes, zebras, rhinos, impalas and hippos. Also of special interest are the zoo's Humboldt penguins, Arctic polar bears and orangutans. The staff is proud of the fact that it has one of the world's most successful Asian elephant–breeding programs. You'll also find an extensive collection of Pacific Northwest animals, including beavers and otters. Admission. ~ 4001 Southwest Canyon Court; 503-226-7627.

Nearby is the **World Forestry Center**. Here's your chance to learn tree nomenclature, logging history and the story of monumental fires like the Tillamook Burn. Kids will enjoy a chat with the 70-foot talking tree. While this center has a pro-logging slant, it does offer a useful perspective on the state's lumber industry. Admission. ~ 4033 Southwest Canyon Road; 503-228-1367.

One way to tell the trees from the forest is to visit the 175-acre **Hoyt Arboretum**. You'll have a chance to see over 850 varieties of shrubs and trees, including one of the nation's largest collection of conifers. ~ 4000 Southwest Fairview Boulevard; 503-823-3654.

North of Washington Park is a favorite Oregon house tour, **Pittock Mansion**. Built by *Oregonian* publisher Henry Pittock and his wife Georgiana, this 16,000-square-foot, château-style residence features an Edwardian dining room, French Renaissance drawing room, Turkish smoking room and Jacobean library. Chandeliers, Italian marquetry, friezes on the doorways, a carved-stone fireplace and bronze grillwork make this 1914 home a treasure. The finest craftspeople of the day used native Northwest materials to make this house Portland's early-20th-century masterpiece. The 46-acre estate, landscaped with roses, azaleas, rhododendrons and cherry trees, has a great view of the city and the mountains. Be sure to stop for lunch or tea at the **Gate Lodge**. Closed the first three weeks of January. Admission. ~ 3229 Northwest Pittock Drive; 503-823-3624.

Rail fans may want to head out to Trolley Park and Museum in Glenwood. Here you'll see a vintage collection of interurban streetcars and trolleys.

Well worth visiting is the **Portland Audubon Society Sanctuary and Wildlife Care Facility**. The 60-acre center helps rehabilitate over 4000 injured animals and birds each year. Visitors can watch the staff handle animals through an observation window and can also view up close a few of the center's permanent creatures: two red-tailed hawks, a barn owl, pygmy owl, acorn woodpecker and brown bat. Naturalist guides often lead tours through the flora and fauna of the sanctuary, and miles of hiking trails here link up with Forest Park. ~ 5151 Northwest Cornell Road; 503-292-6855.

To experience the country's biggest wilderness park fully, continue on Skyline Boulevard along the Tualatin Mountains. Overlooking the Willamette River, Forest Park extends west for eight miles. Turn right at Germantown Road and drive north through Forest Park's woodlands to Route 30. Continue west to the Sauvie Island Bridge. Cross the bridge and proceed one mile to **James F. Bybee House and Howell Territorial Park**. Open only on summer weekends, the Bybee House is a restored 19th-century Classical Revival reflecting the island's culture and development during the 1850–75 period. ~ 13901 Northwest Howell Park Road; 503-621-3344.

On the grounds of the James F. Bybee House is the **Agricultural Museum** displaying pioneer equipment, shops and hands-on exhibits. In addition you'll want to explore the **Pioneer Orchard** containing over 120 varieties of apple trees, as well as pears and plums.

Another attraction in West Portland is the **Children's Museum**, a must for families with small children (infant through nine years of age). This brick building has fun-filled exhibits including a pint-sized grocery complete with a bar-code scanner and a medical center where kids can "operate" on parents and friends. Admission. ~ 3037 Southwest 2nd Avenue; 503-823-2227.

Washington County west of Portland has a number of excellent wineries. **Oak Knoll Winery** is known for pinot noirs and chardonnays. This small vineyard has a white-tiled tasting room and a charming picnic area. ~ 29700 Southwest Burkhalter Road, Hillsboro; 503-648-8198.

Laurel Ridge Winery is on 143 acres of rolling terrain. Set on a hillside with commanding views of Forest Grove and the agricultural valley below, Laurel Ridge features sparkling wines and sauvignon blanc. Closed January. ~ 46350 Northwest David Hill Road, Forest Grove; 503-359-5436.

Traveling south, the **Willamette Shore Trolley** offers a 90-minute, 14-mile roundtrip scenic tour along the Willamette River. Your trip aboard a vintage trolley runs along a section of the Jefferson Street Line built in the late 19th century. ~ 311 North State Street, Lake Oswego; 503-222-2226.

Downtown Cypress Inn offers contemporary rooms. Within walking distance of the popular shops and restaurants in the Nob Hill district, this five-story motel building is tucked into a residential neighborhood. Nondescript from the outside, the inn has attractive carpeted rooms with potted plants, desks and posturepedic beds. Kitchenettes are available in the suites. The upper-story rooms have great views of downtown Portland. ~ 809 Southwest King Avenue; 503-226-6288, 800-532-9543, fax 503-274-0038. MODERATE TO DELUXE.

LODGING

A renovated English Tudor, **Heron Haus** provides a pleasant view of the city, the Cascades and Mt. St. Helens. A blend of country casual and contemporary furniture, the oak-parquet flooring, mahogany library, sun room and pool make the establishment a delight. Fireplaces and quilts add to the comfort of the six spacious rooms. After enjoying the continental breakfast, stroll down to the popular Nob Hill shops and boutiques. ~ 2545 Northwest Westover Road; 503-274-1846, fax 503-532-9543. DELUXE TO ULTRA-DELUXE.

With 250 rooms and suites, **The Greenwood Inn** is a good bet for families or visitors planning long stays. Surrounded by verdant courtyards, the lower-priced rooms have Murphy beds, full kitchens, twig rockers, Berber carpets and sitting areas. Suites feature fireplaces and decks. An atrium restaurant and lounge, two pools, jacuzzi, exercise room and sauna are on the premises. Ask for a room away from the highway. ~ 10700 Southwest Allen Boulevard, Beaverton; 503-643-7444, 800-289-1300, fax 503-626-4553. DELUXE.

HIDDEN ► At **The Yankee Tinker Bed and Breakfast,** three New England–style guest rooms are decorated with handcrafted quilts, antiques, flowers and wallhangings. Blueberry pancakes, muffins, peaches-and-cream french toast and herbed omelettes are on the breakfast menu. Special diets can be accommodated. Ten miles west of Portland, the inn is in the heart of Washington County's wine country and close to farmers' markets. ~ 5480 Southwest 183rd Avenue, Beaverton; 503-649-0932, 800-846-5372. MODERATE.

HIDDEN ► Located southwest of Portland off Route 5, the **Sweetbrier Inn** resides in a park-like stand of fir. King-size beds, wicker furniture, comfortable sitting areas, a garden pool, children's play area and nearby jogging track make this inn a winner. An adjacent building has 32 two-bedroom suites with workstations to accommodate businesspeople. A restaurant, jazz bar and lounge are here, too. ~ 7125 Southwest Nyberg Road, Tualatin; 503-692-5800, 800-551-9167, fax 503-691-2894. MODERATE TO DELUXE.

DINING

You say you were lusting for grilled spring Chinook salmon with an Indonesian sauce of soy, hot peppers, garlic, lime and brown sugar served with sautéed spinach and deep-fried leeks? Then follow the crowds to **Zefiro Restaurant and Bar,** a high-tech make-over of a historic Nob Hill brick commercial building. From the copper tables in the bar area to the black furniture in the oak-floored dining area, this establishment is one of Portland's hottest bistros. The mostly Mediterranean and Southeast Asian menu is filled with imaginative and always changing entrées like saffron risotto with prawns, roasted red peppers and *gremolata*. Closed Sunday. ~ 500 Northwest 21st Avenue; 503-226-3394. MODERATE TO DELUXE.

Café des Amis is a cheery neighborhood restaurant furnished with oak furniture, antique breakfronts and sideboards. In the heart of Nob Hill, the restaurant presents entrées like duck with blackberry sauce, filet of beef with a port garlic sauce, lamb tenderloin with sauce béarnaise and roast rack of lamb with white beans. There's an excellent wine list, and the french rolls are great. Highly recommended. Dinner only. Closed Sunday. ~ 1987 Northwest Kearney Street; 503-295-6487. DELUXE.

Start the day at **Jamie's Great Hamburgers,** a classy Nob Hill diner with booth and counter seating, music from a jukebox and a checkerboard floor. Buttermilk pancakes, french toast made with thick ranch bread, muffins, fresh fruit or orange juice are the perfect way to begin your day. You can also build your own omelette from a list of ten ingredients or choose heavier fare such as grilled chicken and burgers for lunch and dinner. ~ 838 North-west 23rd Avenue; 503-248-6784. BUDGET.

Located in a rustic home, **L'Auberge** is one of Portland's best French restaurants. Dine in front of the fireplace or, in the warm months, on the deck. Wicker furniture, antiques and impression-ist prints grace this three-level restaurant. Specialties include rack of lamb, veal, salmon, sturgeon and scallops. There's also a pop-ular bar menu with lighter fare such as steamed mussels. On Sunday, the dining room is closed, but the bar shows movies and offers barbecued ribs and hamburgers made with gruyère cheese and served on onion buns. ~ 2601 Northwest Vaughn Street; 503-223-3302. DELUXE TO ULTRA-DELUXE.

Yes, there really is a free dinner at **Sayler's Old Country Kitchen**. All you have to do is eat one of the 72-ounce top-sirloin steaks along with a salad, slice of french bread, ten fries or a baked potato, two carrot sticks, two celery sticks, two olives, a bever-age and ice cream—and the house will pick up the tab. You only get one hour to finish, and it is a one-time-only offer. Over 500 customers have won the bet. Strangely enough, the typical win-ner tends to have a slender build. If you're not that hungry try the tenderloin, prime rib, chicken, scallops, prawns or halibut steaks. ~ 4655 Southwest Griffith Drive, Beaverton; 503-644-1492. MODERATE.

◄ HIDDEN

High-tech Mex design is the hallmark of **Macheezmo Mouse**, where the burritos, tacos, salads and other entrées are all listed with their calorie content. There's no deep frying here, and many of the entrées come with brown rice and black beans. The bright decor attracts a budget-minded crowd that's become dependent on this quality fast food. ~ 10719 Southwest Beaverton-Hillsdale Highway, Beaverton; 503-646-6000. BUDGET.

For great views of the Willamette, head for **Ram Big Horn Brewing Company**. The downstairs dining area, with its cherry-

---

✔ CHECK THESE OUT—UNIQUE DINING

- *Budget:* Fill your entire plate with one huge apple-walnut pancake at the **Tabor Hill Café**. *page 289*
- *Moderate:* Join the locals at **Ole's Supper Club**, hidden off the tourist trail in an industrial area of The Dalles. *page 310*
- *Moderate to deluxe:* Discover the creative culinary touches at **Zefiro Restaurant and Bar**, a popular bistro serving Mediterranean and Southeast Asian cuisine. *page 298*
- *Deluxe to ultra-deluxe:* Have a bite of pumpkin risotto while en-joying a view of the Gorge at the **Columbia River Court**. *page 310*

Budget: under $8   Moderate: $8–$16   Deluxe: $16–$24   Ultra-deluxe: over $24

wood paneling, offers American fare in the form of steaks, burgers, salads and daily specials. Alfresco seating is an option in the summer. Upstairs is a 21-and-over game room with pool tables, virtual-reality video games and a wall of TVs broadcasting sporting events. ~ 320 Oswego Point Boulevard, Lake Oswego; 503-697-8818. BUDGET TO MODERATE.

SHOPPING "Escape from the ordinary" is the motto at **Norm Thompson**, where you can find fine-quality clothing in a variety of materials. Enjoy a glass of Oregon wine as you check out the men's and women's apparel, foods and gifts. ~ 1805 Northwest Thurman Street; 503-221-0764.

Pulliam Deffenbaugh Gallery specializes in contemporary Northwest art as well as work from other regions. ~ 522 Northwest 12th Avenue; 503-228-6665.

Another excellent place to look for fine local art is the **Laura Russo Gallery**. Paintings, original prints, drawings, watercolors and sculptures in a variety of media are all shown here. ~ 805 Northwest 21st Avenue; 503-226-2754.

We were impressed by the breadth of the offerings at **Contemporary Crafts Gallery**, a nonprofit organization showcasing everything from ceramic pins and medallions to metal sculpture. Highlighting crafts of the five disciplines (clay, glass, wood, fiber and metal), this eclectic gallery is a great place to shop for a gift. ~ 3934 Southwest Corbett Avenue; 503-223-2654.

NIGHTLIFE Classical-music buffs will enjoy the **Portland Baroque Orchestra**. Make it a point to hear this group if they're performing during your visit (October through April). ~ Trinity Episcopal Cathedral, 147 Northwest 19th Avenue; 503-224-7908.

Mission Theater is a historic movie theater that now doubles as a pub, with seating at tables and couches where you can dine and watch second-run films. There's also traditional theater seating on the balcony level. ~ 1624 Northwest Glisan Street; 503-223-4527.

BEACHES & PARKS **MACLEAY PARK** 🦌 This natural 120-acre park offers several excellent trails, a pond, creek and viewing windows overlooking a bird-feeding area. In addition, it provides stunning views of the city and Mt. St. Helens from Pittock Mansion. There's a good chance you'll spot deer and other wildlife on your walk. Hiking trails lead down to Lower MacLeay Park, which is a gateway to 5000-acre Forest Park. The Portland Audubon Society's headquarters, bookstore and wildlife care center are adjacent to the park. Facilities include restrooms and a playground. ~ Take Lovejoy Street west to Northwest Cornell Road and continue to the park; 503-823-2223.

COUNCIL CREST PARK 🏃 Atop a Tualatin Mountain peak, this forested 42-acre park is a great way to see the Cascades and the Coast Range. Make your way through stands of fir and maple via Marquam Hill Trail. A sculptured fountain of a mother and child, stolen in 1990, has been replaced. Facilities include picnic tables and restrooms. ~ Located on Southwest Council Crest Drive near Fairmount Boulevard; 503-823-2223.

SAUVIE ISLAND WILDLIFE AREA 🏃 🚴 ⛴ 🚣 🛥 🛳 🎣   ◀ *HIDDEN*
This 12,000-acre haven ten miles northwest of Portland is an ideal place to spot great blue heron, bald eagles, sandhill cranes and 160 other bird species. Featuring a sandy beach on the Columbia, the refuge is also home to 37 mammal species including black-tailed deer. The island trails which lead through orchards and gardens are ideal for leisurely exploration on foot. Small craft explore the sloughs while oceangoing freighters cruise by on the Columbia. For fishing, try for catfish, perch and crappie from slough and pond banks. There are portable toilets and bird observation platforms. Some areas are open year-round; other areas are closed October to April. Day-use only; you must obtain a parking permit ($3/day), available at stores on the island or at any Fred Meyer department store or G.I. Joe's Sporting Goods throughout Portland. ~ Take Route 30 west from Portland toward Astoria. Four miles past St. John's Bridge, take the Sauvie Bridge turnoff to the Island; 503-621-3488.

ELK ROCK, THE GARDEN OF THE BISHOP'S CLOSE For more   ◀ *HIDDEN*
than 75 years this refuge has been a favorite of Portland's garden societies. And why not? A terraced 13-acre estate overlooking the Willamette River and Elk Rock Island, the garden is also home to the Episcopal Diocese of Oregon's main office. Formal gardens and native plants, including dozens of magnolia varieties, make this a spot for Zen-like contemplation. Also here are lily ponds, a rock garden and a small spring. Self-guided tour information is available from the visitors center. ~ 11800 Southwest Military Lane; 503-636-5613.

TRYON CREEK STATE PARK 🏃 🚴 🐎 Set in a shallow, steep-walled canyon, this 630-acre suburban park is a hot spot for hiking, biking and horseback riding. Tryon is forested with fir, alder and maple and also has a grassy meadow. Look for beaver and pileated woodpeckers. There's a trillium festival in the spring. Facilities here are restrooms, an observation area and a nature center. ~ Located six miles southwest of downtown Portland. Take the Terwilliger exit off Route 5 and follow signs to the park; 503-636-9886.

MARY S. YOUNG STATE PARK 🏃 🚴 🐎 🎣 A popular day-use area forested in fir, maple, cottonwood and oak, the park sits on the Willamette River. With 133 acres, this leisurely spot is perfect for fishing from the riverbank, riding or walking. There are restrooms and picnic tables. ~ Located nine miles south of Portland on Route 43; 503-636-9886.

▼▼▼▼▼▼▼▼▼▼▼▼
The Columbia River Gorge

All visitors to Portland owe it to themselves to see the Columbia River Gorge. The spectacular scenery includes one of the Northwest's most important historical sites, Fort Vancouver. Heaven for windsurfers, waterfall lovers, hikers and history buffs, this is the ultimate Portland day trip. Of course, if you love it as much as we did, you'll probably want to spend the night.

SIGHTS

Although it's only half an hour from downtown Portland and the logical starting point for touring the Columbia Gorge region, many visitors to the region miss **Fort Vancouver**. What a pity. Located across the Columbia River from Portland, this national historic site is a cornerstone of Pacific Northwest history. Organized by the Hudson's Bay Company in 1825, the fort was a British fur-trading post and focal point for the commercial development of an area extending from British Columbia to Oregon and from Montana west to the Hawaiian Islands.

Nine structures have been reconstructed on their original fort locations. Collectively, they give a feel for life prior to the arrival of the first white settlers. One of the best ways to start your tour is at the visitors center with the introductory video. On your tour you'll see the re-created **Chief Factor's House**, once home to Dr. John McLoughlin, the British agent who befriended American settlers and is remembered as the "Father of Oregon." The phenomenal ability of the British to instantly gentrify the wilderness is reflected in the fine china, copper kettles and elegant furniture of this white clapboard home wrapped with a spacious veranda. You may be surprised to learn that the male officers dined without their wives.

The recently reconstructed **Fur Warehouse** demonstrates how fur was collected and prepared for shipment to England. Also worth a visit are the **Blacksmith's Shop, Bakery, Kitchen, Wash Room, Stockade** and **Bastion**. At the **Indian Trade Shop and Dispensary**, you'll learn how American Indians bartered skillfully with the British. Because most of the items were imported, there was a two-year hiatus between ordering goods and receiving them. Fort Vancouver: Admission May to September. ~ East Evergreen Boulevard, Vancouver, WA; 360-696-7655.

On nearby **Officer's Row**, you'll see 21 grand homes built for American Army leaders who served here during the latter half of the 19th and the early 20th centuries. These charming Victorians are the focus of a rehabilitation program combining interpretive

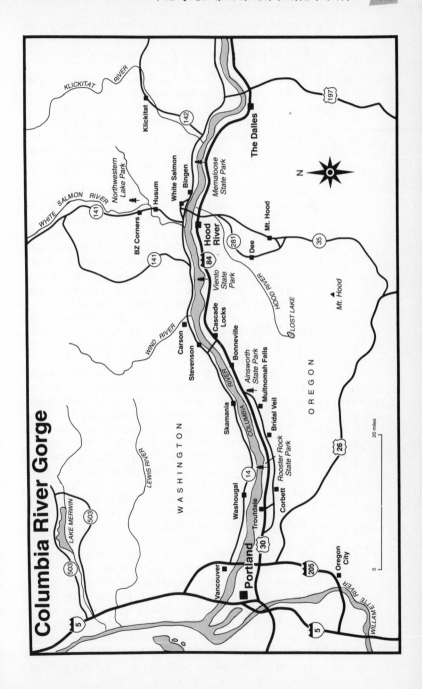

and commercial use. Among the residences you can tour is the **Grant House** (360-694-5252). The **George C. Marshall House** (360-693-3103), an imposing Queen Anne structure, also offers tours.

HIDDEN ▶

Next to Fort Vancouver is **Pearson Air Museum**. Opened in 1905, this is the oldest operating airfield in the United States. Exhibits feature a display on the world's first nonstop transpolar flight (Moscow to Vancouver) in 1937. The Soviet aviators were greeted by General George Marshall, who hosted them at his residence. The airpark exhibit features flyable vintage aircraft. Closed Monday. Admission. ~ 1115 East 5th Street, Vancouver, WA; 360-694-7026.

Originally constructed as a Carnegie Library, **Clark County Historical Museum** has a better than good regional collection—from the American Indian artifacts and handicrafts to the historical doctor's office, general store and type shop. The doll collection includes everything from Eskimo creations to early Barbies. Not to be missed is the downstairs train room with a Pullman unit, railway telegram office, dining car china, a model train layout and photos of noteworthy local derailments. Closed Sunday and Monday. ~ 1511 Main Street, Vancouver, WA; 360-695-4681.

To see more of Vancouver stop by the **Greater Vancouver Chamber of Commerce** and pick up the handy heritage tour brochure. ~ 404 East 15th Street, Suite 11, Vancouver, WA; 360-693-1313, 800-377-7084.

Returning to the Oregon side of the river take Route 84 east up the Gorge to the **Historic Columbia River Highway**. Beginning east of Troutdale (Exit 17), this road ascends the bluff above the river to **Crown Point/Vista House**, a must-see viewpoint. Descending east toward the Gorge you'll find yourself in one of the loveliest regions in the Northwest. With more than 70 waterfalls in the area, it's easy to have one to yourself. ~ Vista House: Corbett, OR; 503-695-2240.

Towering Multnomah Falls is ranked as the fifth-highest waterfall in the U.S.

Among the highlights are **Latourell Falls**, **Bridal Veil Falls** and **Coopey Falls**. You can climb down from the road to explore the base of 250-foot Latourell Falls, the first cascade you'll encounter heading east on the Historic Columbia River Highway.

Perhaps the most popular destination is the **Multnomah Falls** area. Multnomah Falls tumbles about 620 feet, making it the fifth-highest waterfall in the United States. Walk up the paved trail to the observation spot on the bridge between the upper and lower falls; from here you'll get a misty look at this propulsive cascade. In September 1995, a 400-ton rock fell 200 feet from the top of the falls to the upper pool as a result of the ongoing erosion that originally formed the falls. The school bus–sized rock caused about 20 minor injuries due to flying debris, reminding us that the amazing geology here is still experiencing natural transformations on a large scale. From the observation bridge you can hike up a mile to the top of Multnomah Falls; you can also connect with trails leading to other cascades like **Wahkeena Falls** and **Triple Falls**. Perhaps the best way to spend a day is to take the 6.2-mile loop to **Fairy Falls**, a dainty 25-foot drop along a basalt cliff. Near the base of Lower Multnomah Falls is a visitors center, gift shop and restaurant.

The taming of the Columbia River to provide low-cost power is one of the most controversial issues associated with the river. You'll get the pro side of the picture at **Bonneville Lock and Dam**, which is reached by taking Exit 40 off Route 84. ~ Four miles west of Cascade Locks, OR; 541-374-8820.

At the **Bradford Island Visitor Center**, extensive interpretive displays provide an overview of the dam operation and history. You can also learn how the dam operates, see the fish ladders and visit the **Fort Cascades National Historic Site** on the Washington shore. To get there, cross the Columbia River on the **Bridge of the Gods**, named for a natural bridge famous in Indian legend and head west three miles on Route 14. The 59-acre historic site includes part of the old Portage Railroad, a onetime Chinook Indian village and an old military fort.

Retrace your route across the Bridge of the Gods to the Oregon side and stop at the **Cascade Locks Museum** to see exhibits on American Indians, the first Columbia River locks, the portage road, logging and fishwheels. Water powered, these rotating devices scooped so many salmon from the river that they were banned by the state in 1926. The museum is open from May to September only. ~ Marine Park, Cascade Locks, OR; 541-374-8535.

The sternwheeler **Columbia Gorge** is docked in Cascade Locks from June through September. The multidecked old paddlewheel steamboat leads daytime and dinner cruises through the Gorge. ~ 541-374-8619.

On the Washington side of the bridge in Stevenson is the spacious new **Columbia Gorge Interpretive Center**, where the focus is on the cultural and natural history of the Gorge. Located on a ten-acre site overlooking the river, the center includes a 37-foot-high replica of a 19th-century fishwheel, a restored Corless Steam Engine, a theater with a nine-projector slide show re-creating the cataclysmic formation of the Gorge and several exhibits drawn from the oral histories of local American Indians and pioneer settlers. The world's largest rosary collection is also housed here. Admission. ~ 990 Southwest Rock Creek Drive, Stevenson, WA; 509-427-8211, 800-991-2338.

Farther east on Route 14 is **Carson Hot Mineral Springs Resort**. On the Wind River, this resort is well-known by weary travelers for its mineral baths and massages, and can provide a restful stop for those who have been hiking all day. The resort also has beautiful hiking trails and an 18-hole golf course. From here you can drive east along Route 14 to Route 141, which leads north along the White Salmon River Valley to Trout Lake. Then return to Route 14 and the town of White Salmon. ~ Carson, WA; 509-427-8292, 800-607-3678.

Your next stop should be on the Oregon side at **Hood River**, which has become a windsurfing capital thanks to the strong breezes here. Stop at the **Hood River County Visitors Center** for information on this scenic hub. ~ 405 Portway Avenue; 541-386-2000. Nearby is the **Hood River County Historical Museum**, featuring exhibits on American Indian culture, the westward migration, pioneer farming, logging and the Columbia River. Also found here is an extensive collection of period furniture and early 20th-century artifacts. ~ Port Marina Park, Hood River, OR; 541-386-6772.

HIDDEN ►

One of the prettiest drives in Oregon is the 20-mile trip from Hood River to **Lost Lake**. At the lake (elevation 3140 feet) you'll have a stunning angle on Mt. Hood—have your camera ready—and can rent a canoe or paddleboat (motorized boats are banned on the lake). In addition to fishing for rainbow trout, visitors like to walk the three-mile Lakeshore Trail that circles the lake. To reach the idyllic retreat, take Route 281 south to Dee and then follow the signs west to the lake. Do keep an eye out for logging trucks en route.

Although many visitors miss it, we strongly recommend a visit to **The Dalles**, on the Oregon side of the Gorge. The end of the Oregon Trail, where immigrants boarded vessels to float down the Columbia (the Barlow Trail later made it possible to complete the overland journey), this city has a superb old-town walking tour. Pick up a copy of the route map at **The Dalles Area Chamber of Commerce**. ~ 404 West 2nd Street, The Dalles, OR; 541-296-2231.

Highlights on this walk include one of the state's oldest bookstores, **Klindt's**, 315 East 2nd Street, and the circa-1863 **Waldron Brothers Drugstore** nearby.

If you're traveling with children don't miss **WonderWorks A Children's Museum**. A storefront gem, this volunteer organization has hands-on exhibits for kids, a dress-up area, puppeteer area and crafts. The young folk will love it. Closed Sunday. Admission. ~ 419 East 2nd Street, The Dalles, OR; 541-296-2444.

The **Fort Dalles Museum** is a favorite stop. Only one fort building, the Surgeon's Quarters, remains today. But the museum does preserve an excellent collection of pioneer artifacts, rifles, quilts and historic photographs. Open year-round, with reduced winter hours. Admission. ~ 15th and Garrison streets, The Dalles, OR; 541-296-4547.

From here, take Route 30 east to Route 197 north. Cross the freeway to Bret Clodfelter Way and follow signs to **The Dalles Dam**. Perhaps the saddest part of this story, the downside of that pro-dam story you saw at the Bradford Island Visitor Center, focuses on the demise of the Gorge's best-known Indian fishing grounds. Wherever you go along this part of the Columbia River, in coffeeshops and hotel lobbies, phone company offices and visitors centers, you're likely to see classic photographs of Indians dipping their nets into the river at heavenly Celilo Falls. To get the full picture, leaf through the scrapbook of Celilo Falls fishing pictures at the Fort Dalles Museum.

If you continue on Route 84 east of The Dalles for 12 miles you'll come to a small **Celilo Falls Marker**, which indicates where these bounteous fishing waters prospered before being destroyed by the dam in the late 1950s.

A few miles farther east, on the Washington side, is one of the most isolated museums in America. **Maryhill Museum of Art** was ◄ *HIDDEN* designed in 1914 as the mansion residence of eccentric millionaire Sam Hill, and was supposed to oversee a Quaker agricultural town. But the plan for a new town flopped and the house on the hill eventually became a museum. This eclectic assemblage was dedicated in 1926 by Queen Marie of Romania, which helps explain the presence of treasures from that nation's royal collection. Also here are Russian icons, a large number of Rodin sculptures, Charles M. Russell's *Indian Buffalo Hunt*, French decorative arts, a good display of American Indian handicrafts and artifacts, contemporary Pacific Northwest art, as well as one of the world's great chess collections. Views of the Columbia Gorge are spectacular, as are the sunsets. Three miles east of Maryhill is **Stonehenge**, Sam Hill's memorial to local soldiers who died in World War I. Closed mid-November through mid-March. Admission. ~ 35 Maryhill Museum Drive, Maryhill, WA; 509-773-3733.

◆◆◆

THE LITTLE TRAIN THAT COULD

The scenic **Mt. Hood Railroad** excursion train links the Gorge with Mt. Hood along a route pioneered in 1906. The trip climbs up the Hood River Valley through steep canyons, orchards and forests. You'll enjoy panoramic views of the Cascades from the restored coaches on a 44-mile roundtrip journey. Special fall foliage trips are well worth your while. The railroad runs April through October, with selected holiday trips between Thanksgiving and Christmas. ~ 110 Railroad Avenue, Hood River, OR; 541-386-3556.

LODGING   Located just above the Columbia Gorge Interpretive Center in Stevenson, Washington is the **Skamania Lodge**, a modern resort built in the tradition of the grand mountain lodges of a century ago. Guests can congregate in the wood-paneled Gorge Room with its deep sofas and three-story river-rock fireplace. Public areas and the 195 guest rooms are handsomely decorated with mission-style furniture, Pendleton fabrics, petroglyph rubbings and American Indian–inspired rugs. The grounds include an 18-hole golf course, fitness center, whirlpools, swimming pool and more. ~ 1131 Skamania Lodge Way, Stevenson, WA; 509-427-7700, 800-221-7117, fax 509-427-2547. ULTRA-DELUXE.

One of the frustrating facts of life on the road is the Sunday brunch. If you crave broccoli quiche, Italian sausages and eggs, artichoke frittatas, baklava, date tarts, fresh fruit and a dozen other treats, Monday to Saturday just won't do. Fortunately, the

HIDDEN ▶   **Inn Of The White Salmon** has solved this problem in an imaginative way. This lovely bed and breakfast offers brunch seven days a week. All you need do is check in to one of the inn's countrified rooms featuring brass beds and antiques, and this splendid feast is yours. Across the Columbia from Hood River, this inn also features a comfortable parlor. ~ 172 West Jewett Boulevard, White Salmon, WA; 509-493-2335, 800-972-5226. DELUXE.

Located in a quiet residential area near downtown Hood River, **Hackett House** is a 1903 Dutch Colonial surrounded by dogwood trees and red rhododendron bushes. Among the four guest rooms is the pale-green-and-rose-accented Victorian Suite, which has a sitting area and a king-sized bed. The rates include a full breakfast served in a formal dining room. ~ 922 State Street, Hood River, OR; 541-386-1014. MODERATE.

The **Columbia Gorge Hotel** is a 42-room landmark where strains of Bach waft through the halls, sculptured carpets highlight the public areas and the fireplace is always roaring. This Mediterranean-style hotel tucks guests into wicker, brass, canopy or hand-carved antique beds. The dining room, home of a popular five-course farm breakfast, offers splendid riverfront dining. Relax in the Valentino Lounge or take a walk through the manicured gardens. ~ 4000 Westcliff Drive, Hood River, OR; 541-386-5566, 800-345-1921, fax 541-387-5414. ULTRA-DELUXE.

The chandeliered **Hood River Hotel** is a restored brick landmark with 41 rooms and suites. Brightly painted rooms are appointed with oak furniture, four-poster beds, casablanca fans, wing chairs and antiques. Some offer views of the Columbia River. Comfortable sitting areas, a lounge offering jazz music and a cheery café are all part of the charm. Kitchenettes suites are available. ~ 102 Oak Street, Hood River, OR; 541-386-1900, 800-386-1859, fax 541-386-6090. MODERATE TO ULTRA-DELUXE.

Beautifully located overlooking the Columbia, **Vagabond Lodge** offers spacious, carpeted rooms—some opening right on to the riverfront. All feature contemporary furniture, doubles or queens and a secluded garden setting. For the price, it's hard to beat this motel west of town. ~ 4070 Westcliff Drive, Hood River, OR; 541-386-2992, fax 541-386-3317. BUDGET TO MODERATE.

Three miles south of Hood River in the midst of apple and pear orchards is **The Beryl House**, a classic American woodframe farmhouse with a wraparound porch. The four guest rooms are simply decorated with reproduction antique furniture and have views of Mt. Hood, Mt. Adams and the surrounding orchards. Guests have access to a living room with a piano and stereo system; breakfast includes fresh fruit from the Hood River Valley. ~ 4079 Barrett Drive, Hood River, OR; 541-386-5567. MODERATE.

Williams House Inn is a picturesque Victorian on a wooded hilltop. Adjacent to an arboretum and a creek, the home is furnished with Georgian and Victorian antiques as well as Asian art. Upstairs rooms feature canopied beds, a chaise lounge and writing desk. From your balcony you'll enjoy a tremendous panorama of the Klickitat Hills. The three-room main-floor suite is a best buy. ~ 608 West 6th Street, The Dalles, OR; 541-296-2889. MODERATE.

Catering primarily to windsurfers in the summer and other budget-conscious visitors in the spring and fall is the **Condon House**, a spacious Victorian with five hunter-green rooms with brass and iron beds. Out back is a sunny patio area where guests can picnic or barbecue if they wish. The rates do not include breakfast or private bathrooms. ~ 512 Union Street, The Dalles, OR; 541-296-4271. BUDGET.

For contemporary motel accommodations try the **Quality Inn**. The fully carpeted rooms have oak tables and queen beds featuring pink spreads with seashell designs. There's a pool on the premises, as well as Cousins, the only restaurant we know featuring a John Deere tractor in the middle of the dining room. ~ 2114 West 6th Street, The Dalles, OR; 541-298-5161, 800-848-9378, fax 541-298-6411. MODERATE.

DINING

◄ HIDDEN

With a name like **Hidden House**, we couldn't resist. This structure and the adjacent residence (now a retail business) at 110 West 13th Street were built by Lowell M. Hidden and his son Foster. Much of Vancouver was built with Hidden bricks from the family factory, still in operation today. Once the home of Clark College, this handsome red-brick Victorian offers dining upstairs and down. Antiques are an integral part of the decor, which includes three fireplaces, the original stained glass, ash and black-walnut woodwork and a covered veranda ideal for outside dining. The menu features steaks, seafood, chicken Kiev and veal dishes served with homemade poppyseed bread. Northwest wines are featured. Lunch is served weekdays and dinner is served nightly except Monday. ~ 100 West 13th Street, Vancouver, WA; 360-696-2847. MODERATE TO DELUXE.

After a visit to Multnomah Falls it makes sense to dine at **Multnomah Falls Lodge**. The smoked-salmon-and-cheese platter, stew served in a hollowed-out loaf of french bread, and generous salads are recommended. The European-style lodge building with a big stone fireplace, scenic paintings of the surroundings and lovely views will add to your enjoyment of the Gorge. ~ Bridal Veil, OR, off Route 84; 503-695-2376. MODERATE.

About 20 minutes north of the Gorge, and well worth the trip, is one of the Gorge's most intriguing restaurants, **The Logs**. You'll be impressed by the broasted chicken, hickory-smoked ribs, giant fries and huckleberry pie served in this log-cabin setting. The battered and deep-fried chicken gizzards and cheese sticks are a big hit with the regular clientele, which includes locals, rafters, skiers and devotees of the rich mud pie. In business for six decades, this is the place where city slickers will come face to face with their first jackalope, safely mounted on the wall. ~ Route 141, White Salmon, WA; 509-493-1402. BUDGET.

HIDDEN ► Tucked away in the woods, **Stonehedge Inn** is an antique-filled home preparing Continental and Northwest dining at its finest. Set in a beautiful garden, this paneled restaurant has a tiny mahogany bar and a roaring fireplace. Among the dishes are scallop sauté, veal chanterelle, jumbo prawns and filet of salmon. Light entrées, such as a seafood platter, are also recommended. Call for summer hours; open Wednesday through Sunday the rest of the year. ~ 3405 Cascade Drive, Hood River, OR; 541-386-3940. MODERATE TO DELUXE.

Pasquale's Ristorante has breezy indoor and sidewalk seating in the center of this resort town. The heart of the dining room is a handcrafted bar with an etched glass mirror. Entrées include filet of salmon, capellini bolognese and rack of lamb. ~ 102 Oak Street, Hood River, OR; 541-386-1900. MODERATE.

An elegant dining room overlooking the Gorge, **Columbia River Court** is a romantic place to dine on roast pork tenderloin, fresh Oregon salmon, rack of northwest lamb or hazelnut prawns. Done in an Early American design with oak furniture and candlelit tables, this establishment is well known for its lavish farm breakfast. ~ 4000 Westcliff Drive, Hood River, OR; 541-386-5566. DELUXE TO ULTRA-DELUXE.

HIDDEN ► An A-frame tucked away in an industrial area, **Ole's Supper Club** proves that location isn't everything in the restaurant business. The candlelit dining room with wood tables, carpeted floors, wood captain's chairs and works by local artists is jammed with locals who swear by the prime rib, baked ham lorraine and Pacific salmon fresh from the nearby Columbia. Dinners, complete with fresh-baked bread, vegetables, salad and soup, include chicken piccata, fettuccine with fresh scallops and sautéed scampi. The restaurant also boasts an impressive wine list, with over 500 wines to choose from. Dinner only. Closed Sunday and Monday. ~ 2620 West 2nd Street, The Dalles, OR; 541-296-6708. MODERATE.

To the people at **Johnny's Café**, cordon bleu sounds like something you use to tint your fireplace. This temple of American cuisine has made few concessions to the trends of the '90s. Lit with fluorescent bulbs, furnished in formica and vinyl, this eatery is big on macaroni and cheese. For decades, locals have been coming here to feast on broasted chicken, salmon steak, fish-and-chips, pies and puddings. ~ 408 East 2nd Street, The Dalles, OR; 541-296-4565. BUDGET.

Fort Vancouver Gift Shop is the place to go for books, maps and pamphlets on Pacific Northwest history. We recommend picking up a copy of the *Fort Vancouver National Historic Site Handbook* 113. ~ 612 East Evergreen Boulevard, Vancouver, WA; 360-696-7655.

SHOPPING

Aviation buffs will want to stop by the gift shop at **Pearson Air Museum**. The shop has an ace collection of memorabilia and souvenirs for adults and juniors alike. ~ 1115 East 5th Street, Vancouver, WA; 360-694-7026.

Pendleton Woolen Mills and Outlet Store offers big savings on irregulars. Tours of the mill, in operation since 1912, are available, but call first for schedule information. ~ #2 17th Street, Washougal, WA; 360-835-1118.

A good place to select a fine Oregon white or red is **The Wine Sellers**. Also here are fresh french bread, cheese and gifts. ~ 514 State Street, Hood River, OR; 541-386-4647.

Oregon fruit makes a terrific present for the folks back home. **Rasmussen Farms** sells Hood River apples, Comice pears and cherries. They can all be shipped as gift packs. ~ 3020 Thomsen Road off Route 35 south of Hood River, OR; 541-386-4622, 800-548-2243.

GIVE YOURSELF A BREAK

A little Washington gem on the White Salmon River north of the Columbia, **Northwestern Lake Park** is an ideal destination for a day trip where you can swim, fish, hike or just loaf. There are also summer cabins nearby for those who want to stay longer. ~ Head west from White Salmon on Route 14 to Route 141. Continue north five miles to the park.

Columbia Art Gallery represents 200 artists, primarily from the Columbia Gorge region. Featured are the works of photographers, printmakers, potters, glassblowers, weavers and painters. ~ 207 2nd Street, Hood River, OR; 541-386-4512.

The Dalles Art Center, located in the historic Carnegie Library, exhibits work by local and regional artists. Much of this fine art is available for purchase. The gallery showcases pottery, jewelry, paintings, beadwork, calligraphy, wearable art and baskets. ~ 220 East 4th Street, The Dalles, OR; 541-296-4759.

NIGHTLIFE   A popular gay and lesbian nightspot in Vancouver, Washington, is **North Bank Tavern**, which has a video area, dancefloor and outdoor patio. ~ 106 West 6th Street; 360-695-3862.

The **Power Station** is a theater and pub located in the former Multnomah County poor farm. The theater presents movies and occasional special events in the farm's former boiler room. The pub serves a full menu in the converted laundry building. Also on the premises is the Edgefield Brewery and Winery. ~ 2126 Southwest Halsey Street, Troutdale, OR; 503-669-8610.

The **River Rock Lounge** at the Skamania Lodge features live acoustic music on weekends before a woodburning fireplace. ~ 1131 Skamania Lodge Way, Stevenson, WA; 509-427-7700.

Full Sail Brewing Company offers tastings of their very popular microbrewed beers, as well as a pub-style menu and deck seating with fine views of the Columbia. ~ 506 Columbia Street, Hood River, OR; 541-386-2247.

BEACHES   **ROOSTER ROCK STATE PARK** 🏃 🚶 🎣 🏄 🛶 🚤 ⛵
& PARKS   Offering more than three miles of sandy Columbia River frontage, this 872-acre park is near the Gorge's west end. The rock, named for a towering promontory, is adjacent to a camping site chosen by Lewis and Clark in 1805. Well-known for swimming and windsurfing, Rooster Rock also has excellent hiking trails, a small lake and forested bluff. Anglers can fish for salmon. There are picnic tables and restrooms. Day-use fee, $3. ~ Located in Oregon, 22 miles east of Portland on Route 84 at Exit 25; 503-695-2261.

VIENTO STATE PARK 🏃 🚲 🚶 🎣 🛶 Originally a rest stop on the old Columbia River Highway, this 247-acre park includes a riverfront and Viento Creek forest section. Dramatic views of the Columbia River make this a popular camping and picnicking facility. It can get very windy. Facilities include picnic tables, showers and restrooms. ~ On Route 84, eight miles west of Hood River in Oregon, Exit 56; 541-374-8811.

▲ There are 18 tent sites and 57 hookups; $14 to $16 per night.

AINSWORTH STATE PARK 🏃 Ranking high among the treasures of the Columbia River Scenic Highway is this 156-acre park. Near the bottom of St. Peter's Dome, the forested park has a gorgeous hiking trail that connects with a network extending throughout the region. A serene getaway, the only sound of civilization you're likely to hear is from passing trains. Closed from mid-November through mid-March. There are picnic tables, showers and restrooms. ~ Located on Route 30, the Columbia River Scenic Highway, 37 miles east of Portland on the Oregon side; 503-695-2301.

▲ All 45 sites have full hookups; $18 per night.

MEMALOOSE STATE PARK The park is named for an offshore Columbia River island that was a American Indian burial ground. This 336-acre site spreads out along a two-mile stretch of riverfront and is forested with pine, oak and fir. Much of the park is steep and rocky. It can also be very windy. In case you were wondering, "Memaloose" is a Chinook word linked to the sacred burial ritual. There are showers and restrooms. Open April to November only. ~ Located off Route 84, 11 miles west of The Dalles in Oregon. Westbound access only; 541-478-3008.

▲ There are 67 tent sites and 43 hookups; $15 to $19 per night. Contact Reservations Northwest for reservations; 800-452-5687.

▼▼▼▼▼▼▼▼▼▼▼▼▼▼

Outdoor Adventures

SKATING

Skating may not be big-thrills adventure, but it sure is fun. In Portland, rollerskating even takes on an old-fashioned aura when you've got an amusement-park organ playing the music. Skaters are also welcome to use any hard surface in the city's parks. ~ Portland Parks Department; 503-823-2223.

PORTLAND EAST Rollerblade or rollerskate to the strains of the mighty Wurlitzer at the 90-year-old **Oaks Amusement Park** on the east bank of the Willamette. Skate rentals are available. ~ East end of the Sellwood Bridge; 503-236-5722.

At **Skateworld**, you can also rent skates, including inlines. Public skating sessions are held daily. ~ 4395 Southeast Witch Hazel Road; Hillsboro; 503-640-1333.

PORTLAND WEST City ordinance prohibits skaters (and skateboarders) from most city center streets. One happy exception is the esplanade in **Waterfront Park**. When the weather is particularly pleasant, the concrete pathway (it's about ten feet wide) can get congested with cyclists, runners, skaters, skateboarders and strollers. But the mood is always congenial. ~ Front Street, from Southwest Harrison Street to Northwest Glisan Street.

You can rent inline skates just two blocks away at **Sport Works** at the foot of Morrison Bridge. ~ 421 Southwest 2nd Avenue; 503-227-5323.

ICE SKATING

PORTLAND EAST Ice skaters can practice their balance at the Clackamas Ice Chalet. Besides public ice-skating sessions, the center has a live deejay on the weekends. Ice skates are available to rent. ~ Clackamas Town Center, 12000 Southeast 82nd Street; Portland; 503-786-6000.

At **Ice Chalet**, the music is recorded but the fun is genuine. Skate rentals are available here too. ~ 953 Lloyd Center shopping mall, between Northeast Multnomah and Halsey streets and Northeast 9th and 15th avenues, Portland; 503-288-6073.

WINDSURFING

Between the high cliff walls of the Columbia Gorge, east of Portland, winds on the river can hit 60 knots, so it's no wonder this is one of the world's best windsurfing areas, with Hood River its capital. According to a local expert, "Once you learn the tricks and let the wind do the work for you, it's not as hard as it looks." And if you don't mind cool temperatures (50°F and lower) in winter, you can windsurf year round.

COLUMBIA RIVER GORGE If you're experienced and want to rent equipment, or if you're not and want a day of windsurfing lessons in sheltered coves, contact **Hood River Windsurfing**. ~ 101 Oak Street, Hood River; 541-386-5787. The **Rhonda Smith Windsurfing Center** also offers lessons and equipment, and has a beginner beach area in front of the Hood River Inn. ~ Port Marina Park, Hood River; 541-386-9463, 800-241-2430.

FISHING

Imagine catching a 350-pound sturgeon, even if you've never fished before. "Your dream can come true," says one local outfitter. "Your arms will be sore, but you'll have a smile on your face for two days!" You don't have to go far to get your wish. You can haul in these babies, which can come in at seven to ten feet and weigh upward of 300 pounds, year-round, right out of the Columbia. Walleye is another year-round favorite found in the Willamette; Tillamook Bay, about 65 miles west on the coast, is well known for trophy-size fall chinook salmon.

PORTLAND **Page's Northwest Guide Service** can set up a one-day Tillamook Bay fishing trip on a 23-foot, all-weather boat, or arrange an outing on the Willamette, Clackamas, Columbia or Sandy rivers. ~ Portland; 503-760-3373.

PORTLAND EAST If you'd like to have your angling moment of glory videotaped, just say the word to **Portland Fishing Adventures**, which will arrange fishing trips on Tillamook Bay or one of the nearby rivers. The company also runs deep-sea fishing trips. ~ 42500 Southeast Erickson Road, Sandy; 503-668-8541.

Don Schneider's Reel Adventures specializes in full-day fishing trips on the Sandy River but also provides trips on the Columbia and Willamette. Schneider can custom-tailor an outing in a drift boat or, during spring and summer, in an individual miniature "cat" boat along an isolated stretch of the river. ~ 39261 Proctor Boulevard, Sandy; 503-622-5372.

RIVER RUNNING

About 90 minutes from downtown Portland is a whitewater thrill ride—the White Salmon River, just north of the Columbia, in Washington. Designated a Wild and Scenic River, it moves "fast and furious" through the forest canyon. Southeast of Portland is the Clackamas, another popular whitewater river, with some Class III and IV rapids. It's about an hour away. Most whitewater-rafting trips are done in paddleboats (*you* paddle!), holding six to eight people, plus a guide. The passive adventurer who'd like to photograph the gorgeous mountain scenery instead of paddle should ask about oar-powered raft trips.

PORTLAND AREA   About 35 miles southeast of Portland, the Clackamas River is the best bet for a one-day whitewater adventure. From March through July, it runs with some Class III and IV rapids (the water is too low the rest of the year). **River Drifters Whitewater Tours**, the only outfitter operating on the upper Clackamas, can arrange a complete full-day trip. The company also offers trips to the White Salmon River and overnight trips on the Deschutes. ~ 7135 Monte Verde, Gladstone; 503-656-9218, 800-972-0430.

COLUMBIA RIVER GORGE   There are some 30 Class II, III and IV rapids along the short course of the White Salmon River, a pool-and-drop mountain stream that is fed by rainfall and snow-melt from Mt. Adams, 30 miles distant. For a half-day guided whitewater adventure on the White Salmon, call **Phil's White Water Adventure**. ~ 38 Northwestern Lake, White Salmon, WA; 509-493-2641, 800-366-2004.

PARA-GLIDING

With today's lightweight equipment, it's possible for just about anyone to learn to paraglide. Even a one-day introduction gets beginners flying off gentle training slopes or soaring high in tan-

✔ **CHECK THESE OUT—OUTDOOR ADVENTURES**
- Hike the cinder cone of an extinct volcano at Mt. Tabor Park without leaving the Portland city limits. *page 293*
- Don't fall off your bike if you glimpse a bald eagle among the 160 bird species at Sauvie Island Wildlife Area. *page 301*
- Catch the wind at one of the premier windsurfing spots in the world—the Columbia River Gorge. *page 314*
- Climb aboard your inflatable raft and shoot the rapids of the White Salmon River on the Washington side of the Gorge. *page 315*

dem with an experienced instructor. Experienced flyers take off from mountain sites. In the Portland area, contact the **Hang Gliding and Paragliding School of Oregon** to arrange a flying adventure within a two-hour drive of the city. Tandem flights are also offered. ~ 14185 Southwest Yearling Court, Beaverton; 503-223-7448.

SKIING

With Hood River and the Columbia River Gorge practically at the foot of snowcapped Mt. Hood, it's possible to ski in the morning (even in July) and windsurf in the afternoon. In Hood River, see **Hood River Windsurfing** about ski rentals and repairs. (For more information on skiing Mt. Hood, see Chapter Nine.) ~ 101 Oak Street; 541-386-5787.

GOLF

To reserve a tee time at one of several Portland-area courses, call **The Golf Network**. The service is free to golfers. Courses using the service are Persimmon, Glendoveer, Rose City, Eastmoreland and Heron Lakes (all in the Portland area), Indian Creek in Hood River and Mint Valley in Longview, Washington. ~ 503-292-8570.

PORTLAND EAST **Eastmoreland Golf Course** is an 18-hole regulation course rated by *Golf Digest* as one of the country's top-25 public courses. ~ 2425 Southeast Bybee Boulevard, Portland; 503-775-2900. The two 18-hole courses at **Glendoveer Golf Course** are lined with fir trees. ~ 14015 Northeast Glisan Street, Portland; 503-253-7507. Across the state border you can tee off at **The Cedars Golf Club**. ~ 15001 Northeast 181st Street, Brush Prairie, WA; 509-285-7548.

PORTLAND WEST Just 30 minutes from downtown Portland, the four 9-hole greens at **Meriwether National Golf Club** are good walking courses. The club also has an 18-hole championship natural turf putting green. ~ 5200 Southwest Rood Bridge Road, Hillsboro; 503-648-4143. **King City Golf Club** is a challenging, nine-hole, semiprivate course that, says a local golf pro, is "harder than it looks." ~ 15355 Southwest Royalty Parkway, Tagard; 503-639-7986.

COLUMBIA RIVER GORGE It's only nine holes, but **Hood River Golf and Country Club** has full mountain views, pear orchards and a driving range. ~ 1850 Country Club Road, Hood River; 541-386-3009. **Indian Creek Golf Course**, with its gentle rolling hills, is a dry, year-round 18-hole course. ~ 3605 Brookside Drive, Hood River; 541-386-7770.

TENNIS

Among the numerous public clubs is **Portland Tennis Center**, which has four hardtop indoor (hourly per person charge) and eight lighted outdoor courts (free). They also maintain a list of other public tennis courts throughout the city. ~ 324 Northeast 12th Street; 503-823-3189.

To say that the Portland area is bicycle friendly is like saying New York has a lot of tall buildings—so what else is new? There are 260 miles of bike lanes in the metropolitan area (plus 83 miles of multi-use lanes), and city buses all have bike racks. *Bicycle Magazine* has picked Portland as the country's top bicycle city. Morning, afternoon or entire-day bicycling in the area presents a variety of options, from a mountain-bike ride in a city park to a long-distance excursion along the Columbia River.

BIKING

Visitors interested in bicycling in the Portland metropolitan area will find the going easier by first contacting one or more of these resources. The **Portland Bicycle Program** publishes a small map of the city's bikeway system; an accompanying brochure explains how to take your bike along on a bus (you'll need a $5 permit). The map and brochure are free and available at the program's office and in some bike shops. ~ 1120 Southwest 5th Avenue, Room 730; 503-823-2925.

Multnomah County also puts out a map, but it just covers the east county area. ~ 1220 Southeast 190th Avenue; 503-248-5050.

The best resource is *Bike There*, a detailed bicycle map and safety guide for the metropolitan area. Bike and multi-use lanes are color coded to a use-suitability scale (off-street, low-traffic, etc.). *Bike There* is put out by Metro (an elected regional government). You can pick one up at Powell's Bookstore, most bike shops or at Metro headquarters at 600 Northeast Grand Street in Portland.

Just as the riders using them come in a variety of shapes and sizes, bike routes in the area are of varying lengths and distances. Beginners and intermediate riders would do well to contact **The Bike Gallery** (see Bike Rentals, below), which sponsors weekend group rides that are open to the public. Two rides are usually offered: a road ride one day, a mountain ride the next.

City riders will find the northeast and southeast portions of the city more suitable. The terrain is relatively flat, and marked bike routes follow low- or medium-traffic streets.

PORTLAND EAST The **Springwater Corridor** follows an old railroad route along the southern flank of the city. The 16-mile trail extends from Southeast McLoughlin Boulevard east through Powell Butte Nature Park and Gresham to the city of Boring in Clackamas County. Most of this multi-use trail is unpaved.

PORTLAND WEST Mountain bikers will like **Forest Park**, which comprises 5000 acres west of downtown. The park has some rather hilly terrain, perfect for mountain biking, and one multi-use trail, Leif Erickson, is especially popular.

A favorite cycling getaway in the area is **Sauvie Island**, located ten miles northwest of Portland. Light traffic makes it a pleasure to pedal through this wildlife sanctuary. (You can take a Tri-Met bus out to the island.)

More experienced riders, of course, have the option of longer rides, perhaps west to the **vineyards** around Hillsboro. The Bike Gallery in Beaverton (see "Bike Rentals" below) is a good source for information on suggested routes, distances and length of trips.

COLUMBIA RIVER GORGE East of Portland, the Columbia River Gorge along Route 84 is prime cycling territory, particularly along any portion of the 62-mile route from Portland to Hood River. The old Columbia River Highway, which parallels Route 84, is less trafficked, calmer, scenic and a wonderful way to experience the Gorge.

During the summer, full- and half-day guided tours through the Hood River Valley and Columbia Gorge and on Mt. Hood provide a variety of riding options for all experience levels. Contact **Gorge Mountain Velo Mountain Bike Guide Service.** ~ Mt. Hood Meadows; 503-337-2222 ext. 298.

Bike Rentals For rentals of mountain bikes, road bikes and trail maps, try one of **The Bike Gallery**'s three locations in Portland and Beaverton. ~ In Portland at 821 Southwest 11th Avenue, 503-222-3821 and 5329 Northeast Sandy Boulevard, 503-281-9800; in Beaverton at 3645 Southwest Hall Boulevard, 503-641-2580.

In Hood River, **Discover Bicycles** rents and sells mountain bikes and tandems and can provide information about guided bike tours. ~ 1020 Wasco Street; 541-386-4820.

For mountain-bike rentals, sales and repair in The Dalles, see **Life Cycles.** ~ 418 East 2nd Street; 541-296-9588.

HIKING A hiker's paradise, the Portland region has beautiful riverfront walks, urban trails and wilderness loops perfect for a brief interlude or an all-day excursion. Trail information is available from the Portland/Oregon Visitors Association or the **Bureau of Parks and Recreation.** ~ 1120 Southwest 5th Avenue; 503-823-2223. All distances listed for hiking trails are one way unless otherwise noted.

CENTRAL PORTLAND Named for a former governor, **Tom McCall Waterfront Park** offers a 2-mile-long path along the Willamette River. This is an ideal way to get an overview of the downtown area.

PORTLAND EAST The **Springwater Corridor** (15 miles) begins at Tideman-Johnson Park and heads to Gresham and south to Boring, shadowing Johnson Creek. This multi-purpose trail is a converted railway line that's part of the Rails to Trails project.

You don't have to go all the way to Mt. St. Helens to hike a volcano. Just take the **Mt. Tabor Perimeter Loop** (2.7 miles). Your hike on Southeast 60th Avenue, Southeast Yamhill Street, Southeast 72nd Avenue and Southeast Lincoln Street provides a pleasant overview of this landmark.

Another easy route is the loop circling **Powell Butte** (2 miles). You'll ascend the 630-foot summit for a Portland vista you won't soon forget.

PORTLAND WEST   Sauvie Island is ideal for short or long strolls. One of our favorite walks in the region is the hike from parking lot #5 in Crane Unit around **Willow Hole to Domeyer Lake** (1.5 miles). Another good bet is the hike from Walton Beach along the Columbia to **Warrior Rock Lighthouse** (3 miles).

With more than 5000 acres, Forest Park offers over 50 miles of connecting trails. Many of the routes are spurs off **Wildwood Trail** (27 miles), the primary route traversing this vast urban refuge. Depending on your time and mood, hike as much of this trail as you want, connecting easily to other convenient routes. Your starting point for Wildwood is Hoyt Arboretum's Vietnam Memorial. If you're feeling more ambitious, try **Marquam Nature Trail** (5 miles) leading from Hines Park to Washington Park via Terwilliger Boulevard and Council Crest Park.

Two mile-long walks will add to your enjoyment of Hoyt Arboretum. The **Conifer Tour** leads through a forest thick with spruce, fir and redwood. Also well worth your time is the **Oak Tour**.

COLUMBIA RIVER GORGE   Latourell Falls Trail (2 miles), on the Columbia River Highway three miles east of Crown Point, is a moderately difficult walk leading along a streambed to the base of the upper falls. To extend this walk another mile take a loop trail beginning at the top of lower Latourell Falls and returning to the highway at Talbot Park.

Near the Bridal Veil exit off Route 84 is **#415 Angels Rest Trail** (2 miles), an easy hike leading to an overlook. This route can be extended another 15 miles to Bonneville Dam by taking the **#400 Gorge Trail**, an amazing path that passes many of the Gorge's stunning cascades, including Multnomah Falls, Triple Falls and Horsetail Falls.

Eagle Creek Campground at Exit 41 on Route 84 is the jump-off point for the easy **#440 Eagle Creek Trail** to Punch Bowl Falls (2 miles) or Tunnel Falls (6 miles), the latter of which has a man-made tunnel passing behind the cascading water. You can continue to follow the wildflower-riddled path (part of the Pacific Crest Trail) through the Columbia Wilderness, up to Wahtum Lake (13 miles). Four campsites provide rest between Eagle Creek and the lake.

On the Washington side of the river west of Bonneville Dam is the 1-mile trail leading to the top of **Beacon Rock**, an 800-foot monolith noted by Lewis and Clark. Ascended by a series of switchbacks guarded by railings, this trail offers numerous views of the Gorge.

East of Home Valley, Oregon, on Route 14 is the **Dog Mountain Trail** (3.5 miles), a hearty climb up 2900 feet for impressive views of Mt. Hood, Mt. St. Helens and Mt. Adams. During May and June, the surrounding hills are covered with wildflowers, making this an extraordinary time to hike the trail.

▼▼▼▼▼▼▼▼▼▼▼▼
Transportation

CAR

Most visitors to Portland arrive on one of three primary highways. **Route 5** bisects the city and provides access from the north via Vancouver, Washington. This same highway also is the main line from points south like the Willamette Valley and California. From points east, **Route 84** along the Columbia River is the preferred way to enter Portland. From the west, **Route 26** is a major highway into town. Secondary routes include **Route 30** from the west and **Route 99** from the south. For road conditions, call 503-222-6721.

AIR

Portland International Airport is the major gateway. Located ten miles northeast of downtown, it is served by Air B.C., Alaska Airlines, American Airlines, America West Airlines, Delta Air Lines, Hawaiian Airlines, Horizon Air, Northwest Airlines, Reno Air, Southwest Airlines, Trans World Airlines, United Airlines and USAir.

Limousines, vans and buses take visitors to downtown locations, including **Raz Transportation** (503-684-3322) and **Prestige Limousines** (503-282-5009).

BUS

Greyhound Bus Lines (800-231-2222) offers bus service to Portland from across the nation. The main downtown terminal is at 550 Northwest 6th Avenue. ~ 503-243-2316.

TRAIN

Amtrak provides service from Washington and California via the "Coast Starlight." The "Pioneer" serves eastern Oregon, Idaho, Utah and points east. There is also a northerly connection to Spokane on the "Empire Builder." ~ 800 Northwest 6th Avenue; 800-872-7245.

CAR RENTALS

At the airport try **Avis Rent A Car** (800-331-1212), **Budget Rent A Car** (800-527-0700), **Dollar Rent A Car** (800-800-4000) or **Hertz Rent A Car** (800-654-3131). Cars are also available from **Bee Rent A Car** (800-633-7117) and **Enterprise Rent A Car** (800-736-8222).

PUBLIC TRANSIT

Tri-Met Buses/MAX Lightrail (503-238-7433) serve the Portland region. Buses blanket the city, while the MAX Lightrail line extends east from downtown to the Lloyd Center and then on to Gresham. There is free bus service downtown in the "Fareless

Square" region spanning 300 blocks. Hood River is served by the
Hood River County Transportation District (541-386-4202).

Broadway Cab (503-227-1234), **Radio Cab** (503-227-1212) and   **TAXIS**
Yellow Cab (503-227-1234) all provide convenient local service.
In Hood River, call **Hood River Taxi and Transportation** (541-
386-2255).

EIGHT

Oregon Coast

As you take in the wonders of the Oregon Coast, do it with respect, for in a very real sense you are stepping into a paradise borrowed. In 1805, when Lewis and Clark arrived at the mouth of the Columbia River, only about 10,000 American Indians in such coast tribes as the Tillamook and Yaquina called this home. With roughly three square miles per inhabitant, these tribes were undisputed masters of their realm. The American Indians traveled almost entirely by water, were intensely spiritual and had, for the most part, a modest and self-sufficient lifestyle. Working hard during the spring and summer months, they harvested enough from the sea and forests to relax during the winter.

But their world began to change, indeed it was doomed, when distant entrepreneurs set sights on the region's vast resources. These men believed that the Northwest did not belong to its native populace but was instead destined to be claimed by a new master race of settlers thousands of miles away. Among them was John Jacob Astor, the richest man in America. Eager to monopolize the lucrative fur trade in the uncharted Northwest, he dispatched the ship *Tonquin* from New York in the fall of 1810. Then, in the spring of 1811, just about the time the *Tonquin* was sailing across the Columbia River Bar, a second overland group sponsored by Astor left St. Louis. They began by following the river route pioneered by Lewis and Clark but then forged a new trail across the Rockies, eventually reaching the Snake River, where they were turned back by impenetrable rapids. By early 1812, when the party limped into Astoria, the little settlement created by men from the *Tonquin*, it was clear that their patron's great vision remained distant. For one thing, most of the *Tonquin* group had headed north to Vancouver Island, where dictatorial captain Jonathan Thorn spurned the American Indians, triggering a massacre that destroyed almost everyone aboard. In a final insane act of revenge, a surviving crew member lured the American Indians back on the ship, went below and lit the ship's magazine, killing everyone aboard.

In September 1812, not long after they received news of this tragedy, the Astorians left behind at the little Columbia River settlement were visited by a party from the rival North West Fur Company. These newcomers announced that a British warship was en route to seize Fort Astoria. To make matters worse, they declared that the British had just won the War of 1812. Cut off from the news that would have exposed this lie, the Astorians decided to sell off their pelts and the first American settlement west of the Mississippi for pennies on the dollar. Then they began the long journey home.

While the British took over the fur trade, manifest destiny brought the Americans back on the Oregon Trail. In 1846, Oregon Country was returned to the Americans and new settlers gradually returned to the coast. Astoria and other settlements along the coast emerged as fishing, farming and logging centers. The arrival of the railroads spawned the development of resort towns like Newport and Seaside. Boardwalks, modeled after those found on the East Coast, soon sprang up to serve the growing clientele.

The coast may have been the magnet, but it didn't take the new arrivals long to discover that the lofty headlands, picturesque estuaries, rocky points, sand dunes and tidepools were only part of the attraction. Back behind the coastal rhododendron fields were rivers that offered legendary steelheading. Sunny valleys forested with fir, spruce, hemlock and cedar were perfect for camping. Stands of weird carnivorous plants, plunging waterfalls, myrtle groves and pristine lakes were all part of the draw. And the Indians, decimated by white man's diseases, were subjugated by the new settlers and ultimately forced onto reservations.

Having pushed the natives conveniently out of the way, the pioneers soon began reaping nature's bounty from the coastal region. Coos Bay became a major wood-processing center, and commercial fishing dominated the economies of communities like Port Orford. In other towns, such as Tillamook, the dairy trade flourished. And, of course, farming also began to emerge in the sunnier valleys east of the coast.

Today, thanks in part to a comprehensive network of state parks, the coast is equally appealing to motorists, bikers and hikers. While it's hard to improve on this landscape, mankind has done its best to complement nature's handiwork. From bed and breakfasts heavy on chintz and lace to bargain oceanfront motels furnished from garage sales, accommodations serve every taste. Everywhere you turn, another executive chef weary of big-city life seems to be opening a pasta joint or a pita stand. Theater, classical music, jazz, pottery and sculpture galleries have all found a home in towns ranging from North Bend to Cannon Beach. A major aquarium in Newport, a world-class maritime museum in Astoria, a printing museum in Coos Bay, a flyfishing museum in Florence—these are just a few of the special places that are likely to capture your attention.

If you must go down to the sea again, and you must, rest assured that this coast offers the space all of us need. True, some of the northern beaches draw a crowd on weekends and holidays. But traffic is lighter on the South Coast, where beachcombing can be a lonely, at times solitary, experience. With vast national recreation areas, national forests and sloughs, it's easy to get lost in the region. Often foggy, the Oregon coast is hit by frequent storms in the winter months. But this rugged weather is offset by mild periods in the summer or early fall. Even when the coast itself is socked in, inland valleys just a few miles away can be warm and sunny. The contrast continues: Temperatures along the coast seldom fall below freezing, but the adjacent coastal peaks are frequently snowbound in the winter months. And while the surf is bracing, lakes adjacent to the coast feature warmer waters ideal for swimming and waterskiing.

To fully experience the coast, you're well advised to see it border to border, from Astoria to Brookings. But many travelers prefer to focus on one or two areas. If you're history minded, Astoria is a must. For pure scenic grandeur and small-town charm, it's hard to beat the Tillamook–Three Capes area. Another winner in this category is the Otter Rock community north of Newport. Windy Port Orford is a very special place, scenic, uncrowded and ideal for steelheading.

Groups with diverse interests such as surf fishing, arcade games and shopping for folk art will want to consider well-rounded resort towns like Lincoln City, Seaside and Newport. They offer sporting life, cultural attractions and all the cotton candy you can eat. These towns are also convenient to rural gems when you're ready to make a great escape.

One of the most alluring communities on the coast is Florence. A delightful historic district, some of Oregon's finest dunes, a good restaurant scene and easy access to the Willamette Valley make this community a popular getaway. In the same category is Bandon, a charming port with a commercial district that will delight the shoppers in your group. Those who are eager to take a jet boat to the wilderness will doubtless find themselves in Gold Beach, a major fishing center. And Brookings is the gateway to one of our favorites, the Chetco River country.

The Bay Area, Coos Bay/North Bend/Charleston, is an ideal choice for clamming on the tidal flats. The parks, sloughs and country roads south of the area will keep you busy for days. And there is an impressive variety of museums, including one of the state's finest art institutions.

When it comes to a trendy resort atmosphere with tasteful shopping malls, sign ordinances, café au lait, classical music, French cuisine and gallery openings, Cannon Beach is the coast's class act. Every day the tourist tide from the east washes in patrons of the arts and Oregon varietals. This town may set the record for merchant-punsters operating shops with names like "Sometimes a Great Lotion" and "Katz'ndoggers."

There are many other destinations that don't appear on any map. In fact, the best of the Oregon Coast may not be its incorporated cities or parklands. Think instead of rocky points home only to sea lions. Eddies so beautiful you don't care if you catch anything. Offshore haystacks that don't even have names. Dunes that form the perfect backdrop for a day of kite flying. Points that seem to have been created solely for the purpose of sunset watching.

All these possibilities may seem overwhelming. But we believe the following pages will put your mind at ease. An embarrassment of riches, the Oregon Coast is more byway than highway. As you explore the capes and coves, visit the sea-lion caves and sea-cut caverns, you're likely to make numerous finds of your own. Those hidden places we're always talking about will tempt you to linger for hours, maybe even days. And however long you stay, give pause to remember that another people once lived here.

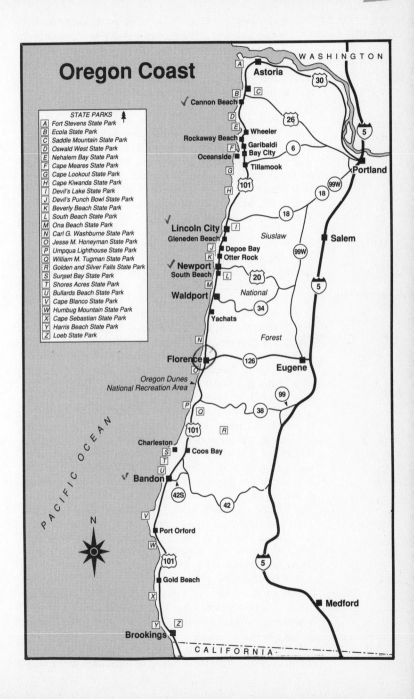

Oregon Coast

WASHINGTON

Astoria

30

✓ Cannon Beach

Wheeler

26

Rockaway Beach

Garibaldi
Bay City

Oceanside

6

Tillamook

Portland

101

18

99W

18

STATE PARKS

A	Fort Stevens State Park
B	Ecola State Park
C	Saddle Mountain State Park
D	Oswald West State Park
E	Nehalem Bay State Park
F	Cape Meares State Park
G	Cape Lookout State Park
H	Cape Kiwanda State Park
I	Devil's Lake State Park
J	Devil's Punch Bowl State Park
K	Beverly Beach State Park
L	South Beach State Park
M	Ona Beach State Park
N	Carl G. Washburne State Park
O	Jesse M. Honeyman State Park
P	Umpqua Lighthouse State Park
Q	William M. Tugman State Park
R	Golden and Silver Falls State Park
S	Sunset Bay State Park
T	Shores Acres State Park
U	Bullards Beach State Park
V	Cape Blanco State Park
W	Humbug Mountain State Park
X	Cape Sebastian State Park
Y	Harris Beach State Park
Z	Loeb State Park

✓ Lincoln City

Gleneden Beach

Siuslaw

Salem

Depoe Bay
Otter Rock

99W

✓ Newport
South Beach

20

Waldport

National

34

5

Yachats

Forest

Florence

126

Eugene

*Oregon Dunes
National Recreation Area*

99

38

101

Charleston

Coos Bay

✓ Bandon

42S

42

Port Orford

101

Gold Beach

Medford

5

P A C I F I C   O C E A N

N

Brookings

CALIFORNIA

North Coast

Oregon's North Coast is one of the most heavily traveled tourist routes in the Pacific Northwest. From June through early October, you can expect to have plenty of company. While most travelers hug the shoreline, some of the best sightseeing is actually found a few miles inland. Less crowded and often sunnier, these hidden spots reward those willing to veer off Route 101.

A special tip for those who prefer to drive during off-peak times: Around 5 p.m. most of the logging trucks are berthed and the RVs are bedded down for the night. In the summer consider allocating a good part of your day for sightseeing. Then, at 5 p.m., when many of the museums and attractions close, take a couple of daylight hours to proceed to your next destination. Not only is the traffic lighter, the sunsets are remarkable. Plus, you'll be able to dine fashionably late.

SIGHTS

Why not follow the path of Lewis and Clark by taking Route 30 west from Portland along the Columbia River to **Astoria**, the first American settlement established west of the Rockies? Set on a hillside overlooking the Columbia River, Astoria is one of the Pacific Northwest's most historic cities. Grand Victorians, steep streets and skies that belong to the gulls and shorebirds make this river town a must. As you enter Astoria, stop at the **Uppertown Firefighters Museum**. The vintage collection includes a classic 1878 horse-drawn ladder wagon, antique motorized pumpers and fire-fighting memorabilia. Open weekends only. Admission allows entry to Flavel house and the Heritage Museum. ~ 30th Street and Marine Drive, Astoria; 503-325-2203.

Continue west to the **Columbia River Maritime Museum**. One of the nation's finest seafaring collections, this 24,000-square-foot building tells the story of the Northwest's mightiest river, discovered in 1792 by Captain Robert Gray and navigated by Lewis and Clark in 1805 on the final leg of their 4000-mile journey from St. Louis. Besides documenting these disasters, the museum offers exhibits on American Indian history, the Northwest fur trade, navigation and marine safety, fishing, canneries, whaling, sailing and steam and motor vessels. And that's not all. Docked outside is the *Columbia*, the last of numerous lightships that provided navigational aid along the Pacific Coast. Admission. ~ 1792 Marine Drive, Astoria; 503-325-2323.

Continue west along Marine Drive to Astoria, the city founded in 1812 by John Jacob Astor as a fur-trading post. Head to the **Astoria–Warrenton Area Chamber of Commerce** to pick up a helpful map and background. ~ 111 West Marine Drive, Astoria; 503-325-6311.

Among the many Astoria Victorians on the National Register of Historic Places is the **Flavel House**, a Queen Anne with Italianate columns and Eastlake-style woodwork around the doors and windows. You can use your Uppertown Firefighters Museum ticket to get in. Featuring six fireplaces, a library, music parlor and three-story octagonal tower, this home is one of the most visited residences on the Oregon coast. For $3 you can pick up a walking-tour guide to Astoria's Victorian homes. Admission. ~ 441 8th Street, Astoria; 503-325-2563.

Your admission ticket to the Uppertown Firefighters Museum and the Flavel House also pays for entrance to the **Heritage Museum**, where you'll see artifacts from the *Peter Iredale*, a ship wrecked in 1906. It remains visible off the beach at nearby Fort Stevens State Park. Other exhibits feature artifacts from local logging camps and a popular saloon called The Louvre. Admission. ~ 16th and Exchange streets, Astoria; 503-325-2203.

You'll also want to visit **Fort Astoria**. This small blockhouse replica was the home base for the Astorians when they settled here in the early 19th century. ~ 15th and Exchange streets, Astoria.

For a good overview, follow the signs up 16th Street to **Coxcomb Hill**. Pictorial friezes wrapping around the 125-foot-high column cover the region's heritage from its American Indian past to modern times. Unless you're prone to vertigo, climb the circular stairway to the top for a panoramic view of Astoria.

About five miles west of Astoria near the town of Hammond is **Fort Stevens Historic Area and Military Museum**. On June 21, 1942, the fort became the first American continental military installation shelled since the War of 1812. Seventeen shots fired by a Japanese raider hit the fort. Fortunately none caused any damage. (The same pilot also dropped a few ineffective bombs near Brookings on the southern Oregon coast.) While visiting, you can tour the fort in a two-and-a-half-ton Army truck or take an underground tour of Battery Mishler (fee; May through October). Don't miss the wreck of the *Peter Iredale*, now a rusty skeleton easily reached by following signs inside the park. Parking fee. ~ Fort Stevens State Park; 503-861-2000.

During the rainy winter of 1805–1806, the 33-member Lewis and Clark party bivouacked at **Fort Clatsop National Memorial**

RADIO FREE ASTORIA

About 20 miles east of Portland you can tune in KMUN (91.9 or 89.5 FM), one of the finest public-broadcasting stations in the Northwest. A kind of Radio Free Astoria, this listener-sponsored station features local kids reading their favorite fiction, opera buffs airing Bellini, river pilots doing variety shows and park rangers playing jazz.

for three months before returning east. Named in honor of the Clatsop tribe, this reconstructed fort has an introductory slide presentation and interpretive displays. In the summertime, buckskin-clad rangers armed with flintlock rifles offer muzzle-loading demonstrations or show how Lewis and Clark's team built canoes, made candles, did woodworking and sewed hides. Admission. ~ Five miles south of Astoria off of Route 101; 503-861-2471.

Oregon's answer to Coney Island, the town of **Seaside** is the kind of place to go when you long for saltwater taffy and game arcades, boardwalks and volleyball. Just head down Broadway to find the carnival atmosphere. By the time you reach the beach you'll feel a restless urge to start building sandcastles. One of the most popular resorts on the coast, it is easy to visit with a little help from the **Seaside Chamber of Commerce**. ~ 7 North Roosevelt Drive, Seaside; 503-738-6391.

The two-mile boardwalk known as the Prom offers a historical look at Seaside. Along the way are Victorian-style homes, arts-and-crafts bungalows, Colonial revivals and English-style cottages. Another highlight is the Prom "Turnaround" marking the end of the Lewis and Clark Trail. At the south end is a reproduction of the cairn where the Lewis and Clark expedition boiled seawater during the winter of 1806 to make salt. More than three-and-a-half bushels were produced for the return trip.

Of special interest is the **Seaside Museum and Historical Society**. Inside are Clatsop artifacts, turn-of-the-century photos of boardwalk hotels and bathhouses, old printing presses, and antique fire-fighting and logging equipment. Admission. ~ 570 Necanicum Drive, Seaside; 503-738-7065.

Also here in town is the **Seaside Aquarium**, where you can see marine mammals and feed local harbor seals. Kids love the hands-on interaction at the touch tank. Closed Monday and Tuesday

✔ CHECK THESE OUT—UNIQUE SIGHTS

- Visit the only two sites in the continental U.S. bombed by the Japanese during World War II, **Fort Stevens** near Astoria and **Forest Service Road 4013** near Brookings. *pages 327, 359*
- Stop by **Tillamook Cheese**, which annually produces 40 million pounds of cheddar cheese—or over ten pounds for every Oregonian. *page 330*
- Get nose to nose with Keiko, the star of *Free Willy*, at the underwater viewing windows in Newport's **Oregon Coast Aquarium**. *page 341*
- Direct your signal to one of the coast's signature **lighthouses**, open for viewing at Cape Meares, Yaquina Bay and Coquille River. *page 343*

from November through February. Admission. ~ 200 North Promenade, Seaside; 503-738-6211.

Eighteen miles east of Seaside on Route 26 is the **Camp 18 Logging Museum**. Steam donkeys, cranes, train cabooses and other vintage equipment are among the exhibits. (There's a restaurant on the premises.) ~ Milepost 18, Route 26; 503-755-2476.

Follow Route 26 east to Jewell Junction and continue north on Fishawk Falls Highway toward Jewell. Just north of town is the **Jewell Meadows Wildlife Area**. Run by the Oregon Department of Fish and Wildlife, the sanctuary is a good place to spot Roosevelt elk, raptors, red-tailed hawks, songbirds and, in winter, bald eagles. ~ Route 202; 503-755-2264.

◄ HIDDEN

Located south of Seaside is **Tillamook Head Trail**, a three-mile route that extends to Cannon Beach's northern edge. Most of the route is within Ecola State Park. A highlight of this park is the tidepools of rocky Indian Beach. From the head you'll enjoy excellent views of the coast and the **Tillamook Rock Lighthouse**.

Cannon Beach, one of the most popular villages on the North Coast, is an artists' colony and home of photogenic **Haystack Rock**. Rising 235 feet ("the third-largest freestanding monolith in the world") and accessible at low tide, this geologic wonder is a marine and bird sanctuary, and a good place to explore tidepools and look for puffins. With its resorts and condos, boutiques and small malls, Cannon Beach (it's named for a cannon that drifted ashore after a shipwreck) can be a busy place, especially in summer when the population increases fourfold. Gallery shows, the Stormy Weather Festival (early November's artist showcase), sandcastle contests and concerts in the park add to the fun.

Twelve miles south of Cannon Beach, **Oswald West State Park** offers a series of beautiful viewpoints. Just south of the park is **Neah-kah-nie Mountain**, a promontory surrounded by a 200-year-old American Indian legend. Indian lore holds that a wrecked Spanish galleon carrying gold and beeswax washed up on the beach and the surviving crew members tucked the treasure into a hole dug at the base of the mountain. But treasure hunters, using everything from backhoes to bare hands, have failed to strike it rich here.

A lovely spot on the North Coast is **Nehalem Bay**, separated from the ocean by a sandspit. The Nehalem River, a waterway filled with Chinook salmon, empties into the bay, making it one of the best fishing spots in the Pacific Northwest. You'll see boats crowding the bay during the prime fall fishing months.

Along the bay are three small resort towns. The northernmost, **Manzanita**, sits amidst trees at the foot of Neah-kah-nie Mountain. Many residents of Portland and Seattle make Manzanita a weekend retreat. In fact, more than 60 percent of the homes here are owned by people who are not residents year-round. A three-block-long strip of gift shops, restaurants and motels make this the bay's center for provisions. The historic **Nehalem** waterfront, located right where the river meets the bay, was a American Indian community before being replaced by canneries, lumber mills and dairy farms. Today it has just a few shops, most of them dealing in antiques. Nearby **Wheeler** is an increasingly popular town situated on a hill sloping down to the Pacific. Boutiques are beginning to sprout up in this town on the southern side of Nehalem Bay.

One of the most treacherous spots on the West Coast, the turbulent Columbia River Bar was a nautical graveyard claiming scores of ships.

Heading south, Route 101 follows the curving shoreline around Tillamook Bay. On your way into **Tillamook** you'll probably want to stop to sample the familiar orange cheddar at **Tillamook Cheese**. A self-guided tour makes it easy to see the Pacific Northwest's largest cheese factory, Tillamook County Creamery, which produces 40 million pounds annually. Overhead walkways offer a bird's-eye view of the cheddaring process. ~ 4175 North Route 101, Tillamook; 503-842-4481.

Next, stop by the **Tillamook Chamber of Commerce** to pick up helpful background information about this area. ~ 3705 North Route 101, Tillamook; 503-842-7525.

Among the musts is the **Tillamook County Pioneer Museum**. Unlike many museums that display only a small portion of their holdings, this one is packed with 35,000 antiques, artifacts, dioramas, mounted animals, gems and gemstones and other items connected with the coast's pioneer life and natural history. Highlights include Tillamook basketry, pioneer implements, antique-clock section and fire-lookout cabin. You'll also learn that the giant hangars south of town berthed blimps that patrolled the West Coast for the Navy during World War II. Among the most recent additions to the military collection is a SCUD fragment retrieved during the 1991 Operation Desert Storm. Admission. ~ 2106 2nd Street, Tillamook; 503-842-4553.

If you'd like to explore the world of dirigibles, head to the **Tillamook Naval Air Station Museum**, housed in a former blimp hangar that dates from 1943. It's the largest wooden clear-span structure in the world. The museum's collection features photographs, artifacts and 25 World War II fighter airplanes, as well as a vintage-aircraft restoration center. Admission. ~ 6030 Hangar Road, Tillamook; 503-842-1130.

HIDDEN ▶ Seven miles south of town via Route 101, take the turnoff to 266-foot-high **Munson Creek Falls**, easily reached via a half-mile trail. This horsetail falls is the highest in the Coast Range, and is a popular spot for picnicking. The creek gorge is lovely.

West of Tillamook is one of the most picturesque drives on the Oregon Coast, 40-mile **Three Capes Loop**. As you follow Bay

Ocean Road along the southern edge of Tillamook Bay, you'll come to one of the region's most fascinating ghost towns, **Bay Ocean Park**. Designed to become a pre-casino Atlantic City of the West, this 1912 subdivision eventually grew to 59 homes. But between 1932 and 1949 the sea cut a half-mile swath across the spit, turning it into an island. Over the next 20 years the ocean eroded the Bay Ocean landscape and one by one homes were swept into the sea. Finally, in 1959, the last five remaining houses were moved. Today only a sign marks the site, which is also commemorated at the Tillamook County Pioneer Museum.

◄ HIDDEN

The Three Capes Loop continues past **Cape Meares Lake**, a haven for waterfowl and shorebirds, before continuing to **Cape Meares State Park**. While here you'll want to visit the Octopus Tree, a legendary Sitka spruce with six trunks extending horizontally for up to 30 feet before making a skyward turn. With just two more limbs this could have been the world's largest Hanukkah menorah. You can also take the short trail to the century-old Cape Meares lighthouse, surrounded by wild roses in the warm months.

Continue south to Oceanside and **Three Arch Rocks Wildlife Refuge**, home of Oregon's largest seabird colony. Half a mile offshore, these islands harbor 75,000 common murres as well as tufted puffins, pigeon guillemots, storm petrels, cormorants and gulls. You might spot a noisy sea-lion colony perched on the rocks below.

At **Cape Lookout State Park**, nature trails and coast walks delight visitors. With 2000 acres of forested headlands abutting sandy dunes, Cape Lookout has some of the best walking trails on the coast (see "Beaches & Parks" below). Dune buffs will enjoy visiting the **Sand Lake Recreation Area** seven miles south of Cape Lookout. These 1000 acres of dunes attract the ATV crowd, who zoom up and over the dunes ceaselessly. **Pacific City**, at the bottom of the Three Capes Loop, is famous for its dory fleet launched into the surf from the Cape Kiwanda beach.

South of Neskowin, Cascade Head Road leads to the **Cascade Head Scenic Research Area** and the **Cascade Head Experimental Forest**. These two areas, run as research facilities by the U.S. Forest Service, are full of colorful wildflowers and birds. The six-mile-long Cascade Head Trail follows the coast and provides plenty of opportunities to whale watch. Because these are special research areas, be sure to stay on the trails and not disturb any flora or fauna.

A neoclassical revival with fir wainscoting, leaded glass, traditional American furnishings and formal dining room, the **Rosebriar Hotel and Conference Center** offers 11 rooms in a renovated former convent. The rooms have wing-back chairs and mahogany

LODGING

furniture; some have fireplaces. One unit is located in a separate carriage house with a kitchenette and jacuzzi. A gourmet breakfast is included. ~ 636 14th Street, Astoria; 503-325-7427, 800-487-0224, fax 503-325-6937. MODERATE TO ULTRA-DELUXE.

East of town, the **Crest Motel** sits on a grassy hilltop overlooking the Columbia River. This trim and tidy establishment has 40 modernized units with watercolor prints and writing desks, a jacuzzi and laundry facilities. Try for one of the quieter rear rooms. ~ 5366 Leif Erickson Drive, Astoria; phone/fax 503-325-3141, 800-421-3141. MODERATE.

Also on the Columbia River is **Bayshore Motor Inn**. The 77 motel units have contemporary furniture and print bedspreads. Some rooms feature bay views, kitchenettes and jacuzzis. There's also a comfortable lounge where complimentary coffee, tea and pastries are served. The indoor pool, sauna and whirlpool are free for guests' use; laundry facilities are a plus. Convenient to Astoria's historic district, this is an ideal spot to watch river traffic or fish. ~ 555 Hamburg Street, Astoria; 503-325-2205, 800-621-0641. MODERATE.

Hillcrest Inn offers 26 attractive, pine-shaded units in a quiet garden setting close to this resort town's beach, shops, restaurants and nightlife. Choose between studios and one- and two-bedroom units with kitchens. Eclectic furniture ranges from fold-out sofas to wicker living-room sets. Some units have fireplaces, decks and spas. Family groups will find this establishment a good value. Barbecue facilities and picnic tables are provided for guest use. Adjacent to the inn is an ultra-deluxe five-bedroom beachhouse that sleeps up to 16 people; it rents weekly and monthly in the summer and requires a two-night minimum in the off-season. ~ 118 North Columbia Street, Seaside; 503-738-6273, 800-270-7659. MODERATE TO DELUXE.

The **Oceanfront Motel** is an older, 35-unit brick motel with two-room suites on the beach. The carpeted rooms have wooden bedframes, refrigerators and picture windows ideal for sunset watching. Kitchenettes are also available. Number 13, a one-bedroom cottage, is a bargain for the budget-minded. ~ 50 1st Avenue, Seaside; 503-738-5661. MODERATE TO DELUXE.

Right on the beach, the three-story **Seashore Resort Motel** has 53 spacious guest rooms with comfortable upholstered furniture, vanities, an enclosed pool, sauna and whirlpool. Within walking distance of Seaside's most popular attractions, it overlooks volleyball courts and the surf. ~ 60 North Promenade, Seaside; 503-738-6368, 888-738-6368, fax 503-738-8314. MODERATE TO DELUXE.

A mix of sleeping rooms and one- and two-bedroom units, the completely non-smoking **McBee Motel Cottages** are conveniently located on the south side of town. Some of the ten units in this older, motel-style complex offer kitchenettes and fireplaces. Large groups may want to take the two-story cottage. ~ 888 South Hemlock Street, Cannon Beach; 503-436-2569. BUDGET TO ULTRA-DELUXE.

Set on a hill with commanding views of Nehalem Bay, the motel rooms at **Wheeler Village Inn** are small, clean and brightly painted. All seven rooms have carpets and kitchenettes. Pull up a chaise longue and enjoy the sunsets or relax outside in the landscaped garden. ~ 2nd and Gregory streets, Wheeler; 503-368-5734. BUDGET.

A white, two-story lodge in a park setting, **View of the West** is one of the coast's authentic treasures. Ten beautifully furnished theme rooms, a great hillside setting, patio decks and flowers everywhere make this resort perfect for a honeymoon. Accommodations include an Early American room with a bent-willow frame bed and a Southwest room with a lodgepole-pine canopy bed as well as American Indian arts and crafts. All rooms open onto porches with panoramic views of the North Coast; some have kitchenettes. There's also a large deck with barbecue. ~ 294 Hall Street, Wheeler; 503-368-5766, fax 503-368-4806. MODERATE.

◄ HIDDEN

On Nehalem Bay, **Wheeler on the Bay Lodge and Marina** certainly is on the bay; it even has its own private docks. Motel-style units and suites, some with spas and kitchenettes, are furnished with fireplaces and VCRs. The lodge runs an on-site video store as well as canoe rentals. Rooms range from Victorian style to art deco; all are carpeted. It's convenient to fishing, clamming, sailboarding, hiking and birdwatching. ~ 580 Marine Drive, Wheeler; 503-368-5858, 800-469-3204, fax 503-368-4204. MODERATE TO DELUXE.

Eclectic is surely the word for **Ocean Locomotion Motel** with ten units overlooking Twin Rocks, a pair of giant rocks rising from the surf facing Rockaway Beach. Eight modernized one-, two- and three-bedroom units have kitchenettes and ocean views and two more-basic units offer beds and refrigerators only. Most have older furniture, but unit six has a contemporary look and qualifies as a best buy. Lawn furniture, barbecues, a fire pit, clam rakes and buckets make this family-oriented establishment appealing. ~ 19130 Alder Avenue, Rockaway Beach; 503-355-2093. MODERATE.

Large, carpeted accommodations in a saltbox-style home make **Pelican's Perch** an excellent choice. Brass beds, panoramic views and kitchenettes add to the charm of this bed and breakfast; all four rooms have private baths. For the elegant B&B touch, a full breakfast is served each morning, with a champagne brunch on Sunday; snacks and hors d'oeuvres are offered in the afternoon. One room has a private jacuzzi, and there is an outdoor hot tub for all guests. Convenient to fishing and an excursion railroad, this is one of our favorite inns on the coast. Reservations recommended. ~ 112 East Cypress Street, Garibaldi; 503-322-3633. MODERATE TO DELUXE.

HIDDEN ▶ The **Blue Haven Inn**, appropriately painted robin-egg blue, is one of the few bed and breakfasts we know that has its own antique shop on the premises. You'll enjoy staying upstairs in one of the cozy rooms individually decorated with French-silk wallpaper. One room, for example, is appointed with a four-poster bed and plates featuring Scarlett O'Hara surrounded by half a dozen admiring beaux. The breakfasts are great. ~ 3025 Gienger Road, Tillamook; phone/fax 503-842-2265. MODERATE.

On the Three Capes Scenic Loop, **Terimore Motel** offers 28 one- and two-bedroom cottages and kitchenettes. Located on the beach, these clean, modernized units are comfortably furnished with lofts, sitting areas and fireplaces. A quiet retreat, it's ideal for fishing, whale watching and agate collecting. ~ 5105 Crab Avenue, Netarts; 503-842-4623, 800-635-1821. MODERATE.

DINING For fish-and-chips you'll have a hard time beating the **Ship Inn**. Huge portions of cod and halibut are served in the waterfront dining room along with chowder, generous salads and desserts. The full bar is one of the town's most crowded gathering places. Nautical decor gives diners the feeling they're out on the bounding main. ~ One 2nd Street, Astoria; 503-325-0033. BUDGET TO DELUXE.

A great spot for river watching, **Pier 11 Feedstore Restaurant & Lounge** is the place to go for seafood, prime rib, crab legs, lobster tail and large salads. This renovated commercial building has picture windows with a wonderful view of the Columbia River. Done in a seminautical style, the dining room offers seating at oak tables on bowback captain's chairs. ~ Foot of 10th Street, Astoria; 503-325-0279. BUDGET TO ULTRA-DELUXE.

The **House of Chan** menu features Cantonese and Mandarin specialties in a large dining room with red booths and carpets, Asian art and vases. Dishes include scallops with mushrooms, onions and vegetables sautéed in wine sauce, beef with orange flavor and pineapple *war shu* duck. You can also enjoy a drink in the Sampan Lounge. Dinner only except for Sunday brunch. ~ 159 West Bond Street, Astoria; 503-325-7289. MODERATE.

One of the most beautiful dining rooms on the coast is found at **Café Uniontown**. An elegant, paneled setting with a mirrored bar, red tablecloths and marine view make this restaurant *the* place to go to enjoy stuffed halibut, filet mignon served with a sauce of shiitake mushrooms and port wine, cioppino, steaks and pasta dishes. Located under the bridge in the historic Uniontown district, this is also a relaxing spot for a drink after a hard day of sightseeing. Closed Sunday and Monday. ~ 218 West Marine Drive, Astoria; 503-325-8708. MODERATE.

Not every pizza parlor can boast a medieval-castle setting with a classic Wurlitzer "Bubbler" jukebox and deck seating overlooking a river that's home to gulls and ducks. But that's what awaits you at **BJ's Pizza Palace**. The "palace" is decorated with booths and murals of jousting knights, and the kitchen prepares 32 kinds of pizza with traditional toppings as well as smoked oysters, shrimp and baby clams. Kids have a ball in the covered play area. Closed Monday during winter. ~ 2490 North Route 101, Seaside; 503-738-7763. BUDGET TO MODERATE.

The **Pig 'N Pancake** can seat over 100 patrons at booths and tables to feast upon Swedish pancakes, crêpe suzettes and strawberry waffles. Lunch and dinner entrées include patty melts, garden sandwiches, halibut and steaks. ~ 323 Broadway Street, Seaside; 503-738-7243. BUDGET TO MODERATE.

Convenient to the city's popular attractions, **Dooger's Seafood and Grill** serves crab legs, prawns, fish and chips, pasta dishes, burgers and steaks. The paneled, carpeted dining room sports oak furniture. Dessert specialties include marionberry cobbler. ~ 505 Broadway Street, Seaside; 503-738-3773. MODERATE.

The menu at **Schooner Bay Restaurant and Lounge** boasts huge salads and a large variety of burgers and sandwiches. Dinner entrées include grilled seafood, halibut, fish and chips and pasta primavera. Closed Thursday. ~ Upstairs in Ecola Square, Hemlock Street at West 1st Street, Cannon Beach; 503-436-9338. MODERATE.

Start your day with an omelette or gingerbread waffles at the **Lazy Susan Café**, a cut above your average café. Or try their seafood salad or seafood stew for lunch or dinner. The paneled dining room with bright-blue tablecloths and watercolor prints on the walls make the Lazy Susan a local favorite. Closed Tuesday. ~ 126 North Hemlock Street, Cannon Beach; 503-436-2816. BUDGET TO MODERATE.

With both take-out and in-house dining at wood tables, **Pizza a fetta** is a good choice for a slice or an entire pie. In addition to regular toppings you can order sun-dried tomatoes, artichoke hearts, pancetta ham or fruits. Cheeses include Monterey jack, Oregon blue, French feta, fontina and Montrachet chèvre. Closed Wednesday during winter. ~ Village Center, 231 North Hemlock Street, Cannon Beach; 503-436-0333. MODERATE.

For elegant Continental dining try the **Bistro Restaurant and Bar**. Set in a small house, this intimate dining room serves specialties like baked blue-cheese halibut, sautéed scampi with garlic and mushrooms and broiled lamb with eggplant relish. ~ 263 North Hemlock Street, Cannon Beach; 503-436-2661. MODERATE.

Many museums have cafés in the basement or out on the patio.

HIDDEN ► But **Artspace** is a rare find, a fine restaurant in an elegant gallery setting. You'll walk past contemporary paintings, prints, sculpture and jewelry by outstanding Northwest artists on the way to the white-walled dining area. At booths and tables, black-and-white-checkered tablecloths, ceiling fans and sunny bay windows add up to an inviting setting for specialties like oysters Italia, vegetarian fettuccine and lemon chicken. Sunday brunch includes treats such as vegetarian eggs Benedict, waffle boats and huevos rancheros. Lunch served Monday through Saturday; dinner served Thursday through Saturday; Sunday brunch. ~ 9120 5th Street, Bay City; 503-377-2782. MODERATE.

If you're looking for good, honest deli fare with soup or salad on the side, head to the **Blue Heron French Cheese Company**. The deli counter in the midst of this jam-packed shop is stocked with goodies such as pastrami and provolone, smoked turkey and creamy brie or roast beef with tangy Cotswold cheese. ~ 2001 Blue Heron Drive, Tillamook; 503-842-8281. BUDGET.

Set in a shingled Craftsman house, **La Casa Medello** is the right place to go when you want south-of-the-border fare on the North Coast. The dark-wood interior featuring beautiful built-in cabinetry and casablanca fans is brightened by floral arrangements and plants. You can dine family-style at the big tables offering specialties like *chile rellenos*, Spanish-rice salad, homemade tamales and generous burritos. If you're hungry try la casa fajita tostada with steak or chicken breast. ~ 1160 North Route 101, Tillamook; 503-842-5768. BUDGET TO MODERATE.

Nautical decor, pink walls and valances, ocean views and an oak counter make **Roseanna's Café** an inviting spot to enjoy Willapa Bay oysters, daily fish specials, vegetable fettuccine, burgers and pesto salmon. This board-and-batten building is packed on the weekend with a loyal clientele that likes to toast those delicious moments when the sun finally burns through the fog. Breakfast is served on weekends. Closed most of December. ~ 1490 Pacific Street, Oceanside; 503-842-7351. MODERATE.

HIDDEN ► A favorite coastal short-order joint is **Wee Willie Restaurant**. Locals and tourists flock to this carpeted, lodge-style building where the menu features burgers, long dogs, short dogs, chili dogs,

DON'T TELL YOUR DENTIST

With more than a dozen varieties of saltwater taffy, as well as caramel apples and caramel corn, **Leonard's** has been an Oregon Coast tradition for nearly 80 years. Popular flavors include peanut butter, banana, licorice, molasses and cinnamon. ~ 111 Broadway Street, Seaside; 503-738-3467.

BLTs and seafood specialties like barbecue crab and cheese, grilled shrimp and cheese, oyster burgers, clam chowder and fresh shrimp salad. Picnic tables indoors and outside on the lawn attract a big beach crowd. Be sure to try the homemade pies or warm gingerbread for dessert. ~ 6060 Whiskey Creek Road, Netarts; 503-842-6869. BUDGET.

M and N Workwear is where you can find flannel shirts, sweaters, jeans and casual menswear. Located beneath the bridge in the old Finnish Hall, this establishment is popular with fishermen, lumberjacks, farmers and tourists in the midst of shopping-mall deprogramming. Located in Astoria's historic Uniontown district, this is not a place for quiche eaters. ~ 248 West Marine Drive, Astoria; 503-325-7610.

Turn back the clock at **Persona Vintage Clothing**. Collectible and antique clothing and accessories for men, women and children span the 1890–1960 era. Also on hand are a large hat section, beaded bags, costume jewelry, linens and laces. ~ 100 10th Street, Astoria; 503-325-3837.

You made it all the way to Cannon Beach and discovered that your bathing suit is too big, last summer's T-shirt has faded and you're out of #15 sunblock. **Clothes Encounters** comes to your rescue with the latest in swimwear, T-shirts, running togs and casual sportswear. If you can wear it near the water, they've got it. ~ 183 North Hemlock Street, Cannon Beach; 503-436-2401.

Our idea of a coastal gallery is **Artspace**. Contemporary Northwest sculpture and painting, jewelry and arts and crafts are all found in this intriguing showplace. WPA art from the '30s, '40s and '50s is also on display. There's a restaurant on the premises. ~ 9120 5th Street, Bay City; 503-377-2782.

Rainy Day Books focuses on new and used titles and has an excellent section on the Pacific Northwest. This is also a good place to pick up inexpensive paperbacks that come in handy when you want to relax by the fireplace. ~ 2015 2nd Street, Tillamook; 503-842-7766.

Located on the waterfront, the **Red Lion Inn** features live comedy on Tuesday and pop music and dancing Wednesday through Sunday. ~ 400 Industry Street, Astoria; 503-325-7373.

Sunsets on Broadway offers rock-and-roll bands every night except Sunday, when locals show off with karaoke. Cover on Friday and Saturday. ~ 311 Broadway Street, Seaside; 503-738-8417.

In Cannon Beach, the **Bistro Restaurant and Bar** has a solo guitarist on the weekends. Take a seat at the bar or order drinks and dessert at one of the adjacent tables. This romantic setting is the ideal way to wind up the evening. ~ 263 North Hemlock Street, Cannon Beach; 503-436-2661.

For musicals and jazz piano, Broadway shows, revivals, comedies and melodramas, check out the **Coaster Theater Playhouse.** Closed in January. ~ 108 North Hemlock Street, Cannon Beach; 503-436-1242.

BEACHES & PARKS

FORT STEVENS STATE PARK 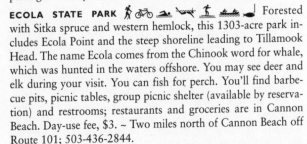 This 3762-acre state park embraces a Civil War–era fort that defended the coast during World War II. The site of a rare coastal attack by a Japanese submarine in 1942, the park includes shallow lakes, dunes, sand flats and a pine forest. Of special interest are the oceanfront remains of a wrecked British ship, the *Peter Iredale.* A museum and guided tours offer historical perspective on the region. Fish the surf for perch. The razor clamming is excellent. Facilities include picnic tables, showers, restrooms and a gift shop; restaurants and groceries are in Hammond. Day-use fee, $3. ~ Take Pacific Drive west from Hammond; 503-861-1671.

▲ There are 262 tent sites and 343 RV hookups; $17 to $20 per night. Nine yurts are also available, $27 per night.

ECOLA STATE PARK Forested with Sitka spruce and western hemlock, this 1303-acre park includes Ecola Point and the steep shoreline leading to Tillamook Head. The name Ecola comes from the Chinook word for whale, which was hunted in the waters offshore. You may see deer and elk during your visit. You can fish for perch. You'll find barbecue pits, picnic tables, group picnic shelter (available by reservation) and restrooms; restaurants and groceries are in Cannon Beach. Day-use fee, $3. ~ Two miles north of Cannon Beach off Route 101; 503-436-2844.

SADDLE MOUNTAIN STATE PARK A 3283-foot twin peak is the heart of this natural heritage site that features unusual plants and flowers. The peak was originally called Swallahoost after a chief who, after being murdered, was said to have returned to life as an eagle. From the mountaintop you can see both the Columbia River's mouth and the Pacific Coast. Douglas fir, spruce, hemlock and alder shade the 2911-acre park. There are picnic tables and restrooms; restaurants and groceries are in Necanicum Junction. Closed in winter from October to April, or until the snow melts. ~ Located off Route 26, eight miles northeast of Necanicum Junction; 503-368-5943.

▲ There are nine primitive sites; $14 per night.

OSWALD WEST STATE PARK With four miles of Pacific shoreline, this 2474-acre park provides great views of Nehalem Bay. Douglas fir, spruce and western red cedar dominate the rainforest in this park bounded on the south by legendary Neahkah-nie Mountain. You'll want to visit the picturesque creeks, coves and scenic Arch Cape. Fishing is good at the beach for cod, perch and bass. You'll find picnic tables and restrooms; restaurants and groceries are located nearby in Manzanita. ~ Located ten miles south of Cannon Beach off Route 101; 503-368-5943.

▲ There are 36 primitive sites accessible by foot with wheelbarrows for walk-in campers; $14 per night.

NEHALEM BAY STATE PARK 🚶🚴🐎 ⛵🚤🛥️🛶 Encompassing a three-mile-long sandspit at Nehalem Bay's mouth, this 889-acre park is a popular recreational area. The open, windswept landscape is ideal for kite flying. Nehalem Bay State Park is also a favorite for horseback riding, cycling and walking. There's good crabbing in the bay and, depending on the season, good fishing for steelhead, cutthroat trout, perch and chinook salmon. You can swim in the bay if you're so inclined. Facilities include picnic tables, restrooms, showers and an on-site airport; restaurants and groceries are nearby in Manzanita. Day-use fee, $3. ~ Located off Route 101, three miles south of Manzanita Junction; 503-368-5943.

▲ There are 278 sites with hookups, $19 per night; ten yurts, $25 per night; and 17 horse camps, $14 per person per night.

CAPE MEARES STATE PARK 🚶 Named for an 18th-century British naval officer and trader, this 94-acre park and adjacent wildlife refuge encompass a spruce-hemlock forest and memorable ocean headlands. While the historic lighthouse no longer shines, the cape remains a landmark for tourists, who come to see the offshore national wildlife refuge and birds. Also here is the Octopus Tree, an exotic Sitka spruce that was once a meeting point for Tillamook American Indian medicine men. There are picnic tables and restrooms; restaurants and groceries are in Tillamook. ~ Located off Route 101, ten miles west of Tillamook.

CAPE LOOKOUT STATE PARK 🚶🛶 With two miles of forested headlands, a rainforest, beaches and sand dunes on Netarts Bay, it's hard to resist this 2000-acre gem. Thanks to an extensive trail network, Cape Lookout is an excellent place to observe sea lions and shorebirds. It is also one of the highlights of the Three Capes Loop. There's excellent crabbing in Netarts Bay. You'll find picnic tables, restrooms and showers; restaurants and groceries are nearby. Day-use fee, $3. ~ Located off Route 101, about 12 miles west of Tillamook; 503-842-4981.

▲ There are 191 tent sites and 53 RV hookups, $16 to $20 per night; a hiker-biker camp, $4 per person per night; and 6 yurts, $25 per night.

CAPE KIWANDA STATE PARK 🚶🛶 This 185-acre headland park has a beautiful, sheltered beach. On the road between Pacific City and Sand Lake, it has wave-sculptured sandstone cliffs, tidepools and dunes. Shore fishing is good. There are picnic tables and restrooms; restaurants and groceries are nearby in Pacific City. ~ Located off Route 101, one mile north of Pacific City.

▼▼▼▼▼▼▼▼▼▼▼
Central Coast

Proceeding down the coast you'll appreciate an impressive state-park system protecting coastal beaches and bluffs, rivers and estuaries, wildlife refuges and forested promontories. With the Pacific to the west and the Siuslaw National Forest to the east, this section of the coast is sparsely populated but has more than its share of state parks and beaches. Anglers and hikers have plenty of options here, with many of the best spots only about 90 minutes away from Salem or Eugene.

SIGHTS
One of the largest communities on the coast, **Lincoln City** stretches along the shore for roughly ten miles. While the coastal sprawl may turn some visitors off, this region offers many fine parks, lakes and restaurants, and seven miles of clean, sandy (not rocky) beaches. Stop by the **Lincoln City Visitors and Convention Bureau** for helpful details on beachcombing, shopping for crafts and recreational activities. ~ 801 Southwest Route 101, Suite 1, Lincoln City; 541-994-8378.

Many visitors flock to **Devil's Lake**, a popular water sports and fishing area. But few of them realize that **D River**, located at the lake's mouth, is reputedly the world's shortest river, just under 500 feet at low tide. This is also a terrific place to fly a kite. At the southern edge of the city, Drift Creek Road leads to **Drift Creek Covered Bridge**, the oldest covered bridge in Oregon. Dating from 1914, the structure is so flimsy that it was removed from the road and placed off to the side. Though you can't drive over it, the bridge still makes for a wonderful photo.

When it's foggy on the coast, it makes sense to head inland where the sun is often shining. One way to do this is to take Route 229 inland along the Siletz River. Six miles beyond the town of Kernville you'll come to **Medicine Rock**, a pioneer landmark. Indian legend held that presents left here would assure good fortune.

HIDDEN ►

Proceed south to **Siletz**, named for one of the coast's better-known American Indian tribes. In 1856, at the end of the Rogue River Wars, the American Army created the Siletz Indian Agency, which became home for 2000 American Indians. Within a year, unspeakable conditions diminished their numbers to 600. The agency closed for good in 1925, and today the Siletz tribe gathers each August for its annual powwow featuring dancing and a salmon bake.

Continue on to visit the popular galleries and antique shops at **Toledo**. This small town operated one of the country's largest spruce mills during World War II.

From Toledo, follow Route 20 west to **Newport**. A harbor town with an array of tourist attractions, Newport is a busy place, especially during the summer. Like Seaside, Newport is filled with souvenir shops, saltwater-taffy stores and enough T-shirt shops to outfit the city of Portland. There are also fine museums, galleries and other sightseeing possibilities. Begin your visit to this popular vacation town with a stop at the **Greater Newport Chamber of Commerce**. ~ 555 Southwest Coast Highway, Newport; 541-265-8801.

A short walk from the chamber is the **Lincoln County Historical Society**. At the Log Cabin Museum and adjacent Burrows House you'll see Siletz basketry, maritime memorabilia, farming, logging and pioneer displays, patterned glass, Victorian-era household furnishings and clothing and many historic photographs. Closed Monday. ~ 545 Southwest 9th Street, Newport; 541-265-7509.

The most popular tourist area in Newport is **Bay Boulevard**, where canneries, restaurants, shops and attractions like **Undersea Gardens** peacefully coexist. Located on Yaquina Bay, this waterfront extravaganza gives you a chance to view more than 5000 species including octopus, eel, salmon and starfish. Scuba divers perform daily for the crowds in this bayfront setting. Admission. ~ 250 Southwest Bay Boulevard, Newport; 541-265-2206.

The OSU **Mark O. Hatfield Marine Science Center** is the coast's premier aquarium with a quarter-mile-long, wheelchair-accessible estuary loop. The center features hands-on displays, aquariums and exhibits interpreting the research being done at the aquarium. Admission. ~ 2030 South Marine Science Drive, Newport; 541-867-0100.

Next door is the **Oregon Coast Aquarium**, which has indoor and outdoor exhibits showcasing seabirds, marine mammals and fish in a re-created natural environment. Children love the inter-

EXTRA! FILM STAR MOVES INTO CUSHY NEW HOME!

The most popular attraction at the Oregon Coast Aquarium is the killer whale Keiko, better known as the star of *Free Willy*. After international protest about his confining tank and unrelenting show schedule at a theme park in Mexico City, a new home for Keiko was found here in a two-million-gallon seawater tank opened for his arrival in January 1996. Not performing anymore, Keiko can be seen through a glass wall and is being rehabilitated to return to the ocean (the target date for his release is in fall of 1998, although it could be later). After that, the tank will be used for rehabilitating other marine mammals.

active exhibits and the touch tank. Admission. ~ 2820 Southeast Ferry Slip Road, Newport; 541-867-3474.

HIDDEN ► As you leave the Hatfield Center and head back up to the bridge you'll pass **Zigzag Zoo/El Fincho Rancho**, a sculpture garden that deserves a place on the Oregon folk-art map. Wood sculptor Loran Finch has blanketed his yard and garden with ships masts, propellers, floats, fishnets, abalone shells and nicely carved figurines. The result is a kind of driftwood fantasia. ~ 2640 Southwest Abalone Street, Newport.

After crossing the bridge, follow the signs west to visit the **Yaquina Bay Lighthouse** in Yaquina Bay State Park. Continue north on Mark Street to **Nye Beach**. Newport's historic beach district is more than a century old, but many of the early-day hotels, cabins and beach houses survive.

In Nye Beach you'll find the **Cloe–Niemela–Clarke Gallery**, where you can familiarize yourself with paintings, handicrafts and photography by members of the Yaquina Art Association. Open daily in summer; weekends only in winter. ~ 839 Northwest Beach Drive, Nye Beach; 541-265-5133.

Drive north on Route 101 to **Agate Beach**, a great spot for rockhounds. Moonstones, jasper and tiger eyes are all found here. Continue north on Route 101 to the Otter Crest Loop. Begin by visiting **Devil's Punchbowl State Park**, near Otter Rock, named after a collapsed cavern flushed by high tides. There's a lovely beach here, and you can shop for a picnic or mask art in the tiny oceanfront hamlet of **Otter Rock**. Continue north past Cape Foulweather, named by Captain James Cook in 1778, to **Depoe Bay**, home of the smallest harbor in the world. This six-acre port is fun to explore on foot thanks to its seafood restaurants and shops.

While the harbor is the heart of this charming seaside village, you may also want to head across Route 101 to the coast, one of the best whale-watching spots in Oregon. A location for the movie *One Flew Over the Cuckoo's Nest*, Depoe Bay is also famous for **Spouting Horn**, where the surf surges above the oceanfront cliffs in stormy weather.

Also worth a visit is **Depoe Bay Aquarium**, which has sea lions, harbor seals and a wide variety of bottomfish. Admission. ~ Route 101 at Bay Drive, Depoe Bay; 541-765-2259.

Return to Newport on Route 101 and continue south ten miles to **Seal Rock State Park**. This wayside park has some of the best tidepools in the area and is a great place to watch the barking pinnipeds and hunt for agates.

Continue south on Route 101 to **Waldport** and **Alsea Bay**, one of the best clamming spots on the coast and easily accessed from numerous parks. The port town is a relatively peaceful alternative to the coast's busy tourist hubs.

Let There
Be Light

No matter where you are on the Oregon Coast, a powerful beacon may be sweeping the high seas and shoreline. From Tillamook to Port Orford, nine of these classic sentinels built since 1857 still stand. Five continue to operate as unmanned Coast Guard stations, and three inactive lighthouses are restored and open to the public.

One of the best, located at **Cape Meares**, five miles south of Tillamook Bay, is a dormant beam that was built in 1890. Special displays offer historical perspective on this beacon. Open year-round for a self-guided look-see, the lighthouse is part of Cape Meares State Park. ~ Off Route 101, ten miles west of Tillamook.

Also open to the public is **Yaquina Bay Lighthouse**, built in 1871. Authentically restored with 19th-century furniture, Yaquina Bay features an interpretive exhibit. ~ Off Route 101, just north of the Yaquina Bay Bridge.

Newport's **Yaquina Head Lighthouse** was constructed in 1873. This automated light flashes every 20 seconds and is supplemented by a powerful radio beacon. There are daily tours; fee. ~ Four miles north of Yaquina Bay.

Coquille River Lighthouse, dating to 1896, was the last lighthouse built on the Oregon Coast. Restored and open to the public, it serves as a public observatory with interpretive displays on the Coquille River region. ~ At the south end of Bullards Beach State Park, a mile north of Bandon.

While they are not open to the public, other lighthouses attract visitors who come to admire the architecture of these whitewashed towers. **Tillamook Rock Lighthouse**, opened in 1881 and the state's only lighthouse that is actually offshore, was built and then ferried to the construction site by tender.

One of the most photographed spots on the coast is **Heceta Head Lighthouse**. At 4.5-million candlepower, this is the brightest beacon on the Oregon Coast. ~ Off Route 101, 13 miles north of Florence. Built in 1857, the **Umpqua Lighthouse** was the coast's first. Destroyed in an 1861 flood, it was replaced in 1894. The 65-foot tower is adjacent to Umpqua Lighthouse State Park. Tours are offered Wednesday through Sunday. ~ Off Route 101, six miles south of Reedsport

The 1934 **Cape Arago Lighthouse** is on a rocky island at the Coos Bay entrance. The unmanned beacon has an automated white light, fog signal and beacon. ~ Next to Sunset Bay State Park off Route 101.

In service since 1870, **Cape Blanco Lighthouse** is the westernmost navigational beacon in Oregon. It is also Oregon's oldest continuously operated light. This 300,000-candlepower light is near Cape Blanco State Park. Open Thursday through Monday from April to October for volunteer-guided tours. ~ Nine miles north of Port Orford off Route 101.

Pick up Route 34 east along the Alsea River for nine miles to
HIDDEN ▶   **Kozy Kove Marina and Travel Park**. You can rent a boat here and
explore this tributary bounded by the Siuslaw National Forest.
It is also the home of the coast's only floating full-service restaurant and lounge, the Kozy Kove Café and Hook Up Lounge. A
great fishing spot, this section of the Alsea can be a sunny alter-
ative to the foggy coast. ~ 9464 Alsea Highway, Tidewater; 541-
528-3251.

For a picturesque, albeit windy, drive, continue east 30 miles
HIDDEN ▶   on Route 34 to the village of Alsea and follow the signs to **Alsea
Falls**. The area around the 35-foot cascade makes a good spot for
a picnic, and there's also three-and-a-half miles of hiking trails
through old-growth forest and Douglas firs. Along the way you
may catch a glimpse of woodpeckers, beavers and white-tailed
deer.

Return to Waldport and continue south to **Yachats** (pronounced "Ya-HOTS"), a classy village with fine restaurants, inns
and shops. This town is also home of the **Little Log Church**.
Surrounded by a charming garden, this tiny house of worship has
a handful of white pews for congregants
warmed by a pioneer stove. ~ Located at
3rd and Pontiac streets.

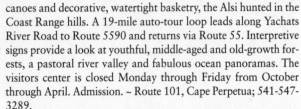

South of Reedsport is one of
the most popular fishing ports
in the dunes region, Salmon
Harbor on Winchester Bay.
The crabbing and rock-
fishing here are top-
notch.

To the south is Cape Perpetua, discovered by
Captain James Cook in 1778. The 2700-acre
Cape Perpetua Scenic Area has miles of trails
ideal for beachcombing, viewing deer and exploring tidepools. The **Cape Perpetua Visitors Center**
is a good place to learn about the region's original
inhabitants, the Alsi. Known for their woodworking,
canoes and decorative, watertight basketry, the Alsi hunted in the
Coast Range hills. A 19-mile auto-tour loop leads along Yachats
River Road to Route 5590 and returns via Route 55. Interpretive
signs provide a look at youthful, middle-aged and old-growth forests, a pastoral river valley and fabulous ocean panoramas. The
visitors center is closed Monday through Friday from October
through April. Admission. ~ Route 101, Cape Perpetua; 541-547-
3289.

Two miles south of Cape Perpetua off Route 101 is **Strawberry
Hill State Park**. The white blossoms of wild strawberries create
a floral panorama in the spring months. This park is also a popular spot for seals that sunbathe on the shoreline's basalt rocks.
The tidepools shelter sea stars, anemones and bright-purple spin
sea urchins. However, the pools are a protected reserve, so re-
moval of anything is strictly forbidden. Down the road another
two miles is the distinctive **Ziggurat**, a pyramid-shaped bed and
breakfast. ~ Ziggurat: 95330 Route 101, Yachats; 541-547-3925.

Just south of Heceta Head Lighthouse is pinniped heaven, **Sea Lion Caves**. Ride the elevator down to the two-story-high cave to see the resident stellar sea lions enjoying a life of leisure. The outside ledges are a rookery where these marine mammals breed and give birth in the spring and early summer. The bulls vigilantly protect their harem's territory. An overlook adjacent to the entrance is a great whale-watching spot. Admission. ~ 91560 Route 101; 541-547-3111.

As you continue on toward Florence, about four miles north of the city is **Darlingtonia Botanical Wayside,** a short path that takes you to see the bog where Darlingtonia, serpent-shaped plants also known as cobra lilies, trap insects with a sticky substance and devour them.

To gain perspective on the region's American Indian and pioneer history, visit the **Siuslaw Pioneer Museum**, a former Lutheran Church. Closed Monday and the month of December. ~ 85294 Route 101, one mile south of Florence; 541-997-7884.

In Florence, the **Chamber of Commerce** will quickly orient you to this Siuslaw River community. ~ 270 Route 101, Florence; 541-997-3128. Then, with the help of a chamber walking-tour guide, explore Florence's old town. A small artists' colony with a gazebo park overlooking the Siuslaw waterfront, **Florence** has a popular historic district centered around Bay Street. Here you can browse, sip an espresso or take in a film at the circa-1938 Harbor Theater, repainted in pink.

Anglers won't want to miss the **Fly Fishing Museum** displaying angling prints and a vintage collection of flies from around the United States as well as 20 foreign countries. Open by appointment only. Admission. ~ 280 Nopal Street, Florence; 541-997-6349.

Floating at the Old Town Docks is a beautifully restored, turn-of-the-century sternwheeler, the **Westward Ho**. It operates year-round and provides history and wildlife tours of the river during the day. Dinner cruises are offered on weekends. ~ Bay Street, Florence; 541-997-9691.

Florence is also the northern gateway to **Oregon Dunes National Recreation Area**. Miles of sandy beaches and forested bluffs laced by streams flowing down from the mountains make this region a favorite Oregon vacation spot. Woodlands and freshwater lakes provide a nice contrast to the windswept beaches. Numerous parks offer access to the dunes. Among them is **Oregon Dunes Overlook**, ten miles south of Florence. Admission. ~ 541-271-3611.

Near Reedsport on Route 38 about three miles east of Route 101 is **Dean Creek Elk Preserve**. The herd of Roosevelt elk make for an unusual photo opportunity.

LODGING The **Inn at Spanish Head** has 120 rooms and suites with kitchens. Furnished with wall-to-wall carpets, contemporary easy chairs, oak tables, nature prints and full ocean views, most of the units feature decks. A pool, spa, recreation room, lounge and restaurant add to the resort atmosphere. ~ 4009 South Route 101, Lincoln City; 541-996-2161, 800-452-8127, fax 541-996-4089. DELUXE TO ULTRA-DELUXE.

Salishan Lodge offers 205 units. In a forested setting above Siletz Bay, this lodge accommodates guests in two- and three-story, hillside buildings. Units all feature stone fireplaces, balconies, contemporary prints and carports. Golf, tennis, a fitness center, library and art gallery are just some of the amenities. ~ Route 101, Gleneden Beach; 541-764-2371, 800-452-2300, fax 541-764-3681. ULTRA-DELUXE.

One of the area's best deals is **Trollers Lodge**. Set on an oceanfront bluff, this 12-unit establishment has clean units with eclectic furniture, picture windows and kitchenettes. Picnic tables and benches ideal for watching whales swim by in season add to the convenience. One- and two-bedroom suites with full kitchens are also available. The location is good for deep-sea fishing trips. ~ 355 Southwest Route 101, Depoe Bay; 541-765-2287, 800-472-9335, fax 541-765-3287. MODERATE.

Modeled after a 19th-century New England–style inn, **Gracie's Landing** overlooks the nation's smallest harbor. Nautical decor, queen and king beds and Early American–style cherry-wood furniture add to the charm of the inn's 13 rooms and suites. All the suites have decks overlooking this picturesque harbor; some have jacuzzis. There is also a parlor with a baby-grand piano and comfortable sofas, and a library with a fireplace. ~ 235 Southeast Bay View Avenue, Depoe Bay; 541-765-2322, 800-228-0448. MODERATE TO DELUXE.

Don't be surprised if you find a couple sitting on an ocean-view bench outside **Alpine Chalets**. They are probably coming back to remember a honeymoon spent at this oceanfront retreat adjacent to Devil's Punchbowl State Park. Blessed with its own private park and beach access, each one- and two-bedroom A-frame chalet has a large, paneled sitting area furnished with contemporary foldout sofas. All 11 units are fully carpeted and come with kitchens and casablanca fans. Four units are pet-friendly. ~ Otter Crest Loop, Otter Rock; 541-765-2572, 800-825-5768, fax 541-765-3135; e-mail alpine@netbridge.net. MODERATE.

The **Inn at Otter Crest** offers 100 rooms including one- and two-bedroom suites with fireplaces, sofa beds, fully equipped kitchens and decks. The semiprivate cove boasts great tidepools; you can look for seals and, in season, migrating gray whales. Set in a fir forest, with duck ponds and wild rhododendron, the inn also sports tennis courts, a pool and sauna. There's also a restaurant and lounge on the premises. ~ Otter Crest Loop off Route 101, Otter Rock; 541-765-2111, 800-452-2101, fax 541-765-2047. DELUXE TO ULTRA-DELUXE.

The four-story **Sylvia Beach Hotel**, a honeymoon haven that had degenerated into a flophouse, was renovated and renamed for the proprietor of Shakespeare and Co. and first publisher of James Joyce's *Ulysses*. Her Paris bookstore and coffeehouse was a home away from home for writers like Joyce, Ernest Hemingway, T. S. Eliot and Samuel Beckett. Twenty rooms, each themed after an author, now accommodate guests. Our favorites are the ornate Oscar Wilde room featuring garish Victorian wallpaper (while dying in a Paris hotel room his last words were: "Either this wallpaper goes or I do"), the Dr. Seuss room (*The Cat in the Hat* is front and center), the Mark Twain room (fireplace, deck, antique school seat) and the Emily Dickinson room (marble dresser, green carpet, beautiful antique desk). While Henry Miller (*Tropic of Cancer*) didn't get his own quarters, this man of letters is appropriately commemorated in the basement restrooms. Incidentally, we'd love to see the owners add a James Joyce room in the years ahead. The hotel is completely nonsmoking and Jersey, the house cat, lives there. Breakfast is included. ~ 267 Northwest Cliff Street, Newport; 541-265-5428. MODERATE TO DELUXE.

The **Summer Wind Motel** offers fully carpeted rooms and kitchenettes with woodframe beds, sofas, pine coffee tables and stall showers. One of many Route 101 strip motels serving the Newport crowd, it's set back from the highway, and the rear rooms are relatively quiet. ~ 728 North Coast Highway, Newport; 541-265-8076. BUDGET TO MODERATE.

The **Cliff House** is a bed and breakfast on the ocean. It features a baby-grand piano, big fireplace in the living room and gazebo

---

✔ CHECK THESE OUT—UNIQUE LODGING

- *Budget:* Enjoy hilltop views of Nehalem Bay from your perch at **Wheeler Village Inn.** *page 333*
- *Moderate:* Sprawl out on a lodgepole-pine canopy bed at the two-story **View of the West,** a resort in a hillside park setting. *page 333*
- *Moderate to deluxe:* Spot whales using the binoculars found in your cozily decorated room at the **Home by the Sea** in Port Orford. *page 360*
- *Deluxe to ultra-deluxe:* Keep an eye out for seals and gray whales at **The Inn at Otter Crest**'s semiprivate cove before settling down in front of the fireplace. *page 346*

Budget: under $50   Moderate: $50–$90   Deluxe: $90–$130   Ultra-deluxe: over $130

in the front yard. Convenient to 16 miles of walking beach, the inn also offers a jacuzzi, sauna and an on-call masseuse. Some of the four themed rooms have chandeliers, down comforters and wall-to-wall carpeting. Reservations highly recommended. Gay-friendly. ~ 1450 Southwest Adahi Street, Waldport; 541-563-2506, fax 541-563-4393. DELUXE TO ULTRA-DELUXE.

Romantic, secluded accommodations on three-and-a-half forested acres above the ocean can be found at **The Oregon House**, an inn with cottages, guest rooms, suites and townhouse units, some with kitchens, fireplaces, marble bathrooms and jacuzzis. One of the most charming is Clementine's Cabin, which has red-and-white-checked curtains, a red fireplace, a hot tub and a brass-and-iron bed. The grounds include a private beach, trails and a creek. Gay-friendly. ~ 94288 Route 101, Yachats; 541-547-3329. BUDGET TO DELUXE.

Built in the 1940s to resemble a horse ranch, the **Yachats Inn** has 19 pleasant motel accommodations with a rustic knotty-pine look and superb ocean views. Especially nice are the upstairs units, which include a glassed-in sunporch, great for watching a winter storm roll in. There is an indoor swimming pool and a lounge with stone fireplace, piano, books, games, puzzles and free coffee. Gay-friendly. ~ 331 South Coast Highway, Yachats; 541-547-3456. MODERATE TO DELUXE.

HIDDEN ▶

Set in a sunny valley surrounded by the Siuslaw National Forest, a wildlife refuge and the Yachats River, **Serenity Bed and Breakfast** lives up to its name. Six miles from the coast, this resort is a verdant country retreat ideal for hiking, biking or birding. The Alt Heidelberg Room features an oak-frame double bed imported from a German castle; you can listen to a vintage collection of Bavarian music in the—what else—Bavarian room. Or perhaps you'd prefer to try one of this ten-acre bed and breakfast's other rooms featuring canopied beds, French-provincial furniture, Italian writing desk and two-person jacuzzi. The full gourmet German breakfast is accompanied by uplifting German music. ~ 5985 Yachats River Road, Yachats; 541-547-3813. MODERATE TO ULTRA-DELUXE.

On a 40-foot cliff overlooking the Pacific six and a half miles south of Yachats, **See Vue** offers 11 units. Each is individually named and themed. All have plants and antiques. Weekend reservations recommended well in advance. Gay-friendly. ~ 95590 Route 101, Yachats; 541-547-3227. BUDGET TO MODERATE.

Turn up the Vivaldi and step right in to the circa-1914 **Edwin K Bed and Breakfast**, where the six rooms are named for six seasons (including Autumn and Indian Summer). As you might expect, Winter features a white Battenberg bedspread, while Fall has a flowered down comforter. Furnished with oak armoires, chandeliers and white carpets, this elegant home has a backyard waterfall and Siuslaw River views. ~ 1155 Bay Street, Florence; 541-997-8360, 800-833-9465. DELUXE.

On the Siuslaw River, the 40-unit **River House Motel** is a one-block walk from this popular town's historic shopping district. Many of the units have decks overlooking the river traffic and drawbridge. Immaculate rooms feature oak furniture and queens and kings with floral-print bedspreads. Some rooms have jacuzzis and overlook the waterfront. ~ 1202 Bay Street, Florence; 541-997-3933. MODERATE TO DELUXE.

If you're interested in cetaceans, consider checking in to **Driftwood Shores Resort & Conference Center**. An estimated 21,000 whales migrate south past this inn each winter and return northward in the spring. Overlooking Heceta Beach, the 127-unit establishment has rooms and kitchenette suites featuring nautical prints, stone fireplaces, picture windows, decks and contemporary furniture. An indoor pool, hot tub and restaurant are located on the premises. ~ 88416 1st Avenue, Florence; 541-997-8263, 800-422-5091, fax 541-997-5857. MODERATE.

DINING

The Noodle is one of those Italian restaurants you might buzz right by were it not for a book like this one. Located at the north end of town, it is favored by locals who enjoy this cross between a trattoria and a yacht club. Take a seat on one of the deck chairs beneath a sailboat photo and order lasagna made with ricotta and mozzarella cheeses and sausage. Or try the Florentine ravioli or fettuccine alfredo. Garlic bread and salad come with all dinners. Dinner only. ~ 2185 Northwest Route 101, Lincoln City; 541-994-8800. BUDGET TO MODERATE.

Kernville Steak and Seafood is known for its reasonably priced, hearty meals. Dine in the paneled dining room beneath a vaulted ceiling. Sea-green linen, captain's chairs, blue-heron pictures and a touch of greenery set the scene. Known for its generous bacon-wrapped filet mignon, prime rib, steamers and scallops, the restaurant also has an excellent vegetarian menu, seafood pasta salad and smaller portions for those who don't arrive famished. No lunch on Sunday. ~ 186 Siletz Highway, Lincoln City; 541-994-6200. MODERATE TO ULTRA-DELUXE.

Salishan Lodge's **Sun Room** lives up to its name, a bright, paneled dining room with cedar tables, Windsor chairs and garden views. This lodge-style restaurant offers seafood specialties, natural veal stew, butter clams steamed in a broth of thyme, garlic and Weinhard's Ale, shrimp-salad pita sandwiches, oyster stew and chilled gazpacho. ~ Route 101, Gleneden Beach; 541-764-2371. MODERATE.

For a step above in price, try the **Dining Room**, Salishan's romantic, tri-level gourmet restaurant with one of the biggest wine lists on the coast. Specialties include lamb chops with garlic-roasted pepper butter, grilled Pacific halibut with shellfish sausage and a summer vegetable plate. ~ Route 101, Gleneden Beach; 541-764-2371. DELUXE.

Chez Jeannette is French dining with an Oregon twist. Nestled in the woods, this pastoral, candlelit restaurant has a cozy fireplace, burgundy carpet and high-backed oak chairs. Reservations are a good idea at this establishment, where you might start with smoked salmon served with a horseradish, sour-cream caper, dill-and-brandy sauce and then enjoy specialties like wild mushroom ragoût, rack of lamb in pinot noir sauce and filet mignon. They also have an excellent wine cellar. For lighter appetites there's a shrimp salad. Dinner only. ~ 7150 Old Route 101, Gleneden Beach; 541-764-3434. DELUXE TO ULTRA-DELUXE.

If you've had it with minimalist nouvelle cuisine, head straight for the **Whale Cove Inn**. Half the customers leave with doggie bags, proof positive that few establishments offer more generous helpings of fresh salmon, cod or halibut. Also on the menu are vegetarian fettuccine dishes, steamed clams, clam chowder, beef marsala, scallops poached in white-wine sauce and a towering crab and shrimp Louie. Friday night offers all-you-can-eat barbecue beef ribs. The dining room is a blend of semicircular booths and plastic tables with a panoramic view of this first-rate whale-watching spot. Ask for a pair of binoculars. A prime choice for sunset dining. Breakfast, lunch and dinner. Closed first two weeks of January. ~ Route 101, two miles south of Depoe Bay; 541-765-2255. BUDGET TO DELUXE.

Shrimp cocktail with ale sauce, a pizza crust made with stout, bangers with beer mustard, oysters with ale sauce—do we detect a trend here? **The Rogue Ales Brewery and Public House** serves these specialties with its golden ales, stouts, lagers, award-winning Old Crustacean barley wine and gold medal–winning Rogue Smoke in a wood-paneled lounge. Tiffany-style lamps illuminate the booths, and the walls are decorated with classic advertising signs. The gameroom in the rear is good for a game of pool or darts. Specialties include sandwiches, salads and fresh fish-and-chips. ~ 748 Southwest Bay Boulevard, Newport; 541-265-2537. BUDGET TO MODERATE.

Gino's Seafood and Deli offers crab and deli sandwiches, chowder and fish-and-chips. You can dine alfresco on picnic tables. A good bet for picnic fare. ~ 808 Southwest Bay Boulevard, Newport; 541-265-2424. BUDGET.

The Whale's Tale serves excellent breakfasts, vegetarian lasagna, cioppino, hamburgers, seafood poorboys and fish filets with mushrooms, lemon butter and wine. This dark-wood café has an open-beam ceiling, inlaid mahogany and oak tables and Tiffany-style lamps. A kayak frame, harpoon, whale's vertebrae and tail suspended from the ceiling complete the decor. Breakfast, lunch and dinner are served. Closed in January and on Wednesday from fall through spring. ~ 452 Southwest Bay Boulevard, Newport; 541-265-8660. MODERATE TO DELUXE.

Canyon Way Bookstore and Restaurant serves up a host of delectables in a contemporary setting. Choose between a cozy, bistro-style room adjoining the bar, a main room with wood tables with inlaid tiles, a garden room and, best of all, a handsome, enclosed brick patio with booths and tables in a garden setting. Dinner features bouillabaise bacon-wrapped filet mignon, grilled seafood and chicken. The restaurant is closed all day Sunday and Monday evening. ~ 1216 Southwest Canyon Way, Newport; 541-265-8319. MODERATE TO DELUXE.

If you're looking for a sushi bar, try **Yuzen Japanese Cuisine**. Set in a former rathskeller with leaded glass windows and Tiffany-style lamps, the restaurant has been redecorated with red paper lanterns, paper screens and a wooden sushi bar. The menu includes tempura, sukiyaki, *katsu don*, bento dinners, sashimi deluxe and, by reservation, *shabu shabu nabe*. Closed Monday. ~ 10111 Northwest Route 101, Seal Rock; 541-563-4766. MODERATE TO ULTRA-DELUXE.

For the ultimate waterfront-dining experience, try **Kozy Kove Café**. Built on a dock, this floating restaurant continues a century-old tradition in an open-beamed dining room with handcrafted tables and casablanca fans. The menu features steamer clams, oysters, steaks, smoked salmon chowder and vegetarian dishes. Deer and otter are frequently visible from a restaurant that rises and falls with the tides. Breakfast and lunch are served Friday through Monday; lunch and dinner are served Tuesday through Thursday. ~ 9464 Alsea Highway, Tidewater, nine miles east of Waldport; 541-528-3251. MODERATE.

◄ *HIDDEN*

While some restaurants may be advertising "fresh crab" just flown in from Anchorage, **La Serre** insists on truth in labeling. Only fresh local fish and crab off the boat are served in the contemporary dining room decorated with oak tables and chairs, oil lamps, potted plants and polished-hardwood floors. A bistro with a fireplace and full bar also provides a relaxed setting for drinks or dinner. La Serre specializes in seafood like razor clams, scallops, bay oysters, vegetarian entrées, chicken pot pies, steaks and fresh pastries. Dinner only; Sunday breakfast. Closed Tuesday. ~ 2nd and Beach streets, Yachats; 541-547-3420. MODERATE TO DELUXE.

Lotus Seafood Palace has two kitchens; one to prepare the Chinese menu, another to whip up the American. Chinese seafood dishes include steamed crab, prawns with mild chili sauce and clams with black-bean sauce, as well as Mongolian beef, mu shu pork and crispy duck. The American menu features steak, pork chops and seafood. The rose-carpeted dining room is landscaped with hanging and potted plants. Guests dine at oak tables overlooking the Siuslaw River and Oregon Dunes. ~ 1150 Bay Street, Florence; 541-997-7168. MODERATE TO DELUXE.

SHOPPING   The **Oregon Surf Shop** both sells and rents surfboards, boogie boards, skimboards, wet suits and beach toys for fun outside the water. There are also good beachwear and swimwear departments. ~ 4933 Southwest Route 101, Lincoln City; 541-996-3957.

The town of Toledo is home to one of the best galleries along the coast, **Michael Gibbons Gallery**. Located in the old vicarage of the city's Episcopal church, the gallery is both home and workspace for noted landscape painter Michael Gibbons. ~ 140 Northeast Alder Street, Toledo; 541-336-2797.

The **Wood Gallery** offers beautiful wooden sculptures, myrtlewood bowls, cherry-wood cabinets and jewelry boxes. Also here are metal sculptures, elk antler knives, jewelry, ceramics, pottery and stained glass. Handmade children's toys, furniture and ceramic tables are all worth a look. ~ 818 Southwest Bay Boulevard, Newport; 541-265-6843.

Oceanic Arts has innovative water fountains as well as limited-edition prints, pottery, jewelry and decorative basketry. ~ 444 Southwest Bay Boulevard, Newport; 541-265-5963.

Forget your kite? For stunt, quad-line, box, delta, cellular, dragon and diamond kites try **Catch The Wind**. A full line of accessories, repairs and free advice are also available from the resident experts. ~ 1250 Southwest Bay Street, Florence; 541-997-9500.

The **Bay Window** will delight antiquarians in the market for old and rare prints, books and antiques. Classic maps and historic photographs are found in this charming waterfront shop. ~ 1308 Bay Street, Florence; 541-997-2002.

NIGHTLIFE   To enjoy rock and jazz you can dance to, try the second-story lounge at **Salishan Lodge**. When you're tired of the dancefloor, take a table by the fireplace or at the bar. There are also billiard tables as well as a deck overlooking the golf course. Contemporary painting completes the decorating scheme. ~ Route 101, Gleneden Beach; 541-764-2371.

The **Newport Performing Arts Center** presents a variety of concerts, dance programs and theatrical events in the Alice Silverman Theater and the Studio Theater. Both local groups and touring companies perform. ~ 777 West Olive Street, Newport; 541-265-9231.

At **Rookie's Sportsbar** in the Holiday Inn Newport, nine televisions project every sporting event imaginable. There's a pool table, sports memorabilia, darts and a relaxing view. They have deejay music Friday and Saturday nights and occasional pop and rock bands in the summer. ~ 3019 North Coast Highway, Newport; 541-265-9411.

For live rock-and-roll, dancing and low-stakes blackjack, try **Pip Tide's Restaurant and Lounge**. Across the street from the waterfront, Pip Tide's has a fireplace lounge with dark-wood booths and casablanca fans to beat the heat. There's also a gameroom upstairs. Cover on weekends. ~ 836 Southwest Bay Boulevard, Newport; 541-265-7796.

The **Lotus Lounge** presents live music, dancing and light shows Thursday through Sunday. In addition to bands performing at this nightplace, you can join the laser karaoke singalong craze. Just follow the bouncing ball on the television monitor, bellow into the microphone and you'll be serenading the crowd. A traditional mounted moose head surveys the party atmosphere. ~ 1150 Bay Street, Florence; 541-997-7168.

DEVIL'S LAKE STATE PARK   Is there really a devil in the deep blue sea? That's what American Indian legend says right here in Lincoln City. Find out for yourself by visiting this 109-acre spot offering day-use and overnight facilities. The camping area is protected with a shore-pine windbreak. A day-use area is available at East Devil's Lake down the road. Fish for bass and trout. Facilities include picnic tables, restrooms, showers, kayak rentals and a boat moorage; restaurants and groceries are nearby. ~ The West Devil's Lake section is at 1450 Northeast 6th Drive off Route 101. The day-use section is located two miles east of Route 101 on East Devil's Lake Road; 541-994-2002.

▲ There are 68 tent sites and 32 RV hookups in the Devil's Lake section; $16 to $20 per night. Some camp sites are wheelchair accessible.

DEVIL'S PUNCHBOWL STATE PARK   Don't miss this one. The forested, eight-acre park is named for a sea-washed cavern where breakers crash against the rocks with great special effects. Besides the thundering plumes, the adjacent beach has impressive tidepools. There are picnic tables, barbecue pits and restrooms; restaurants and groceries are in Otter Rock. ~ Located off Route 101, eight miles north of Newport.

BEVERLY BEACH STATE PARK   Numerous coastal creeks make ideal fishing, hiking and camping areas. Among them is Spencer Creek, part of this 130-acre refuge. The windswept beach is reached via a highway underpass. Some of Oregon's best surf fishing is found here. You'll find picnic tables, restrooms and showers; restaurants and groceries are nearby. ~ Located seven miles north of Newport on Route 101; 541-265-9278.

▲ There are 252 developed sites, 52 with full hookups, 75 with partial hookups; $16 to $20 per night; 20 yurts are available,

$26.50 per night; hiker-biker sites are also available, $4 per person per night.

SOUTH BEACH STATE PARK 🚶 🐎 ⛵ 🚤 🛶 South of Newport's Yaquina Bay Bridge, this 434-acre park includes a sandy beach and a forest with pine and spruce. Extremely popular in the summer months, the park includes rolling terrain and a portion of Yaquina Bay's south-jetty entrance. For anglers, try for striped perch in the south jetty area. You can also ride horses on the jetty. Boat ramps at the marina make it possible to boat in the bay. Facilities include picnic tables, restrooms and showers; restaurants and groceries are nearby. ~ Located on Route 101, two miles south of Newport; 541-867-4715.

▲ There are 244 sites with partial hookups, $19 per night; a hiker-biker camp, $4.25 per person per night; primitive sites, $13 per night; and 10 yurts, $27 per night.

ONA BEACH STATE PARK 🛶 🎣 🚤 🛶 Beaver Creek winds through this forested, parklike setting to the ocean. Picturesque bridges, broad lawns and an idyllic shoreline are the draws of this 237-acre gem. Good fishing can be found in the river for perch or trout in season, and from the shore. There are picnic tables and restrooms; restaurants and groceries are nearby. ~ Located on Route 101, eight miles south of Newport.

CARL G. WASHBURNE STATE PARK 🚶 🛶 A mile of sandy beach with excellent tidepools and forested, rolling terrain make this park yet another coastal gem. Elk are often sighted at 1089-acre Washburne Park. The south end of the park connects to Devil's Elbow State Park's Cape Creek drainage. Fishing is excellent: there's tuna, bass and snapper in the sea, and several streams offer trout, salmon and steelhead. Clamming is also good. There are picnic tables, restrooms and showers; restaurants and groceries are in Florence. ~ Located on Route 101, 14 miles north of Florence; 541-997-3851.

▲ There are 66 sites (58 with full hookups), two drive-in and six walk-in sites; $16 to $20 per night.

SIUSLAW NATIONAL FOREST 🚶 🚴 🐎 🏕 🛶 🎣 🚤 🚢 🛶 With two sections on the coast, this 630,000-acre region has more seacoast, 43 miles, than any other national forest in the United States. The terrain includes the Coast Range, Mt. Hebo and Mary's Peak. Oceanfront areas include the Cascade Head Scenic Area, Umpqua Spit wilderness and the Cape Perpetua Visitors Center. While hiking some of the forest's 113 miles of trails, you may see deer, elk, otter, beaver, fox and bobcat. Northeast of Waldport, several trails lead into the old-growth forests of the Drift Creek Wilderness Area. Furthermore, there's cross-country skiing in the winter, boating and horseback riding in the summer. Incidentally, Siuslaw is taken from a Yakona Indian word meaning "far away waters." Over 200 species of fish including salmon, perch and trout can be caught in local streams and along the coast. Facilities include picnic areas, restrooms, showers and horseback riding rentals; restaurants and groceries are in nearby towns. ~ Route 101 passes through the Siuslaw in Tillamook, Lincoln and Lane counties; 541-750-7000.

▲ There are 41 campgrounds, some with RV sites and hookups; $5 to $15 per night. Two of the best known are the Blackberry Campground between Corvallis and the coast on Route 34 (32 tent/RV sites at $8 per night; no hookups) and the Tilicum Beach site on the coast near Westport (59 tent/RV sites at $12 per night; no hookups). The former is situated on the Siuslaw River near a boating area and hiking trails; the latter is right beside a nice beach.

JESSIE M. HONEYMAN STATE PARK

This park is richly endowed with 500-foot-high sand dunes, forested lakes, rhododendron and huckleberry. Bisected by Route 101, 522-acre Honeyman is ideal for water sports, dune walks and camping. As far as we know, it has the only bathhouse on the National Register of Historic Places. A stone-and-log structure at Cleawox Lake, the unit now serves as a store and restaurant. Anglers can find bass, trout, perch, bullhead and bluegill at Cleawox and Woahink Lake. Boating and waterskiing are allowed at Woahink. Picnic tables, restrooms, showers, a store and restaurant are the facilities here. Day-use fee, $3. ~ Located three miles south of Florence on Route 101. 541-997-3641.

▲ There are 238 tent sites, 54 sites with full hookups, 89 sites with partial hookups, $19 to $20 per night; and a hiker-biker camp, $4 per person per night. A group camp that accommodates up to 30 people is also available, $64 per night.

UMPQUA LIGHTHOUSE STATE PARK

South of Winchester Bay, this park offers beautiful sand dunes and a popular hiking trail. Forested with spruce, western hemlock and shore pine, the 450-acre park is at its peak when the rhododendron bloom. Trout are common catches. Great views of the Umpqua River are available from the highway. The lighthouse was built to signal the river's entrance; catch a tour Wednesday through Saturday. You'll find picnic tables, restrooms and showers; restaurants and groceries are in Reedsport. ~ Located off Route 101, six miles south of Reedsport; 541-271-4118.

▲ There are 44 tent sites and 22 sites with full hookups; $13 to $17 per night.

WILLIAM M. TUGMAN STATE PARK

This 560-acre park includes Eel Lake, cleaned of logging debris and turned into a popular recreational area. An excellent day-use area, Tugman is ideal for swimming and boating. Restrooms and showers are the facilities here; restaurants and groceries are in Reedsport. ~ Located on Route 101, eight miles south of Reedsport; 541-888-3778.

▲ There are 115 sites with partial hookups, $15 per night; and a hiker-biker camp, $4 per person per night.

HIDDEN ►   **GOLDEN AND SILVER FALLS STATE PARK** 🚶‍♂️ ⏚ A pair of 100-foot-high waterfalls, old-growth forest including myrtlewood trees, and beautiful trails make this 157-acre park an excellent choice for a picnic. Cutthroat trout is a common catch here, as are crawdads. There are picnic tables and restrooms. ~ Located off Route 101, 24 miles northeast of Coos Bay.

▼▼▼▼▼▼▼▼▼▼

South Coast

The quietest part of the Oregon coastline, Oregon's South Coast offers miles of uncrowded beaches, beautiful dunes and excellent lakes for fishing or waterskiing. The smaller towns make an excellent base for the traveler who appreciates fine restaurants, museums, festivals and shopping. The Rogue and Chetco rivers offer rugged detours from the coast, ideal for the angler or rafter.

SIGHTS   A real sleeper, the **Coos Bay/North Bend/Charleston Bay area** is the coast's largest metropolitan area, a logging center, college town and fishing center. Historic residential districts, a grand harbor and towering piles of logs awaiting their turn to be sliced into lumber make this working-class town an intriguing place. The **Bay Area Chamber of Commerce** is the ideal place to orient yourself. ~ 50 East Central Avenue, Coos Bay; 541-269-0215.

One of our favorite galleries in the Pacific Northwest is the **Coos Art Museum**, where 20th-century American paintings, sculpture and prints form the heart of the collection. Special exhibits feature well-known local artists. Closed Sunday and Monday. ~ 235 Anderson Avenue, Coos Bay; 541-267-3901.

The art museum is just one of 22 landmarks on the chamber of commerce's self-guided walking-tour brochure. This route includes Victorian homes, Greek Classic commercial buildings and the Myrtle Arms Apartments, a rare Oregon building done in the Mission/Pueblo style.

A landmark in Coos Bay is the **Marshfield Sun**. This museum preserves the *Sun* printing office with its antique handset presses, typecases, proof press and other tools of the trade. The building, with an oak floor and potbelly stove, is a delightful period piece. Second-story exhibits cover the history of printing. Open Tuesday through Saturday from Memorial Day to Labor Day; otherwise by appointment. ~ 1049 Front Street, Coos Bay; 541-888-0158.

Also worth a visit is the **Coos Historical Society Museum**, where you'll see American Indian baskets, tools and dugout canoes. Pioneer logging and mining equipment and a homestead kitchen are also found here, along with a hands-on exhibit that gives you an opportunity to touch a variety of artifacts. You can learn about tidewater highways as well. Closed Sunday and Monday. Admission. ~ 1220 Sherman Avenue, North Bend; 541-756-6320.

A popular recreational region, the Bay Area offers watersports and fishing at **Tenmile Lakes**. The **Charleston Boat Basin** is ideal for sportfishing, clamming, crabbing, birdwatching and boating.

From Charleston, continue south four miles to **Shore Acres State Park**. Although the mansion of lumberman Louis Simpson burned down years ago, the grand, seven-acre botanical garden, including a 100-foot lily pond, is preserved. Admission. ~ 10965 Cape Arago Highway, Charleston; 541-888-3732.

From here, head south to **Cape Arago State Park**, your best bet for local tidepools and seal watching. The road into the park is closed to vehicle traffic, but you can still walk in, feet willing.

Return toward Charleston and head south on Seven Devil's Road to **South Slough National Estuarine Research Reserve**. An extension of the Coos Bay Estuary, this splendid nature reserve is a drowned river mouth where saltwater tides and freshwater streams create a rich estuarine environment. Even if you only have time to stop at the Interpretive Center, don't miss South Slough. Easily explored on foot, thanks to a network of trails and wooden walkways, the estuaries, tideflats, salt marshes, open water and forest communities are a living ecology textbook. A major resting spot for birds like the great blue heron, the slough can also be navigated by canoe. Open year-round, but the interpretive center is closed on weekends from Labor Day to Memorial Day. ~ Charleston; 541-888-5558.

Back at Charleston and Coos Bay, pick up Route 42 south to **North Bank Road** and drive west along the Coquille River. This pastoral route, one lane at times, is the hidden Northwest of your dreams. You'll see farms, pastureland, orchards, towering stands of fir and an array of birdlife. Tread lightly.

◄ HIDDEN

Bandon is one of those popular resort towns that seems to have everything. From myrtlewood and cranberry bogs to salmon

COOS BAY'S LEGENDARY RUNNER

Of special interest in the Coos Art Museum is the **Prefontaine Memorial Room**, a collection honoring the life and times of Steve Prefontaine, the distance runner who died in a 1975 car accident at the age of 24. During his short life Prefontaine set 11 United States indoor and outdoor records including several that still stand. Every year, a running event commemorates the memory of this Coos Bay native.

bakes and dune lakes, it's hard to be bored in Bandon. Swing by the **Bandon Chamber of Commerce** for brochures and information. ~ 300 2nd Street, Bandon; 541-347-9616.

Bandon's **Old Town** is an engaging neighborhood where you can shop for cranberry treats and pottery or visit one of the local art galleries. Also here is the **Bandon Driftwood Museum**. Located in an old general store, the museum features driftwood sculptures well worth a look. ~ 1st and Baltimore streets, Bandon; 541-347-3719.

Harbor seals and sea lions breed on offshore rocks near Port Orford known as the "Thousand Island Coast."

One of the town highlights used to be **Tupper Rock**, a site sacred to the Coquille tribe and returned to them in 1990. Unfortunately, most of this blue-colored rock was removed 40 years ago to build the town jetty, and what was left of it now lies buried underneath a new rest home operated by the Coquille. South of town, **Beach Loop Road** leads past Bandon's scenic trio—Table Rock, Elephant Rock and legendary Face Rock. One of Oregon's most photographed spots, the offshore seastacks make an ideal backdrop at sunset.

West Coast Game Park Safari, located seven miles south of Bandon, gives visitors a chance to see more than 75 species including lions, tigers, snow leopards, bison, zebras and elk. On their walk through the park, children can pet cubs, pups and kits in the company of attendants. Many endangered species are found at this wooded, 21-acre site. Open seven days a week March through November; in winter, open weekends and holidays, weather permitting. Admission. ~ Route 101; 541-347-3106.

Port Orford, the first townsite on the Oregon Coast and westernmost town in the continental United States, is a major commercial and sportfishing center. Windsurfers flock to local Floras and Garrison lakes. The Sixes and Elk rivers are popular salmon and steelhead fishing spots.

Six miles south of Port Orford is **Humbug Mountain State Park**, where hiking trails offer majestic views of the South Coast. ~ 541-332-6774.

Continue another six miles to the **Prehistoric Gardens**. Filled with life-size replicas of dinosaurs and other extinct species, this touristy menagerie includes the parrot-beaked *Psittacosaurus*, an ancestral form of the horn-faced dinosaur. Open year-round, weather permitting. Admission. ~ 36848 Route 101, Port Orford; 541-332-4463.

At **Gold Beach**, a settlement at the mouth of the Rogue River, you'll find yourself on the edge of one of the coast's great wilderness areas. Here you can arrange an ocean-fishing trip or a jet boat ride up the wild and scenic Rogue River. Along the way, you may see deer, bald eagle, bear or otter. Accessible only by water, some of the rustic Rogue lodges are perfect for an overnight getaway. It's also possible to drive along the Rogue to Agness. For more details, check with the **Gold Beach Chamber of Commerce**. ~ 29279 Ellensburg Avenue #3, Gold Beach; 541-247-7526.

Fifteen miles south of Gold Beach is Samuel H. Boardman State Park, where you'll begin a ten-mile stretch that includes **Arch Rock Point**, **Natural Bridges Cove**, **House Rock** and **Rainbow Rock**. Many visitors and locals agree this is the prettiest stretch on the Oregon coastline.

Just when you thought it would never end, the Oregon Coast comes to a screeching halt. The end of the line is Brookings, the Chetco River port town that produces 75 percent of the Easter lilies grown in America. They are complemented by daffodils raised commercially in the area. **North Bank Chetco River Road** provides easy access to the fishing holes upstream. One of the most popular destinations is **Loeb State Park** ten miles east of Brookings. Redwood and myrtlewood groves are your reward. You can loop back to Brookings on South Bank Road. En route consider turning off on **Forest Service Road 4013** and take the trail to one of only two continental United States locations bombed by a Japanese pilot during World War II. The other location, bombed by the same raider, is farther up the Oregon coast at Fort Stevens. The raider, who used a plane built aboard an offshore submarine, returned years later to give the city a samurai sword as a peace offering.

◄ HIDDEN

The **Brookings/Harbor Chamber of Commerce** can provide additional information on visiting this region. ~ 16330 Lower Harbor Road, Brookings; 541-469-3181.

Shortly before reaching the California line, you'll see the Blake House, site of the **Chetco Valley Historical Society Museum**. The oldest standing house in the region, visitors can check out a turn-of-the-century kitchen, antique sewing machines, Lincoln rocker, patchwork quilts dating back to 1844 and American Indian artifacts. Once a trading post and way station, the old home is filled with period furniture. The world's largest Monterey Cypress is found here. Closed Monday and Tuesday in the summer; closed Monday through Thursday in winter. ~ 15461 Museum Road, Brookings; 541-469-6651.

A 1912 Colonial-style house, **Coos Bay Manor** has five rooms (three with private baths) themed in Victorian, regal and country-casual style. Also here are a Colonial room with twin-poster or king beds and a garden room furnished with white wicker furniture. A rhododendron garden, redwoods and a delicious breakfast add to the fun. The ten-minute walk to downtown Coos Bay and the boardwalk is a bonus. ~ 955 South 5th Street, Coos Bay; 541-269-1224, 800-269-1224. DELUXE.

LODGING

If you're eager to crab or clam, consider unpretentious **Captain John's Motel**. On the small boat basin, this establishment is within walking distance of fishing and charter boats. Special facilities are available to cook and clean crabs. Forty-seven rooms and kitchenettes are fully carpeted and feature contemporary motel furniture. Other accommodations include deluxe-priced condos and apartments. ~ 8061 Kingfisher Drive, Charleston; 541-888-4041, fax 541-888-6563. BUDGET TO DELUXE.

One block from Bandon's old-town district, **Sea Star Guest House** offers four modern, carpeted units with brass or step-up beds, quilts and harbor views. Two are regular rooms and two are suites, with living rooms, kitchens and lofts. ~ 370 1st Street, Bandon; 541-347-9632, fax 541-347-9533. MODERATE.

In the same complex is the **Sea Star Youth Hostel**. The two dorms are sex-segregated and feature ten bunk beds; you'll be asked to do minor chores in the morning. There are also five family/couple rooms that should be reserved in advance. No curfew. ~ 375 2nd Street, Bandon; 541-347-9632. BUDGET.

You can hear the foghorn from the **Bandon Beach Motel** where many of the 28 units have balconies overlooking the ocean. Nautical decor, wood paneling and vanities make these rooms appealing. There's also a pool. Pets are welcome. ~ 1110 11th Street, Bandon; 541-347-4430. MODERATE.

American Indian legend tells us that Ewauna, the willful daughter of Chief Siskiyou, wandered too far out into the surf and was snatched up by Seatka, the evil spirit of the sea. Today, Bandon visitors learn that images of all the protagonists in this tragedy have been frozen in stone at Face Rock. That may be one of the reasons proprietors of **The Inn at Face Rock** caution guests to be wary of the local surf. Adjacent to a public golf course, this 60-unit resort—including 20 suites and mini-suites with fireplaces and balconies—also has ocean views. Wallhangings, comfortable sofas, fireplaces and decks make the king- and queen-bedded rooms appealing. There's a restaurant on the premises. ~ 3225 Beach Loop Road, Bandon; 541-347-9441, 800-638-3092, fax 541-347-2532. MODERATE TO DELUXE.

Castaway-by-the-Sea Motel offers rooms and suites overlooking one of the South Coast's most picturesque, albeit windblown, beaches. Kitchenettes, glassed-in decks, contemporary upholstered furniture, wall-to-wall carpeting and easy access to fishing make this 13-unit motel a popular place. ~ 545 West 5th Street, Port Orford; 541-332-4502, fax 541-332-9303. BUDGET TO MODERATE.

HIDDEN ▶

Breathtaking views of the coast are found at **Home by the Sea**. Ceramic tile floors, myrtlewood beds with quilted spreads, a leather loveseat, rocking chair, oriental carpets and stained glass add to the charm of these units. Rooms include private baths, mini-refrigerators and phones; every room in this bed and breakfast comes with binoculars perfect for whale watching through the picture windows. Laundry access is available. ~ 444 Jackson Street, Port Orford; 541-332-2855; e-mail alan@homebythesea. com. MODERATE TO DELUXE.

If you're an adventurer eager to go deep-sea fishing, raft the Rogue, go boating, cycling or hike the coastal mountains, consider **Jot's Resort**. Jot's has 140 attractive, contemporary rooms and suites with pink wall-to-wall carpet, oak furniture, vanities and decks featuring river views. Crabbing and clamming are great here. A full-service resort, there's a jacuzzi, sauna and two pools, an indoor and outdoor. ~ 94360 Wedderburn Loop, Gold Beach; 541-247-6676, 800-367-5687, fax 541-247-6716. MODERATE TO DELUXE.

On the Rogue River, **Tu Tu Tun Lodge** can be a sunny alternative to the cloudy coast. Seven miles upriver from Gold Beach, this lodge offers 16 rooms with 12-foot-window walls, refrigerators, lounge chairs and decks or patios overlooking the water. Several have fireplaces and outdoor soaking tubs. There are also two houses for rent and two suites with kitchen facilities. Amenities here include hiking trails, horseshoes and, in the main lodge, an antique pool table, player piano and game tables. ~ 96550 North Bank Rogue Road, Gold Beach; 541-247-6664, 800-864-6357, fax 541-247-0672. DELUXE TO ULTRA-DELUXE.

Located in a Craftsman-style home designed in 1917 by Bernard Maybeck, **South Coast Inn Bed & Breakfast** is an inn with three guest rooms in the main house and a separate private cottage; both share use of an indoor sauna and spa area. Especially choice is the Rose Room, which has a large picture window framing the Pacific, a highrise four-poster bed, and an old-fashioned clawfoot tub in the bathroom. A gourmet candlelit breakfast is included. Gay-friendly. ~ 516 Redwood Street, Brookings; 541-469-5557, 800-525-9273. MODERATE.

At **Best Western Beachfront Inn**, more than a hundred units, all with ocean views and some with kitchenettes, offer a quiet resting place. Furnished with contemporary oak dressers and tables, the king- and queen-bedded units come with microwaves, refrigerators, sofas and decks. Suites and some rooms offer jacuzzis. ~ 16008 Boat Basin Road, Brookings Harbor; 541-469-7779, 800-468-4081, fax 541-469-0283. MODERATE TO ULTRA-DELUXE.

A one-lane road leads you to **Chetco River Inn Bed and Breakfast**, a get-away-from-it-all establishment on 35 wooded acres. ◄ HIDDEN An ideal retreat for fishing, swimming, hiking through myrtle groves or loafing on the riverbank, this contemporary solar-, propane- and battery-powered home furnished with antiques and eclectic furniture, the inn has down comforters and large brass beds, casablanca fans and, by advance request, dinner. The cooking is innovative, and portions are generous. Special discounts are offered for anglers who agree to catch and release their fish. ~ 21202 High Prairie Road, 17.5 miles east of Brookings on the Chetco River; 541-670-1645, 800-327-2688. DELUXE.

DINING

For *chile rellenos*, *chilaquiles*, chicken *mole* and *carne asada*, try **Playa Del Sol**. Spanish carvings, sombreros and photographs of Mexico give this popular little restaurant a festive feel. Closed Sunday. ~ 525 Newport Avenue, Coos Bay; 541-267-0325. BUDGET TO MODERATE.

If you've been looking for Korean, Japanese or Chinese dishes, stop by **Kum-Yon's**. *Bulgoki*, *ton katsu*, *yakitori*, mongolian beef, tempura *udon* and tofu dishes are just a few of the enticing specialties. Like the menu, the decor is pan-Asian with Japanese-shell plaques, Korean wedding decorations and Chinese fans accenting the brick dining room. ~ 835 South Broadway, Coos Bay; 541-269-2662. BUDGET TO MODERATE.

To get a big laugh at **Portside Restaurant and Lounge**, just ask if the fish is fresh. Grilled sole, deep-fried scallops, steamed clams, salmon and Coquille St. Jacques are among the specialties, as well as Maine lobster and Dungeness crab. Also recommended is the cucumber boat, a salad with shrimp, crab and smoked salmon and served with cucumber dressing and garlic toast. The contemporary dining room features photos of the fishing industry. ~ Charleston Bay Boat Basin, Charleston; 541-888-5544. MODERATE TO ULTRA-DELUXE.

At **Andrea's Old Town Café**, you can breakfast on fresh-baked pastries and omelettes, return for pizza or burgers at lunch and then choose from specialties at dinner such as fresh seafood, pasta, steak and Creole dishes. An extensive wine list, fruit pies or cheesecake will round out your day at this eclectic, oak-furnished café. From November to June, dinner is served on Friday and

---

✔ CHECK THESE OUT—UNIQUE DINING

- *Budget:* Sample the barbecue crab and cheese or an oyster burger at **Wee Willie Restaurant**, a North Coast favorite. *page 336*
- *Moderate:* Try a tasty gourmet meal at **Café Uniontown**, located under a bridge in Astoria's historic Uniontown district. *page 334*
- *Moderate to deluxe:* Munch on a seafood poorboy underneath a ceiling festooned with a whale's vertebrae at **The Whale's Tale**. *page 350*
- *Deluxe to ultra-deluxe:* Savor the wild mushroom ragoût by candlelight at **Chez Jeannette**, serving French cuisine in a woodsy setting. *page 350*

Budget: under $8   Moderate: $8–$16   Deluxe: $16–$24   Ultra-deluxe: over $24

Saturday only. ~ 160 Baltimore Street, Bandon; 541-347-3022. MODERATE.

Spaghetti West, where the dimly lit bar and knotty pine–paneled dining room are decorated with local art for sale, offers an interesting mixture of artsy bohemian culture. You'll find pasta, steak, seafood and chowder on the menu; the kitchen accepts special requests from guests who want something not found on the menu. Dinner only. Closed Tuesday and Wednesday. ~ 236 6th Street, Port Orford; 541-332-9327. MODERATE.

For waterfront dining, try the **Nor'wester Seafood Restaurant**. Cedar woodwork, local artwork on the walls and a large fireplace create an inviting and cozy atmosphere. Sample the fresh fish, seafood, steaks, pasta or chicken. Dinner only. ~ 10 Harbor Way, Gold Beach; 541-247-2333. MODERATE TO DELUXE.

When the natives get restless for logger breakfasts, fish and chips, burgers, clam chowder, shrimp cocktails or homemade chili, they head for **Marty's Pelican Bay Seafood**. This modest establishment seats customers at pine tables in the nautically themed dining room featuring fishing photos. ~ 16403 Lower Harbor Road, Brookings; 541-469-7971. BUDGET TO MODERATE.

A culinary time warp on the coast, **O'Holleran's Restaurant and Lounge** serves middle-of-the-road entrées in a modest dining room with wood tables and pictures on the wall. You'll find few bells or whistles on the traditional menu featuring steaks, prime rib and seafood. While you can't get blackberry catsup on the side, the food is well prepared. Dinner only. ~ 1210 Chetco Avenue, Brookings; 541-469-9907. MODERATE TO DELUXE.

You say Mexican food, we say **Rubio's**. A bright red-and-yellow bungalow decorated with piñatas and casablanca fans, this affordable stop also offers picnic-table seating outside beneath patio umbrellas. An extensive menu features burritos, enchiladas verde, chicken fajitas and fresh fish. A brunch specialty is *huevos rancheros*. Burgers and sandwiches are also available for yankee appetites. Closed Monday. ~ 1136 Chetco Avenue, Brookings; 541-469-4919. BUDGET TO MODERATE.

Katydid, the nonprofit gift shop at the Coos Art Museum, offers a selection of jewelry, glassware, pottery, sculptures, baskets, carvings, cards and works by local artists. Closed Sunday and Monday. ~ 235 Anderson Avenue, Coos Bay; 541-267-3901.

SHOPPING

And now let's hear it for **Margaret Brinegar, "The Bird Lady."** This folk artist, operating out of her garage, produces outstanding wind-powered whirlygigs perfect for your yard. You can choose between sprinklers, birds and other colorful Rube Goldberg–like contraptions. ~ 6943 Beacon Street, Coos Bay; 541-888-3549.

For beaded earrings, silver and turquoise, dance regalia and other American Indian arts and crafts, visit **Klahowya!** They also carry American Indian art originals, pottery, ceramics and gifts celebrating the natural world. ~ 175 2nd Street, in the Continuum Center Plaza, Bandon; 541-347-5099.

If you're looking for smoked salmon, smoked albacore, crab or shrimp, head for **Bandon Bay Fisheries**. Viewing windows allow you to see the seafood industry at work. Appointments are required. ~ 250 Southwest 1st Street, Bandon; 541-347-4454.

Oregon Myrtlewood Factory is the place to see the owner creating dinnerware, vases, sculptures, clocks and other popular souvenirs. Closed in the winter. ~ Route 101, six miles south of Bandon; 541-347-2500.

Weaver Ellen Warring's beautiful baskets incorporate a variety of weaves, including the distinctive, geometric-patterned Cherokee weave. Her **Basket Studio** is a good place to browse and learn about this delicate art. ~ 736 Route 101, Port Orford; 541-332-0735.

Jerry's Rogue River Museum and Gift Shop offers a broad selection of locally made arts and crafts. There is also an extensive collection of artifacts, photos and natural-history exhibits on the Rogue River area. ~ Port of Gold Beach; 541-247-4571.

For wall masks, magical creatures like dragons and wizards or bisque pieces, try **Dragon Stone Ceramics**. Handpainted gifts and American Indian pieces are also available. ~ South Route 101 and Winchuck Road, Brookings; 541-469-9534.

NIGHTLIFE On Broadway Thespians presents classical and contemporary drama and musical theater in an intimate 90-seat auditorium. ~ 226 South Broadway, Coos Bay; 541-269-2501.

We were impressed by the performances at **Timber Inn Lounge**. Live country, rhythm-and-blues and rock bands that perform Wednesday through Saturday are all popular in this big, second-story room heavy on silver foil and lumberjack photos. The bartenders are cordial, and you can really jam on the spacious dancefloor. The ground-floor lounge features karaoke nightly. ~ 1001 North Bayshore Drive, Coos Bay; 541-267-4622.

For music and dancing weekends, try the **Portside Lounge**. Bands and combos offer '60s and '70s hits, easy listening and jazz on Friday and Saturday nights. You can enjoy the performers from the patio on warm nights. Great sunsets and harbor views. ~ Charleston Boat Basin, Charleston; 541-888-5544.

Lloyd's offers rock-and-roll bands on weekends year-round. There's a large dancefloor on which to let loose. Occasional cover. ~ 119 Southeast 2nd Street, Bandon; 541-347-4211.

Lord Bennett's offers jazz, country and pop in their antique-filled lounge on weekends throughout most of the year. ~ 1695 Beach Loop Road, Bandon; 541-347-3663.

Jot's Rod and Reel Restaurant occasionally offers country-and-western, pop, jazz and oldies ideal for dancing weekends. Their contemporary lounge enjoys a Rogue River view. ~ 94360 Waterfront Loop, Gold Beach; 541-247-6823.

When it's time for live tunes, head for the **Rascals Lounge**. The bands play every weekend to a dimly lit room with café seating and a full bar. If you don't want to dance, head on over to the low-stakes blackjack tables and struggle against the odds. There's a two-drink minimum. Cover. ~ Lower Harbor Road, Brookings; 541-469-5503.

SUNSET BAY STATE PARK 🏃 🚴 🏊 ⛱ 🛶 🚤 ⛴ ⚓ A splendid park on dramatic headlands, Sunset is forested with spruce and hemlock. Highlights include Big Creek, a popular stream flowing into the bay. As the name implies, this is the place to be when the sun sets. Swimming, canoeing, boating, clamming and other crabbing are also popular activities. Picnic tables, restrooms and showers are the facilities here; restaurants and groceries are in Charleston or Coos Bay. ~ Located off Route 101, 12 miles southwest of Coos Bay; 541-888-4902.

▲ There are 74 tent sites, 29 sites with full hookups, and 35 sites with partial hookups, $16 to $19 per night; and a hiker-biker camp, $4 per person per night.

SHORE ACRES STATE PARK 🏃 Let's skip the superlatives and get to the point: Visit Shore Acres. This 745-acre estate was once the site of a timber baron's mansion. Although the house burned down, the formal garden remains a showcase. Planted with azaleas, rhododendrons, irises, dahlias and roses, Shore Acres also offers trails on the forested bluffs. There are picnic tables, restrooms, an observation shelter and a gift shop; restaurants and groceries are nearby. Day-use fee, $3. ~ Located off Route 101, 13 miles southwest of Coos Bay; 541-888-3732.

BULLARDS BEACH STATE PARK 🏃 🚴 🐎 ⛱ 🛶 🚤 ⛴ ⚓ All good things come to an end, even the Coquille River. Fortunately, this 1289-acre park makes it possible to enjoy the tail end of the stream as it flows into the estuary and the Pacific opposite the city of Bandon. The Coquille River lighthouse is located in the park. A great recreation area, the park has fine dunes, beaches and forested lowlands. It's also ideal for crabbing and clamming. Fish for steelhead, silver and chinook salmon. Facilities include picnic tables, restrooms and showers; restaurants and groceries are nearby in Bandon. ~ Located off Route 101, two miles north of Bandon; 541-347-2209.

▲ There are 8 primitive horse-camp sites, $13 per night; 7 yurts, $25 per night; 92 sites with full hookups and 100 sites with partial hookups, $19 per night; and a hiker-biker camp, $4 per person per night.

**BEACHES
& PARKS**

CAPE BLANCO STATE PARK 🚶 🚲 🐎 ⛵ Settled by an Irish dairy farmer, these dramatic, pastured headlands include the westernmost lighthouse in Oregon. A windswept, 1894-acre retreat, Cape Blanco welcomes visitors to the Hughes House, built by a pioneer family in 1898. There's good surf fishing. You'll find picnic tables, restrooms and showers; restaurants and groceries are in Port Orford. ~ Located nine miles north of Port Orford off of Route 101; 541-332-2973.

▲ There are 6 horse-camp sites, 58 sites with water and electric hookups, $16 to $18 per night; and a hiker-biker camp, $4 per person per night.

PORT ORFORD HEADS STATE WAYSIDE 🚶 You'll love this windblown and unforgettable 96-acre wayside. It encompasses the ocean bluff as well as Nellies Cove. The park protects marine gardens and prehistoric archaeological landmarks. There are picnic tables and restrooms. ~ Located off Route 101 at Port Orford.

HUMBUG MOUNTAIN STATE PARK 🚶 🚲 ⛵ A 1750-foot peak forested with fir, spruce, alder and cedar, Humbug is one of the coast's finest parks. Hiking trails, viewpoints, Brush Creek and ocean frontage make the 1842-acre sanctuary a great retreat. If you're feeling ambitious, why not take the three-mile hike up the wildflower-lined trail to the summit? You'll find picnic tables, restrooms and showers; restaurants and groceries are in Port Orford. ~ Located off Route 101, six miles south of Port Orford; 541-332-6774.

▲ There are 78 tent sites and 30 sites with water and electrical hookups; $16 to $18 per night; and a hiker-biker camp; $4 per person per night.

CAPE SEBASTIAN STATE PARK 🚶 This narrow park includes several miles of exceptional coastline. The centerpiece of the 1104-acre place is the cape, carpeted with wildflowers and rhododendron in the spring. Views are magnificent. Old-growth Douglas fir and shore pine form a handsome backdrop. Restaurants and groceries in Gold Beach. ~ Located seven miles south of Gold Beach off of Route 101. Not recommended for long RVs or vehicles towing trailers.

HARRIS BEACH STATE PARK 🚶 🐋 🎣 ⛱ 🏄 ⛵ Named for a butte rising above the coast, this one-time sheep-and-cattle ranch is the southernmost state camping facility on the coast. The 172-acre park offers sandy beaches and great sunsets. The shoreline is punctuated with dramatic, surf-sculptured rocks, which make kayaking and surfing challenging. There's good fishing for salmon and perch. There are picnic tables, restrooms and showers; restaurants and groceries are in Brookings. ~ 1655 Route 101, Brookings; 541-469-2021.

▲ There are 69 tent sites, 34 sites with full hookups and 53 sites with partial hookups (cable TV in some sites), $16 to $19 per night; four yurts, $25 per night; and a hiker-biker camp, $4 per person per night.

LOEB STATE PARK 🏃 🛶 🎣 On the Chetco River, this   ◄ *HIDDEN*
park can be a warm place when the coast is not. A one-mile trail leads to Loeb's redwood grove. There's also a myrtle grove here. A popular fishing region, particularly during the steelhead season, the Chetco is one of Oregon's special havens. With 320 acres, the park provides easy access to a prime stretch of this river canyon. Picnic tables, firepits, restrooms and showers are some of the facilities; restaurants and groceries in Brookings. ~ Located eight miles northeast of Brookings along the Chetco River; 541-469-2021.

▲ There are 53 sites; $16 per night, partial hookups available for no extra charge.

Well known for salmon, Oregon's coastal waters are also fished for ling cod, capizon (a big, ugly bottom fish), sea bass, red snapper, albacore and halibut. From mid-May or June through September or mid-October, charter companies and outfitters up and down the coast regularly run ocean fishing trips: from a half day of bottom fishing to longer reef-fishing outings. Tackle is usually provided, but a fishing license is required (you can purchase it through charter operators). And don't forget to bring lunch.

Outdoor Adventures

SPORTFISHING

NORTH COAST **Charleton Deep Sea** accommodates up to 15 people, May through September, for trips for salmon, sturgeon and a variety of bottomfish. ~ 45 Northeast Harbor Street, Warrenton; 503-861-2429. **Garibaldi/D&D Charters** runs an annual trip each May for halibut; it's so popular, however, it's booked a year in advance. They offer several other trips, so you should have no trouble getting a spot on the salmon, light-tackle or deep-reef bottomfish trips. The 38-foot boat fits up to 15 anglers, the 32-footer fits 12. ~ 607 Garibaldi Avenue, Garibaldi; 503-322-0007, 800-900-4665.

CENTRAL COAST **Deep Sea Trollers** specializes in full-party charters of up to six people for a half-day of reef fishing (sea bass, cod, snapper), June through September. ~ Depoe Bay; 541-765-2248. **Bayfront Charters** runs half-day trips for bottomfish, ling cod and chinook salmon on 40- to 65-foot boats. The halibut trip is out for 12 hours while the albacore trip is out for 24. Box lunches can be provided. ~ 1000 Southeast Bay Boulevard, Newport; 541-265-7558, 800-828-8777.

SOUTH COAST In Charleston, **Betty Kay Charters** has year-round half-day bottomfishing trips, as well as seasonal runs for tuna and halibut. You'll be fishing with 15 others on the 50-foot boat. ~ 7788 Albacore Street; 541-888-9021, 800-752-6303. Besides halibut fishing in May, **Bob's Sportfishing** offers several other trips on the 40-foot boat, including a half-day bottomfishing excursion. ~ Charleston; 541-888-4241.

FISHING   You can rent a small boat and row out into a bay, such as Yaquina or Nehalem, for year-round recreational crabbing (always call first for tide information), as well as seasonal catches of perch, flounder, bass and salmon. Near Coos Bay, Ten Mile Lake is stocked with trout, crappie and catfish.

NORTH COAST **Jetty Fisheries** rents 16-foot aluminum Smokercraft boats. August through November, a run of salmon moves through the bay to spawn in the Nehalem River. Crabbing is good year-round. Crab-cooking and fish-cleaning facilities are provided. ~ Route 101 at Nehalem Bay, Rockaway; 503-368-5746.

CENTRAL COAST On Yaquina Bay, **Embarcadero Marina** rents 14-foot fiberglass boats (Livingston). Expect to catch perch, flounder and small bass, April through November; crabbing is year-round. Fish-cleaning and crab-cooking facilities are provided. If you've forgotten your tackle, you can rent some and buy bait here. ~ 1000 Southeast Bay Boulevard, Newport; 541-265-5435.

SOUTH COAST For a day of fishing for trout, crappie, bass, bluegill and catfish, rent an aluminum fishing boat at **Tenmile Marina, Inc.** The famous tall dunes separating the lake from the ocean are visible from the lake. ~ 7th and Park streets, Lakeside; 541-759-3137.

WHALE WATCHING   The Oregon Coast provides a front-row seat to one of nature's magnificent shows: the annual migrations of the California gray whales. Although the southbound leg of the mammals' trip peaks in late December, it continues until February. Then, with calves in tow, the mammals begin the northbound journey in March. It continues through May. This is an excellent time to take a whale-watching tour: during this leg of the trip, the whales travel closer to shore and more slowly.

CENTRAL COAST Depoe Bay calls itself the whale-watching capital of the Oregon Coast. Several California gray whales have taken up summer residence in local waters—one, at least, has returned to Depoe Bay over the last 15 years and has been christened "Spot." The mammals are probably attracted to the bay because of a unique environment that provides plenty of "feed" for the whales. Whale-watching here is almost a year-round activity.

Dockside Charters runs daily whale-watching tours of between one and two hours. Once the boat reaches the migration route—usually about a mile or two offshore—it will stop and drift for a while so visitors can watch the whales feed. Owner Jim Tade will also take up to six people out in inflatable zodiac boats for up-close looks at the mammals ("We've even petted them," says Tade). ~ Depoe Bay; 541-765-2545. **Tradewinds Charters** also operates daily one-hour whale-watching trips on the 50-foot *Kingfisher*, which can accommodate up to 40 people. ~ Depoe Bay; 541-765-2345, 800-445-8730.

Surfing in Oregon hasn't reached the crescendo of activity that it has in California. Nevertheless, there are local contingents of surfers up and down the coast. Ecola State Park, Indian Beach and Oswald West State Park are recommended North Coast surfing spots, and good for all skill levels. Along the Central Coast, Otter Rock, south of Newport, is good place for beginners. But only a few shops rent surfboards, wetsuits and various other "board" sports equipment.

SURFING

NORTH COAST   **Cleanline Surf Shop** in Seaside started out nearly 20 years ago renting wetsuits to diehard surfers ready to brave the cold winter waters. Now it rents just about everything, including wetsuits, surfboards, snowboards and skateboards. ~ 719 1st Avenue, Seaside; 503-738-7888.

CENTRAL COAST   **Safari Town Surf Shop** rents wetsuits, surfboards, bodyboards and skimboards. The shop is about a half-hour's drive north of Otter Rock. ~ 3026 Northeast Route 101, Lincoln City; 541-996-6335.

Kayaking is popular on Coffenberry Lake at Fort Stevens State Park in Astoria. And in Langlois, on the South Coast, there's a windsurfing bed-and-breakfast inn, where you can take lessons after your continental breakfast.

WIND-SURFING & KAYAKING

NORTH COAST   For kayak rentals, contact **Pacific Wave Limited**. The shop also offers kayaking lessons, as well as guided kayak tours of the area's rivers, bays and estuaries. ~ 2021 Route 101, Warrenton; 503-861-0866.

✔ **CHECK THESE OUT—UNIQUE OUTDOOR ADVENTURES**

- Canoe through tideflats and salt marshes harboring protected birds at South Slough National Estuarine Research Reserve. *page 357*
- Drop a line in the Chetco River for salmon and steelhead in a grove surrounded by redwoods at Loeb State Park. *page 368*
- Grab a prime viewing spot along the ship's rail on a whale-watching tour during the peak months from December through May. *page 368*
- Follow the scenic coastal route at a leisurely pace as you bike the 367-mile-long Oregon Coast Bike Route. *page 371*

SOUTH COAST A sandspit separates the freshwater, spring-fed Floras Lake from the ocean. At the **Floras Lake House**, a bed and breakfast that sits just off the lake, the owners also operate a wind-surfing school (equipment and wetsuit included). Mornings are best for lessons (steady northwest winds blow during the after-noon) on the lake, which is shallow and warm. ~ 92870 Boice Cope Road, Langlois; 541-348-9912.

RIDING STABLES

Look no further than the Oregon Coast for a more impressive scenic backdrop for a half-day's guided ride through a coastal mountain pine forest, an open ride along beach dunes, or a moun-tain trail ride near the mouth of the Rogue River.

NORTH COAST For a guided one-hour mountain ride, contact **Faraway Farms**. They also have a horse motel. ~ Seaside; 503-738-6336.

CENTRAL COAST **C&M Stables** has two ride times—around noon and 2 p.m. (adjusted seasonally, with the change in daylight hours)—for guided rides through the dunes and along the beach or the mountains. Longer (half- or full-day) rides through the mountain pine forests can also be arranged. A meal is served on the full-day ride. Maximum group is 12 unless arranged in ad-vance. ~ 90241 Route 101, Florence; 541-997-7540.

SOUTH COAST **Bandon Beach Riding Stables** specializes in open hour- and hour-and-a-half-long rides along the beach, and oper-ates year-round. Maximum group of 16 people. Reservations rec-ommended. ~ Beach Loop Drive, Bandon; 541-347-3423. A bit farther south, **Indian Creek Trail Rides** will take you up into the mountains for a two-and-a-half-hour trail ride, lunch, and a chance to see wild turkey, deer, elk and, reportedly, an occasional bear. ~ 94680 Jerry's Flat Road, Gold Beach; 541-247-7704.

GOLF

When rainfall along the coast can measure 60, 70, even 80 inches a year, good drainage is important for a golf course. The courses listed here all report good drainage, making them playable year-round.

NORTH COAST For a round of nine holes, try the public **High-land Golf Course**. It's a fun but challenging course, with ocean views from some holes. They rent clubs and handcarts. ~ 1 High-land Road, Gearhart; 503-738-5248. At the 18-hole **Gearhart Golf Links**, ocean views are obscured by a condominium com-plex, but the terrain is relatively flat, making this public course quite walkable. Clubs and carts are rentable. ~ North Marion Street, Gearhart; 503-738-3538.

CENTRAL COAST The scenic nine-hole, privately owned but publicly accessible **Agate Beach Golf Course** is fairly flat and walk-able, with ocean views from some holes. Designed by the Martin family, this 3002-yard-long course has a driving range and rents power cart. ~ 4100 North Coast Highway (Route 101), Newport; 541-265-7331. In Florence, **Sand Pines Golf Links** was named by *Golf Digest* magazine in 1993 as the country's best new public course. The 18-hole course was built on sand dunes, which provide excellent drainage and spectacular scenery. You can rent clubs and carts here. ~ 1201 35th Street; 541-997-1940. There's a "wee bit o' Scotland" in Florence at the 18-hole, public **Ocean Dunes Golf Links**, an older, well-known, "true" links course, with high slope and difficulty ratings. Carts and clubs are available for rent. ~ 3345 Munsel Lake Road; 541-997-3232.

Every year, thousands of bicyclists hit the Oregon Coast Bike Route, which largely parallels Route 101 as a shoulder bikeway.

SOUTH COAST **Sunset Bay Golf Course** is adjacent to Sunset Bay; it's public, nine holes, walkable and "about the only course in the area playable in the winter," according to a local pro. Clubs and carts can be rented at this John Zahler–designed course. ~ 11001 Cape Arago Highway, Coos Bay; 541-888-9301. About 12 miles north of Gold Beach, the nine-hole, public **Cedar Bend Golf Course** is set in a valley with a creek winding through it. Alder, hemlock and fir trees add to the scenic beauty. You can rent carts and clubs here. ~ 34391 Squaw Valley Road, Ophir; 541-247-6911.

Even for nonbicyclists, the 368-mile **Oregon Coast Bike Route** is well known. There are numerous sections that take in scenic and quiet county and city streets that have low volume traffic and slow traffic speeds. There are also backcountry sites and facilities that cater to the cycling crowd.

BIKING

If you're thinking about making the ride, get hold of the **Oregon Coast Bike Route Map**. It's free and published by the Oregon Department of Transportation. The department also publishes the **Oregon Bicycling Guide** that maps out bike routes throughout the state and provides information on various route conditions. It should be noted that Oregon Coast Bike Route is really for experienced cyclists. Besides the length of the trip (it takes about six or eight days to make the journey), the route rises and falls 16,000 feet along the way. ~ Oregon Department of Transportation Bikeway Program: 355 Capitol Street Northeast, Room 210, Transportation Building, Salem, OR 97310; 503-986-3400.

Bicycling along the spectacular Oregon Coast sounds like great fun, even for the weekend recreational cyclist. But the problem is unless you come to Oregon with your own bike, you're going to have a hard time renting one the farther south you travel along the coast.

NORTH COAST An eight-mile paved route through **Fort Stevens State Park**, west of Astoria, passes through the park's historic section, then leads into a wooded area before crossing to parallel the ocean and looping back into the park. In Seaside you can ride along the two-mile boardwalk or head back into the Lewis and Clark area for rides along paved roads and some old logging roads.

Bike Rentals   In Seaside, **Prom Bike and Hobby Shop** is just three blocks from the beach. The shop rents three-speed cruisers, mountain bikes, kids' bikes, tandems and beach tricycles. Or you might try a surrey, rollerskates or inline skates. Rentals come with helmets and locks. They also sell and repair. ~ 622 12th Avenue, Seaside; 503-738-8251. A few miles south, **Mike's Bike Shop** in Cannon Beach rents "fun-cycles"—big three-wheelers—for riding on the fairly level wide beach at low tide. Otherwise, you can rent mountain bikes to ride on nearby logging trails (they're private, however) or up to Ecola State Park, about a mile away. You may also rent beach cruisers. Sales and repairs are available. Rental bikes include helmets and locks. ~ 248 North Spruce Street, Cannon Beach; 503-436-1266.

HIKING

All distances listed for hiking trails are one way unless otherwise noted.

NORTH COAST   **Fort Stevens State Park** has several easy trails, including the 1.8-mile stroll from Battery Russell to the wreck of the *Peter Iredale*.

Saddle Mountain Trail (2.5 miles) ascends the highest mountain on the coastal range. A challenging climb offering great views. It's located off Route 26 near Necanicum.

Tillamook Head Trail (3 miles) begins south of the town of Seaside and ascends to 1200 feet on the route to Ecola State Park's Indian Beach. This is believed to be the route followed by Lewis and Clark when they journeyed to Ecola Creek.

HIDDEN ▶   Inland from Tillamook on Route 6 is the moderate-to-difficult **Kings Mountain Trail** (5.4 miles). This route takes you through the area of the famed Tillamook Burn, a series of 1939, 1945 and 1951 fires that took out enough lumber to build over one million homes. While the area, now the Tillamook State Forest, is covered with younger timber, some evidence of the old burn can still be seen.

Neah-kah-nie Mountain Trail (1 mile) is a challenging climb that begins 2.6 miles south of Oswald West State Park's Short Sands parking area. Great views of the coast.

HIDDEN ▶   **CENTRAL COAST**   In the Siuslaw National Forest east of Pacific City, the **Pioneer Indian Trail** (8 miles) is highly recommended. This moderately difficult trail runs from Itebo Lake to South Lake through a fir forest and a meadow that has a wide array of wildflowers in the summer.

Otter Creek State Park has an easy 1-mile hike along the beach to the base of the Devil's Punchbowl.

The **Estuary Trail** (.25 mile) at the Hatfield Marine Science Center is a great introduction to local marine life. This posted route is wheelchair accessible. ~ 2030 South Marine Science Drive, Newport; 541-867-0100.

Captain Cook's Trail (.6 mile) leads from the Cape Perpetua visitors center below Route 101 past American Indian shell middens to coastal tidepools. At high tide you'll see the spouting horn across Cook's Chasm. Far more challenging is the **Cummins Creek Loop** (10 miles) up Cook's Ridge to Cummins Creek Trail and back down to the visitors center. Enjoy the old-growth forests and meadows.

At the southern end of the Oregon Dunes National Recreation Area, **Bluebill Trail** (1 mile roundtrip), two-and-a-half miles off Route 101 near Horsefall Beach Road, offers a beautiful loop hike around the marshy area once known as Bluebill Lake. It includes an extensive boardwalk system.

SOUTH COAST   The **Estuary Study Trail** at South Slough National Estuarine Research Reserve south of Coos Bay (1.5 miles) is one of the finest hikes on the Oregon Coast. Leading down through a coastal forest, you'll see a pioneer log landing, use a boardwalk to cross a skunkcabbage bog and visit a salt marsh.

Shrader Old Growth Trail (1.5 miles) off Jerry's Flat Road, east   ◄ *HIDDEN* of Gold Beach, is a pleasant loop where you'll see rhododendron, cedar, streams and riparian areas. The marked route identifies coastal species along the way.

To really get away from it all, hike the **Lower Rogue River**   ◄ *HIDDEN* **Trail** (12.2 miles) south from Agness. You'll pass American Indian landmarks, see picturesque bridges and spot wildlife as you hike this wild and scenic canyon.

Bandon to Fourmile Creek (8.5 miles) is one of the coast's most scenic walks. Begin at Bandon Harbor and head south past the Bandon Needles, dunes, ponds and lakes to the creek. Of course you can abbreviate this hike at any point. One easy possibility is to head south on Beach Loop Drive to the point where it swings east toward Route 101. Park here and take the short .2-mile walk through the woods and up over the dune to Bradley Lake, a good swimming hole.

Redwood Trail (1 mile) north of Loeb State Park, ten miles east of Brookings, is a beautiful streamside walk leading past rhododendron, myrtlewood and towering redwoods.

From Northern California or Washington, the coast is   ▼▼▼▼▼▼▼▼▼▼ easily reached via **Route 101**. Within Oregon, many   **Transportation** roads link Portland and the Willamette Valley to resort destinations. **Routes 30** and **26** provide easy access to the North   **CAR** Coast communities of Astoria and Seaside, while **Route 6** connects with Tillamook. **Route 18** leads to Lincoln City, and **Routes**

20 and 34 connect with the Central Coast region in the vicinity of Newport and Waldport. **Route 126** is the way to Florence. **Route 38** heads to Reedsport. To reach Bandon and the South Coast, take **Route 42**.

AIR

Horizon Air flies to **North Bend Airport** and Harbor Airlines goes to **Astoria General Airport**. The **Portland International Airport** and **Eugene Airport**, described in other chapters, also provide gateways to the coast.

BUS

Greyhound Bus Lines (800-231-2222) serves many coast destinations. There is a highway stop in Lincoln City, along with stations in Newport at 956 Southwest 10th Street, 541-265-2253; in Waldport at 230 Route 101, 541-563-3883; in Gold Beach at 310 Colvin Street, 541-247-7710; and in Brookings at 601 Railroad Street, 541-469-3326.

CAR RENTALS

Hertz Rent A Car has two branches at the Astoria and North Bend airports, as well as one at 1492 Duane Street in Astoria. ~ 800-654-3131.

PUBLIC TRANSIT

In Otis, Lincoln City, Newport, Waldport, Yachats and Siletz, local service is provided by **Lincoln County Transit** (541-265-4900). The same company provides service from Siletz and Yachats to Newport, and from Newport to Lincoln City. Connections can be made from Bend, Corvallis, Salem and Albany through **Valley Retriever Bus Lines** (541-265-2253).

TAXIS

For service in Seaside, try **Seaside Cab Co.** (503-738-5252). On the South Coast, **Yellow Cab** (541-267-3111) operates in Coos Bay/North Bend. Gold Beach is served by **Gold Dust Taxi** (541-247-8294).

NINE

Oregon Cascades

Some questions are impossible to answer. Here's one that came to mind while we traveled the highways and byways of the Oregon Cascades, swimming in crystal-clear pools, basking at alpine resorts, fishing pristine streams, dining on fresh salmon and cooling off beneath the spray of yet another waterfall: Why isn't this heavenly space positively jammed with people who want to get away from it all?

Except for a handful of places, such as Mt. Hood on a Saturday afternoon, Route 97 in the vicinity of Bend or Crater Lake's Rim Drive, it's often hard to find a crowd in this seemingly inexhaustible resort area. Sure there's a fair number of timber rigs out on major routes. And the no-vacancy sign does pop up a good deal at popular resorts during the summer and weekends. But who cares when you can head down the road half a mile and check into a glorious streamside campground where the tab is rock-bottom and there's no extra charge for the nocturnal view of the Milky Way? The fact is that mile for mile, the Oregon Cascades offer some of the best wilderness and recreational opportunities in the Pacific Northwest.

To really get a feel for the area, you need a week or longer. But even if you only have time to buzz up to Mt. Hood for an afternoon, this is the best place we know to gain perspective on the volcanic history of the Pacific Northwest. A chain of peaks topped by 11,235-foot Mt. Hood, the Cascades have an average elevation of about 5000 feet. Heavily forested, these mountains are the headwaters for many important rivers such as the Rogue, the Umpqua and the McKenzie. Klamath Falls is the principal southern gateway to the region, and Bend and Redmond provide easy access from the east. Within the mountains are a number of charming towns and villages such as Sisters, McKenzie Bridge and Camp Sherman. While the summer months can be mild and sunny, winter snowfalls blanket the western slopes with 300 to 500 inches of snow.

For some perspective on the Cascades, take a look at the area's good-old days. Begin with the evolution of one of the Northwest's signature attractions, Crater

Lake. Looking at this placid sea, it's hard to imagine what this region looked like 60 million years ago during the late Cretaceous period. As Lowell Williams has written: "At that time the Coast Ranges of Oregon . . . were submerged and the waves of the Pacific lapped against the foothills of the Sierra Nevada and the Blue Mountains of Oregon. Where the Cascade peaks now rise in lofty grandeur, water teemed with shellfish . . . giant marine lizards swam in the seas, and winged reptiles sailed above in search of prey."

Later, in the Eocene and Oligocene periods, roughly 25 million to 60 million years ago, the Crater Lake region became a low plain. Throughout this period and the late Miocene, volcanoes erupted. Finally, about one million to two million years ago, in the last great Ice Age, the Cascades were formed. The largest of these peaks became 12,000-foot Mt. Mazama. About 7000 years ago, this promontory literally blew its top, leaving behind the caldera that is now Crater Lake.

The American Indians, who viewed this area as a sacred and treacherous place, went out of their way to avoid Crater Lake. It was only after the white man arrived in the 19th century that it became a tourist attraction and eventually a national park. Today the lake is considered a unique national treasure.

Because they provided a tremendous challenge to settlers heading toward the Pacific Ocean on the Oregon Trail, the Cascades also gained an important place in the history of the West. Landmarks surrounding Mt. Hood tell the dramatic story of pioneers who blazed time-saving new routes to the promised land across this precipitous terrain. Of course, their arrival permanently altered American Indian life. Inevitably, efforts to colonize the Indians and turn them into farmers and Christians met with resistance. American Indian leader Captain Jack led perhaps the most famous tribal rebellion against the miseries of reservation life in the 1872–73 Modoc War. This fighting raged in an area that is now part of the Lava Beds National Monument across the border in California. Captain Jack and his fellow renegades were ultimately hanged at Fort Klamath.

While logging became the Cascades' leading industry, tourism emerged in the late 19th century. Summer resorts, typically primitive cabins built at the water's edge, were popular with the fishing crowd. Later, the arrival of resort lodges like the Timberline on the slopes of Mt. Hood drew a significant winter trade. But even as Oregon's best-known mountain range evolved into a major resort area, it was able to retain carefully guarded secrets. Little-known fishing spots, obscure trails, waterfalls absent from the maps—this high country became Oregon's private treasure.

Today, Oregon, one of the nation's most environmentally conscious states, is trying to find peaceful coexistence between the logging industry and environmentalists. The "spotted owl" controversy led to new logging restrictions in the fight to save old-growth forests for future generations. You'll be able to take a first-hand look at the subject in question on some of our recommended walks through old-growth preserves. Because logging has traditionally been such an important component of the local economy, many residents worry that further restrictions will threaten their livelihood.

A new forest plan, implemented in 1994 by the Forest Service under Bill Clinton, has remapped the Pacific Northwest, dividing it into sections of environmen-

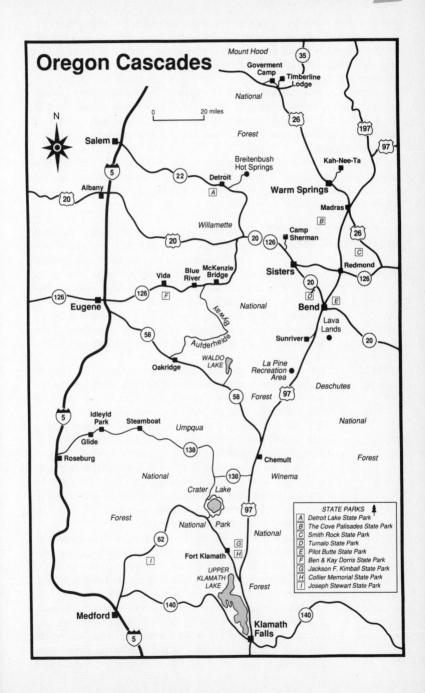

Oregon Cascades

N

0   20 miles

Mount Hood

35

Goverment Camp

Timberline Lodge

National

26

197

97

Salem

5

Breitenbush Hot Springs

22   Detroit

A

Albany

20

Kah-Nee-Ta

Warm Springs

Madras

B

26

Willamette

20

20   126

Camp Sherman

C

Redmond

126

Vida

Blue River

McKenzie Bridge

Sisters

20

D

126

126

F

Eugene

National

E

Bend

58

Lava Lands

Sunriver

20

Aufderheide

WALDO LAKE

La Pine Recreation Area

Deschutes

Oakridge

58

97

Forest

National

5

Idleyld Park

Steamboat

Umpqua

Forest

Glide

138

Roseburg

Chemult

National

138

Winema

Crater Lake

97

Forest

62

National

Park

National

G

H

Fort Klamath

I

UPPER KLAMATH LAKE

Forest

140

Medford

5

Klamath Falls

140

STATE PARKS

A Detroit Lake State Park
B The Cove Palisades State Park
C Smith Rock State Park
D Tumalo State Park
E Pilot Butte State Park
F Ben & Kay Dorris State Park
G Jackson F. Kimball State Park
H Collier Memorial State Park
I Joseph Stewart State Park

tal reserve and areas open to logging. The protection of the riparian reserves (areas around rivers and streams) and late-successional reserves (sections of nearly old-growth forest) has caused the logging industry to shift some of its priorities. The plan, however, is not a law nor legally binding, and logging companies are waging persistent battles against it.

Although in many ways the lumber companies continue to practice business as usual, the rate of forest depletion has slowed. As you travel through the Cascades, realize that your economic contribution, in the form of tourist dollars, is helping local residents make the transition from a lumber economy to a diverse recreational region.

Walking into the Cascades backcountry, you can easily spend hours on a road or trail looking for company. This solitude is the area's greatest drawing card. Appreciate the fact that the only lines you'll have to bother with most of the time are the kind with a hook on the end.

▼▼▼▼▼▼▼▼▼▼▼▼▼▼

Northern Cascades

Given their proximity to the state's major urban centers such as Portland and Eugene, the Northern Cascades are a popular destination, particularly on weekends and during the summer months. Most of the highlights, in fact, can be reached within a couple of hours. Pioneer history, American Indian culture and scenic wonders are just a few of the Cascades' treasures. And if you're looking for uncrowded, out-of-the-way places, relax. Those hidden spots are easily located, often just a mile or two off the most popular routes.

SIGHTS
Our visit to the **Mt. Hood** region begins on Route 26. Portions of this road parallel the time-saving trail first blazed in 1845 by pioneer Samuel Barlow. The following year he and a partner turned this discovery into a $5 toll road at the end of the Oregon Trail, the final tab for entry to the end of the rainbow. Today a series of small monuments commemorates the **Barlow Trail**. At Tollgate campground, a quarter-mile east of Rhododendron on the south side of Route 26, you'll want to visit a reproduction of the historic Barlow Tollgate. Continue five miles east of Rhododendron to the **Laurel Hill Chute** marker. You can take the short, steep hike to the infamous "chute" where wagon trains descended the perilous grade to Zigzag River Valley.

Two of the region's most popular fishing streams, the **Salmon River** and **Sandy River** are convenient to old-growth forests, waterfalls and hiking trails. The lower Sandy is also good for swimming. Continuing east, you'll reach Zigzag and **Lolo Pass Road**. This backcountry route on the west side of Mt. Hood leads to **Lost Lake**, a great escape (see Chapter Seven for more on the lake).

After returning to Route 26, drive east to Government Camp and head uphill to Mt. Hood's **Timberline Lodge**, one of the Northwest's most important arts and crafts–style architectural landmarks. Massive is the word for this skiing hub framed with giant timber beams and warmed by a two-level, three-sided stone fireplace. In the summer you can hike the wildflower trails surrounding the lodge. Be sure to check out the lower-level display on the lodge's fascinating history and current restoration. ~ Timberline Ski Area; 503-272-3311, 800-547-1406.

Two miles east of Government Camp turn south on Route 2656 to picturesque **Trillium Lake**, a popular fishing, swimming and sailboat spot created by the damming of Mud Creek. This is an ideal place for a picnic and wildlife viewing.

For more information on the area surrounding the great mountain, call the **Mt. Hood Information Center**. ~ Located 15 miles east of Sandy on Route 26. ~ 503-622-3017.

Returning to Route 26, pick up Route 35 over Barlow Pass. East of the junction of these two highways, you'll pass a stone cairn marking a **Pioneer Women's Grave**. It commemorates the heroism of all the women who bravely crossed the Oregon Trail. Continue another one-and-three-quarters miles to Forest Road 3530 and the **Barlow Road Sign**. Hand-carved by the Civilian Conservation Corps, this marker is a short walk from the wagon ruts left behind by the pioneers.

Half a century after the pioneers arrived, tourism began to put down roots on this Cascades Peak. Overnight guests were accommodated at the turn-of-the-century **Cloud Cap Inn**, the first structure built on Mt. Hood. Although it no longer accepts the public, the shingled inn is on the National Register of Historic Places. Today, it serves as a base for a mountain-climbing-and-rescue organization and provides views of Mt. Hood's north side. It is accessible in late summer and early fall via a washboard dirt road. ~ Located 10.5 miles north of Route 35, Mt. Hood.

Return south to Route 26 and continue southeast to Warm Springs and **Kah-Nee-Ta**, one of the Pacific Northwest's most intriguing American Indian reservations. Near the lodge entrance an interpretive display offers background on the Confederated

✔ **CHECK THESE OUT—UNIQUE SIGHTS**

- Chisel colorful stones at the world's largest pick-and-pay "thunder egg" farm, **Richardson's Recreational Ranch**. *page 380*
- Wend your way along old logging roads through wilderness areas and 5700-foot peaks on the **Aufderheide National Scenic Byway**. *page 385*
- Don a sweater for a chilly but fascinating spelunking trip through Oregon's longest lava tube, the **Lava River Cave**. *page 387*
- Explore the crystalline waters of **Crater Lake**, situated inside the caldera of an exploded volcano. *page 396*

Tribes of Warm Springs. Indian dance performances and a traditional Salmon bake are held at the lodge each Saturday in the summer months. Tribe members skewer Columbia River salmon on cedar sticks and cook it over alderwood coals. The hot springs are also highly recommended. ~ 541-553-1112, 800-554-4786.

Richardson's Recreational Ranch could also be called the world's largest pick-and-pay thunder-egg farm. Formed as gas bubbles in rhyolite flows and filled with Silica, these colorful stones range from the size of a seed to 1760 pounds. You can pick up, chisel or dig your thunder eggs out of 12 beds spread across this 4000-acre rock ranch. ~ Located 11 miles north of Madras on Route 97, at milepost 81 turn right and continue southeast three miles; 541-475-2680.

Thanks to dependable snowpack throughout the summer months, it is possible to spend the morning skiing on Mt. Hood and devote the afternoon to swimming in the warm waters of nearby Cascade Lake.

The 31-mile **Cove Palisades Tour Route** off Route 97 is also a worthwhile excursion. Just southeast of Madras, the route circles Lake Billy Chinook, a popular place for recreational watersports. Three major rivers, the Deschutes, Crooked and Metolius, have cut canyons through this Oregon plain and merged at Lake Billy Chinook behind Round Butte Dam. Be sure to visit the observatory viewpoint and museum on the lake's Metolius River arm. In addition to memorable views of **Deschutes Canyon**, you'll have a chance to learn about local wildlife and American Indian artifacts. Adjoining the lake is **Cove Palisades State Park**, a mostly arid landscape interrupted by towering volcanic cones. Begin by picking up a brochure that details this excursion at the **Madras-Jefferson County Chamber of Commerce**. ~ 197 Southeast 5th Street, Madras; 541-475-2350.

After completing this tour, return to Route 97. Continue south 12 miles to Terrebonne. Then head east three miles to **Smith Rock State Park**, a favorite of world-class rock climbers. Don't worry if you forgot to bring your spikes and pitons. You can still enjoy the Cascades scenery from your vantage point along the Crooked River Gorge. ~ 541-548-7501.

LODGING   When it comes to architecture, history, location and ambience, few hotels in the Cascades match **Timberline Lodge**. A veritable museum of Northwest arts and crafts, the lodge was built in 1937 by the Works Progress Administration on the slopes of Mt. Hood. All of the 71 rooms have handwoven draperies, bedspreads and rugs featuring a variety of themes; there are iron-and-oak beds, writing desks, WPA watercolors and views of the valley and mountain. While the rooms are small, there is nothing modest about the public areas, which feature a two-level, three-sided stone fireplace and banisters decorated with handcarved owls and beavers. Perfectly situated for skiing, hiking or climbing. ~ Timberline; 503-272-3311, 800-547-1406, fax 503-272-3710. MODERATE TO DELUXE.

Huckleberry Inn offers 17 accommodations in varying price ranges. The units are spare and woodsy, and are popular with hikers scaling Mt. Hood. Moderate-priced standard rooms sleep small groups, while deluxe rooms with spiral staircases leading up to sleeping lofts accommodate more. Budget dorm rooms are sometimes available as well. The inn's restaurant is also worth checking out for its wide selection of dishes using locally grown huckleberries. ~ Route 26 at Government Camp Business Loop, Government Camp; 503-272-3325. BUDGET TO ULTRA-DELUXE.

Fernwood at Alder Creek Bed and Breakfast is a historic log home in the Mt. Hood foothills. The two moderate rooms have antique furnishings, sitting rooms, oak rocking chairs, whirlpools and decks overlooking the creek and ponds. Guests can enjoy a main living room with a fireplace and wood stove, as well a reading room with books and magazines dating back to the 1920s and 1930s. An early breakfast is served family-style each morning. ~ 54850 Route 26; 503-622-3570. MODERATE.

In the mid-1960s the federal government built the Dalles Dam on the Columbia River, submerging the ancestral fishing grounds of local Indians. The Confederated Tribes of Warm Springs used their compensation to pay for **Kah-Nee-Ta Resort**. Located in the midst of the 600,000-acre reservation, this resort offers visitors a variety of lodging choices. There are 139 rooms at the lodge, 30 guest rooms at the village, an RV park, and teepees with cement floors. The rooms have been recently remodeled with wall-to-wall carpets, vanity areas, easy chairs and decks. Set in a red-rock canyon about an hour southeast of Mt. Hood, this resort offers rafting, golfing, horseback riding, swimming pools, fishing, tennis, a water slide, bike rentals and gambling in a casino. ~ Warm Springs; 541-553-1112, 800-554-4786. MODERATE TO DELUXE.

If you don't try the **Cascade Dining Room** in the Timberline Lodge, you'll be missing one of the best meals in the Pacific Northwest. Liveried waiters and waitresses preside over this arts-and-crafts establishment with a stone fireplace and views of the Cascade Mountains. On a frosty morning there's no better place to down *birchermuesli* (oats and yogurt with fresh fruit) or apple oat cakes. Dinner entrées include prime rib, sea bass, chicken and vegetarian specialties. ~ Timberline; 503-272-3311. DELUXE.

DINING

Convenient to the Timberline area is **Mt. Hood Brewing Company and Brew Pub**. Located in a three-story, stone-and-wood building, this establishment features a flyfishing motif with knotty-pine paneling, a red-quarry tile floor and a 43-foot-long copper bar. Through the large windows you can see the beer-brewing kettles. (Brewery tours are available on a limited basis.) The family-style menu offers gourmet pizza, pasta, steaks, salads and hamburgers served on sourdough rolls. ~ Route 26 at Government Camp Business Loop Road, Government Camp; 503-272-3724. MODERATE.

At the Kah-Nee-Ta Lodge, try the informal **Pinto Grill** for moderately priced entrées such as burgers, sandwiches, soups and salads in a contemporary café-style dining room. The **Juniper Room** has deluxe-priced specialties like venison steak, prawns, halibut, steamed clams blended in a seafood pot and birds in clay, a specialty that is cooked for three hours. ~ Warm Springs; 541-553-1112. MODERATE TO DELUXE.

SHOPPING   **Oregon Candy Farm** is the place to shop for homemade hand-dipped chocolates. Even the nutmeats are roasted in-house. Part of the fun is watching the candy-making process through big windows. Sugar-free chocolate is available. ~ 48620 Southeast Route 26, five and a half miles east of Sandy; 503-668-5066.

For limited-edition prints, posters, books, cards and other high-country souvenirs, visit the **Wy'East Store** adjacent to Timberline Lodge. A cross between a gift shop and a mountain outfitter, this is also a good place to find sportswear that will make you even more stylish on your way down the slopes. ~ Timberline; 503-272-3311.

When it comes to shopping for American Indian arts and crafts, why not go to the source? At **Kah-Nee-Ta**, both the Lodge and Village have gift shops offering beautiful basketry, handicrafts, blankets and jewelry. Many are made right on the reservation. ~ Warm Springs; 541-553-1112.

Richardson's Recreational Ranch Gift Shop has a wide variety of polished spheres, as well as rocks from around the world. Choose from agates, jasper, marble, petrified wood, novelty items and jewelry. ~ Located 11 miles north of Madras on Route 97, at milepost 81 turn right and continue southeast three miles; 541-475-2680.

NIGHTLIFE   On weekends live bands play rhythm-and-blues at **Charlie's Mountain View**. This rustic mountain lodge offers booth and table seating. The walls and ceilings are appointed with old-time skis, boots, snowshoes, ski bibs and other high-country memorabilia. Cover. ~ Government Camp Loop off Route 26, Government Camp; 503-272-3333.

At the **Appaloosa Lounge** at Kah-Nee-Ta, you can dance to live bands in a disco setting. It's also fun to enjoy the music outside on the adjacent deck. When the stars are out this is a particularly romantic setting. ~ Warm Springs; 541-553-1112.

MT. HOOD NATIONAL FOREST 🧍🚴🐎🎣🏕️⛵🚤⛵ PARKS

This one-million-acre national forest is named for the 11,235-foot Cascades peak that dazzles newcomers and natives alike. Extending from the Columbia River Gorge south to the Willamette National Forest boundary, the resort region includes four major wilderness and roadless areas. Popular destinations include the Olallie scenic area, known for its beautiful lakes and wildflowers, and the Mt. Hood Loop, a 150-mile scenic drive circling Oregon's highest peak. Along the way, you'll see mountain meadows, waterfalls, scenic streams, major ski areas and the magical Columbia River Gorge. More than 4500 miles of rivers and streams and 167 lakes and reservoirs will delight anglers seeking trout, salmon or steelhead. There are picnic tables, visitors center and restrooms. ~ Access is by Routes 84, 30, 35, 224 and 26; 503-622-3360.

🔺 Permitted in 107 campgrounds; $6 to $15 per night; RV sites without hookups are available. Three of the best sites for tent/RV camping are on Timothy Lake: the Gone Creek, Hood View and Oak Fork sites. Or try Trillium Lake, with 54 tent/RV sites close to boating and fishing. No hookups are available at any of the sites. For reservations call 800-280-2267.

COVE PALISADES STATE PARK 🧍🏊🎣⛵🚤⛵ Located at

the junction of the Crooked, Deschutes and Metolius rivers, this 4129-acre park encompasses two arms of Lake Billy Chinook. The cove is set beneath towering palisades and located on benchland punctuated by volcanic cones. Rich in petroglyphs and American Indian history, this region is a geological showcase. Fishing is excellent for smallmouth bass, trout and kokanee. Three miles of hiking trails offer excellent panoramic views and opportunities to see wildlife. There is also a picnic area, restrooms, a marina, a playground, nature trails and concessions; restaurants and groceries are in Madras. ~ Located off Route 97, 15 miles southwest of Madras; 541-546-3412.

🔺 There are 94 tent sites, 87 sites with full hookups and 91 sites with partial hookups; $16 to $20 per night.

▼▼▼▼▼▼▼▼▼▼▼▼

Central Cascades

One of Oregon's top recreational areas, the Central Cascades include some of the state's finest museums and interpretive centers. A year-round getaway for hiking, fishing, climbing and skiing, this area is also famous for its volcanic scenery, mountain lakes and rafting. Within the national forests are some of the West's leading wilderness areas and great opportunities for wildlife viewing. The region is an ideal family resort and also boasts one of the best scenic drives in the Northwest, the Cascades Loop Highway.

Although none of the peaks have the name recognition of Mt. Hood, the Central Cascades are by no means inferior mountains.

A trio known collectively as the Three Sisters rise above 10,000 feet, while relatively diminutive Mt. Bachelor (a mere 9065 feet) provides some of the Northwest's best alpine skiing. The topography is so daunting, in fact, that not many roads cross the Central Cascades, although a few open up in the summer to provide access to the area's voluminous mountain lakes and rivers. Still, plenty of destinations can be reached year-round, and there are enough outdoor activities to keep you busy for weeks.

SIGHTS
A good way to begin your visit is by heading west from Redmond 20 miles on Route 126 to **Sisters**. Gateway to some of the Cascades' most memorable scenery, this small town has a Wild West–style main street that delights tourists driving between the Willamette Valley and the Bend area.

After pausing to shop, dine or provision, head west nine miles on Route 20 and then turn north to the **Metolius River Recreation Area**. Here you can enjoy flyfishing, horseback riding and, in the winter, cross-country skiing. You can also sign up for a river trip. ~ 541-595-6117.

Nearby **Black Butte Ranch** is a resort area (see "Lodging" below) named for a towering volcanic cone. ~ Route 20, eight miles west of Sisters; 541-595-6211. To the west off Route 20, **Blue and Subtle lakes** are resort destinations, as well, with easy access to the scenic treasures of the Mt. Washington Wilderness to the south. Continue west on Route 20 past Lost Lake to Route 22 and **Detroit Lake**, a recreational area ideal for waterskiing.

HIDDEN ▶
This area is also home of the **Shady Cove Bridge**, an unusual, three-span, wooden-truss structure. Handcut and hand-assembled using hundreds of small interlocking pieces, the bridge links French Creek Road with Little North Santiam drainage.

From Detroit Lake, take Route 46 northeast ten miles to **Breitenbush Hot Springs**, a New Age wilderness resort. Yoga, guided forest hikes, meditation, hot-springs pools, steam saunas and massage therapy are all part of the fun. The artesian hot springs boast 30 minerals said to have curative powers. Before the arrival of the white man, American Indians conducted rituals and ceremonies at this soothing spot. ~ 503-854-3314.

HIDDEN ▶
Return to Route 22 and head east. When you reach Route 126, go west three miles to **Sawyer's Ice Cave**, a lengthy lava tube that served as a refrigerator for the pioneers. If you plan to explore the cave, bring a flashlight and warm clothing.

HIDDEN ▶
Another major volcanic landmark, located three miles southeast via Route 126, is **Clear Lake**, the source of the McKenzie River. Created when lava blocked a canyon, this lake lives up to its name in every respect.

Continue south on Route 126 to **Sahalie Falls**, a wheelchair-accessible spot where the McKenzie River cascades 100 feet over lava cliffs. A short drive south is **Koosah Falls**, which plunges more than 80 feet. In the fall this waterfall divides into several sections. Southeast on Route 126 another 17.6 miles is the hamlet of **McKenzie Bridge**, gateway to many scenic highlights of the Central Cascades. The town proper consists of little more than the Log Cabin Inn and a small market.

Head west to the **Blue River Ranger Station** (541-822-3317) and pick up the **Aufderheide National Scenic Byway** audio tape. ◄ *HIDDEN*
Following old logging roads, the byway winds through the Three Sisters Wilderness, passing mid-size peaks like Olallie Mountain (5708 feet) and Grasshopper Mountain (5651 feet). The byway parallels the south fork of the McKenzie River for much of the way. You can also begin this 70-mile tour from the south end at the **Westfir Lodge Bed and Breakfast Inn**. The same tape is available here. ~ Route 58, three miles west of Oakridge; 541-782-3103.

The Central Cascades is an ideal area for a family getaway.

Before returning north to the McKenzie Bridge area, take a look around the Oakridge area. We enjoyed visiting **Oakridge Pioneer Museum**. Even if you're not into chainsaws—one of the Northwest's best collections is found here—you'll enjoy seeing the antique farm implements, grocery displays and vintage crockery. Parked in the courtyard are an antique logging truck, fire truck and caboose. The museum is open Saturday from 1 to 4 p.m., but will open its doors anytime with advance notice. ~ 76433 Pine Street; 541-782-2885, 541-782-3904.

Twenty miles east of Oakridge is pristine **Waldo Lake** (Route ◄ *HIDDEN*
58). Clean enough to qualify as distilled water, the six-mile-long lake has astonishing visibility. Out on the water you can see down 100 feet to the bottom. While there are facilities, the lake, one of Oregon's largest, also has wilderness on the west and north shores.

Heading north to the McKenzie Bridge area again, pick up Route 126 east to Route 242 (a narrow route not recommended for long motor homes) up McKenzie Pass to the **Dee Wright Observatory**, where a half-mile paved trail leads through one of the Cascades' largest lava fields. From the observatory you can see 11 mountain peaks. Also worth a visit nearby is **Black Crater**, a volcanic summit close to North Sister Mountain.

Continue east to Sisters and pick up Route 20 east to **Bend**. One of Oregon's fastest-growing resort communities and a sunny alternative to the more drizzly parts of the Northwest, this town has become a year-round recreational center.

As you drive into town, be sure to stop at the **Bend Chamber of Commerce**. Extensively decorated by Oregon artists (even the restrooms feature artwork), this is the best place to orient your-self. ~ 63085 North Route 97, Bend; 541-382-3221.

In the center of Bend, **Drake Park** on Riverside Boulevard shouldn't be missed. On the Deschutes River, this urban sanctuary features picturesque **Mirror Pond**. Put out a blanket on the lawn, have a picnic, feed the ducks and study your own reflection.

Although strip development along Route 97 is changing Bend's small-town character, the past is well preserved at the **Deschutes Historical Center**. Located in the Reid School building on the south end of downtown, the museum features exhibits on American Indian history, early-day trappers and explorers, pioneer trails, the lumber industry and the tourist business. Admission. ~ 129 Northwest Idaho Street, Bend; 541-389-1813.

One piece of Devils Hill Flow volcanic rock was flown to the moon by Apollo astronaut James Irwin.

Three miles south of Bend is the **High Desert Museum**. One of the finest collections in the Pacific Northwest, the indoor galleries are complemented by 20 acres of nature trails and outdoor exhibits including a high-desert stream and pond. Permanent exhibits include exploration and settlement, natural history and a walk-through hard-rock mine that authentically re-creates life underground. A nice display here is a dawn-to-dusk "walk through time" that showcases the past. Along the way you'll have a look at American Indian history and the 19th-century heyday of the cowboy. After seeing Indian exhibits, crafts and quilting displays, visitors head outdoors to view the river-otter pool, hand-feeding of native porcupines and a birds-of-prey show. Hands-on activities and demonstrations at the Changing Forest exhibit; a sheepherder's wagon and settler's cabin make the museum a major pioneer-history center. Admission. ~ 59800 South Route 97; 541-382-4754.

Continue south on Route 97 to the **Lava Lands Visitors Center**. This small museum is one of Oregon's geologic showcases, the product of more than 500,000 years of volcanic eruptions. Part of the Deschutes National Forest, Lava Lands encompasses numerous volcanic landmarks. At the visitors center, you'll find interpretive exhibits, dioramas, slide talks and rangers who can suggest a variety of nature trails that lead through the lava flow. Admission. ~ 58201 Route 97; 541-593-2421.

Within this ten-square-mile lava flow are highlights like 6100-year-old **Lava Butte**, which changed the course of the Deschutes River. Reached by a paved road (open to vehicles only during the winter months, accessed by shuttle only Memorial Day to Labor Day) from the visitors center, the butte offers a 360-degree view of the Cascades and Lava Lands. You'll have to hike the final 200 yards to the summit. After enjoying the vista, you can continue west four miles from the visitors center (follow the signs saying

"Deschutes River Views") to reach **Benham Falls**, a popular picnic spot next to roaring Deschutes whitewater.

Much of the best sightseeing in Lava Lands is found on the
east side of Route 97. Two worthy spots in this fascinating region
are **Lava River Cave** and **Lava Cast Forest**. The former, a lava
tube, is great for spelunkers. Flashlight in hand, you can walk a
mile down this eerie tunnel (Oregon's longest uncollapsed lava
tube), but bring warm clothing since it stays around 40° in the
tube. The latter, explored via a mile-long trail, is a unique piece
of Oregon scenery, a forest created out of lava. This unusual landscape was shaped when lava swept across a stand of pine 6000
years ago, creating molds of each tree.

The region's largest geologic feature is 500-square-mile **Newberry Volcano**, created by eruption from more than 400 cinder
cones in the area just south of Bend. **Paulina and East lakes**, two
popular resort areas for anglers, are found in the five-mile-wide
Newberry Caldera. Also worth a visit is the crater's shiny, black
obsidian flow.

West of Bend is **Mt. Bachelor**, central Oregon's premier ski
area (see "Outdoor Adventures" below). Continue up the **Cascade Lakes Highway** to tour one of the region's most idyllic resort regions. Todd, Sparks, Devils, Elk, Hosmer, Lava, Cultus and
Davis lakes are a few of the popular spots for fishing, boating,
swimming and camping. For those eager to head for the outback,
there's easy access to high-country lakes, streams and creeks in the
Three Sisters Wilderness.

Scenic highlights in this region include spots like **Devils Garden**, a beautiful meadow where you can spot pictographs left behind by Warm Springs Indians.

◀ *HIDDEN*

Sisters Motor Lodge offers comfortable motel-style accommodations with country-inn decor. Four of the 11 rooms have kitchenettes; two-bedroom units are available. Breakfast includes fresh
muffins and scones. ~ 511 West Cascade Street, Sisters; 541-549-
2551. BUDGET TO MODERATE.

LODGING

When it comes to lodging, you really can get just about anything you want at **Black Butte Ranch**. This 1850-acre resort offers
more than 100 hotel rooms, condos, cabins and private homes.
Chalet-style accommodations nestled in the pines have paneled
walls and ceilings, decks, fireplaces and, in some condos, fully
equipped kitchens. Choose between two golf courses, four swimming pools, 23 miles of bike and jogging trails and 19 tennis
courts. There's canoeing in a chain of spring-fed lakes, as well as
skiing, hiking, fishing, boating and horseback riding. ~ Route 20,
eight miles west of Sisters; 541-595-6211, 800-452-7455. MOD-
ERATE TO DELUXE.

The **Metolius River Lodges** in Camp Sherman include four studios, six cabins and one duplex where you can flyfish off your deck. Located about 15.5 miles northwest of Sisters, this wooded retreat is in an area ideal for mountain biking, rafting, cross-country skiing and water sports. The wood-paneled units have carpeting, fireplaces, barbecues and rustic cabin furniture. ~ Five and a half miles north of Route 20, Camp Sherman; 541-595-6290, 800-595-6290. MODERATE TO DELUXE.

A small lake created by a dammed stream is just one of the attractions at Camp Sherman's **Lake Creek Lodge**. Sixteen one-, two- or three-bedroom knotty pine–paneled cabins feature Early American furniture, full kitchens, fireplaces and decks. Near the Metolius River, this 60-acre resort has tennis courts, a swimming pool, bike and hiking trails and serves meals family style. There are special activities for children. ~ Camp Sherman Road, four miles north of Route 20, Camp Sherman; 541-595-6331, 800-797-6331. ULTRA-DELUXE.

Possibly the only resort in Oregon with a resident channel offering metaphysical counseling, **Breitenbush Hot Springs** has it all. Located about ten miles northeast of Detroit in the western Cascades, this retreat provides everything from massage therapy to yoga to a spiritual/self-help workshop. Guests bring their own bedding and are housed in spartan, cedar-shake cabins paneled with fir. Platform tents and campsites are also available. Geothermal heat and electricity from hydropower provide energy self-sufficiency. Guests can choose between hot tubs, *au naturel* hot springs overlooking the river and mountains and a hot natural-steam sauna complete with a cold-water tub. Vegetarian meals included. ~ 503-854-3314. BUDGET TO DELUXE.

Herbert Hoover, Clark Gable and Sean Penn have all stayed at the century-old **Log Cabin Inn**. A 19th-century stagecoach stop, this three-story log building replaced the original building that burned down in an 1896 fire. Although the second-story bordello is now only a gift shop, many other traditions endure at the cedar-paneled dining room, bar and wraparound porch. Eight log cabins (two with kitchenettes) on this six-and-a-half-acre site face the McKenzie River. The units have period furniture, quilts, rockers, fireplaces, braided rugs and decks. There are also six teepees overlooking the river. ~ 56483 McKenzie Highway, McKenzie Bridge; 541-822-3432, 800-355-3432. MODERATE.

HIDDEN ► Nestled in an orchard, the **McKenzie River Inn** provides three spacious, paneled rooms and a cottage on the water. Just steps from the river, this two-and-a-half-acre retreat has a library and piano in the main living room, peacock chairs and ceiling fans in the bedrooms and kitchen facilities in the cottage. ~ 49164 McKenzie Highway, Nimrod; 541-822-6260. BUDGET.

Holiday Farm has roomy, knotty pine–paneled cabins on the McKenzie River complete with fireplaces, decks and kitchenettes. The units make an ideal fishing retreat—you can cast for trout from your porch! This 90-acre resort has two private lakes and serves meals in a farmhouse that was once a stagecoach stop. ~ 54455 McKenzie River Drive, Rainbow; 541-822-3715. DELUXE.

On a lake created by a lava dam, **Clear Lake Resort** offers six units with kitchens, baths and showers. Sixteen rustic cabins without bath facilities are also available. There are no electric outlets in these units, and generator-powered lights are shut off at 10 p.m. You must provide your own bedding. Clear Lake is limited to rowboats that can be rented at the resort. ~ Located 19 miles northeast of McKenzie Bridge on Route 126; reservations by mail, c/o Santiam Fish & Game Association, P.O. Box 500, Lebanon, OR 97355; information, 541-258-3907. BUDGET.

The Riverhouse in Bend is one of over a dozen motels on the city's main drag. There are 220 rooms featuring contemporary furniture, floral-print bedspreads and sitting areas. In the evening you can relax in front of the fireplace or have a drink on your deck overlooking the Deschutes River. Deluxe-priced suites are also available with kitchen facilities. An 18-hole golf course, jogging trail, two pools, a sauna and whirlpool make this a good place to relax. ~ 3075 North Route 97, Bend; 541-389-3111, 800-547-3928. MODERATE TO ULTRA-DELUXE.

In the same part of Bend is the **Travelers Inn**, located directly beside the Bend Welcome Center and featuring 36 uniform motel rooms, a swimming pool and a hot tub. Continental breakfast served. ~ 3705 Route 97 North, Bend; 541-382-2211. BUDGET TO MODERATE.

The **Dunes Motel**, with 30 rooms, is close to downtown Bend. There's an indoor hot tub. ~ 1515 Northeast 3rd Street, Bend; 541-382-6811. MODERATE.

▲▲▲

✔ CHECK THESE OUT—UNIQUE LODGING

- *Budget:* Retreat with a book to the **McKenzie River Inn**, tucked away in a riverside orchard. *page 388*
- *Moderate to deluxe:* Experience a piece of history at the museum-like **Timberline Lodge**, built in 1937 by the WPA. *page 380*
- *Deluxe:* Take in breathtaking views of America's deepest lake from the **Crater Lake Lodge.** *page 401*
- *Ultra-deluxe:* Join in the family-style meals at **Lake Creek Lodge** after a hard day of playing in the Metolius River. *page 388*

Budget: under $50 Moderate: $50–$90 Deluxe: $90–$130 Ultra-deluxe: over $130

Located across from Drake Park, **Lara House Bed and Breakfast** hosts guests in six big, carpeted rooms with easy chairs, antiques, colorful quilts and private baths, some with clawfoot tubs. You can take your full breakfast on the sun porch. This 1910 Colonial also has a comfortable living room and an outdoor hot tub. ~ 640 Northwest Congress Street, Bend; phone/fax 541-388-4064. MODERATE.

The **Bend Riverside Motel** offers 193 budget rooms, moderately priced studios and deluxe suites with park or river views. The studios and suites have fireplaces, kitchen facilities, sauna, hot tub and tennis facilities. Convenient to downtown in a secluded setting. ~ 1565 Northwest Hill Street, Bend; 541-389-2363, 800-284-2363. BUDGET TO DELUXE.

At the 3300-acre **Sunriver Lodge and Resort**, you can choose between 300 rooms and suites featuring pine furniture, brass beds, fireplaces, wall-to-wall carpets and decks with views of the Cascades. Condos and homes are also available. All guests can take advantage of pools, tennis courts, bicycles, canoes, racquetball, skiing and other facilities. ~ Fifteen miles south of Bend on Route 97, Sunriver; 541-593-1221, 800-547-3922. DELUXE.

In the wooded Cascades foothills, **The Inn of the Seventh Mountain** is the only resort in Oregon with its own skating rink and waterslide. The 327 rooms, suites and apartments have queens and Murphy beds, knotty-pine paneling, fireplaces and contemporary prints. Convenient to Mt. Bachelor, the inn is ideally located for horseback riding, whitewater rafting and mountain biking. ~ 18575 Southwest Century Drive, seven miles west of Bend; 541-382-8711, 800-452-6810. MODERATE TO DELUXE.

HIDDEN ► Built around a circa-1923 lodge, nine-unit **Elk Lake Resort** is a forested retreat ideal for fishing, boating, swimming and loafing. The knotty-pine cabins, with two bedrooms, kitchens and small decks, are near wilderness hiking, Nordic skiing and horseback riding. For the adventurous, the resort is accessible only by snowmobile in the winter months. ~ Cascade Lakes Highway, 30 miles west of Bend; 541-317-2994. MODERATE TO DELUXE.

DINING In Sisters, **Ali's** provides a convenient solution for those who can't decide between a sandwich or a salad. Generous sandwiches served on an open-faced bagel or wrapped pita bread include curry chicken, dilly tuna, lemon-ginger chicken and Mexican chicken olé. A wide variety of vegetarian sandwiches and smoked-turkey sandwiches are offered, as well as soups, bagels and coffee drinks like the mocha-mint espresso float. ~ Town Square, Sisters; 541-549-2547. BUDGET.

One of the most popular pizza parlors in these parts is **Papandrea's**. The modest board-and-batten establishment has indoor seating and patio service on picnic tables covered with green-and-white-checkered tablecloths. Antique farm implements decorate the dining room. All dough and sauces are homemade, and the tomatoes are fresh. ~ 442 East Cascade Street, Sisters; 541-549-6081. BUDGET TO MODERATE.

For dining in a contemporary setting, consider the **Lodge Restaurant at Black Butte Ranch**. This split-level establishment has cathedral ceilings, picture windows and Early American furniture. While enjoying the panoramic Cascades view, you can order prime rib, roast duck, halibut filet, pasta primavera with chicken or vegetables. Closed on Monday and Tuesday during the winter. ~ Route 20, eight miles west of Sisters; 541-595-1260. MODERATE TO DELUXE.

Located in a shingled lodge-style building adjacent to the Metolius River, **Kokanee Café** is recommended for fresh seafood dishes, venison medallions and quail, fresh salmon or steaks accompanied by soup and a garden salad with the house vinaigrette. The desserts are exceptional. Worth a special trip. Closed from late October to early April. Call ahead for hours. ~ Camp Sherman; 541-595-6420. MODERATE TO DELUXE.

◄ HIDDEN

Whether you choose one of the porch lunches served alfresco or head in to the paneled dining room for supper, the historic **Log Cabin Inn** offers fine dining in a traditional setting. This three-story log building, originally a stagecoach stop, erected in 1886, was rebuilt in 1906 after a fire. Specialties include barbecued salmon, baby-back ribs, quail, rainbow trout fresh from the McKenzie River and pioneer game stew. ~ 56483 McKenzie Highway, McKenzie Bridge; 541-822-3432. MODERATE.

◄ HIDDEN

In a café-style dining room situated in an old church, the family-run **Ernesto's Italian Restaurant** serves up rich, homemade lasagna, veal parmigiana and calzone. ~ 1203 Northeast 3rd Street, Bend; 541-389-7274. MODERATE.

A Bend tradition since 1936 and one of our Oregon favorites, **Pine Tavern** has an enviable location overlooking Mirror Pond. Built around 200-year-old ponderosa pines, the restaurant prides itself on home-cooked dishes like steamed vegetables and fettuccine, pork back ribs, fish-and-chips, Cobb salad and their specialty, prime rib using grain-fed beef. A special, heart-healthy menu features entrées such as halibut filet and herbed chicken. Seafood specials are offered each evening; there's also a children's menu. ~ Foot of Northwest Oregon Street, Bend; 541-382-5581. MODERATE.

For some different fare, head for **Deschutes Brewery and Public House**. This microbrewery, known for its Cascade Golden Ale and Black Butte Porter, homemade root beer and ginger ale, serves upscale pub fare like a pastrami Reuben, Buffalo wings and vegetarian chili. ~ 1044 Bond Street, Bend; 541-382-9242. MODERATE.

HIDDEN ▶ Located in a chalet-style building behind a gasoline station, **Marcello's Italian Cuisine and Pizzeria** proves that location isn't everything. Locals pack this carpeted brick dining room decorated with stained glass and hanging flower pots. Their reward is pasta, veal and chicken specialties, as well as calzones, seafood and, of course, a dozen varieties of pizza. ~ Beaver Drive and North Ponderosa Road, Sunriver; 541-593-8300. MODERATE.

For dining with a view of the Cascades, a good choice is **The Meadows**. The restaurant serves fresh seafood and northwestern cuisine. Closed for renovations until May 1998. ~ Sunriver Lodge, Sunriver; 541-593-1221. MODERATE TO DELUXE.

Also at Sunriver Lodge is the more casual **Merchant Trader Café**, with outdoor patio seating. The breakfast menu includes homemade scones and granola. Baby back ribs or a number of gourmet salads are offered for lunch and dinner. ~ Sunriver Lodge, Sunriver; 541-593-1221. MODERATE.

With picture windows and patio seating, **Poppy Seed Café** offers dining at the Inn of the Seventh Mountain. Fettuccine dishes, shrimp salads, steaks, burgers and sandwiches are all popular here. ~ 18575 Southwest Century Drive, seven miles west of Bend; 541-382-8711. MODERATE.

HIDDEN ▶ If you're looking for a hearty breakfast or coffee-shop lunch fare, try the counter at the rustic **Elk Lake Resort**. The knotty pine–paneled dining area is a great place for bacon and eggs, pancakes or french toast. Burgers, salads and sandwiches fill the lunch menu. Although table service is available, we recommend taking a stool for the maximum waterfront view. Dinner entrées include soup, salad and dessert. Dinner by reservation only. ~ Cascade Lakes Highway, 30 miles west of Bend; 541-317-2994. BUDGET TO MODERATE.

SHOPPING Pine Tree Square is home to **Something Special**, which carries expressive home decor, music, crafts and antique furniture. ~ West Cascade Avenue at South Oak Street, Sisters; 541-549-3579.

If you're in the market for jewelry, wood sculpture, pottery or basketry, try the **Folk Arts Gallery**. More than 80 Pacific Northwest artists are represented. ~ 183 East Hood Street, Sisters; 541-549-9556.

You say it's hot out there and you left your bandanna back home? Those storm clouds are threatening and you forgot your rain jacket? About to head uphill on your 18-speed and your handlebars need adjustment? Then head to **Sisters Mountain Supply**. This hiking, biking and camping supply store also sells Patagonia shirts, topo maps, sunglasses and, for those who know when to quit, a hammock. ~ 143 East Hood Street, Sisters; 541-549-3251.

HIDDEN ▶ Stop by the **Blue Spruce Gallery**, which carries a beautiful collection of pottery, ceramic vases, candlesticks, custom-made lamps and dinnerware, paintings, jewelry and decorative art. ~ 61021 South Route 97, Bend; 541-389-7745.

The **High Desert Museum Store** is a great place to browse for American Indian basketry, nature books, handmade jewelry, cards and photographs. It also offers birdfeeders, mobiles, wildflower seeds and posters. ~ 59800 South Route 97, Bend; 541-382-4754.

For live Top-40 and classic-rock music, head to the **River House**. This contemporary lounge has a roomy dancefloor, full bar and spacious deck overlooking the Deschutes. In warm weather you can enjoy the music from the deck. ~ 3075 North Route 97, Bend; 541-389-3111.

NIGHTLIFE

The **Community Theatre of the Cascades** has presented musicals, dramas, comedies and Broadway hits since 1978. This intimate, live theater offers six shows from late August to late June. ~ 148 Northwest Greenwood, Bend; 541-389-0803.

At Inn of the Seventh Mountain, **Josiah's** has live music in the lounge during the summer months, ranging from jazz to country to rock. ~ 18575 Southwest Century Drive, seven miles west of Bend; 541-382-8711.

DETROIT LAKE STATE PARK This 104-acre park is a popular day-use and overnight facility on the shore of one of the busier Cascade Lakes. A forested spot on the north shore of Detroit Reservoir, the park is divided into two units. The smaller Mongold is for day-use picnicking and swimming. To the east is the Detroit Lake State Park campground. You can fish for trout and kokanee salmon. There are restrooms and picnic areas; restaurants and groceries are nearby in Detroit. ~ Located on Route 22, two miles west of Detroit; 503-854-3346.

PARKS

▲ There are 134 tent sites, 107 sites with full hookups and 70 sites with partial hookups; $17 to $22 per night.

WILLAMETTE NATIONAL FOREST This 1.6-million-acre region (larger than the state of Connecticut!) covers from 10,495-foot Mt. Jefferson to the Calapooya Mountains northeast of Roseburg. Diverse terrain ranges from volcanic moonscapes to wooded slopes and cascading rivers. One of the world's purest bodies of water, Waldo Lake, is found here. More than 380,000 acres of wilderness encompass seven major Cascade peaks. Home to more than 300 animal species, including deer, cougar, grouse and Roosevelt elk, this forest also boasts more than 600 varieties of rhododendron. There are over a thousand miles of hiking trails here, and mountain bikers cluster near the town of Oakridge to ride the foothills. In the winter months, heavy snowfall blankets the popular Nordic and alpine skiing areas at Willamette Pass and Mt. Bachelor. More than 1500 miles of rivers and streams, as well as 375 lakes, offer countless opportunities for fishing. You'll find picnic tables, interpretive centers and restrooms. ~ Access is via Routes 22, 20, 126, 46, 242 and 58; 541-465-6522.

▲ Permitted at over 80 campgrounds; free to $10 per night; RV sites available at most campgrounds. Some of the most popular sites are the Hoover Campground at Detroit Reservoir, and the Paradise and McKenzie Bridge campgrounds near the town of McKenzie Bridge along Route 126. Some of the more secluded sites (like the Homestead Campground) can be accessed by Forest Service Road 19 near Blue River.

> Several state parks, botanical areas, nature sites, canoe trails and waterfowl observation points make the Upper Klamath Lake Tour Route a winner.

BEN AND KAY DORRIS STATE PARK 🏃 🚤 🛥 🎣

A picturesque, 92-acre park at the head of Martin Rapids blending river frontage with an old orchard, this park is shaded by Douglas fir and big-leaf maple that add color to the region in the fall months. While a mile of river frontage is the park's leading attraction, the "Rock House," an outcropping that provided shelter for pioneers traveling the historic wagon road, is also worth a visit. This is one of Oregon's better places to catch trout. Facilities include picnic areas and restrooms. ~ Located on Route 126, 31 miles east of Eugene; 541-548-7501.

SMITH ROCK STATE PARK 🏃 🎣

Along steep Crooked River canyon, this day-use park is popular with climbers. They enjoy scaling striated Smith Rock, a formation rising several hundred feet above the tributary's north bank. Named for John Smith, a 19th-century pioneer, the park includes a forested bluff on the river's south bank. For anglers, there's decent fishing for rainbows and smallmouth bass. There are picnic areas and restrooms. ~ Located on Northeast Crooked River Drive, east of Route 97, nine miles northeast of Redmond; 541-548-7501.

▲ Permitted in the Bivouac Area for primitive hike-in camping. Space limited by parking (53 spaces); $4 per person per night.

TUMALO STATE PARK 🏃 🎣

Convenient to the Bend area in Deschutes River Canyon, it is forested with juniper, ponderosa pine, willow and poplar. Named for "temolo," the Klamath Indian word for wild plum, the 333-acre park has handsome basalt bluffs above the canyon. There's good trout fishing, too. Facilities include a picnic area, restrooms, showers, a playground and nature trails; restaurants and groceries are in Bend. ~ Located four miles north of Bend on O. B. Riley Road off Route 20; 541-388-6055.

▲ There are 68 tent sites and 20 full RV hookups; $15 to $19 per night.

DRAKE PARK 🏃

This verdant, 12-acre park is along the Deschutes River and includes a riverfront strollway and footbridge across the river. Beloved by the local populace, the park is home to most of Bend's community events. Stroll alongside the river and be serenaded by geese and ducks. Adjacent to downtown Bend, it includes picturesque Mirror Pond, actually just a part of the river that was widened and made into a peaceful place to sit beside. You'll find picnic areas and a playground (across the bridge at Harmon Park). ~ Take Franklin Avenue west from Route 97 into downtown Bend where it becomes Riverside Boulevard. Continue west to the park; 541-388-5435.

PILOT BUTTE STATE PARK 🏃 A cinder cone that served as a landmark for Oregon pioneers is the heart of this 100-acre urban park. The 511-foot-high volcanic dome is located on the east side of Bend and is a very popular climb (it takes only about 15 minutes to scale). Ascend the spiral road to the top of this pine-covered butte to enjoy great views of the Cascades from Mt. St. Helens to the Three Sisters. ~ Located on Greenwood Avenue (Route 20) in Bend; 541-388-6055.

LA PINE STATE PARK 🏊 🚣 ⛵ This rolling Deschutes River   ◀ HIDDEN
Valley park is shaded by pine and old-growth forest. Expect to spot mule deer as you explore this uncrowded 2333-acre getaway. It's ideal for boating and a good base for visiting the surrounding volcanic landmarks including Newberry Crater. Anglers can fly cast for rainbow and brown trout. There are picnic areas, restrooms and showers; restaurants and groceries are in La Pine. ~ Located west of Route 97 on La Pine State Park Road, 27 miles south of Bend; 541-388-6055.

▲ There are 145 sites with hookups; $13 to $15 per night.

DESCHUTES NATIONAL FOREST 🏃 🚴 🏕 🛶 🚣 ⛵ Named for the popular river that descends the east slope of the Cascades, this 1.6-million-acre forest embraces Mt. Bachelor, the Three Sisters Wilderness, the Cascade Lakes region and Newberry National Volcanic Monument. Many popular resorts and five wilderness areas are found in the Deschutes forests, meadows and high country. Climbing from 2000 to 10,358 feet, the forest is dominated by ponderosa pine. You can climb up to the South Sister via the Green Lakes Trail, a popular three-mile hike, and on the way explore the Three Sisters Wilderness. The forest is known for its raftable rivers, spelunking and skiing. There are innumerable places to ski cross-country, including Dutchman Flat, Edison Butte and the Skyliner/Meissner area. Bend is the most convenient jump-off point. More than 240 miles of streams and 158 lakes and reservoirs make for ideal fishing. Picnic tables, interpretive centers, marinas and restrooms are facilities here. ~ Access via Routes 126, 242, 58, 97, 31, 20 and 46; 541-388-2715.

▲ There are over 100 campgrounds for tents and RVs throughout the national forest; $5 to $13 per night; call for details. The best camping is found off the Cascade Lake Highway near one of the many lakes in the area. Paulina Lake near the Newberry National Volcanic Monument has tent/RV sites ($11 to $13; no hookups). South of Elk Lake, the Hosmer campground has two campgrounds with lots of room for both tent and RV camping ($5; no hookups).

▼▼▼▼▼▼▼▼▼▼▼▼▼
Southern Cascades

Blessed with several major wilderness areas that are great for viewing wildlife or birdwatching, the Southern Cascades are also the home of Oregon's only national park, Crater Lake. In addition to being drop-dead gorgeous—its chilly waters are an extraordinarily piercing shade of blue—the lake offers many recreational possibilities, from Nordic skiing to snowshoeing to hiking. The Southern Cascades also include a real sleeper, the Klamath Lake area.

SIGHTS

CRATER LAKE One of the world's most famous mountain lakes, tucked inside the caldera of an exploded volcano, Crater Lake is known for its shimmering vistas and dark, cold depths. The best way to see this geologic wonder is to take **Rim Drive**, the 33-mile road circling Crater Lake. With more than 50 turnouts, it provides a thorough overview of this mountain-rimmed, deep-blue lake. Vertical lava flow patterns add to the majesty of the volcanic scenery. The drive is seasonal; call the visitors center (541-594-2211) to be sure the road is open.

While the crystal-clear waters are the prime attraction, the 1000-foot-high rim walls create an excellent cutaway view of the remains of Mt. Mazama. Allow at least five hours for this trip around the 20-square-mile, 1000-foot-deep lake (the road itself is about 33 miles around). You'll want to begin your tour at the **Visitors Center** (open June through September) located across from **Rim Village**. A short walk below the crater rim is **Sinnott Memorial**. There's a small museum on this rock ledge where rangers give geology talks during the summer months. Continue clockwise around the lake to **Discovery Point**, where in 1853 explorer John Wesley Hillman became the first white man to spot this treasure. ~ Visitors Center: 541-594-2211.

From here you'll want to go to major viewpoints. About three miles past Discovery Point is a turnout ideal for seeing one of the park's major volcanoes, **Union Peak**. Continue another seven-tenths of a mile to **Wizard Island** overlook. It's named for the small Crater Lake island that is actually the top of a small volcano. For a panoramic view of the lake, perfect for photographs, pull off at **Steel Bay**. Rim Drive's highest viewpoint is **Cloudcap**. This is a great spot to see how part of Mt. Mazama was sliced away by the caldera's collapse. Also of special interest is **Pumice**

Castle, an orange and pink landmark sculpted by the elements into a fortress-like formation.

The only access to the lakeshore is found at **Cleetwood Cove Trail.** This steep route takes you down to Cleetwood Boat Landing, where you can tour the lake by boat (admission). On this two-hour tour you'll be able to explore **Wizard Island,** a 700-foot-high cinder cone and see remnants of an older volcano called the **Phantom Ship.** ~ Boat tours: 541-594-2511.

Although America's deepest (1932 feet) lake is the centerpiece of this national park, other attractions are well worth your time. Southeast of Rim Village you'll find **Steel Visitors Center** (open year-round), where you can see an 18-minute video on the lake, as well as interpretive exhibits.

We also recommend visiting **The Pinnacles** area on the park's east side. Pumice and ash left behind by the Mt. Mazama collapse were gradually eroded by rain and snow. These formations evolved into rock pinnacles, further eroded by the elements into weird, hoodoo shapes. Today, hiking through these colorful canyons is one of the park's great pleasures.

Sixteen miles west of Crater Lake National Park in the vicinity of Union Creek is **Rogue River Gorge.** Here this mighty river is channeled into a beautiful little canyon easily accessed on foot. It's a must for whitewater fans. In the same area, a mile west of Union Creek, is **Natural Bridge** where the Rogue flows into a lava tube for a short distance before reappearing. The bridge is well worth a visit and an easy walk.

KLAMATH LAKE REGION   Although not in the mountains, its proximity to the high country makes the area around Upper Klamath Lake a favorite of travelers coming or going to them.

One of the best ways to explore the Klamath Lake area is via the **Upper Klamath Lake Tour Route.** Take Route 97 south to Chiloquin and then turn north on Route 62 to Fort Klamath. (If you're coming direct from Crater Lake simply take Route 62 south.)

Your first stop is **Fort Klamath Museum.** Built in 1863, this frontier post tells the story of the 1872–73 Modoc Indian War. Captain Jack and three other American Indians executed after this uprising are buried here. Open June 1 through Labor Day. Closed Tuesday and Wednesday. ~ Route 62, south of Fort Klamath; 541-381-2230.

Farther south is the **Klamath Indian Tribal Museum,** distinguished by its basketry and arrowhead exhibits. ~ Route 97, Chiloquin; 541-783-2218.

The centerpiece of your tour is **Upper Klamath Lake.** At roughly 64,000 acres, this is one of the state's largest lakes, extending south nearly 25 miles to the town of Klamath Falls. The

Text continued on page 400.

Gorges in
the Mist

The land of falling waters, the Pacific Northwest is the
place to go for plunging rivers. Thousands of waterfalls
are found here, often convenient to major highways or
trails. Reached via fern canyons, paths through old-growth
forests and along pristine streams, waterfall hunting is great sport,
even on a rainy day. And part of the fun is getting misted or sprayed
by the raging waters.

In the Oregon Cascades, these falls are at their peak in late spring or
early summer. But even if you come later in the summer or fall, there will
still be plenty to see: deep, plunging streams, tiered falls that split into roaring ribbons before converging in swirling pools, horsetails that drop at a 90-
degree angle while retaining contact with bedrock. And, of course, you can
count on frequently spotting the distinctive waterfall that gives this region
its name—the Cascades that drop down in a series of steps.

The Mt. Hood area offers some of the loveliest falls. Among the easiest
to reach is **Yocum Falls**, on Route 26 seven miles east of Rhododendron.
Here, Camp Creek drops several hundred feet. Continue east to Route 35
and the entrance to Mt. Hood Meadows ski area. You'll see a sign marking
the .2 mile trail to **Umbrella Falls**. Although these falls drop only about 60
feet, the verdant setting and fields of wildflowers make this an excellent
choice, especially for families with small children. In early summer, the falls
trail is reached via a hike through fields of wildflowers. Return to Route 35
and continue 1.4 miles east to **Switchback Falls**. At its peak, in the late
spring, North Fork Iron Creeks drops 200 feet.

To the south, the McKenzie River has two highly recommended falls accessible via Route 126. Located five miles south of the Route 20 junction,
the river drops 140 feet at **Sahalie Falls**. Continue south another .4 mile
to **Koosah Falls**. A trail takes you down the river canyon to enjoy the view
from a series of overlooks. Continue another 5.2 miles south to a road that
heads to the McKenzie River Trailhead. After hiking upriver for two miles
you'll discover that **Tamolitch Falls** have now run dry. Although the river
has been diverted to a reservoir at this point, it remains a scenic spot.
Thanks to local springs, the river begins anew at this location.

The Bend area is an excellent choice for waterfall lovers. **Tumalo
Falls**, 15 miles west of town, is reached via Galveston Avenue and Route
1828. The falls drop nearly 100 feet in an area badly damaged by a fire in
1979. South of town, off Route 97, is **Paulina Creek Falls**. Located in

Newberry Crater, this 100-foot drop is an easy walk from Paulina Creek Falls picnic ground.

Century Drive, the beginning of the Cascade Lakes Highway west of Bend, provides easy access to **Lava Island Falls** on the Deschutes River. Take this road to Route 41 and drive south for .4 mile. Go left on Route 620 for .8 mile to reach the falls. If you take Route 41 south from Century Drive three miles and pick up Route 500 for .9 mile you'll reach Dillon Falls. Take Route 620 south about three miles from the intersection of Route 500 to see a 50-foot cataract called **Benham Falls**.

Off Cascade Lakes Highway, **Fall Creek Falls** is another fine choice. Take Century Drive 28 miles west of Bend to Route 46. Drive .2 mile on the road to Green Lakes Trail and then hike the last .3 mile to the falls.

In the Umpqua River Valley, Route 138 gets you to a number of beautiful falls. Among them is **Susan Creek Falls**, located via a trail seven and a half miles east of Idleyld Park. You'll hike one mile north of the highway to reach the falls. Drive Steamboat Road northeast from Steamboat 4.2 miles to reach **Steamboat Falls**. Located at a forest-service campground, this small waterfall is circumvented by fish that use an adjacent ladder. Near mile marker 42 about three miles southeast of Steamboat are **Jack Creek** and tiered **Jack Falls**. These three falls are particularly rewarding for photo buffs.

Also popular are **Toketee Falls**. To see this 90-foot drop, take Route 138 to the Toketee Lake turnoff. Continue north .3 mile to the trail leading west .6 mile to the falls. East of Toketee Lake is Lemolo Lake, a popular resort destination. From here, Thorn Prairie Road leads to Lemolo Falls Road. Hike the Lemolo Falls Trail one mile west to this cataract.

Off Route 62, the main highway from Medford to Crater Lake, is one of the Cascades' grander waterfalls, 175-foot **Mill Creek Falls**. Accessible by Mill Creek Road, this scenic spot is an easy .3 mile hike from the Mill Creek Falls Scenic Area trailhead on the south side of Prospect. Also accessible on this hike are **Barr Creek Falls**, **Prospect Falls**, **Pearsoney Falls** and **Lower Red Blanket Falls**.

Within Crater Lake National Park, **Annie Falls** is off Route 62, 4.7 miles north of the park's southern entrance. Because this falls is located in an unstable canyon-rim area, visitors should approach it with extreme caution. Also in the park, close to Applegate Peak, is **Vidae Falls**.

To get a complete rundown on these watery delights, check with local park or ranger offices. Or pick up a copy of the definitive guide to this subject, *A Waterfall Lover's Guide to the Pacific Northwest* by Gregory A. Plumb (The Mountaineers).

shallow waters here are prime fishing territory and a major wild-life refuge. One of the best birdwatching areas in the Pacific Northwest, these wetlands and marsh are also home to otter, beaver and muskrat.

In Klamath Falls, the **Senator Baldwin Hotel Museum** has been restored to its turn-of-the-century heyday. A guided tour shows off the four-story building's architectural gems and historic memorabilia. Open June through September. Closed Sunday and Monday. Admission. ~ 31 Main Street, Klamath Falls; 541-883-4207.

At the **Klamath County Museum**, flora and fauna and American Indian and pioneer history are all on display. There's also a special exhibit on geothermal energy. Closed Sunday. Admission. ~ 1451 Main Street, Klamath Falls; 541-883-4208.

Also in the Klamath Falls area is the **Favell Museum of Western Art and Indian Artifacts**. The contemporary building features American Indian art and artifacts, art of the West, taxidermy and a vast collection of miniature firearms. You won't have trouble finding arrowheads because more than 60,000 are on display. Closed Sunday. Admission. ~ 125 West Main Street, Klamath Falls; 541-882-9996.

LODGING   For cabins in a wooded setting, head for **Cultus Lake Resort**. Twenty-three spacious, pine-paneled units equipped with brick fireplaces, alcove kitchens and drop-beam ceilings are set in a forest glen. The four-mile-long lake is great for sailing, fishing and kayaking. There's also a beach popular for sunbathing and swimming. Closed mid-October through April. ~ Located 50 miles southwest of Bend off Cascade Lakes Highway; radio phone 541-389-5125, tone, 037244. MODERATE.

Midway between Bend and Crater Lake in the small highwayside town of Chemult is the **Dawson House Lodge**, a 1929 train station boarding house that has been converted into a rustic yet cozy inn. Choose from five upstairs hotel rooms furnished with antiques, including one double unit featuring log-framed four-poster beds and a tub and shower. The inn also offers three motel-style rooms and a second-story pine veranda. A continental breakfast awaits in the fireplace-warmed lobby each morning. ~ Route 97 at 1st Street, Chemult; 541-365-2232. BUDGET TO MODERATE.

Zane Grey loved the north Umpqua River, and today a 31-mile stretch has been limited to "flyfishing only." In the heart of the river region 18 miles east of Idleyld Park is **Steamboat Inn**. An eclectic mix of streamside cabins, hideaway cottages, river suites and ranch-style homes, the inn serves meals family style in the main lodge. Some of the 19 units are pine paneled; others offer river views, mini-kitchens, fireplaces, soaking tubs, quilted comforters and paintings by leading Northwest artists. Closed in

January and February. ~ Route 138, Steamboat; 541-498-2230, 800-840-8825, fax 541-498-2411. DELUXE TO ULTRA-DELUXE.

Crater Lake Lodge is a magnificent wood and stone structure built between 1909 and 1924 on the rim overlooking Crater Lake. The lodge has 71 rooms including a few lofts, all with natural-wood furnishings and many with views of the lake. Other superb views can be enjoyed from the lodge's Great Hall, which has a massive stone fireplace, historic photographs, three Douglas fir trees and floor-to-ceiling windows framed in rustic wood bark. Open mid-May through mid-October. ~ Crater Lake National Park; 541-830-8700, fax 541-830-8514. DELUXE.

Additional lodging in the national park can be found at **Mazama Village Motor Inn**. Forty modern units are available from early June to early October. Board-and-batten exteriors, paneled interiors and wall-to-wall carpeting make these gray-toned accommodations rather appealing. ~ Crater Lake National Park, Route 62; 541-830-8700, fax 541-830-8514. MODERATE.

With 92 units, **Diamond Lake Resort** is the largest hostelry in the Crater Lake region. This complex includes 40 motel rooms, 10 studios and 42 cabins, all a short walk from the busy waterfront. Expect paneled, carpeted rooms with fireplaces, Franklin stoves and marine views. The studios and cabins come with kitchen facilities and, in some cases, private decks. An 11.5 mile biking trail circles the lake, and there are boat and bike rentals and hiking trails as well. While some find Diamond Lake too crowded for their tastes, it is convenient to many beautiful wilderness areas. ~ Route 138, five miles north of the Crater Lake entrance; 541-793-3333, 800-733-7593, fax 541-793-3309. MODERATE.

If you like the ambience of a historic inn but prefer the comfort of motel-style units, the **Prospect Historical Hotel and Motel** may be just the place. Located just a mile off Route 62 and 38 miles from the west entrance to Crater Lake National Park, the white frame hotel has eight cozy rooms with Early American furniture, watercolor prints, quilts, vanities and access to a pleasant front porch. There are also 14 motel rooms. ~ 391 Mill Creek Drive, Prospect; 541-560-3664, 800-944-6490. BUDGET TO MODERATE.

◄ *HIDDEN*

Motel-style units and cabins convenient to Upper Klamath Lake's Pelican Bay are found at **Rocky Point Resort**. Set in a fir forest frequented by elk and deer, this waterfront resort is a good place to photograph bald eagles, osprey and white pelican colonies. The paneled rooms are clean and comfortable. Cabins offer kitchen facilities. Camping (33 RV hookups, 4 tent sites), boat rentals, moorage, fishing tackle and guide service are all available on the premises. ~ 28121 Rocky Point Road, Klamath Falls; 541-356-2287, fax 541-356-2222. BUDGET TO MODERATE.

For inexpensive lodging try the **Maverick Motel**. Forty-nine carpeted guest rooms are brightly painted and furnished with dark-wood furniture. There's a pool here. ~ 1220 Main Street, Klamath Falls; 541-882-6688, 800-404-6690. BUDGET.

DINING

With American Indian decor, a menu featuring specialties like the buckaroo breakfast, and a parking lot filled with diesel rigs, station wagons and motorcycles, it's obvious that the **Wheel Cafe** cultivates an eclectic clientele. Take a seat at the counter and order turkey, swiss cheese, bacon and tomato on a sourdough roll, a chef's salad or plantation chicken. The peaches in the pie tasted like they had been picked the same morning. ~ Route 97, Chemult; 541-365-2284. BUDGET.

You'll have a hard time beating the **Steamboat Inn**. This establishment is famous for its fisherman's dinner. After enjoying apéritifs in the library, guests head inside to the lodge where dinner is served family-style on gleaming wood tables illuminated by the glow of the fireplace. Appetizers are followed by salad, soup and homemade bread. One set dinner menu is served nightly. Entrées may include beef, fish, lamb or pork. Breakfasts here are also memorable. Don't miss the fruit rollups, an inn tradition. Dinner by reservation only. ~ Route 138, Steamboat; 541-498-2230. DELUXE.

For Mexican food, hamburgers, sandwiches and homemade soups, try **Munchies**. This full-service restaurant also serves fresh-baked pie. ~ 20142 Route 138, Glide; 541-496-3112. BUDGET.

HIDDEN ►

An Early American setting makes the carpeted **Prospect Historical Hotel and Motel Restaurant** a comfortable dining spot. From the combination seafood plate to the pasta and chicken dishes, this establishment will challenge any dieter's willpower. The ambience is elegant. ~ 391 Mill Creek Drive, Prospect; 541-560-3664. MODERATE.

✔ **CHECK THESE OUT—UNIQUE DINING**

- *Budget:* Roll into the **Wheel Cafe** alongside folks in diesel rigs and station wagons for classic American diner specialties. *page 402*
- *Budget to moderate:* Savor made-from-scratch pizza amid antique farm equipment at the board-and-batten **Papandrea's**. *page 390*
- *Moderate:* Whup yer appetite into shape before unhitching at McKenzie Bridge's **Log Cabin Inn**, originally built as a stagecoach stop. *page 391*
- *Deluxe:* Begin a frosty morning with delicious apple oat cakes at the classy **Cascade Dining Room** in the Timberline Lodge. *page 381*

Budget: under $8 Moderate: $8–$16 Deluxe: $16–$24 Ultra-deluxe: over $24

With its beautiful setting overlooking Klamath Lake, rustic **Rocky Point Resort** is best known for its steaks and seafood. Reservations are suggested. Open from Labor Day to Memorial Day, on weekends only. ~ 28121 Rocky Point Road, Klamath Falls; 541-356-2287. MODERATE.

When an Oregon restaurant boasts of its "San Francisco Bay Area atmosphere," you know you're in for a real dining experience. **Alice's Saddle Rock Café and Pub** is as unpretentious as the town it calls home. But the interior is a fine example of adaptive reuse with handsome brick walls and modern art. Go for the rotisserie meats, homemade soups, sandwiches and pastas. ~ 1012 Main Street, Klamath Falls; 541-883-3970. BUDGET.

SHOPPING

An excellent collection of limited-edition prints, American Indian and Western art, American Indian jewelry and arrowheads is found at the **Favell Museum Gift Shop**. Exhibited in an attractive, two-story shop, this store features many one-of-a-kind pieces, as well as a multitude of "made in Oregon" products like jams, syrups and candies. ~ 125 West Main Street, Klamath Falls; 541-882-9996.

For knives, cutlery, beads and beading supplies, American Indian earrings, buckskins and leather goods, visit **Oregon Trail Outfitters**. This board-and-batten building is extremely popular with visitors searching for a piece of the Old West. The owners frequently help stage historic rendezvous. Participants clad in traditional buckskin costumes demonstrate muzzle loading, knife and tomahawk throwing, fire-starting with flint steel and cannon shoots. Closed Sunday. ~ 5728 South 6th Street, Klamath Falls; 541-883-1369.

NIGHTLIFE

Ross Ragland Theater hosts touring theater companies, country-and-western bands, jazz and blues and classical performers. The year-round calendar also includes special children's shows and, in the summer, locally produced musicals. ~ 218 North 7th Street, Klamath Falls; 541-884-5483.

The Linkville Playhouse offers a variety plays and musicals throughout the year. The local productions feature classics ranging from *The Crucible* to *Blithe Spirit*. The company is known for its comedies. ~ 201 Main Street, Klamath Falls; 541-884-6782.

PARKS

UMPQUA NATIONAL FOREST 🚶 🚲 🎣 ⛺ 🛶 ⛵ 🚤
Named for the Umpqua Indians, this forest spans almost a million acres and embraces three wilderness areas, numerous secluded waterfalls and high-country trails. Within the Umpqua are volcanic ridges, pine benches, alpine forests and meadows laced by snow-fed streams. Among the Umpqua landmarks are the world's tallest sugar pine, bedrock gorges and volcanic-rock

arches. Major destinations include the scenic Umpqua River Canyon and Diamond, Lemolo and Toketee lakes. Most lakes allow swimming; only Lemolo Lake allows waterskiing. The forest is also convenient to Crater Lake. Canoeing and rafting are popular on the North Umpqua River. Mt. Bailey near Diamond Lake has downhill skiing, while the areas around Diamond and Lemolo lakes offer good cross-country trails. Hundreds of miles of streams and numerous lakes make this a great spot for angling, especially in the North Umpqua River. There are picnic tables, history programs, pack stations and restrooms. ~ You can access the forest by Routes 138, 227, 1, 62 and 230; 541-672-6601.

▲ There are 46 sites in the forest; $15 per night; RV sites without hookups are available. The Diamond Lake area is probably the most developed for camping, with three campgrounds around the lakeshore. Even better for those who want to be away from drive-in sites is the Twin Lakes campground (43 miles east of Glide), a walk-in (or bike-in) campground two and a half miles from Route 138. You'll be camping in a primitive site under the stars amidst cold, clear high mountain lakes.

HIDDEN ► **MILL POND PARK** 🔄 With half a mile of frontage on Rock Creek, this serene campground is a beautiful getaway on the edge of the Umpqua National Forest near Idleyld Park. It has a picturesque swimming hole and towering, moss-covered trees, and is the small Oregon park at its finest. Closed October through late May. You'll find picnic areas, a playground, a softball field and restrooms; groceries and restaurants are in Idleyld Park. ~ From the town of Idleyld Park take Route 138 east to Route 78 (Rock Creek Road) and head north six miles; 541-440-4930.

▲ There are 12 tent/RV sites (no hookups); $8 per night.

CRATER LAKE NATIONAL PARK 🏃 🚲 🛶 ⤵ One of the unique geologic features of the Pacific Northwest, Crater Lake is irresistible. The 183,224-acre park offers hundreds of miles of hiking and cross-country skiing trails, a fascinating boat tour of this volcanic lake and opportunities for biking, fishing and backpacking. For anglers there's nothing to get excited about though there are rainbow, kokanee and brook trout off Wizard Island. There are picnic areas, restaurants, motel units and museums. ~ On Route 62, 54 miles northwest of Klamath Falls; 541-594-2211.

▲ There are 200 sites at Mazama Campground; $13 to $14 per night with hookups. There are 16 tent sites at Lost Creek; $11 per night, no hookups. Backcountry camping by permit. Closed in winter.

WINEMA NATIONAL FOREST 🏃 🏕 🚤 ⤵ Between Crater Lake National Park and Upper Klamath Lake, this national forest is famous for its fishing and waterfowl habitat. Although the forest elevation ranges from roughly 4100 to 9200 feet, much of the eastern portion of this semiarid region is high-plateau country. The Winema is forested with pine and fir and has several roadless places including the Mountain Lakes Wilderness Area. More than 200 bird species have been identified on this Pacific Flyway. In addition, elk, deer, bear, coyote, bobcat, beaver, otters and many other species live here. Forty lakes and rivers like the Sycan, Sprague and Williamson offer good opportunities to catch trout and mullet. Rock hounds can be happy here. Picnic tables and restrooms are facilities here. ~ Routes 97, 138, 62 and 140 all provide easy access; 541-883-6715.

▲ Camping is permitted anywhere in the forest and there are 11 developed campgrounds with tent/RV sites costing $8 to $11 per night.

JACKSON F. KIMBALL STATE PARK ◢ This 19-acre Oregon   ◀ HIDDEN
state park is a scenic, forested spot on the headwaters of the Wood River. It's ideal for those seeking a quiet getaway. There's good flyfishing for rainbow and brown trout. There is a picnic area; restaurants and groceries are in Fort Klamath. ~ On Route 232, three miles north of Fort Klamath; 541-783-2471.

▲ There are seven primitive sites; $10 per night.

COLLIER MEMORIAL STATE PARK ◢ Set in a ponderosa-pine forest at the junction of Spring Creek and Williamson River, this 655-acre park is a perfect place to spend the day or the night. The park is also a logging heritage site, filled with important mementos and lumberjack equipment. There's good trout fishing in the streams. You'll find picnic tables, restrooms, playground and a museum; gas, restaurant and groceries are located five miles south in Chiloquin. ~ Located 35 miles north of Klammath Falls on Route 97; 541-783-2471.

▲ There are 18 tent sites and 50 sites with full hookups; $14 to $17 per night.

JOSEPH STEWART STATE PARK ⚐ ⚓ ⚑ ⚓ ◢ A lush lawn leads down to Lost Creek Lake, making this park on the road to Crater Lake particularly inviting on a warm day. With 910 acres, there's room to spare for day and overnight use. Take a seat on a blanket beneath one of the pine groves and watch the waterskiers slalom their way to happiness. Or toss in a line and wait for the big ones to nibble. With more than a mile of waterfront, this Rogue River Canyon park is a great place to take the kids. There's excellent fishing for bass, rainbow, brook or brown trout. Facilities include a picnic area, restrooms and a marina. ~ Located 35 miles north of Medford on Route 62; 541-560-3334.

▲ There are 50 sites with partial hookups and 151 sites with full hookups; $14 to $15 per night.

▼▼▼▼▼▼▼▼▼▼▼▼▼▼

Outdoor Adventures

FISHING

The Oregon Cascades are famous for rivers and lakes brimming with trout, salmon, bass and steelhead. Now that more and more people are trying to fish these waters, "We've got a shrinking resource," as one guide says; that's why you'll find him and others encouraging a catch-and-release policy for all fish caught. The point is that you can still wade out into the Deschutes to flyfish for wild trout or pull steelhead out of the Umpqua from aboard a drift boat and have the kind of experience immortalized in the fiction of Zane Grey.

NORTHERN CASCADES Whether you're an experienced fisher or a beginner, **Wy'East Expeditions** can arrange a day-long Deschutes River flyfishing trip for fall steelhead or, in the spring, wild rainbow trout. Overnight trips let you get out into areas that are a bit more remote. ~ 6700 Cooper Spur Road, Mt. Hood; 541-352-6457.

So far, the national forest service has not issued permits to any guides or outfitters to take you fishing to mountain lakes in this part of the Cascades. You may, however, fish the lakes on your own. If you need gear, contact **Gorge Fly Shop** in Hood River. Besides renting gear and obtaining information, you can set up a guided trip on the Deschutes River, the John Day River, and other prime fishing spots in the area. ~ 201 Oak Street; 541-386-6977. In Maupin, **Michael McLucas** has been a fishing guide for 25 years. He'll take you out on the Deschutes for trout or steelhead fishing trips. ~ Oasis Resort; 541-395-2611.

CENTRAL CASCADES Although there's no commercial use permitted on the Metolius River (that is, no guided trips), it's a very popular flyfishing spot. **Fly Fisher's Place** can rent or sell you gear or arrange a guided trip on the McKenzie, the Deschutes or, near Pineville, on the Crooked River, where you can catch wild trout. ~ 151 Main Street, Sisters; 541-549-3474. **High Desert Drifters, Guides, & Outfitters** specializes in flyfishing float trips for trout and steelhead on the Deschutes for either one day or several days. ~ Bend; 541-389-0607, 800-685-3474. **Sunriver Fly Shop**, also a fly shop and guide service, offers fishing classes if you want to learn more. Some of its popular trips are to the Davis, Hosmer and Crane Prairie lakes, where you will catch a variety of trout between April and November. ~ 1 Venture Lane, Sunriver; 541-593-8814.

SOUTHERN CASCADES Bill Conner of **North River Guide Service** primarily fishes the Umpqua, specializing in drift boat trips for two people. ~ Glide; 541-496-0309. In Klamath Falls, call **Siens Guide Service** for trips on the Williamson and Wood rivers as well as Klamath Lake and Agency Lake, the latter of which is popular for large rainbow trout. ~ Klamath Falls; 541-883-2642, fax 541-883-1418.

The increasing popularity of whitewater rafting in the Northwest means that a river like the Deschutes, where access is less restricted than on the North Umpqua and other rivers, can get pretty crowded with individual and guide-led groups of rafters. That, of course, is especially the case in the summer. Still, the fun and excitement of a day of whitewater rafting is hard to beat, even with a crowd. Guided full-day trips usually include a riverside lunch stop along the way.

RIVER RUNNING

CENTRAL CASCADES From May through October, **Jim's Oregon Whitewater** leads full- and half-day rafting and kayaking trips on the McKenzie River and full-day trips on the Deschutes and North Umpqua, which has several Class IV rapids and has limited access for guide-led groups. ~ 56324 McKenzie Highway, McKenzie Bridge; 541-822-6003, 800-254-5467. For a 17-mile run through Class III and IV rapids on the Deschutes, **Rapid River Rafters** puts in at Maupin, about 89 miles north. Other whitewater trips include the McKenzie River (Class III) and the calmer Santiam River. ~ Bend; 541-382-1514, 800-962-3327. **Sun Country Tours and Cascade River Adventures** rafts only on the Class IV rapids of the Deschutes, specializing in half-day, full-day and overnight expeditions. ~ Bend, 541-382-6277; and Sunriver Village Mall, Sunriver; 541-593-5710.

In the Cascades, where resort courses comprise most of the golf options, forested mountain sides, emerald meadows, rivers coursing through fairways, elk lingering on the perimeters and wild geese flying overhead add a unique dimension to the experience.

GOLF

NORTHERN CASCADES **Resort at the Mountain** has three nine-hole courses open to the public. The mountain setting makes all three scenic; the first nine is the longest, but fair and forgiving; the third nine, Fox Glove, is fairly narrow and the most challenging. ~ 68010 East Fairway Avenue, Welches; 503-622-3101. Located on an American Indian reservation, the championship 18-hole **Kah-Nee-Ta Golf Course** is a fairly flat course, set in a valley. This location is often sunny, so the course is open year round. ~ Off Route 26, Warm Springs; 541-553-1112.

CENTRAL CASCADES The resort of **Black Butte Ranch** has two 18-hole courses: Big Meadow (flat and open) and Glaze Meadow (hilly and narrow). The courses are open mid-March through late October. ~ Route 20, eight miles west of Sisters; 800-399-2322 for tee times, 541-595-1500 for pro shop. At the semiprivate **Widgi Creek Golf Club**, an 18-hole championship course meanders beneath huge pine trees along the rim of the Deschutes River canyon. Open April through October. ~ Century Drive, five miles west of Bend; 541-382-4449. Probably the most famous course in the Cascades and certainly one of the most picturesque in the Northwest, **Tokatee Golf Club** is set majestically in the McKenzie

River Valley. "It's a walk with nature," says the pro. Tokatee, which is considered among the nation's top public courses, is open February through November. Walk-ins are welcome during the week. ~ 54947 McKenzie Highway, Blue River; 541-822-3220.

SOUTHERN CASCADES The 18-hole public **Harbor Links Golf Course** isn't near a harbor, but it is near a lake. It's a short course, fairly flat and narrow, and has lots of water. This course is set in a more developed region. ~ Harbor Isles Boulevard, Klamath Falls; 541-882-0663.

TENNIS

Many resorts in the Cascades have tennis courts available to guests; the public is permitted access sometimes as well.

CENTRAL CASCADES The **Bend Metro Park and Recreation District** maintains a number of courts in the city. None of them are nightlighted, but they're free and available on a first-come, first-serve basis (access to the courts at schools, however, may be restricted due to school-related activities). There are four courts at **Juniper Park** (Franklin Avenue and Northwest 8th Street); two courts at **Summit Park** (Three Sisters Drive at Fairwell Drive, on the north side of Aubrey Butte); two courts at **Sylvan Park** (Summit and Promontory drives); and four each courts at **Bend High School** (230 Northeast 6th Street), **Mountain View High School** (2755 Northeast 27th Street) and **Central Oregon Community College** (2600 Northwest College Way). ~ Call 541-389-7275 for more information.

SOUTHERN CASCADES In Klamath Falls, three courts are available at **Moore Park**. ~ Lakeshore Drive; 541-883-5391. You can also play one of the four lighted courts at **Hilyard Park**. ~ Hilyard Avenue and Crest Street; 541-882-3193. If you time it right you may get on one of the two lighted courts at **Wiard Park**. ~ Wiard Street at Hilyard Avenue; 541-882-3193.

SKIING

Skiing in July? It's possible in Oregon's endless winter. With one of the longest ski seasons in the West, the Cascades offer a ton of alpine and Nordic opportunities.

NORTHERN CASCADES In the Northern Cascades, the best-known resorts are found on the slopes of Mt. Hood. They include the venerable **Timberline Lodge and Ski Area,** with six chairlifts serving open-bowl and tree-lined runs. Three lifts operate at night. From May to September, the resort offers a summer season at the 8500-foot level. ~ Timberline; 503-272-3311.

Another resort serving the same area is **Mt. Hood Skibowl,** with nearly 100 trails, one-third lit for night skiing. ~ 503-272-3206. **Mt. Hood Meadows** offers ten chairlifts serving 82 trails, rated 15 percent beginner, 50 percent intermediate and 35 percent expert. This resort offers runs for the physically challenged in conjunction with area organizations. ~ 503-337-2222, 800-754-4663.

CENTRAL CASCADES On Route 20's Santiam Pass west of Sisters, **Hoodoo Ski Bowl** is a good bet for families looking for alpine or Nordic skiing. ~ 541-882-3799. **Mt. Bachelor** west of Bend is Oregon's largest ski area, offering dry powder and a season extending to July. Eleven chairs serve 3686 skiable acres, and there are 56 kilometers of groomed Nordic trails. ~ 800-829-2442.

SOUTHERN CASCADES **Crater Lake National Park** has extensive Nordic trails with views of the blue water beneath the snowcapped rim. ~ 541-594-2511. Diamond Lake Resort also has Nordic trails, as well as snowcat skiing on **Mt. Bailey**. The latter, limited to just a dozen people per day, transports skiers uphill to enjoy 3000 feet of deep-powder terrain. ~ 541-793-3333.

RIDING STABLES

NORTHERN CASCADES From March to the end of November, guided hourlong rides wind through the hills of scenic red-rock country at **Kah-Nee-Ta** resort. ~ Warm Springs; 541-553-1112.

CENTRAL CASCADES In the Sisters area, guided half-hour to all-day trail rides and overnight pack trips into the Cascades are operated by Equine Management, Inc., which operates stables at **Black Butte Ranch**. ~ Route 20, eight miles west of Sisters; 541-595-2061, 800-743-3035. **River Ridge Stables** takes up to eight riders into the forest and then back up the Deschutes River for an hour or more. ~ Inn of the Seventh Mountain, 18575 Century Drive, Bend; 541-389-9458.

BIKING

From easy town rides to mountain biking on rugged backcountry trails, the Oregon Cascades offer thousands of miles of scenic cycling.

NORTHERN CASCADES Mountain-bike trails in the Zigzag Ranger District invite cyclists with scenic views of the Mt. Hood region. Among the best is the 12-mile **Still Creek Road**. This rarely

✔ **CHECK THESE OUT—UNIQUE OUTDOOR ADVENTURES**

- Revisit the classic flyfishing waters immortalized by Zane Grey on the Umpqua River. *page 406*
- Enjoy alpine and Nordic skiing at Oregon's largest ski area, Mt. Bachelor, where the season often extends as late as July. *page 409*
- Explore one of the Northwest's largest Indian reservations, Kah-Nee-Ta, on a guided horseback ride. *page 409*
- Blaze a trail up 11,235-foot Mt. Hood, Oregon's tallest mountain. *page 411*

traveled route connects Trillium Lake with the town of Rhodo-dendron. The ten-mile **Sherap Burn Road/Veda Lake** trail leads up to outstanding viewpoints.

CENTRAL CASCADES   In the Bend area, take **West Newport Avenue** for a six-mile trip to Shevlin Park or follow **O. B. Riley Road** five miles to Tumalo State Park. Another possibility is to take the road south 23 miles from Route 97 to **Newberry Volcano**.

At Black Butte Ranch, 16 miles of bike paths include the **Lodge Loop** (5 miles), the scenic **Glaze Meadow Loop** (4 miles) and the **Aspen Loop** (1.6 miles).

Near Sisters, **Suttle Lake**, with its "upsy-daisy" loop of about ten miles, is a pleasant outing of moderate exertion for most people.

A popular **Cascades Loop** trail begins in Bend, heads west on Century Drive to Mt. Bachelor and then continues on Cascades Lakes Highway to Route 58. Allow several days to enjoy these demanding 74 miles.

SOUTHERN CASCADES   One of the most popular biking trails in the Southern Cascades is the 11.5-mile **Diamond Lake Bike Path**. This level route is ideal for the whole family. The route takes cyclists from Thielsen View Campground to Silent Creek. Complete the loop on the highway returning to Thielsen View. A two-mile section of this route is wheelchair accessible.

The ultimate biking experience at Crater Lake is **Rim Drive**, offering the complete 33-mile overview of this volcanic landmark. Another excellent possibility is **Grayback Trail**, a scenic, unpaved route ideal for mountain bikes. In Klamath Falls, **Nevada Avenue** and **Lakeshore Drive** provide convenient bike-touring access to Upper Klamath Lake. This route continues west to Route 140 along the lake's west shore. **Kit Carson Way** also has a separated bike path.

Bike Rentals   In Sisters, **Eurosports** rents mountain bikes as well as children's bikes. The shop also has bike route maps and suggestions for rides in the area. ~ 182 East Hood Avenue, Sisters; 541-549-2471. For mountain-bike rentals in Bend, as well as advice about where to ride (and directions on how to get there), visit **Skjersaa's**. ~ 130 Southwest Century Drive, Bend; 541-382-2154. The **Chrome Pony** in Sunriver can rent you a bike, give you directions to the 30 miles of paved trails crisscrossing the resort or point you in the right direction to other mountain trails. ~ 1 West Mall, Sunriver; 541-593-2728.

In the Bend area, **Paulina Plunge**, as it's known, is a six-mile downhill mountain-bike tour that descends 3000 feet on groomed trails, with stops along the way at several waterfalls in the Newberry Crater region. **High Cascade Descent** operates this activity, taking up to 15 people, late March through late October. ~ Bend; 541-389-0562.

With hundreds of miles of trails, including many in wilderness areas, the Oregon Cascades are ideal for relaxed rambles or ambitious journeys. All are best tackled in the warmer seasons and not recommended to try in the winter months. All distances listed for hiking trails are one way unless otherwise noted.

HIKING

NORTHERN CASCADES   Zigzag Trail (1 mile) takes you across the Hood River's east fork via a drawbridge (closed in winter). You'll continue up the canyon to Dog River Trail, which leads to a viewpoint overlooking Mt. Hood and the Upper Hood River Valley.

Tamanawas Falls Loop (5.5 miles) leads along the north bank of Mt. Hood National Forest's Cold Spring Creek. After hiking to scenic Tamanawas Falls, you'll return to the trailhead via Elk Meadows Trail.

Also in Mt. Hood National Forest is Castle Canyon Trail (2 miles) climbing out of the Rhododendron area to rocky pinnacles. Views of the scenic Zigzag Valley are your reward.

Another relatively easy possibility is Bonney Meadow Trail, reached by taking Route 35 to Bennett Pass and then following Routes 3550 and 4891 to Bonney Meadows Campground. Take trail #473 east along the ridge (3.5 miles) to enjoy the views of Boulder and Little Boulder lakes. Return to the campground by turning right on trail #472.

CENTRAL CASCADES   Located 33.4 miles west of Sisters off Route 20 is the Black Butte Trail (2 miles), a steep route to the top of a volcanic cone.

About one mile farther west on Route 20 is Blue Lake, where Crater Rim Trail (2.5 miles) offers an easy ramble around this scenic landmark.

In the Detroit Lake area, you might want to try Tumble Ridge Trail (5.3 miles), which begins on Route 22. This demanding trek heads up through second-growth forest, past Dome and Needle rocks to Tumble Lake.

Built along the Little North Santiam River, the Little North Santiam Trail (4.2 miles) crosses eight tributaries with stringer bridges. Fishing and swimming holes are easily reached from this trail leading through some old-growth forests.   ◀ *HIDDEN*

Return east on Route 20 and turn south on Route 126. Continue for eight miles to Robinson Lake Road and go east 4.4 miles to Robinson Lake Trail (.3 mile). It's an easy family hike leading to a pleasant hideaway.   ◀ *HIDDEN*

In the McKenzie Bridge area, the Olallie Trail (9.7 miles) is an all-day hike offering memorable views of the Three Sisters, Mt. Washington, Mt. Jefferson and Bachelor Butte. Take this trail in the summer and fall. The trailhead is three miles from Horse Creek Road.

For an easier hike off McKenzie Pass Highway (Route 242), take the **Lava River Trail** (.5 mile). This interpretive trail beginning near the Dee Wright Observatory leads through lava flows. Signs add to your understanding of this moonscape's volcanic past. Wheelchair accessible.

Crater Lake National Park rangers lead free snowshoe ecology walks on Saturday and Sunday (they will provide the snowshoes).

To the south, the Willamette National Forest's Oakridge Ranger District offers many fine hikes including **Fisher Creek Trail** (6.5 miles). A great way to see a primitive-forest region, you'll get a closeup view of old-growth trees. The silence is deafening. The **Waldo Lake Trail** (21.8 miles) is a challenging route around this incredibly pure lake.

The **Lava River Cave Trail** (.9 mile) is an easy, rather chilly trail through the state's largest lava tube. It's south of Bend off Route 97, one mile south of Lava Lands Visitors Center, which is an excellent place to stop for some information on the area. Lanterns are available (seasonally) close to the parking lot.

Fourteen miles south of Bend off Route 97, **Lava Cast Forest Nature Trail** (.9 mile) takes you through one of the Pacific Northwest's weirdest landscape. You'll see tree molds created when molten lava destroyed a forest thousands of years ago.

SOUTHERN CASCADES Off Route 62, the road from Medford to Crater Lake, the **Upper Rogue River Trail** (6.5 miles) is an easy ramble. Begin at the Prospect Ranger Station and make your way through sugar pines, pausing along the way to cool off in the stream.

Toketee Lake Trail (.4 mile) runs parallel to this spot. Short spurs lead to the waterfront where you'll find otter, beaver and ducks complementing the scenery.

The **North Umpqua Trail** (77 miles) offers a wide variety of hiking opportunities. Skirting both the Boulder Creek and Mt. Thielsen wilderness areas, most of this route is easy to moderate. Spur trails lead to waterfalls, fishing spots and campgrounds. Among the North Umpqua's most popular segments are **Panther Trail** (5 miles), beginning at Steamboat, and **Lemolo Trail** (6.3 miles), starting at Lemolo Lake.

Mt. Bailey Trail (5 miles) is a steep route west of Diamond Lake. Your reward for climbing 3000 feet is a panoramic view of Diamond Lake, Mt. Thielsen and the Southern Cascades.

Running 2570 miles from Canada to Mexico, the **Pacific Crest Scenic Trail** is western America's back door to the wilderness, the kind of place John Muir lived for. Scenic, uncrowded, larger than life, it's worth a special trip. You can pick up a 30-mile segment at the North Crater Trailhead, a mile east of the Crater Lake National Park Trailhead on Route 138. Hike as much of this section as you care to. You can exit via the Tipsoo, Howlock Mountain, North Umpqua or Mt. Thielsen trails.

CRATER LAKE NATIONAL PARK Watchman Peak Trail (.7 mile) is a steep route up Watchman Peak. From the top you'll have a great view of Wizard Island.

It's ironic that most visitors to Crater Lake never actually reach the shore. Doing so requires a steep descent on **Cleetwood Cove Trail** (1 mile). This is the route that leads to boat tours of Wizard Island. Bring water and good shoes.

For a good workout, try the **Mount Scott Trail** (2.5 miles). Along the way you'll spot many small animals and birds. The gnarled whitebark pines make a good photographic backdrop. On top you'll have a 360-degree view of the park.

To see the national park's impressive pinnacles, take **Godfrey Glen Trail** (1 mile). This route leads through a hemlock and red-fir forest to Sand Creek Canyon.   ◄ *HIDDEN*

Located east of Crater Lake Lodge, **Garfield Peak Trail** (1.7 miles) is a fairly steep route offering views of the lake. Look for eagles and hawks along the way.

A short walk in the park is **Castle Crest Wildflower Trail** (.4 mile). This easy loop is the best way to sample Oregon wildflowers in mid-summer. An eden-like setting with small streams trickling down the hillside, the trail is one of Oregon's best-kept secrets.   ◄ *HIDDEN*

Sevenmile Trail/Pacific Crest Trail (15 miles) west of Fort Klamath off Route 3334 West leads through the Sky Lakes Wilderness south of Crater Lake National Park. Sevenmile Trail hooks up with the Pacific Crest Trail for a 2.5-mile stretch and then cuts off to Seven Lakes Basin. You can also follow the Pacific Crest Trail to Devil's Pass and the steep ascent of Devil's Peak.

▼▼▼▼▼▼▼▼▼▼

Transportation

The Oregon Cascades are a 50-to-100-mile-wide band extending almost the entire length of the state. They begin on the eastern edge of the Willamette Valley and Ashland-Rogue River area and extend to the high-desert region of central Oregon.

CAR

Route 26 travels east from Portland to the Mt. Hood area. You can also reach Mt. Hood by taking **Route 35** south from the Hood River area.

From Salem, take **Route 22** east to the Detroit Lakes and Santiam Pass area. **Route 20** east of Albany leads to the same destination, while **Route 126** is Eugene's mainline east to the McKenzie Bridge and McKenzie Pass area. **Route 58** southeast of Eugene is convenient to the Deschutes National Forest, and **Route 138** takes you from Roseburg to the Umpqua River Canyon.

From Medford, take **Route 62** northeast to Crater Lake. An alternate route to Crater Lake is **Route 97** north of Klamath Falls. This same highway also provides access to the Bend area and the Central Cascades. If you're coming from the east, Routes 20 and 26 are the most convenient ways to reach the mountains.

AIR

Redmond Airport, 16 miles north of Bend, is served by Horizon Airlines, Reno Air and United Express. **Klamath Falls Airport** is served by Horizon Airlines and United Express. The **Portland International Airport**, **Eugene Airport** and **Medford Airport** are also convenient to the Cascades.

Redmond Airport Shuttle provides service from the Redmond Airport to Bend and Cascades destinations like Sunriver, Mt. Bachelor, Sisters and Black Butte Ranch. ~ 541-382-1687.

Luxury Accommodations offers limousine van service from the Portland airport to popular Northern Cascades recreation areas. ~ 503-668-7433.

BUS

Greyhound Bus Lines (800-231-2222) offers service to depots at Klamath Falls and Bend, as well as stops at Chemult and Government Camp. ~ Klamath Falls: 1200 Klamath Avenue; 541-882-4616. Bend: 2045 East Route 20; 541-382-2151. Government Camp: 503-272-3325.

TRAIN

Amtrak's "Coast Starlight" is a scenic and comfortable way to reach the Cascades. It serves stations in Klamath Falls, Chemult, Eugene, Salem, Albany and Portland, all convenient starting points for the mountain resorts. ~ 800-872-7245.

CAR RENTALS

Arriving passengers at the Redmond Airport are served by **Budget Rent A Car** (800-527-0700), **Hertz Rent A Car** (800-654-3131) and **National Interrent** (800-328-4567).

Car-rental agencies at the Klamath Falls Airport are **Avis Rent A Car** (800-331-1212), **Budget Rent A Car** (800-527-0700) and **Hertz Rent A Car** (800-654-3131).

In Bend, you can rent from **Budget Rent A Car** (800-527-0700), **Cheap Wheels Car Rental** (541-389-8893), **Hertz Rent A Car** (800-654-3131) and **All Star Car Rental** (541-385-7711).

PUBLIC TRANSIT

Lane Transit District (541-687-5555) serves McKenzie Bridge. **Basin Transit Service** (541-883-2877) operates in the Klamath Falls area.

TAXIS

For taxi service, contact **City Cabs** (541-548-0919) in Redmond. In Klamath Falls, call **A B Cab** (541-885-5607).

TEN

The Heart of Oregon

Drivers in a hurry barrel down Oregon's 280-mile Route 5 corridor in about five hours. Incredibly, that's the way many people see the region that lies at the end of the fabled Oregon Trail. Tempted by free land or the prospect of finding gold, the pioneers risked everything to get here. Today a new generation, rushing to reach Crater Lake, Mt. Hood or the Oregon Coast, speeds through, never knowing what they've missed.

That's progress. Fortunately, all it takes is a trip down a Route 5 offramp to get hooked on the Heart of Oregon, the 60-mile-wide region that extends from Salem to the California border. With the freeway left behind in the rearview mirror, you may understand why residents say God spent six days creating the Earth and on the seventh He went to Oregon.

Framed by the Klamath and Coast ranges on the west and the Cascades on the east, this is the place to find peaceful covered bridges and exciting rafting runs, the nation's oldest Shakespeare festival and a legislature that has made Oregon America's most environmentally conscious state. Home to two major universities, the center of Oregon agriculture and some of its most historic towns, the Heart of Oregon is where you'll find many of the state's best-known writers, poets, artists and artisans.

Just an hour from the state's famous mountain and seaside resorts, the Willamette Valley and the Ashland–Rogue River areas are the primary destinations in the Heart of Oregon. Fields of wildflowers, small towns with falsefront stores and gabled homes, businesses with names like "Wild and Scenic Trailer Park," pies made with fresh-picked marionberries—this is the Oregon found in the postcard rack. Soda fountains with mirrored backbars, jazz preservation societies, old river ferries, museums built out of railroad cars, music festivals and folk-art shrines—you'll find them all and even more here.

In many ways this area's heritage, touted by writers ranging from Washington Irving to Zane Grey, sums up the evolution of the West: American Indians followed by British fur traders, American explorers, missionaries, pioneer settlers, gold miners and the merchants who served them. The 19th-century nouveau riche tapped the hardwood forests to create Victorian mansions. As the mines were played out, lumber and agriculture became king. Strategically located on the main stage and rail lines to California and Washington, this corridor also became the principal gateway to most of Oregon's cities, as well as its emerging mountain retreats and coastal beaches.

But the Heart of Oregon story also has a special dimension, one told at local museums and historic sites. The fatal impact of American expansion on the American Indian culture began with the arrival of missionaries, who preached Christianity but left behind diseases that decimated their converts. In 1843 the promise of free land triggered a stampede as "Oregon or bust" pioneers sped west. Many became farmers who prospered in the California trade after gold was discovered in 1848 at Sutter's Mill. Three years later, after gold was found closer to home near Jacksonville, many settlers put down their plows and made a beeline for the mines. A new boom brought instant prosperity to this sleepy town as millions in gold dust poured through banks on California Street and miners dazzled their brides with mansions shipped in piecemeal from Tennessee.

Not sharing in this windfall were American Indians pushed from their ancestral lands by the settlers and miners. The Indians fought back in the Rogue River Wars between 1851 and 1856. But they were ultimately forced onto reservations, easing the path to statehood in 1859. Settled by Methodist missionaries in 1840, Salem was one of several towns that emerged as a regional supply center. Others included Eugene and Corvallis.

As the railroad improved access, businessmen discovered there was more to sell in Oregon than gold, lumber, dairy products and bountiful crops. Visitors began to explore the fishing streams, caves and forests. Chautauqua tents brought intellectuals and entertainers to Ashland, as Jacksonville offered a different kind of nightlife that gave preachers something to denounce on their pulpits. When Zane Grey showed up to fish the Rogue and the Umpqua rivers, the entire country read about it in his articles. As the good word spread, more visitors began arriving to raft these and other rivers, to see the waterfalls and photograph the vernacular architecture.

Although it was a long way from Middle America, tourists loved the Main Street look and unspoiled countryside of the Heart of Oregon. Culturally it became a hub for social experiments and alternative lifestyles, happily exported by local celebrities like Ken Kesey, who took his famous traffic-stopping bus on a national tour with the "Merry Pranksters" in the 1960s.

Although the Heart of Oregon can be overcast and wet during the winter months, summers tend to be sunny and hot, particularly in the Ashland–Rogue River area. While Route 5 is the mainline, Route 99 is a pleasant alternative. Because the Willamette Valley is flat, it's ideal terrain for cyclists. South of Eugene, the Klamath mountains frame picturesque valleys and towns such as Medford, Ashland and Jacksonville. At the bottom of the state the Siskiyous form the backdrop to the California border.

Because this is the state's primary transportation corridor, it's convenient to scores of popular attractions. Since you're only an hour from the beach or the

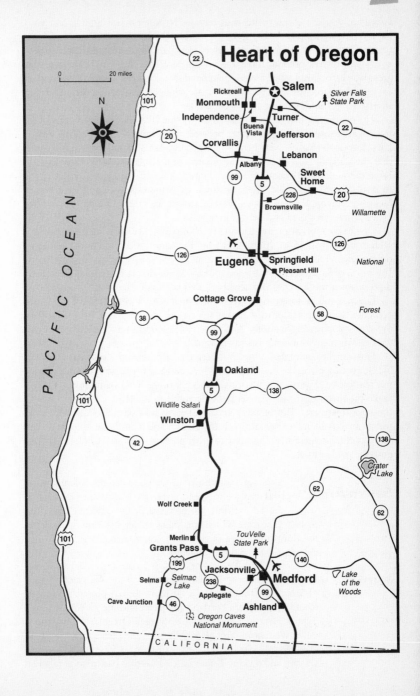

Heart of Oregon

0 _____ 20 miles

N

PACIFIC OCEAN

22

101

Rickreall
Monmouth
Independence
Buena Vista
Corvallis
Albany
99
5
20

Salem
Silver Falls State Park
Turner
Jefferson
Lebanon
Sweet Home
228
Brownsville
22
20

Willamette

126
Eugene   Springfield
Pleasant Hill

126

National

Cottage Grove
58

Forest

38
99

Oakland
5
138

Wildlife Safari
Winston

42

138

Crater Lake

Wolf Creek
62

62

Merlin
Grants Pass
5
199
Selma   Selmac Lake
Jacksonville
238
Applegate
Cave Junction   46
Oregon Caves National Monument

TouVelle State Park

140
Medford
99
Ashland

Lake of the Woods

CALIFORNIA

Cascades, you can easily spend your days waterskiing or spelunking and your nights enjoying *King Lear*. Blessed with some of the state's finest resorts and restaurants, the Heart of Oregon also offers plenty of birdwatching thanks to several wildlife preserves found along the Willamette River. Here you're likely to spot great blue herons, red-tailed hawks, quails and woodpeckers. Deer, fox, opossums, coyotes and raccoons abound in the valley, while elk, bobcats, bear and flying squirrels are found in the southern mountains.

The region's highlands are pocketed by pristine lakes, hundreds of miles of remote hiking trails and resort lodges paneled in knotty pine. There's even downhill skiing on the highest peak here, 7533-foot Mt. Ashland. But there's little doubt that the signature attractions between Salem and Ashland are the river valleys. From the Willamette wetlands to the swimming holes of Applegate River, it's hard to beat the streamside life. Rushing down from the Cascades, roaring through Hellgate Canyon, flowing through restaurants at the Oregon Caves, these tributaries define every area and delight every visitor.

One of the most attractive features is the proximity to the wilderness. You are seldom more than 15 or 20 minutes from the countryside, and even the bigger towns, such as Eugene and Salem, have major greenbelts within the city limits. Just north of Salem is Oregon's wine country. While the state capitol is the biggest draw, many historic homes and neighborhoods add to the charm of the central city.

Eugene's college-town status gives it the amenities you would expect in a larger community. Its central location makes the city an ideal base for visiting most of the state's popular destinations. And the city's Ecotopian fervor shows what can happen when environmentalists take control.

Jacksonville, a city that boomed during the rollicking gold rush days, is a delightful period piece, the kind of town where bed and breakfasts outnumber motels ten to one. The tree-lined streets, red-brick office blocks and dusty old bars make the town a favorite. Artists flock here and to Ashland, an Oregon mecca for the dramatic arts. Thoroughly gentrified, heavily booked and loaded with great restaurants, Ashland is the state's last temptation and a hard one to leave on the route south. No mere stepping stone to other parts of the state, the Heart of Oregon is an end in itself.

▼▼▼▼▼▼▼▼▼▼▼
Salem Area

Although best known as Oregon's capital, Salem is a desirable place to spend a day for many other reasons. A short drive from Oregon's wine country, Salem is also close to several historic Willamette Valley ferries. Near the Willamette, the downtown area is rich with restored buildings, museums, churches and a pioneer cemetery.

SIGHTS   Most travelers from Portland drive down the Willamette Valley to Salem via Route 5. But a far more scenic approach is to exit Route 5 in southern Portland and pick up **Route 99 West** through Tigard. Here you can continue through Oregon's wine country on 99 West, head through McMinnville and then cut east to Salem at Rickreall. Even better, turn off Route 99 West at the town of Dayton and pick up **Route 221**, a beautiful backroad paralleling the Willamette River. Near Hopewell it's fun to cross the river on the Wheatland Ferry.

In Salem, you'll find **Mission Mill Museum**, a historic restoration that turns back the clock to Oregon's pioneer days. Built in the 19th century is the Thomas Kay Woolen Mill, a factory-turned-museum. Adjacent are the Jason Lee House, the oldest residence standing in the Pacific Northwest, and the John Boon House, where you'll learn what family life was like in the mid-19th century. The 1841 Methodist Parsonage is open for tours. Enjoy a picnic here by the millstream. The **Salem Convention and Visitors Association** (503-581-4325) has an office in the complex. Fee for guided tours. ~ 1313 Mill Street Southeast, Salem; 503-585-7012.

Two blocks south in Bush's Pasture Park is the **Deepwood Estate**. With its stained-glass windows, oak woodwork and solarium, this Queen Anne is a monument to turn-of-the-century craftsmanship. Of special interest are the formal gardens. A nature trail leads through the adjacent wildlife area. Admission. ~ 1116 Mission Street Southeast, Salem; 503-363-1825.

Court-Chemeketa Residential Historic District showcases 117 historic Queen Anne, Italianate, gothic, Craftsman and saltbox homes. On this mile-long walk you'll see many of the fine homes built by the city's founders. ~ Court and Chemeketa streets, Salem; 503-581-4325.

The **Oregon State Capitol** is a four-story Greek-style structure boasting half a dozen bronze sculptures over the entrances. Built from Vermont marble, the state building is crowned by the 23-foot-high gilded statue *The Oregon Pioneer*. The tower and rotunda have recently reopened after repairs were made to fix damage caused by the March 1993 earthquake (the quake measured 5.5 on the Richter scale). Tours up the 121 stairs of the tower run every half-hour. Surrounding Wilson Park has a pretty fountain and gazebo. ~ Court Street, Salem; 503-986-1387.

◆◆◆

✔ CHECK THESE OUT—UNIQUE SIGHTS

- Nip your blues in the bud with a bloomin' good visit to **Schreiner's Iris Garden** during the May to June flowering. *page 420*
- Exit Route 5 and take one of the rural side roads leading to historic **covered bridges**. *page 431*
- Burrow your way through the Northwest's grandest spelunking adventure at the **Oregon Caves National Monument**. *page 433*
- Discover how they orchestrate stage magic at the Oregon Shakespeare Festival's **Backstage Tour and Exhibit Center**. *page 435*

Across from the capitol, **Willamette University** is the state's oldest institution of higher learning (founded in 1842). On this shady campus you'll want to see the exhibit on the history of the school (which in many ways mirrors the history of Salem) at venerable **Waller Hall**. Cone Chapel (also in Waller Hall) is the place of worship for this onetime Methodist school. The campus is also home to an unusual formation of five giant sequoias known as the **Star Trees**; if you stand in the middle of them and look upwards, you'll see the shape of a star. The trees are near the **Sesquicentennial Rose Garden**, a blooming place for a walk across State Street from the capitol. ~ Willamette University: 900 State Street, Salem; 503-370-6300.

NORTH OF SALEM The byways and secondary highways of the Willamette Valley north of Salem offer great possibilities for a day of sightseeing. Many of Oregon's best wineries are along Route 99 West—a rural and scenic alternative to Route 5.

In the spring, don't miss **Schreiner's Iris Garden** five miles north of Salem. Although there are over 250 acres here, only ten of them are open to the public, and that is only during the May-to-June blooming season. Still, a visit to this photographer's dream is a must during those months; the rest of the year, the gardens are closed while Schreiner's ships irises all over the world through its catalog business. ~ 3625 Quinaby Road Northeast, Salem; 503-393-3232.

HIDDEN ►

Mt. Angel Abbey is a century-old Benedictine monastic community 18 miles northeast of Salem. On tours, arranged by advance appointment, you'll visit the Romanesque church and retreat houses. A small, newly remodeled museum focuses on the Russian Old Believer community, while another building emphasizes the ancient history of the region. The beautiful library, designed by Alvar Aalto, features a display of rare handprinted books. Near the top of a 300-foot butte is the grotto of Our Lady of Lourdes. In July, the retreat hosts the Abbey Bach Festival. ~ 1 Abbey Drive, St. Benedict; 503-845-3030.

Wineries are one of the true delights of the Salem area. Many are found along Route 99 West in the Willamette Valley north and west of the city. All the establishments mentioned below offer tours; call ahead to confirm visiting hours.

Rex Hill Vineyards is a beautifully landscaped 25-acre winery with an inviting terraced picnic area. Furnished with antiques, the tasting room has a warm fireplace. Try the pinot noir or the chardonnay. ~ 30835 North Route 99 West, Newberg; 503-538-0666.

One of Oregon's older vineyards, **Erath Winery** is set high above the Willamette Valley in the lovely Dundee Hills. You can sample the winery's pinot noir, cabernet sauvignon and white riesling in a rustic, wood-paneled tasting room. ~ Worden Hill Road, Dundee; 503-538-3318, 800-539-9463.

A relatively new player receiving high marks on the Oregon wine scene is **Argyle**. Located at a onetime hazelnut processing plant, this winery makes excellent sparkling wines and a variety of still wine. The inviting tasting room is in a restored Victorian farmhouse. ~ 691 Route 99 West, Dundee; 503-538-8520.

Among the most scenic vineyards in Oregon is **Sokol Blosser Winery**. Here you'll enjoy great views of the Willamette Valley, along with a pleasant picnic area and contemporary tasting room. The tasting room stocks a full range of Oregon products such as smoked salmon, fruit preserves, gourmet mustards, salad dressings and candies. Ask for a brochure outlining a self-guided walking tour. ~ 5000 Sokol Blosser Lane, Dundee; 503-864-2282.

McMinnville's **Yamhill Valley Vineyards** is on a 300-acre estate in the Coast range foothills. Specializing in pinot noir and pinot gris wines, Yamhill has an elegant tasting room set in an oak grove. The cathedral ceiling, stained-glass windows and balcony overlooking the vineyard add to the charm. ~ 16250 Southwest Oldsville Road, McMinnville; 503-843-3100.

SOUTH OF SALEM Heading south from Salem, you may want to skip Route 5 altogether. A fun loop drive, beginning in Albany (about 25 miles south of Salem), leads through Corvallis, home to one of Oregon's biggest universities, as well as through some accommodating rural towns and sights.

Take the kids to **Enchanted Forest**, located in a park setting seven miles south of Salem on Route 5. The dream of creator Roger Tofte, this family fun spot has fairytale attractions like a crooked house, Seven Dwarfs' cottage, an Alice in Wonderland rabbit hole, old-lady's-shoe slide, haunted house and the Big Timber log ride. Plays are performed in an outdoor theater. Closed October through mid-March, and weekdays in September. Admission. ~ 8462 Enchanted Way Southeast, Turner; 503-363-3060.

Heading southeast from Salem on Route 51, continue past the town of Independence and follow the signs seven miles south to the historic **Buena Vista Ferry**, which carries a handful of cars and cyclists across the Willamette in the time-honored manner. No trip to Oregon is complete without a ride on one of these old-timers. Closed Monday and Tuesday. ~ 503-588-7979.

Proceed south to Albany, where you can begin a circular drive of the area north of Eugene. South of Albany, Route 34 leads east to the town of Lebanon. Continue east to Sweet Home and one of the Northwest's better pioneer museums. In a 19th-century woodframe church, the **East Linn Museum** collection is big on logging equipment, antique dolls, quilts, butter churns, linotypes and saddles. There's also a full blacksmith shop here. Closed Monday from May through August, and Monday through Wednesday from September through April. ~ 746 Long Street, Sweet Home; 541-367-4580.

The **Sweet Home Chamber of Commerce** provides information on this Cascades gateway. ~ 1575 Main Street, Sweet Home; 541-367-6186.

Green Peter Reservoir offers the kind of views you'd expect to find in Switzerland.

Perched in the foothills ten miles east of the town of Sweet Home are **Foster Reservoir** and the adjacent **Green Peter Reservoir** on Quartzville Road.

Brownsville, west of Sweet Home on Route 228, is one of the valley's most charming small towns. The **Linn County Historical Museum,** in the Oregon and California Railroad depot, is flanked by boxcars and a caboose. American Indian, natural history, manufacturing and agricultural exhibits are on display. ~ 101 Park Avenue, east of Main Street, Brownsville; 541-466-3390.

You can pick up a walking-tour brochure at the museum that guides you to other local museums, including the century-old **Moyer House.** Built from lumber milled in John Moyer's own sash and door factory, this Italianate home features 12-foot ceilings. Landscapes are painted on the walls and window transoms. ~ 204 Main Street at Kirk Avenue, Brownsville.

HIDDEN ►

Howard Taylor and his wife, Faye, devoted 20 years to the creation of the folk-art capital of central Oregon, the **Living Rock Studios.** Howard created this memorial to his pioneer ancestors with 800 tons of rock. The circular stone building is inlaid with pioneer wagon-wheel rims, an American Indian mortar and pestle, fool's gold, obsidian and coffee jars filled with crystals. A series of illuminated biblical pictures are displayed downstairs, while a circular staircase leads upstairs to a display of Taylor's carvings. Closed Sunday and Monday. Admission. ~ Highway 228, West Brownsville; 541-466-5814.

A popular Oregon college town located on the west side of the valley at the edge of the coast range, **Corvallis** is also the seat of Benton County. A prominent landmark here is the **Benton County Courthouse.** The building, dating to 1887 and still in use, has an impressive clock tower. Guided tours are available. Closed weekends. ~ 120 Northwest 4th Street, Corvallis; 541-757-6831.

On the 500-acre **Oregon State University** campus in Corvallis, you'll find the OSU art department's **Fairbanks Gallery** in Fairbanks Hall (541-737-4745) and **Giustina Gallery** at 26th and Western streets (541-737-2402), two small gallery spaces that usually feature rotating exhibits, often by the university's students. ~ OSU: Campus Way, Corvallis; 541-737-0123.

For information on other local attractions, contact the **Corvallis Convention and Visitors Bureau.** ~ 420 Northwest 2nd Street, Corvallis; 541-757-1544.

East of Corvallis on Route 20 is **Albany,** where you'll find nearly 500 Victorian homes. One of the best is the **Monteith**

House, which is a frame residence with period 19th-century furnishings. Dressed in Victorian costumes, docents lead intriguing tours. ~ 518 Southwest 2nd Avenue, Albany. At the **Albany Regional Museum** are an old-time general store, barber shop and doctor's office. ~ Located at 3rd and Ferry streets, Albany.

To arrange tours of either location contact the **Albany Visitors Association**, where you can pick up a helpful walking-tour map. ~ 300 Southwest 2nd Avenue, Albany; 541-928-0911.

LODGING

State House Bed and Breakfast, a refurbished 1920s Craftsman on Mill Creek, has four rooms appointed with brass fixtures and quilts. Enjoy breakfast, featuring homemade sausage, bacon and eggs, on the newly added porch or in the garden. You can feed the ducks and geese in the pond, relax in the spray of the waterfall or grab a tube and float down the creek. ~ 2146 State Street, Salem; 503-588-1340, 800-800-6712, fax 503-585-8812. MODERATE.

Convenient to Route 5, the **Best Western Mill Creek Inn** has 109 units including junior suites with microwaves, refrigerators and wet bars. The large rooms have contemporary furniture and ample closet space. ~ 3125 Ryan Drive Southeast, Salem; 503-585-3332, 800-346-9659, fax 503-375-9618. MODERATE.

Econolodge offers lodging just 50 yards from the Willamette River. Clean, air-conditioned rooms are furnished in modern decor. The price is right for this motel convenient to downtown. ~ 345 Northwest 2nd Street, Corvallis; 541-752-9601. BUDGET.

The **Sweet Home Inn** has clean, newly redecorated rooms with white and pink brick walls and contemporary furniture. A small pond and garden are located on the premises, which is a block away from the museums and shops of this gateway to some of the valley's best boating and fishing. ~ 805 Long Street, Sweet Home; 541-367-5137, 800-367-8859. BUDGET.

DINING

The ambience and setting are deluxe at the **Inn at Orchard Heights**. Prime rib, fresh salmon, stuffed shrimp, pasta and chicken sautéed with seasonal fruits are a few of the entrées on the extensive menu. Indian artifacts, wallhangings, plants and pottery decorate the elegant, pine-paneled dining room. On warm days, ask for patio seating. Dinner only. Closed Sunday. ~ 695 Orchard Heights Road Northwest, Salem; 503-378-1780. MODERATE TO DELUXE.

There's no MSG at **Kwan's**, a Chinese establishment with seating for 400 at comfortable booths and large tables ideal for the whole family. Specialties like imperial fried rice and garlic chicken have won a loyal following. Entering this pagoda-style building, you'll find a 15-foot-tall redwood Buddha in the lobby. ~ 835 Commercial Street, Salem; 503-362-7711. MODERATE.

Just when you're about ready to give up on McMinnville as another franchise landscape, the chain stores of Route 99 give way to the town's well-preserved downtown. Tucked away in a storefront is **Nick's Italian Café**, where the kitchen prepares memorable dishes such as smoked salmon and homemade lasagna with pesto, mushrooms and Oregon filberts. Don't despair if you can't get a reservation because there's nearly always seating available at the counter. Dinner only. Closed Monday. ~ 521 East 3rd Street, McMinnville; 503-434-4471. DELUXE TO ULTRA-DELUXE.

Michael's Landing offers rock shrimp fettuccine, red snapper, a seafood salad and Monte Cristo sandwiches in the restored Southern Pacific Station. One of the city's most popular restaurants, it has a great view of the Willamette. ~ 603 Northwest 2nd Street, Corvallis; 541-754-6141. MODERATE TO DELUXE.

For steaks, lamb chops, prime rib, scallops or oysters, try **The Gables**. Portions are generous, and there's an extensive wine cellar. Dinner only. ~ 1121 Northwest 9th Street, Corvallis; 541-752-3364. MODERATE TO ULTRA-DELUXE.

HIDDEN ▶ Located in a strip shopping center, **Amador's Alley** is one of the most popular Mexican restaurants in the area. Huge portions of *huevos con chorizo*, chile colorado and enchiladas rancheros are served up steaming. Diners are seated at plastic tables and chairs. Arrive early or be prepared to wait. ~ 870 North Main Street, Independence; 503-838-0170. BUDGET.

Take one of the window booths at **The Point Restaurant and Lounge** and enjoy a perfect waterfront view. Fresh fish, steak, prawns, lobster and generous salads are a few of the specialties. A fresh-baked loaf of bread comes with every meal. ~ 6305 Route 20, Sweet Home; 541-367-9900. BUDGET TO MODERATE.

SHOPPING **Mission Mill Village**'s warehouse complex has a half-dozen shops, including the **Salem Audubon Society** (503-585-5689), which has birdfeeders and books on birds. Also here is **Temptations** (503-585-8773), where you'll be able to purchase Mary Engelbreit cards, gifts and collectibles, Raggedy Ann handcrafted dolls, Boyd bears, miniatures and a wide variety of children's books. ~ 1313 Mill Street Southeast, Salem.

An excellent place for regional arts and crafts—pottery, sculpture, paintings, prints and jewelry, for example—is the **Bush Barn Art Center**. ~ 600 Mission Street Southeast, Salem; 503-581-2228.

NIGHTLIFE The **Oregon Symphony Association** offers classical concerts, as well as a pops series. ~ 707 13th Street Southeast, Salem; 503-364-0149.

Pentacle Theater is a well-established community theater with several plays each season. ~ 324 52nd Avenue Northwest, Salem; 503-364-7121.

For belly dancing, big band music, folk, reggae, rock or blue-grass, check out **Boon's Treasury**. This circa-1860 two-story brick building has a small dancefloor. Artworks by local artists are frequently exhibited. Cover on weekends. ~ 888 Liberty Street Northeast, Salem; 503-399-9062.

For live rhythm-and-blues, try **Lenora's Ghost**. Cover. ~ 114 Main Street, Independence; 503-838-2937.

BUSH'S PASTURE PARK   The Bush Collection of old garden roses is one of the highlights in this 89-acre park south of the capital. They were originally collected from pioneer homesteads to represent roses brought west on the Oregon Trail. Also here are natural wildflower gardens and the **Bush Conservatory**, the West's second-oldest greenhouse. Facilities include a picnic area, restrooms and tours of the house and gardens; restaurants and groceries are nearby. ~ 600 Mission Street, entry off High Street, Salem; 503-588-2410.

PARKS

WILLAMETTE MISSION STATE PARK   et in orchards and hop fields south of Wheatland's landing, this 1686-acre Willamette River park is the site of an 1830s Methodist Mission. A monument commemorates these early settlers. In the midst of the park are the historic Wheatland Ferry landings. This shady spot is a delightful retreat on a warm day. Try for trout in the river. There are picnic tables, kitchen shelter areas, restrooms, and bike and equestrian trails; groceries and restaurants are nearby. Parking fee, $3. ~ On Wheatland Road, 12 miles north of Salem; 503-393-1172.

SILVER FALLS STATE PARK   If you're addicted to waterfalls, look no further. Located in twin lava-rock gorges created by Silver Creek's north and south forks, the 8700-acre park has ten waterfalls. Also here are bike and equestrian trails leading through an old-growth fir forest with towering maples and quaking aspen ideal for fall-color buffs. South Falls, a seven-mile roundtrip hike from the highway, has the biggest drop, 178 feet, or 25 feet more than Niagara Falls. You'll find picnic tables, restrooms, rustic group lodging, a nature lodge, a jogging trail and a horse camp. Parking fee, $3. ~ Located 25 miles east of Salem on Highway 214; 503-873-8681.

▲ There are 51 developed tent sites and 53 RV sites with hookups; $16 to $20 per night.

McDOWELL CREEK FALLS PARK   This forested glen is a perfect refuge. An easy hike across the creek and up through a fir forest takes you to a pair of scenic falls. On a weekday you may have this park to yourself. There are picnic tables and restrooms; restaurants and groceries are in Lebanon. ~ Located 12 miles southeast of Lebanon via Berlin Road and McDowell Creek Drive; 541-967-3917.

◄ *HIDDEN*

LEWIS CREEK PARK 🏃 🏊 🎣 🚣 🛥 ⚓ On the north shore of Foster Lake, Lewis Creek Park is a good spot to swim and enjoy other water sports. Troll for bass and trout in the lake. This day-use park includes 20 acres of open space and 20 acres of brush and forest, as well as plenty of fine views of the Cascades. Picnic tables and a boat dock are the facilities here; restaurants and groceries are in Sweet Home. Parking fee, $2. ~ Four miles northeast of Sweet Home. Take Route 20 east to Foster Dam and turn left at Quartzville Road. At North River Road turn left to the park; 541-967-3917.

CASCADIA STATE PARK 🏃 🏊 🎣 ⚓ On the South Santiam River Canyon, this 253-acre park has a beautiful one-mile trail leading to a waterfall. Pump your own soda water from a spring. Largely forested with Douglas fir, the park also has an open meadow on the north river bank. You can fish for trout in the river. Facilities include restrooms and picnic tables. ~ Located on Route 20, 14 miles east of Sweet Home; 541-367-6021.

⛺ There are 26 primitive sites; $9 per night; closed in winter.

HIDDEN ► **WHITCOMB CREEK COUNTY PARK** 🏃 With its stunning rainforest terrain on the shores of ten-mile-long Green Peter Reservoir, this 328-acre park in the foothills east of Sweet Home is a winner. It offers spectacular views of the Cascades and good trout fishing. The park is forested with fir and deciduous trees. You'll find picnic tables and pit-toilet restrooms; restaurants and groceries are in Sweet Home. ~ From Sweet Home take Route 20 east to Foster Dam and turn left at Quartzville Road. Continue north 15 miles to the park; 541-967-3917.

⛺ There are 38 tent/RV sites (no hookups); $9 per night.

▼▼▼▼▼▼▼▼▼▼
Eugene Area

College towns are often inviting and Eugene is no exception. Climb one of the town buttes and you'll find the city surrounded by rich farmland and beckoning lakes and streams. With the Cascades and the McKenzie River Valley to the east and the Coast Mountains to the west, Eugene has an ideal location. The city, used for the filming of the movie *Animal House*, offers sidewalk cafés, malled streets and upscale shops.

SIGHTS
Pick up touring ideas at the **Convention and Visitors' Association of Lane County Oregon**. ~ 115 West 8th Avenue, Suite 190, Eugene; 541-484-5307.

Stop by the **University of Oregon's** (541-346-3111) 250-acre campus. You'll find an arboretum with over 2000 varieties of trees; weekday tours for prospective students are offered from Oregon Hall at 13th and Agate streets (541-346-3091).

Among the campus highlights is the **Museum of Natural History**. This collection is a good way to orient yourself to the state's geology and anthropology. Permanent exhibits cover Oregon's fossil history and archaeology. Closed Monday and Tuesday. ~ 1680 East 15th Avenue, Eugene; 541-346-3024.

Also recommended is the **Museum of Art**. The colonnaded sculpture court with pool adjacent to the entrance is one of the campus's architectural highlights. The collection, one of the best in the state, displays Northwest art and photography, as well as Asian and other international artworks. Closed Monday and Tuesday. ~ Just east of 14th and Kincaid streets, Eugene; 541-346-3027.

Eugene is at its best in the fall when maples, black walnuts, chestnuts and cottonwood brighten the landscape.

Eugene is big on adaptive reuse of commercial buildings like the **5th Street Public Market**, home to dozens of shops, two restaurants, fourteen food stands and a courtyard that's a popular venue for local musicians, artists and acrobats. ~ 296 East 5th Avenue, Eugene; 541-484-0383.

The prime attraction in the neighboring town of Springfield is the **Springfield Museum**, which has a section detailing the history of this timber-industry town (the first mill opened in 1853) and a gallery with changing exhibits of artwork, antique collections and Americana. ~ 590 Main Street, Springfield; 541-726-2300.

No trip to the Eugene area is complete without an excursion into the nearby countryside. You can head east on **Route 126** along the McKenzie River or southeast on **Route 58** to Lookout Point Reservoir, Oakridge and Salt Creek Falls. **Route 5** takes you south to Cottage Grove. Government Road leads east past Dorena Reservoir and several covered bridges to the historic **Bohemia Mining District**. This mountainous region was the scene of a mid-19th-century gold rush that proved to be a bust. Today, tourists roam the district by car and four-wheel-drive vehicles to see lost mines, ghost towns like Bohemia City and covered bridges.

Before setting out for this national forest area be sure to check with the Cottage Grove Ranger Station (541-942-5591). Because there are active mining claims in the area, it is important not to trespass. The **Cottage Grove Historical Museum** has a major exhibit on the Bohemia District, as well as displays on the *Titanic* and a covered bridge. ~ Birch and H avenues, Cottage Grove; 541-942-3963.

The **Willamette Valley Scenic Loop** is a 195-mile adventure. It begins and ends in Cottage Grove, looping through Corvallis, Salem and Albany. This backroad journey includes historical sites, museums, covered bridges, ferries, parks, gardens and wineries. A detailed brochure is available at the **Convention and Visitors' Association of Lane County Oregon**. ~ 115 West 8th Avenue, Suite 190, Eugene; 541-484-5307.

The **Roseburg Visitors and Convention Bureau** offers a handy city tour guide. ~ 410 Southeast Spruce Street, Roseburg; 541-672-

9731. Highlights include the **Roseburg Historic District** in the Mill Street/Pine Street neighborhood. You'll find many modest cottages built in the late 19th century. The **Floed-Lane House** is a Classic Revival featuring a full-length, two-tier veranda with half a dozen square columns supporting each level. It's open for tours on Sunday. ~ 544 Southeast Douglas Street, Roseburg.

The **Douglas County Museum of History and Natural History** features American Indian and pioneer artifacts, and a 19th-century railroad depot. Admission. ~ Douglas County Fairgrounds, 123 Museum Drive, Roseburg; 541-440-4507.

Wildlife Safari is Oregon's drive-through adventure, a 600-acre park where over 550 animals and birds roam freely. Visitors motor past Bactrian camels, hippopotamuses, lions, and scores of other species. In addition to the self-paced driving tour, the Safari Village has a petting zoo and newborn nursery. Elephant rides are also available. Admission. ~ Safari Road, Winston; 541-679-6761.

LODGING   **Valley River Inn** enjoys an enviable view of the Willamette River. Adjacent to the 140-store Valley River Center, this 257-room hotel features Indian quilts hanging over the big lobby fireplace that faces a conversation pit. Large rooms, decorated with wicker furniture and impressionist prints, open onto small patios. Bicycling and jogging paths are adjacent to the inn, which rents bikes and has its own workout room. ~ 1000 Valley River Way, Eugene; 541-687-0123, 800-543-8266, fax 541-683-5121. DELUXE TO ULTRA-DELUXE.

The 66-unit **Best Western Greentree Inn** offers attractive, contemporary rooms with sitting areas and balconies, some with a creek view. Most units have refrigerators. Adjacent to the University of Oregon campus, this establishment has a pool, jacuzzi, exercise center, restaurant and sports bar. Continental breakfast is included. ~ 1759 Franklin Boulevard, Eugene; 541-485-2727. BUDGET TO MODERATE.

✔ CHECK THESE OUT—UNIQUE LODGING

- *Budget:* Unpack your bags at **Sweet Home Inn** before heading out on the town. *page 423*
- *Moderate:* Reserve a room at **Wolf Creek Tavern**, a beautifully restored 1850s stage stop where Jack London once stayed. *page 435*
- *Deluxe:* Dive into the **Oregon Caves Lodge**, a spelunker's getaway surrounded by waterfalls. *page 436*
- *Ultra-deluxe:* Gaze up at the stars from your private deck at the Victorian **Fox House Inn**. *page 437*

Budget: under $50 Moderate: $50–$90 Deluxe: $90–$130 Ultra-deluxe: over $130

Overlooking Eugene, **The Campbell House** offers peaceful and elegant accommodations within walking distance to both city center and outdoor pursuits. The 17 rooms are individually decorated, though all have a Victorian flavor. You'll also find a comfortable parlor and library. ~ 252 Pearl Street, Eugene; 541-343-1119, 800-264-2519, fax 541-343-2258. MODERATE TO DELUXE.

A 1900-vintage farmhouse has been transformed into the **Tuscany Inn** on the outskirts of Eugene, set amid fields, gardens and orchards. Much of the farm's produce winds up in the breakfasts offered to guests—raspberry syrup on whole-wheat pancakes, for instance. The four rooms share bathroom facilities; beds are comfortable, furnishings rustic. The cost is remarkably reasonable. ~ 33461 Bloomberg Road, Eugene; 541-747-4586. BUDGET TO MODERATE.

◄ HIDDEN

Located in the historic town of Oakland, the Classic Revival **Beckley House Bed and Breakfast** is furnished with oak furniture and early 1900s antiques. The bright decor and comfortable sun porch make this a cheerful spot, even on a gray Oregon day. ~ 338 Southeast 2nd Street, Oakland; 541-459-9320. MODERATE.

◄ HIDDEN

The emphasis at **Sweetwaters** is on Oregon cuisine featuring locally grown veal, lamb, lettuce, herbs, mushrooms and fruits. Seafood entrées include grilled fresh Chinook salmon, Dungeness crab chowder and fresh swordfish. This contemporary dining room overlooking the Willamette River is complemented by a deck ideal for drinks before or after dinner. ~ Valley River Inn, 1000 Valley River Way, Eugene; 541-341-3462. DELUXE.

DINING

Ambrosia prepares Italian specialties in a red-brick building distinguished by leaded glass, a mirrored oak and mahogany backbar, Tiffany-style lamps and a tintype ceiling. You'll find pizza and calzone made with a plum tomato sauce, pasta and entrées like grilled fresh lamb and fresh seafood. There are 325 vintages on the wine list, including 25 ports. Outdoor dining is available. ~ 174 East Broadway, Eugene; 541-342-4141. MODERATE.

For pasta dishes, fresh salmon, lamb, steaks and generous salads, the **Excelsior Café** is a good choice. Located in a Victorian near the university, this pleasing restaurant also has an excellent Oregon wine list and a generous brunch on Sunday. Ask for a table in the greenhouse. ~ 754 East 13th Street, Eugene; 541-342-6963. MODERATE.

Café Zenon, an elegant, yuppified establishment with slate floor, marble tables, white tile and outdoor seating, has an eclectic menu featuring items such as oysters Bienvielle, fettuccine rustica and Tuscan roast rabbit. There's an extensive wine list. ~ 898 Pearl Street, Eugene; 541-343-3005. MODERATE TO DELUXE.

Mekala's Thai Cuisine is on the second floor of the 5th Street Public Market. They serve authentic Thai recipes and boast nearly

100 items, including traditional curries, noodle dishes, stir frys, soups and seafood. There is seasonal outdoor seating. ~ 296 East 5th Street, Eugene; 541-342-4872. BUDGET TO MODERATE.

Live jazz and blues is performed on weekend nights at the **Oregon Electric Station Restaurant and Lounge**, a historic building magnificently reborn as a clublike dining and entertainment venue with oak paneling, high-backed tapestry chairs and antique train cars serving as dining areas. Fresh grilled seafood and prime rib highlight the menu. ~ 27 East 5th Avenue, Eugene; 541-485-4444. DELUXE.

HIDDEN ► **Tolly's Soda Fountain** is one of the most inviting lunch counters in Oregon. Located in a brick building, Tolly's is an architectural landmark with a mirrored backbar, varnished fir counters and stools, brass footrests and Tiffany lamps. Enjoy a soda, milkshake or banana split. Also available are breakfast hash and eggs, as well as Reuben sandwiches, croissants, a Cobb salad, lasagna and fresh strawberry pie. The budget-priced breakfasts and lunches are bargains; dinner brings a higher price tag. ~ 115 South Locust Street, Oakland; 541-459-3796. MODERATE TO DELUXE.

SHOPPING Eugene's **Saturday Market** is an open-air marketplace held weekly from April through November, with over 150 vendors selling everything from handcrafted furniture to quilts to floral arrangements. There is an also an international food court and live music. ~ 8th and Oak streets, Eugene; 541-686-8885.

The **5th Street Public Market** has an impressive collection of shops and galleries. Among the best is **Twift** (541-342-8686). ~ 296 East 5th Street, Eugene; 541-484-0383.

Dozens of other arts-and-crafts galleries are found in the Eugene area. **Opus 5 Gallery of Crafts** offers paintings, ceramics, handblown glass, metal works and jewelry by several noted Northwest artists. ~ 136 East Broadway, Eugene; 541-484-1710. **Criterion Gallery** focuses on wildlife, Western outdoors and maritime art. ~ 35 West 8th Avenue, Eugene; 541-683-8474. **Ruby Chasm** sells necklaces, books, ceramics and tribal art. ~ 152 West 5th Street, Eugene; 541-344-4074.

If you're searching for shells, American Indian art or books on Northwest natural history, head for the **University of Oregon Museum Store**. ~ 1680 East 15th Avenue, Eugene; 541-346-3024.

One of the most comprehensive women's bookstores in the Northwest is **Mother Kali's Books**. ~ 2001 Franklin Boulevard, Eugene; 541-343-4864.

NIGHTLIFE The **Hult Center for the Performing Arts** is the home of the summer Oregon Bach Festival, Eugene's symphony, opera and ballet, as well as visiting artists from around the world. Performances

Bridging the Past

Oregon takes pride in the fact that it has more covered bridges (53) than any other state west of the Mississippi. Most of these wooden spans are found in the Willamette Valley, although a handful are scattered along the coast, in the Cascades, the Ashland–Rogue River area and around Bend. Although some have been retired from active duty and now serve only pedestrians and cyclists, all these bridges are worth a special trip.

Originally the idea of covering a bridge was to protect its plank deck and trusses from the elements. But aesthetics eventually proved as important as engineering, and Oregon's beautiful hooded spans became one of the state's signature attractions.

Highly recommended is the Calapooia River's **Crawfordsville Bridge** (Route 228) east of Brownsville. Clustered around the nearby agricultural communities of Crabtree and Scio are many other "kissing bridges" such as **Shimanek**, **Larwood**, **Gilkey** and **Hannah**.

To the south, Lane County is home to 18 covered bridges, all listed on the National Register of Historic Places. The Lowell area, on Route 58 southeast of Eugene, has four of these spans, including the **Lowell Bridge**, which crosses a river later flooded to create a lake. Other bridges are at **Pengra**, **Unity** and **Parvin**. A highlight in the Cottage Grove area is **Chamber's Bridge**, the only "roofed" railroad bridge on the West Coast. In the same region, south of Dorena Reservoir, is **Dorena Bridge**. Other covered bridges in the same area are found at **Mosby Creek**, **Currin**, **Stewart** and **Chambers**.

Douglas County has a number of fine spans. One is **Mott Bridge**, 22 miles east of Glide. Constructed in the '30s, this on-deck wood-truss arch bridge may be the only bridge of this type in the country. The **Rochester Bridge** (County Road 10A) west of Sutherlin also has some history behind it. After county highway workers burned down a bridge in the late 1950s, residents feared the beloved Rochester Bridge nearby was destined for the same fate. Armed with shotguns, they kept an all-night vigil and saved the span.

Take the time to visit **Weddle Bridge** in Sweet Home. In 1987, after 43 years of service, it was damaged but, thanks to strong protests, the county wisely decided to take the bridge apart piece by piece and put it in storage. Donations and promotions raised $190,000 to reassemble the bridge, originally built in 1937 for $8500.

Great guides to these spans are *Roofs Over Rivers* (Oregon Sentinel Publishing) by Bill & Nick Cockrell and *Oregon Covered Bridges: An Oregon Documentary In Pictures* (Pacific Northwest Book Company) by Bert & Margie Webber. Or contact the **Covered Bridge Society of Oregon** (503-399-0436).

take place in Silva Hall or the smaller Soreng Theater. ~ Between 6th and 7th avenues and Willamette and Olive streets, Eugene; 541-682-5000.

Three theater companies make their home in Eugene. The **University Theater** stages full-scale productions in the Robinson Theater and smaller plays in the Arena Theater. ~ Villard Hall; 541-346-4191. The **Very Little Theater** is considered one of the best community theaters in the Eugene area. ~ 2350 Hilyard Street; 541-344-7751. The **Actors Cabaret/Mainstage Theater** presents Broadway and off-Broadway comedies and musicals. ~ 996 Willamette Street; 541-683-4368.

The **Traditional Jazz Society of Oregon** is dedicated to preserving the American jazz tradition. ~ P.O. Box 7432, Eugene, OR 97401; 541-746-1097.

Allann Brothers Coffee House hosts an array of live performances including zydeco, blues, reggae, salsa, jazz, folk and classical trios. ~ 152 West 5th Street, Eugene; 541-342-3378.

One of Eugene's premier brewpubs is **Steelhead Brewery & Café**, which has a handsome brick interior filled with large palms and ficus trees, marble tables and a mahogany bar. The pub offers satellite sports stations, beers from the adjoining microbrewery and a casual menu featuring calamari, Buffalo wings and other items. ~ 199 East 5th Avenue; 541-686-2739.

For jazz, try **Jo Federigo's Café & Jazz Bar**. An intimate cellar setting with hanging plants, fans and modern art provides the background for some of the region's finest musicians. Cover on Sunday. ~ 259 East 5th Avenue, Eugene; 541-343-8488.

The Valley River Inn's **Sweetwaters** presents live entertainment in a fireplace lounge setting. On warm nights the strains of rhythm-and-blues, rock and standards drift out to the big deck overlooking the Willamette. ~ 1000 Valley River Way, Eugene; 541-341-3462.

PARKS

BROWNSVILLE PIONEER PARK 🏃 ⛵ ⛵ ⌐ The forested, ten-acre city park along the banks of the Calapooia River is a short walk from the center of a historic Willamette Valley community. Big playfields, shady glens and a spacious picnic area will add to your enjoyment. Facilities include picnic tables and restrooms; restaurants and groceries are in downtown Brownsville. ~ Take Route 5 north from Eugene 22 miles to Route 228 and continue east four miles. An alternative scenic loop heads north from Springfield via Mohawk, Marcola and Crawfordsville; 541-466-5666.

▲ Permitted, though there are no formal sites; $4 to $7 per night.

HENDRICKS PARK AND RHODODENDRON GARDEN A glorious springtime spot when over 3000 rhododendrons brighten the landscape. The 81-acre park is shaded by Oregon white oaks and maples. There are picnic tables, restrooms, trails and Sunday tours during bloom season. ~ Located at the east end of Summit Avenue, Eugene; 541-687-5333.

▼▼▼▼▼▼▼▼▼▼

Ashland–Rogue River Area

If your vision of a good vacation is rafting by day and Shakespeare by night, look no further. With the Klamath-Siskiyou mountains providing a rugged backdrop, this section of southern Oregon supports an array of fun activities: river rafting, downhill skiing, and, yes, the West Coast's best Shakespeare festival. Home of the largest concentration of bed and breakfasts in Oregon, Ashland is also your gateway to backcountry famous for its hidden gems.

The wild and scenic Rogue River is one of Oregon's signature attractions. It is also convenient to wilderness areas, mountain lakes, thundering waterfalls, marble caves and popular resort communities.

SIGHTS

A good place to orient yourself is the **Grants Pass Visitors and Convention Bureau**. ~ 1995 Northwest Vine Street at 6th Street; 541-476-5510. **Wildlife Images** is a fascinating animal rehabilitation center. Each year more than 150 injured animals are nursed back to health by veterinary staff and volunteers. Among the creatures you can see being treated are owls, eagles, weasels, black bears and cougars. Highly recommended. Tours by appointment. ~ 11845 Lower River Road, Grants Pass; 541-476-0222.

◄HIDDEN

Pottsville Powerland has a vintage collection of tractors, farm and logging equipment, antique cars and fire trucks. It's five miles north of Grants Pass. ~ Pleasant Valley Road west of Monument Drive, Pleasant Valley; 541-479-2981.

Although it's far from the core of Oregon's wine country, **Bridgeview Vineyards** is attracting a loyal following. Situated on 74 acres in the Illinois Valley, this European-style winery offers tastings. Try the gewürztraminer, chardonnay or riesling. ~ 4210 Holland Loop Road, Cave Junction; 541-592-4688.

◄HIDDEN

The **Oregon Caves National Monument** is the Pacific Northwest's grandest spelunking adventure. Fifty miles southwest of Grants Pass, it's reached by taking Route 199 to Cave Junction and then continuing east on Route 46. Guided tours are led through the cave, which has over three miles of damp and dripping passageways lined with stalagmites, flowstone, translucent draperies and cave coral. If you visit on a summer weekend, go early in the day or be prepared to wait an hour or more to join a tour. Be sure to wear sturdy walking shoes that you don't mind getting a bit muddy. The tour is not recommended for those with respiratory or heart problems. Admission. ~ 20000 Caves Highway, Cave Junction; 541-592-3400.

Southeast of Grants Pass is **Jacksonville**, a 19th-century mining town that has clung to its legendary frontier tradition. The entire town has been designated a National Historic Landmark with over 80 homes, stores and public buildings. Stop at the **Jacksonville Chamber of Commerce** to pick up a walking-tour map of the town's tree-lined streets. ~ Oregon and C streets, Jacksonville; 541-899-8118.

Along the way you'll want to stop at the **Jacksonville Museum of Southern Oregon History**. Among the exhibits are gold-mining artifacts and the Miner Baker furniture display about early valley history. In the same complex is the **Children's Museum**. Kids, take your parents to this former jail filled with "please touch" exhibits including a miniature kitchen and 1890s general store. There's also a major exhibit on Jacksonville native Vance Colvig, who provided the voice for many Disney characters (Goofy and Grumpy, for starters) and who later became the first—and best-known—Bozo the Clown. Closed Monday and Tuesday in winter. Separate admission for both museums. ~ 206 North 5th Street, Jacksonville; 541-773-6536.

California Street, the heart of Jacksonville, is a step back in time. The graceful balustraded brick buildings have been lovingly restored. Worth a visit is the gothic **C. C. Beekman House**. The living history tour re-creates the lifestyle of the rich and famous, circa 1876. Along the way you see banker Beekman's carved oak bedframe, overstuffed furniture, lap desk and summer kitchen. Nearby at California and 3rd streets, visit the Beekman Bank, one of the first buildings in Jacksonville to be restored. Closed in winter. Admission. ~ 352 East California Street east of Beekman Square, Jacksonville; 541-773-6536.

Route 238 southwest of Jacksonville leads to the picturesque **Applegate Valley**, a two-mile-wide, fifty mile-long canyon with memorable views and few tourists. After reaching the town of Applegate you can continue south on Applegate Road to the foot of the Siskiyous. Alternatively, Little Applegate and Anderson Creek roads loop back to Route 99.

Located about ten miles west of Jacksonville via Route 238, Medford is by far the largest city in the vicinity of Ashland and the Rogue River. A much-frequented stop in the area is **Harry and David's Original Country Store**, famous for its gift packs shipped nationwide. The store has a fruit stand, gourmet pantry, gift shop, coffee corner and deli. Tours of the packinghouse depart from the gift store. ~ 1314 Center Drive, Medford; 541-776-2277.

The **Medford Visitors and Convention Bureau** is an excellent source of information on southern Oregon. ~ 101 East 8th Street, Medford; 541-772-5194.

The nearby **Southern Oregon Historical Society's Historical Center** has an extensive collection of artifacts featuring furniture, shawls, saddles and agricultural tools. ~ 106 North Central Avenue, Medford; 541-773-6536.

Twelve miles north of Medford off Route 62, **Butte Creek Mill**   ◀ *HIDDEN*
has been producing stone-ground products since 1872. Occasionally you may see the miller grinding wheat, rye and corn on giant white stones quarried in France, assembled in Illinois, shipped around the Horn to California and finally brought over the Siskiyous by wagon. ~ 402 Royal Avenue North, Eagle Point; 541-826-3531.

Next door to the mill is the **Oregon General Store Museum**. Set up as an 1890s shop, this fascinating collection features over-the-counter medicines, hardware, toys, clothing, Coca-Cola signs, tobacco tins and a variety of unusual memorabilia. The delightful period piece is open only on Saturday in the summer months.

While **Ashland** is best known for the Oregon Shakespeare Festival, the play is not the only thing here. From shopping to restaurants to biking, this city offers plenty of diversions. Home to more bed and breakfasts than any other city in the state, Ashland has strict zoning controls that protect the architectural landscape.

To explore the possibilities, stop by the **Ashland Chamber of Commerce**. ~ 110 East Main Street, Ashland; 541-482-3486. A good place to begin your visit is the downtown plaza and verdant Lithia Park (see "Parks" below).

> Ashland is heavily booked during the Shakespeare season (mid-February through late October) when street vendors are out in force selling espresso.

Across the street is the **Oregon Shakespeare Festival** and the fascinating **Backstage Tour**. This excellent behind-the-scenes program is a helpful introduction to stagecraft. Members of the theater company guide you through the making of a play on this 90-minute look at the dramatic arts. Also worth a visit is the festival's **Exhibit Center**, where you can see, and try on, costumes and props. Closed November through mid-February. Admission to Backstage Tour. ~ 15 South Pioneer Street, Ashland; 541-482-4331.

Most people come to Ashland for the plays, but the mountain lakes east of town are a tempting day trip. Take Route 5 north and pick up Route 140 east to Dead Indian Road. Turn south to the first and most picturesque of these retreats, **Lake of the Woods**, an ideal place for a picnic, swimming or sunbathing. Continue southeast to **Howard Prairie Reservoir** and **Hyatt Reservoir**, both popular for water sports and fishing. Return to Dead Indian Road for the cliffhanging descent back into Ashland, an entrance that rivals anything you're likely to see on the Elizabethan stage.

An 1850s stage stop, **Wolf Creek Tavern** now operates as a state historic property. Handsomely restored and run by a staff in 19th-   **LODGING** century-style attire, the tavern offers eight rooms with private baths. You'll find antiques, old photographs and brass beds in the medium-sized rooms. You can also see the room where Jack London stayed on his visit. ~ 100 Front Street, Wolf Creek; 541-866-2474. MODERATE.

The **Pine Meadow Inn** is a relaxing bed-and-breakfast retreat surrounded by five acres of private pine forest. Four upstairs guest rooms are furnished with antiques and cozy comforts like fresh flowers and private baths. Enjoy the gardens, sit by the koi pond and waterfalls, or soak in the outdoor hot tub. ~ 1000 Crow Road, Merlin; 541-471-6277, 800-554-0806. MODERATE TO DELUXE.

A glorious view of the Coastal Mountain range is just one of the pluses at the **Paradise Resort**. Whether you arrive by plane on the ranch's runway or come by car, expect a great escape at this Rogue Valley resort. One of 15 motel-style rooms or the cottage with Early American furniture and pond views, will be your base. A house is also available for families. You can photograph swans on the pond, fish for bass (catch-and-release) at three-acre Paradise Lake, golf or enjoy tennis, hiking and biking. ~ 7000 Monument Drive, Grants Pass; 541-479-4333, fax 541-479-0218. DELUXE.

The **Riverside Inn** is the largest motel in town with an enviable location on the Rogue River across from Riverside Park. This 174-unit inn's large rooms and kitchenette suites are furnished with comfortable sofas and easy chairs. Most rooms have private balconies overlooking the river. In some cases you can pick blackberries from your deck. A Rogue jet-boat dock is next door, and there is some highway noise from the bridge traffic. ~ 971 Southeast 6th Street, Grants Pass; 541-476-6873, 800-334-4567, fax 541-474-9848. MODERATE TO DELUXE.

The **Oregon Caves Lodge**, in a wooded glen surrounded by waterfalls, is an ideal place to spend the night after a visit to the Oregon Caves National Monument. Faced with cedar shakes, this National Historic Landmark has two big marble fireplaces framed with fir timbers in the lobby. Moderate-sized rooms with 1930s furnishings and Pendleton bedspreads offer forest and pond views in this serene setting. Closed November through April. ~ 20000 Caves Highway, Cave Junction; 541-592-3400. DELUXE.

For women only, **Mountain River Inn** is a secluded bed-and-breakfast inn located on 27 forested acres above the Illinois River near Grants Pass. The main house is a two-story, woodframe passive solar structure with three sunny guest rooms and a living room with TV, stereo and exercise equipment. Also on the grounds are a private cabin with kitchen and sundeck, as well as campsites, a hot tub, sauna, private swimming hole and hiking trails. Closed for renovation until the end of 1998. ~ P.O. Box 34, O'Brien, OR 97534; 541-596-2392. BUDGET.

The historic red-brick **Jacksonville Inn** offers nicely restored rooms with oak-frame beds, quilts, wall-to-wall carpets, antiques, gas-style lamps and floral-print wallpaper. ~ 175 East California Street, Jacksonville; 541-899-1900, 800-321-9344, fax 541-899-1373. DELUXE.

Convenient to downtown Jacksonville, the **McCully House Inn** is a charming 19th-century home where a grandfather clock sounds the hour and guests sip wine around the fireplace. This immaculate white house has hardwood floors, painted friezes on the walls and rooms big on lace, walnut furniture and clawfoot tubs. ~ 240 East California Street, Jacksonville; 541-899-1942, 800-367-1942, fax 541-899-1560. DELUXE.

Take a 125-year-old country estate, complete with a three-story barn, add a redwood deck, flower garden and orchard and what do you get? **Under the Greenwood Tree Bed and Breakfast Inn**. Overfurnished with Persian rugs, Chippendale and chintz, this is the place for travelers who want to wind down with a full afternoon tea or sherry and pluck a truffle off their pillow before climbing into bed. A regional three-course farm-fresh breakfast prepared by a Cordon Bleu chef is included. ~ 3045 Bellinger Lane, Medford; 541-776-0000. DELUXE.

◄ HIDDEN

Reached via a redwood staircase, the **Columbia Hotel** is a comfortable European-style inn. Rooms are furnished with brass beds, floral-print drapes, fans and wall-to-wall carpet. Some provide views of the surrounding mountains. ~ 262½ East Main Street, Ashland; 541-482-3726, 800-718-2530. MODERATE.

Devotees of Craftsman-style architecture will love the **Redwing Bed and Breakfast**. Gleaming fir woodwork and original lighting fixtures detail the interior. Queen beds, wicker furniture, antiques, and country quilts make the rooms welcoming. ~ 115 North Main Street, Ashland; 541-482-1807, 800-461-6743, fax 541-488-1433. DELUXE.

The **Queen Anne Bed and Breakfast** has fine views of the Cascades and the Coast Range. In the library you can choose from several of the Bard's works. A beautiful English garden behind the inn, near the waterfall and gazebo, is a great place to read the play you're about to see at the Shakespeare Festival. Two rooms and two suites feature queen-sized beds (naturally), handmade quilts bay windows, and clawfoot tubs. ~ 125 North Main Street, Ashland; 541-482-0220, 800-460-6818, fax 541-732-1718. DELUXE.

The **Fox House Inn** is a restored early Victorian with stained-glass windows, dark-wood wainscotting and oriental rugs. Choose a room or suite with a queen canopied bed, ceiling windows and a clawfoot tub. The upstairs suite has floor-to-ceiling windows and a private deck, while the downstairs room opens onto a flower garden. Each has a private hot tub. ~ 269 B Street, Ashland; 541-488-1055, 800-488-1055, fax 541-482-6940. ULTRA-DELUXE.

One block from the Shakespeare Festival, **Will's Reste** is an inviting cottage with kitchen facilities and housekeeping services. You'll enjoy the hot spa and the deck with views of the Siskiyou and Cascade ranges. Gay-friendly. ~ 298 Hargadine Street, Ashland; 541-482-4394. MODERATE.

Cedarwood Inn of Ashland is one of several modern motels found south of downtown. Choose between wood-paneled rooms with queens and courtyard family units with kitchens and decks. All 64 rooms have contemporary oak furniture. Pools, saunas and barbecue facilities are available. ~ 1801 Siskiyou Boulevard, Ashland; 541-488-2000, 800-547-4141, fax 541-482-2000. MODERATE TO DELUXE.

For information on Ashland bed and breakfasts, and other inns across Oregon, send a large self-addressed, stamped envelope to **The Oregon Bed and Breakfast Guild**. ~ P.O. Box 3187, Ashland, OR 97520. You may also call **Ashland's Bed and Breakfast Network**. ~ 541-482-2337, 800-944-0329.

DINING

Clam chowder is the staple at **The Laughing Clam**. Stop by for lunch or dinner and choose from sandwiches, large salads, fresh seafood and pasta, including the Seafood Mama (shrimps, scallops and clams in a cream sauce over lemon linguine). ~ 121 Southwest G Street, Grants Pass; 541-479-1110. BUDGET TO MODERATE.

For dining in a glorious country setting, consider **Paradise Resort**. Garlic-roasted rack of lamb, fresh halibut filet and manicotti florentine top the menu. There's also a Sunday brunch serving petite steak and eggs, lingonberry crêpes and french toast with cream cheese and fruit. ~ 7000 Monument Drive, Grants Pass; 541-479-4333. MODERATE TO DELUXE.

Traversing a stream, the **Oregon Caves Lodge Restaurant** offers steaks, seafood, chicken and pasta dishes. Downstairs is a 1930s-style soda fountain. Scores of patrons seated on red stools enjoy sundaes, omelettes, french toast, salads, deli sandwiches and burgers. Don't miss this knotty-pine-paneled classic. ~ 20000 Caves Highway, Cave Junction; 541-592-3400. MODERATE.

The **Jacksonville Inn** serves breakfast, lunch, dinner and Sunday brunch in the restored 19th-century Ryan and Morgan general-store building. The dimly lit, brick-walled dining room with red carpets and tablecloths creates a great setting for vast, seven-course dinners or a la carte dishes. A large menu features Oregon cuisine, including razor clams, scallops, prime rib and vegetarian dishes. The wine list is endless. ~ 175 East California Street, Jacksonville; 541-899-1900. DELUXE.

For patio dining, it's hard to beat the **McCully House Inn**. Entrées served outside or in the lovely dining room include wild-mushroom fettuccine, grilled New York steak and sautéed prawns with peanut sauce and . You'll find Oregon wildflowers on every

table. ~ 240 East California Street, Jacksonville; 541-899-1942.
MODERATE TO DELUXE.

Phoenix-like, the **Bella Union** has risen from the ashes of one
of Jacksonville's best-loved 19th-century saloons. Like its prede-
cessor, this establishment is an important social center. On the
menu you'll find pizza, seafood, pasta, and sandwiches. You have
your choice of several noisy dining rooms or the more serene
heated patio out back. ~ 170 West California Street, Jacksonville;
541-899-1770. MODERATE.

On a warm evening, the garden patio at the **Winchester Country Inn** is an ideal place to enjoy Teng Dah beef, duck à la Bigarade
and lamb du jour. This opulent Victorian, surrounded by a colorful garden, also has gazebo seating and a dining room decorated
in burgundy tones with accents of blue. Dinner only. ~ 35 South
2nd Street, Ashland; 541-488-1115. DELUXE.

Whether you choose a seat at the counter or one of the glass-
paneled booths, you'll find the country-casual **Geppetto's** a comfortable place to enjoy Italian and Ashland cuisine like linguine,
five-spice chicken and snapper. Try the fresh fruit pies. ~ 345 East
Main Street, Ashland; 541-482-1138. MODERATE.

Looking for Asian cuisine served at a creekside setting? Consider **Thai Pepper**. Step into the romantic gray-walled dining room,
take a seat on the wicker furniture and order such dishes as green
chicken curry, yellow shrimp curry and crispy fish served with
cold Singha beer. But your best bet, especially on a warm evening,
is a seat on the shady patio next to the creek. ~ 84 North Main
Street, Ashland; 541-482-8058. MODERATE.

A French bistro with stained-glass windows and dark wood-
booths illuminated by Tiffany-style lamps, **Chatêaulin Restaurant**
prepares such dishes as veal and pork sausage with Dijon mustard,
pan-roasted rack of lamb with garlic mashed potatoes, and spinach linguine. In addition to deluxe-priced dinners, the bistro menu
offers moderately priced dishes such as rotini pasta with smoked

---

✔ CHECK THESE OUT—UNIQUE DINING

- *Budget:* Reserve your appetite for a huge serving of enchiladas rancheros
  at **Amador's Alley**, a local favorite. *page 424*
  - *Moderate:* Savor innovative Asian cuisine on the creekside patio at **Thai
    Pepper** on Ashland's Main Street. *page 439*
    - *Deluxe:* Sample fresh Northwest seafood—salmon from the Chinook
      River, clams from Dungeness Spit—at Eugene's **Sweetwaters**. *page 429*
      - *Deluxe to ultra-deluxe:* Refuel with smoked salmon at **Nick's Italian
        Café**, located in McMinnville's well-preserved downtown. *page 424*

Budget: under $8 Moderate: $8–$16 Deluxe: $16–$24 Ultra-deluxe: over $24

salmon and shrimp with roasted tomato and basil coulis. Dinner only. ~ 50 East Main Street, Ashland; 541-482-2264. MODERATE TO DELUXE.

Alex's Plaza Restaurant has a good house pizza topped with fontina cheese, mushrooms and leeks. Also on the menu is a vegetarian wild-mushroom lasagna. Located in the first brick building built following the disastrous 1879 downtown fire, this second-story dining room still has its original fir floors. It's flanked by patios. ~ 35 North Main Street, Ashland; 541-482-8818. MODERATE TO DELUXE.

Mediterranean, Italian and vegetarian fare served in a creekside setting make the **Greenleaf Restaurant** worth a visit. Specialties include breakfast dishes like mushroom frittatas and tofu scrambles with sausage. For lunch or dinner, try pasta primavera, fruit salad or red snapper. An excellent choice for to-go fare, they will also prepare picnic baskets. ~ 49 North Main Street, Ashland; 541-482-2808. BUDGET TO MODERATE.

Brother's Restaurant and Delicatessen has an eclectic menu including shrimp omelettes, *huevos rancheros*, bagels and lox, and caesar and Greek salads. The carpeted, wood-paneled dining room with indoor balcony seating puts Brother's a cut above your average deli. Breakfast and lunch only. ~ 95 North Main Street, Ashland; 541-482-9671. BUDGET TO MODERATE.

SHOPPING Stop, look and listen. **Walker's Antique Radio** sells early wood consoles and classic "tombstone" table models, as well as novelty and shortwave radios. ~ 300 Merlin Road, Merlin; 541-476-1259.

HIDDEN ► **Windy River Farms** has culinary and medicinal herbs, organic teas, and vegetables. It is 15 miles northwest of Grants Pass. ~ 348 Hussey Lane, Grants Pass; 541-476-8979.

A good place to search for country kitchenware and antiques, jewelry, quilts, rare books, children's books and toys, Americana and Western memorabilia is **Turner House Antiques**. ~ 120 North 5th Street, Jacksonville; 541-899-1936.

Tudor Guild Gift Shop, adjacent to the Elizabethan Theatre, sells all the Bard's works, as well as brass rubbings, jewelry and pull toys with a dramatic flair. ~ 15 South Pioneer Street, Ashland; 541-482-0940.

The Northwest Nature Shop is a wonderful place to shop for birdhouses, minerals, wind chimes, hiking maps and nature and travel books. In a Craftsman-style house near downtown, this shop has a good selection of nature-oriented children's games. ~ 154 Oak Street, Ashland; 541-482-3241.

For locally made products, **Oregon Store Ashland** is a good bet. You can sample smoked salmon or Oregon jam and chutney.

Scores of other local products such as wooden toys and handicrafts are also sold here. ~ 242 East Main Street, Ashland; 541-482-5453.

Mick's Ale House and Restaurant at the Riverside Inn has digitally spun music overlooking the Rogue River. You can also enjoy music and drinks outdoors on the deck. ~ 971 Southeast 6th Street, Grants Pass; 541-476-6873.

NIGHTLIFE

    Britt Festivals offers classical, jazz, folk, theater and dance performances from late June through August. Headliners such as the Indigo Girls, Wynonna and Grover Washington Jr. make this event a worthy companion to the nearby Oregon Shakespeare Festival. At this outdoor theater, you can choose between lawn and reserved seating in the natural setting of the historic Britt estate. ~ Britt Pavilion, Jacksonville; 541-773-6077, 800-882-7488.

> Prior to evening shows at the Elizabethan, the Green Show Renaissance Musicians and Dancers offer free half-hour performances in the Oregon Shakespeare courtyard.

    The Oregon Shakespeare Festival is the nation's oldest annual Shakespeare celebration and one of the largest regional theaters in the country, attracting more than 100,000 people each season. The most popular venue is the **Elizabethan Theatre**, which stages plays during summer. The indoor **Angus Bowmer Theatre** also presents Shakespearian performances, as well as classics by Shaw and Wilder and contemporary playwrights. Experimental works are presented at the **Black Swan Theater**. The season runs from mid-February through late October. Advance reservations are strongly recommended in peak season. ~ 15 South Pioneer Street, Ashland; 541-482-4331.

    The **Oregon Cabaret Theatre** holds professional productions including musicals, reviews, comedies, original works and the best of Broadway in a renovated church complete with stained-glass windows, wooden balustrades and a crystal chandelier from an old movie palace. Dinner theater also available. ~ 1st and Hargadine streets, Ashland; 541-488-2902. The **Actor's Theater** is an off-Broadway–style community theater group performing at the Minshall Playhouse in Talent. ~ 101 Talent Avenue, Talent; 541-535-5250.

    The lounge at the **Mark Antony Hotel** hosts live music and dancing in an elegant setting Thursday through Saturday. Cover. ~ 212 East Main Street, Ashland; 541-482-1721.

    Siskiyou Micro Pub features a deck overlooking Lithia Creek, 14 brews on tap and live entertainment nightly. Catch blues on Tuesday, open-mike readings on Thursday, and a variety of bands on Wednesday, Friday and Saturday. Occasional cover. ~ 31-B South Water Street, Ashland; 541-482-7718.

PARKS

VALLEY OF THE ROGUE STATE PARK 🚶 🚲 ⛵ 🚤 🎣 ⚓
This 316-acre park on the Rogue River is convenient to the Grants
Pass Area. Near the interstate, it's central to many rafting operators. Trout, steelhead and chinook salmon are caught in the Rogue
River. The grassy, mile-long riverfront park is shaded by madrone,
black locust and oak. Facilities include picnic areas and restrooms;
restaurants and groceries are in Grants Pass. ~ Off Route 5, 12
miles east of Grants Pass; 541-582-1118.

▲ There are 21 developed sites, 55 with partial hookups and
97 with full hookups; $15 to $17 per night. Showers available to
all sites.

BEN HUR LAMPMAN STATE PARK 🎣 ⚓ On the south bank of
the Rogue River opposite Gold Hill, the 23-acre wayside park is
named for the late Ben Hur Lampman, a popular Oregon newspaper editor, fisherman and poet laureate. Emulate his fishing
prowess by angling for trout and steelhead in the Rogue. There
are picnic tables; restaurants and groceries are located nearby in
Grants Pass; day-use only. ~ Located off Route 5, 16 miles east of
Grants Pass; 541-582-1118.

HIDDEN ► **INDIAN MARY PARK** 🎣 🚤 🎣 ⚓ This half-mile-long park
on the Rogue River west of Merlin is another ideal retreat for the
entire family. Kids can play on the sandy beach or enjoy themselves at the playground. If you're towing a boat or raft, you can
launch it here. You can also fish from the beach. You'll find picnic
areas, restrooms, playgrounds and a sand volleyball court; restaurants and groceries are ten miles away in Merlin. ~ From Grants
Pass take Route 5 north to the Merlin exit. Continue west ten
miles on Merlin-Galice Road; 541-474-5285.

▲ There are 32 tent sites and 60 sites with full hookups; $12
to $15 per night.

LAKE SELMAC 🚶 🚲 🐎 🎣 ⛵ 🚤 🎣 ⚓ A large Illinois
Valley lake convenient to the Grants Pass area, this is a popular
summer resort. The 160-acre lake near Selma is a good choice for
fishing (trout, bass and crappie), canoeing and sailing. The waters
here tend to be warmer than the nearby rivers. Facilities are limited to picnic tables are restrooms; restaurants and groceries are
in Selma. ~ Located 2.3 miles east of Selma via Upper Deer Creek
Road; 541-474-5285.

▲ There are 80 developed sites and 35 sites with full hookups; $12 to $17 per night at Lake Selmac Campground.

ILLINOIS RIVER STATE PARK 🚶 🎣 ⚓ The largely undeveloped
511-acre day-use park at the junction of the east and west forks
of the Illinois River is a secluded spot perfect for trout and steelhead fishing and birdlife and wildlife viewing. You'll find picnic
tables and restrooms; restaurants and groceries are nearby in Cave

Junction. ~ On Route 199, one mile south of Cave Junction; 541-582-1118.

▲ Permitted in nearby U.S. Forest Service campgrounds in the Illinois Valley. Among them are Grayback and Cave Creek campgrounds (541-592-3400), respectively 12 and 17 miles east of Cave Junction on Oregon Caves Highway. Grayback has 38 self-contained tent sites and one site with full hookups; Cave Creek has 18 tent sites; $8 to $12 per night.

TOUVELLE STATE PARK 🏊🚤⛵🛶 The 54-acre day-use facility is adjacent to Table Rock, an 1890-acre biologic, geologic and historic preserve forested with Pacific madrone, white oak and ponderosa pine. In the park you can swim or fish for salmon and trout. Facilities include picnic tables, restrooms and wildlife viewing; restaurants and groceries are in Medford. Parking fee, $3. ~ Take Route 62 nine miles north of Medford to Table Rock Road; 541-582-1118.

CANTRALL-BUCKLEY PARK 🚶🏊🛶 Just eight miles southwest   ◀ HIDDEN
of Jacksonville on a wooded hillside above the Applegate Valley, Cantrall-Buckley extends half a mile along the inviting Applegate River and offers beautiful views of this farming region. Swimmers head to the small cove, while anglers try for trout in the river. There are picnic areas, barbecue pits, showers and restrooms; restaurant and groceries are in Jacksonville. Parking fee, $3. ~ Take Route 238 eight miles southwest from Jacksonville and turn right on Hamilton Road; 541-776-7001.

▲ There are 42 primitive tent sites; $10 per night.

ROGUE ELK PARK 🏊🚤⛵🛶 The nearly mile-long park on the Rogue includes a warm creek ideal for swimming, and the kids can swing out into the river Tarzan-style on a rope hanging from an oak limb. There's good rafting and fishing (steelhead and trout) in the Rogue. Shade trees make this park a good choice on warm days. An ideal stopover en route to Crater Lake. You'll find picnic tables, restrooms and showers. Parking fee, $3. ~ Located eight miles north of Shady Cove on Route 62; 541-776-7001.

▲ There are 22 developed sites and 15 sites with full hookups; $14 to $15 per night.

LITHIA PARK 🚶🏊 Ashland's 100-acre urban forest was originally designed by John McLaren, the creator of Golden Gate Park in San Francisco. A beautiful place to walk or jog, the park is filled with towering maples, black oaks, sycamore, sequoia, bamboo, European Beech, flowering Catalpa and the Chinese Tree of Heaven. Also here are a Japanese garden, rose garden and two duck ponds. Facilities include picnic tables, a playground, a tennis court, a swimming hole, a band shell, a fountain and restrooms. ~ On the south side of the Ashland Plaza in Ashland; 541-488-5340.

▼▼▼▼▼▼▼▼▼▼▼▼▼▼
Outdoor Adventures

FISHING

In a Northwest wonderland of sparkling lakes, rivers and mountain streams, it's no surprise that fishing is such a part of the scene. Even novice anglers should try casting a line; they're bound to catch something: fall salmon from coastal rivers and streams in October and November; winter steelhead, from December through March. Spring and summer bring trout (try Detroit Lake, or the McKenzie River for huge rainbow trout) and summer steelhead (the North and South Santiam rivers are the best spots).

SALEM AREA　Bill Kremers arranges daily fishing trips on the west side of the Cascades, longer excursions elsewhere. ~ 29606 Northeast Pheasant Street, Corvallis; 541-754-6411. **White Water Warehouse** runs one-day fishing trips to the Umpqua and Deschutes rivers from mid-May to mid-September (salmon, steelhead, trout; novice to expert; fly or spin cast) and to the Alsea and Siletz rivers from October through March (fall salmon and winter steelhead). ~ 625 Northwest Starker Avenue, Corvallis; 541-758-3150, 800-214-0579.

EUGENE RIVER AREA　Wilderness River Outfitters runs one-day and overnight fishing trips locally on the Willamette, Umpqua and McKenzie rivers and throughout Oregon. ~ 1567 Main Street, Springfield; 541-726-9471.

ASHLAND–ROGUE RIVER AREA　For fishing tackle and helpful advice, contact **Specialty Tackle Shop**. ~ 5274 Crater Lake Avenue, Central Point; 541-772-7375. For salmon and steelhead fishing, contact **Rogue Wilderness Inc.**, which has specialized in drift-boat fishing for 25 years. Trips of one to four days can be arranged, with a one-guide to two-passenger ratio. ~ 325 Galice Road, Merlin; 800-336-1647. For a day trip to fish for salmon and steelhead on the Chetco near Brookings or the Rogue estuary at Gold Beach, contact **Rogue River Guide Service**. ~ 1684 Axtell Drive, Grants Pass; 541-476-7288.

RIVER RUNNING

A rafting or kayaking adventure can take you from the wild and scenic whitewater ruggedness of the Rogue River (where some of the rapids are Class III and IV) to an outing on the more gentle Willamette River or one of the local lakes. With dozens of rivers in the foothills surrounding Salem, Eugene and Ashland, you're never far from an enjoyable stretch of river. The North Santiam River near Salem is popular for both its rapids and views of the surrounding woods, while the McKenzie and Willamette near Salem lean more towards the serene than the adventurous. But by far the most popular area is around Ashland. Here the Rogue River offers everything from casual floats to spectacular rapids, like those in Hellgate Canyon.

Kayakers should look for a copy of the book *Soggy Sneakers*, a regional guide to kayaking published by the Willamette Kayak and Canoe Club. The book is sold locally for about $18.

One of the best regional resources for outdoor adventurers interested in fishing, hunting and rafting is the **Oregon Outdoors Association** in Eugene. The group publishes an extensive directory of guides and outfitters throughout the state and will have a home page on the Internet. ~ 541-683-9552, 800-747-9552.

SALEM AREA   **White Water Warehouse** can set you up with hardshell kayaks (including Perception and Wave Sport), sea kayaks, canoes and rafts. Instruction in whitewater kayaking is also available. The company also runs day raft trips locally on the North Santiam River, a fast-moving, clear river with rapids and lots of scenery. (The company also runs longer raft trips to the MacKenzie and Rogue rivers farther south.) ~ 625 Northwest Starker Avenue, Corvallis; 541-758-3150, 800-214-0579.

EUGENE AREA   Scenic day or overnight float trips (you can sit back and be a passenger or help paddle) on the McKenzie, Umpqua and Deschutes rivers can be arranged with **Northwest Whitewater Float & Fishing Excursions**. ~ Eugene; 541-334-5122. **Wilderness River Outfitters** runs a starlit evening float along serene stretches of the Willamette. ~ 1567 Main Street, Springfield; 541-726-9471.

ASHLAND–ROGUE RIVER AREA   Whether you paddle your own kayak or float with a guide, rafting is the ideal way to see the Rogue's wild and scenic sections. Choose between one-day trips and overnight trips. **Orange Torpedo Trips Inc./Grants Pass Float Co.** specializes in inflatable kayaking, with one-day and multiday whitewater trips on the Rogue, Klamath and North Umpqua. ~ 210 Merlin Road, Merlin; 541-479-5061. **Rogue Wilderness Inc.** can set you up for a one-day, 13-mile scenic adventure in an inflatable kayak or an oar or paddle raft, and also arrange longer

✔ **CHECK THESE OUT—UNIQUE OUTDOOR ADVENTURES**

- Hike, bike or horseback ride through Silver Falls State Park to its dramatic South Falls, a 178-foot cascade. *page 425*
- Cast a line in the Rogue, Umpqua and McKenzie rivers, all legendary for salmon and steelhead fishing. *page 444*
- Join the flotilla of rafters and kayakers on a wild ride down the Rogue River. *page 445*
- Pedal the eight miles of off-road mountain-bike trails at the hilly, occasionally muddy Fox Swale Area south of Eugene. *page 449*

wilderness trips on the Rogue. ~ Merlin; 541-479-9554, 800-336-1647. For a full- or half-day whitewater adventure led by a naturalist along the middle Rogue (water ratings range from Class I to IV) or the upper Klamath in a six-person paddleboat, contact **The Adventure Center**. Multiday rafting and camping trips are also available. ~ 40 North Main Street, Ashland; 541-488-2819.

The Rogue River's Hellgate Canyon—where sheer rock walls rise 250 feet—was the setting for the Meryl Streep film *The River Wild*. **Hellgate Jetboat Excursions** will take you through this rugged wilderness on one of several jet-boat tours it operates. ~ 966 Southwest 6th Street, Grants Pass; 541-479-7204, 800-648-4874.

SKIING

ASHLAND–ROGUE RIVER AREA   Although most of the Heart of Oregon lies in a valley between the Cascades and the Coast Range, the southern section of the Route 5 corridor passes through the Klamath-Siskiyou Mountains. Skiers in that area head for **Mt. Ashland**. At 7500 feet, it's the highest peak in the range and just 18 miles south of Ashland off Route 5. Facilities include a lodge, rental shop, four chairlifts and 23 ski runs. Both alpine and cross-country (ungroomed) trails are found here. ~ Exit 6, Route 5; 541-482-2897, 541-482-2754 for recorded ski-condition information.

BALLOON RIDES

SALEM AREA   The quiet exhilaration of floating above it all—wine country, the river, rolling farmland—explains why ballooning is popular in the Salem area (the annual Northwest Natural Gas Hot Air Balloon Championships are held here each September). From April to November, **Vista Balloon Adventures** operates one-hour flights over the wine country of Newburg (about 25 minutes north of Salem). The company has five balloons and can fly six to ten passengers in each. If you're the participatory type, you can put on some gloves and help inflate the balloon. ~ Sherwood; 503-625-7385, 800-622-2309.

ASHLAND–ROGUE RIVER AREA   Sunrise Balloon Adventures flies from late April to mid-October. From Touvelle State Park, the one-hour flights ascend between 2000 and 3000 feet, offering spectacular views of the nearby flat Table Rocks mountains; on a clear day, Mt. Shasta (a two-hour drive away in California) is visible. ~ Medford; 541-776-2284.

RIDING STABLES & LLAMA TREKS

Along the western slopes of the Cascades, within a 30-mile drive of the Willamette Valley, lie some of the most pristine wilderness areas in the state, much of them U.S. Forest Service land. One of the best ways to explore these alpine meadows, old-growth forests and scenic mountain peaks is on a guided day-long or multiday trail ride from a local outfitter. Even if you only have a couple of hours, Mt. Pisgah just outside Eugene provides a good opportunity for a casual ride.

SALEM AREA Pack trips with llamas allow hikers to explore the wilderness with trusty companions. For one- to three-hour day trips in Silver Falls State Park, contact **Salem Trek**. ~ 555 Howell Prairie Road Southeast, Salem; 503-362-0873.

EUGENE AREA Three Sisters Wilderness, just east of Eugene in Willamette National Forest, takes its name from the North, Middle and South Sisters, three 10,000-foot-plus peaks that define the area. **Outdoor Adventures Plus Guide Service**, the only licensed guide for this wilderness area, runs overnight packhorse trips for four to six people during spring and summer, as well as horseback hunting trips. For less rugged adventurers, the company can also arrange a few hours' ride through Mt. Pisgah in Eugene. ~ Eugene; 541-344-4499.

Public courses in the area offer a variety of landscapes, course lengths, and difficulty ratings.

GOLF

SALEM AREA Built in 1928, **Salem Golf Course** is a lush, old-style Northwest course: 18 holes with meandering greens and big old fir trees. ~ 2025 Golf Course Road South, Salem; 503-363-6652. Near Stayton, 18-hole **Santiam Golf Course** has lots of water and trees and is nice for walking because it's fairly flat. ~ 8724 Golf Club Road Southeast, Aumsville; 503-769-3485.

EUGENE AREA The relatively flat 18-hole **Fiddler's Green** is known for its famous pro shop. ~ 91292 Route 99 North, Eugene; 541-689-8464. The 75-year-old, nine-hole **Hidden Valley Golf Course** is tucked away in a picturesque little valley and lined with mature fir and oak trees. ~ 775 North River Road, Cottage Grove; 541-942-3046.

ASHLAND–ROGUE RIVER AREA Oak Knoll Golf Course is only nine holes, but they're regulation length and set on gently rolling greens. ~ 3070 Route 66, Ashland; 541-482-4311. The 18-hole, par-70 **Cedar Links Golf Course** is 6000 yards but an easy walk for the most part. The back nine crosses a pear trees and offers good views of the valley. ~ 3155 Cedar Links Drive, Medford; 541-773-4373.

SALEM AREA If you'd like to swing a racket, the Salem Parks and Recreation Department (503-588-6261) operates plenty of free courts in the capital. At **Bush's Pasture Park** (Mission and High streets) there are four lighted courts; **Highland School Park** (Broadway and Highland Avenue Northeast) has two lighted courts; and there are four lighted courts at **Orchard Heights** (Orchard Heights and Westhaven streets). Courts are also available at **Hoover School/Park** (1104 Savage Road Northeast), **River Road Park** (3005 River Road) and **Woodmansee Park** (4635 Sunnyside Road Southeast).

TENNIS

EUGENE AREA   Eugene Parks and Recreation (541-687-5333) operates four hardtop courts at **Churchill Courts** (1850 Bailey Hill Road), two lighted courts at **Washington Park** (2025 Washington Street) and four lighted courts at each of the following locations: **Amazon Courts** (Amazon Parkway and 24th Avenue), **Sheldon Courts** (2445 Willakenzie Road), **Echo Hollow Courts** (1501 Echo Hollow Road) and **West Mooreland Courts** (20th and Polk streets).

For $16 per hour, both indoor and outdoor courts are available to nonmembers at **Willow Creek Racquet Club**, which also has a pro shop. ~ 4201 West 13th Avenue, Eugene; 541-484-7451.

ASHLAND–ROGUE RIVER AREA   The Medford Parks Department operates eight (unlighted) courts at **Fitchner Mainwaring Park** (Stewart Avenue and Holly Street), four lighted courts at **Bear Creek Park** (Siskiyou Boulevard and Highland Drive) and 16 lighted courts at **North Medford High School** (Keene Way Drive and Crater Lake Road).

BIKING

For recreational bicyclers, there are hundreds of miles of relatively flat, scenic bike trails that parallel beautiful rivers, parks and lakes throughout the valley. Experienced, active riders will enjoy the more challenging mountain trails or some of the longer loops in and around the region.

SALEM AREA   The **Salem Bicycle Club** publishes a monthly newsletter that includes a two- or three-page "Ride Sheet," which lists club-sponsored rides and is usually posted in bike shops around town. Club rides vary from beginner (15 to 20 miles) to expert (100-mile loops to the coast). Weekend rides are held year-round; in the summer, evening rides are held during the week. ~ P.O. Box 2224, Salem, OR 97308; 503-588-8613.

The **Oregon Trans-America Trail** from the Dallas area near Salem heads south through the scenic wine country to Corvallis. Four miles of bike trails traverse **Willamette Mission State Park** (503-393-1172), which is surrounded by orchards and farm fields. **Silver Falls State Park** (503-873-8681), with its waterfalls and gorges carved out of lava, has a popular four-mile paved bike trail. Work is nearing completion of a 27-mile perimeter trail as well. East of the city, there are trails "all over **Lyons and Detroit lakes**," according to one local enthusiast.

Near Corvallis, Oregon State University has its own gated research forest called **McDonald Forest** (541-737-4434). It's a hilly tract, but not steep, and its 15-mile trail system is very popular. From the top of Dimple Hill, which gains 800 feet in about four miles, there's a good view of the surrounding area. OSU maintains several trails and outlines them in a map widely available at bike shops.

About 15 miles southwest of Corvallis, **Mary's Peak**, the highest peak in the Coast Range, rises over 4000 feet. You can drive to a parking lot about three miles from the top. From there you can bike along the pavement to the summit, from which you'll get great views of the ocean and mountains to the east. When you're ready to descend, you can can follow one of several trails down.

Bike trails can be found in state parks throughout the area, including **Holman** (four miles west of Salem) and **Willamette Mission State Park** (eight miles north of Salem), the latter of which features a four-mile trail.

EUGENE AREA Eugene is one of the nation's top biking cities: more than 8500 people commute to school and work on bikes, and there are 200 miles of bike paths. All this in a city with a population of only 120,000.

Eugene's **Willamette River Recreation Corridor** offers five bridges that connect the north and south bank bike trails. The flat 15-mile loop from Knickerbocker Bridge to Owosso Bridge takes you through or past parks and rose gardens, shops and restaurants in downtown Eugene, and the University of Oregon campus.

Eight miles south of Eugene, the **Fox Swale Area** has eight miles of off-road trails ideal for mountain biking. Ride the Fox Hollow Road nine-and-a-half miles over the summit and down into the valley to BLM Road 14-4-44. Muddy during the rainy season.

ASHLAND–ROGUE RIVER AREA From the town of Rogue River, east of Grants Pass on Route 5, head north eight miles along Evans Creek to Wimer and the glorious **Evans Valley**. It's a scenic, relatively easy four-mile ride out Pleasant Creek Road to the covered bridge. Look for elk in the meadows alongside the road.

If you'd like to join an escorted downhill bike tour on Mt. Ashland, contact **The Adventure Center**. Beside bike rentals (and insider tips about the more pleasant route past small rural farms and ranches for a two-hour loop to Emigrant Lake), this outfitter offers several different off-road bike tours, all guided, with extras like picnic brunch . ~ 40 North Main Street, Ashland; 541-488-2819.

Another resource for information on cycling routes and events is the Southern Oregon Cycling Association. ~ P.O. Box 903, Ashland, OR 97520; 541-488-2453.

Bike Rentals Bike rentals in Salem are hard to come by. Try **South Salem Cycleworks** for tandem, mountain and road bikes. ~ Sunnyslope Shopping Center, 4555 Liberty Road, Salem; 503-399-9848. About 15 minutes east of Salem, **Upper Eschelon** rents mountain bikes, tandems and bike racks. You can also pick up local and regional bike trail maps at this shop. ~ 267 East Washington Street, Stayton; 503-769-9789.

Pick up mountain and cruise bikes at **Peak Sports**, the only rental shop in the city. The shop also still has a few three-speeds, which are perfect for an easy afternoon ride around town. ~ 129 Northwest 2nd Street, Corvallis; 541-754-6444.

Eugene Mountain Bicycle Resources Group publishes *Mountain Bike Ride Guide*, available at bike shops in the Eugene area. Of the more than 14 bike shops in Eugene, there are only two places to rent. **Pedal Power Bicycles** has mountain bikes, hybrids, tandems and trailers for rent. ~ 535 High Street, Eugene; 541-687-1775. **Blue Heron Bicycles** rents mountain bikes and six-speed city bikes in the spring and summer (complete with fenders and baskets). ~ 877 East 13th Avenue, Eugene; 541-343-2488.

HIKING

Hiking does not necessarily mean huffing and puffing up steep mountain slopes. Several of the hikes mentioned here may be more aptly described as "walks." In any event, a hike or a walk along the river or through a park is a great way to get some exercise and to get to know the area. All distances listed for hiking trails are one way unless otherwise noted.

SALEM AREA   **Riverfront Trail** (4 miles) in Willamette Mission State Park offers a secluded stretch of river.

The Loop Trail (7 miles) at Silver Falls State Park reaches all ten waterfalls along Silver Creek Canyon. Shorter hikes (less than 2.5 miles) can also be taken from roadside trailheads to the individual falls.

Salem's **Rita Steiner Fry Nature Trail** (.3 mile) offers a pleasant stroll through Deepwood Park, adjacent to the historic Deepwood Estate.

On River Road South, a mile south of downtown, **Minto-Brown Island Park** has 15 miles of trails and paths.

HIDDEN ►   **EUGENE AREA**   Convenient to Eugene, the **Fall Creek National Recreation Trail** (14 miles) is ideal for day hikes and overnight trips in the hardwood and conifer Willamette National Forest. Pristine Fall Creek is visible from most of the trail, which begins west of the Dolly Varden Campground. The short, paved Johnny Creek Nature Trail, a spur located off Road 1821, is ideal for the physically challenged. Wildflowers abound in the spring.

Eugene's **Mount Pisgah Arboretum** has seven miles of hiking trails. You can enjoy a lovely walk through oak savanna, a Douglas fir forest or along a seasonal marsh.

Pre's Trail is a Eugene memorial to legendary Oregon runner Steve Prefontaine. This all-weather trail through the woods and fields of Alton Baker Park offers parcourse-style routes ranging from .5 to 1.5 miles.

HIDDEN ►   The **Kentucky Falls Recreation Trail** (2 miles) runs along Kentucky Creek through a forest of Douglas fir and western hemlock. Located 41 miles southwest of Eugene, it leads down 760 feet to the twin falls viewpoint. ~ 541-268-4473.

ASHLAND–ROGUE RIVER AREA   More than 30 trail systems are found in the **Illinois Valley Ranger District** surrounding the Cave

Junction/Oregon Caves area. Trails run from half a mile to 15 miles. Possibilities include **Tin Cup Gulch**, the **Kalmiopsis Wilderness**, **Black Butte** and **Babyfoot Lake**. ~ 541-476-3830.

Try Medford's **Bear Creek Greenway Trail** (5.5 miles), beginning at Bear Creek Park and running north through Medford to Pine Street in Central Point. The trail has three segments. One is near the Route 5 south interchange off Table Rock Road. A series of 18 interpretive stations points out more than 20 kinds of trees and berries as well as landmarks along the creek. The other trail segment (3.5 miles) is in the Talent area with the trailhead in Lynn Newbry Park. The trail runs south toward Ashland, passing wetland habitats and historical sites, with an interpretive guide available. ~ 541-776-7268.

▼▼▼▼▼▼▼▼▼▼

Transportation

CAR

From Northern California, **Route 5** runs north over the border to Ashland and the Rogue River Valley. Route 5 also takes you southbound from Washington across the Columbia River into Portland. If you're arriving from the Northern California coast, pick up **Route 199**, which heads northeast through the Siskiyous into Southern Oregon and Grants Pass. Many other highways link the Willamette Valley with the Oregon Coast and central Oregon, including **Routes 126, 20** and **22**.

AIR

Two airports bring visitors to the Heart of Oregon: Eugene and Medford. In addition, the big **Portland International Airport** an hour north of Salem has convenient connections to all major cities and is serviced by Air Canada, Alaska Airlines, America West, American Airlines, Delta, Hawaiian Airlines, Horizon Air, Northwest Airlines, Reno Airlines, Southwest Airlines, Trans World Airlines, United Airlines and United Express.

Eugene Airport is served by American Airlines, Horizon Air, United Airlines and United Express. **Medford Airport**, near Ashland, is currently served by the Funjet, Horizon Air, United Airlines and United Express.

For ground transportation to and from the Eugene Airport call **Airport City Taxi & Limo**. ~ 541-484-4142.

In Medford, **Yellow Cab** serves the airport and links the Shakespeare capital with the Medford Airport. ~ 541-772-6288.

BUS

Greyhound Bus Lines (800-231-2222) serves the Willamette Valley and Ashland–Rogue River area, with stations in Salem, Corvallis, Albany, Eugene, Grants Pass and Medford. ~ Salem: 450 Church Street; 503-362-2428. Corvallis: 153 Northwest 4th Street; 541-757-1797. Albany: 108 Southeast 4th Avenue; 541-926-2711. Eugene: 987 Pearl Street; 541-343-2578. Grants Pass: 460 Agness Avenue; 541-476-4513. Medford: 212 North Bartlett Street; 541-779-2103.

TRAIN   Amtrak's (800-872-7245) "Coast Starlight" provides daily service
to the Willamette Valley, with stations in Eugene at 4th Avenue;
in Albany at 110 West 10th Street; and in Salem at 13th and Oak
streets.

CAR   You'll find many of the major agencies at the airports in Eugene
RENTALS   and Medford. In Eugene, airport agencies include **Avis Rent A
Car** (800-331-1212), **Budget Rent A Car** (800-527-0700) and
Hertz Rent A Car (800-654-3131). In Medford, try **Avis Rent A
Car** (800-331-1212), **Budget Rent A Car** (800-527-0700), **Hertz
Rent A Car** (800-654-3131) and **National Interrent** (800-328-
4567).

PUBLIC   All the major Willamette Valley and Ashland–Rogue River cities
TRANSIT   have local public transit systems. While there are bus connections
to many of the smaller towns, you'll need to rent a car to see many
of the rural highlights.

The Salem area is served by **Cherriots** (503-588-2877). Contact the **Corvallis Transit System** (541-757-6998) in Corvallis. In
Eugene, the **Lane Transit District** (541-687-5555) blankets the
city. Medford, Jacksonville and Ashland are served by the **Rogue
Valley Transportation District** (541-779-2877).

TAXIS   In Eugene, **Airport City Taxi** (541-484-4142) or **Yellow Cab** (541-
746-1440) can take you downtown. In Medford, call **Yellow Cab**
(541-772-6288).

ELEVEN

Vancouver and
the Sunshine Coast

Mother Nature went all out in British Columbia, a Canadian province larger than California, Oregon and Washington combined. Stretched along the upper west coast of North America, the coastline is dotted by thousands of islands, only a few inhabited. Inland are thick forests, rugged mountain ranges and high deserts. The more remote northern regions contain vast, pristine wildernesses.

Bordered by the Pacific to the west, the United States to the south and the Coastal Range to the east, the southwestern corner of the province, including Vancouver, Whistler and the Sunshine Coast, contains unrivaled scenic splendors. The waters of the region, fed by heavy rains (60 inches annually in Vancouver, more at higher elevations), shape this land: the ocean, high lakes, mountain streams, broad rivers, inlets and fjords carve through alpine meadows and mold shorelines.

Nature has long provided for human needs here. Myriad indigenous tribes, living in peaceful coexistence with the earth, thrived in the mild climate of the region for centuries, hunting and camping in verdant forests, fishing salmon-filled waters and traversing the many streams and rivers. Europeans made an appearance in the 1770s, when Captain James Cook sailed through searching for the Northwest Passage and stopped to trade with the native inhabitants. Britain didn't lay claim to the area until Captain George Vancouver's visit in 1792.

Stories of the incredible abundance of wildlife brought in trappers and traders; a string of posts established by Hudson's Bay Company soon followed, with a steady flow of settlers not far behind. Friction arose when American settlers moved in and sought United States government authority. Eventually, the boundary between the United States and British Columbia was settled in 1846 by the Oregon Treaty.

As the fur trade began to wane, the Fraser Gold Rush of 1858 was just gaining speed, so the stream of settlers continued. Logging took off not long after the gold petered out. Gastown, the first settlement in what is now Vancouver, grew around an early saw mill. The city's future was ensured with the arrival of the transcontinental railroad in 1887 and, with its natural harbor, its importance as a shipping center soon became evident.

Industry in British Columbia is still largely based on what the land provides—logging, fishing and mining—with Vancouver the processing and shipping center. Since the Vancouver World's Fair in 1986 focused worldwide attention on all the region had to offer, tourism has grown to become the second major industry in the province, after logging. Add to this mix Swiss-style banking regulations that attract investment from around the world and you have a truly dynamic city.

Canada's Pacific gateway in fact as well as image, Vancouver is one of the economic centers of the Pacific Rim, and a major North American shipping center. It's also a bustling cruise-ship departure port. The city has long attracted immigrants from Asia, most recently from Hong Kong, although that tide has slowed now that control of the colony has reverted to China. Even so, Vancouver's Chinatown is one of the three largest in North America, behind New York and San Francisco. The city also has strong Italian, Greek, French, Indian, Japanese and Russian communities, and is a popular destination for European travelers. The West End (adjoining Stanley Park) is the most densely populated urban district in North America, much resembling a European city neighborhood with its residential towers, streetside shops and cafés. The Vancouver visitor can hear more than a dozen languages in a day's journey through the city, a reflection of its vital, cosmopolitan nature.

The combination of exceptional scenery, heady cultural life, economical production costs and attractive exchange rates has made Vancouver a film-industry center that ranks with San Francisco. *The X Files* was taped here, along with a half-dozen other American TV shows and, sometimes, literally dozens of films a year. Aside from the cachet this brings the city, it's an economic boon—more than $530 million a year.

Whistler, 75 miles northeast of Vancouver, is close enough for a day trip from the city (though there's too much to see and do in just one day). With island-dotted Howe Sound to the west and the verdant Coastal Range to the east, there are enough sights along the picturesque Sea to Coast Highway to make driving the narrow, winding road slow but enjoyable. Parks and scenic pullouts along the way are perfect for a picnic or stretch.

The first settlers to arrive in Whistler in the early 1900s realized right away the potential in the area's beauty, so it comes as no surprise that some of the first structures were built as vacation retreats, most geared toward fishing and hunting. Skiing began in earnest in 1966 with the opening of the Garibaldi Lift Company in Whistler. A stylized European village resort was constructed 12 years and $550 million later at the convergence of the Blackcomb and Whistler mountains. In its short time, this ski destination has gained a strong international reputation and is now among the top attractions in North America. The resort is consistently rated number 1 in North America by *Ski Magazine*—ahead of such better-known destinations as Aspen, Vail and Sun Valley.

Although summer used to be the slow season at Whistler, an explosion of golf development is attracting a rapidly growing crowd of warm-weather visitors. Hiking, tennis, sailing, fishing, biking and horseback riding are among the other activities that occupy visitors; lodging and dining rates are still somewhat lower than in winter. Boutiques and eateries line the cobbled walkways of Whistler Village, which are often alive with street entertainers, from jugglers and clowns to dancers and musicians. The warmer months (June–September) are a favorite time to visit since crowds are minimal, prices for accommodation are drastically lower and there are so many outdoor activities to enjoy in the area's quiet alpine meadows, dense green forests and cool mountain lakes. However, even during ski season (November–May), you'll find no shortage of parking—a big problem at many resorts—because the main village of this carefully planned resort is built atop a massive underground garage.

With approximately 2400 hours of sunshine each year, the Sunshine Coast lives up to its well-deserved name. It is made up of small, quiet fishing and logging communities strung along a 90-mile coastline. These pleasant sights lie between Langdale, a short ferry ride from Horseshoe Bay in West Vancouver, and Lund, the gateway to Desolation Sound Marine Park. Another short ferry ride between Earls Cove and Saltery Bay connects the northern and southern sections of the coast. The ferry trips give visitors the sense that they are touring a series of islands even though the Sunshine Coast is firmly attached to the mainland.

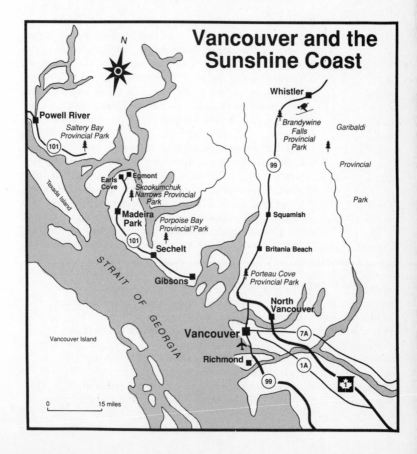

The region is a gem for anyone who loves the great outdoors, with mild weather and enough hiking, camping and water activities—fishing, diving, canoeing, kayaking, sailing or simply lounging on one of many beaches—to please one and all. The locals, mainly loggers, anglers and artists, are friendly and upbeat, willing to share recommendations for what to see and do in their neck of the woods. Except for warm summer weekends, the Sunshine Coast is not yet inundated by tourists and retains a rustic, provincial air.

Southwestern British Columbia offers something for everyone tucked into a neat package: the urbane and worldly pleasures of Vancouver, the bustle and excitement of resort life at Whistler and the undeveloped, uncrowded scenic beauty of the Sunshine Coast. Simply put, it is a vacationer's paradise in the Pacific Northwest.

▼▼▼▼▼▼▼▼▼▼▼▼
West Side– Granville Island

If museums are your passion, this is a good place to start your visit to Vancouver. A number of the city's leading facilities are found here. Marvelous Granville Island offers some cultural attractions as well.

SIGHTS

Begin your visit with a pleasant stroll through several of the city's leading museums. One of the finest is the University of British Columbia's **Museum of Anthropology**, with sunlit galleries of Northwest Coastal First Nation totems, chests, canoes, jewelry, ceremonial masks, clothing and contemporary native artwork. There's no charge to visit the true-to-life Haida longhouse and totems behind the museum; you may even find a carver at work on a totem there. Closed Monday from September through May. Admission. ~ 6393 Northwest Marine Drive; 604-822-5087.

Further samples of First Nation artifacts along with intriguing collections of European costumes, tools, furniture and relics portraying the rapid colonization of the area are at the **Vancouver Museum**, located on a small green peninsula in English Bay known as Vanier Park. The **H. R. MacMillan Planetarium** (604-738-7827) upstairs stages regular astronomy programs and musical laser light shows. Closed Monday in winter. Separate admission to museum and planetarium. ~ 1100 Chestnut Street; 604-736-4431.

✔ CHECK THESE OUT—UNIQUE SIGHTS

- Dig deep into the Pacific Northwest's human history at the University of Vancouver's **Museum of Anthropology**. *page 456*
- Discover the unique offerings found at **Granville Island**'s craft studios, parklands and enormous public market. *page 457*
- Tread lightly through the **Dr. Sun Yat Sen Classical Chinese Garden**, the first such classical garden built outside China. *page 463*
- Wander through acres of thick forest without leaving downtown Vancouver at the pride of the city, **Stanley Park**. *page 464*

Nearby is the **Vancouver Maritime Museum,** documenting the maritime history of British Columbia including the glory of international steamship travel. Housed in the connected A-frame is the Royal Canadian Mounted Police supply ship, the **St. Roch,** now a National Historic Site since it was the first ship to pass successfully through the Northwest Passage in both directions. Closed Monday in winter. Admission. ~ 1905 Ogden Avenue; 604-257-8300.

Across a short bridge from downtown Vancouver lies **Granville Island.** Refurbished by the federal government, Granville contains everything from parkland to craft studios to a cement factory. Once an industrial area, today it is a classic example of native funk gone chic. Corrugated-metal warehouses have been transformed into sleek shops, while rusting cranes and dilapidated steam turbines have become decorative pieces. There are several **working studios** to view. The focal point is the **Granville Public Market,** a 50,000-square-foot collection of stalls selling fresh fish, fruits, vegetables and other goodies.

A quick stop at the **InfoCentre** to see the orientation film and pick up a map helps you focus on what you want to see and do. ~ 1592 Johnston Street; 604-666-5784.

Leave time for an informal 30-minute tour of the **Granville Island Brewing Company,** the first microbrewery in Canada and home of the popular Island Lager. Daily tastings are offered. ~ 1441 Cartwright Street; 604-687-2739.

Of course, getting to the market is half the adventure: you can walk, drive or catch the **False Creek Ferry** from behind the Vancouver Aquatic Center (south end of Thurlow Street). ~ 604-684-7781.

Throughout the year there are affordable rooms available at the **Walter Gage Residence,** part of the University of British Columbia's conference center. Single and twin rooms in the dorm buildings are generally full of students during the school term but are available in the summer. "Triple suites" (one-bedroom apartments with kitchenette and private bath) are always available. Guests can get an inexpensive meal in the Student Union Building cafeteria. ~ 5961 Student Union Boulevard; 604-822-1010. BUDGET TO MODERATE.

LODGING

The **Hostelling International—Vancouver,** the second-largest youth hostel in North America, enjoys a prime setting on English Bay at lovely Jericho Beach. Housed in what was once military barracks, there is space here for over 275 hostelers in the many dorm-style rooms with shared baths; the few couple/family rooms go quickly. With fully equipped communal kitchens, laundry facilities, cafeteria (closed in winter) and lounge with big-screen television, this is easily one of the fanciest hostels you could hope to visit. ~ 1515 Discovery Street; 604-224-3208, fax 604-224-4852. BUDGET.

The welcoming glass lobby full of greenery bustles with businesspeople, the majority of the clientele at the **Executive Inn**. This quiet, friendly hotel near the airport has 30 standard rooms and 130 suites in pastel tones with breakfast bars, mini-refrigerators and modern furnishings in separate seating and sleeping areas. Rooms with jacuzzis or kitchenettes are also available. ~ 7211 Westminster Highway, Richmond; phone/fax 604-278-5555, 800-663-2878. DELUXE.

HIDDEN ► Although it's on a back street in a quiet neighborhood, nearby public transportation makes **Beautiful Bed & Breakfast** accessible to Vancouver's main attractions, including downtown and the UBC, both of which are just minutes away by bus. Housed in a spacious, attractive colonial-style home, the inn's four rooms include a honeymoon suite with marble fireplace and a large balcony. Breakfast is served to order in a formal dining room with silver service. ~ 428 West 40th Avenue; 604-327-1102, fax 604-327-2299. MODERATE TO DELUXE.

DINING

The Kitsilano neighborhood, a long, narrow district that runs from around Burrard Street to Alma Street and features commercial corridors along 4th Avenue and Broadway, boasts many excellent, small restaurants.

Tropika offers a fine introduction to Malaysian cuisine. If you really don't know what you're getting into, order satay (marinated meat skewered and grilled over charcoal); if you've had some exposure, you'll appreciate the spicier starred selections. They specialize in curries. ~ 3105 West Broadway; 604-737-6002. MODERATE.

HIDDEN ► The last time we stopped by **Sophie's Cosmic Café**, diners were lined up outside the door. Inside, people were piling into Naugahyde booths and gazing at the pennants, pictures and antique toys that line this quirky café. There are tofu omelettes and high-fiber Belgian waffles for breakfast, and falafel and burgers later in the day. Dinner gets downright sophisticated as Sophie cooks up Cajun prawns, oysters and chicken Rouchambeau. A scene. ~ 2095 West 4th Avenue; 604-732-6810. BUDGET TO MODERATE.

Shijo Japanese Restaurant, atmospherically appointed with tatami, bronze lamps and black wood accents, is popular with the downtown crowd. Sushi, vegetarian dishes and traditional Japanese fare are prepared with an innovative twist. Delicate broiled eggplant morsels topped with miso paste and barbecued shiitake mushrooms are among the standout dishes. ~ 1926 4th Avenue; 604-732-4676. MODERATE.

Set near the conservatory at the peak of Queen Elizabeth Park, the elegant **Seasons in the Park Restaurant** enjoys sweeping views of the Vancouver skyline and the mountains towering above the

North Shore. The seafood and Continental dishes are seasonal, and specials from the daily menu are always on a par with the outstanding view. ~ Cambie Street at 33rd Avenue; 604-874-8008. MODERATE TO DELUXE.

A just-for-fun diner is **Fogg 'n' Suds**, a fancified hamburger joint with relaxed atmosphere and a friendly crowd. You probably won't have time to try each of the 250 beers from around the globe, but regulars get a chance to fill out a stylized passport of brews. ~ 500 West Broadway; 604-872-3377. BUDGET.

Spicy northern Chinese cuisine is showcased brilliantly at **Kirin Mandarin**, a large, stylish restaurant handsomely adorned with gray-green walls and Chinese ceramics. An emphasis on fresh local seafood is evidenced by well-stocked fish tanks at the rear of the dining area. Shellfish dishes are especially noteworthy, including lobster and crab prepared with ginger sauce or chili-spiked sea scallops. ~ 1166 Alberni Street; 604-682-8833. MODERATE.

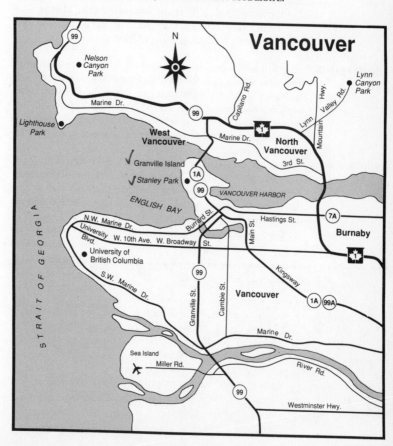

Tandoori fans will appreciate the hearty East Indian fare at **Da Tandoor**, where flavorful spices wake up those bored taste buds. Favorites from the authentic earthenware oven include leavened breads, lamb curry, India spice chicken and other tandoori specialties marinated in yogurt and spices. ~ 819 Pacific Street; 604-684-2529. MODERATE TO DELUXE.

Another spot for a fine view of the city lights, this time from water level on the Granville Island Wharf, is **Bridges**. The restaurant is one of the current hot spots of the dining elite who have the choice of the refined elegance of the dining room, the relaxed bistro or the convivial pub. The fare here ranges from standard and nouvelle preparations of seafood and meats to basic pasta and finger foods. Reservations recommended for the dining room. ~ 1696 Duranleau Street; 604-687-4400. MODERATE TO DELUXE.

Inevitably you are going to end up on Granville Island. Should hunger strike while you're touring the shops and artist studios, check out the food stalls at the **Granville Public Market**. Here you'll find a fish-and-chips shop, souvlaki stand, juice and salad bar, deli, even a fresh soup outlet. All are BUDGET.

SHOPPING A strip of intriguing shops lies along **4th Avenue** between Burrard and Alma streets. Situated between Granville Island and the University of British Columbia campus, this is the Kitsilano neighborhood. Back in the 1960s and 1970s, it was a center for Vancouver's counterculture. Since then, time and gentrification have transformed the area into a spiffy district of smart shops and comfortable homes.

HIDDEN ► Just off 4th is **T**, one of the district's more intriguing shops. Devoted entirely to teas, T has two dozen black-tea varieties, ranging from common types such as Earl Grey to rarities such as a robust Tanzanian leaf. Fruit and herbal teas and pastries round out the offerings. ~ 2460 Heather Street; 604-874-8320.

The main draw on Granville Island is the **Public Market**, with rows of vendors selling fresh produce, flowers, pastas, wines, baked

TIMING IS EVERYTHING

July, August and early September are the peak tourist times in the lower mainland of southwestern British Columbia, and that is indeed when the weather is most reliable. However, visitors would do well to consider off-season travel—that's when local hotels offer special packages that can be incredible bargains. Luxury accommodations are sometimes half-price—which, when you take into account the favorable exchange rate, can mean a super-deluxe room can be had for less than US$100. For more information call Tourism Vancouver (604-682-2222) or SuperNatural BC (800-663-6000).

goods, seafood and meats, along with the section brimming with fast-food outlets proffering an international array of delectables. The **Kids Only Market** within the market is a mall full of toy stores, children's clothing shops and a tykes' beauty salon. ~ 1496 Cartwright Street; 604-689-8447. **Christmas Presence** showcases yuletide ornaments and decorations all year. ~ 1551 Johnston Street; 604-684-9922. The market's **Cartoon Corner Art Gallery** carries limited-edition animation cels that go for a pretty penny. ~ 1406½ Old Bridge Street; 604-683-8989.

There is plenty of innovative theater to choose from on Granville Island. The **Carousel Theatre** offers family-oriented classical and contemporary productions. ~ 1411 Cartwright Street; 604-669-3410. There's a wide variety of shows with a multicultural flair at the nearby **Waterfront Theatre**. ~ 1410 Cartwright Street; 604-685-6217. The **Playwrights Theatre Center** hosts the Annual Vancouver New Play Festival, showcasing the works of Canadian playwrights. ~ 1405 Anderson Street; 604-685-6228. One of the largest nonprofit theaters in Canada, the **Arts Club Theatre** has afternoon performances followed by high tea. ~ 1585 Johnston Street; 604-687-1644.

    Bridges, a subdued but trendy bistro on Granville Island, is fairly quiet and a good place to savor a glass of wine and the lights of the city dancing on the water of False Creek. ~ 1696 Duranleau Street; 604-687-4400.

NIGHTLIFE

QUEEN ELIZABETH PARK Taking the place of two stone quarries that once supplied building materials for the city, this 130-acre park now features various ornamental gardens showcasing the indigenous plants of the coast along with two rock gardens that reflect the land's past. At 501 feet above sea level, the park affords some of the best views of downtown Vancouver, crowned by the mountains of the North Shore. Bloedel Conservatory rests at its peak. You'll find a restaurant, restrooms, picnic facilities, 18 tennis courts, lawn bowling lanes, frisbee golf and a pitch-and-putt golf course. ~ Located at Cambie Street and 33rd Avenue.

BEACHES & PARKS

WRECK BEACH Of the many beaches in and around Vancouver, this highly undeveloped (and unspoiled) sandy stretch across from the University of British Columbia on the tip of Point Grey Peninsula is the only *au naturel* spot in town. Students make up the majority of the sun worshippers here. There are outhouses, seasonal concession services and a telephone at the top of the trail; restaurants are nearby at the university. ~ Located south of Nitobe Garden and the Museum of Modern Art off Northwest Marine Drive; a steep, twisting trail opposite the university residences leads from the road to the beach; 604-224-5739

◄ *HIDDEN*

ENGLISH BAY BEACHES (SOUTHERN SHORE) ⚓ Stretched around the north face of Point Grey Peninsula on the opposite side of the bay, Kitsilano Beach, Jericho, Lacarno and Spanish Banks beaches attract hordes of windsurfers, sunbathers, picnickers and swimmers, but are spacious enough not to feel overcrowded. There is a heated outdoor saltwater pool at Kitsilano Beach in case the sea is too nippy. You'll find restrooms, lifeguards (in summer), changing rooms and intermittent food stalls; restaurants and groceries are nearby. ~ Kitsilano Beach is at Cornwall Avenue and Arbutus Street; Jericho, Lacarno and Spanish beaches are accessible off of Northwest Marine Drive; 604-257-8400.

▼▼▼▼▼▼▼▼▼▼▼▼▼▼▼▼
Downtown Vancouver

If your vision of downtown is an office world that rolls up the sidewalk at 6 p.m., get ready for a pleasant surprise. A beautiful harbor setting, intriguing historic districts, galleries and gardens set downtown Vancouver apart from most cities.

SIGHTS   **Tourism Vancouver** offers detailed information to visitors. ~ Plaza Level, Waterfront Centre, 200 Burrard Street; 604-683-2000. The best guide to Vancouver dining, theater, music and other events is the *Georgia Straight*, a free weekly with comprehensive coverage of the city's cultural life. It's available at most coffee shops, bookstores, hotels, restaurants and newsstands.

The **Vancouver Cultural Alliance** maintains an arts-event clearinghouse that offers comprehensive information on musical, theatrical, cultural and artistic happenings in the city. Tickets are available for some events. ~ 938 Howe Street; 604-684-2787.

The shining geodesic dome so prominent on the Vancouver skyline as you approach the city from the south was Expo Centre during the 1986 Exposition and is now home to **Science World British Columbia**. Fascinating hands-on exhibits let you bend light, fondle a tornado, dance on a giant synthesizer keyboard and more. The **OMNIMAX Theatre** (604-268-6363) upstairs features a variety of exciting films shown on the largest screen in the world. Separate admission to museum and theater. ~ 1455 Quebec Street; 604-268-6363.

Dedicated in 1995, **Library Square** is a stunning architectural highlight of Vancouver's decade-long building boom. Vancouver Public Library's Central Branch is the centerpiece: a fascinating oval building cast in reddish concrete, designed by famed Canadian architect Moshe Safdie to hint at the Roman Coliseum. Its many windows and unusual angles capture and reflect light like a prism. With eight floors of books and reference materials, the library is one of the largest in North America. ~ 350 West Georgia Street; 604-331-3600.

There are numerous photo-worthy spots in **Chinatown**, which stretches along Pender Street between Carrall and Gore streets.

North America's third-largest Chinese community, this crowded neighborhood is particularly festive during holiday periods. Among the most remarkable sites is the extremely narrow **Sam Kee Building**, Pender and Carrall streets, listed in the *Guinness Book of World Records* as the skinniest building in the world at just six feet wide. Along the way you'll also see brightly colored, elaborately carved facades of buildings housing herbalists, bakeries, dim sum parlors, silk or souvenir shops and open-front produce stands. Also be sure to stop by the **Dr. Sun Yat Sen Classical Chinese Garden** ✓ (see "Vancouver in Bloom" below), a unique garden that seems to have been magically transported to Vancouver from China.

A bit farther on Pender Street is the old **Sun Tower Building** ◄ *HIDDEN* which, at 272 feet, was once the tallest building in the British Empire and site of a daring escape stunt pulled off by Harry Houdini during the height of his career. ~ 100 West Pender Street; 604-683-2305.

Colorful **Gastown**, named after saloon keeper "Gassy" Jack Deighton whose statue stands in Maple Tree Square (Alexander

Downtown Vancouver

and Carrall streets), is where the original townsite began in 1867. This touristy heritage area of cobbled streets, Victorian street lamps and storefronts, charming courtyards and mews is chock-full of antique and souvenir shops and international eateries. On the corner of Cambie and Water streets is the world's first **steam-powered clock** wheezing out musical chimes on the quarter hour. ~ 604-683-5650.

A few steps farther on Carrall there's a great view of the harbor from **Canada Place**, Vancouver's trade-convention center and cruise-ship terminal, complete with hotel and IMAX theater. From the bow of this landlocked behemoth you can scan the waterfront, taking in the broad sweep of North Vancouver and the spectacular mountains behind it. Bridges arch to port and starboard, ships lie at anchor in the harbor and an occasional ferry plies the narrow waterway.

There's hardly a native tree to be seen in downtown Vancouver. However, the furor over B.C.'s forests can be encountered at the **Forest Alliance Visitors Center** in the financial district, where visitors will discover the timber industry's take on forest management. Its displays about wood fiber growth, harvest and use are attractive but quite one-sided; however, it does convey the economic and political significance of the province's vast forests. ~ 1055 Dunsmuir Street; 604-685-7507.

Nearby, a glass elevator zips you up to the aptly named **Lookout!** circular viewing deck high atop Harbour Centre. With a tremendous 360-degree view of Vancouver and environs, plaques pointing out all the major sights, guides present to answer all questions and a brief multimedia presentation on the highlights of the city, this is one of the best places to get your bearings. Admission. ~ 555 West Hastings Street; 604-689-0421.

Housed in what was once the central courthouse, the **Vancouver Art Gallery** has four floors of galleries showcasing the works of international masters alongside popular contemporary Canadian artists; the Emily Carr Gallery, featuring many of her drawings and paintings of the coastal rainforests is a must-see. Closed Monday and Tuesday in winter. Admission. ~ 750 Hornby Street; 604-662-4700.

Adjacent **Robson Square**, below the current government offices and courts, is the site of frequent concerts and lectures and has a skating rink. ~ 800 Robson Street; 604-660-2830.

STANLEY PARK Easily ranked as one of the most outstanding city parks in the world, 1000-acre Stanley Park offers more recreational and entertainment options than you can imagine. Only the outer 20 percent of this green grove poking out into Burrard Inlet at the head of the downtown peninsula is developed for recreational use. ~ 604-257-8400.

Vancouver
in Bloom

Rain is a common sight in this neck of the woods during the winter months, but the payoff bursts forth in the spring. Vancouver is a green, green city overflowing with international parks and gardens that are a flourishing testament to the forethought of the city's founders.

Rose aficionados will want to stroll through Stanley Park's lovely **Rose Garden**, crowning glory of the city's parks. The fragrant collection in this mid-size formal garden is sure to contain one or two specimens you'd like to have in your own yard. Late summer is the best time to visit for the full effect. ~ Located near the park's entrance just off Georgia Street; 604-257-8400.

There's also a wonderful rose garden in Queen Elizabeth Park, but it is often overshadowed entirely by the star of the show here, the **Bloedel Conservatory**. Set at the crown of Little Mountain, the conservatory houses over 500 tropical plant species under a 70-foot-high triodetic geodesic dome. Admission. ~ 604-257-8570.

With over 16,000 species, the award for variety goes to the **University of British Columbia Botanical Garden**. This 70-acre research facility is filled with exotic and familiar specimens separated into alpine, Asian, British Columbian natives and food gardens. Summer admission. ~ 6804 Southwest Marine Drive; 604-822-9666.

VanDusen Botanical Garden runs a close second with over 6500 species of plants from six continents divided into theme areas. It takes a full day (and a great deal of staying power) to make it through the entire 55-acre complex, but you can hit the major sites—the Elizabethan hedge maze, the hanging basket display, rock and stone gardens, Canadian Heritage garden, fragrance garden and herb garden—in two to three hours. Admission. ~ 5251 Oak Street; 604-878-9274.

Nitobe Memorial Garden is an authentic Japanese strolling garden with teahouse. Narrow paths wind through two-and-a-half acres of serene traditional Japanese plantings and across gracefully arched bridges over the still pond. Folks come here for the cherry blossoms in April, irises in June and flaming red Japanese maples in October. Closed weekends in winter. Summer admission. ~ University of British Columbia campus, 1903 West Mall; 604-822-6038.

The jewel of Chinatown is the multimillion-dollar **Dr. Sun Yat Sen Classical Chinese Garden**. Designed and constructed by craftsmen brought in from China, this Ming Dynasty–style garden is the first such classical garden to be built outside China. Many of the elements, including the architectural and artistic components, rocks and pebbles (but not the plants) were shipped in from China. Admission. ~ 578 Carrall Street; 604-662-3207.

Within the park you'll find the **Vancouver Aquarium**, where you can view the resident orca whales, as well as nearly 700 species of marine life in the museum's numerous tanks. Then stroll through the tropical rainforest room and listen to the birds chitter while peering at crocs or piranhas. An outdoor viewing deck on the west side of the compound allows free looks at the seal and beluga whale pools. Admission. ~ 604-685-3364.

You can enter the nearby **Children's Farm Yard** to frolic with the llamas, goats and other little critters. You can also ride the miniature railway, a scaled-down version of the first train to cross Canada. Admission. ~ 604-257-8530.

The best way to take in all the sights is to bike or hike along the divided six-mile **seawall promenade** (see "Outdoor Adventures" for more information). If you're pressed for time or just not up for the several-hour jaunt around the perimeter path, hop in the car and follow the one-way **scenic drive** signs from the park's main entrance off Georgia Street to hit most of the highlights.

Making your way around the promenade, you'll pass a statue of Lord Stanley, the rose gardens, the Royal Vancouver Yacht Club, Deadman's Island, the Nine O'Clock Gun, an array of Kwakiutl and Haida totem poles and the "girl in a wetsuit" statue next to the historic figurehead from the S.S. *Empress* of Japan.

Continue along the promenade to **Prospect Point Lookout**, at the far northern tip of the park, which boasts a great view of the **Lions Gate Bridge**. One of the longest suspension bridges in the world, it stretches over Burrard Inlet to the slopes of West Vancouver. Siwash Rock, the hollow tree and Second, Third and English beaches, extremely popular among sunbathers and water enthusiasts, finish out the seawall route. Second Beach has a heated outdoor pool.

To get to know the wild interior of the park, visit the **Nature House**, an interpretive center at the northeast edge of Lost Lagoon where visitors learn about the flora and fauna in the park, or join one of the **summer nature walks**. Hikers will enjoy the miles of trails through thick coniferous forest while birdwatchers will probably prefer to perch quietly at the edge of **Beaver Lake** or **Lost Lagoon** to peer at Canadian geese, rare trumpeter swans and other waterfowl. For children, there's the **Variety Kid's Water Park** (a wonderful, watery play area complete with slides, water cannons and a pint-size, full-body blow drier), a miniature steam locomotive, pony rides, Kids Traffic School and a fire-engine playground. Admission.

LODGING
SuperNatural B.C. operates a free reservation hotline to assist visitors in arranging for accommodations in all price categories. It's expensive to stay in the city, especially in the downtown core.

If you bring your car, expect to pay an additional $10–$15 per day to park at most downtown hotels. You will also pay the Goods and Services Tax (17 percent) on all hotel accommodations; if 7 percent of this tax amounts to over $7, you can claim a rebate for this percentage by filling out a form (available from your hotel) and mailing it to Revenue Canada. ~ 800-663-6000.

Located in the heart of the business and entertainment district of cosmopolitan Vancouver, the luxurious **Sutton Place Hotel** offers five-star accommodations at prices comparable to (and in some cases lower than) other top hotels in town, while assuring guests more for their money in terms of space and personal attention. Needless to say, rooms are elegant, with classical decor punctuated by a blend of antique reproductions and fine botanical prints; marbled bathrooms are enormous, with deep European-style tubs and separate showers. Personal service is the signature here. ~ 845 Burrard Street; 604-682-5511, 800-961-7555, fax 604-682-5513. ULTRA-DELUXE.

Home away from home for the British royal family since it opened in 1939, the **Hotel Vancouver**, peaked by a château-style oxidized-copper roof, is a landmark. The calling card of this posh property is Old World elegance. Rooms are spacious and well appointed with polished antiques, plump chairs, large writing desks and tall windows that open to the surrounding scenery. Bathrooms are a bit small (typical of the period in which it was built) but elegant nonetheless. ~ 900 West Georgia Street; 604-684-3131, 800-441-1414, fax 604-662-1929. ULTRA-DELUXE.

There's a reason the **Four Seasons Vancouver** consistently shows up in top-ten rankings for North America. The service here is incomparable, composed of dozens of tiny details that escape the average hotel. Head out the door to go jogging, for instance, and the doorman will greet your return with a dry towel. The decor is a bit dated—'70s metallic shine—but the location is superb and the 385 spacious rooms are well equipped for business travelers. The extensive second-floor fitness center opens onto a remarkable waterfall garden, perfect for contemplation. ~ 791 West Georgia Street; 604-689-9333, 800-268-6282, fax 604-689-3466. ULTRA-DELUXE.

The view from the **Waterfront Centre Hotel** captures the essence of Vancouver: In the foreground is the commercial hubbub of Canada Place; beyond that is Burrard Inlet, with sailboats and container ships; beyond that, the Lion's Gate Bridge and Grouse Mountain. More than half the 489 rooms in this deluxe business-class hotel are positioned to look out on this vista; be sure to ask for one. There's also an extensive herb garden on the patio adjoining the swimming pool. ~ 900 Canada Place Way; 604-691-1991, 800-441-1414, fax 604-691-1999. DELUXE.

The **Coast Plaza** is by far the best lodging after Stanley Park. With 267 airy, large rooms and suites looking out over the park, its location is unsurpassed for West End visitors. ~ 1733 Comox Street; 604-688-7711, fax 604-688-5934. MODERATE TO DELUXE.

If prime downtown location and lots of room space are important to you, check into **Pacific Palisades**. The well-furnished studios and suites are roomy with modern, pastel decor; all are equipped with kitchenettes, and many have breezy patios with grand views of the harbor. Triple-sheeted beds are turned down as part of the pampering service that includes pluses like thick robes, French milled soaps and other extras travelers have come to expect from the Shangri-La hotel chain. Prices drop drastically during periodic off-season promotions. ~ 1277 Robson Street; 604-688-0461, 800-663-1815, fax 604-688-4374. ULTRA-DELUXE.

The **West End Guest House**, a pink Victorian a block off bustling Robson Street, offers a more personable alternative to the area's hotels and motels. Each of the eight guest rooms filled with a mixture of antiques has a personality of its own. All have private bath and romantic four-poster brass beds with plush feather mattresses, duvets and luxurious linens. Meals here, from the afternoon sherry with nuts and pâté to the multicourse morning repast, are a gourmand's delight. Free bike rentals. Gay-friendly. ~ 1362 Haro Street; 604-681-2889, fax 604-688-8812. DELUXE TO ULTRA-DELUXE.

It's not hard to tell from its layout that the three-story **Barclay Hotel** was at one time an apartment building, though renovations have really spruced up the public areas. Rooms are a bit tight, with mix-and-match furniture, minuscule bathrooms, refrigerators, air-conditioning and painted walls. The suites provide an affordable (though not cheap) alternative for families. Facing on

---

✔ CHECK THESE OUT—UNIQUE LODGING

- *Budget to moderate:* Stay in the heart of Vancouver without paying a fortune at the **Kingston Hotel Bed and Breakfast**, a European-style B&B. *page 469*
- *Moderate to deluxe:* Transport yourself to the Alps via **Edelweiss**, a European-style pension catering to ski enthusiasts. *page 480*
- *Deluxe:* Luxuriate at the **Villa Marisol**, where windows serve as frames for fabulous scenescapes. *page 490*
- *Ultra-deluxe:* Make yourself at home as the British royal family does on occasion—at the elegant **Hotel Vancouver**. *page 467*

Budget: under $50   Moderate: $50–$90   Deluxe: $90–$130   Ultra-deluxe: over $130

Robsonstrasse near all the restaurants and boutiques, the location is its best attribute. ~ 1348 Robson Street; 604-688-8850, fax 604-688-2534. MODERATE TO DELUXE.

Heritage House Hotel offers 110 rooms in an older brick building shaded by green awnings. Thoroughly renovated, the rooms feature refrigerators, wall-to-wall carpeting and contemporary furniture. Centrally located, the hotel is convenient to Gastown, Chinatown and major shopping districts. ~ 455 Abbott Street; 604-685-7777, fax 604-685-7067. MODERATE.

The **Burrard Motor Inn** has standard, motel-style accommodations in a good central location. A crotchety old elevator takes guests to upper-level, medium-size rooms arranged in a quadrangle around the carport hidden under a rooftop garden. Furnishings are run of the mill, but parking is free, virtually unheard of in downtown Vancouver. There are a few kitchenette units available. ~ 1100 Burrard Street; 604-681-2331. MODERATE.

Offering five guest rooms, **Nelson House** is a three-story Edwardian located near Barclay Heritage Square. Each room is individually decorated. Lounge by the cozy fireplace in the living room. Enjoy the full breakfast. Nonsmoking; children by prior arrangement only. Gay-friendly. ~ 977 Broughton Street; 604-684-9793, fax 604-684-4141. MODERATE TO ULTRA-DELUXE.

The **Kingston Hotel Bed and Breakfast** is an unusual find in downtown Vancouver. This 1910 woodframe with the large green awning and red neon sign was recently renovated inside and out to look more like a European bed and breakfast. The tiny rooms are clean and offer the bare necessities—vanity sink, dresser, bed, small closet—and a shared bath down the hall; eight rooms with private bath and television are larger. A continental breakfast is served in the lobby. ~ 757 Richards Street; 604-684-9024, fax 604-684-9917. BUDGET TO MODERATE.

Hostelling International's downtown Vancouver lodge is perfectly located—10 to 15 minutes' walk from Stanley Park, Granville Island, Gastown and the business district. With space for more than 200 hostelers, its rooms are clean and functional; a few offer private or ensuite bath. Laundry, recreation, cooking, meeting and studying facilities are available. Dozens of organized activities are offered every day, but wanderers will find almost limitless opportunities within easy reach. ~ 1114 Burnaby Street; 604-684-4565, fax 604-684-4540. BUDGET.

Housed in a huge, exquisitely renovated century-old Victorian home, **O Canada House's** six elegant, comfortable rooms all feature private bath and are furnished with period antiques. Guests are served a gourmet three-course breakfast. It's just a ten-minute walk to the Granville Island ferries, and 15 minutes to Stanley Park. Gay-friendly. ~ 1114 Barclay Street; 604-688-0555. DELUXE.

DINING

Dining in Chinatown is spelled dim sum. And the **Pink Pearl Restaurant** is a dim sum emporium, a cavernous dining room where black-clad waiters and waitresses roll out dozens of steam-tray delectables on trundle carts. Dine on this finger food while enjoying the Chinese artwork adorning the walls. ~ 1132 East Hastings Street; 604-253-4316. MODERATE.

HIDDEN ►

The decor at **C**, the snazzy seafood restaurant overlooking False Creek, is flashy—lots of metal and glass, exposed pipes and modern furniture, along with kitschy touches such as fishing lures on the restroom doors. But the food is quite down-to-earth, based on rich-stock soups, hearty breads and delights such as deep-fried salmon-skin crisps. Fish dishes are cooked to perfection; the menu offers a dozen types of caviar; and you can round off dinner with one of C's 20 types of tea. ~ 1600 Howe Street (on the False Creek Pier); 604-681-1164. MODERATE TO DELUXE.

Some of the food at **900 West** is so rich and delectable that you'll want to ask the chef exactly what went into it. No problem: He's standing right there along the dining bar. And the line cooks are hard at work behind the bar. These two innovations make 900 West an ideal place for the single traveler seeking a little conversation while dining. The airy, high-ceilinged room has two dozen tables, which seem surprisingly intimate in the big, open space. Lamb, poultry and salmon dishes, many of them rotisseried, are especially good. Desserts are as sumptuous as the main courses. ~ In the Hotel Vancouver, 900 West Georgia Street; 604-669-9378. DELUXE.

When wandering around Gastown, it's hard to miss the rotund, dancing monks touting their "scrumptious spaghetti, super salmon, ravishing ravioli and fabulous fondues" painted on the side of **Brother's Restaurant**. Waiters in Franciscan habits fit right in with the dark, monastical decor of this fun, family-style eatery. As promised, the food is good (especially the seafood and prime rib). ~ 1 Water Street; 604-683-9124. MODERATE.

When the wallet is plump and it's time to indulge the taste buds, head for longtime favorite **The William Tell**, poshly appointed with fine European art and a few antique crossbows in keeping with its name. Your gastronomic experience might start with smoked B.C. salmon or Cajun oyster chowder, followed by veal chop with Portobello mushrooms or roast duck breast in sun-dried cranberry and mango sauce. Items on the seasonal menu insert are always good choices, as are the extraordinary set meals presented in conjunction with shows at the Queen Elizabeth Theatre. Reservations recommended. ~ Georgia Court Hotel, 765 Beatty Street; 604-688-3504. DELUXE TO ULTRA-DELUXE.

Bandi's is a charming home-turned-restaurant serving authentic Hungarian fare such as pork tenderloin, crispy duck and red cabbage, marinated veal, robust goulash and peasant bread. On fine days, the best seats in the house are actually outside in the garden. There's usually no problem finding a table at lunch, but reservations are recommended for dinner. ~ 1427 Howe Street; 604-685-3391. MODERATE TO DELUXE.

If you're in the mood for Italian food, you can't go wrong by heading to one of Vancouver's five restaurants in the Umberto dynasty. The service and decor are impeccable and the food always tasty: Caprese salad, antipasti and pasta are reliable choices. For alfresco dining on sunny days, we recommend the villa-style, terra-cotta courtyard of **Il Giardino**. Check the phone book for addresses and phone numbers of other Umberto locations. ~ 1382 Hornby Street; 604-669-2422. MODERATE TO DELUXE.

Café Fleuri, well known for outstanding Continental cuisine,   ◄ HIDDEN
also serves an incredible Chocoholic Bar from 6 to 10 p.m. each Thursday, Friday and Saturday night that attracts hordes of sweet-toothed locals. There are 16 to 20 different chocolate items on the buffet (crêpes, fondues, cakes, covered fruits) that change daily. They also feature Sunday brunch, a seafood buffet on weekends and high tea Monday through Saturday. ~ Sutton Place Hotel, 845 Burrard Street; 604-682-5511. MODERATE TO DELUXE.

Success can be a dangerous thing. Long cited as the premier French restaurant in Vancouver, **Le Crocodile** shows the signs of complacency: Service is a bit snotty, the bread can be stale, portions are shrinking. Champagne glasses are not much larger than thimbles, but the prices aren't equally minuscule! However, the French provincial main dishes, such as cassoulet, remain hearty and rich, the nightly specials are inviting, and the crowded buzz of the place creates an energizing, cosmopolitan air. ~ 909 Burrard Street; 604-669-4298. DELUXE.

At **Villa del Lupo**, chef Julio Gonzalez-Perini practices food as art. Each dish is not only exquisitely flavorful, it's visually striking —swirls of sauce, artfully layered dashes and splashes of ingredi-

✦✦

✔ CHECK THESE OUT—UNIQUE DINING

- *Budget:* Order a shrimp sandwich for lunch at **Sundowner** then ask for Indian candy (honey-cured salmon) when you leave. *page 478*
- *Moderate:* Enjoy "ravishing ravioli and fabulous fondues" in a monastic setting at **Brother's Restaurant**, where waiters dress as monks. *page 470*
- *Deluxe to ultra-deluxe:* Enter **Delilah's**, a local favorite, for Northwest haute cuisine accented with bordello decor. *page 473*
- *Moderate to deluxe:* Feast on generous portions of French cuisine at **Les Deux Gros**, where the motto is "Never trust a skinny chef." *page 481*

Budget: under $8   Moderate: $8–$16   Deluxe: $16–$24   Ultra-deluxe: over $24

ents. The pastas, all handmade, are especially fine. The basement wine cellar (which guests can sometimes use for very intimate private parties) is extensive. ~ 869 Hamilton Street; 604-688-7436. DELUXE.

HIDDEN ►   Art is the decor theme at **Uforia**, an unobtrusive cubbyhole in the downtown business district. Sculptures, collages, paintings and found objects in dizzying array entertain the eyes, while an equally inventive blend of Mediterranean and Northwest cuisines tempts the palate. Desserts are lavish, delicious and visually memorable. ~ 860 Burrard Street; 604-685-7770. MODERATE TO DELUXE.

Although fine sandwiches and soups are available at **Miriam's**, this small chain of cafés is best known for its pies and baked goods. On Tuesday, a slice of pie is just $1.85—and it's not the sticky-sweet Stuckey's kind. Apple/rhubarb, bumbleberry and tart blueberry typify the savory offerings. ~ 2 Water Street in Gastown; 604-685-9985. Also in the West End at 105-1184 Denman, 604-683-7624; and in the downtown core at 148-757 West Hastings (Sinclair Centre), 604-683-4232. BUDGET.

Vancouver's explosion of coffee shops has become, if anything, greater than Seattle's. There are many fine local purveyors;
HIDDEN ►   the best downtown is **Trees**, a small enclave in the financial district just a couple of blocks from Canada Place. They roast their own all-organic coffees; even better, the very best muffins in town are baked in the kitchen out back. ~ 450 Granville Street; 604-684-5060. BUDGET.

Of the dozens of cafés and small eateries along Denman, near Stanley Park, **Bojangles** is a bit snazzier than most, but still offers an economical lunch for visitors who've spent the morning in the park. The deluxe sandwiches are exceptionally good; soups and salads are dependable. A small outdoor seating area faces south, into the sun, along a side street. ~ 785 Denman Street; 604-687-3622. BUDGET TO MODERATE.

If a customer fails to finish the food ordered at the Elbow Room Cafe, he or she is required to give a donation to a local charity. How much? Past donations have ranged from 50 cents to $50.

For more refined dining, turn to the **Monterey Lounge and Grill**, a romantic spot with candlelit tables, soft piano serenades and expansive window views of the endless parade on bustling Robson Street. The restaurant features a West Coast menu that changes every three months. ~ Pacific Palisades Hotel, 1277 Robson Street; 604-684-1277. MODERATE TO DELUXE.

Generous breakfasts and lunches attract a mixed clientele to the **Elbow Room Cafe**, which is decorated with autographed photos of movie stars. Start your day with the lumberjack or English breakfast, eggs Benedict, pancakes or an omelette. For lunch try a Monte Cristo, clubhouse or shrimp sandwich. Hamburgers are big and popular. The owners say you have to have personality to fit in. Weekend breakfasts are popular. ~ 560 Davie Street; 604-685-3628. BUDGET.

Local office workers line up on the sidewalk at lunchtime to get a table at **Stepho's**, a fairly traditional Greek taverna which serves up heaping platters of excellent roast lamb or fish. One platter is a huge meal at a most reasonable price—about U.S. $6. ~ 1124 Davie Street; 604-683-2555. BUDGET TO MODERATE.

Don't miss **Liliget Feast House**, a "longhouse" serving the native cuisine of the Pacific Northwest. You'll feast your eyes on Vancouver's most unique menu, then fill your belly with venison soup, barbecued duck breast, clam fritters and alder-barbecued salmon. On the side are steamed fern shoots and wild rice. For dessert, how about cold raspberry soup or whipped soapallalie (Indian ice cream), washed down with a cup of juniper tea? ~ 1724 Davie Street; 604-681-7044. MODERATE TO DELUXE.

◄ HIDDEN

With its bordello decor and prime Northwest haute cuisine, funky **Delilah's** in the West End is one the locals usually prefer not to share. As you arrive, you'll be handed a seasonal menu—perhaps tempura trout, Szechuan rack of lamb, Chilean sea bass with orange-ginger glaze and New York steak with a bourbon cream sauce. Next, sidle up to the bar for one of their famous martinis to keep you happy during the longish wait to be seated and served. Dinner only. ~ 1789 Comox Street; 604-687-3424. DELUXE TO ULTRA-DELUXE.

There are enough shops in Vancouver to overwhelm even the most serious of the "I'd-rather-be-shopping" crowd. Here are a few in the most popular shopping districts.

SHOPPING

In Chinatown, the **Beijing Trading Company** carries an intriguing selection of herbs, teas and food products. ~ 89 East Pender Street; 604-684-3563. Also in Chinatown, **Cheng Kiu** is an emporium of Chinese vases, brassware and collectibles. ~ 8105 Main Street; 604-327-1381.

Nearby, Gastown teems with souvenir shops full of T-shirts, totems, maple sugar, smoked salmon and other regional items; **Canadian Impressions** seems to have the widest selection. ~ 321 Water Street; 604-689-2024. In the same area is the **Inuit Gallery**, with high-dollar Northwest Coast First Nation and Inuit art. ~ 345 Water Street; 604-688-7323. **Polo/Ralph Lauren**, also in Gastown, has high-quality clothes. ~ 375 Water Street; 604-682-7656.

Located on the edge of Gastown, **Sikora** is a modern oddity, a store with just one type of merchandise—classical music. But what a selection! With thousands of CDs, classical music lovers will find artists and versions of standards that you'll never see in mainstream American music stores, no matter how large. ~ 432 West Hastings Street; 604-685-0625.

It seems like there are a zillion antique and curio shops in the Gastown area; one of the best is **Salmagundi West**, an engaging collection of clothes, jewelry, household goods and such. The owner has a fetish for horns, so if you need an antique trumpet or other heraldic instrument, this is the place. ~ 321 West Cordova Street; 604-681-4648.

The dark and passionate swirls of First Nations art have been incorporated by designer **Dorothy Grant** into a line of fine women's apparel, available only at her store in downtown's Sinclair Centre, near Canada Place. Her garments are truly distinctive and richly attractive. ~ 250-757 West Hastings Street; 604-681-0201.

Lush is exactly what its name implies—a redolent profusion of lotions, emollients, soaps, oils and other cosmetics and body-care products. It's an outpost of a popular European chain; all its products are natural and organic; Vancouverites voted it the best new store in town in 1997. ~ 1118 Denman; 604-608-1810. Also in the Robson Street shopping district at 100-1025 Robson; 604-687-5874.

Another popular downtown shopping area is Robson Street. It's nicknamed Vancouver's Rodeo Drive because of the sheer number of see-and-be-seen sidewalk cafés and upscale boutiques. **Robson Fashion Park** has a number of boutiques selling high fashion. ~ 1131 Robson Street. There are also several souvenir shops scattered along the strip along with some fun places such as the **Robson Public Market** with over two dozen retail stores. ~ 1610 Robson Street; 604-682-2733.

Vancouver is a chocoholic's paradise, with an unusual number of fine chocolate shops throughout the city. A downtown favorite is **Le Chocolat Belge Daniel**, which uses top-quality Belgian chocolate to create truffles and other confections. ~ 1105 Robson Street; 604-688-9624.

A high-style boutique on the west side of town, **Boboli** features imported European clothing for men and women. ~ 2756 Granville Street; 604-736-3458.

NIGHTLIFE The **Vancouver Opera Association** (604-682-2871) stages productions about five times a year at the Queen Elizabeth Theatre and Playhouse, also home to **Ballet British Columbia** (604-732-5003) as well as major theater productions and visiting musicals. ~ Theatre and Playhouse: Hamilton Street between Georgia and Dunsmuir streets; 604-665-3050.

The **Vancouver Symphony Orchestra** (604-684-9100) provides first-rate entertainment at The Orpheum, a multilevel vaudeville theater built in the mid-1920s that's worth a visit in itself. ~ Orpheum: 884 Granville Street.

The **Ford Centre for the Performing Arts**, opened in 1996 across the street from Library Square, is a glittering venue dedicated to touring Broadway shows and other musical extravaganzas such as *Sunset Boulevard* and Riverdance. ~ 777 Homer Street; 604-280-2222.

There are hundreds of clubs, discos, cabarets, lounges, pubs and taverns in Vancouver; we touch on only a few popular selections here. **Richard's on Richards**, the city's current "in" place, with its refined wood, brass and stained-glass decor, adult-oriented rock and live Top-40 bands on weekends, attracts a mixed crowd, predominantly upscale businesspeople. Wednesday is salsa night. ~ 1036 Richards Street; 604-687-6794.

For an unhurried drink and quiet conversation, your best bet is the **Gérard Lounge**, a genteel gentlemen's-style club; this is the place to spot visiting celebrities as well. ~ Sutton Place Hotel, 845 Burrard Street; 604-682-5511.

The **Hot Jazz Society** presents swing and modern jazz. ~ 2120 Main Street; 604-873-4131. The **Coastal Jazz and Blues Society Hotline** lists what's going on in the numerous jazz clubs around town. ~ 604-682-0706.

Of the local gay haunts, **Celebrities Night Club** is open to both men and women. ~ 1022 Davie Street; 604-689-3180.

Charlie's Lounge offers soft jazz in a chandeliered room warmed by a fireplace and decorated with traditional paintings. Downstairs, at the same location is **The Lotus Club**, with music played by a deejay. A mixed gay and lesbian crowd frequents the dancefloor at this contemporary lounge. Friday and Wednesday nights (women only) the club features Top-40 music. Cover on Friday. The third venue at this location is **Chuck's Pub**, where you'll find drag shows on the weekends. This male-oriented room offers a large oak bar, pool table, dartboards and contemporary music. ~ 455 Abbott Street; 604-685-7777.

Casino gambling is legal here, with half the profits going to local charities; for a little roulette, sic bo or blackjack action, try the **Great Canadian Casino**. ~ 2477 Heather Street; 604-872-5543. The **Royal Diamond Casino** also offers the gambling experience. ~ Plaza of Nations, 750 South Pacific Boulevard; 604-685-2340.

ENGLISH BAY BEACHES (NORTHERN SHORE) ~ Connected by Stanley Park's seawall promenade, silky English Bay Beach and broad Sunset Beach Park are prime candidates for a long sunset stroll. Within walking distance of the city center, they are a favorite of businesspeople out for a lunch break or there to catch

BEACHES & PARKS

the last rays after work during the week. There are restrooms, changing rooms and intermittent food stalls; restaurants and groceries are nearby. ~ Off Beach Avenue on the southwest side of town; 604-257-8400.

STANLEY PARK 🚶 🚴 ⚓ Beautiful Stanley Park is a green oasis in downtown Vancouver. Highlights include the aquarium, children's farmyard, seawall promenade, children's water park, a miniature railway, scenic lighthouses, totem poles and statues, pitch-and-putt golf, shuffleboard, tennis courts, an evening gun salute (each day at 9 p.m.), open-air theater, a swan-filled lagoon, nature house and miles of trails through thick coniferous forest. Second and Third bathing beaches are extremely popular among sun lovers and water enthusiasts. Second Beach boasts a new heated outdoor pool. Facilities include restaurants and concession stands, restrooms, showers and picnic facilities. ~ Follow Georgia Street heading west through downtown to the park entrance; 604-257-8400.

▼▼▼▼▼▼▼▼▼▼
North Shore

One of Vancouver's best features is its proximity to nature. Just a few minutes from the heart of town is this lush, green slope with scenic beaches, ecology centers and campgrounds. Easily reached by transit, this area also offers a great bird's-eye view of the metropolitan district.

SIGHTS

There are several sights of interest on the North Shore, beginning with **Capilano Suspension Bridge and Park**, a swaying footbridge stretched over the chasm 230 feet above the Capilano River; you will pass through a park complete with totem poles and souvenir-filled trading post to reach the bridge. Admission. ~ 3735 Capilano Road, North Vancouver; 604-985-7474.

Up the road a bit is the **Capilano Salmon Hatchery**, where the public can take a self-guided tour and learn about the life cycle of this important fish. ~ 4500 Capilano Park Road, North Vancouver; 604-666-1790.

Up farther still is **Grouse Mountain,** the top of Vancouver, where visitors catch the Skyride gondola to the mountain peak complex to ski, hike, see the incredible high-tech mythology and history presentation about Vancouver in "The Theatre in the Sky" or settle in for a meal at one of the restaurants. Admission. ~ 6400 Nancy Greene Way, North Vancouver; 604-984-0661.

HIDDEN ►

Even the floor—9000 pieces of Brazilian polished agate—is eyecatching at the **Sri Lankan Gem Museum,** a unique enclave in a suburb north of Vancouver. This small but breathtaking attraction has samples of every precious and semiprecious stone known to man, ranging from brilliant emeralds, rubies and sapphires to a massive, 20,000-carat topaz. Founder Shelton da Silva's jewelry store is next door, but the museum stands alone as testament to the mineral wonders of nature. Admission. ~ 2770 Mount Seymour Parkway, North Vancouver; 604-929-7110.

Since 1985, the **Bed and Breakfast at Laburnum Cottage** has been a breath of fresh air in North Vancouver, offering welcome respite for weary travelers. There are three posh, deluxe-priced guest rooms (each with private bath) on the second floor of the elegant, antique- and art-filled main house. Of the two ultra-deluxe housekeeping cottages on the grounds, the larger has an extra sleeping loft making it suitable for families. The smaller, nestled in the prim English garden, is designed for romance. The food here is also a memorable experience. ~ 1388 Terrace Avenue; phone/fax 604-988-4877, 888-676-4877. DELUXE TO ULTRA-DELUXE

LODGING

The **Grouse Inn**, near the north end of the Lions Gate Bridge not far from shopping, dining and sightseeing spots, offers 79 tidy but plain, motel-style rooms decorated in earth tones. Standard rooms have the basics—full bath, queen bed, cable television, small table and chairs—though a few are set up as family suites and others are equipped with kitchenettes. ~ 1633 Capilano Road, North Vancouver; 604-988-7101, 800-779-7888, fax 604-988-7102. MODERATE.

If you're looking for quiet, **Bay View B&B's** perch in an exclusive residential neighborhood above West Vancouver is the place. A spacious, neat home at the end of a little-traveled cul-de-sac, Bay View has a four-room suite on the main floor and two three-room suites upstairs. All offer nice views down to the water a mile below, and the Lion's Gate Bridge beyond. Guests are greeted with a plate of steaming fresh cookies. Despite its bucolic locale, it's just 15 minutes from downtown Vancouver. ~ 1270 Netley Place, West Vancouver; 604-926-3218, 800-208-2204, fax 604-926-3216. MODERATE TO DELUXE.

◄ *HIDDEN*

For that million-dollar view of the city and outstanding seafood to match, **The Salmon House on the Hill**, perched on a North Shore hill in what is actually referred to as West Vancouver, fits the bill. The specialty here is fresh British Columbia salmon grilled over alderwood, but the prawns and scallop brochettes and rack of lamb are also worth trying. Lunch, dinner and Sunday brunch; reservations recommended. ~ 2229 Folkestone Way, West Vancouver; 604-926-3212. MODERATE TO DELUXE.

DINING

Chesa, yet to be discovered by the "in" crowd that tends not to stray from downtown, has built a solid reputation on extremely friendly service and delicious Swiss fare. Our favorite here is *emincé* of veal à la Zurichoise (sautéed morsels of veal, mushrooms and onion in a light, creamy, white-wine sauce), though the par-

◄ *HIDDEN*

fait of duck liver and chicken Ossi are also tempting. The garden decor and wicker furniture are conducive to a leisurely meal. Closed Monday. ~ 1734 Marine Drive, West Vancouver; 604-922-2411. MODERATE TO DELUXE.

The coffee at **Savary Island** is fine, but it's the secondary attraction after a sumptuous array of baked goods that make a perfect breakfast, on the way to Whistler, say. The pecan/cranberry muffins are unbelievably good. ~ 1533 Marine Drive, West Vancouver; 604-926-4021. BUDGET.

Sundowner is a traditional seafood store much favored by locals. It also serves up fantastic lunch selections, including excellent freshly made sushi and crab and shrimp sandwiches. Ask for some Indian candy (honey-cured salmon) to take with you as you leave. ~ 1482 Marine Drive, West Vancouver; 604-922-4332. BUDGET.

Beach Side Café offers outstanding, original dishes. The menu is an imaginative mix of such entrées as grilled beef tenderloin medallion with leeks and halibut wrapped in pancetta. The decor is a simple combination of white tablecloths and straight-back chairs. ~ 1362 Marine Drive, West Vancouver; 604-925-1945. MODERATE TO DELUXE.

HIDDEN ►   Strange as it sounds, **Capers Café** is a waterfront restaurant tucked into the back of a health-food store. The accent falls on quiche dishes, fresh seafood, pasta, salads and vegetarian plates. There is outdoor patio seating with views of Burrard Inlet. ~ 2496 Marine Drive, West Vancouver; 604-925-3374. MODERATE.

SHOPPING   Across Burrard Inlet in North Vancouver, **Lonsdale Quay Market** is a tri-level atrium mall on the waterfront. In addition to postcard views of the Vancouver skyline, this bustling shopping center combines trendy stores with a farmer's market. A great place to spend money, people watch and survey the shoreline. ~ End of Lonsdale Avenue; 604-985-6261.

BEACHES & PARKS   **LYNN CANYON PARK** 🏃 Though it's much shorter but slightly higher than the Capilano Suspension Bridge, there is no charge to venture out onto Lynn Canyon Suspension Bridge stretched 240 feet above the rapids of Lynn Canyon. There is also a fine ecology center in this pretty, 617-acre park. Facilities include restrooms, picnic facilities, nature trails, a concession stand and an ecology center; restaurants and groceries are nearby. ~ In North Vancouver at 3663 Park Road; 604-981-3103.

CAPILANO RV PARK 🏃 Located under the north end of Lions Gate Bridge, this private venture is the closest camping option you will find. While it's primarily set up for recreational vehicles, there are a few grassy tent sites; reservations can be made for hookups only, and are essential during the busy summer months. There are restrooms, showers, picnic tables, a playground, a lounge, a laundry, a pool, and a whirlpool; restaurants and groceries are nearby. ~ In North Vancouver at 295 Tomahawk Avenue; 604-987-4722.

▲ There are 8 tent sites and 125 sites with hookups; Can. $22 to Can. $32 per night. Pet charge; Can. $2 per day.

One of Vancouver's best day trips leads to Whistler, a resort area famous for its skiing and après-ski life. Snow lovers are drawn to the region's crystalline lakes and lofty mountains as well as its alpine trails and cosmopolitan ski village. Located 79 miles northeast of Vancouver, the Whistler area has a number of British Columbia's best-known provincial parks that make the area ideal for fishing, windsurfing, swimming and, of course, loafing.

▼▼▼▼▼▼▼▼▼▼
Whistler

On your way up to Whistler, stop for a tour through the **B.C. Museum of Mining**, which takes you deep into the workings of what was once the highest-yielding copper mine in the British Empire. The kids will enjoy panning for gold in the small pool set up for just that purpose. Open May 20 through Thanksgiving. Admission. ~ Route 99, Britannia Beach; 604-896-2233.

SIGHTS

As you're cruising farther up the Sea to Coast Highway, you'll pass a couple of sights worth a detour near the town of Squamish. First will be **Shannon Falls**, a high, shimmering ribbon of tumbling water immediately off the highway. Next you'll come to **The Chiefs**, the second-largest monolith in the world after the Rock of Gibraltar; on a fine day there will be climbers dangling all about the face of this mountaineer's dream.

One of the more interesting heritage sites in Whistler is at **Rainbow Park**, the site of the area's first vacation retreat and now a day-use park. This is also the best spot for a view of the valley and the Blackcomb and Whistler mountains. ~ Alta Lake Road.

For an in-depth look at the history of the area, visit the **Whistler Museum and Archives Society**, a quaint museum next to the public library in Whistler Village that houses relics and artifacts and an interesting slide presentation. Call ahead for hours. ~ 4329 Main Street; 604-932-2019.

North of Whistler past the logging and farming town of Pemberton is **Meager Creek Hot Springs**, a series of pools, each varying in temperature, set in a pristine grove of evergreens. To get there, take Route 99 to the Pemberton Meadows Road and follow it north to Hurley River Road. After 45 minutes on this logging road, you'll come to the springs. It's possible to drive all the way through in summer, but a snowmobile trip is required to

◀ HIDDEN

reach it during winter. The public is advised not to use the springs due to contamination. A clean-up is under way, though the project's completion date has not yet been determined. ~ 604-898-2100.

LODGING
The **Whistler Hostel** on Alta Lake is a convenient location for those arriving by train (which passes immediately in front of the hostel twice each day and stops on request). Accommodations are basic here, with men's and women's dorms and a private room upstairs, and a kitchen, dining room and gameroom downstairs overlooking the lake. ~ Alta Lake Road; 604-932-5492, fax 604-932-4687. BUDGET.

A nicer alternative is the UBC **Whistler Lodge**. You still need to provide your own food and bedding and will share cubicles with other hostelers, but this rustic lodge set above a quiet residential section offers lots of pleasant extras like a sauna and jacuzzi, barbecue and fire pit off the large deck, ski-equipment/bike storage locker, kitchen, laundry, game lounge and separate television/movie room. Book well in advance for ski season. ~ 2124 Nordic Drive; 604-932-6604, 604-822-5851. BUDGET.

Whistler is considered by many to be one of North America's top ski areas.

If you seek an all-out alpine experience, you'll do well to choose **Edelweiss**, a charming, European-style pension complete with window boxes and rosemaling on the chalet-like exterior. There are eight simply furnished guest rooms with private bathrooms and down comforters. A small guest lounge shares space with the sunny breakfast room where guests are treated to a hearty breakfast. The French and German proprietors are avid skiers who post a ski bulletin daily for guests. There's even a whirlpool and sauna for post-slope relaxation. ~ 7162 Nancy Greene Way; 604-932-3641, fax 604-938-1746. MODERATE TO DELUXE.

The Whistler Fairways Hotel is farther from the lifts but has resort amenities like a dining room, pub, fitness room, sauna, jacuzzi, shiatsu massage clinic and a heated pool. Rooms are boxy, with basic, light-wood furniture, mini-fridges and cramped bathrooms; some have built-in window seats to take advantage of the views. Request a corner unit or one with vaulted ceilings, which seem to be roomier and are the same price. ~ 4005 Whistler Way; 604-932-2522, 800-663-5644, fax 604-932-6711. DELUXE.

Lifestyles of the Rich and Famous dubbed the **Château Whistler**, located at the base of Blackcomb Mountain, "Whistler's premier address" with good reason. The property is strikingly elegant and brimming with Old World charm. Guests enjoy inspiring alpine views from more than 500 rooms, all smartly furnished with country-style wood furniture, double sleeper sofas, queen or king beds, mini-bars and large bathrooms. They also have an 18-hole golf course. ~ 4599 Château Boulevard; 604-938-8000, 800-441-1414, fax 604-938-2055. ULTRA-DELUXE.

Le Chamois, Whistler's newest full-service luxury hotel, shares the same prime ski-in, ski-out location at the base of the Black-comb runs. However, its smaller proportions (only 50 rooms) al-low for a high degree of personal attention. The guest rooms are spacious, with big bathrooms, kitchenettes and designer touches evident throughout the decor; the studio rooms are especially wonderful, with two-person jacuzzi tubs in the living room area set before bay windows overlooking the slopes and lifts. ~ 4557 Blackcomb Way; 604-932-8700, 800-777-0185, fax 604-932-2176. ULTRA-DELUXE.

"Never trust a skinny chef" is the motto at Les Deux Gros, which the staff translates to mean "the two fat guys." The focus here is on country French cuisine, and portions are generous in-deed. The steak tartare, juicy rack of lamb and salmon Welling-ton are all superbly crafted and presented, well worth the price. Located just about a mile southwest of the village, this is the spot for that special, romantic dinner. Dinner only. ~ 1200 Alta Lake Road; 604-932-4611. MODERATE TO DELUXE.

DINING

◄ HIDDEN

The abundance of fresh seafood at the Crab Shack is com-plemented by nautical decor and an oyster bar. In addition, you can order pasta, steak or chicken while cracking jokes with the entertaining waitstaff. There's occasional live music in the bar. ~ 4005 Whistler Way; 604-932-4451. MODERATE TO DELUXE.

To complete that alpine experience, you might want to head to Aviano for a cheese or meat fondue. Other picks you might want to try from the far-reaching Continental menu include pizza and pasta choices. The wooden tables are a bit crowded here, and the bar is often packed, so this is no place for private con-versation. ~ Whistler Village Square; 604-932-2112. MODERATE TO DELUXE.

Araxi's, a bright and airy restaurant with congenial staff, has been a dependable favorite in town since its beginning. The menu features creative Italian cuisine. Breads, sausages and pasta are all house-made. The dining room is often overflowing with custom-ers, while the bar is best for a rousing drink with your friends. ~ Whistler Village Square; 604-932-4540. MODERATE TO DELUXE.

There are also several delis in the village, and the one the lo-cals recommend most is Chalet Delicatessen, occupying a street-level corner on Sundial Place. Offerings here are breakfast, gour-met soups, salads, sandwiches, pastries, cookies and homemade ice cream. On nice days there are plenty of tables set out front; otherwise you'll be lucky to get one of the few stools at the ta-bles along the front windows. ~ Saint Andrews House; 604-932-8345. BUDGET.

Amazingly, there are five Japanese restaurants in little Whistler Village, and of those five, **Sushi Village** is the one the locals most often visit. This place is busy, so service can be slow to a fault, but the atmosphere is serene, the decor clean-cut and the food quite good, especially the tasty tempura and à la carte sushi items. ~ 4272 Mountain Square; 604-932-3330. MODERATE TO DELUXE.

Another romantic spot slightly removed from the bustling activities of the central village is **The Wildflower**, an elegant restaurant decorated to echo the Old World charm of its setting in the Château Whistler. The award-winning chef focuses on fresh Pacific Northwest cuisine featuring organically grown regional herbs, veggies, fruits, eggs and meat. Seafood is also a specialty of the house, and on Friday and Saturday nights there is an Asian buffet. The Sunday seafood brunch is a bargain considering the quality, as is the breakfast buffet. ~ 4599 Château Boulevard; 604-938-2033. MODERATE TO ULTRA-DELUXE.

SHOPPING   Most of the great shopping in Whistler is done in the village, at specialty shops like **Christmas at Whistler**. ~ 4293 Mountain Square; 604-932-3518. Outdoor-lovers will appreciate the assortment of climbing gear and back-country equipment available at **The Mountain Shop**. ~ Delta Mountain Plaza; 604-932-2203. **Escape Route** also carries the latest in adventure gear. ~ #113-4350 Lorimer Road; 604-938-3338. Chocoholics will be in seventh heaven at the **Rocky Mountain Chocolate Factory**. ~ 4190 Spring Lane; 604-932-4100. **The Snoboard Shop** offers all the latest equipment and clothing for the serious snow shredder. ~ 4205 Whistler Village Square; 604-932-4440.

Few artists call Whistler home, but the works of those who do are shown alongside contemporary pieces by Inuit and Northwest Coast artists at the **Whistler Inuit Gallery** in the lower level of the Château Whistler. ~ 4599 Château Boulevard; 604-938-3366.

Another gallery showcasing works of local artists is **Mountain Craft Gallery**, located in the lobby level of the Delta Whistler Resort. Here you'll find a wide range of items in glass, bronze, ceramic, wood, textile and new media. ~ 4050 Whistler Way; 604-932-5001.

NIGHTLIFE   You'll find a good selection of lounges, taverns and discos in Whistler Village (not surprising for a resort destination). The après-ski scene is big everywhere, though one of the most popular spots is the **Longhorn Saloon**, with a deejay nightly and one of Whistler's largest dancefloors. ~ Carleton Lodge; 604-932-5999.

Rustic and rowdy **Garfinkel's** offers a wide variety of music, including reggae and jazz. Cover for live shows. ~ 14308 Main

Street; 604-932-2323. The glitzier **Savage Beagle Club** has an eclectic mix of sounds: hip-hop, house, classic rock and salsa. ~ 4316 Skier's Approach; 604-938-3337.

The Hard Rock Café, like all Hard Rock Cafés, offers a bar and restaurant with walls filled with rock memorabilia. Concerts and music videos are presented on big-screen TVs. ~ 4295 Blackcomb Way; 604-938-9922.

The refined **Mallard Bar**, with a large fireplace, soft piano music and expansive views of the Blackcomb Mountain base, is infinitely suitable for a quiet drink with friends. ~ Château Whistler, 4599 Château Boulevard; 604-938-8000.

PORTEAU COVE PROVINCIAL PARK This
is a favorite among scuba enthusiasts because of its wooden-hulled minesweep ship and concrete reefs full of marine life located not far off the rocky beach. Porteau Cove is a long, narrow park stretched along the B.C. Rail tracks on the east shore of picturesque Howe Sound. Swimmers and kayakers are also welcome. Restrooms, showers, picnic facilities, an amphitheater, and a divers' changing room are available. ~ Located off Sea to Sky Highway 15 miles north of Horseshoe Bay; 604-898-3678.

▲ There are 59 developed sites for tents and RVs (no hookups); Can. $15.50 per night; and 15 walk-in sites; Can. $7 per night.

GARIBALDI PROVINCIAL PARK Named for Mt. Garibaldi, its crowning point, this awe-inspiring park is made up of 480,000 acres of intriguing lavaland, glaciers, high alpine fields, lakes and dense forests of fir, cedar, hemlock, birch and pine. Thirty-six miles of developed trails lead into the five most popular spots—Black Tusk/Garibaldi Lake, Diamond Head, Singing Pass, Cheakamus and Wedgemont Lake. You can try for rainbow trout in Mamquam Lake (Diamond Head area), but swimming is very cold throughout the park. You'll find restrooms, picnic tables, shelters and nature, bike and cross-country ski trails; restaurants and groceries are nearby. ~ Located 40 miles north of Vancouver off the Sea to Sky Highway (Route 99), north of Squamish; 604-898-3678.

▲ Permitted at Diamond Head, where there is a hike-in shelter with propane stoves (seven-mile hike); you must bring your own gear; Can. $10 per night. There are two hike-in campgrounds at Garibaldi Lake (four-mile hike) with propane stoves; Can. $7 per night.

BRANDYWINE FALLS PROVINCIAL PARK The highlight of this small park is its 230-foot waterfall; winding nature trails are also close at hand. Swimming is permitted in Daisy Lake. Perched alongside the highway, the sparsely wooded campsites can be a

BEACHES & PARKS

bit noisy at high-traffic times (weekends). There are restrooms, picnic facilities, fire pits and nature and hiking trails; restaurants and groceries are nearby. ~ Located approximately 60 miles north of Vancouver on the Sea to Sky Highway (Route 99); 604-898-3678.

▲ There are 15 developed sites; Can. $9.50 per night.

▼▼▼▼▼▼▼▼▼▼▼▼▼
Sunshine Coast

With a 100-mile shoreline that stretches along the northeast side of the strait of Georgia, the Sunshine Coast is bordered by sandy beaches, secluded bays and rugged headlands. It reaches from Howe Sound in the south to Desolation Sound in the north. This area is rustic, even a bit worn around the edges, but don't let that stop you. There are pleasant sites, plus a good number of artists in residence whose work is worth checking out.

SIGHTS

As you leave the ferry at Langdale and begin to wind your way up the Sunshine Coast along Route 101, one of the first areas of interest is the port town of **Gibsons**. Be sure to stop at **Molly's Reach** on Route 101, for years the set for a popular Canadian television series and now a restaurant.

The **Elphinstone Pioneer Museum** maps the history of European pioneers in the area. Artifacts from the daily life of these settlers are on display. The museum also houses a massive collection of seashells. ~ Winn Road; 604-886-8232.

Next stop on the lower coast is the **House of Héwhîwus**, or House of Chiefs, the center of government, education and entertainment for the self-governing Sechelt Indian band. Photographs and artifacts relating the history of the tribe are on display in the **Tems Swîya Museum** (604-885-4592). Ask for directions to the totems and grouping of carved figures behind the complex. Closed Sunday in winter. ~ 5555 Route 101, Sechelt; 604-885-2273.

HIDDEN ▶

If you have an interest in archaeology, rent a boat and head north up the inlet from Porpoise Bay to view ancient Indian **pictographs** on the faces of the cliff walls looming above the water.

From the trailhead near the town of Egmont, it takes approximately an hour to stroll the well-posted trail in to see **Skookumchuk Narrows**, a natural phenomenon of rapids, whirlpools and roiling eddies created by massive tidal changes pushed through the narrow inlet. If you arrive at low tide you can view the fascinating marine life trapped in tidal pools near Roland Point.

HIDDEN ▶

Taking the next ferry hop, from Earls Cove to Saltery Bay, brings you to the **Lang Creek Salmon Spawning Channel** about midway to Powell River. During the peak spawning season (September to November) you can get a close look at pink or chum salmon making the arduous journey upstream. ~ Route 101.

Nearby at **Mountain Ash Farm** the kids can play with little potbellied pigs, chickens, goats, sheep, emus and llamas while you visit the country store for a look at kitchenware, specialty foods and the farm's own products. Closed Monday and Tuesday. Admission. ~ 10084 Nassichuk Road, Kelly Creek; 604-487-9340.

The tourism boom has yet to hit the Sunshine Coast, which is rather surprising since nature has provided so much to admire here.

The **Powell River Historical Museum**, an octagonal building just across from Willingdon Beach, houses a fine collection of regional memorabilia including furniture, utensils and hand tools of pioneers and indigenous people along with a photo and print archive with material dating back to 1910. Closed weekends in winter. Admission. ~ 4800 Marine Avenue, Powell River; 604-485-2222.

For a further lesson in the history of the area, take the **heritage walk** through the Powell River Townsite to view the early-1900s homes, churches and municipal buildings of this old company town. Maps are available from the **Travel InfoCentre**. ~ InfoCentre: 4690 Marine Avenue, Powell River; 604-485-4701.

During the months of June, July and August you can take a free two-hour tour of the **MacMillan Bloedel Pulp and Paper Mill**, the lifeblood of Powell River. The tour gives you an inside view on the process of turning logs into lumber and paper products, from water blasting the bark off through forming pulp sheets to rolling the finished newsprint. No children under 12 permitted. Closed weekends. ~ 6270 Yew Street, Powell River; 604-483-3722.

There's a great hilltop view of the "Hulks," a half-moon breakwater of ten cement ships protecting the floating logs waiting to be processed in the mill, at the **Mill Viewpoint** on Route 101. Interpretive signs give a bit of history about the ships and the mill.

LODGING

There are no big resorts or major chain hotels yet. Motels, inns and lodges are sometimes a shade worn but generally are friendly and inexpensive.

A bed and breakfast since 1922, **Bonniebrook Lodge** is a charming yellow clapboard house overlooking the Strait of Georgia. Four guest rooms, each with a different color motif, feature flocked wallpaper and Victorian-style furnishings such as marble-topped tables and hand-carved beds. Two of the rooms have water views. Fifty campsites for tents and RVs (half of the sites have hookups) are also available on the grounds behind the house. ~ 1532 Ocean Beach Esplanade, Gibsons; 604-886-2887. BUDGET TO MODERATE.

The **Royal Reach Motel and Marina** offers clean, basic accommodations in 32 simple rooms that are pretty much the same. Nondescript furnishings include one or two double beds, a long desk/television stand, plain bedside table and lamps, a mini-fridge, electric kettle and a small bathroom. Ask for one of the waterfront rooms that looks out over the marina and Sechelt Inlet. ~ 5758 Wharf Road, Sechelt; 604-885-7844. BUDGET.

Lowes Resort, a Pender Harbor institution since 1952, offers a range of accommodation options including 18 housekeeping cottages and 12 tent and RV spaces among the permanent mobile-home units on the grounds. White paint, blue trim and flower baskets adorn the rustic, little housekeeping cottages, each furnished with vinyl couch and chairs, laminated table, blond-wood furniture and quilted bedspread in the separate bedroom. The bathrooms are tiny. This is a suitable spot for families on a budget. The marina makes it a good choice for fishing and diving fans as well. ~ Lagoon Road, Madeira Park; 604-883-2456, fax 604-883-2474. BUDGET TO MODERATE.

With furniture that appears to be stuck in at odd angles to make it all fit, the motel-style rooms at the **Beach Gardens Resort,** are nothing special, equipped with the basics. There are also cabins and kitchenette units available. What qualifies this as a resort are amenities such as the private marina, dining room, lounge, indoor pool, weight room and sauna. ~ 7074 Westminster Avenue, Powell River; 604-485-6267, 800-663-7070, fax 604-485-2343. BUDGET TO DELUXE.

Within moments of arriving at the charming **Beacon Bed and Breakfast** and getting settled into one of the two inviting bedrooms or roomy downstairs suite, you'll begin to unwind and feel right at home. It's hard to tell whether to attribute this to the genuine hospitality or the cozy, down-home decor. Whatever the case, the congenial hosts, large hot tub, great ocean view, proximity to the beach and thoughtful touches like plush robes and made-to-order breakfasts make this one of the most delightful lodging options in the region. ~ 3750 Marine Avenue, Powell River; 604-485-5563. MODERATE TO DELUXE.

DINING

HIDDEN ►

Gibsons Fish Market, a smallish outlet on the main drag above the landing, does a booming business with tasty takeout fish-and-chips. It may not look like much, but there's usually a crowd lined up on the front sidewalk. ~ 294 Gower Point Road, Gibsons; 604-886-8363. BUDGET.

The **Harbour Café,** a few doors down is your best bet for breakfast. This multilevel, wood-paneled diner serves fine omelettes and pastries throughout the morning and afternoon; they also add a selection of burgers, soups and salads to the lunch menu. ~ Gower Point Road, Gibsons; 604-886-6882. BUDGET.

The **Blue Heron Inn,** a delightful waterfront home-turned-restaurant on picturesque Porpoise Bay, is home to masterful creations. The daily menu uses fresh regional produce and seafood in the dishes. Closed Monday and Tuesday. Reservations are required. ~ East Porpoise Bay Road, Sechelt; 604-885-3847, 800-818-8977. DELUXE.

Folks over 19 can stop by the **Royal Canadian Legion Hall Branch 112** for a super-cheap supper of prawns or chicken and chips, Salisbury steak or juicy burgers. This is actually one of the nicest (and only) places in town to get a meal, but the bar inside means that only those of legal drinking age can enter. The salt-of-the-earth folks here might even let you in on a hand of cards or a fevered dart or shuffleboard game. ~ Lily Road, Madeira Park; 604-883-0055. BUDGET.

For homemade Mediterranean and Greek cuisine, try **The Sea House**. Entrées include seafood, souvlaki, steak, foccacia and brick-oven pizza. ~ 4448 Marine Avenue, Powell River; 604-485-5163. MODERATE.

The **Shingle Mill Restaurant**, situated at the tip of Powell Lake, has large windows on three sides so the views of this beautiful, pine-trimmed lake are not wasted. It's no surprise that they serve grilled B.C. salmon in this waterfront eatery, but the steak *au poivre*, chicken in puff pastry, and fusilli primavera are unexpectedly good. Items from the dinner menu are available in the relaxed bistro. ~ 6233 Powell Place, Powell River; 604-483-2001. MODERATE TO DELUXE.

SHOPPING

There is an abundance of artists living in small communities all along the Sunshine Coast, many willing to open their studios to tours available through the **Sunshine Coast Arts Council**. Closed Monday. ~ Corner of Trail and Medusa streets, Sechelt; 604-885-5412.

You'll find fine representations of local art (serigraphs, pottery, woodwork, watercolors, jewelry, sculpture) at Gibson's **Show Piece Gallery** at 444 Gower Point Road (604-886-9213), at Sechelt's **Dream Shoppe** at Trail Bay Mall (604-885-1965) and at Powell River's **Gallery Tantalus** at 4555-C Marine Avenue (604-485-9412).

◄ *HIDDEN*

Cranberry Pottery, a working studio, offers functional and affordable handmade stoneware in varying designs and glazes. Closed Sunday. ~ 6729 Cranberry Street, Powell River; 604-483-4622.

For arts and crafts of Northwest First Nations including masks, drums, totems and baskets, visit the Sechelt Indian Band's **Cultural Center Gift Shop**. Closed Sunday in winter. ~ 5555 Route 101, Sechelt; 604-885-4592.

NIGHTLIFE

Along the Sunshine Coast you'll find slimmer after-hours pickings, limited primarily to friendly, no-airs local taverns and pubs that occasionally have a dance space, live music and great water views.

A popular neighborhood hangout, **The Cedars Pub** has occasional live music and karaoke. ~ 920 Route 101 at Show Road; 604-886-8171. Thursday to Saturday night you can shake your thang to live rock and R&B at Sechelt's **Wakefield Inn**. ~ 6529 Sunshine Coast Highway; 604-885-7666.

Powell River has two amiable establishments in which to spend a comfortable evening after canoeing the lakes. The **Marine Hotel Pub** has live rock-and-roll and Top-40 on Friday and Saturday. ~ 4429 Marine Avenue; 604-485-4881. Kick back with a brew and a view overlooking Powell Lake at the **Shinglemill Pub**. ~ Powell Lake; 604-483-3545.

BEACHES & PARKS

PORPOISE BAY PROVINCIAL PARK 🏃 🏊 ⛴ 🍴 One of the prettiest parks along the coast, Porpoise Bay has a broad, sandy beach anchored by grass fields and fragrant cedar groves. This is a favorite base for canoeists who come to explore the waterways of the Sechelt Inlets Marine Recreation Area. You'll also find excellent sportfishing. The park has restrooms, showers, picnic tables, an adventure playground, an amphitheater, nature trails, visitor programs and a fall salmon run; restaurants and groceries are nearby. ~ Located northeast of Sechelt off Porpoise Bay Road; 604-898-3678, 800-689-9025.

▲ There are 86 sites for tents and RVs (no hookups); Can. $14.50 per night. They also have cyclist campsites with showers; Can. $7 per night.

SALTERY BAY PROVINCIAL PARK 🏊 🎣 ⛴ 🚤 🍴 Named for the Japanese fish-saltery settlement located in this area during the early 1900s, this lovely oceanside park with twin sandy beaches enjoys grand views of Jervis Inlet, where sharp-eyed visitors often catch glimpses of porpoises, whales, sea lions and seals. Scuba divers flock to the park to visit the nine-foot bronze mermaid resting in 60 feet of water not far offshore from the evergreen-shrouded campground. Swimming and offshore salmon fishing are excellent. There are restrooms, picnic sites, fire pits and disabled diving facilities; restaurants and groceries are nearby. ~ Located off Sunshine Coast Highway 17 miles south of Powell River; 604-898-3678, 800-689-9025.

▲ There are 42 developed sites; RVs are allowed (no hookups); Can. $9.50 per night.

HIDDEN ►

POWELL RIVER CANOE ROUTE 🏃 🚣 🍴 There are 12 fjord-like lakes interconnected by rivers, streams and 50 miles of hiking trails making it possible to make portage canoe trips of anywhere from three days to a week in this beautiful Northern Sunshine Coast recreational area. There are over 80 miles of hiking trails around Powell River. Best time to make the trip is between April and November; lakes at upper elevations tend to freeze, and roads are inaccessible during winter months. Obtain a map from the Powell River Forest Service (7077 Duncan Street, Powell River, BC V8A 1W1; 604-485-0700) to plan your circuit. Facilities include outhouses, picnic tables, hiking trails (the Inland Lake trail is wheelchair accessible), and a camping supply store; restaurants and groceries are nearby. ~ Jumpoff point for the canoe route is Lois Lake, accessed by the Canoe Mainline; 604-485-4701.

> A total of 50 miles of canoeing and five miles of portaging are available on the Powell River Canoe Route.

▲ Permitted at any of the 30 recreation sites. Prices vary from free (at forestry-run campgrounds) to Can. $12 at some of the municipal and provincial campsites around the area.

WILLINGDON BEACH MUNICIPAL CAMPSITE 🏃 🛶 The sandy, log-strewn, crescent beach bordered by wooded acres of campsites draws a big summertime crowd to this comfortable municipal site in Powell River. Some of the campsites are right up on the beach, while others in a grove of cedar are more secluded. The site has great, though unsupervised, swimming. You'll find restrooms, showers, a laundry, a barbecue area, playgrounds, a nature trail and a seasonal food stall; restaurants and groceries are nearby. ~ Located immediately off of Marine Avenue in the Westview section of Powell River; 604-485-2242.

▲ There are 79 sites, half with full hookups; Can. $11 to Can. $18 per night. Extended stay discounts are available.

DESOLATION SOUND MARINE PARK 🛶 🐟 🚤 ⚓ Made up of 37 miles of shoreline and several islands, this is the largest marine park in British Columbia. The waters here are very warm and teem with diverse marine life, making the area ideal for fishing (excellent for cod or salmon), swimming, boating and scuba diving. The park is wild and undeveloped, with magnificent scenery at every turn. There are a few onshore outhouses and numerous safe anchorages. ~ Boat access only from the coastal towns. Easiest access is from Powell River; 604-898-3678.

▲ There are several walk-in wilderness campsites; no charge.

White Rock

Perhaps because it is so close to the border that they whiz right on by, U.S. travelers overlook White Rock, a peaceful seaside town about 40 minutes from downtown Vancouver that claims Canada's best climate—and has a couple palm trees growing right along the main drag for proof. Canadians and European visitors to Canada flock to White Rock's small inns, motels and B&Bs; on summer weekend afternoons the town is astir with people using the beachside promenade, or strolling the avenue of small shops, cafés and restaurants behind it.

There isn't anything particularly glamorous about White Rock. In fact, it seems ever so much like the small British beach towns from which it drew its inspiration. That's what makes it charming —no big resorts, no famed sights, no fancy shops. Facing south into the sun, with a Mediterranean cast to the houses climbing the slope that fends off northerly storms, it does offer a balmier clime than most of the rest of B.C. Innumerable places offer fish and chips, and lots of happy couples stroll hand in hand along the promenade. For a tourist destination, it's charmingly low-key.

SIGHTS

Built in 1986 with assistance from the national and provincial governments, the **White Rock Promenade** spans one and a quarter miles of the town's gray-sand beach. Paved in brick, with numerous benches, it's a great place for a walk or a run; the sun keeps it warm, but the harbor breeze prevents excess warmth. When the tide's out a truly vast expanse of gray sand beach lies exposed, attracting many sandcastle builders young and old. A pier leads a quarter-mile out into deeper water; you can toss crab pots in the water here if you're interested in hand-caught seafood. Not far south of the pier, the White Rock that lent the city its name sits on the slope above the beach. At 486 tons, it's staying put. If it was not truly white historically, liberal coats of paint ensure that it is now. ~ Along Marine Drive in downtown White Rock.

Built into the handsome, restored 1912 railroad depot, the **White Rock Museum and Archives** offers revolving exhibits to explain just how a timber-shipping outpost became a weekend beach enclave. There's also a visitor information booth just south of the depot. ~ 14970 Marine Drive; 604-541-2222.

LODGING

Perched halfway up the hill from the Promenade, **Villa Marisol** has one of the finest vantages you could expect from a B&B, with distant islands and peaks jutting into the sunset. It also offers luxurious modern accommodations in a California-style house; the two guest suites have superlative views, expansive bedrooms and baths, cushy beds and balconies. One has its own fireplace and solarium, the other is right by an outdoor hot tub. For those in mauve moods, pastel color schemes dominate. An elegant breakfast is part of the tab. ~ 1389 Archibald Road; 604-535-9735. DELUXE.

The **Seaside Inn** is about as close to the water as you can get in White Rock—the Promenade and beach are across the street. The two bedroom units have queen-size beds; there is also an 1100-square-foot suite with living room, dining room, kitchen, fireplace and laundry facilities. The modern house is a handsome, white stucco Mediterranean design and affords fine harbor views. Rooms include a full English breakfast (think sausage and biscuits). ~ 14619 Marine View Drive; 604-538-1222, fax 604-599-9209. MODERATE.

Elmo Berlinghof used to run the snazziest restaurant in White Rock. Then he "retired"—to help his wife Margo run their B&B in the countryside near White Rock, just north of the U.S. border. Thus at **St. Elmo's Inn** you get breakfast cooked by a chef who once served the British royal family, and a fine breakfast it is too. The four regular rooms are European-style B&B accommodations: basically just beds crammed in fairly small rooms. There's also a honeymoon suite with a private bath. Either choice is quite economical. Call for directions, it's hard to find. ~ 678 176th Street; 604-538-7585. MODERATE.

Tapas are the fare at **Cielo**, one of the Mediterranean-style eateries on Marine Drive, White Rock's main drag. But the restaurant's chefs have expanded the usual range of these Spanish appetizer plates to include such nontraditional items as breaded eggplant, calamari and grilled chorizo. Three plates is an ample amount for two, and the atmosphere is a bit more elegant than the typical pub eatery found on Marine. ~ 15069 Marine Drive; 604-538-8152. MODERATE.

DINING

Following the smell of roasting coffee is the best way to pick out **Peach's Brew Coffeehouse** among the storefronts on Marine Drive. Its coffee is roasted daily and made expertly, and the muffins, scones and pastries make an excellent breakfast. ~ 14961 Marine Drive; 604-535-6944. MODERATE.

If it's a full-scale breakfast you're after, you want "The Big One" at **Holly's Poultry in Motion**. The plate comes piled high with eggs, hash browns, toast and ham or bacon. Lunch entrées, sandwiches and burgers are similarly generous. There's an oyster bar Wednesday through Sunday, and Holly rents rooms and suites upstairs. ~ 15491 Marine Drive; 604-538-8084. BUDGET.

If you can hold off on breakfast, lunch and dinner, your reward ought to be a leisurely visit to **White Mountain Ice Cream**, where they advertise homemade product, and deliver the best you can imagine. The acid test is vanilla—it's practically perfect at White Mountain. In fact, it's almost cause to visit the town just for the ice cream. ~ 14909 Marine Drive; 604-538-0171. BUDGET.

▼▼▼▼▼▼▼▼▼▼▼▼▼▼
Outdoor Adventures

WATER SPORTS

With 5000 miles of sheltered water within easy reach, Vancouver and southwestern British Columbia afford many opportunities to get out on the water. You can rent a powerboat or a sailboat and head north to the Sunshine Coast, where Desolation Sound has the warmest waters north of Mexico, or you can hop into an inflatable raft and paddle the Chilliwack River whitewater.

DOWNTOWN VANCOUVER   Although Canada does not require a license to operate either a powerboat or a sailboat, **Blue Pacific** requires that you prove your expertise before you rent one of its vessels. Otherwise, Blue Pacific will set you up for a three- to five-day skippered cruise; you can learn sailing basics or laze around on the deck. ~ 1519 Foreshore Walk; 604-682-2161.

English Bay is downtown's most popular beach. That's why Peter Rainier set up his **Ocean West** kayak operation here, but it also happens to be the best set-off point for a wonderful half-day trip around Stanley Park, or around the bay to the UBC campus and Wreck Beach. Rainier leads guided trips, including a picnic lunch. The company also has extended trips into the islands along the Sunshine Coast. ~ At the English Bay Beach Bath House, corner of Denman and Davie streets; 604-688-5770, 800-660-0051.

WHISTLER   Canoeing and kayaking are very popular on Whistler's five beautiful lakes. Rentals and tours are available through **Whistler Outdoor Experience Co.** from mid-May to mid-October. Rent a canoe or kayak and take a self-guided tour of the Serene River of Golden Dreams; see waterfalls and bird life. ~ Château Whistler; 604-932-3389.

SUNSHINE COAST   Desolation Sound Marine Park and the 50-mile Powell Forest Canoe Route, which includes eight breathtaking lakes and lush, interconnecting forests, are ideal spots for canoes and kayaks. "Powell Forest Canoe Route is as beautiful as the more popular Bowron Lake Route in northern British Columbia, but it's less populated by people in canoes," explains a local outfitter. Maps for the canoe route are available from the **Powell River Forest Service**. ~ 7077 Duncan Street, Powell River; 604-485-0700.

To rent a canoe for a day or eight days, contact **Wolfson Creek Canoe Rentals** in Powell River. You can go it alone or take along a guide as you explore the Powell Forest Canoe Route. ~ 9537 Nassichuk Road, Powell River; 604-487-9670. Experienced kayakers can rent craft for the day from **Sunshine Kayaking Ltd.** in

---

HELI-ADVENTURES

Quick trips to the backcountry for hiking, fishing, skiing or other activities are possible via helicopters. **Mountain Heli-Sports Inc.** will arrange skiing trips to the Sea-to-Sky Corridor near Whistler. ~ 604-932-2070. **Blackcomb Helicopters** arranges fishing and hiking trips during the summer. ~ 604-938-1700, 800-330-4354. **Vancouver Helicopters Inc.** specializes in drop-off service to the Tantalus Range, a rugged area with glaciers, lakes and the highest concentration of bald eagles in North America. ~ 604-898-9688, 800-894-3919.

Gibsons, on Howe Sound. Longer tours and kayaking classes are also offered. ~ RR4 S12 C18, Gibsons, BC V0N 1V0; 604-886-9760.

Scenic floats and whitewater rafting are also immensely popular around Vancouver, especially on the Chilliwack River, 65 miles east of the city. Near Whistler, the Green and Birkenhead rivers are popular, as are the Thompson, Squamish and Elaho rivers.

RIVER RUNNING

DOWNTOWN VANCOUVER Hyak Wilderness Adventures runs guided whitewater-rafting trips on the Chilliwack River in the spring, when snow still caps surrounding mountains. By summer, focus shifts to the Thompson River, with its desert scenery. Rapids along these rivers range from Class II to Class V. You can actively participate by paddling or go the lazy route and let the guides do the work. ~ 1975 Maple Street; 604-734-8622.

WHISTLER There are mountains, glaciers and waterfalls to observe on guided raft trips on several local rivers, including the Green and Squamish. Jet boat trips (on the Green and Lillooet rivers) are also arranged by **Whistler River Adventures** from April to September. ~ P.O. Box 202, Whistler, BC V0N 1B0; 604-932-3532.

The tremendous variety of fish in southwestern British Columbia waterways affords an array of exciting challenges for the angler. In the mountain country, you can flyfish or spin-cast in high alpine lakes and streams for rainbow trout, Dolly Varden, steelhead or kokanee salmon. On the coast, you'll find chinook, coho, chum, pink and sockeye salmon and bottom-dwelling halibut, sole and rockfish. Licenses for both fresh- and saltwater fishing are required (charter operators usually can provide them); regulations change frequently. **Saltwater licenses** are issued by the federal government's Recreational Fisheries Division. ~ Department of Fisheries and Oceans, 555 West Hastings Street, Vancouver, BC V6B 5G3; 604-666-5835, 604-666-2074.

SPORT-FISHING

Freshwater licenses are issued through the provincial government and can be bought at most sporting goods stores. **The Ministry of Environment, Lands and Parks (B.C. Environment)** maintains a list of licensed **freshwater fishing guides**. For a copy, call 604-582-5200.

WHISTLER Besides half-day and full-day freshwater fishing charters in local waters, **Whistler Backcountry Adventures** can send you off on a helicopter to isolated alpine lakes for overnight or longer trips. Gear and licenses are available. ~ #36 4314 Main Street; 604-932-3474, 888-932-9998.

SUNSHINE COAST Lowes Resort operates eight-hour fishing charters in Pender Harbor for salmon, rock cod and snapper.

Gear and license are available. ~ Lagoon Road, Madeira Park; 604-883-2456.

SCUBA DIVING

A thick soup of microscopic plant and animal life attracts and feeds an abundance of marine life that in turn attracts divers in numbers that continue to grow. This area is home to the largest artificial reef in North America, a 366-foot destroyer that sank and is now a diver's paradise. Add to this the array of wrecks and underwater sights (such as a nine-foot bronze mermaid in the Powell River) and it's easy to understand the popularity of scuba diving around Vancouver and the Sunshine Coast.

DOWNTOWN VANCOUVER   Dive charters to local waters, the Gulf Islands and Port Hardy are arranged by **Canadian Diving Center**. Transportation from store to dive spot is provided, as is unlimited air. Equipment rental is also available. ~ 288 West Esplanade, North Vancouver; 604-988-6134. **Aqua Sapiens** charters excursions in British Columbia and Washington. Gear and lessons (from resort to technical instructor certification) are available. ~ 1386 Main Street, North Vancouver; 604-985-3483.

SKIING

NORTH SHORE   The majestic range crowning Vancouver's North Shore offers three fine ski areas within minutes of the city center. **Cypress Bowl**, with 23 groomed runs on two lift-serviced mountains, boasts the longest vertical run of the local Vancouver resorts. Snowboarders share the runs with downhills skiers. A third area features groomed cross-country trails tracked for both classic and skate skis. Night skiing and backcountry skiing trails are available in the provincial park. ~ 604-926-5612.

The glittering string of lights visible each night on the North Shore across the inlet from downtown Vancouver marks the arc-lit runs of **Grouse Mountain**, where residents head after work to get in some slope time. The resort offers 22 runs (30 percent beginner, 50 percent intermediate, 20 percent expert), a variety of lifts, a snowboard park, a snowshoeing park and cross-country skiing. There's also outdoor skating on a pond. ~ 6400 Nancy Greene Way, North Vancouver; 604-984-0661.

On a clear, fogless day, Burnaby and Richmond are visible from the 20 ski runs at **Mt. Seymour**. Good novice runs make this a best bet for beginners or those who want to avoid hot doggers. Downhill runs are serviced by a network of chairlifts and tows and are open for night skiing. Though the skiing here is mainly beginning and intermediate (80 percent of the runs), Mt. Seymour attracts international professional snowboarders who come for the natural terrain in its three parks. Hilly cross-country trails run through the adjacent Mt. Seymour Provincial Park. ~ 1700 Mt. Seymour Road, North Vancouver; 604-986-2261.

WHISTLER Whistler Resort, located 75 winding miles north-east of Vancouver at the base of Whistler and Blackcomb mountains, is a world-class resort and one of the top ski destinations in the world. The resort offers over 200 marked runs and the longest lift-serviced ski runs in North America, with a drop of one vertical mile. The official season runs from late November through May, then starts again for glacier skiing in mid-June. ~ 4165 Springs Lane, Whistler; 604-932-3434, 888-588-3434.

WHISTLER Whistler Outdoor Experience Co. leads guided rides during the summer through the Pemberton Meadows and along Ryan Creek and the Lillooet River. Winter sleigh rides provide views of glacier-fed Green Lake and a ring of mountains. ~ Edgewater Lodge; 604-932-3389.

RIDING STABLES

Golf in Vancouver is bound to involve water in some way. Even if there isn't much of it on the course, the location or the view will likely encompass a body of water—English Bay, the Strait of Georgia, one of the rivers.

GOLF

DOWNTOWN VANCOUVER There are dozens of golf courses and practice facilities in and around Vancouver and Richmond. Near the Fraser River, **Fraserview Golf Course** is an 18-hole public course that will have a brand-new design come June 1998, when it reopens after a year of renovation. ~ 7800 Vivian Street, Vancouver; 604-280-1818. The semiprivate **Mayfair Lakes Golf and Country Club** has lots of water—14 out of 18 holes have water, including the heavily bunkered 18th with water right up to the green. ~ 5460 Number 7 Road, Richmond; 604-276-0505.

WHISTLER In Whistler you can tee off amid the splendid terrain at the **Whistler Golf Course**, an 18-hole public course. ~ 4010 Whistler Way; 604-932-4544. ~ Or you can swing and putt at the 18-hole **Château Whistler Golf Club**. This narrow mountainous course is surrounded by trees and has scenic views of

✔ **CHECK THESE OUT—OUTDOOR ADVENTURES**

- Mountaineers enjoy ascending The Chiefs, the second-largest monolith in the world after the Rock of Gibraltar. *page 479*
- Your energy is the only limitation as you canoe across eight lakes on the 50-mile Powell Forest Canoe Route. *page 492*
- Alpine scenery, an upscale village and challenging downhill trails make Whistler Resort one of the world's top ski destinations. *page 495*
- Mountain bikers wheel over to Whistler in summer for some of the most dizzying mountain descents imaginable. *page 496*

Blackcomb and Whistler Mountains. ~ 4612 Blackcomb Way; 604-938-2095.

SUNSHINE COAST Open year-round, the 18-hole **Myrtle Point Golf Club** also has splendid views of Texada and Vancouver islands. ~ C-5 McCausland Road, RR #1, Myrtle Point; 604-487-4653. An occasional elk can be seen emerging from the surround lush vegetation to wander across one of the fairways at the nine-hole **Pender Harbor Golf Club**. ~ Sunshine Coast Highway, Pender Harbor; 604-883-9541. The **Sunshine Coast Golf and Country Club** is an 18-hole semiprivate course. With challenging greens, the tree-lined course isn't too long and is good for the average golfer. ~ 3206 Sunshine Coast Highway, Roberts Creek; 604-885-9212.

TENNIS

There are over 80 locations in the Vancouver area with tennis courts: most are free and first-come, first-serve; all are open for play year-round, weather permitting. Call the Park Board (604-257-8400) for a list of locations other than those listed here. Of course, many of the area's resorts provide tennis facilities for guests as well.

WEST SIDE/GRANVILLE ISLAND **Kitsilano Beach Park** has ten public courts charging minimal fees (only during warm weather months). ~ Cornwall Avenue and Arbutus Street. Other parks with courts include **Queen Elizabeth Park**, just off Cambie Street, and **Jericho Beach Park**, off Northwest Marine Drive.

DOWNTOWN VANCOUVER Of the 21 courts in **Stanley Park**, six charge minimal fees for reserved playing times; the rest are free.

BIKING

WEST SIDE/GRANVILLE ISLAND To avoid busy streets, try the shoreside paths at **Jericho Beach** and **English Bay** and the pathways that parallel Chancellor and University boulevards and 15th Avenue on the scenic campus of the **University of British Columbia**.

DOWNTOWN VANCOUVER Because of heavy traffic in Vancouver, cyclists are better off sticking to the protected 5.5-mile seawall path around the perimeter of **Stanley Park**.

WHISTLER Biking is popular in Whistler, especially mountain biking on rough alpine trails or paved trails around **Lost Lake** and along the **Valley Trail**, which connects the village with the nearby residential areas, parks and lakes. Daredevils go for the **mountain descents**, often taking a helicopter or gondola to the peaks so that they don't expend the energy needed for zooming down the dry ski runs. At ungodly speeds they follow an experienced trail leader who knows how to run the slopes safely.

Whistler Outdoor Experience Co. offers a guided descent on Blackcomb Mountain as well as slower-paced bike tours of parks and lakes. ~ Edgewater Lodge; 604-932-3389.

For a "heli-biking" adventure (a helicopter will fly you into a wilderness area for single-track mountain biking), contact **Whistler Backroads Mountain Bike Adventures**. ~ P.O. Box 643, Whistler, BC V0N 1B0; 604-932-3111.

SUNSHINE COAST   There is no protected bike path along **Route 101**, the main artery of the Sunshine Coast, and the rocky shoulder drops off entirely at times, forcing bikers onto the highway. However, the moderately challenging trip from Langsdale to Earls Cove is popular nonetheless. The backcountry of the entire coast is laced with marked and unmarked **logging trails** leading off Route 101 just waiting to be explored by intrepid mountain bikers; a detailed map of the trails between Jervis Inlet and Lund is available from the Powell River Travel InfoCentre (604-485-4701).

Bike Rentals   **Spokes Bicycle Rentals** has a large selection of bike rentals; they arrange group tours to nearby Stanley Park. ~ 1798 West Georgia Street, Vancouver; 604-688-5141. **Recreation Rentals** rents bikes as well as inline skates. ~ 2560 Arbutus Street, Vancouver; 604-733-7368. For bike rentals in Whistler, from May through the fall, turn to **Tracks and Trails**. They also offer tours and bike descents of Whistler Mountain. ~ Base of Whistler Mountain Gondola; 604-938-2017. **Whistler Backroads Mountain Bike Adventures** also rents during the warm months. ~ Westbrook Hotel Base; 604-932-3111. On the Sunshine Coast, rent bikes at **Taws Cycle and Sports**. ~ 4597 Marine Avenue, Powell River; 604-485-2555.

All distances listed for hiking trails are one way unless otherwise noted.

HIKING

WEST SIDE/GRANVILLE ISLAND   Pacific Spirit Regional Park (30 miles) crisscrosses 1000 acres of parkland on Point Grey Peninsula, offering easy-to-moderate hikes of varying length through this largely unmarked ecological reserve. Here you're more likely to run into a blacktail deer or bald eagle than another hiker. A map is available from the Greater Vancouver Regional Parks office (604-432-6350).

◄ *HIDDEN*

DOWNTOWN VANCOUVER   Stanley Park Seawall Path (5.5 miles), carefully divided to accommodate both cyclists and pedestrians, is easily the most popular hike in town. There are also numerous paths that plunge into the thickly forested acres of the park.

NORTH SHORE   Capilano Pacific Trail (4.5 miles), in North Vancouver's Capilano River Regional Park, passes from massive Cleveland Dam to Ambleside Park through sections of coastal rainforest and offers great views of the Lions, the twin mountain peaks soaring majestically above the dam.

Norvan Falls (9.5 miles) offers a more rugged backcountry trek for the experienced hiker through the wilderness areas of Lynn Headwaters Regional Park. The shorter **Lynn Loop Trail** (3 miles) affords views of Lynn Valley and passes an abandoned cabin. Call 604-985-1690 for trail conditions.

WHISTLER There are trails in Whistler for all levels. **Valley Trail** (15 miles roundtrip) is a bustling paved walkway/bike path/cross-country ski trail that winds through town, connecting Alpha, Nita, Alta, Lost and Green lakes, the village and the various residential areas.

Lost Lake Trails (9 miles, all together) serve as cross-country ski trails during the winter and make for fairly level summer hiking paths (with some paved areas) through the forested area between Lost and Green lakes.

Singing Pass-Russet Lake (6.75 miles), an alpine hiking trail just behind Whistler Village, and the graded **Garibaldi Lake Trail** (5.5 miles), located off Route 99 south of town, are prime options for experienced hikers interested in heading into the steep fringes of incredible Garibaldi Park.

SUNSHINE COAST The **Soames Hill Mountain Trail** (1.5 miles), otherwise known as "The Knob" because of its appearance to passengers on ferries approaching Langdale, is a brisk stair climb to an elevation of 800 feet followed by expansive views of Howe Sound, the surrounding mountains and villages.

Smuggler's Cove Marine Park Trail (.5 mile) is an easy walk leading from the parking lot off Brooks Road approximately six miles north of Sechelt to the cove once used to smuggle in Chinese immigrants and other contraband and now home to an array of seabirds.

Mt. Valentine Trail (approximately 1 mile) offers a short walk up a gravel path followed by a steep climb up a stone staircase leading to panoramic views of Malaspina and Georgia straits, Vancouver Island and the surrounding town of Powell Lake.

Inland Lake Trail (8 miles), just north of Powell River, offers a longer hike over a well-maintained circuit of boardwalks and bridges through scenic swamp areas and skirting lovely Inland Lake. The entire trail is wheelchair accessible, and several handicap shelters and fishing wharfs are along the way.

▼▼▼▼▼▼▼▼▼▼
Transportation

CAR

From the West Coast of the United States, **Route 5** turns into **Route 99** after crossing the Canadian border at Blaine and proceeds northwest through Vancouver's suburbs and into the city core where the name changes once again, this time to **Granville Street**. The **Trans-Canada Highway** (**Route 1**) connects Vancouver with points east in Canada.

Route 99, referred to as the **Sea to Sky Highway** from Horseshoe Bay northward, picks up again in North Vancouver, hugs the rugged coastline and continues north into the mountains to Whistler.

Route 101, the only major thoroughfare through the Sunshine Coast, connects Langdale to Earls Cove and Saltery Bay to Lund, the northernmost point of this long, transcontinental highway with southern terminus in Chile.

AIR

Vancouver International Airport services domestic charters and flights by Air B.C., Canada 3000, Harbour Air and Royal Airlines. International airlines include Air Canada, Air China, Air New Zealand, Alaska Airlines, American Airlines, British Airways, Cathay Pacific, Continental Airlines, Delta Airlines, Horizon Air, Japan Air Lines, KLM Royal Dutch Airlines, Korean Air, Lufthansa, Mandarin Air, Northwest Airlines, Qantas, Singapore Airlines and United Airlines.

Airport express buses operated by **The Airporter** depart every 15 minutes or so from Level II of the Main Terminal building and stop at the bus station and most major hotels in downtown Vancouver. ~ 604-244-9888, 800-668-3141. **B.C. Transit** buses also serve the airport; catch #100 from either terminal and then transfer to #20 at Granville Street and 71st Avenue, which will take you to Granville Mall in the heart of Vancouver. ~ 604-521-0400.

FERRY & BOAT

Between May and October, cruise ships call regularly at the terminal at **Canada Place**, an architectural stunner under Teflon-coated white "sails." ~ 999 Canada Place, Vancouver; 604-666-6068.

B.C. Ferries provides service between Vancouver Island and Tsawwassen (an hour south of downtown Vancouver), Horseshoe Bay (half an hour northwest of downtown) and Langdale on the southern Sunshine Coast and Earls Cove and Saltery Bay on the northern Sunshine Coast. ~ 604-277-0277.

BUS

Greyhound Lines Incorporated offers service to and from the United States. ~ 1150 Station Street, Vancouver; 800-231-2222 from the U.S., 800-661-8747 from Canada. **Maverick Coach Lines** also provides bus service from Vancouver to Whistler. ~ 1150 Station Street, Vancouver; 604-255-1171.

TRAIN

Via Rail Canada at 1150 Station Street in Vancouver (604-669-3050) provides rail service throughout Canada and connects with **Amtrak** (800-872-7245) to points within the United States.

From North Vancouver, **B.C. Rail** runs daily roundtrip service to Whistler. Intriguing whistle- and flag-stops along the way remind you of the casual nature of British Columbia. ~ 1311 West 1st Street; 604-984-5246.

CAR RENTALS

Rental agencies at Vancouver International Airport include **Avis Rent A Car** (800-331-1084), **Budget Rent A Car** (800-527-0700), **Hertz Rent A Car** (800-654-3001), **Thrifty Car Rental** (800-367-2277) and **Tilden** (800-387-4747).

ABC **Rent A Car** (604-276-0108) and **Discount Car Rentals** (604-273-8322) have offices in the neighboring suburb of Richmond and offer free airport pickup.

PUBLIC TRANSIT

B.C. Transit governs Vancouver's expansive transit system, with buses, the SkyTrain and the SeaBus covering all the main arteries within the city and fanning out into the suburbs. Running on a 16-mile, mostly elevated track between Canada Place downtown and the suburb of Surrey, the SkyTrain is a good way to see some of the major sights of the city. You can also get a great view of the skyline from the water aboard the SeaBuses that cross Burrard Inlet between downtown and the North Shore. The handy "Discover Vancouver on Transit" tour guide, day passes and timetables are available from Travel InfoCentres. ~ 604-521-0400.

Whistler Transit (604-938-0388), the local operator for B.C. Transit, runs five buses connecting Whistler Creek and Whistler Village every half hour. B.C. Transit is also responsible for transit service along the Sunshine Coast; for more information dial 604-485-4287 for municipal areas and 604-483-2008 for rural areas.

TAXIS

Cab companies serving the airport include **Bel-Air Taxi** (604-433-6666), **Black Top and Checker Cabs** (604-731-1111), **Vancouver Taxi** (604-255-5111) and **Yellow Cab** (604-681-1111).

TWELVE

Victoria and Southern Vancouver Island

I say, do you want a taste of veddy proper Britain without having to fly across the Atlantic? Then step into Victoria, a city of stately government buildings, picture-perfect lawns and fascinating glimpses of the British influence. Shorn, manicured and embellished, Victoria is called more British than Britain itself. But have no fear: This is not stiff-upper-lip territory. Travel out of Victoria and you will find the rest of Vancouver Island an untamed land. Stretching 280 miles along the rugged Pacific coastline of Canada and the United States it occupies some 12,400 square miles. Most of this mass protects the lower mainland of British Columbia from torrential rains and gale-force winds of the open ocean. However, the island does cross the 49th parallel, the general boundary between the United States and Canada, and its southern one-fifth, including the city of Victoria, is on the same latitude as parts of Washington State.

Much of the island lies in its natural state with beaches, forests, mountains and meadows. Rains nurture thick, sometimes ancient forests, and over centuries the ocean has carved out sandy beaches. The area is a stunning contrast of the rugged, mountainous and relatively uninhabited west coast to sleepy seaside villages, farms and bucolic islands on the southeastern shore. On the west coast, winds and rains can be brutal. Mountains drop right into a raging Pacific Ocean. Many remote settlements or camps—too small even to be called villages—have scant road access and rely on freighters, boats or float planes to deliver everything from apples to asphalt.

Geography and the elements have conspired to make the southern part of the island a relative haven where farming, tourism and commerce thrive. A number of picturesque villages and towns are perched on the coast. The Malahat Drive offers fabulous views of Washington's Olympic Mountains and the Saanich Peninsula, which is dotted with small farms, orchards and forests.

For the most part, the island's climate is gentle, thanks to the warmth from the Japanese current. A majestic range of mountains divides the island into a dense rainforest on the west coast and the drier lowlands on the east coast. The eastern summers can be blissful with long, sunny days. The climate of Victoria and the southeastern part of the island is akin to that of the Mediterranean—dry, cool summers and mild winters. It is no accident that many Canadians choose to retire there.

Not all of Vancouver Island is so bucolic. The west coast is rugged with craggy mountains, a rugged coastline and often brutal weather. Starting in September, the winter rains start to pour, and blustery winds are not uncommon.

In contrast to the rugged side of Vancouver Island, Victoria emerges gracious and genteel. On the island's southern shore, this is the seat of the provincial government, but there is also a cozy and quaint look to the place. It overflows with flowers, the lawns graced with tulips, rhododendrons and roses, the window boxes and hanging planters filled with geraniums and lobelia. Victoria's economy rests on the shoulders of government and tourism. Although heightened in summer, tourism is a year-round activity in this city.

Prior to settlement by white explorers, the island's people lived in harmony with nature. Natives lived in bands of the Nootka or Nuu-chah-nulth on the west, the Coast Salish to the south and east and the Southern Kwakiutl to the north. These people lived off the bounty of the land, principally the salmon, cedar and wild berries. Spanish explorers first came to the island in 1592, followed by Captain James Cook in 1778. Vancouver Island is the namesake of George Vancouver, British naval captain, who negotiated the island away from Spain in 1795.

In 1843 James Douglas, a representative of the Hudson's Bay Company, established a fort, named after the British queen, Victoria, where Bastion Square sits on Wharf Street today. Coal mining, fishing, logging and fur trading brought settlers to other parts of the island.

Fortunately, the island's wealth of wildlife has not all been hunted away. Home to several species of salmon, the waters surrounding the island make for excellent fishing and offer a supply of natural food for orca whales, sea lions and seals. These waters also contain a wide variety of seabirds. The mountains and highlands contain Roosevelt elk, black bears, black tail deer, marmots, wolves and cougars.

It's all waiting for you. Ta-ta!

▼▼▼▼▼▼▼▼▼▼▼▼▼▼

Downtown Victoria

Victoria combines a rich, British heritage with a relaxed lifestyle and climate of the North American West Coast. Winsome, gracious and colorful, the city comes alive with sights that illustrate its history, customs and ties with the sea. Sightseeing in Victoria veers in the direction of its British influence, its natural history and the residents' passion for gardening.

SIGHTS
The place to get information is the **Travel InfoCentre**, on the Inner Harbour. ~ 812 Wharf Street; 250-953-2033.

The **scenic marine drive** along the coast is the best route to see views of the water, the coast, the Olympic Mountains and some of Victoria's most elegant homes. Starting at Mile 0, the end of the Trans-Canada Highway, (at the intersection of Dallas Road

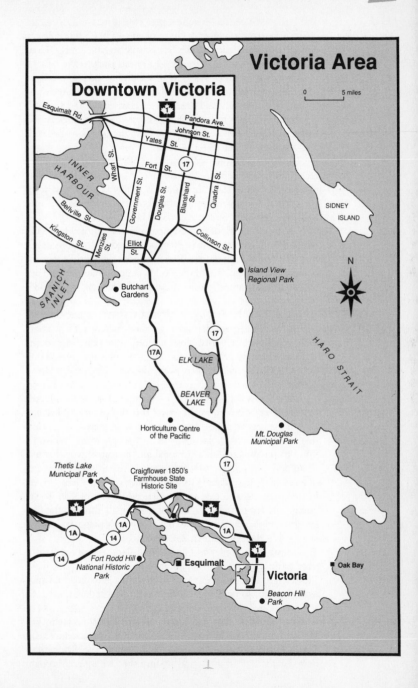

Victoria Area

Downtown Victoria

Esquimalt Rd.

Pandora Ave.

Johnson St.

Yates St.

INNER HARBOUR

Wharf St.

Fort St.

(17)

Government St.

Douglas St.

Blanshard St.

Quadra St.

Bellville St.

Kingston St.

Menzies St.

Elliot St.

Collinson St.

0   5 miles

SIDNEY ISLAND

N

Island View Regional Park

SAANICH INLET

Butchart Gardens

HARO STRAIT

(17)

(17A)

ELK LAKE

BEAVER LAKE

Horticulture Centre of the Pacific

Mt. Douglas Municipal Park

(17)

Thetis Lake Municipal Park

Craigflower 1850's Farmhouse State Historic Site

(1)

(1)

(1A)

(1A)

(1A)

(14)

(14)

Fort Rodd Hill National Historic Park

Esquimalt

Victoria

Oak Bay

Beacon Hill Park

and Douglas Street), follow the signs as the drive winds along the coast. You pass through Oak Bay, around part of Cadboro Bay, to Mount Douglas Park and the Saanich Peninsula. At Elk Lake, you can turn left onto Highway 17 to head back to Victoria.

Visitors get a good overview of the city by taking a **Tallyho Horsedrawn Tour**, whose steeds have been clip-clopping their way through the streets since 1903. ~ Inner Harbour; 250-383-5067.

Another tour company offering horse-drawn outings is **Victoria Carriage Tours**. ~ Tours leave from the corner of Belleville and Menzies streets; 250-383-2207.

The **Empress Hotel** is Victoria's unofficial central landmark facing the Inner Harbour. Opened in 1908, it reflects the gentility of an earlier time. The Palm Court, with its magnificent stained-glass dome, is renowned for its afternoon teas and tropical plants. ~ 721 Government Street; 250-384-8111.

On the ground floor of the Empress Hotel, you will find **Miniature World**, with more than 80 miniaturized illustrations of history and fantasy. Miniature World includes the world's smallest operational sawmill, two of the world's largest dollhouses and one of the world's largest model railways. Admission. ~ 250-385-9731.

Just east of the Empress is **Crystal Gardens**, a one-time enclosed swimming pool that now is a glass-roofed tropical aviary with hundreds of colorful blossoms and more than 75 varieties of birds including penguins and flamingos, plus the world's tiniest butterflies in the summer. Admission. ~ 713 Douglas Street; 250-381-1213.

Walk across Belleville Street, just south of the Empress Hotel, to a complex anchored by the **Royal British Columbia Museum**. One of the best on the continent, the museum focuses on the history of British Columbia—its land and people from prehistoric times to the present—in a personal and evocative way. Visitors sit among totem poles, walk inside a longhouse and learn stories of native people struggling to survive once white settlers arrived. Museum guests also can stroll down the streets of Old Town, plunge into the bowels of a coal mine and walk through the *Discovery*, a replica of the ship used by Captain Vancouver. Admission. ~ 675 Belleville Street; 250-387-3014.

Part of the complex is **Thunderbird Park**, a postage stamp–sized park covering only a quarter of the block. The park is the site of ten or so magnificent totem poles and a longhouse in which natives demonstrate the crafts of carving and beading during the summer. ~ Belleville and Douglas streets.

Just behind the park and adjacent to the museum is **Helmcken House**, built in 1852 for pioneer doctor J. S. Helmcken. This is British Columbia's oldest residence on its original site. Rooms decorated in the style of the period are furnished with pieces brought around Cape Horn from England by Victoria's founding families. The library includes Dr. Helmcken's medicine chest and medical instruments. Recorded audio presentations relate colorful stories about the house and family narrated by various family members. Admission. ~ 10 Elliott Street beside the Royal British Columbia Museum; 250-361-0021.

From here you can take a detour (just a couple blocks south) to a Victorian Italianate cottage known as **Carr House,** where British Columbia landscape painter Emily Carr was born in 1871 and lived her girlhood years. Historians have restored the home with period wall coverings and furnishings to look as it did when she lived there. Carr was also an author, and her gardens have been re-created from her books, excerpts of which stand on plaques among the vegetation. Closed mid-October through mid-May except the month of December. Admission. ~ 207 Government Street; 250-383-5843.

The **Parliament Buildings** are in the next block west of the Royal British Columbia Museum. The legislative buildings are Francis Rattenbury's architectural salad of Victorian, Romanesque and Italian renaissance styles with 33 copper-covered domes. At night they are outlined with more than 3000 twinkling lights. A statue of Queen Victoria stands in front of the buildings, and one of Captain George Vancouver tops the main copper dome. Guided tours explain historic features and the workings of the provincial government. Closed weekends between Labor Day and mid-May. ~ 501 Belleville Street; 250-387-3046.

Across the street is the **Royal London Wax Museum,** also designed by Rattenbury as the ticket office for the Canadian Pacific Railroad. The Acropolis-style building now contains wax sculptures of the Princess of Wales, President Bill Clinton and some 250 other Josephine Tussaud figures. The likenesses of the American figures are lacking, but the Royal Family is very lifelike. You will want to keep young children out of the Horror Chamber with its

◆◆

✔ CHECK THESE OUT—UNIQUE SIGHTS

- Sit among totem poles at the regal **Royal British Columbia Museum** and study the evocative and personal history of the province. *page 504*
- Be dazzled by the 3000 twinkling lights that illuminate 33 copper-colored domes at Victoria's **Parliament Buildings** at night. *page 505*
- Escape British-styled Victoria to **Duncan,** with its large native population and 60 totem poles. *page 521*
- Stay dry while watching the world's largest firefighting planes at **Martin Mars Water Bombers** drop 6000 gallons of water on Sproat Lake. *page 529*

gruesome depictions of decapitations and other methods of torture, but adolescents love it. Admission. ~ 470 Belleville Street; 250-388-4461.

On the water side of the Wax Museum is the **Undersea Gardens**, a salute to British Columbia life below water. At regularly scheduled intervals, divers swim behind huge windows in the enclosed aquarium tanks to show and tell visitors (comfortably dry in the underwater auditorium) information about sea creatures within the province. Admission. ~ 490 Belleville Street; 250-382-5717.

You can continue out Belleville Street by car, cab, bus or bicycle to picturesque **Fisherman's Wharf**, a working fishing pier. Moorage allows for up to 400 boats, but the little bay often is jammed with many more, tied up to one another. If the fishing fleet is in, visitors can buy fresh fish from the docks. ~ Corner of Dallas Road and Erie Street. A walk in the **James Bay neighborhood**, one of the city's more fashionable areas, takes you past several restored Victorian and Edwardian homes.

Continue back around the Inner Harbour past the Empress and the Travel InfoCentre heading north on Wharf Street to **Bastion Square**. In 1843–44, James Douglas established Fort Victoria here, but the buildings there now, including warehouses, offices, saloons and waterfront hotels, were constructed in the late 1800s, the city's boom period. The buildings, many of them red brick, have been restored and now house restaurants, shops and art galleries. ~ Off Wharf Street between Fort and Yates streets.

The **Maritime Museum** is housed in a large, turreted building that was originally the Provincial Court House. The museum depicts British Columbia's maritime history from its early days to the present. It includes nautical charts, an extensive model ship collection, brassware from old ships, Navy uniforms and two incredible vessels—*Tilikum*, a 38-foot dugout canoe that sailed from Victoria to England at the turn of the century, and *Trekka*, a 20-foot ketch that sailed single-handedly around the world. The museum's new lighthouse includes both old and new apparatus, along with the history of the characters who ran the equipment. Admission. ~ 28 Bastion Square; 250-385-4222.

Walk over to Government Street and continue north to Johnson Street. Here you will find **Market Square**. Market Square incorporates the original Occidental Hotel, the choice of many Klondike gold miners in 1898, now a favorite area for shopping and dining. ~ Government and Johnson streets.

Take Fan Tan Alley north another block to **Chinatown** at Government and Herald streets. In the late 19th century, Victoria's Chinatown was second largest on the continent, only trailing that of San Francisco. The Chinese immigrants headed to British Columbia to work on the railroad and to mine for coal and gold.

Approaching Chinatown from Government Street, you see the ceramic-tiled Gate of Harmonious Interest with two hand-carved stone lions standing guard. Fan Tan Alley, dubbed Canada's narrowest street, contains boutiques and artists' studios.

LODGING

The problem with lodging in Victoria is the same as elsewhere in popular cities—it's expensive. Several luxurious hotels line the Inner Harbour. Several others charge luxurious prices for mediocre to shoddy rooms. Budget prices can be found, but those accommodations are often farther from downtown.

Like Vancouver's, Victoria's high season is the end of June to mid-September. And like Vancouver's, the city's hotels offer superlative off-season lodging packages that often bring room rates down to near 50 percent of the summer tariff. The weather isn't as dependable, but the streets aren't thronged with crowds of bus-borne tourists. For more information, call **Tourism Victoria,** whose accommodation line provides travelers with current rates and availability at a full range of places. ~ 800-663-3883.

Also contact **All Seasons Bed and Breakfast Agency** (250-655-7173) or the **Garden City Bed and Breakfast Reservation Service** (250-479-1986).

The dominant sight in Victoria's Inner Harbour is the stately, Neo-Gothic **Empress Hotel**. Canadian Pacific Railways commissioned architect Francis Rattenbury to design this magnificent hotel. In 1989 a $45 million renovation improved all 475 guest rooms. Other amenities include a swimming pool, sauna, health club, lobby and lovely grounds. This grande-dame hotel is known throughout the world for its British-style elegance and wonderful afternoon teas. ~ 721 Government Street; 250-384-8111, 800-230-6922, fax 250-381-4334. ULTRA-DELUXE.

Even after renovating its 50 rooms, the **James Bay Inn** still fills the bill for price-minded travelers. It is located in a residential area among heritage homes and small cafés but is pretty convenient to downtown. The hotel, which opened in 1913, features light-oak paneling and period furnishings in the lobby. Guest rooms are small but have been updated with new wallpaper, paint, carpet and linens. Pub and restaurant are on the premises. ~ 270 Government Street; 250-384-7151, 800-836-2649, fax 250-385-2311. MODERATE.

For luxury accommodations along the Inner Harbour near the Parliament Buildings, **Hotel Grand Pacific** is one of the city's finest. The lobby and other public areas feature rich, mahogany paneling and millwork. The 145 rooms offer views of the harbor or downtown. Amenities include an indoor swimming pool, sauna, whirlpool, health and fitness facilities, restaurant and lounge. ~ 450 Quebec Street; 250-386-0450, 800-663-7550, fax 250-385-6579. ULTRA-DELUXE.

Admiral Motel, on the Inner Harbour, is a very basic motel with 32 straightforward, clean rooms, all with refrigerators, 25 with kitchenettes. ~ 257 Belleville Street; 250-388-6267. DELUXE.

Just a brisk walk or shuttle or ferry ride from the downtown attractions, the **Coast Victoria Harbourside Hotel** opened in 1991 and faces a 42-slip marina. Marine colors of teal blue, dark mahogany, original art and watery motifs are found throughout the hotel. The 132 rooms and suites, each with private balcony, come with all the amenities of a top-rate hotel, including bar and computer hookup. Pick your view: the harbor or the Olympic Mountains. The hotel features an indoor/outdoor pool and deck, with whirlpool, sauna and exercise room. They also offer free parking and a courtesy van to downtown. ~ 146 Kingston Street; 250-360-1211, 800-663-1144, fax 250-360-1418. ULTRA-DELUXE.

One of the most comfortable, luxurious hotels in an ideal location downtown, across from Victoria Eaton Centre, is the **Bedford Regency Hotel.** The large open lobby is furnished with comfortable rattan pieces. Done in vibrant Southwest colors, the hotel's 40 individually decorated guest rooms feature marble fireplaces, comfortable beds complete with down comforters and pillows, cotton sheets and window boxes overflowing with colorful flowers. A complimentary full breakfast is served in the hotel's Red Currant Dining Room and fresh coffee or tea is placed outside each room in the morning. ~ 1140 Government Street; 250-384-6835, 800-665-6500, fax 250-386-8930. DELUXE TO ULTRA-DELUXE.

The place for basic accommodations is the **Victoria Hostel,** sandwiched between historic buildings and offices in the downtown area. The hostel features two kitchens, gameroom, lounge, eating area, library, bicycle-storage area, laundry facilities and hot showers. There are 108 beds, dormitory-style, and five small fam-

✔ CHECK THESE OUT—UNIQUE LODGING

- *Budget:* Start your day off with a full breakfast after a good night's rest at the **Cherry Bank Hotel.** page 509
- *Moderate:* Stay in a one-time boys' school, the Tudor-style **Qualicum College Inn,** offering stunning views of Georgia Strait. page 524
- *Deluxe to ultra-deluxe:* Settle into a cabin near the beaches of Pacific Rim National Park at the **Pacific Sands Beach Resort.** page 532
- *Ultra-deluxe:* Tempt yourself at the British-style High Tea before checking into Victoria's landmark **Empress Hotel.** page 507

Budget: under $50   Moderate: $50–$90   Deluxe: $90–$130   Ultra-deluxe: over $130

ily rooms. Private double-occupancy rooms are available with reservation. ~ 516 Yates Street; 250-385-4511. BUDGET.

Swans Hotel is a small, 29-room hotel in a restored brick heritage building along the harbor in downtown Victoria offering a colorful pub and restaurant. Each contemporary unit, ranging from studios to two-bedroom suites, features designer decor and includes a kitchenette, dining area and original art on the walls. ~ 506 Pandora Avenue; 250-361-3310, 800-668-7926, fax 250-361-3491. DELUXE TO ULTRA-DELUXE.

If you want low-cost accommodations close to downtown but with more privacy than you'd find at a hostel, the **Cherry Bank Hotel**, a hotel/rooming house, is a possibility. The full breakfast included with your room is the best part of the deal. The dining room is cozy, clean and attractive, which is more than can be said for the rooms, which, at their best, feature an eclectic mix of cast-off furniture, draperies and bedspreads. ~ 825 Burdett Street; 250-385-5380, 800-998-6688, fax 250-383-0949. BUDGET.

Abigail's is just four blocks east of downtown. This Tudor inn has a European ambience with colorful, well-kept gardens and a light, bright interior. The foyer features hardwood floors and an open oak staircase to the guest rooms. The sitting room is luxurious with hardwood floors, leather sofa, piano, game table, fireplace and fresh flowers. Each of the 16 rooms and suites features down comforters and antiques, and some have whirlpool baths, fireplaces and vaulted ceilings. Included in the room rate is an evening sherry hour in the library and a gourmet breakfast served in the dining room. ~ 906 McClure Street; 250-388-5363, 800-561-6565, fax 250-388-7787. DELUXE TO ULTRA-DELUXE.

A truly hidden discovery for couples seeking a romantic getaway is **Humboldt House**, which looks like a private residence. ◄ HIDDEN
A Victorian home built in 1895 and tastefully renovated in 1988, it includes five suites. The library offers walls full of books and a fireplace. Guests are served champagne and truffles on arrival. The rooms are individually decorated with stained glass and have jacuzzis and fireplaces. Guests have breakfast delivered to their room via a two-way compartment. ~ 867 Humboldt Street; 250-383-0152, 888-383-0327, fax 250-383-6402. DELUXE TO ULTRA-DELUXE.

A large old Edwardian-style home, the **Beaconsfield Inn** has a turn-of-the-century ambience with antique pieces, stained glass, oak fireplace, 14-foot beamed ceiling and the original, dark paneling. Millionaire R. P. Rithet built it in 1905 as a wedding present for his daughter, Gertrude. The nine guest rooms vary in charm, but all include down comforters and antiques. Many feature canopy beds, jacuzzis and fireplaces. Guests also can enjoy afternoon tea, sherry hour in the library and a full gourmet breakfast in the original dining room or sun room, all included in the room rate.

~ 998 Humboldt Street; 250-384-4044, fax 250-384-4052. DE-LUXE TO ULTRA-DELUXE.

Dashwood Manor Bed and Breakfast, a gracious Tudor mansion built in 1912, sits next to Beacon Hill Park and offers unobstructed views of the Strait of Juan de Fuca and the Olympic Mountains. This is not the place to hang out and meet other bed-and-breakfast aficionados. Unfortunately, the only place for guests to mingle is a little office. Breakfast is make-it-yourself with ingredients provided in the kitchenettes in each of the rooms. Three of the 16 rooms have fireplaces. The grounds are impeccable, the rooms are clean, but industrial-grade carpeting in the hallways is grimy. ~ 1 Cook Street; 250-385-5517, 800-667-5517, fax 250-383-1760. DELUXE TO ULTRA-DELUXE.

DINING

The menu at **The Water Club** is determinedly mainstream—pastas, pizza, roast chicken, seafood, sandwiches. But the overall quality is quite good (it's operated by the same folks that run the highly regarded Herald Street Caffe), the prices are reasonable, and the location at Crystal Gardens, just opposite the Royal BC Museum, is visitor-friendly. ~ 703 Douglas Street; 250-388-4200. MODERATE.

How can anything at the Empress Hotel be hidden? Easy: So much attention focuses on the hotel's lobby, tea service and up-

HIDDEN ►

scale shops, that visitors overlook the **Bengal Lounge**, a curry bar par excellence. Once the hotel's library, the lounge is decorated with curios reflecting the British Empire's colonial era—a tiger-skin wall hanging, Indian ceiling fans. The curry is served buffet-style at lunch, à la carte in the evenings, and it's a welcome contrast to the monotony of British pub fare that tends to overwhelm Victoria dining. ~ Empress Hotel, 721 Government Street; 250-384-8111. MODERATE TO DELUXE.

James Bay Tea Room and Restaurant is a homey place with photographs of English royalty overlooking tables set close together with hand-crocheted tea cozies insulating every teapot. This place is popular with the older set. Afternoon tea is served daily. Dinner entrées include homemade potpies, rib-eye roast with Yorkshire pudding and bangers and mashed potatoes. ~ 332 Menzies Street; 250-382-8282. MODERATE.

A charming and graceful Japanese restaurant is **Yokohama**. Its large sushi bar with an extensive menu is deemed the best place in town for such fare. The restaurant features authentic Japanese entrées as well as familiar favorites of tempura, sukiyaki and ginger pork in the main dining area or in private tatami rooms. ~ 980 Blanshard Street; 250-384-5433. MODERATE TO DELUXE.

The Keg Steakhouse and Bar is an informal restaurant, one of the most popular, reasonably priced places in downtown. Its dining room offers great views of the Inner Harbour. Entrées include prime rib and grilled shrimp. Try the Classic Meal, a sirloin or New York steak served with sautéed mushrooms, oven-roasted vegetables and Caesar salad or salad bar. Dinner only. ~ 500 Fort Street; 250-386-7789. MODERATE TO DELUXE.

Historic Bastion Square contains two of Victoria's best restaurants. **Camille's Restaurant** is romantic and elegant with brick walls, balloon curtains and linen tablecloths. This intimate restaurant prepares delicious West Coast and Pacific Rim cuisine, such as caramel and almond duck with cranberry champagne sauce and roast venison with mushroom risotto. The breads and desserts are heavenly. Camille's also has an extensive wine cellar. Dinner only. ~ 45 Bastion Square; 250-381-3433. MODERATE TO DELUXE.

The other Bastion Square restaurant is **La Ville Di's**. Set in an ivy-covered brick building, the atmosphere is cozy and friendly with soft lighting and classical music. Seafood, rabbit, beef and lamb entrées are prepared in a Brittany style. Try the *langoustines polinac*, tiger prawns with mushrooms and shallots in Calvados and Muscadet sauce, or the soufflé *de homard*, lobster soufflé with prawns. The restaurant features an extensive list of French wines. From May to October, more casual dining is available for lunch in the outside café. Closed Sunday. ~ 26 Bastion Square; 250-388-9414. DELUXE.

Delicious Greek food, including moussaka, souvlaki and spanakopita, along with standard steaks and seafood are served at **Periklis**, a convivial, Taverna-style restaurant with dining areas on three levels and Greek posters on the walls. Greek and belly dancing draws big crowds on the weekends in winter and seven nights a week during the summer. Closed for lunch on weekends. ~ 531 Yates Street; 250-386-3313. MODERATE.

Siam Thai serves up some of the best Thai food in Victoria. The atmosphere is dark and quiet, with soft lighting lending a bit of mystery to this ethnic eatery. Only fresh ingredients are used in the entrées, such as *larp gai*, diced chicken in spicy lime juice, onions and vegetables, or scallop *prik paow*, sautéed scallops with green-red peppers, onions, mushrooms and chili paste. ~ 512 Fort Street; 250-383-9911. MODERATE.

The **Fowl & Fish Cafe, Ale & Oyster House** offers a convivial ambience with huge vases of fresh flowers and a display of colorful local artwork against brick walls of the historic building that was once a grain warehouse. They specialize in fresh seafood, particularly oysters. Try the cassino oysters with bacon in sweet garlic butter and chablis sauce, the black bean fettuccine or homemade beer bread. Dinner only. ~ In the Swans Hotel, 506 Pandora Avenue; 250-361-3310. MODERATE TO DELUXE.

A traditional Chinese restaurant, in the heart of Chinatown, is **Don Mee**. Go through the door under the neon sign and walk up a long, green-carpeted staircase to the large dining area. The food here is good, portions are ample and the presentation is upscale. People come for the Cantonese-style seafood dishes like lobster in ginger sauce or crab with black beans. Favorites include Szechuan chicken and fresh vegetable dishes. The dim sum, served for lunch daily, is especially good. ~ 538 Fisgard Street; 250-383-1032. MODERATE.

> Vancouver Island is North America's largest Pacific Island.

Two intimate dining rooms with candlelit tables, lace curtains and mauve accents form the interior of **Chez Daniel**, a restaurant in northeast Victoria devoted to classic French cuisine. Rabbit in white wine sauce, trout with slivered almonds and roast lamb with ginger, shallots and brandy cream sauce are among chef-owner Daniel Rigollet's signature dishes. The wine list is one of the most extensive on the island. Dinner only. Closed Sunday and Monday. ~ 2522 Estevan Avenue; 250-592-7424. DELUXE.

Outdoor dining made warm and cozy by fireplaces and overhead heaters is offered by **Il Terrazzo**. Here they serve sophisticated Northern Italian cuisine on a brick plant-filled terrace off Waddington Alley. Daily specials yield such possibilities as grilled lamb chops seasoned with garlic and fresh mint or baked halibut with fresh raspberry sauce. ~ 555 Johnson Street; 250-361-0028. MODERATE TO DELUXE.

SHOPPING
Victoria's downtown is chock full of fascinating shops. Best buys are locally made candies, Indian-made sweaters, carvings and silver, British Columbia jade, weavings and pottery, books on Canada and goods imported from Britain. Shopping starts with tiny shops in the Empress Hotel and extends north on Government Street.

Roger's Chocolates is *the* place for connoisseurs of fine chocolates. Housed in a 1903 building with a tiled floor, dark-oak paneling and oak-and-glass display cases, the shop is full of Dickensian charm. ~ 913 Government Street; 250-384-7021.

Even if you brought all your reading with you, stop at **Munro's Books** to see this neoclassical heritage building with high ceilings and carved details, formerly the head office of the Royal Bank. It is one of the finest bookshops in western Canada. The shop holds more than 50,000 titles of Canadian, British and American works. ~ 1108 Government Street; 250-382-2464.

The purveyor of fine teas and coffees is **Murchies**, where you also can pick up some delectable pastries. This importer also has one of the largest stocks of china and porcelain in the province. ~ 1110 Government Street; 250-383-3112.

For Battenburg lace, linen damask tablecloths, fine handkerchiefs and natural-fiber lingerie, visit the **Irish Linen Store**. ~ 1019 Government Street; 250-383-6812.

For a look at another beautifully restored old building, stop by **The Spirit of Christmas**. It is located in an 1886 bank building with high ceilings, large, arched windows and dark-oak and glass display cases containing thousands of whimsical ornaments, music boxes, nutcrackers, Disney characters and collectibles. ~ 1022 Government Street; 250-385-2501.

Eaton Centre, a multilevel shopping mall located in the heart of Victoria, has more than 100 shops and opens to an interior courtyard with a fountain under skylights and arches. Eaton's offers goods from all over the Commonwealth, especially china and woolen products. ~ Government and View streets; 250-389-2228.

The Canadian company that pioneered settlement of the west is the **Hudson's Bay Company**. It still carries the famous Hudson's Bay point blankets and top brands of English china and woolens, as well as contemporary works by local artists and artisans. ~ 1701 Douglas Street; 250-385-1311.

Fort Street between Blanshard and Cook streets is known as Antique Row with antique maps, stamps, coins, estate jewelry, rare books, crystal, china, furniture and paintings. **Victoria Limited Editions** offers a large selection of china, crystal and collectors plates. ~ 919 Fort Street; 250-386-5155.

In the Empress Hotel, the **Bengal Lounge**, with its high ceilings, potted plants and rattan furnishings, is fit for the raj. It is a comfortable, old-money place for a drink. ~ 721 Government Street; 250-384-8111.

NIGHTLIFE

Rumours, a gay dance bar, features progressive music. Disco lights illuminate the dancefloor at this contemporary club with bare, black walls. Sunday is *déjà vu* night, featuring top hits from the '70s. There's also a pool room on the premises. Every second Sunday is a drag show. ~ 1325 Government Street; 250-385-0566.

For a more cultured evening, Victoria offers several options. The well-respected **Pacific Opera** performs at the **Royal Theatre** at 805 Broughton Street (250-385-0222) and the **McPherson Playhouse** at 3 Centennial Square at Government and Pandora streets (250-386-6121).

The **Victoria Symphony** offers concerts featuring international conductors and artists, from September through May. They also do a summer pop series, and on the first weekend in August hold the celebrated "Symphony Splash," a free, open-air concert where the orchestra plays from a barge in the harbor. ~ 846 Broughton Street; tickets, 250-386-6121; information, 250-385-6515.

Planet Harpo's features an eclectic mix of live music, ranging from blues to jazz to rock. The decor isn't much, but the nightclub does have a large dancefloor. ~ 15 Bastion Square; 250-385-2626.

Sweetwater's offers contemporary rock music for dancing. Cover. ~ Market Square; 250-383-7844.

Victoria's pubs offer an alternative to the expensive price of having a drink in the hotel lounges. Some of these pubs feature beers made on the premises, while others stock a wide variety of local and imported beers and ales. Whether in historic buildings or cottage breweries, you also are apt to find a game of darts and a number of skilled competitors. One of the liveliest pub crowds is found at the **Swans Hotel,** where you can hear great local jazz combos several nights a week and see a changing and colorful collection of local and international art. ~ 506 Pandora Avenue; 250-361-3310.

Centennial Square arts center includes the original City Hall (1878) and the **McPherson Playhouse.** The playhouse is a restored baroque and Edwardian-style Pantages Theatre seating 800. It hosts stage plays, classical and pops concerts, dance performances, films and touring lectures. ~ Government and Pandora streets; 250-386-6121.

Kaleidoscope Theatre Productions presents cabaret and family entertainment. ~ 520 Herald Street; 250-475-4444.

A favorite spot for karaoke singalongs is the **Karaoke Club** in Paul's Motor Inn. ~ 1900 Douglas Street; 250-382-9231.

PARKS

BEACON HILL PARK This sedate park near downtown, founded in 1882, contains forest, open grassy areas, ponds and Goodacre Lake, a wildfowl sanctuary. Among gardens blooming nearly year-round, you also will find one of the tallest totem poles in the world, lawn bowling, a 100-year-old cricket pitch, the Mile 0 marker of the Trans-Canada Highway and a children's petting zoo in the summer, all at the southwestern corner where Dallas Road and Douglas Street meet. Facilities include restrooms, picnic areas, tennis courts, playground, lawn bowling, baseball and soccer fields, a children's wading pool and water play area. ~ Along Douglas Street, only a ten-minute walk from the Empress Hotel; 250-361-0600.

▼▼▼▼▼▼▼▼▼▼▼▼▼▼▼▼▼▼
Victoria Neighborhoods

Beyond the heart of Victoria are some of the city's most important landmarks including a castle fit for a queen and the house where Her Majesty really stays on her visits. Your itinerary also features Victoria's major art gallery and a leading museum of Victoriana. If you have half a day at your disposal, just follow our lead.

SIGHTS

You'll need your own or public transportation to head out east on Fort Street to **Craigdarroch Castle.** Robert Dunsmuir had the house built for his family after new coal deposits were found in 1869, making him, the overseer of the Hudson's Bay Company, British Columbia's first millionaire. Today, visitors can tour Craigdarroch, furnished in turn-of-the-century style featuring 39 rooms on five floors with stained-glass windows, intricate woodwork, original furniture and turrets. Admission. ~ 1050 Joan Crescent; 250-592-5323.

Just a couple of blocks southeast of the castle is the **Art Gallery of Greater Victoria**. One of Canada's finest art museums, this gallery features Canadian art, European pieces from the 15th through 20th centuries and the only Shinto shrine outside Japan, plus a large Oriental art collection. A portion of the gallery is housed in Spencer Mansion, built in 1890, which features a dramatic staircase, Jacobean ceiling and a dollhouse with many intricate details. Admission (Monday is free). ~ 1040 Moss Street; 250-384-4101.

> Take a few minutes to explore Rockland Avenue, home of many mansions built during the 1880s and 1890s.

Just a couple of blocks southwest is **Government House**, where the Queen of England and her family stay when they visit Victoria. It is the official residence of the Lieutenant Governor, the Queen's representative in British Columbia. When royalty is not visiting, the public can stroll through the formal lawns and gardens, complete with a lily pond and waterfall. ~ 1401 Rockland Avenue; 250-387-2080.

If you enjoy Victorian furnishings, you will want to see **Point Ellice House**, which contains British Columbia's most comprehensive collection of Victorian furnishings and art in its original setting. The house was built around 1862. Visitors also can stroll through a wonderful 19th-century garden where afternoon tea is served daily (reservations required) throughout the summer. The house can be reached by a ten-minute ferry ride from Victoria's Inner Harbour (ferry information, 250-480-0971). Admission. ~ 2616 Pleasant Street off Bay Street; 250-380-6506.

LODGING

Claddagh House Bed and Breakfast offers three rooms, a hearty Irish breakfast and a patio and garden open to guests. Although tucked away in a quiet residential area, it is convenient to tourist attractions, shopping and the ocean. Gay-friendly. ~ 1761 Lee Avenue; 250-370-2816. BUDGET TO MODERATE.

Oak Bay Guest House is a turn-of-the-century bed and breakfast furnished with period antiques. The 11 rooms offer garden views and private baths, some with clawfoot tubs. Relax by the living-room fireplace or enjoy a book in the sun room. Gay-friendly. ~ 1052 Newport Avenue; 250-598-3812, 800-575-3812, fax 250-598-0369. MODERATE TO DELUXE.

If you don't mind student housing without frills, the **University of Victoria Housing Services**, 20 minutes north of downtown, offers over 800 rooms, including breakfast in the residence dining room, from May 1 to August 30. ~ P.O. Box 1700, Finnerty Road, Victoria, BC V8W 2Y2; 250-721-8395. BUDGET TO MODERATE.

About one-quarter of the way from Victoria to Sidney in a quiet residential area on the edge of the park by the same name is the **Mount Douglas Park Resort**. The contemporary lodge, built on the side of a hill, features large relief carvings of birds and marine life. The 42 rooms are contemporary and comfortable. Suites have balconies with ocean or park views, and some have fireplaces, jacuzzis and kitchenettes. Breakfast is included in the tab. ~ 4550 Cordova Bay Road; 250-658-2171, 800-222-2221, fax 250-658-4596. MODERATE TO ULTRA-DELUXE.

The Gorge Waterway extends northwest from the Inner Harbour. Here you will find a number of less expensive motels. Hidden among the many motels lining Gorge Road, the **Travelodge** is one that offers the most quality and service for your money. The motel appeals to families because of its indoor pool, twin saunas, restaurant and lounge. Just a few minutes drive from downtown, the motel has 73 newly renovated rooms that are clean, decorated in cool colors and feature oak trim. Some rooms and 12 one-bedroom suites feature kitchenettes. ~ 229 Gorge Road East; 250-388-6611, 800-565-3777, fax 250-388-4153. DELUXE.

DINING

For a truly English dinner or afternoon tea, meander out to Oak Bay to the **Blethering Place**. There you will find the silver-haired set gossiping over hours-long tea, and families stopping by for supper. The fare includes crumpets, tarts, scones, Welsh rarebit, steak-and-kidney pie and decadent desserts. ~ 2250 Oak Bay Avenue; 250-598-1413. BUDGET TO MODERATE.

Located in the Tudor-style Oak Bay Beach Hotel on the southwest side of the peninsula, **Bentley's on the Bay** offers a romantic dining experience. Bay views through the leaded-glass windows, a baronial fireplace and tables with candles and green and white linen napery set the scene. The traditional fare is highlighted by grilled fresh salmon and halibut and a variety of pasta dishes. ~ 1175 Beach Drive; 250-598-4556. DELUXE.

✔ CHECK THESE OUT—UNIQUE DINING

- *Budget to moderate:* Unwind at the **Six Mile Pub**, a one-time carriage-house offering time-honored pub grub and beer. *page 517*
- *Moderate to deluxe:* Relish the caramel and almond duck with champagne sauce at the peaceful and romantic **Camille's Restaurant** in Bastion Square. *page 511*
- *Deluxe to ultra-deluxe:* Savor seafood caught in the harbor below **Sooke Harbor House**, which has meals as dazzling as the views. *page 532*
- *Ultra-deluxe:* Fly into **The Aerie** and enjoy gourmet creations and panoramic views. *page 517*

Budget: under $8   Moderate: $8–$16   Deluxe: $16–$24   Ultra-deluxe: over $24

The name, **Ceccone's Pizzeria & Trattoria**, implies a more casual atmosphere than you will find in this upscale bistro in the Shelbourne area. Soft lighting, decorator colors and window seats with cushions and pillows lend a feeling of intimacy. Ceccone's turns out wood-oven pizzas and calzones, pastas, homemade desserts and tasty entrées and specials like rack of lamb. Weekend reservations are a must. Closed for lunch on Sunday. ~ 3201 Shelbourne Avenue; 250-592-0454. MODERATE TO DELUXE.

The **Marina Restaurant** not only has a smashing view of Oak Bay and the Lower Mainland in the distance, it offers excellent seafood and pastas, along with house-made breads. There's also a very fine sushi bar making good use of local fish and shellfish. It's extremely popular with residents. ~ 1327 Beach Street; 250-598-8555. MODERATE TO DELUXE.

Located in an 1855 carriagehouse six miles from downtown, **Six Mile Pub** is the picture of an old English pub with hanging lamps, oak moldings, dart boards and stained-glass windows. At lunch expect traditional pub fare such as Cornish pasties or steak-and-kidney pie. Changing specials at dinner may include charbroiled salmon or vegetable stir-fry. ~ 494 Island Highway; 250-478-3121. BUDGET TO MODERATE.

The **Aerie** is one of Victoria's most elegant restaurants, sitting atop the Malahat summit. Located outside greater Victoria on the way to Duncan, this eatery's dining room has a 23-carat-gold-leaf ceiling, with panoramic views stretching from the Gulf Islands to the Olympic Mountains. The menu changes, depending on availability of the very freshest local ingredients. Entrées such as sage-and-pancetta-crusted pheasant breast or roasted venison loin with a matsutake mushroom sauce attract enough high-flying guests that a helicopter pad was added to the restaurant and 29-room guest house. ~ 600 Ebedora Lane, Malahat; 250-743-7115. ULTRA-DELUXE.

SHOPPING

The municipality of Oak Bay offers an array of boutiques and specialty stores on Oak Bay Avenue featuring designer clothing, English toffees, New Age toys and games, crafts and jewelry. Be sure to stop by the **Teddy Bears Picnic** with a selection of toys appealing to the child in each of us. ~ 2250 Oak Bay Avenue; 250-598-5558.

Mayfair Shopping Center is one of the largest and most upscale shopping centers on the island. It contains more than 100 shops specializing in men's and women's fashions. ~ A mile from downtown near Douglas Street and Finlayson Avenue; 250-383-0541.

NIGHTLIFE

In Oak Bay, east of downtown Victoria, the **Snug** at the Oak Bay Beach Hotel attracts locals and visitors alike. It has a warm, British atmosphere with plaster walls, dark-wood beams, a large bar and fireplace. In the summer, the balcony overlooks the ocean. ~ 1175 Beach Street; 250-598-4556.

BEACHES & PARKS

THETIS LAKE MUNICIPAL PARK 🏃 🏊 ⛵ Just five miles from the city center, this park offers opportunities for walking, hiking and solitude on more than 1600 acres of rolling hills, fir and cedar forest and lake frontage. You can swim in the lake during the summer. There are picnic areas and restrooms; restaurants and groceries are nearby. ~ Located about five miles northwest of downtown Victoria off Route 1; 250-478-3344.

MOUNT DOUGLAS MUNICIPAL PARK 🏃 🏊 On the east side of the Saanich Peninsula is this 500-acre park with forests of arbutus, fir and cedar, a beach and Mount Douglas peak. Visitors can drive a one-and-a-half-mile paved route to a parking area and then hike a short distance to the peak where the view stretches in all directions. You can swim here in summer. You'll find picnic areas and restrooms; restaurants and groceries are nearby. ~ Located about five miles northeast of downtown Victoria off Route 17 and Royal Oak/Cordova Bay Road; 250-475-1775.

▼▼▼▼▼▼▼▼▼▼▼▼▼
Saanich Peninsula

One of Vancouver Island's leading tourist attractions, Butchart Gardens, is the Saanich Peninsula's primary draw. This area also offers a host of other garden retreats featuring exotic fauna from all over the world.

SIGHTS

Traveling north on Route 17 from Victoria toward Sidney, signs direct you to **Butchart Gardens**, a must for anyone who ever dreamed of having a green thumb. Dating back to 1904, the industrious wife of the manufacturer of Portland Cement turned a quarry pit created by her husband into a fabulous sunken garden. Today, Jennie Butchart's project is a world-famous, 50-acre botanical showcase, which includes the Rose Garden, the Italian Garden, the Japanese Garden, the Star Pond and the Ross Fountains. The gardens, joined by a series of walkways, display masses of color and rare and exotic plants. See fantastic fireworks displays every Saturday night in July and August. Admission. ~ 800 Benvenuto Drive; 250-652-5256.

Returning south on Route 17, you can stop at the **Horticulture Centre of the Pacific** where perennial displays are all labeled. You walk on forest paths to see a fabulous display of Asian lilies, a rose garden with more than 100 kinds of miniature roses, a creek flanked with ferns and hostas and the rhododendron vale. They have winter garden of fruit trees and a fuchsia arbor, giving the center flowers year-round. Admission. ~ 505 Quayle Road; 250-479-6162.

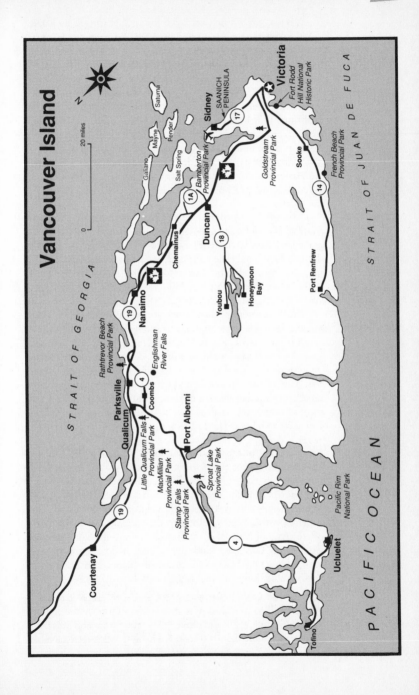

Vancouver Island

When Route 17 intersects with Route 1, head west on Route 1 and follow the signs to **Craigflower 1850's Farmhouse Historic Site**. Craigflower grew out of the requirement that in order to have a lease on Vancouver Island, the Hudson's Bay Company had to colonize it. Craigflower is one of four farms planned by the company. Some 25 families arrived from Scotland in 1853 to live on and work the farm. Visitors can tour the Georgian-style farmhouse built for bailiff Kenneth McKenzie in 1856, which contains furnishings and articles brought from Scotland. Craigflower Schoolhouse is the oldest school building in western Canada. There is also a heritage garden with heirloom plants and farm animals. Admission. ~ 110 Island Highway, corner of Craigflower and Admirals roads; 250-383-4627.

LODGING

Near Butchart Gardens, ferries and the airport, the **Best Western Emerald Isle Motor Inn** appeals to families because it is convenient and rooms have kitchenettes. No decorator interiors here, but the decor is functional. The 63 rooms, some of which are nonsmoking, are clean. Restaurant, whirlpool baths, sauna, health spa. ~ 2306 Beacon Avenue, Sidney; 250-656-4441, 800-315-3377, fax 250-655-1351. MODERATE TO DELUXE.

The three cabins at **Rusty Duck** are not only waterfront: They are over the water on pilings, facing south on Brentwood Bay just north of Butchart Gardens. Each cabin is a clean, light and airy space with a loft bedroom, and sitting, dining and cooking areas downstairs. Full meal service is available at an adjoining restaurant. Guests can rent canoes and kayaks on-site, either for a leisurely cruise on the bay, or a crowd-free quick trip to the back entrance at Butchart Gardens. ~ 799 Verdier Avenue, Brentwood Bay; 250-544-1441, fax 250-544-1015. MODERATE TO DELUXE.

BEACHES & PARKS

ISLAND VIEW BEACH REGIONAL PARK 🏃 ⛵ 🚤 🚤 On the eastern shore of the Saanich Peninsula, the weather has molded this relatively flat park with rolling sand dunes at the north end and a long, accretion beach at the water's edge. The beach, full of fine, white sand, is strewn with sculpture-like driftwood. The water, however, is cold, although some do swim in it. The park offers views of Mt. Baker, de Haro Strait and the San Juan and Gulf islands. Facilities include picnic areas, hiking, restrooms and a boat launch. ~ Located northeast of Victoria on the Saanich Peninsula off Route 17 and Island View Road; 250-478-3344.

ELK/BEAVER LAKE REGIONAL PARK 🏃 🚲 🐎 ⛵ 🏊 🚤 🚤 🛶 Rolling hills, lush wetlands, tranquil forests and hilltop vistas surrounding Elk and Beaver lakes (good trout and bass fishing) provide more than 1000 acres of habitat at this regional park for many birds, including owls, woodpeckers and ducks. There are picnic areas and restrooms. ~ Located north of Victoria off Route 17 and Beaver Lake Road; 250-478-3344.

GOLDSTREAM PROVINCIAL PARK 🏃 🛶 🛶 This park provides two distinct vegetation zones—dry ridges with dogwood, lodgepole pine and arbutus, and wetter areas with 600-year-old Douglas fir, western red cedar, western hemlock, western yew, black cottonwood and big-leaf maple, as well as many wildflowers. A salt marsh, where the Goldstream River flows into Finlayson Arm, contains mosses, lichens and liverworts. Each October, the river draws thousands of salmon returning to spawn. The river got its name after gold was discovered there, but the find was a small one. You'll find picnic areas and restrooms; restaurants and groceries are nearby. ~ Ten miles northwest of Victoria off Route 1; 250-391-2300.

▲ There are 159 sites for tents and RVs (no hookups available); Can. $15.50 per night.

Esquimalt Area

Swing west of Victoria along Esquimalt Harbour to visit one of the region's most important landmarks, **Fort Rodd Hill National Historic Park**, a 44-acre park of rolling hills, an open, parade-grounds area, woods and beach. The fort was built in 1895 to protect the entrance to the Royal Navy Yards in Esquimalt Harbor. It became a park in 1962. Visitors can see restored batteries and the restored Fisgard Lighthouse, the oldest lighthouse on the Pacific Coast, which features exhibits on shipwrecks and navigation. There is a film at the entrance of both sites. Admission. ~ Ocean Boulevard off the Old Island Highway; 250-478-5849.

Also in the Esquimalt area is **English Village and Anne Hathaway's Cottage**. The village occupies five acres and includes replicas of William Shakespeare's birthplace and other English sites, such as the Garrick Inn and Plymouth Tavern. The replica of Anne Hathaway's Cottage is authentically furnished with 16th-century antiques and surrounded by colorful gardens of flowers and herbs. Tour guides are garbed in period costumes. Admission. ~ 429 Lampson Street; 250-388-4353.

Southeast Island

Vancouver Island's southeast region is a great place to learn about the area's native heritage and logging industry as well as swim at surprisingly warm beaches such as those on Qualicum Bay.

SIGHTS

The towns on the island's protected southeastern shore tend to be more low key than the proper British Victoria. The town of **Duncan** is the site of a collection of some 60 totem poles, ten of which are along the highway and the others scattered about town.

This logging community is the site of the **British Columbia Forest Museum**, where you ride the rails behind a steam locomotive through a typical Northwest forest, across a trestle over Somenos Lake to the train station. Once there you can walk around the 100-acre park to see early logging equipment, the Log Museum exhibiting logging artifacts, the Jones Building with historic photos and displays explaining the history of logging. There's also a picnic area and playground. Closed mid-October through March. Admission. ~ 2892 Drinkwater Road, RR #4, Duncan; 250-715-1113.

Visitors have an opportunity to experience authentic traditions of the Cowichan people at the **Cowichan Native Village** in Duncan. Today, the Cowichan Band, with about 4000 members, is the largest group of native peoples in British Columbia. You can see carvers at their work and watch women as they spin and knit authentic Cowichan sweaters. Call to make a reservation for the midday salmon barbecue with two shows of interpretive dancing. An audio visual presentation gives a sense of the Cowichan spiritual traditions so closely tied with the earth and nature. The center also includes a fine-art gallery and a smaller gift shop. Admission. ~ 200 Cowichan Way, Duncan; 250-746-8119.

HIDDEN ► **Nanaimo**, population 60,000, is a hidden destination right under the noses of visitors who pass through it on their way from the ferry landing. The city's name grew out of its native title, "Snenymo" meaning "great and mighty people." White pioneers came to the area after large deposits of coal were discovered in 1851. The city was incorporated in 1874, and today, its economy rests on fishing, forestry, port business and tourism.

The **Nanaimo District Museum** gives visitors an experience of the city's past by taking them through a coal-mining tunnel, a blacksmith's shop, general store, and barbershop in a turn-of-the-century town, a restored miner's cottage, dioramas depicting the history and culture of the Nanaimo First Nations people and an area focusing on Chinatown. Closed Sunday and Monday during the winter. Admission. ~ 100 Cameron Road, Nanaimo; 250-753-1821, fax 250-753-1777.

◆◆◆

PICTURES OF THE PAST

Chemainus is known as the little town that did. Instead of allowing unemployment to turn Chemainus into a ghost town when the local mill closed, residents hired well-known artists to paint murals all over the town. Yellow footprints on the sidewalks direct visitors past images of native chiefs, loggers felling huge trees and locomotives hauling logs through the forest. The murals have drawn tourists from around the world, creating a new industry there.

There's a self-guided, historical walking tour of Nanaimo detailed in a map available at the **Tourism Nanaimo Beban House**. ~ 2290 Bowen Road, Nanaimo; 250-756-0106, 800-663-7337.

The **Hudson's Bay Bastion**, a 30-foot-tall building, was built on the waterfront in 1852, ostensibly to protect white settlers from the natives. But because the Indians proved to be peaceful, the fort really didn't protect anything. Since 1910 it has been a museum depicting Nanaimo's heritage. ~ Just south of the Seaplane Terminal along the harbor.

In the Parksville-Qualicum area, you can visit **St. Anne's/St. Edmund's Anglican Church**, one of the oldest churches on the island. A group of 45 farmers in the area used oxen to haul the logs for building it. The log church features stained-glass windows. Closed weekends. ~ 407 Wembley Street at Church Road, Parksville; 250-248-3114.

The **Craig Heritage Park and Museum** displays artifacts from the local area, including an old schoolhouse, fire engine and period cottages. Open during the summer only.~ 1245 East Island Highway, Parksville; 250-248-6966.

If you visit the **Big Qualicum Fish Hatchery** during spawning season, you can watch the salmon thrashing their way upstream to lay their eggs. After the staff "milk" the salmon eggs, they are placed under controlled conditions for hatching. There are hiking trails and a picnic area on the grounds. ~ Off the East Island Highway north of Qualicum Beach; 250-757-8412.

Just a few miles west of Parksville is the little town of **Coombs** with its Old West look of boardwalks and hitching posts. In the summer, goats graze on the thatched roofs of some of the shops.

West of Coombs is **Butterfly World**, where visitors can see all stages of butterfly life, including egg laying and caterpillar rearing. The most colorful area is the tropical indoor garden where butterflies sip nectar, court and flit among colorful blossoms. Also check out the aviary, koi pond and gift shops. Closed November through mid-March. Admission. ~ Route 4; 250-248-7026.

LODGING

The Victorian **Pacific Shores Inn** offers three suites (sleeping two to four people) with kitchens and private entrances. Two of the suites feature washers and dryers, making them ideal choices for families. For a romantic getaway, rent the Fairy Tale Cottage with its unique stonework and wood detailing, fireplace and private deck and yard. ~ 9847 Willow Street, Chemainus; 250-246-4987, fax 250-246-4785. MODERATE TO DELUXE.

The **Coast Bastion Inn** is one of the most luxurious hotels in the area. Rooms feature wood furniture, designer color schemes and views of the water. The inn has a sauna, whirlpool and exercise room, restaurant, café and pub. ~ 11 Bastion Street, Nanaimo; 250-753-6601, 800-663-1144. MODERATE TO DELUXE.

The **Dorchester Hotel** offers oceanfront views from most of its 70 newly refurbished units with a Victorian theme. Built on the former site of the old Windsor Hotel and Opera House near the Bastion, the hotel also has a restaurant, rooftop garden and a library. ~ 70 Church Street, Nanaimo; 250-754-6835, 800-661-2449, fax 250-754-2638. MODERATE TO DELUXE.

Surrounded by woods on three sides, **Beach Acres Resort Hotel** opens onto a large, secluded beach. The 55 beachfront or forest cottages or oceanview condominiums with kitchens are clean, comfortably furnished and all feature fireplaces. Amenities include an indoor pool, whirlpool, sauna, tennis courts, laundry and a restaurant. ~ 1015 East Island Highway, Parksville; 250-248-3424, 800-663-7309, fax 250-248-6145. ULTRA-DELUXE.

The **Island Hall Beach Resort** is in downtown Parksville on nearly 1000 feet of sandy beach. This resort opened its doors in 1917 with 24 rooms. Now it has grown to 49 units. Rooms are light and bright with a pleasing mixture of older and contemporary furnishings. The resort also features an indoor pool, sauna, whirlpool, tennis courts, restaurant, pub and lounge. ~ 181 West Island Highway, Parksville; 250-248-3225, 800-663-7370, fax 250-248-3125. MODERATE.

Wood paneling, plush carpets and water views mark the 50 rooms at the **Parksville Beach Motel**, right on the beach in this sunny resort town north of Nanaimo. Rooms have either two queen or two double beds, and some include kitchenettes. The resort itself has two beach volleyball courts, a whirlpool and sauna, an indoor pool, horseshoe pits and tennis courts. A playground and water park are next door. ~ 161 West Island Highway, Parksville; 250-248-6789, 888-248-6789, fax 250-248-4789. MODERATE TO DELUXE.

Once a private boys' school, the old-English, Tudor-style **Qualicum College Inn** sits on five acres on a bluff overlooking Georgia Strait. Half the inn's 70 attractive rooms have water views, and some include fireplaces. Amenities include five nearby golf courses, an indoor pool, whirlpool, lounge, dining room, neighborhood pub and beach access. ~ 427 College Road, Qualicum; 250-752-9262, 800-663-7306, fax 250-752-5144. MODERATE.

DINING

The **Lighthouse Bistro** is designed to look like a lighthouse built into a white, Cape Cod–style building with light blue trim. The restaurant offers a great view of the harbor, especially from the tables on their large deck, and a menu that changes with the local fish in season, such as blue marlin or trout. The pub upstairs serves the same menu, including the smoked salmon corn chowder. ~ 50 Anchor Way at the Seaplane Terminal, Nanaimo; 250-754-3212. MODERATE TO DELUXE.

Jim and Sam's Original Chowder House is just a quarter mile from the B.C. Ferry Terminal. This eatery offers nautical charm as a backdrop to a variety of the freshest seafood, including prawns, crab, fish, clams and oysters. Vegetarian and chicken dishes are also served. ~ 1340 Stewart Avenue, Nanaimo; 250-754-6611. MODERATE TO DELUXE.

The name of Qualicum is derived from a native word that means "where the dog salmon run."

The Grotto pegs itself as a Nanaimo waterfront tradition. It resembles a sprawling, wooden beach house surrounded by gardens of driftwood, shells and plants. Here you can dine on fresh seafood, sushi, chicken, steak, ribs, pasta or stir-fry. ~ 1511 Stewart Avenue, Nanaimo; 250-753-3303. MODERATE TO DELUXE.

In Parksville, visit **Kalvas**, a large, log-beam building, for fine French and German fare. You can feast on East Coast lobster, fresh local crab and oysters. Lunch and dinner. ~ 180 Moilliet Street; 250-248-6933. DELUXE.

For English-style fish and chips, try Parksville's **Spinnaker Seafood House**. The comfortable restaurant features a nautical theme, and the eclectic menu includes fresh seafood, pizza, hamburgers and salads for eating in or taking out. ~ 625 East Island Highway; 250-248-5532. BUDGET TO MODERATE.

SHOPPING

In Duncan, the **Quamichan House** at the Cowichan Native Village offers one of the largest selections of authentic native arts and crafts on the island, including original paintings, jewelry, carvings, masks, rattles, drums, Cowichan knitted items and books on the culture and art of native Northwest coastal peoples. ~ 200 Cowichan Way; 250-746-8119, fax 250-746-4143.

Hill's Indian Crafts features Cowichan sweaters, small replicas of totem poles, carvings, jewelry and prints. ~ 20 Commercial Street, Nanaimo; 250-755-7873.

NIGHTLIFE

Nightlife isn't plentiful outside Victoria, but that doesn't mean you can't have an enjoyable time in some of the island's southeastern communities. Try Nanaimo's **Dinghy Dock Pub**, reached by a ten-minute ferry ride (ferry information, 250-753-8244). The pub offers locally brewed beers and other spirits and spectacular views of Nanaimo, its harbor and Newcastle Island. Closed mid-October to spring. ~ 8 Pirate's Lane, Protection Island; 250-753-2373.

Nanaimo also has a handful of **theater companies**, including the Nanaimo Theatre Group, Yellow Point Drama Group and Malispina College Drama Group. For information on all groups, call 250-756-0106.

Text continued on page 528.

The Gulf
Islands

Ready for some island-hopping? Whether you're into beaches, arts and crafts, birdwatching, dining or just plain looking around, there is something here for everyone. The Gulf Islands provide plenty of activities—swimming, windsurfing, scuba diving, beachcombing, boating, bicycling, hiking and horseback riding—to suit families and outdoor enthusiasts of all abilities.

These islands are isolated places where residents enjoy a bucolic lifestyle. At sunset, basking like a group of sea turtles in the water, the islands are like shadows, amorphous shapes in muted shades of blue, mauve and gray stacked up behind one another. The islands, sisters of the San Juan Islands in Washington State, include mountain peaks, sandy beaches, and pastoral farms. The climate is Mediterranean-like—mild and dry. The archipelago includes almost 200 islands, but only five have a population of more than 250—Salt Spring, Pender, Galiano, Mayne and Saturna. **B.C. Ferries** plies the waterways between Tsawwassen, just south of Vancouver, and the Gulf Islands and Vancouver Island's Swartz Bay and the islands. ~ 250-386-3431.

Salt Spring Island, named for a series of briny springs at the island's north end, is the largest with a population of about 9500. The first non-native settlers were blacks escaping slavery in the United States in 1859. Once supported by an agrarian economy, the island now thrives on tourism and the arts. In fact, the Gulf Islands are believed to be home to more artists per capita than most other regions in Canada.

The largest village on Salt Spring is Ganges, a pedestrian-oriented, seaside hamlet, where visitors flock to a summer-long arts-and-crafts fair, art galleries and the Saturday morning market.

Another attraction is Cusheon Lake, a popular, freshwater lake with a large swimming area—and the water is warm. The island also offers popular oceanside beaches; Vesuvius and Bader's beaches on the island's west side have the warmest water. Because it sits at the edge of the forest, Bader offers much more privacy, but the sandy beach is small.

Pender Island, population 1500, is really two islands connected by a narrow, wooden bridge that affords splendid views of Browning and Bedwell harbours. Medicine Beach in Bedwell Harbour and Hamilton Beach in Browning Harbour are popular picnic spots. The Driftwood Centre and Port Washington are locations of several galleries.

Birdwatching is a prime activity on the Gulf Islands. Cormorants, harlequin ducks, gulls, oyster catchers, turkey vultures, ravens and bald eagles are commonly seen. Other birds include tanagers, juncos, bluebirds, flycatchers, black-birds and sparrows. Many of these birds can be seen in the island's parks.

Mouat Provincial Park (Seaview Avenue, Ganges) on Salt Spring Island is a pleasant, wooded park with camping and picnicking facilities. **Prior Centennial Provincial Park** is near Bedwell Harbour on Pender Island. It features good fishing, swimming, a boat launch, picnic areas and restrooms. The islands also are sites of several marine parks. One of the largest is **Beaumon Marine Park** on South Pender Island and sheltered by Bedwell Harbour. It includes upland forest, picnic areas, campsites and hiking trails.

If you are a diver, the Gulf Islands provide a number of good locations. Divers often see octopi, wolf eels, sea cucumbers, sea stars, sea urchins and sea pens. Shore dives include Vesuvius Bay on Salt Spring Island for sighting octopus and ling cod; Fulford Harbour opposite the ferry terminal with a shallow area perfect for seeing crabs and starfish; and Tilley Point on North Pender Island for interesting kelp beds. Near Thetis Island, the *Miami*, a steel-and coal-carrying freighter that sunk in 1900, is covered with interesting vege-tation and marine life. The *Del Norte*, a 190-foot side-wheel passenger steam-ship that sank in 1868, is between Valdez and Galiano islands and appropriate only for more advanced divers.

Visitors can find a variety of accommodations on Salt Spring and Pender islands. **The Inn on Pender Island**, with nine rooms, three cabins and a hot tub, sits on seven acres of wooded tranquility near Prior Centennial Provincial Park, where hiking, bicycling and beachcombing are in abundance. Breakfast is included in the price. ~ 4709 Canal Road; 250-629-3353, 800-550-0172, fax 250-629-3167. MODERATE.

The Plumbush Inn on Salt Spring Island is a country-house B&B on nearly 1000 feet of private oceanfront that each unit faces. ~ 600 Walker Hook Road, Ganges; phone/fax 250-537-4332. MODERATE.

The **Applecroft Heritage Family Farm** is an elegant, 20-acre 1893 family farm featuring a self-contained two-bedroom cottage, complete with fireplace and a tub-for-two. Organic gourmet breakfast is delivered to your door. ~ 551 Upper Ganges Road, Ganges; phone/fax 250-537-5605. MODERATE.

Cusheon Lake Resort has fully equipped log and A-frame chalets, all with kitchens and water views, some with fireplaces, and an outdoor jacuzzi. Fishing, swimming and boating are available. ~ 171 Natalie Lane, Salt Spring Island; phone/fax 250-537-9629. MODERATE TO DELUXE.

BEACHES & PARKS

BAMBERTON PROVINCIAL PARK 🏃 ⛵ 🛶 🎣 🏊 🚤 The warm waters of the Saanich Inlet make this park, with a 750-foot sandy beach, attractive to swimmers. The park contains many arbutus trees in a second-growth forest. The Saanich Peninsula, Mt. Baker and the Gulf Islands form the backdrop to water and mountain views from this park. Picnic areas and restrooms are the only facilities. ~ Located northwest of Victoria off Route 1 at the northern foot of Malahat Drive; 250-391-2300.

▲ There are 50 tent/RV sites (no hookups); Can. $9.50 per night. For camping reservations, call 800-689-9025.

NEWCASTLE ISLAND PROVINCIAL MARINE PARK 🏃 🚲 ⛵ 🛶 🎣 🚤 Over 750 acres of woods and sandy beaches on an island in Nanaimo Harbor afford views of Vancouver Island and the mainland's Coast Mountains. The park features sandstone ledges and sandy, gravel beaches. The area was a site for coal mining and sandstone mining in the mid-to-late 1800s. Cast a rod for salmon. There are picnic areas, a playground, restrooms, a visitors center and a snack bar in the summer. ~ In summer, scheduled foot passenger ferry service departs from behind the Nanaimo Civic Arena off Route 1, north of downtown. Cars are not allowed; 250-391-2300. (For off-season ferry service, phone 250-753-5141.)

▲ There are 18 tent sites available on a first-come, first-serve basis; Can. $9.50 per night.

RATHTREVOR BEACH PROVINCIAL PARK 🏃 🚲 ⛵ 🎣 🏊 🚤 Located between Nanaimo and Parksville, this park's popularity lies within its sandy beach. There are also a wooded upland area, excellent birdwatching during the spring herring spawn and views of Georgia Strait. There are picnic areas, restrooms and showers; restaurants and groceries are nearby. ~ It's about two miles south of Parksville off Route 19; 250-954-4600.

▲ There are 179 sites for tents and RVs (no hookups); Can. $15.50 per night; and 100 walk-in sites; Can. $7 per night. Reservations: 604-689-9025, 800-689-9025.

ENGLISHMAN RIVER FALLS PROVINCIAL PARK 🏃 🚲 ⛵ ⛵ Forests of huge cedar trees surround a large, crashing waterfall in this lush park that encompasses 240 acres. Large groves of hemlock and fir also can be found in the park. A good time to visit is in autumn when the maple trees offer a colorful contrast to the evergreens. You'll find picnic areas and restrooms. ~ Located west of Parksville off Route 4; 250-954-4600.

▲ There are 105 sites for tents and RVs (no hookups); Can. $12 per night. Reservations: 604-689-9025, 800-689-9025.

LITTLE QUALICUM FALLS PROVINCIAL PARK 🏃 ⛵ 🎣 Although a neighbor to Englishman River Falls Park, this park is much drier. Consequently, visitors see more pine, Douglas fir and arbutus trees in this park that straddles the Little Qualicum River. A must-see are the impressive waterfalls splashing down a rocky gorge. Fish for salmon and take a dip in Cameron Lake or one of the pools around the falls. Picnic areas and restrooms are the only facilities. ~ Located 11 miles west of Parksville off Route 4; 250-954-4600.

▲ There are 94 sites for tents and RVs (no hookups) available on a first-come, first-served basis; Can. $12 per night.

STRATHCONA PROVINCIAL PARK 🏃 🐾 ⛵ This is British Columbia's oldest provincial park, a half-million-acre enclave in the middle of Vancouver Island four hours north of Victoria. It offers a popular day hike from Paradise Meadows to the Forbidden Plateau; this can also serve as the starting point for extensive backcountry pack trips. Intrepid hikers might want to try for 1443-foot Della Falls, one of the ten highest waterfalls in the world, accessible only by boat and foot. Less determined visitors can simply relax in the Buttle Lake campground. ~ The park is an hour east of Campbell River on provincial Highway 28; 250-337-2400.

◄ HIDDEN

▲ Campsites at Buttle Lake (86 sites) or Ralph River (60 sites) are on a first-come, first-served basis; Can. $12 and Can. $9.50 per night from Memorial Day through September, free the rest of the year. The nearby Strathcona Park Lodge (250-286-8206, fax 250-286-6010) offers simple rooms (budget to deluxe) and cabins (deluxe to ultra-deluxe).

▼▼▼▼▼▼▼▼▼▼▼
Southwest Island

Whether you come by land or sea, southwest Vancouver Island is one of the Pacific Northwest's most accessible wilderness regions. With its national parks, wildlife and snow-capped peaks, this is a favorite getaway.

SIGHTS

Board the **M. V. Lady Rose** for a unique experience traveling the Alberni Inlet aboard a freighter, the likes of which have served the hidden, remote communities on the island's west coast for over 50 years. Passengers on the day-long trips can see deliveries of fish food to commercial fish farms, asphalt shingles to individuals reroofing their homes and mail to residents of communities such as Bamfield and Kildonan. Kayakers can be dropped off at the Broken Group Islands. Tourists should be forewarned that the boat is primarily a freighter, so don't expect a naturalist or interpretive guide with fascinating commentary. ~ Alberni Harbour Quay; 250-723-8313, 800-663-7192.

Just outside Port Alberni at Sproat Lake, take the time to view a hidden attraction, the **Martin Mars Water Bombers**, owned by Forest Industries Flying Tankers Ltd., a private fire protection serv-

◄ HIDDEN

ice. Although not regularly scheduled, and certainly not developed for tourists, the sight of the largest firefighting aircraft in the world dropping 6000 gallons of water on the lake in a test run is almost too impressive for words. ~ 9350 Bomber Base Road, off Lakeshore Road; 250-723-6225.

The most popular wildlife of Pacific Rim National Park is the Pacific gray whale, seen during spring migration between mid-March and mid-April.

Pacific Rim National Park, comprising three units, protects the windswept and jagged west coast of Vancouver Island. The three parts of the park are distinctly different. The West Coast Trail should be traveled only by experienced hikers. The Broken Group Islands unit can be reached by boat, canoe or kayak. The Long Beach unit, the most accessible, includes a six-mile-long sandy beach. There, between Ucluelet and Tofino, you will find the Wickaninnish Centre, an interpretive center that displays exhibits on Pacific Ocean history. Here visitors can see powerful waves rolling up on the beach, watch nature presentations, participate in day hikes and view whales, seals and sea lions. There's also a restaurant with views of the surf and spectacular sunsets. The center is closed from October through mid-March. ~ 250-726-7721.

Most of the park includes a rocky shoreline that supports tidepools with barnacles, mussels, starfish, hermit crabs and anemones. Sitka spruce thrive just behind the pockets of sandy beaches and the rocky outcroppings. Farther inland are cedar, hemlock, fir and areas of bog and muskeg with pine and laurel. The forest floor is redolent with moss, ferns, huckleberry and salmonberry. The park also offers sightings of sea lions, harbor seals, river otter, mink and a vast array of resident and migrating birds (see "Beaches & Parks" for more information).

The **Eagle Aerie Gallery** is as much a cultural experience as it is an art gallery. The building was designed by native artist Roy Henry Vickers and constructed by his brothers. The gallery is built in the longhouse style with adzed cedar paneling and massive totem cornerposts. Effective lighting, evocative subject material and a background of taped native chanting and drumming inspire a spirit of reverence unlike almost any other place. The gallery represents Vickers's art only. ~ 350 Campbell Street, Tofino; 250-725-3235, 800-663-0669.

LODGING A bed and breakfast that started as a 1940s log cabin and grew to include a cedar addition with five guest rooms, **Ocean Wilderness** offers travelers a secluded seaside retreat. Set on five oceanfront acres just outside Sooke, the original log cabin is now the inn's breakfast area, and accommodations in the addition are adorned with romantic canopy beds and eclectic antiques. Decks overlook the water or garden. During the summer, the inn offers clambakes on the beach with barbecued salmon and other fresh seafood. ~ 109 West Coast Road, Sooke; 250-646-2116, 800-323-2116, fax 250-646-2317. MODERATE TO DELUXE.

The Barclay with 88 rooms is one of the largest hotels in town. It features an attractive lobby, a coffee shop, dining room, sports bar and lounge. Accommodations are clean, fairly standard rooms and suites. Amenities include a heated outdoor pool, whirlpool and sauna. ~ 4277 Stamp Avenue, Port Alberni; 250-724-7171, 800-563-6590, fax 250-724-9691. MODERATE.

Coast Hospitality Inn may be the best place to stay in town if you don't mind the absence of a pool. The lobby features comfortable seating in front of a fireplace. The inn offers 50 rooms in soft, attractive colors with firm beds and standard motel furniture. ~ 3835 Redford Street, Port Alberni; 250-723-8111, 800-663-1144, fax 250-723-0088. MODERATE.

The **Canadian Princess Resort** is unique in that 30 of its 76 rooms are aboard the ship of the same name (which serviced from 1932 to 1975 as a hydrographic survey vessel). Consequently, these moderately priced staterooms are small, and many share a bath. Three buildings contain 46 spacious, contemporary rooms and loft suites with fireplaces, decks and views of the ship and the harbor. The resort also includes ten fishing boats and a nautical-themed restaurant and lounge for guests. ~ Ucluelet Harbor, Ucluelet; 250-726-7771, 800-663-7090. MODERATE TO ULTRA-DELUXE.

Just a block from the Ucluelet marina is the **Thornton Motel** with 19 rooms and suites with standard furnishings, some with kitchenettes. It is popular with the fishing crowd. ~ 1861 Peninsula Road, Ucluelet; 250-726-7725, fax 250-726-2099. MODERATE TO DELUXE.

At the **West Coast Motel**, views of the harbor from some of the 21 rooms make up for the rather standard motel decor. Non-smoking rooms are available. Added advantages are an indoor swimming pool, sauna and tanning salon. The dining room (open summer only) overlooks the harbor. ~ 247 Hemlock Street, Ucluelet; 250-726-7732, fax 250-726-4662. MODERATE TO DELUXE.

If you want a more personal experience, try **Chesterman Beach Bed and Breakfast,** which offers three private units with fireplaces, including a charming cottage, a spacious suite and a cozy honeymooner's room, on the beach by the same name. After a visit to the island's west coast, owner Joan Dublanko fell in love with the place. Her hospitality and tasty breakfasts match her enthusiasm. ~ P.O. Box 72, Tofino, BC V0R 2Z0; phone/fax 250-725-3726. DELUXE.

The best thing about **Duffin Cove Resort** is that it offers views of the ocean from a bluff a block away from downtown. Eleven suites and kitchen units with garage-sale furniture and two cottages with fireplaces on the beach are a winter storm-watcher's delight. ~ 215 Campbell Street, Tofino; 250-725-3448, 800-222-3588, fax 250-725-2390. DELUXE.

Ocean Village Beach Resort is a nest of 51 comfortably rustic duplex and single cedar chalets on McKenzie Beach, a quarter-mile of safe, sandy beach facing the Pacific Ocean. The units feature an eating area with table and benches, sitting area and a sleeping area or separate bedroom and bath. The resort also includes an indoor swimming pool, hot tub and laundromat. ~ 555 Hellesen Drive, Tofino; 250-725-3755. MODERATE.

Pacific Sands Beach Resort is one of the best resorts on the west coast. Located on Cox Bay, bordering Pacific Rim National Park, the resort offers 10 two-bedroom cedar cottages just a few feet from the beach and 54 housekeeping suites with contemporary furnishings, fireplaces and views of the beach and the ocean. Two of the suites have hot tubs. ~ 1421 Pacific Rim Highway, Tofino; 250-725-3322, 800-565-2322, fax 250-725-3155. DELUXE TO ULTRA-DELUXE.

Perched on a rocky point thrusting out into the Pacific, not far from Pacific Rim National Park and Clayoquot Sound, the **Wickaninnish Inn** has a spectacular setting under any circumstances. During the West Coast's sometimes phenomenal winter storms, it's an unparalleled natural experience. Each of the 46 spacious rooms faces the ocean, and includes a soaking tub, large-screen television, refrigerator, fireplace, and furniture made from recycled old-growth fir, cedar and driftwood. Full communications technology, including high-speed dual-line phones, makes it possible to use the inn as an executive retreat. ~ Osprey Lane at Chesterman Beach, Tofino; 250-725-3100, 800-333-4604, fax 250-725-3110. DELUXE.

DINING

Some of the finest dining in British Columbia is offered by **Sooke Harbor House**, a white clapboard inn surrounded by colorful gardens on a bluff above Sooke Harbor's Whiffen Spit. In a setting of handsomely refinished pine and maple furnishings with whimsical folk art accents, the dining room offers a changing menu. There's an emphasis on fresh seasonal ingredients and local seafood that might include such unusual delicacies as sea urchin roe or fresh skate served with cranberry vinegar. Suckling kid, duck and rabbit are among the possible meat choices. ~ 1528 Whiffen Spit Road, Sooke; 250-642-3421, 800-889-9688, fax 250-642-6988. DELUXE TO ULTRA-DELUXE.

It would be hard to leave hungry after a meal at **Little Bavaria**, which seduces local appetites with huge plates of traditional German favorites such as schnitzel, as well as local seafood such as salmon and crab. The Bavarian Platter offers meat, sausage, potatoes, noodles, rolls and vegetables for two at about $35. ~ 3035 4th Avenue, Port Alberni; 250-724-4242. MODERATE.

The Harbour View Restaurant, located on the second story of the West Coast Motel, features large, log-beamed ceilings and panoramic views of the Ucluelet harbor and the mountains beyond. The menu features seafood, steaks, and salads. Closed in winter. ~ 247 Hemlock Street, Ucluelet; 250-726-3441. MODERATE.

The **Maquinna Lodge Restaurant** is housed in a fairly nondescript building in downtown Tofino, but the dining room offers splendid views of the harbor and kayakers returning at dusk. The mostly Greek menu offers souvlakia with a choice of beef, chicken or prawn filling, moussaka and calamari, as well as pastas, steaks and pizzas. An equally distracting view is the dessert table with an array of baked-on-the-premises cakes, pies and cheesecakes. Entrées are carefully prepared and come in generous servings. ~ 120 1st Street, Tofino; 250-725-3261. BUDGET TO MODERATE.

Perched on a knoll above the harbor, the **Schooner Restaurant** is a cozy place with a slate of excellent food. Cedar plank walls and a nautical decor are the backdrop to an array of entrées such as poached salmon in a yogurt-dill caviar sauce, pepper steak, ribs, salads and seafood, all carefully prepared and attractively presented. Breakfast is served in summer. Closed January. ~ 331 Campbell Street, Tofino; 250-725-3444. MODERATE.

SHOPPING

Ucluelet's **Du Quah Gallery** is a native-owned gallery featuring impressive carved masks with real animal fur and shredded cedar bark, fine jewelry, bentwood boxes and more. ~ 1971 Peninsula Street; 250-726-7223.

In Tofino, the **House of Himwitsa** gallery offers a good selection of native art including limited-edition prints, silver jewelry, weavings, carvings, beaded items and pottery. ~ 300 Main Street; 250-725-2017.

Nearby, the **Eagle Aerie Gallery** features works by Roy Henry Vickers, a native artist who has found international acclaim for his works that integrate the contemporary and traditional. ~ 350 Campbell Street, Tofino; 250-725-3235.

NIGHTLIFE

You won't find nightclubs on the rugged west coast. Some bars and lounges offer sunset views. The bar at **The Loft Restaurant** is not on the water, but it has a casual, nautical theme and lots of fishing tales told 'round its bar, attracting locals and visitors alike. ~ 346 Campbell Street, Tofino; 250-725-4241.

The bar at the **Maquinna Lodge** offers magnificent harbor views. ~ 120 1st Street, Tofino; 250-725-3261.

BEACHES & PARKS

EAST SOOKE PARK 🚶 🛶 🦐 🎣 This regional park is where the west coast begins. The 3500-acre park encompasses beautiful arbutus trees clinging to the windswept coast. You'll find small pocket beaches, rocky bays and islets for beachcombing and tidepooling. It features six miles of rugged coast trails and 30 miles of trails through forest, marsh and field with opportunities to view orca whales, sea lions, harbor seals, Columbian black-tailed deer and cougar. In September, check out the large number of bald eagles, hawks and other raptors that stop here during their migration. The park has views of the Strait of Juan de Fuca and the Olympic Mountains. You'll find picnic areas and restrooms. ~ Located about 25 miles southwest of Victoria off East Sooke Road on Becher Bay Road; 250-478-3344.

FRENCH BEACH PROVINCIAL PARK Visitors have the opportunity to see whales in the spring from this mile-long, sand-and-gravel beach on the Strait of Juan de Fuca. The park also contains second-growth forest. There are picnic areas and restrooms. ~ Located west of Sooke off Route 14 near Jordan River; 250-391-2300.

There are 69 sites for tents and RVs (no hookups); Can. $9.50 per night; reservations 800-689-9025.

PACIFIC RIM NATIONAL PARK   Cliffs, islands, bog and beach are just some of the topography visitors discover at this vast, 158,400-acre park. The reserve is divided into three areas: Long Beach, the Broken Group Islands and the West Coast Trail.

Long Beach   The most accessible section of the reserve, Long Beach is a six-mile stretch of sand and surf between rocky outcroppings. Beach hiking is excellent. Nine marked trails traverse old-growth rainforest. Facilities include picnic areas, restrooms and a restaurant. ~ Located on Route 4 (Pacific Rim Highway), 67 miles west of Port Alberni; 250-726-7721.

Green Point Campground has 55 primitive walk-in sites on the beach and 94 inland tent/RV sites with beach access; Can. $14 to $20 per night; 250-726-4214. To reserve a drive-in site, call 800-689-9025.

Broken Group Islands   With more than a hundred islands and islets in Barkley Sound, this is kayak and sailboat territory. Accessible only by boat, these remote islands offer up wildlife ranging from sea lions to eagles. Composting toilets are available in the camping areas. ~ The M. V. *Lady Rose*, a mail boat that also takes passengers and kayaks, makes trips to Bamfield, the Broken Group Islands and Ucluelet; 250-723-8313, 800-663-7192.

There are primitive campsites on eight of the islands; Can. $5 per night.

West Coast Trail   This demanding 47-mile stretch between Bamfield and Port Renfrew follows a turn-of-the-century trail constructed to aid shipwrecked mariners. Only experienced backpackers should undertake this grueling five- to eight-day trek. Expect to see coastal rainforests, the remains of early settlements, ship-wrecks and a plethora of marine life. The number of hikers on the trail is regulated. Reservations and permits are required. Closed from October through April. ~ Land access to the Bamfield and Port Renfrew trailheads is by logging roads only. The M. V. *Lady Rose* (250-723-8313, 800-663-7192) drops hikers at Bamfield. For reservations and permits, call 800-663-6000.

MACMILLAN PROVINCIAL PARK On the shores of Cameron Lake, this 336-acre park, available for day-use only, provides access to Cathedral Grove, a large stand of giant, old-growth Douglas fir. Some of the trees are 800 years old, and the largest are nearly 250 feet tall and nearly ten feet in diameter. These trees are believed to have survived a fire some 300 years ago because of their fire-resistant bark, nearly a foot thick on some of the trees now. Walking through this ancient forest can be a spiritual experience, but the area is so popular it is being "loved to death" by tourists. ~ Located west of Parksville, about 11 miles east of Port Alberni off Route 4; 250-954-4600.

SPROAT LAKE PROVINCIAL PARK On the north shore of Sproat Lake just west of Port Alberni, this park is a water enthusiast's paradise. The lake is warm and sunny, perfect for summer swimming. Fishing is excellent for steelhead, trout and salmon. Visitors can walk a short distance through the woods to see prehistoric petroglyphs. Facilities are limited to picnic areas and pit toilets; restaurants and groceries are nearby. ~ Eight miles northwest of Port Alberni off Route 4; 250-954-4600.

There are 59 sites for tents and RVs (no hookups); sites available on a first-come, first-serve basis; Can. $12 to $14.50 per night.

STAMP FALLS PROVINCIAL PARK This park offers pleasant walks among the stands of cedar and fir, and an area for contemplation near the waterfall. Visitors can view salmon jumping up the fish ladders in summer and fall. Steelhead and cutthroat trout also invite anglers. Picnic areas are the only facilities; restaurants and groceries are nearby. ~ Located about eight-and-one-half miles north of Port Alberni off Route 4 on Beaver Creek Road; 250-954-4600.

There are 22 tent/RV sites (no hookups); sites available on a first-come, first serve basis; Can. $9.50 a night.

Victoria has incredible sportfishing for salmon, primarily, but also for bottom fish like rock cod and red snapper and the occasional halibut. Besides the great angling possibilities, there's the unsurpassable natural backdrop of scenery and wildlife: snowcapped mountains, old lighthouses, sea lions, whales, bald eagles, herons and other water

Outdoor Adventures

SPORT-FISHING

birds. **Saltwater licenses** are issued by the federal government. Charter operators will usually sell the license to you. ~ Information: Department of Fisheries and Oceans, 555 West Hastings Street, Vancouver, BC V6B 5G3; 604-666-2074. **Freshwater licenses** are issued through the provincial government and can be bought at most sporting goods stores. The Ministry of Environment, Lands and Parks (B.C. Environment) maintains a list of licensed **freshwater fishing guides**. For a copy, call 604-582-5200.

DOWNTOWN VICTORIA It's just a few minutes' walk from downtown Victoria to the marinas where charter outfits operate saltwater fishing trips. **Oak Bay Charters** provides bait and tackle for up to six people on charter trips into the protected waters around Victoria. Charter sightseeing excursions are also available. ~ Oak Bay Marina, 2141 Newton Street; 250-598-1061. **Adam's Fishing Charters** has a standard charter package for a minimum of four hours for up to four people, as well as more customized trips. ~ Inner Harbour; 250-370-2326. **A-1 Island Charters** provides the usual bait, tackle and license for a minimum four-hour charter for up to four people. ~ Inner Harbour; 250-479-7640.

SOUTHWEST ISLAND   As you angle along the west coast of the island, you might even see an occasional bear walking along the coast. **Bamfield Inn** runs charters in the sound and the ocean, and provides the usual bait, tackle and license for groups of two or three. ~ 75 Boardwalk, Bamfield; 250-728-3354. Located right next to the Pacific Rim National Park, **Weigh West Marine Resort** offers charters for fishing trips and whale watching. ~ 634 Campbell Street, Tofino; 250-725-3277, 800-665-8922.

WHALE WATCHING   The southern part of Vancouver Island is known for orca (or killer) whales, porpoises, harbor seals, sea lions, bald eagles and many species of marine birds. Watch also for the occasional minke whale, gray whale or elephant seal. Whale-watching season extends from April through September. June is the best time to see the orcas. By July and August, cruise operators are very busy, so try to call a day or two ahead for reservations.

DOWNTOWN VICTORIA   Look for little black-and-white Dall's porpoises that play off the bow or follow behind in the wake when you're out on one of these whale-watching trips. **Seacoast Expeditions Ltd.** can accommodate 12 people per boat (for a total of up to 36 people) on its whale-watching cruises, which begin in April. Cruises last about three hours. ~ Ocean Pointe Resort Hotel, 45 Songhees Road; 250-383-2254, 800-386-1525. **Seaker Adventure Tours** takes up to 12 passengers per boat out to look for whales. They're able to accommodate a group of up to 200. ~ 950 Wharf Street; 250-480-0244, 800-728-0244.

Kayaking is an up-close way to explore the coastal inlets of Vancouver Island, where there's plenty of sea mammals, birds and other wildlife to keep you company.

DOWNTOWN VICTORIA Ocean River Sports will rent single or double kayaks to individuals, but only to those with kayaking experience. During the summer the store offers a three-hour "get your feet wet" introductory class for people who want to find out more about kayaking. Experienced kayakers can join one of the scheduled two- to three-day trips to the southern Gulf Islands or inquire about customized trips to other locales. ~ 1437 Store Street; 250-381-4233, 800-909-4233.

SOUTHWEST ISLAND No experience is necessary to join one of the guided day trips or overnight excursions into Clayoquot Sound, along the island's west coast offered by **Tofino Sea Kayaking Co.** Longer excursions, lasting six days, head farther into Clayoquot Sound. Closed from mid-October to mid-March. ~ 320 Main Street, Tofino; 250-725-4222, 800-863-4664.

There are several popular and worthwhile dive spots around Victoria and Sidney. Easily accessible from downtown Victoria, **Ogden Point Breakwater** on Dallas Road is a marine park where diving depths range from 20 to 100 feet. Not the best dive spot, but one that's great for snorkeling and exploring tidepools is **East Sooke Park**, between Victoria and Sooke. For advanced deep-sea diving, try **Race Rocks**, also a marine park, where high-current activity stirs up much marine life.

Between Victoria and Sidney, on the Saanich Peninsula, there's good shore access at **10-Mile Point**, the ecological reserve, although it has strong currents and is not for beginners. **Saanich Inlet** is several hundred feet deep with a sharp 200-foot drop and little tidal exchange, so there's no current.

DOWNTOWN VICTORIA Frank White's Scuba Shop rents equipment and can provide information and directions for you and your

✔ **CHECK THESE OUT—UNIQUE OUTDOOR ADVENTURES**

- Catch a breeze with your sailboard at Elk/Beaver Lake Regional Park. *page 520*
- Maneuver the inlets of Vancouver Island via kayak and get an eyeful of coastal creatures. *page 537*
- Dive in for a close-up view of wildlife at 10-Mile Point, the Saanich Peninsula's ecological reserve. *page 537*
- Scale fjordlike cliffs and wade through tidepools—all on the challenging and lengthy West Coast Trail. *page 541*

diving buddy or buddies. The shop sponsors group shore dives every Saturday at 10 a.m. and monthly night dives on the third Thursday. You can also arrange a private dive trip with a dive master. ~ 1855 Blanshard Street, Victoria; 250-385-4713, 800-606-3977. **Ocean Centre** rents gear and operates a dive charter vessel for full-day trips to the lower Gulf Islands, Race Rocks and wreck dives along the artificial reefs off Sidney. ~ 800 Cloverdale Avenue, Victoria; 250-475-2202, 800-414-2202.

SAANICH PENINSULA   For rentals and instruction, visit **Frank White's Scuba Shop**. On Sunday, the shop sponsors a drop-in dive. ~ 2200 Keating Crossroad, Saanichton; 250-652-3375.

SOUTHEAST ISLAND   Besides equipment rental and training, **Octopus Adventures Dive Center** offers certification classes and can arrange boat dives. ~ 4924 Argyle Street, Port Alberni; 250-723-3057. **Seafun Divers** offers dive charters, rentals and instruction, including certification classes. ~ 300 South Terminal Avenue, Nanaimo; 250-754-4813.

BOATING

Boating and sailing are popular all around Victoria, the southeastern side of Vancouver Island and in the waters surrounding the Gulf Islands. The waters off the west coast are often too rough for relaxed boating, but some pleasure charters are available.

SAANICH PENINSULA   For bareboating rentals (without a guide) of sailboats or powerboats, contact **Bosun's Charters Ltd**. Closed weekends in the winter. ~ Bosun's Landing, Sidney; 250-656-6644. Besides bareboat rentals, **Seahorse Sailing Inc. Sailing School and Yacht Charters** runs three-day to six-day charters up to the wilderness area of Desolation Bay and over to the Gulf Islands. ~ 2075 Tryon Road, Sidney; 250-655-4979, 800-667-9833.

SOUTHWEST ISLAND   There are no unsupervised rentals available on the west side of the island, but **Nootka Charters** offers skippered charter tours on a 35-foot sailboat, for two or three days and longer, to Clayoquot Sound and Barkley Sound, and longer charters to other areas. Closed mid-September through May. ~ Box 348, Tofino, B.C., V0R 200; 250-725-3318.

HANG GLIDING

Air Dreams Hang Gliding School offers special introductory hang-gliding tandem flights to beginning fliers. The tandem flights with a qualified instructor take off from a 2000-foot peak in an area north of Victoria. Paragliding instruction is also available for everyone from beginners to advanced fliers. Flying is offered from late February to December. ~ 615 Brookleigh Road, Victoria; phone/fax 250-658-0119. By calling the **British Columbia Hang Gliding/Paragliding Association**, you can get more information about the sport in the province and referrals to other resources. ~ 250-767-6717.

Golf is very popular in Canada, and Vancouver Island is no exception.

GOLF

DOWNTOWN VICTORIA   There's a "mean" 16th hole at **Cedar Hill Municipal Golf Course**. It's a par-four downhill, with a two-tiered elevated green. ~ 1400 Derby Road; 250-595-3103. The nine-hole par-three **Henderson Park Golf Course** is fun for beginners. You'll only need three clubs to play this course, and you can rent them there. ~ 2291 Cedar Hill Road; 250-370-7200. Just as the name suggests, **Olympic View Golf Club** offers views of the Olympic Peninsula from its 18 holes. It's cut right out of the wilderness, about 25 minutes from Victoria. ~ 643 Latoria Road; 250-474-3671. The nine-hole **Prospect Lake Golf Club** is a challenging course set on the shore of Prospect Lake. ~ 4633 Prospect Lake Road; 250-479-2688. The executive nine-hole **Royal Oak Golf Course** is just minutes from the ferry. ~ 540 Marsett Place; 250-658-1433.

SAANICH PENINSULA   **Glen Meadows Golf and Country Club** is a public 18-hole championship course that has hosted the World Lefthanders Golf Tournament. Also available are three tennis courts and a curling rink. ~ 1050 McTavish Road, Sidney; 250-656-3136.

SOUTHEAST ISLAND   For some beautiful views of southeast Vancouver Island, try the 18-hole **Eaglecrest Golf Club** in the Parksville-Qualicum neighborhood. ~ 2035 Island Highway West, Qualicum Beach; 250-752-6311, 800-567-1320. **Morningstar International Golf Course** hosts one of the events on Canada's professional golf tour. The holes have four sets of tees, so this course can provide a challenge to most golfers. ~ 525 Lowry's Road, Parksville; 250-248-8161.

DOWNTOWN VICTORIA   Although Victoria's terrain is perfect for cycling, the city's streets and walkways are often very crowded; there are no official bike paths, and many walking paths prohibit bicycles. One of the best bets for great views of the water and the Olympic Mountains is Victoria's **Beach Drive**, a six-mile route that passes through lovely Victorian neighborhoods near the ocean. It's an easy ride, with only a few low hills. But use caution on Beach Drive; it is winding and there is often considerable motor traffic. The **Galloping Goose Trail** is a multi-use section of the Trans-Canada Trail. You can pick it up in downtown Victoria and head west toward Sooke and beyond into the mountains. For a map of bike routes in the area, contact the **Greater Victoria Cycling Coalition**. ~ 1275 Oscar Street; 250-381-2453.

BIKING

Bike Rentals   In Victoria, **Budget Rent A Car Victoria Ltd.** has been renting bikes to visitors for nearly two decades. ~ 727 Courtney Street; 800-668-9833. **Sports Rent** rents bikes and inline skates, as well as equipment for camping and water sports. ~ 611 Discovery Street; 250-385-7368. For another mode, rent a scooter at **Island Boat Rentals**. ~ 950 Wharf Street; 250-995-1661. **Pembrook Motorcycles** rents, well, motorcycles. ~ 250-384-2133. In Nanaimo, mountain-bike rentals are available at **Chain Reaction**. The staff will also recommend mountain trails suitable for your skill level. ~ 12 Victoria Crescent, Nanaimo; 250-754-3309.

HIKING   All distances listed for hiking trails are one way unless otherwise noted.

DOWNTOWN VICTORIA   The **Greater Victoria Greenbelt Society** is developing a trail system through the greater Victoria area. For more information, write 3873 Swan Lake Road, Victoria, BC V8X 3W1. Another resource is the **Capital Regional District**, with good trail information about trails in Victoria (see below). ~ 490 Atkins Avenue, Victoria, BC V9B 2Z8; 250-478-3344. For information on trails outside the Greater Victoria area, call B.C. Parks at 250-391-2300.

For an easy stroll (just over 2 miles) around the Inner Harbour take the **Westsong Way Walk**. From there you can watch all kinds of water vessels, including float planes, passenger catamarans, fishing boats and yachts.

VICTORIA NEIGHBORHOODS   There is a maze of trails in **Thetis Lake Park**. Trails loop around Upper Thetis and Lower Thetis lakes and along Craigflower Creek.

The **Norn Trail** (less than 1 mile) at Mount Douglas Municipal Park (information, 250-744-5343) is an easy walk on a well-marked route with plenty of trees. It joins the **Irvine Trail** to reach the summit of Mount Douglas. Hikers can access the Norn Trail from the parking lot at the intersection of Cordova Bay Road and Ash Road.

SAANICH PENINSULA   On the **Island View Beach Regional Park Loop** (1.5 mile roundtrip), visitors can take an easy hike from the parking lot at Island View Park that loops through fragile sand dunes and provides views of the beach and Haro Strait.

The **Lakeside Route** (6.3 miles) at Elk/Beaver Lake Regional Park is a shaded and well-groomed trail of wood chips and wooden bridges through the beaches surrounding Elk and Beaver lakes.

The trail system within **John Dean Provincial Park** (total of 6 miles of trails) provides views of Saanich Inlet, fertile farmland and orchards. Take East Saanich Road to Dean Park Road.

The **Goldmine Trail** (1 mile) at Goldstream Provincial Park is a dirt pathway that travels past a miner's spring and out to Squally Reach Lookout.

SOUTHEAST ISLAND   For an easy walk in Nanaimo, take the **Harbourside Walkway** (2.5 miles) around the harbor with views of Protection Island and the Coast Mountains.

The **Galloping Goose Regional Trail** (37 miles) is a popular multi-use path. Favored by hikers, bicyclists and horses, it begins in downtown Victoria, winds through farmland of Metchosin, then into the semi-wilderness of the Sooke River Valley and up the hills providing ocean views.

SOUTHWEST ISLAND **Gold Mine Trail** (approximately 1 mile) begins just west of the Pacific Rim National Park information center on Route 4 for a nonstrenuous hike through a forest of amambilis fir, red cedar, hemlock, Douglas fir and red alder. The remains of mining machinery, including part of a dredge, can still be found on the beach.

South Beach Trail (approximately .5 mile) starts behind the Wickaninnish Centre and winds through a stand of Sitka spruce. Side trails lead to rocky or sandy coves surrounded by headlands. At the far end of Lismer Beach, a boardwalk climbs over a bluff to South Beach. At the top of this bluff, the **Wickaninnish Trail** leads to the left, but continuing to the right takes hikers past groves of moss-enshrouded Sitka spruce and western hemlock.

The **Wickaninnish Trail** (1.5 miles) links Long Beach to Florencia Bay. Hikers can access this trail via the South Beach Trail or from the Florencia Bay parking lot. This trail is a part of the early Tofino-Ucluelet land route that used beaches, forest trails and sheltered inlets to link the two towns before a road was built farther inland.

The most arduous trek on Vancouver Island is the **West Coast Trail** (47 miles), stretching along the west coast. Hikers need to be prepared for five to eight days traveling on an irregular slippery trail. There are tidepools, fjordlike cliffs, opportunities to see Pacific gray whales, sea lions, harbor seals, shorebirds and seabirds. Access to the southern trailhead is at Port Renfrew. The northern trailhead access is at Bamfield.

Transportation

Vancouver Island lies across the Strait of Juan de Fuca from the state of Washington and west of mainland British Columbia. Victoria and the southeastern communities are accessible from either. **Route 14** runs from Victoria through Sooke to Port Renfrew on the west coast. The **Trans-Canada Highway (Route 1)** goes from Victoria to Nanaimo. **Route 4** goes from the Parksville-Qualicum area west to Port Alberni, leading to the west coast communities of Ucluelet and Tofino.

CAR

The **Victoria International Airport** is 20 minutes from Victoria in Sidney. Carriers include Air B.C., Canada 3000, Canadian Airlines, Canadian Regional Airlines, Royal Airlines, Time Air and Westjet.

AIR

Airport bus service between downtown Victoria and the Victoria International Airport is provided by the **Victoria Airporter**. ~ 250-386-2525.

Helijet Airways offers jet helicopter service into downtown Victoria from downtown Vancouver, and from Victoria Harbour to Vancouver Airport. ~ 250-382-6222; 800-665-4354.

The airport in Nanaimo, **Cassidy Airport**, is served by Air B.C., Canadian Regional and Timberline.

Floatplanes offer a unique experience as they take off on the water and land directly in Victoria's Inner Harbour. **Kenmore Air Harbor** has a daily schedule to Victoria from the Seattle area and also goes to Nanaimo in the summer. ~ 206-486-1257, 800-543-9595.

FERRY

Ferries provide daily, year-round sailings to Victoria and Nanaimo. The number of sailings daily usually increases in the summer, but it is advisable to call for up-to-date schedules and rates.

Travelers wishing to depart from the United States can take Black Ball Transport, Washington State Ferries or Victoria Clipper to Victoria. **Black Ball Transport** takes vehicles and foot passengers from Port Angeles to Victoria's Inner Harbour. ~ Port Angeles, WA, 360-457-4491; Victoria, BC, 250-386-2202. **Washington State Ferries** takes vehicles and foot passengers on a scenic route through Washington's San Juan Islands between Anacortes, WA, and Sidney, BC, and buses take foot passengers to downtown Victoria from Sidney. ~ Seattle, WA, 206-464-6400; Victoria, BC, 250-381-1551. The **Victoria Clipper** ships are 300-passenger, high-speed jet catamarans that run year-round between Seattle's Pier 69 and Victoria's Inner Harbour with stops in the San Juan Islands from May through September. ~ U.S., 800-888-2535; Seattle, WA 206-448-5000; Victoria, BC, 250-382-8100.

B.C. Ferries travels year-round from Tsawwassen, just south of Vancouver, to Swartz Bay, a scenic, half-hour drive by car or bus from Victoria. ~ Victoria, BC, 250-386-3431; within B.C., 888-223-3779.

TRAIN

VIA Rail provides Vancouver Island rail service between Victoria and Courtenay, with stops at Nanaimo. ~ 800-561-3949.

CAR RENTALS

Agencies in downtown Victoria and at the Victoria airport include **Avis Rent A Car** (800-331-1084), **Budget Rent A Car** (800-268-8900), **Hertz Rent A Car** (within the U.S., 800-654-3001; within Canada, 800-263-0600), **Island Auto Rentals** (250-384-4881), **Rent A Wreck** (250-384-5343, 800-809-0788) and **National Tilden Interrent** (800-328-4567).

PUBLIC TRANSIT

Island Coach Lines (250-385-4411) has bus service between Victoria and other points on Vancouver Island. B.C. Transit (250-382-6161) provides local bus service throughout the greater Victoria area. B.C. Transit and Victoria Regional Transit Commission offer public transit service to the disabled called **Handy** DART (250-727-7811).

In the Victoria area, you will find **Bluebird Cabs** (250-382-4235, **TAXIS** 800-665-7055), **Empress Taxi** (250-381-2222, 800-808-6881) and **Victoria Taxi** (250-383-7111, 888-842-7111).

Index

Lodging Index

LODGING SERVICES

Dining Index

Notes

Notes

Notes

Notes

HIDDEN GUIDES

Adventure travel or a relaxing vacation?—"Hidden" guidebooks are the only travel books in the business to provide detailed information on both. Aimed at environmentally aware travelers, our motto is "Adventure Travel Plus." These books combine details on unique hotels, restaurants and sightseeing with information on camping, sports and hiking for the outdoor enthusiast.

THE NEW KEY GUIDES

Based on the concept of ecotourism, The New Key Guides are dedicated to the preservation of Central America's rare and endangered species, architecture and archaeology. Filled with helpful tips, they give travelers everything they need to know about these exotic destinations.

ULTIMATE FAMILY GUIDES

These innovative guides present the best and most unique features of a family destination. Quality is the keynote. In addition to thoroughly covering each destination, they feature short articles and one-line "teasers" that are both fun and informative.

Order Form

HIDDEN GUIDEBOOKS

____ Hidden Arizona, $13.95
____ Hidden Bahamas, $12.95
____ Hidden Baja, $14.95
____ Hidden Boston and Cape Cod, $11.95
____ Hidden Carolinas, $16.95
____ Hidden Coast of California, $16.95
____ Hidden Colorado, $13.95
____ Hidden Florida, $16.95
____ Hidden Florida Keys & Everglades, $11.95
____ Hidden Hawaii, $16.95
____ Hidden Idaho, $13.95
____ Hidden Maui, $12.95
____ Hidden Montana, $13.95

____ Hidden New England, $17.95
____ Hidden New Mexico, $13.95
____ Hidden Oahu, $12.95
____ Hidden Oregon, $13.95
____ Hidden Pacific Northwest, $17.95
____ Hidden Rockies, $16.95
____ Hidden San Francisco and Northern California, $16.95
____ Hidden Southern California, $16.95
____ Hidden Southwest, $17.95
____ Hidden Tahiti, $16.95
____ Hidden Tennessee, $15.95
____ Hidden Utah, $13.95
____ Hidden Wyoming, $13.95

THE NEW KEY GUIDEBOOKS

____ The New Key to Belize, $14.95
____ The New Key to Cancún and the Yucatán, $14.95
____ The New Key to Costa Rica, $16.95

____ The New Key to Ecuador and the Galápagos, $16.95
____ The New Key to Guatemala, $14.95

ULTIMATE FAMILY GUIDEBOOKS

____ Disneyland and Beyond, $12.95

____ Disney World and Beyond, $13.95

Mark the book(s) you're ordering and enter the total cost here ⇨ [   ]

California residents add 8% sales tax here ⇨ [   ]

Shipping, check box for your preferred method and enter cost here ⇨ [   ]

❑ BOOK RATE   **FREE! FREE! FREE!**

❑ PRIORITY MAIL $3.00 First book, $1.00/each additional book

❑ UPS 2-DAY AIR $7.00 First book, $1.00/each additional book

[   ]

Billing, enter total amount due here and check method of payment ⇨ [   ]

❑ CHECK   ❑ MONEY ORDER

❑ VISA/MASTERCARD_____ EXP. DATE _____

NAME _____ PHONE _____

ADDRESS_____

_____

CITY_____ STATE _____ ZIP_____

MONEY-BACK GUARANTEE ON DIRECT ORDERS PLACED THROUGH ULYSSES PRESS.

ABOUT THE AUTHORS & ILLUSTRATOR

ERIC LUCAS, the update author for this edition, is a freelance writer and editor. He has been a newspaper editorial columnist, travel writer, magazine editor and business journalist. An avid gardener, fisherman, backpacker and runner, he lives on Vashon Island outside Seattle.

STEPHEN DOLAINSKI, a regular contributor to *Westways* and *Avenues*, is a freelance travel editor and writer living in Southern California. He has written about travel and business for magazines, and has contributed to several travel guidebooks, including *Hidden Southern California*.

JOHN GOTTBERG has traveled and worked all over the world. The former chief editor of the Insight Guide series and the travel news and graphics editor for the *Los Angeles Times*, he has written eight travel guides and been published in *Travel & Leisure* and *Island* magazines.

MARIA LENHART has been a freelance writer specializing in travel for nearly two decades. She has contributed to *Travel/Holiday*, *Travel & Leisure*, *Odyssey*, *Business Travel News*, the *Christian Science Monitor* and many other publications.

MARILYN McFARLANE, a member of the Society of American Travel Writers, contributed to the chapter on Seattle. A Northwest native, she is the author of *Best Places to Stay in the Pacific Northwest*, *Quick Escapes in the Pacific Northwest* and *Northwest Discoveries*.

JIM POTH, co-author of the Seattle chapter, is a native of the Northwest who spent 21 years reporting in the region for *Sunset* magazine, where he became both bureau chief and senior editor. Jim is a writer, editor and photographer for the Washington State Tourism Division.

ROGER RAPOPORT has written numerous other travel guides including *Great Cities of Eastern Europe*. He has written extensively on the Pacific Northwest for such publications as *Outside* and the *Oregonian*.

MELISSA RIVERS wrote the introductory, Puget Sound/San Juan Islands and Vancouver chapters. She has collaborated on many guides including Fodor's books on the Caribbean, Canada, the United States, Hong Kong and Mexico.

ARCHIE SATTERFIELD, a member of the Society of American Travel Writers, resides in Edmonds, Washington. In addition to the Central Washington and East of the Cascades chapters of this book, he has authored two dozen books on travel and history.

CATHERINE ROSE CROWTHER is an award-winning illustrator whose work has appeared in numerous books and national magazines including *The Atlantic Monthly*, *Utne Reader*, *Parenting*, *Moosewood Restaurant Book of Desserts* and *Yoga Journal*. She lives and works in Berkeley, California.